RAILROAD PROPERTY.

LETTER

FROM

THE SECRETARY OF WAR,

IN ANSWER TO

A resolution of the House of June 4, relative to railroad property in the possession of the government.

JULY 27, 1866.—Laid on the table and ordered to be printed.

WAR DEPARTMENT,
Washington City, July 26, 1866.

SIR: In reply to a resolution of the House of Representatives of June 4, 1866, respecting railroad property which was in possession of the government on May 1, 1865, &c., &c., I have the honor to transmit herewith the Quartermaster General's report of July 23, with accompanying papers, which contains all the information on the subject which the department can furnish at present.

Very respectfully, sir, your obedient servant,

EDWIN M. STANTON,
Secretary of War.

Hon. S. COLFAX,
Speaker of the House of Representatives United States.

QUARTERMASTER GENERAL'S OFFICE,
Washington, D. C., July 23, 1866.

SIR: I have the honor to return herewith resolution of the House of Representatives of June 4, 1866, referred by the War Department to this office June 5 for report.

A copy of the resolution was transmitted, June 6, to General D. C. McCallum, director and general manager of military railroads of the United States, for report from the files of his office of the information called for. Herewith is respectfully forwarded, under date of July 19, the full report of General McCallum, embracing that of Brevet Major F. J. Crilly, assistant quartermaster United States army, under whose supervision the transfer of all the railroad property in the military division of the Tennessee and in the military division of the Mississippi was effected.

In addition thereto is respectfully forwarded a report with schedules of railroad property in the possession of the United States May 1, 1865, prepared from reports received at this office from officers in the military division of the Gulf, showing the disposition of such property, with the authority therefor, and steps taken to recover the value thereof, appended in each case; altogether comprising, it is believed, a full schedule of all railroad property in the possession of the government on May 1, 1865, whether held by right of capture or purchase; also, what disposition has been made of such property—if sold, whether for cash or credit; and if for credit, under what law or authority.

Attention is invited to the letters of General McCallum and Major Crilly, transmitting their respective reports, and especially to the statements contained therein, that, owing to the large amount of property transferred, and the many different sources from which it was derived, it would be impossible, in every case, to trace each separate item back to its original purchase-bill within the present session of Congress, and consequently so much of the resolution requiring the original cost of the property held by the United States by right of purchase has not been fully complied with. For information on this subject, the following extract from the letter transmitting General McCallum's report is quoted:

"The greater portion of this property had been on hand and in use a long time, and though the prices obtained were below the cost, with some exceptions, they are believed to be very favorable to the government; this is particularly true with the property sold on credit, the companies purchasing it paying better prices than when sold for cash."

Upon an examination of the prices obtained for the railroad property in the military division of the Gulf, a similar state of circumstances is found to exist.

The following is a statement of the amounts of sales of railroad property:

For cash	$3, 403, 412 22
On credit	7, 418, 962 30
Total	10, 822, 374 52

Attention is invited to the enclosed consolidated statement of the indebtedness of railroad companies, May 31, 1866, for the purchase of railway material of the United States on credit, prepared from reports transmitted to this office by quartermasters in obedience to General Orders No. 80, Quartermaster General's office, December 22, 1865, (accompanying.)

In order to secure payment of the indebtedness of railroads for the purchase of property of the United States, every railroad company to which sales have been made on credit is required to give bond in double the amount of the value of the property transferred to it, as per form contained in Executive Order of October 14, 1865, (accompanying,) by the terms of which the United States has a lien upon the property transferred, and each company is required to make prompt payments of the instalments as they fall due. These bonds, with lists and receipts of the property transferred, have, in every instance, been executed, and are on file in this office.

A great number of these roads have failed to comply strictly with the terms of their bonds; but owing to the devastating effects of the war, and the great expenses incurred in repairing the roads by rebuilding bridges, trestles, &c., and the prostrate condition of the southern roads, it is believed that they are actually unable to meet their engagements with the United States, and that to attempt to enforce prompt payments would be to arrest the operations of the roads, and thus to defeat the object of the Executive in the policy which dictated Executive Orders relative thereto. A general willingness to meet their engagements with the government appears to be manifested, however, by the greater number of the roads purchasing property, and a very large proportion of the payments already made have been in *cash*. All moneys accruing to their credit for the transportation of troops and supplies have been stopped against them and applied in liquidation of their indebtedness to the government; and arrangements have been made with the Post Office Department by which all payments for mail services performed by indebted railroads are withheld and placed to the credit of such roads on account of the purchase of military railroad property.

It is believed that these arrangements are sufficient to secure, ultimately, the payment of the indebtedness, with interest in full, of all railroads for the purchase of railway material of the United States.

Respectfully, your obedient servant,

M. C. MEIGS,
Quartermaster General, Brevet Major General U. S. A.

Hon. EDWIN M. STANTON,
Secretary of War, Washington, D. C.

REPORT

Of all railroads operated and controlled by the military railroad department during the war, and of all railroad property on hand the 1*st day of May,* 1865, *and not embraced in the report of Major F. J. Crilly; also, copies of the letters of the Quartermaster General to the Hon. Edwin M. Stanton, Secretary of War, dated May* 19 *and July* 17, 1865, *and of Executive Orders of August* 8 *and October* 14, 1865. *Prepared in accordance with resolution of the House of Representatives of June* 4, 1866.

WAR DEPARTMENT,
OFFICE OF DIRECTOR AND GENERAL MANAGER
OF MILITARY RAILROADS UNITED STATES,
Washington, D. C., July 10, 1866.

GENERAL: I have the honor to return herewith the copy of the resolution of the House of Representatives of June 4, 1866, referred to this office June 6, 1866, in the following words, to wit:

"On motion of Mr. Kelley,

"*Resolved,* That the Secretary of War be directed to furnish to the House of Representatives a schedule of all railroad property which was in the possession of the government May 1, 1865, whether held by right of capture or by purchase, and if by purchase, stating what it cost. Also, what disposition has been made of such property; if sold, whether for cash or credit, and if for credit, under what law or authority; and whether the purchase-money has been paid, or what steps have been taken to recover it."

And to transmit, in answer thereto, the following reports, to wit:

1st. Reports numbered from 1 to 9, inclusive, being reports relative to railroad property in the military division of the Tennessee, transmitted to this office by Major F. J. Crilly, assistant quartermaster.

2d. Letter of Major Crilly of July 9, 1866, transmitting and explaining the above reports.

3d. Report of all railroads operated and controlled by the military railroad department during the war, and of all railroad property on hand on May 1, 1865, subject to the control of the military railroad department, and not embraced in the report of Major Crilly, showing how the same was obtained; how and by what authority disposed of, with copies of the letters of the Quartermaster General to the Hon. Edwin M. Stanton, Secretary of War, dated May 19 and July 17, 1865, and indorsements thereon, and of Executive Orders of August 8 and October 14, 1865.

These papers are arranged as follows, to wit:

1st. The letters and orders above referred to.

2d. Reports of all railroads operated and controlled by the United States at any time during the war, under my direction, giving the name of the road, number of miles operated, estimated value, how held, and how disposed of.

3d. A condensed statement showing the value of the property sold on credit to railroad companies in the departments of Virginia and North Carolina, payments made, and amount remaining unpaid.

4th. A schedule of property sold on credit to railroad companies in the departments of Virginia and North Carolina.

5th. A schedule of property sold at aution for cash, by General H. L. Robinson, assistant quartermaster, and Captain J. D. Stubbs, assistant quartermaster, since May 1, 1865.

6th. A schedule of property used in repairing and operating railroads in the departments of Virginia and North Carolina, since May 1, 1865.

7th. A schedule of property transferred to officers not connected with military railroads, since May 1, 1865.

8th. A schedule of captured property, showing how and by what authority disposed of.

9th. A schedule of property not yet disposed of.

In preparing this report it was not possible to give the cost of all the articles. The amount of property on hand was large, and having been received from so many different sources, it could not, at this date, be traced back to the purchase bills. This is particularly true with regard to the property in the military division of the Tennessee; and in the other departments, I could only give the average cost price, or no price at all.

The amount received from sales of property is as follows, to wit:

For cash	$3, 403, 412 22
And on credit	7, 192, 855 63
Total	10, 596, 267 85

The greater part of this property had been on hand and in use a long time, and though the prices obtained were below the cost, with some exceptions, they are believed to be very favorable to the government. This is particularly true with the property sold on credit, the companies purchasing it paying better prices than were obtained when sold for cash.

Though all the railroads in the States lately in rebellion were virtually in the possession of the government on the 1st of May, 1865, only those necessary for military purposes were at any time formally taken possession of and controlled and operated by it; and when the necessity for military occupation ceased, they were either abandoned or turned over to the board of public works of the State, or to their former owners, in accordance with instructions from the general commanding the department, or from the Secretary of War, or Executive Orders of August 8 and October 14, 1865.

Under these orders, control of each road was relinquished so soon as the necessary steps could be taken and the proper persons found to receive and operate it in such a manner as to secure the speedy movements of all military stores and troops.

I have the honor to be, very respectfully, your obedient servant,

D. C. McCALLUM,

Brevet Brigadier General, Director, and General Manager of Military Railroads United States.

Brevet Major General M. C. MEIGS,

Quartermaster General U. S. A., Washington, D. C.

THIRTY-NINTH CONGRESS, FIRST SESSION.

IN THE HOUSE OF REPRESENTATIVES,
June 4, 1866.

On motion of Mr. Kelley,

Resolved, That the Secretary of War be directed to furnish to the House of Representatives a schedule of all railroad property which was in the possession of the government on May 1, 1865, whether held by right of capture or by purchase; and if by purchase, stating the cost. Also, what disposition has been made of such property; if sold, whether for cash or credit; and if for credit, under what law or authority, and whether the purchase money has been paid, or what steps have been taken to recover it.

Attest: EDWARD McPHERSON, *Clerk,*
By CLINTON LLOYD, *Chief Clerk.*

Respectfully referred to the Quartermaster General for report, to be sent to me, with this paper.

By order of the Secretary of War:

EDMUND SCHRIVER,
Inspector General.

W. D., *June* 5, 1866.

A true copy :

ALEXANDER BLISS,
Colonel Quartermaster's Department.

WAR DEPARTMENT, *June* 5, 1866.

Refers for report, to be sent to General Schriver, with the enclosed papers, resolution of the House of Representatives calling for information relative to railroad property.

QUARTERMASTER GENERAL'S OFFICE,
Washington, D. C., June 6, 1866.

Respectfully referred to Brevet Brigadier General D. C. McCallum, general superintendent United States military railroads, Washington, D. C., for report as early as practicable.

The schedule required should embrace all the railroads in the possession of the United States at the date named, as well as movable railroad property, and show the disposition made of both.

By order Quartermaster General:

ALEXANDER BLISS,
Colonel Q. M. Dep't, in charge 4th Division.

No. 1.

REPORTS NUMBERED FROM 1 TO 9, INCLUSIVE, BEING REPORTS RELATIVE TO RAILROAD PROPERTY IN THE MILITARY DIVISION OF THE TENNESSEE, TRANSMITTED BY MAJOR F. J. CRILLY.

[Enclosure No. 1.]

Report showing the disposition of United States military railroad property in the military division of the Tennessee, for which Brevet Colonel John Parks, A. Q. M., is responsible.

[The property sold under Executive Orders of August 8 and October 14, 1865, was appraised by a board convened by Major General G. H. Thomas, commanding military division of the Tennessee. Copy of order herewith.]

Running number.	Articles.	Captured property on hand May 1, 1865.	Property purchased by the United States on hand May 1, 1865.	Total amount of property on hand May 1, 1865.	Property sold on credit to railroad companies under Executive Orders of August 8 and October 14, 1865.					Property captured and returned to owners.				Sold at public auction for cash.	Transferred to officers.	Lost or expended in public service.
					Memphis and Charleston railroad.	Memphis and Little Rock railroad.	Mobile and Ohio railroad.	Memphis and Ohio railroad.	Mississippi and Tennessee railroad.	Memphis and Little Rock railroad.	Mobile and Ohio railroad.	Memphis and Charleston railroad.	Memphis and Ohio railroad.			
1	Books, time......number..					18										174
2	Books, blank......do....	231	55	286							231					55
3	Books, memorandum......do....		12	12												12
4	Books, freight......do....															2
5	Blanks, quartermaster's......quires..		185	185												194
6	Blanks, freight......number..															500
7	Blotting board......sheets..		4	4												52
8	Coal, bituminous......bushels..		4, 673	4, 673		50	100									7, 208
9	Charcoal......do....					25										25
10	Coke......do....															500
11	Wood......cords..		647	647		960	80							19¼		3, 259¼
12	Dividers......pairs..		1	1	6	7										
13	Envelopes, assorted......number..		18, 450	18, 450											12, 100	17, 200
14	Erasers, steel......do....		7	7											7	
15	Files, wire......do....		12	12											12	
16	Files, paper......do....		18	18											18	
17	Ink......bottles..															12
18	Ink, copying......do....															12
19	Ink, carmine......do....															18

20	Ink, blue ....do..															2
21	Inkstands ....number..														32	
22	Lead-pencils ....do..															192
23	Mucilage ....bottles..															12
24	Paper, abstract ....quires..		2	2												2
25	Paper, cap ....do..															160
26	Paper, envelope ....do..		3	3												5
27	Paper, drawing ....do..															5
28	Paper, folio post ....do..		1½	1½												1½
29	Paper, letter ....do..		55	55												165
30	Pens, steel ....number..															26
31	Pens, ruling ....do..		1	1											1	
32	Penholders ....do..														24	
33	Pencils, slate ....box..															1
34	Racks, pen ....number..		3	3											9	
35	Rulers ....do..		3	3											3	
36	Rulers, boxwood ....do..		12	12											12	
37	Rulers, rubber ....do..		1	1											1	
38	Tape, office ....pieces..		19	19												19
39	Wafers ....ounces..		18	18											18	
40	Weights, paper ....number..														6	
41	Oats ....pounds..															1,170
42	Brushes, counter ....number..					6								41		
43	Brushes, dusting ....do..		6	6										8		
44	Brooms ....do..		220	220		41	12							326		
45	Cutter, paper ....do..														1	
46	Chairs, assorted ....do..	5	6	11								5		4	3	
47	Balances, counter ....do..		1	1												1
48	Balances, post office ....do..		1	1											1	
49	Balances, spring ....do..		2	2										17		
50	Clocks ....do..	2		2		1					1	1				
51	Candlesticks ....do..					40										
52	Desks, counting ....do..	4	3	7								4		3		
53	Desks, office ....do..	2	3	5			1					2		2		
54	Elbows, stove pipe ....do..		10	10		16								7		
55	Dusters, feather ....do..		12	12												15
56	Lamp chimneys ....do..		6	6												6
57	Money trays ....do..		2	2											1	1
58	Paper cases ....do..	1	1	2								1		1		
59	Paper cases, secretary ....do..	3		3								3				
60	Presses, letter ....do..	3	3	6		1	1					3		8		
61	Punches, paper ....do..		1	1											1	
62	Safes, iron, assorted ....do..	3	7	10		2	1					3		6	3	
63	Safes, match ....do..		8	8												9
64	Slates ....do..		12	12			3									11
65	Stoves ....do..		29	29		21	8							27		
66	Stove pans ....do..		1	1											1	
67	Stove pipe ....joints..		152	152		174								76		
68	Tables, draughting ....number..	1		1								1				
69	Tables, office ....do..	4	1	5			2					4				
70	Water-coolers ....do..		2	2										1	1	
71	Wick, candle ....balls..															8

Report showing the disposition of United States military railroad property in the military division of the Tennessee, &c.—Continued.

Running number.	Articles.	Captured property on hand May 1, 1865.	Property purchased by the United States on hand May 1, 1865.	Total amount of property on hand May 1, 1865.	Property sold on credit to railroad companies under Executive Orders of August 8 and October 14, 1865.					Property captured and returned to owners.				Sold at public auction for cash.	Transferred to officers.	Lost or expended in public service.
					Memphis and Charleston railroad.	Memphis and Little Rock railroad.	Mobile and Ohio railroad.	Memphis and Ohio railroad.	Mississippi and Tennessee railroad.	Memphis and Little Rock railroad.	Mobile and Ohio railroad.	Memphis and Charleston railroad.	Memphis and Ohio railroad.			
72	Wick, lamp ... balls															48
73	Wick, flat ... number															42
74	Wick, candle ... do					6										24¾
76	Ambulances ... do		1	1											1	
77	Brushes, horse ... do		2	2		3										2
78	Bridles, riding ... do					2										
79	Cars, passenger, 1st class ... do		2	2	3	1									1	
80	Cars, passenger, 2d class ... do		6	6	7	1										
81	Cars, baggage ... do														1	
82	Cars, boarding ... do		1	1											1	
83	Cars, caboose ... do		13	13											15	2
84	Cars, freight ... do	2	116	118	39	56	40	23	7			2			13	
85	Cars, hand ... do		11	11	11	11	3		1							
86	Cars, platform ... do	4	49	53	27	28	13	11	16		2	2			20	
87	Cars, pay ... do		1	1	1											
88	Cars, truck ... do		3	3	3		1		1							
89	Chains, bearing ... do		2	2												4
90	Chains, breast ... do		8	8												10
91	Chains, fifth ... do		1	1												1
92	Chains, halter ... do		10	10												13
93	Chains, stretcher ... do		1	1												1
94	Combs, curry ... do		2	2		1										5
95	Check lines ... do					4										
96	Drays ... do					1										
97	Engines, portable ... do		2	2	1		1									
98	Engines, stationary ... do		1	1	1	1										
99	Engines, locomotive ... do	16	22	38	6	4	1		2	6	2	3	5		20	
100	Harness, wheel, S. S. ambulance ... do		2	2										2		
101	Harness, wheel-horse ... do					3										1
102	Halters, head ... do		2	2												2
103	Halters, strap ... do		2	2												2
104	Horses ... do		6	6		1									6	

105	Harness, dray ....do					2										
106	Lines, lead ....do		2	2											2	
107	Lines, 2-horse ....do		1	1											1	
108	Mules ....do					5										1
109	Neck straps ....do		10	10		3										10
110	Poles, coupling ....do		1	1												1
111	Sticks, jockey ....do		3	3												3
112	Saddles, riding ....do					2								3		
113	Tenders, locomotive ....do		17	17	6	4	1		2						8	
114	Trucks, baggage ....do	6		6								6				
115	Trucks, hand ....do	16		16								16				
116	Trucks, timber ....do		8	8	8											
117	Trucks, tender ....do		2	2	2											
118	Trucks, W. house ....do	2		2								2			5	
119	Wagons, 2-horse ....do		1	1		1									1	
120	Wagons, army ....do					1										
121	Wagon tongues ....do		3	3												3
122	Whips, wagon ....do		3	3												3
123	Brick ....do															15,000
124	Brick, fire ....do		400	400		1,000										2,400
125	Butts and screws ....pairs		197	197	70	110										202
126	Butts and screws, brass ....do		120	120	45											82
127	Cement, roofing ....sq. feet					2,730										29,153
128	Glass ....feet		2,690	2,690	1,550	1,300										1,236½
129	Glass, plate ....boxes						4 5-6							18		11 1-6
130	Glass, plate ....circles				31											5
131	Glue ....pounds		117	117		40	3							46		52
132	Hinges, strap ....pairs		48	48	14½	21	6½									82
133	Locks, car ....number		142	142	126	120	24									
134	Locks, cupboard ....do		15	15												17
135	Locks, door ....do		13	13	6	1	3									49
136	Locks, desk ....do		35	35	30											5
137	Locks ....do		41	41		7										34
138	Locks, drawer ....number				54	18										25
139	Locks, chest ....do				12											24
140	Lumber ....feet		26,300	26,300												238,238
141	Lumber, oak ....do				26,309	32,010										
142	Lumber, clear pine ....do				14,000											
143	Lumber, ash ....do				3,600	350										
144	Lumber, pine siding, matched ....do				1,800	4,500										
145	Lumber, poplar ....do				4,240	3,034										
146	Lumber, walnut ....do				2,792	128										
147	Lumber, pine sills ....do				18,096											
148	Lumber, common boards ....do				80,000											
149	Lumber, pine and poplar ....do				1,500											
150	Lumber, pine ....do					10,255										
151	Lumber, yellow pine ....do					6,956										
152	Lumber, cypress ....do					2,196										
153	Paper, sand ....quires		594	594	370	38	5									249¾
154	Padlocks ....number		66	66	60	8										25
155	Putty ....pounds		130	130	135	100										54
156	Screws ....number		288	288	14,688	34,792										10,224

Report showing the disposition of United States military railroad property in the military division of the Tennessee, &c.—Continued.

Running number.	Articles.	Captured property on hand May 1, 1865.	Property purchased by the United States on hand May 1, 1865.	Total amount of property on hand May 1, 1865.	Property sold on credit to railroad companies under Executive Orders of August 8 and October 14, 1865.					Property captured and returned to owners.				Sold at public auction for cash.	Transferred to officers.	Lost or expended in public service.
					Memphis and Charleston railroad.	Memphis and Little Rock railroad.	Mobile and Ohio railroad.	Memphis and Ohio railroad.	Mississippi and Tennessee railroad.	Memphis and Little Rock railroad.	Mobile and Ohio railroad.	Memphis and Charleston railroad.	Memphis and Ohio railroad.			
157	Sand .... loads															8
158	Screws, brass .... number		1,008	1,008	3,456	576										3,687
159	Lime .... barrels															9
160	Anvils, blacksmith's .... number		16	16	7	12	3							6		
161	Aprons, blacksmith's .... do		6	6	6	6										
162	Bellows, blacksmith's .... do		8	8	1	10	2							4		
163	Blocks, swedge, blacksmith's .... do		3	3	2		1									
164	Blades, hacksaw, with carpenter's tools .... do															
165	Blacksmith tools, steel .... pounds						1,115									
166	Blacksmith tools, iron .... do						2,131									
167	Chisels, cold .... number		35	35	40	147	44									
168	Chisels, track .... do		4	4												11
169	Dies, plates, and taps .... do						2									
170	Drills .... do						12									
171	Face plates, blacksmith's .... do		4	4	2	2										
172	Flatters, blacksmith's .... do		6	6	6											
173	Fullers, blacksmith's .... do		62	62	62											
174	Farrier's knives .... do				1	1										
175	Forges, portable .... do					1										
176	Friction drills .... do				1	2										
	Files issued to railroads .... do		2,503	2,503										2,406		
177	Files, square bastard, 14-inch .... do					6										
178	Files, millsaw, 12-inch .... do					16										
179	Files, round bastard, 16-inch .... do					28										
180	Files, flat bastard, 16-inch .... do					6										
181	Files, millsaw, 16-inch .... do					6										
182	Files, smooth edge, 12-inch .... do					6										
183	Files, smooth edge, 14-inch .... do					2										
184	Files, old .... do					600										
185	Files, bastard square, 12-inch .... do				27	8										
186	Files, bastard hand, 12-inch .... do				19											

187	Files, bastard flat, 6-inch	do				19											
188	Files, bastard hand, 8-inch	do				12											
189	Files, bastard hand, 10-inch	do				12											
190	Files, mill-saw, 14-inch	do				84	6										
191	Files, flat, 12-inch	do				88											
192	Files, smooth hand, 12-inch	do				6		1									
193	Files, smooth hand flat, 10-inch	do				18											
194	Files, bastard half round, 10-inch	do				65	15										
195	Files, bastard flat, 16-inch	do				18											
196	Files, bastard flat, 8-inch	do				36		12									
197	Files, bastard three-square, 7-inch	do				3											
198	Files, bastard round, 7-inch	do				7											
199	Files, bastard smooth half r'd, 14-in	do				13	54										
200	Files, bastard flat, 7-inch	do				22											
201	Files, bastard round, 12-inch	do				19	31										
202	Files, bastard half round, 6-inch	do				59											
203	Files, bastard half round, 12-inch	do				29	19										
204	Files, second cut flat, 8-inch	do				21											
205	Files, smooth half round, 6-inch	do				10		1									
206	Files, bastard half round, 8-inch	do				17		2									
207	Files, smooth flat, 12-inch	do				48											
208	Files, smooth half round, 12-inch	do				4		10									
209	Files, second cut half round, 12-in	do				13											
210	Files, bastard half round, 14-inch	do				3		3									
211	Files, handsaw, 5-inch	do				108	11										
212	Files, bastard flat, 10-inch	do				72											
213	Files, handsaw, 8-inch	do				12											
214	Files, bastard round, 15-inch	do				10											
215	Files, bastard flat, 15-inch	do				16											
216	Files, smooth hand, 14-inch	do				19		8									
217	Files, smooth round, 12-inch	do				12											
218	Files, bastard handsaw, 6-inch	do				26											
219	Files, bastard square, 8-inch	do				28											
220	Files, smooth flat, 16-inch	do				6											
221	Files, bastard flat, 14-inch	do				48	8										
222	Files, bastard round, 10-inch	do				6	12										
223	Files, bastard round, 14-inch	do				54	101										
224	Files, mill-saw, 13-inch	do						13									
225	Files, half round, 14-inch	do						13									
226	Files, ⅜-inch square, 12-inch	do						4									
227	Files, handsaw, 4-inch	do						7									
228	Files, flat tine, 8-inch	do						1									
229	Files, square bastard, 10-inch	do					24										
230	Files, square bastard, 12-inch	do					18										
231	Files, square bastard, 8-inch	do					43										
232	Files, square bastard, 16-inch	do					15										
233	Hammers, machinist's	do		5	5		3	2									
234	Hammers, shoe	do		1	1		1										
235	Hammers, blacksmith's	do						10									
236	Hammers, hand	do				1											
237	Hammers, assorted	do				22	4	7									
238	Hammers, engine	do			2	2									1		

Report showing the disposition of United States military railroad property in the military division of the Tennessee, &c.—Continued.

Running number.	Articles.	Captured property on hand May 1, 1865.	Property purchased by the United States on hand May 1, 1865.	Total amount of property on hand May 1, 1865.	Property sold on credit to railroad companies under Executive Orders of August 8 and October 14, 1865.					Property captured and returned to owners.				Sold at public auction for cash.	Transferred to officers.	Lost or expended in public service.
					Memphis and Charleston railroad.	Memphis and Little Rock railroad.	Mobile and Ohio railroad.	Memphis and Ohio railroad.	Mississippi and Tennessee railroad.	Memphis and Little Rock railroad.	Mobile and Ohio railroad.	Memphis and Charleston railroad.	Memphis and Ohio railroad.			
239	Hammers, sledge ....number..		11	11	9		5							6		
239½	Hammers, claw ....do....				10	11										
240	Hammers, hand ....do....		1	1	1											
241	Hammers, assorted ....do....				22	4	7									
242	Hand-press drill ....do....						1									
243	Mandrels ....do....		150	150	145									5		
244	Mandrels, saw ....do....		1	1	1											
245	Pincers, shoe ....pair..		1	1	1											
246	Punches, blacksmith's ....number..		30	30	3		50									
247	Punches, cold ....do....		3	3	3											
248	Ratchet drills ....do....		9	9	11	5	1									
249	Stock and dies ....sets..		1	1		7	2									
250	Swedges, blacksmith's		32	32			68									
251	Screw cutter				1											
252	Screw plate and dies				1											
253	Tools, blacksmith's ....sets..		1	1		2										
254	Tools, heading, blacksmith's ....number..		30	30	17		20									
255	Tools, lathe and planer ....pounds..		160	160	160											
256	Tongs, engine ....pairs..						1									
257	Tongs, gas-pipe ....do....						2									
258	Fans ....number..						1									
259	Tongs, blacksmith's ....pairs..		116	116	70		46							9		
260	Vices, blacksmith's ....number..		26	26	14	16	4							8		
261	Wrought drills				2											
262	....															
263	Adzes, foot ....number..		42	42	52	20	13									
264	Adzes, truck ....do....				2									22		
265	Axes ....do....		340	340	352	69	14							46		
266	Axes, broad ....do....		6	6		3	7									
267	Augers, assorted ....do....				148	17	14							102		
268	Augers, bits ....set..		½	½	9½									9		
269	Augers, bridge ....lot..													1		

270	Axes, hand .... number				5	8										
271	Awls, scratch .... do				1	2										
272	Awls, scribe .... do				1											
273	Blades, hack-saw .... do													4		
274	Braces, carpenter's .... do					2	1									
274½	Bevels, carpenter's .... do					1										
275	Blades, saw-buck .... do				5									7		
276	Chisels .... do		48	48	95	93	75							34		
277	Compasses .... pairs		3	3	11											
278	Clamps, carpenter's .... number					11										
279	Glazier's diamond .... do		1	1	1	1										
280	Gouges, flat				2	1										
281	Gouges, turning					2										
282	Hatchets, broad		6	6	6											
283	Hatchets				15	12										
284	Knives, draw		9	9	9	8								1		
285	Knives, putty		2	2	8											
286	Lines, chalk				71			13								2
287	Level, spirit					1										
288	Machine and bits, boring .... number		1	1	1											
289	Mallets .... do		4	4	6											
290	Planes, moulding .... do		19	19										19		
291	Planes, assorted .... do				13	12										
292	Planes, jack .... do					15										
293	Planes, smooth .... do					10										
294	Planes, jointer .... do					6										
295	Pencils, carpenter's .... do															24
296	Saws, cross-cut .... do		52	52	27	3	5							21		
297	Saws, hand .... do		26	26	77	22	3							4		
298	Saws, whip .... do		5	5		1								5		
299	Saws, compass .... do					2										
300	Screws, bench .... do					6										
301	Saws, hack .... do				2	2										
302	Saws, buck .... do				1	1										
303	Saws, rip .... do					3										
304	Squares, steel .... do				30	15								15		
305	Tools, carpenter's .... sets					5										
306	....															
307	Barrels .... number		2	2												2
308	Bars, claw .... do		28	28	50	39	13									
309	Bars, clamp .... do		2	2	1									11		
310	Bars, timber .... do		10	10	9		1									
311	Bars, tamping .... do		51	51	145	117	6									
312	Bars, pinch .... do		13	13	41	39	12									
313	Bells, engine alarm .... do		2	2												2
314	Bench, draw .... do		1	1	1											
315	Bits, machine, boring .... sets		2	2	2	2										
316	Blocks, assorted .... number		10	10	8	5								27		
317	Blocks and falls .... sets		3	3	3											
318	Blocks, pulley .... number		4	4	4		10									
319	Blower .... do		1	1	1											
320	Boiler, stationary .... do		2	2	2											

Report showing the disposition of United States military railroad property in the military division of the Tennessee, &c.—Continued.

Running number.	Articles.		Captured property on hand May 1, 1865.	Property purchased by the United States on hand May 1, 1865.	Total amount of property on hand May 1, 1865.	Property sold on credit to railroad companies under Executive Orders of August 8 and October 14, 1865.					Property captured and returned to owners.				Sold at public auction for cash.	Transferred to officers.	Lost or expended in public service.
						Memphis and Charleston railroad.	Memphis and Little Rock railroad.	Mobile and Ohio railroad.	Memphis and Ohio railroad.	Mississippi and Tennessee railroad.	Memphis and Little Rock railroad.	Mobile and Ohio railroad.	Memphis and Charleston railroad.	Memphis and Ohio railroad.			
321	Brushes, paint	number		48	48	175	143										
322	Brushes, artist's	do		24	24	34									2		
323	Brushes, sash	do		12	12	12											
324	Brushes, whitewash	do		5	5	11	6										
325	Brushes, striping	do		12	12	54	24										
326	Brushes, camel's hair	do		13	13	37											
327	Brushes, flat wheel	do		3	3	3											
328	Brushes, scrub	do		24	24	54	6										
329	Brushes, varnish	do		10	10	30	8										
330	Brushes, marking	do				1	1										
331	Buckets, water	do		155	155	303	60	18							13		
332	Buckets, paint	do				2	2										
333	Buckets, tallow	do				1											
334	Brier hooks	do		6	6			6									
335	Basins, wash	do				6	6										
336	Blocks, double	do				4	6										
337	Boiler, steam	do				1	1										
338	Boxes, pepper	do					12										
339	Boxes, emery	do				6	6										
340	Buckets, well	do				1	1										
341	Barrels, oil	do				40									13		
342	Blocks and fall, endless chain	do					1										
343	Bits, car	sets					2										
344	Benches, wood	feet					175										
345	Buildings	number					18										
346	Cans, tin	do		4	4	5	5										
347	Cans, oil	do		4	4		15	7									
348	Cans, tallow	do						3									
349	Clamps, timber	do		3	3	1		2									
350	Clamps, bench	do						5									
351	Clamps and axes	do															1
352	Coal hods	do		4	4	4											

353	Cups	do		24	24	12	15										
354	Cups, tin	do		30	30	45											
355	Cups, paint	do				8	8										
356	Coffee mills	do		1	1										7		
357	Crowbars	do		4	4	4											
358	Cricket frames	do		23	23										23		
359	Cupolas	do		2	2										2		
360	Chest, tool	do													1		
361	Chisels, turning	set				1	1										
362	Chucks	number				4	3										
363	Counter shaft	do						1									
364	Crucibles	do				3	6										
365	Castings, iron tools	pounds					2, 297										
366	Coppersmith tools, iron	do					75										
367	Couplings, brass	do						4									
368	Camp kettles	number		93	93	93	86										
369	Checks	lot		1	1										1		
370	Coal grinder	number	1		1								1				
371	Demijohns	do		2	2	2											
372	Dippers, tin	do		2	2	2											
373	Dutch oven	do		1	1	1											
374	Drills, upright	do				1	1										
375	Dusters, painter's	do				6											
376	Drivers, screw	do					4										
377	Doors, round-house	do					4										
378	Edges, straight	do		2	2	2											
379	Engine oilers	do				14	47										
380	Engine scrapers	do					1										
381	Faucets	do		5	5	5											
382	Fitches	do		4	4	4											
383	Flags	do		30	30	11	4	19									
384	Furnace, brass	do	1		1									1			
385	Frogs, chilled	do															5
386	Frogs, plated	do															4
387	Fire irons	do				6									2		
388	Froes, splitting	do					5										
389	Funnels	do						2									
390	Grindstones	do		7	7	2	2	1							6		
391	Gauges, track	do		16	16	16	12										
392	Gauges, wire	do		2	2	3											
393	Gauges, carpenter's	do					4										
394	Glue kettle	do				1	1										
395	Hangers, drop, cast iron	pounds				910	852										
396	Hoes	number		136	136	27									115		
397	Hooks, cant	do		10	10	9		1									
398	Hooks, packing	do						3									
399	Horse power	do					3										
400	Hinges, drop	do					13										
401	Jacks, car	do		10	10	6	2	4									
402	Jacks, hydraulic	do		6	6	6	4										
403	Jacks, lever	do		4	4	4	2										
404	Jacks, screw	do		13	13	15	23	6							6		

Report showing the disposition of United States military railroad property in the military division of the Tennessee, &c.—Continued.

Running number.	Articles.	Captured property on hand May 1, 1865.	Property purchased by the United States on hand May 1, 1865.	Total amount of property on hand May 1, 1865.	Property sold on credit to railroad companies under Executive Orders of August 8 and October 14, 1865.					Property captured and returned to owners.				Sold at public auction for cash.	Transferred to officers.	Lost or expended in public service.
					Memphis and Charleston railroad.	Memphis and Little Rock railroad.	Mobile and Ohio railroad.	Memphis and Ohio railroad.	Mississippi and Tennessee railroad.	Memphis and Little Rock railroad.	Mobile and Ohio railroad.	Memphis and Charleston railroad.	Memphis and Ohio railroad.			
405	Knives and forks .... sets		7	7		8								7		
406	Knives, butcher .... number				12	1										
407	Knives, pallet .... do				2											
408	Lamps, car .... do		34	34	30		3							2		
409	Lamps, carbon oil .... do		7	7										7		
410	Lamps, hand, assorted .... do		85	85	93		4									
411	Lanterns .... do													9		
412	Lights, white .... do				61	41	18							24		
413	Lights, red .... do				19	24	12									
414	Lathes, engine .... do		2	2	2	3										
415	Lathes, hand .... do		1	1	1											
416	Lathes, driving wheel .... do		1	1	1											
417	Lathes, locomotive .... do		1	1											1	
418	Lathes, screw-cutting .... do		1	1	1											
419	Lathes, turning .... do		1	1	3		1									
420	Lathes .... do						1									
421	Lamps, caboose oil .... do													8		1
422	Lamp fillers .... do				3	7										
423	Levers, hand-car .... do		7	7	3											4
424	Levels, machinist's .... do				6	6										
425	Lead ladle .... do						1									
426	Mill, coal-black .... do	1		1								1				
427	Machine, bolt-cutting .... do		1	1	1	1										
428	Machine, boring .... do		6	6										7		
429	Machine, wheel-boring .... do		1	1	1	1										
430	Machine, circular saw .... do						1									
431	Machine, gumming .... do					1										
432	Machine, slotting .... do				1											
433	Measures .... do		3	3	2	3	2									
434	Mauls, spike .... do		141	141	151	54	16							9		
435	Mills, paint .... do				1											
436	Mess pans .... do					66								26		

No.	Article	Unit	1	2	3	4	5	6	7	8	9	10	11	12	13	14	15
437	Nippers, cutting	pairs		2	2	2											
438	Pile-driver, steam	number		1	1					1							
439	Punches, belt	do		6	6	6											
440	Pans, fry	do		2	2		3								2		
441	Pans, dish	do		1	1		6								1		
442	Pans, tin	do													8		
443	Picks	do		184	184	169	33								21		
444	Plates	do		24	24	18	2								4		
445	Plates, tin	do		36	36	55	42										
446	Plyers	pairs		2	2	4											
447	Presses, vertical drill	number		2	2	1	1										
448	Presses, wheel	do	2	1	3		1						1	1			
449	Press, drill, upright	do					1										
450	Pumps, rotary	do		2	2	1	1										
451	Pumps, station	do		5	5	3	2								4		
452	Planes, iron	do				2											
453	Pulleys	do				25											
454	Pumps, McGowan's	do				3	7	2								1	
455	Punches, railroad	do					120	20									
456	Planer, sink	do				1											
457	Planer, compound	do				1											
458	Pincers	do					4										
459	Patterns	lot					1										
460	Rasps, wood	number		72	72	53									19		
461	Riddles, sand	do		7	7	7											
462	Rollers, boiler	set				1	1										
463	Saws, circular	number		8	8	6									6		
464	Saw-mill	do				1											
465	Scales, Howe's army	do		5	5	6	3	1									
466	Scales, counter	do						1							1		
467	Shears, tinner's	do		2	2	3											
468	Shears, bench	do				2		1									
469	Shears, lever	do				1											
470	Shovels	do		269	269	414	306	32							77		
471	Spades	do		68	68		8								71		
472	Signal lights	do		1	1										1		
473	Snips, round	pair		1	1	1											
474	Snips, straight	do		1	1	1											
475	Spoons, table	sets		3	3	5	8										
476	Spoons, tea	do		5	5	6	7										
477	Sets, rivet	number				2											
478	Spatchel knife	do				1	1										
479	Sieves, brass	do				1	2										
480	Shafting	pounds					2,070										
481	Shafting	sections				12											
482	Screws, hand	number				6									6		
483	Stall fork	do					1										
484	Shackle bars	do						1									
485	Solder irons	do					3										
486	Stable	do				1											
487	Turn-table	do				1											
488	Tape lines	do				7	7										

Report showing the disposition of United States military railroad property in the military division of the Tennessee, &c.—Continued.

Running number.	Articles.	Captured property on hand May 1, 1865.	Property purchased by the United States on hand May 1, 1865.	Total amount of property on hand May 1, 1865.	Property sold on credit to railroad companies under Executive Orders of August 8 and October 14, 1865.					Property captured and returned to owners.				Sold at public auction for cash.	Transferred to officers.	Lost or expended in public service.
					Memphis and Charleston railroad.	Memphis and Little Rock railroad.	Mobile and Ohio railroad.	Memphis and Ohio railroad.	Mississippi and Tennessee railroad.	Memphis and Little Rock railroad.	Mobile and Ohio railroad.	Memphis and Charleston railroad.	Memphis and Ohio railroad.			
489	Tents, common .... number													8		
490	Tent poles, common .... do													8		
491	Tools, coppersmith .... set		1	1	1											
492	Tools, grainer's .... do		1	1	1											
493	Tools, sash .... dozen		1 1-12	1 1-12	1 1-12											
494	Tools, machinist's iron .... pounds					2, 131										
495	Tools, machinist's steel .... do					1, 115										
496	Trucks, baggage .... number					2										
497	Tank valves .... do				4	2										
498	Tallow, tin, pots .... do					9										
499	Taps and dies .... pounds					86										
500	Trucks, timber .... number													4		
501	Tuel irons .... do				6									2		
502	Water spouts and valves .... do		4	4	4											
503	Wheelbarrows .... do		6	6	29	12								9		
504	Wrenches .... do		3	3	28		31									
505	Wrenches, bridge .... do		40	40	15		5							27		
506	Wrenches, iron .... do		36	36	25		24									
507	Wrenches, monkey .... do		32	32	120	48	5							37		
508	Water tanks .... do				4	6										
509	Wheel press .... do														1	
510	Shears, tummer .... do				1											
511	....															
512	Acid, muriatic .... pounds		21	21	6											15
513	Acid, nitric .... do		25	25	9										1	15
514	Acid, sulphuric .... do		40	40	22											18
515	Axe handles .... number		61	61		36	9									97
516	Adze handles .... do		15	15												39
517	Axe handles, broad .... do		30	30												30
518	Alcohol .... gallons		50	50	20	5										30
519	Antimony .... pounds		264	264	169	70										165
520	Axles, car .... number	72	8	80	92	1	72					72				11

521	Axles, driving ....do		6	6	3											3
522	Axles, locomotive ....do		2	2		1										1
523	Axles, tender ....do		14	14	4											10
524	Axles, truck ....do				10	17										8
525	Asphaltum ....gallons		40	40	6	37										5
526	Babbit metal ....pounds		9	9	10	182										83
527	Balances, steam ....number		1	1		15										11
528	Belting ....feet		804	804	1, 017											
529	Benzine ....gallons		194	194	130									32		116
530	Belting, rubber ....feet		6	6		102										112
531	Belting, leather ....do		2, 124	2, 124	2, 056	571	130									264
532	Bonnets, smokestack ....number		3	3	3											
533	Borax ....pounds		118	118	73½											59½
534	Boxes, car ....number		3	3												3
535	Boxes ....do		1	1												1
536	Brads ....papers		348	348	380	42	23									114
537	Brads ....pounds		300	300	168	7	100									34
538	Brass, roll ....do		161	161	259	43										263
539	Brass, sheet ....do		106	106	73	94										247
540	Brass ....do														197½	
541	Blue black ....tubes		8	8												8
542	Blue, new ....do		3	3												3
543	Bunting, red ....yards		40½	40½	15½	10										20
544	Boxes, driving ....number		4	4	4											4
545	Boxes, packing ....do													5		
546	Branch pipe, copper ....pounds													14		
547	Bib cocks, brass ....number				7	6										
548	Bronze, gold ....papers				2											4
549	Brake beams and blocks ....number						9									
550	Bolts, carriage ....pounds					137										
551	Brake shoes ....do						4									
552	Boiler bands ....number													4		
553	Bolt heads ....pounds													230		
554	Bolts, scrap ....do													340		
555	Candles ....do		163	163												163
556	Castings, bridge ....tons		1	1												1
557	Castings, car ....pounds		25, 000	25, 000	14, 000	12, 508										9, 616
558	Castings, engine ....do		2, 500	2, 500	2, 000	3, 595	175									1, 104⅓
559	Castings, brass ....do					256	175									
560	Castings, brass gauge cocks ....do						19									
561	Chairs, railroad ....do		27	27		5, 440	800									1, 927
562	Chalk, white ....do		48	48		7	20									53
563	Chalk, red ....do		5	5	1											4
564	Chrome yellow ....do		71	71	202	18										37
565	Chrome green ....do		61	61	68	31	8									36
566	Chrome yellow ....tubes		15	15											3	12
567	Chrome green ....do		13	13											2	11
568	Chimneys, head light ....number		12	12	1	41	19									11
569	Chrome orange ....tubes		7	7												7
570	Crimson lake ....do		7	7												7
571	Copper, bar ....pounds		178	178	98										4	76
572	Copper, sheet ....do		2, 596	2, 596	2, 387	151½	10								100	310

Report showing the disposition of United States military railroad property in the military division of the Tennessee, &c.—Continued.

Running number.	Articles.	Captured property on hand May 1, 1865.	Property purchased by the United States on hand May 1, 1865.	Total amount of property on hand May 1, 1865.	Property sold on credit to railroad companies under Executive Orders of August 8 and October 14, 1865.					Property captured and returned to owners.				Sold at public auction for cash.	Transferred to officers.	Lost or expended in public service.
					Memphis and Charleston railroad.	Memphis and Little Rock railroad.	Mobile and Ohio railroad.	Memphis and Ohio railroad.	Mississippi and Tennessee railroad.	Memphis and Little Rock railroad.	Mobile and Ohio railroad.	Memphis and Charleston railroad.	Memphis and Ohio railroad.			
573	Copper, ingot .... pounds	....	2, 815	2, 815	1, 601	1, 300	....	....	....	....	....	....	....	....	....	3, 864
574	Copper, tubing .... do	....	384	384	1, 126	1, 126	....	....	....	....	....	....	....	....	....	53
575	Copper, bolt .... do	....	....	....	....	19½	....	....	....	....	....	....	....	....	....	13¼
576	Copper pipe .... feet	....	....	....	....	14	....	....	....	....	....	....	....	....	....	....
577	Cord, bell .... pounds	....	70	70	48	....	....	....	....	....	....	....	....	....	....	81
578	Couplings, gas pipe .... number	....	5	5	....	....	4	....	....	....	....	....	....	....	....	1
579	Car wheels .... do	....	274	274	134	195	2	....	....	....	....	....	....	....	....	41
580	Car wheels and axles .... do	134	91	225	71	....	7	....	....	....	....	43	91	80	....	9
581	Car window catches .... do	....	....	....	....	....	19	....	....	....	....	....	....	....	....	....
582	Car-spring sockets .... pounds	....	....	....	....	....	225	....	....	....	....	....	....	....	....	....
583	Car-seat braces .... lot	....	....	....	....	....	....	....	....	....	....	....	....	1	....	....
584	Crossheads .... number	....	2	2	....	....	....	....	....	....	....	....	....	....	....	2
585	Colors, assorted .... lot	....	2	2	....	....	....	....	....	....	....	....	....	....	....	2
586	Chain brake .... pounds	....	....	....	....	41	15	....	....	....	....	....	....	....	....	....
587	Crucibles .... number	....	12	12	3	6	....	....	....	....	....	....	....	....	....	3
588	Cylinder .... do	....	1	1	....	....	....	....	....	....	....	....	....	....	....	1
589	Canvas .... yards	....	....	....	....	....	....	....	....	....	....	....	....	....	4⅜	113⅝
590	Chains, log .... number	....	....	....	....	1	....	....	....	....	....	....	....	....	....	....
591	Cross-ties .... do	....	....	....	2, 000	5, 940	....	....	....	....	....	....	....	....	....	21, 776
592	Concentrated lye .... boxes	....	....	....	....	....	....	....	....	....	....	....	....	....	....	12
593	Cast steel, forged .... pounds	....	....	....	....	31	....	....	....	....	....	....	....	....	....	....
594	Drop block .... do	....	64	64	69	28	....	....	....	....	....	....	....	....	....	13
595	Driving wheels and axles .... set	....	1	1	....	....	....	....	....	....	....	....	....	....	1	1
596	Doors, box car .... number	....	....	....	....	5	....	....	....	....	....	....	....	....	....	....
597	Elbows, gas pipe, assorted .... do	....	19	19	7	....	....	....	....	....	....	....	....	....	....	12
598	Emery cloth .... reams	....	....	....	....	....	1	....	....	....	....	....	....	....	....	¼
599	Emery .... pounds	....	111	111	194	47	30	....	....	....	....	....	....	....	....	141
600	Frames, door .... number	....	5	5	....	....	....	....	....	....	....	....	....	....	....	5
601	Flues, boiler .... feet	....	1, 178⅔	1, 178⅔	....	....	....	....	....	....	....	....	....	1, 178⅔	....	....
602	Flues, copper .... do	....	1, 644	1, 644	1, 484	390	....	....	....	....	....	....	....	....	....	160
603	Feed pipes, copper .... number	....	1	1	....	....	....	....	....	....	....	....	....	....	....	1
604	Flues, sheet .... do	....	....	....	....	....	....	....	....	....	....	....	....	....	....	1

605	Felting, hair	feet					37										271
606	Fire clay	loads															3
607	Flannel, cotton	yards				8	10										25
608	Frames, car door	number						14									
609	Frogs	do	4		4		6							4			
610	Gas pipe	feet		800	800	614	310	38									359½
611	Gas pipe	pieces		8	8												8
612	Glasses, head-light	number		11	11	7											4
613	Gold leaf	books		37	37	28											9
614	Gauges, steam	number		5	5	4	3	1							12		
615	Gum shellac	pounds		29	29		23	3									24
616	Gongs, locomotive	number		2	2		4								4		2
617	Globe valves	do				6	5										1
618	Glazier's points	papers															7
619	Hammer handles, sledge	number		2	2		2										2
620	Handles, file	do				17	68										79
621	Handles, auger	do					6								125		
622	Handles, adze	do					36	9									
623	Hooks, screw	dozen		½	½												½
624	Hose, rubber	feet		1,329	1,329	1,305½											123½
625	Hose, gum and rubber	pounds													266		
626	Hose, gum	feet		1,147	1,147	472	539½	298									122
627	Hose, rubber	pounds															
628	Head lights	number		3	3	8	10										3
629	Iron, assorted	pounds		161,614	161,614	76,620	60,000	11,200							107,300	164	55,330
620	Iron, boiler	do		5,400	5,400	1,275	1,820								4,213	298	3,214
631	Iron, hoop	do		230	230	1,410									97		253
632	Iron, pig	do		47,308	47,308	34,680									186	81	13,953
633	Iron, Russia	do		773	773	324	265										449
634	Iron, sheet	do		443	443	3,921	19,597	60								25	4,572
635	Iron, scrap	do	760,000	649,880	1,409,880		40,000						760,000		608,800		1,080
636	Iron, tank	do		18,010	18,010	9,325	14,005	587							3,136		6,142
637	Iron, wrought	do														40,000	
638	Iron, railroad	bars															370
639	Iron, angle	pounds					1,500										
640	Iron, truck frame	do					1,771										
641	Iron, forge	do					784										
642	Iron, scrap, forged	do					808										
643	Iron, mandrel	do					206										
644	India red	do		284	284	251	45										76½
645	India red	tubes		1	1												1
646	Jet black	do		5	5												5
647	Lines, sea-grass	number		6	6												6
648	Lampblack	pounds		37	37	8	14										39
649	Lamp-burners	number		36	36	36											
650	Lead, pig	pounds		5,170	5,170		145	23							5,030		385
651	Lead, red	do		390	390	316	175										174
652	Lead, white	do		1,071	1,071	553	231									2	984
653	Line, shafting	feet		150	150	150											
654	Lead pipe	pounds				823											1,701
655	Lead, black	do					8										3½
656	Leather, whang	sides				9	7										10

Report showing the disposition of United States military railroad property in the military division of the Tennessee, &c.—Continued.

Running number.	Articles.	Captured property on hand May 1, 1865.	Property purchased by the United States on hand May 1, 1865.	Total amount of property on hand May 1, 1865.	Property sold on credit to railroad companies under Executive Orders of August 8 and October 14, 1865.					Property captured and returned to owners.				Sold at public auction for cash.	Transferred to officers.	Lost or expended in public service.
					Memphis and Charleston railroad.	Memphis and Little Rock railroad.	Mobile and Ohio railroad.	Memphis and Ohio railroad.	Mississippi and Tennessee railroad.	Memphis and Little Rock railroad.	Mobile and Ohio railroad.	Memphis and Charleston railroad.	Memphis and Ohio railroad.			
657	Leather, sole ....pounds..					50	13									123
658	Lafarge ....do...					45										
659	Lime ....barrels..					5										20
660	Matches ....gross...		2½	2½												4½
661	Maul handles, spike ....number..		15	15												15
662	Nails, cut........pounds..		8, 100	8, 100	3, 500	853	980									10, 297
663	Nails, finishing........do...				42	58										86
664	Nails, wrought........do...					242										300
665	Nails, clinch........do...				100											
666	Nuts ....do...		2, 335	2, 335	3, 536	2, 708	1, 739									3, 223
667	Naples yellow ....tubes..		8	8												8
668	Nipples ....number..		2	2												2
669	Ochre ....tubes..		3	3												3
670	Ochre, Roman........do...		10	10												10
671	Ochre, yellow........pounds..		320	320	277										1	142
672	Oil, coal........gallons..		761	761	810	101½	5									237¼
673	Oil, lard........do...		812	812	1, 593	20	130									2, 248
674	Oil, linseed........do...		50	50	15	74½	2									183½
675	Oxalic acid ....pounds..		7	7												27
676	Oil, head-light........gallons..				140	145										433½
677	Packing gum ....pounds..		232	232	32	391	15							29		179½
678	Pencils, sable hair........number..		4	4	4											
679	Pencils, striping........do...		48	48	48											
680	Pick-handles ....do...		88	88	39	37										164
681	Potash ....pounds..		12	12		3½										17
682	Prussian blue ....do...		32	32	10	2	6									17
683	Pumice-stone........do...		5	5		7										5
684	Purple lake ....do...		9	9												9
685	Pins, crank ....set ...		1	1		1										
686	Packing, hemp ....pounds..				50									84		
687	Pipe, brass........feet..				69											133½
688	Paper, emery........quires..															10

689	Paint, mineral .... pounds					184	20									200
690	Pins, wrist .... number					160										
691	Rivets .... papers		3	3												3
692	Rivets .... number		5,369	5,369	28,500	2,907	174									9,910
693	Rivets, copper .... pounds		37	37	30											70
694	Rivets and burrs .... do		7	7												7
695	Rope .... do		3,355¼	3,355¼	1,233	1,341¼	180							1,497		1,319
696	Rose pink .... do		35	35	15	3½										23
697	Rags .... do															536
698	Rosin .... do					285										
699	Smokestacks .... number		3	3	3	1									1	3
700	Spikes, boat .... pounds		3,394	3,394	1,736											1,658
701	Spikes, cut .... do		130	130												130
702	Spikes, railroad .... do		10,426	10,426	9,000	15,300	900								672	25,064
703	Spelter .... do		37	37	18	31½										34
704	Steel .... do		2,194	2,194										1,927		267
705	Steel, cast .... do		764	764	2,434	5,297	1,385							4,180		2,884
706	Steel springs .... do					1,380										
707	Springs, spiral .... number					48										
708	Springs, volute .... pounds					677										
709	Sulphur .... do						50									
710	Springs, rubber .... do		184	184	255	105	177									148
711	Screws, lag .... do		628	628	112		375									141
712	Screws, wood .... number		15,284	15,284			9,072									15,284
713	Steam gauge-cocks .... do		1	1	1											
714	Straps, eccentric .... do		2	2												2
715	Sponge .... pounds		47	47	43											9
716	Sienna, raw .... tubes		6	6												6
717	Sienna, burnt .... pounds		4	4												4
718	Straps and rods, eccentric .... sets		1	1												1
719	Saw-handles, cross-cut .... number		8	8												8
720	Switch ropes .... do				3	2										
721	Soap .... pounds															364
722	Skins, chamois .... number															6
723	Springs, bolster .... do				68	12										4
724	Tacks .... papers		3,648	3,648	3,335	217	29									269
725	Timber .... feet				4,478	4,992	186									13,209
726	Tallow .... pounds		9,983	9,983	6,224	750	500									3,637
727	Tin .... do		219	219	98		10									111
728	Tin, plate .... boxes		2¼	2¼		7										1⅓
729	Tin, block .... pounds				289½		10									350½
730	Tire, locomotive .... do		3,267	3,267											3,267	
731	Tire, locomotive .... number				12											
732	Turpentine .... gallons		23	23	19¼	6	1½								9	47
733	Thread, cutting .... lot		1	1												1
734	Tire, flanged .... pounds														4,045	
735	Tripoli .... papers															48
736	Twine, hemp .... pounds				1½											
737	Tube, colors assorted .... dozen				15	3¼										6¼
738	Umber, burnt .... pounds		9	9	4	5										5
739	Umber, raw .... do		20	20	20											
740	Umber, burnt .... tubes		9	9												9

Report showing the disposition of United States military railroad property in the military division of the Tennessee, &c.—Continued.

Running number.	Articles.	Captured property on hand May 1, 1865.	Property purchased by the United States on hand May 1, 1865.	Total amount of property on hand May 1, 1865.	Property sold on credit to railroad companies under Executive Orders of August 8 and October 14, 1865.					Property captured and returned to owners.				Sold at public auction for cash.	Transferred to officers.	Lost or expended in public service.
					Memphis and Charleston railroad.	Memphis and Little Rock railroad.	Mobile and Ohio railroad.	Memphis and Ohio railroad.	Mississippi and Tennessee railroad.	Memphis and Little Rock railroad.	Mobile and Ohio railroad.	Memphis and Charleston railroad.	Memphis and Ohio railroad.			
741	Umber, raw ....tubes		4	4												4
742	Ultra-marine blue ....pounds		23	23	12	2										11
743	Valves, check ....number		6	6												6
744	Varnish ....gallons		94	94	71		2									21
745	Varnish, Japan ....do				33	14								31		24
746	Varnish, coach ....do				68	14										33½
747	Vermillion ....pounds		147	147	125	24										46
748	Vermillion ....tubes		5	5												5
749	Van Dyke brown ....do		9	9												9
750	Venetian red ....do		9	9												9
751	Vitriol ....pounds		158	158	145											13
752	Washers, assorted ....number		1,461	1,461		259	1,176								1	1,157½
753	Whistles, locomotive ....do		2	2		2										1
754	Wire ....pounds		332½	332½	216	42								8		58½
755	Wire, brass ....do		117	117	123	15	2½									26
756	Wire, copper ....do		95	95	79	11										30¼
757	Wire, locomotive bonnet ....square feet					180										
758	Wheels, truck ....number		53	53	20	14	16									17
759	Whiting ....pounds				120	30										34
760	Waste ....do				487	90	120									1,536
761	Wool ....do					389										153
762	Wick, lamp ....do															4
763	Yarn, packing ....do		636	636	326	114	150									164
764	Zinc ....do		56	56	257											
765	Zinc, sheet ....do		282½	282½	253½											29
766	Zinc, French ....do		188	188	188											
767	Zinc, slab ....do		65½	65½		419										292½

[Enclosure No. 2.]

Report showing the disposition of United States military railroad property in the military division of the Tennessee for which Captain W. R. Hopkins, A. Q. M., is responsible.

[The property sold under the Executive Orders of August 8 and October 14, 1865, was appraised by a board convened by Major General G. H. Thomas, commanding military division of the Tennessee; copy of order herewith.

The property sold to the Southwestern Iron Company was a few items for which they were charged by the United States in excess of the price paid by them for the rolling mill at Chattanooga, as per public advertisement. The prices were fixed by the board convened by Major General G. H. Thomas, commanding military division of the Tennessee, to assess the value of property sold to railroads.

The property sold at auction was in accordance with the authority of the Secretary of War, communicated through the Quartermaster General.

The captured property was returned to the owner by instructions received from Major General G. H. Thomas, commanding military division of the Tennessee.]

Running number.	Articles.	Captured property on hand May 1, 1865.	Property purchased by the United States on hand May 1, 1865.	Total amount of property on hand May 1, 1865.	Property sold on credit to railroad companies under the Executive Orders of August 8 and October 14, 1865.				Captured property returned to owners.		Sold to the Southwestern Iron Company.	Sold at public auction for cash.	Lost or expended in public service.	Transferred to officers.
					Western and Atlantic Railroad Company.	East Tennessee and Virginia Railroad Company.	East Tennessee and Georgia Railroad Company.	Wills Valley Railroad Company.	Western and Atlantic Railroad Company.	East Tennessee and Virginia Railroad Company.				
1	Ambulances .... number	....	1	1	....	....	....	....	....	....	....	....	....	1
2	Anvils .... do	....	59	59	2	6	2	2	....	....	4	....	....	105
3	Axes .... do	....	2, 455	2, 455	64	95	146	24	....	....	25	....	773	3, 944
4	Axes, broad .... do	....	255	255	48	3	2	6	....	....	....	....	12	526
5	Axes, hand .... do	....	3	3	....	....	4	....	....	....	....	....	30	221
6	Adzes .... do	....	102	102	....	....	32	....	....	....	....	....	263	228
7	Adzes, railroad .... do	....	598	598	24	3	59	12	....	....	2	....	....	597
8	Augers .... do	....	1, 231	1, 231	1	25	31	....	....	....	9	....	93	1, 462
9	Awls, brad .... do	....	99	99	....	9	31	....	....	....	....	....	262	54
10	Awls, scratch .... do	....	350	350	....	....	7	....	....	....	12	....	110	554
11	Awls, saddlers' .... do	....	30	30	....	....	....	....	....	....	....	....	30	....
12	Alcohol .... gallons	....	19	19	½	8	....	....	....	....	....	....	243	5
13	Acid, sulphuric .... pounds	....	16	16	....	....	....	....	....	....	....	....	16	166
14	Acid, oxalic .... do	....	....	....	....	....	....	....	....	....	....	....	12	5
15	Acid, muriatic .... do	....	6	6	....	....	....	....	....	....	....	....	6	11
16	Alum .... do	....	....	....	....	....	....	....	....	....	....	....	50	96
17	Axes, ship .... number	....	....	....	....	....	....	....	....	....	....	....	....	17

Report showing the disposition of United States military railroad property in the military division of the Tennessee, &c.—Continued.

Running number.	Articles.	Captured property on hand May 1, 1865.	Property purchased by the United States on hand May 1, 1865.	Total amount of property on hand May 1, 1865.	Property sold on credit to railroad companies under the Executive Orders of August 8 and October 14, 1865.				Captured property returned to owners.		Sold to the Southwestern Iron Company.	Sold at public auction for cash.	Lost or expended in public service.	Transferred to officers.
					Western and Atlantic Railroad Company.	East Tennessee and Virginia Railroad Company.	East Tennessee and Georgia Railroad Company.	Wills Valley Railroad Company.	Western and Atlantic Railroad Company.	East Tennessee and Virginia Railroad Company.				
18	Axles, tender .... number						7						12	
19	Augers, machine boring .... do													10
20	Axles, engine truck .... do												4	
21	Books, blank, 2-quire .... do					3	18	6						106
22	Books, blank, 3-quire .... do		41	41		2	18						18	30
23	Books, blank, 4-quire .... do		27	27		3	15						30	4
24	Books, blank, 12-quire .... do		1	1									1	
25	Books, memorandum .... do		125	125	7	3	36	13					122	
26	Books, time .... do		160	160		7	24	6					349	188
27	Blanks, quartermasters' .... quires		696 1-12	696 1-12									1,921	200
28	Bands, rubber .... number		144	144									144	
29	Baskets, scrap .... do		2	2										3
30	Boxes, post office .... do		26	26		1							7	18
31	Bells, call .... do		1	1										1
32	Brushes, copy .... do		7	7		2	6	1			3		3	16
33	Blankets, saddle .... do		10	10									12	2
34	Books, copy .... do				2		6	2					24	7
35	Bars, engine coupling .... do													13
36	Bolts, king .... do		20	20									20	19
37	Bows, ox yoke .... do		275	275										852
38	Bows, wagon .... do		572	572										651
39	Boxes, feed .... do		60	60									64	35
40	Bridles, wagon .... do		30	30									12	42
41	Bridles, riding .... do		5	5									10	3
42	Brushes, horse .... do		271	271							34		30	274
43	Buckets, water .... do		1,962	1,962	13	70	105	12			103		994	991
44	Buckets, tender .... do		12	12									4	8
45	Bellows, blacksmith's .... do		39	39	2	6	3	4			2			76
46	Bellows, hand .... do		18	18									2	25
47	Bevels .... do		95	95			12				1		14	112
48	Bevels, T .... do												31	8
49	Bits, car .... sets		37	37		13	5	1			1		37	53

50	Bits, auger ....number						3	2						150
51	Braces and bits ....sets		61	61			1				3		49	9
52	Braces, iron ....number		72	72		12	3	2			2		10	117
53	Bars ....do		722	722							14		708	
54	Bars, timber ....do		70	70									60	14
55	Bars, claw ....do		256	256	116	36	54	10			3		40	480
56	Books, requisition ....do												5	
57	Books, blank, 6-quire ....do												4	
58	Bars, lining ....do		105	105			19						22	172
59	Bars, tamping ....do		409	499		104	159				6		16	625
60	Bars, pinch ....do		227	227	50	56	74	12					36	395
61	Basins, wash ....do		873	873	1	3	10	1			66		128	789
62	Bits, Mullen Japan ....do												24	
63	Bells, signal gong ....do		6	6									6	
64	Bells, engine alarm ....do		10	10			6	3			2		10	16
65	Balances, spring ....do		1	1										23
66	Balances, spring and dish ....do		20	20		3					1		11	25
67	Blocks, swaged chittled ....do		12	12									10	2
68	Blocks, double tackle ....do		24	24	1		7	4			6			18
69	Blocks, iron pulley ....do		9	9			2	1					3	3
70	Blocks, snatch ....do		67	67			3				2		17	70
71	Blocks, pillow ....do		9	9							3		6	
72	Blocks, rigging ....do		34										34	
73	Blocks, triple ....do		23	23	1	5		2			2		14	6
74	Blocks, tackle ....do		74	74			5						6	183
75	Blower & demple, No. 39, & 2 pulleys ....do		1	1							1			
76	Boilers, steam ....do		1											1
77	Boilers, coffee ....do		47	47										86
78	Boxes, emery ....do		253	253			1				2		28	243
79	Benches, carpenters' ....do													2
80	Boxes, brass, for rollers ....do		8	8									8	
81	Boxes, pepper ....do		283	283		1	2				20		31	468
82	Boxes, grindstone ....do		1	1									1	
83	Boxes, twine ....do		1	1										1
84	Boxes, machinery ....do		1	1										1
85	Boxes, cast ....do		2	2							2		2	
86	Boxes, blast ....do		6	6							6			
87	Bolts for rollers ....do		6	6									6	
88	Bolts for pillows ....do		48	48							6		48	
89	Bolts for curving plates ....do		57	57							57			
90	Borers, tap ....do		4											4
91	Binders, wrought ....do		458	458							458			
92	Brasses for stands ....do		4	4							4			
93	Brushes, bench ....do		10											10
94	Brooms, corn ....do		425	425	12	28	9				115		344	722
95	Brooms, splint ....do		48	48	8								12	35
96	Brushes, scrub ....do		110	110			2				5		81	49
97	Brushes, C. H ....do		22	22									55	
98	Brushes, counter ....do		22	22		1							21	
99	Brushes, marking ....do		12	12		4							15	
100	Boxes, salt ....do										10		52	2
101	Belting, gum ....feet												653	2

Report showing the disposition of United States military railroad property in the military division of the Tennessee, &c.—Continued.

Running number.	Articles.	Captured property on hand May 1, 1865.	Property purchased by the United States on hand May 1, 1865.	Total amount of property on hand May 1, 1865.	Property sold on credit to railroad companies under the Executive Orders of August 8 and October 14, 1865.				Captured property returned to owners.		Sold to the Southwestern Iron Company.	Sold at public auction for cash.	Lost or expended in public service.	Transferred to officers.
					Western and Atlantic Railroad Company.	East Tennessee and Virginia Railroad Company.	East Tennessee and Georgia Railroad Company.	Wills Valley Railroad Company.	Western and Atlantic Railroad Company.	East Tennessee and Virginia Railroad Company.				
102	Brushes, paint ... number		188	188	53	8	48				27		22	213
103	Brushes, striping ... do		12	12										15
104	Brushes, varnish ... do		79	79		9					3		82	
105	Brushes, W. W ... do		143	143			6				12		33	105
106	Burners, C. O ... do		25	25		2					5		22	
107	Buggies, timber ... do		4	4				2			4		1	19
108	Buggies, iron ... do		8	8							4		4	
109	Bars, grate ... pounds		3, 258	3, 258							3, 258			
110	Belting, leather ... feet		2, 112	2, 112	1, 549	396½		949					4, 943	3, 633
111	Bolts, carriage ... number		26	26		230	600						2, 368	10, 900
112	Bolts and washers ... do		8	8							8			
113	Bolts, wrought stud ... do		6	6							6			
114	Borax ... pounds		37	37	10	20	30						132	
115	Brads, assorted ... papers		175	175									277	27
116	Butts, cast ... pairs		112	112			48						1, 099	
117	Butts, brass ... do		84	84		25	253						918	564
118	Bunting, red ... yards		107	107	76½	40½	64½	10					608	54
119	Bricks, fire ... number		2, 011	2, 011									62, 664	
120	Brass, sheet ... pounds		38	38		22	1, 770		11				710	2
121	Burlaps ... yards		5	5		50							5	
122	Bolts, brass barrel ... number												32	4
123	Benches, work ... do													22
124	Burs, copper ... pounds		5	5			1						51	1
125	Books, day ... number												4	
126	Books, discharge ... do												7	2
127	Blue, Prussia ... pounds				25	6	3						16	4
128	Blue, ultramarine ... do				18¾	29							31	4
129	Black, India ... do					17¾	24						17	49
130	Butts, wrought ... pairs					89							1, 086	6
131	Beams, scale ... number												4	
132	Brushes, sash tool ... do												7	
133	Bolts, log ... do												375	

134	Barn and ice-house ..... do											1		
135	Buildings, frame ..... do						4					5		
136	Bolts, hexagon ..... do													75
137	Bolts, tank hook ..... do													110
138	Bolts, bridge ..... pounds											20, 264		3
139	Braces, jointer ..... number													5
140	Boats, row ..... do													2
141	Bars, wrench ..... do													11
142	Bars, hand, steel ..... do													1
143	Boilers, iron wash ..... do													7
144	Boilers, wash ..... do													118
145	Brooms, scrub ..... do													2
146	Brushes, dusting ..... do													7
147	Buckets, fire ..... do													1
148	Boxes, packing ..... do													25
149	Beds, coal, 200 by 41 feet ..... do										1			
150	Bridge, McCallum truss ..... do										1			
151	Buildings, privy ..... do										1			
152	Building, 14 by 19 ..... do										1			
153	Building, office ..... do										1			
154	Boiler-house ..... do										1			
155	Buildings, rolling-mill ..... do										1			
156	Block and pillow, iron chain ..... do										1			
157	Bolts ..... do										48			
158	Buggies, cable ..... do										1			
159	Bells, locomotive ..... do										1			
160	Boxes, brass ..... do										8			
161	Braces and bits, iron ..... do						2							
162	Brass, old ..... pounds												1, 370	80
163	Brakes, finished ..... number						42							
164	Beams and head brake ..... do						95							
165	Bars, draw ..... do						245							
166	Books, oil and tallow ..... do						6							
167	Bars, raising ..... do						6				1		49	
168	Bits, copper hatchet ..... do							2						
169	Brakes, car ..... do					15								
170	Benzine ..... gallons					1½								
171	Buts, iron ..... number						42							
172	Braces, ratchet ..... do				2									
173	Boards, bulletin ..... do				2									4
174	Boxes, trackman's tool ..... do				18									57
175	Brasses, car ..... pounds				2, 569									
176	Boilers, 40 by 42 feet in diameter ..... number										6			
177	Boxes, tin ..... do													11
178	Bits, brace ..... do													305
179	Belting, rubber ..... feet				22			100						1, 791
180	Bits, rose ..... number													25
181	Braces, wood ..... do													11
182	Bricks, fire, half ..... do												198	
183	Bolts, door ..... do												4	28
184	Boxes, glass ..... do												8	
185	Boilers, tin ..... do												2	

Report showing the disposition of United States military railroad property in the military division of the Tennessee, &c.—Continued.

Running number.	Articles.	Captured property on hand May 1, 1865.	Property purchased by the United States on hand May 1, 1865.	Total amount of property on hand May 1, 1865.	Property sold on credit to railroad companies under the Executive Orders of August 8 and October 14, 1865.				Captured property returned to owners.		Sold to the Southwestern Iron Company.	Sold at public auction for cash.	Lost or expended in public service.	Transferred to officers.
					Western and Atlantic Railroad Company.	East Tennessee and Virginia Railroad Company.	East Tennessee and Georgia Railroad Company.	Wills Valley Railroad Company.	Western and Atlantic Railroad Company.	East Tennessee and Virginia Railroad Company.				
186	Balances, locomotive spring .... number					4	6	24			20		8	28
187	Barges .... do													1
188	Buildings and sheds .... do											2		
189	Brass, roll .... pounds												13	
190	Brick, soap .... number												2,000	
191	Brick, split .... do												3,000	
192	Books, ration .... do												5	2
193	Bars, crow .... do													75
194	Blocks, single .... do				1		1	2			1			2
195	Boilers, iron .... do													2
196	Boilers, tin .... do						1						3	10
197	Brown, Spanish .... pounds						30	24					41	42
198	Bronze, gold .... papers												6	
199	Brown, Van Dyke .... pounds					19	24						20	50
200	Brick .... number											2,000	220,923	
201	Brick, bull-head .... do												500	
202	Brick, key .... do												1,000	
203	Brass, scrap .... pounds													73
204	Buckets, tin water .... number						1							2
205	Bits, panel plough .... do													21
206	Black drop .... pounds						19							34
207	Boxes, tool machine .... number					20					1			
208	Brakes, head .... do						144							
209	Brasses, truck .... do				12		10							
210	Bowls, whistle .... do						2							
211	Bolts, unfinished .... do						700							
212	Boards, poplar .... feet						4,000							
213	Corn .... pounds		39,692	39,692							11,000		617,454	48,766
214	Calenders .... number		22	22			4				1		8	10
215	Cases, tin drawer .... do		12	12										15
216	Clips, letter .... do		30	30	2								19	9
217	Clips, board .... do		3	3										12

218	Clips, brass	do		9	9									9	
219	Cutters, paper	do		54	54							5		25	28
220	Chairs, office	do		139	139		4					12		27	110
221	Clocks, office	do		53	53		1					8		23	21
222	Cups and sponges	do		3	3									3	
223	Cups, water	do		1	1										1
224	Cars, box	do	16		16					16					
225	Cars, dump	do	7		7					7					
226	Coal	bushels					1,914					26,604	100	134,014	
227	Coke	do												5,535	
228	Cars, flat	number	15		15					15					
229	Cars, passenger	do	4		4					4					
230	Cars, truck	do				4	16	19	2						21
231	Carts	do		29	29									13	16
232	Cards, horse	do		1	1									1	
233	Chains, bearing	do		72	72									81	24
234	Chains, breast	do		44	44									30	80
235	Chains, fifth	do		181	181									153	61
236	Chains, halter	do		642	642									627	158
237	Chains, spreader	do		38	38									38	
238	Chains, stretcher	do		80	80									13	67
239	Collars, horse	do		14	14									12	6
240	Collars, mule	do		6	6										6
241	Combs, curry	do		142	142							19		23	681
242	Covers, wagon	do		110	110										122
243	Covers, pack-saddle	do		6	6									6	
244	Chisels, cold	do		579	579			52						39	1,102
245	Chisels, split	do		1	1									1	
246	Crucibles, black lead	do		32	32		1							23	10
247	Coal	tons					9							5	35
248	Chisels, assorted	number		272	227							1		271	
249	Chisels, framing	do		891	891		7	33				7		12	1,382
250	Compasses	do		79	79			12						28	79
251	Chisels, firmer	do		4	4			6				2		1	299
252	Compasses, wing	do		24	24							3		7	14
253	Chisels, chip	do		3	3										315
254	Cans, assorted	do		216	216		2					35		116	788
255	Cans, half-gallon	do		46	46									46	
256	Cans, one-gallon	do		292	292	3	26	42				3		230	2
257	Cans, two-gallon	do		335	335	6	14	21	6			6		164	230
258	Cans, five-gallon	do		11	11									20	1
259	Cans, ten-gallon	do		17	17		1	2				2		9	18
260	Cans, fifty-gallon	do		4	4			6	1						5
261	Cans, tallow	do		120	120	9		5							190
262	Candlesticks	do		225	225							37		221	283
263	Cases, needle	do		1	1									1	
264	Cellars, oil	do		56	56									56	
265	Chains, log	do		168	168									4	275
266	Chisels, track	do		100	100										100
267	Collars, fast	do		5	5									5	
268	Cocks, stop	do										11	9	10	28
269	Castings, brass	pounds					1,253	309							490

Report showing the disposition of United States military railroad property in the military division of the Tennessee, &c.—Continued.

Running number.	Articles.	Captured property on hand May 1, 1865.	Property purchased by the United States on hand May 1, 1865.	Total amount of property on hand May 1, 1865.	Property sold on credit to railroad companies under the Executive Orders of August 8 and October 14, 1865.				Captured property returned to owners.		Sold to the Southwestern Iron Company.	Sold at public auction for cash.	Lost or expended in public service.	Transferred to officers.
					Western and Atlantic Railroad Company.	East Tennessee and Virginia Railroad Company.	East Tennessee and Georgia Railroad Company.	Wills Valley Railroad Company.	Western and Atlantic Railroad Company.	East Tennessee and Virginia Railroad Company.				
270	Chests, saddler tool .... number		1	1									1	2
271	Collars, loose .... do		1	1									1	
272	Couplings, patent .... do		13	13									13	
273	Crane, on four wheels .... do		1	1							1			
274	Chucks .... do		3	3									1	2
275	Cocks, 2-inch .... do		2	2							2			
276	Cocks, duplicate .... do		1	1							1			
277	Cocks, brass .... do		240	240		5	2				225		149	21
278	Cocks, gauge .... do		18	18							18			
279	Columns, furnace .... do		1	1							1			
280	Chains for plates .... do		13	13							13			
281	Cutters, Stanwood, No. 2 .... do		1	1							1			
282	Cups, tin .... do		3, 748	3, 748	21	44	67				363		789	6, 174
283	Cylinders, screw and steam-pump .... do		1	1									1	
284	Candles, star .... pounds		½	½		160	40	720					1, 730	
285	Candles, car .... do						117	25					666	
286	Chains, switch .... do				14	4	20						921	1, 068
287	Chain, cable .... do		1, 120	1, 120									798	5, 000
288	Chalk, white .... do		275	275	357	100	390	50					267	180
289	Chalk, red .... do		40	40									27	50
290	Cement .... barrels					2							29	3
291	Chains, trace .... number													21
292	Copper, ingot .... pounds		3, 230	3, 230		518							5, 012	
293	Copper, tinned .... do		30	30									75	29
294	Clay, fire .... sacks		186	186									186	
295	Cord, bell .... feet		85	85	86	24	47	20					524	55
296	Chimneys, lamp .... number		20	20	19	4	6						352	
297	Chimneys, headlight .... do		59	59	62	20	57	1					577	15
298	Cloth enamelled .... yards		7	7	108	3	60	12					245	
299	Cloth, emery .... do				18	10	40						57	140
300	Chairs, frog .... number												13	
301	Chairs, guard rail .... do												17	

302	Chairs, railroad .... do		1,130	1,130	2,536	1,000	1,200						19,278	
303	Copper, sheet .... pounds				68	257							1,089	141
304	Chrome, yellow .... do					14	13¾						108	41
305	Calipers .... number		23	23							1		12	10
306	Cans, oil .... do												13	107
307	Cans, tin .... do												4	
308	Casting .... pieces												32	
309	Cocks, brass rack .... number					2	4				10		15	1
310	Chrome, green .... pounds					11	15						41	1
311	Cans, 40-gallon .... number													3
312	Chisels, mortise .... do													3
313	Chain, coil .... pounds												3,360	
314	Covers, wagon .... number												2	
315	Clamps, screw .... do													10
316	Chests, field .... do												4	5
317	Cans, 3-gallon .... do												5	1
318	Cabs, locomotive .... do													3
319	Chains, brake .... pounds					200	200							100
320	Crucibles .... number													13
321	Cans, oil, 22-gallon .... do				1									
322	Cans, oil, 800-gallon .... do				2									
323	Cans, oil, 20-gallon .... do					5								1
324	Clamps, switch .... do				28									3
325	Cars, hand .... do				14	16								6
326	Cutters, iron .... do				2	100	140				13			471
327	Castings, car .... pounds						4,909						2,846	
328	Chains, log .... do						1,000	50			125			810
329	Chisels, hand, tinners' .... number						6							
330	Chucks, universal .... do					3								
331	Cans, 8-gallon .... do					1								
332	Cans, 15-gallon .... do					1								
333	Catchers, brass seat .... do					40								
334	Crayons, chalk .... gross					¾								
335	Cranes, driving, wheel .... number					1								
336	Chairs, pine .... do					6								
337	Castings, iron .... pounds					33,403								20,870
338	Chains, pulley .... do					1					3			
339	Clay, fire .... tons										9½			
340	Collars, cast .... number										12			
341	Castings, R. mil .... pounds										104,647			
342	Coolers, water .... do										1			2
343	Copper, old .... pounds													145
344	Copper, scrap .... do													264
345	Copper, bar .... do													60
346	Coppers, soldering .... do													8
347	Dies .... do										40			
348	Chains, lock .... number													4
349	Chains, stay .... do													20
350	Chains, tongue .... do													5
351	Couplings, 3-link .... do													6
352	Chisels, tinner's .... do													10
353	Covers, cylinder-head .... do													6

Report showing the disposition of United States military railroad property in the military division of the Tennessee, &c.—Continued.

Running number.	Articles.		Captured property on hand May 1, 1865.	Property purchased by the United States on hand May 1, 1865.	Total amount of property on hand May 1, 1865.	Property sold on credit to railroad companies under the Executive Orders of August 8 and October 14, 1865.				Captured property returned to owners.		Sold to the Southwestern Iron Company.	Sold at public auction for cash.	Lost or expended in public service.	Transferred to officers.
						Western and Atlantic Railroad Company.	East Tennessee and Virginia Railroad Company.	East Tennessee and Georgia Railroad Company.	Wills Valley Railroad Company.	Western and Atlantic Railroad Company.	East Tennessee and Virginia Railroad Company.				
354	Cranks, iron	number													5
355	Cranes, iron	do													2
356	Clamps, iron	do													4
357	Cans, 30-gallon	do													1
358	Cases for blanks	do													8
359	Chairs, splint-bottom	do													4
360	Chests, horse medicine	do													2
361	Cranes, water	do													15
362	Chicken coops	do													2
363	Desks, field	do		2	2			2				3			31
364	Desks, office	do		5	5	5	2	3	1						33
365	Dividers	do		2	2									7	5
366	Drills	do		3	3										55
367	Drills, ratchet	do		21	21		3	4	2			1		23	52
368	Dadoes	do		7	7										7
369	Drivers, screw	do		37	37			22				1		62	117
370	Dampers	do		6	6							6		3	
371	Diamonds, glaziers'	do		4	4			1							
372	Dippers, iron	do		2	2									3	
373	Dippers, tin	do		606	606			2				28		117	507
374	Drills, upright	do		1	1		1								2
375	Drippers, oil	do		4	4	3									10
376	Dusters	do		2	2									2	
377	Dusters, feather	do		9	9		2					6			12
378	Dusters, painters'	do												10	6
379	Dogs, lathe	do													17
380	Drills for drill press	do													25
381	Drills, hand	do													1
382	Drier, patent	pounds						3							
383	Dishes, deep	number						4							
384	Doubletrees	do													23
385	Drills, churn	do													1

386	Desks, field, and tables	do													2
387	Envelopes, letter	do					125	5,000						24,092	
388	Envelopes, O. B	do					625	2,500						6,085	1,000
389	Erasers, rubber	do		38	38									80	
390	Engines, 20-horse power	do		1	1							1			
391	Engines, stationary	do		4	4	2						2			
392	Engine wagons	do		1	1							1			
393	Engine, truck, wheel	do		8	8										8
394	Ears, kettle	gross		14	14									105	
395	Elbows, tee, water-pipe	pounds		1,233	1,233									1,233	
396	Elbows, gas-pipe	number		99	99									238	33
397	Elbows, wrought	do		12	29									12	
398	Elbows, assorted	do		174	174							174			
399	Emery	pounds		9	9	7	27½	6	4					89	175
400	Erasers, steel	number										4		17	4
401	Elbows, stove-pipe	do					14	1	5						28
402	Ears, kettle	do													2,160
403	Elbows, tin, assorted	do													30
404	Engines, single steam	do													1
405	Engines, rotary fire	do						1				1			1
406	Engines, D, stationary	do													1
407	Facing stone	barrels												1	
408	Files, paper	number		60	60									49	11
409	Forges	do		47	47		10								37
410	Forges, portable	do		2	2		1		2			2		31	35
411	Files, hand-saw	do		352	352	324	99	84						1,100	2,235
412	Files, mill-saw	do		829	829	72	37	54						397	1,122
413	Files, taper	do		515	515									44	509
414	Files, assorted	do		2,543	2,543	32		30	42			277		1,950	254
415	Files, basfnrd	do		1,003	1,003									571	577
416	Files, flat bastard	do		69	69	138	138	182						56	12
417	Files, hand bastard	do		360	360									624	12
418	Files, square bastard	do		255	255										467
419	Files, ½-round bastard	do		152	152										349
420	File, hand, smooth	do		174	174									363	6
421	Files, ½-round, smooth	do					12								6
422	Files, round	do		5	5		67	95	12			18			223
423	Files, round bastard	do		9	9									435	30
424	Fixtures, cook.stove	sets		156	156		2	3	3			10		131	25
425	Fixtures, grindstone	do		84	84		1	2	2			3		54	16
426	Fillers, lamp	number		173	173	13	31	30				1		110	95
427	Folders, tin, No. 1	do		3	3			1						2	
428	Facing, charcoal	barrels												2	
429	Folders, squaring	number		1	1									1	
430	Folders, roofing	do		1	1									1	
431	Forks	do		1,610	1,610			99				206		4,556	2,860
432	Forks, flesh	do		168	168							8		22	236
433	Forks, rail	do		121	121							6		49	66
434	Frames, cast damper	do		6	6							6			
435	Frogs, chilled	do		37	37	13			7					37	20
436	Frogs, wrought	do												1	
437	Funnels	do		29	29	4	3	1				5		2	62

Report showing the disposition of United States military railroad property in the military division of the Tennessee, &c.—Continued.

Running number.	Articles.	Captured property on hand May 1, 1865.	Property purchased by the United States on hand May 1, 1865.	Total amount of property on hand May 1, 1865.	Property sold on credit to railroad companies under the Executive Orders of August 8 and October 14, 1865.				Captured property returned to owners.		Sold to the Southwestern Iron Company.	Sold at public auction for cash.	Lost or expended in public service.	Transferred to officers.
					Western and Atlantic Railroad Company.	East Tennessee and Virginia Railroad Company.	East Tennessee and Georgia Railroad Company.	Wills Valley Railroad Company.	Western and Atlantic Railroad Company.	East Tennessee and Virginia Railroad Company.				
438	Furnaces, bolt ... number												1	
439	Fasteners, car window ... sets		98	98									98	69
440	Flannel, Canton ... yards		4	4	11	11	25	19½					216	15
441	Fuze, safety ... feet		4, 937	4, 937									1, 720	5, 000
442	Fasteners, metallic ... number		864	864									864	
443	Flags and staffs ... do					31	20						4	
444	Fodder ... pounds												6, 000	
445	Figures ... sets												1	
446	Flasks, iron ... number													14
447	Forges, cast B. S ... do													20
448	Files, flat ... do													2, 259
449	Files, ½-round ... do				97	99	56	4					954	
450	Flasks, moulders' ... do													5
451	Frames, hand-car ... do													2
452	Frames, engine truck ... do													1
453	Frames, window ... do													17
454	Frames, hanging lamp ... do													4
455	Flags, red ... do													177
456	Furnace plates and cups ... do										12			
457	Flake white ... pounds						7½						7½	8
458	Files, square ... number				60	56	66							155
459	Files, flat smooth ... do				18	24	76							
460	Frogs, cast plated ... do				4		4							
461	Faucets, brass ... do				2						4			1
462	Faucets, oil ... do				6									
463	Frame & foundation blacksmith shop ... do					1								
464	Foundry, brass, and tools complete ... do					1								
465	Fencing, 10 feet high ... feet					600								
466	Flooring, dressed ... do				300									
467	Furnaces, complete ... number										6			
468	Furnace columns ... pounds										18, 391			
469	Froes ... number													19

470	Fences, board	do											1		
471	Fence, picket, 8 feet high	do											1		
472	Flooring, tent	lot											1		
473	Fitches, painters'	number												6	
474	Flatters	do												5	
475	Glass, assorted	boxes												160	
476	Gauges, marking	number		226	226			14				2		20	339
477	Gauges, firmer	do		1	1			3				1			
478	Gauges, thumb	do		32	32									57	
479	Gauges, paring	do		2	2									2	
480	Gimlets	do		132	132			7						30	96
481	Gauges, track	do		98	98	22	28	29				2		19	160
482	Gauges, saddlers' slit	do		1	1									1	
483	Grovers and stands	do		1	1									1	
484	Glass, 10 x 12	boxes		37	37		15	7						17	75
485	Glass, 10 x 14	do		109	109			16						48	55
486	Glass, 12 x 16	do		6	6		1	7						6	1
487	Glass, 24 x 28	do		1	1		5							3	
488	Glue	pounds		178	178	150	4	190						503	330
489	Gauges, mortise	number		81	81							1		20	64
490	Grease, wagon	pounds												1,005	
491	Green, chrome	do												30	
492	Green, Paris	do					4½							51	
493	Green verdigris	do												6	
494	Gates, oil	number						1						12	5
495	Glass, 10 x 16	boxes					12	10							16
496	Glass, 8 x 10	do					1								2
497	Gridirons	number													53
498	Guides, roll	do										3,430			
499	Glass, 20 x 24	boxes					1	5							1
500	Gouges, firmer	number													5
501	Gauges, steam	do				5	5	10							30
502	Grease, car	gallons				162½	332	200							
503	Grease, car	pounds												2,740	
504	Gauges, brass	number				3									
505	Griddles, stove	do							2						166
506	Glass, 24 x 24	boxes						6							
507	Glass, 12 x 14	do					5								
508	Glass, 22 x 26	do					1								
509	Hay	pounds												556,725	14,775
510	Holders, pen	number		2	2		48	296				48		226	62
511	Halters, head and rope	do		1	1										1
512	Halters, head	do		314	314									326	214
513	Harness, lead	sets		43	43										94
514	Harness, wheel	do		8	8										12
515	Harness, lead horse	do		4	4										4
516	Harness, lead mule	do		153	153										190
517	Harness, saddle mule	do		33	33										30
518	Harness, wheel horse	do		10	10									3	16
519	Harness, wheel mule	do		40	40										100
520	Harness, six-mule	do		5	5									1	5
521	Horses	number		32	32									14	27

Report showing the disposition of United States military railroad property in the military division of the Tennessee, &c.—Continued.

Running number.	Articles.	Captured property on hand May 1, 1865.	Property purchased by the United States on hand May 1, 1865.	Total amount of property on hand May 1, 1865.	Property sold on credit to railroad companies under the Executive Orders of August 8 and October 14, 1865.				Captured property returned to owners.		Sold to the Southwestern Iron Company.	Sold at public auction for cash.	Lost or expended in public service.	Transferred to officers.
					Western and Atlantic Railroad Company.	East Tennessee and Virginia Railroad Company.	East Tennessee and Georgia Railroad Company.	Wills Valley Railroad Company.	Western and Atlantic railroad Company.	East Tennessee and Virginia Railroad Company.				
522	Hammers, light ...number		2	2									2	
523	Hammers, blacksmiths' ...do		8	8										8
524	Hammers, shoeing ...do		2	2										3
525	Hammers, sledge ...do		66	66										83
526	Hammers ...do		5	5									1	4
527	Hammers, claw ...do		263	263			4				9		72	221
528	Hatchets ...do		259	259	2	13	60	2			24		170	750
529	Hatchets, broad ...do		194	194			5						199	
530	Hatchets, shingling ...do		601	601									505	96
531	Hammers, chip ...do		276	276	55		24	3			3			221
532	Hammers, mason ...do		1	1			6				8			83
533	Hammers, stone ...do		58	58		10	7				13			59
534	Hammers, raising ...do		2	2			1						1	
535	Hammers, engine ...do		136	136			2				3		107	24
536	Hammers, machine ...do		1	1			1							26
537	Hammers, patent steam engine ...do		1	1										1
538	Hammers, rivet ...do		2	2										82
539	Hammers, tinners' ...do		3	3			2							4
540	Hatchets, copper ...do		2	2										2
541	Hatchets, railroad ...do		6	6									6	
542	Hangers ...do		1	1									1	
543	Handles, auger ...do		244	244		25	2				9			973
544	Handles, axe ...do		452	452	60	24	161	48			32			1, 527
545	Handles, adze ...do		200	200	24	18	24	12						413
546	Handles, broad-axe ...do		174	174	20			1						416
547	Handles, chisel ...do		30	30		12	87							1, 024
548	Handles, pick ...do		296	296	440	92	10	100						1, 438
549	Handles, file ...do		11	11									171	365
550	Heads, letter ...do												1, 000	
551	Handles, hammer ...do		40	40									12	75
552	Handles, stone maul ...do		486	486	100		13	18			24		324	488
553	Hollows, tinners' ...do		1	1		4							1	

No.	Article	Unit	1	2	3	4	5	6	7	8	9	10	11	12	13
554	Hollows and rounds	sets		4	4									4	
555	Hooks	pounds		44	44							44			
556	Hooks, fire	do		270	270							270			
557	Hooks, sand	do		76	76							76			
558	Hooks, turning	do		1,073	1,073							1,073			
559	Hooks, clevis	number		4	4							4			
560	Hooks, patent	do		48	48									48	
561	Hooks, shave	do		2	2			1						1	
562	Hooks and thimbles	do		8	8									8	
563	Horns, blow	do		1	1									1	
564	Horns, buck	do		1	1									1	
565	Hinges, strap	pairs		284	284		39	59						939	46
566	Hooks, tank and bolt	sets		4	4									17	
567	Hose, rubber	feet		10	10	200	94	50	50					200	333
568	Hose, fire	do		1,700	1,700			900				1,000		776	1,000
569	Hooks, cant	number							12					6	176
570	Hinges, hasp, assorted	do												108	2
571	Hasps and staples	do		200	200									151	210
572	Handles, cant-hook	do													63
573	Handles, brad-awl	do													103
574	Handles, hatchet	do					12								264
575	Hounds, wagon	do												12	
576	Hames	do													28
577	Houses, lime	do										2			
578	Hubs and collars	sets										1			
579	Hooks, roller	pounds										432			
580	Hooks and straps	number										35			
581	Hasps	do						12							20
582	Holders, stake	do						1							
583	Heads, stake	do						2							1
584	Houses, frame	do						1							
585	Houses, store	do						1							
586	Hair, curled	do					177	55							
587	Hose, gum	feet													13
588	Hammers, hand	number										6		47	47
589	Hammers, trip	do													1
590	Handles, sledge	do												24	2
591	Handles, heavy axe	do													18
592	Handles, brad-awl	do												52	
593	Hoops, belt	do					3								
594	Hammers, spike	do				1									
595	Handles, hammer	do				8	150								
596	Houses, tool	do				2									
597	Houses, mess	do				1		7				8			
598	Hose, gum, assorted	feet				102	199	68							
599	Hoods, smokestack	number													14
600	Hoops, tank	do													57
601	Harness, cart	do													16
602	Houses, large	do											1		
603	Houses, small	do											1		
604	Houses, spring	do											1		
605	Houses, ice, large	do											1		

Report showing the disposition of United States military railroad property in the military division of the Tennessee, &c.—Continued.

Running number.	Articles.	Captured property on hand May 1, 1865.	Property purchased by the United States on hand May 1, 1865.	Total amount of property on hand May 1, 1865.	Property sold on credit to railroad companies under the Executive Orders of August 8 and October 14, 1865.				Captured property returned to owners.		Sold to the Southwestern Iron Company.	Sold at public auction for cash.	Lost or expended in public service.	Transferred to officers.
					Western and Atlantic Railroad Company.	East Tennessee and Virginia Railroad Company.	East Tennessee and Georgia Railroad Company.	Wills Valley Railroad Company.	Western and Atlantic Railroad Company.	East Tennessee and Virginia Railroad Company.				
606	Heaters, iron .... number												9	
607	Heads, draw .... do													2
608	Houses, bunk .... do					15								
609	House and oven, bake .... do					1								
610	House, oil .... do					1								
611	Hammers, copper .... do													2
612	Hose, leather .... feet													24
613	Horses, saddlers' stitch .... number													2
614	Handles, assorted .... do													365
615	Hooks, switch rope .... do													42
616	Hooks, tackle .... pounds													500
617	Ink, black .... bottles		35	35		3	25						73	4
618	Inkstands, glass .... number		87	87	5	2	2				12		20	42
619	Inkstands, wood .... do		59	59		6	1						20	98
620	Irons, tweer .... do		33	33									12	52
621	Injectors, iron body .... do		3	3							3			
622	Irons, soldering .... do		5	5		1	2						1	1
623	Iron, assorted .... pounds		43, 324	43, 324	1, 363	23, 162	172	300					6, 713, 833	411, 905
624	Iron, railroad, (new) .... do		960, 720	960, 720									370, 996	2, 062, 000
625	Iron, sheet .... do		1, 528	1, 528									1, 528	
626	Ink, carmine .... do					8	12						68	24
627	Ink, copy .... bottles						24	3					3	12
628	Iron, pig .... pounds												100, 000	
629	Iron, Russia .... do					264	343						2, 140	
630	Iron, scrap .... do												125, 700	
631	Iron, railroad, (old) .... do												1, 329, 735	
632	Iron, railroad .... bars												1, 350	
633	Iron, boiler .... pounds					1, 241	1, 731						220	2, 125
634	Irons, balance-beam .... number												2	
635	Iron, round .... pounds				7, 202	2, 270	16, 303							1, 981
636	Irons, branding .... number													1
637	Irons, large or wheel-press .... do													1

638	Irons, angle	do													2
639	Iron, T railroad	pounds				934, 400							4,892,209		90, 230
640	Iron, tank	do						1, 554							4, 240
641	Iron, square	do				4, 105		1, 010							
642	Iron, sheet	do					624	365							2, 304
643	Iron, bar	do				2, 000		6, 266							
644	Irons, dog	number					182	30				50			8
645	Irons, switch-rod	sets					3								
646	Irons, head-groving	number						1							4
647	Irons, truck	do						340							
648	Irons, smoke-stack	do													50
649	Irons, roofing, double seamer	do													3
650	Instruments, Swiss	sets												3	
651	Jacks, hydraulic	number		37	37	6	2	6	4						66
652	Jacks, screw	do		36	36	30								38	75
653	Jacks, screw-lever	number		4	4										4
654	Jacks, loco-lever	do		30	30									15	15
655	Joints, union with iron yokes	do		8	8							8			
656	Journals, wrought	do										12			
657	Jacks, ratchet	do				4	4	4				1			53
658	Keys, car-lock	do												52	
659	Kettles, tea	do					2		1						100
660	Knives, paper	do		6	6									6	
661	Kettles, camp	do		125	125			8				8		26	250
662	Kettles, cast	do		1	1									2	1
663	Keys, steel	do		2	2									2	
664	Keys, wrought	do		2	2							2			
665	Knives	do		7, 102	7, 102									335	6, 767
666	Knives, butcher	do		479	479		2	1				15		65	480
667	Knives, putty	do		6	6		4	11				3		6	12
668	Knives, mahogany	do		344	344									898	
669	Knives, draw	do		79	79			9				3		4	249
670	Knobs, door and lock	do												232	
671	Knives and forks	do					15	12							
672	Kettles and furnace, iron	do										1			
673	Knobs, door	do													108
674	Knobs, drawer	do													540
675	Ladles	do												7	18
676	Leather, sole	pounds						10						83	14
677	Locks, door	number					26	7						15	127
678	Lamps, office	do		6	6										27
679	Lines, check	do		22	22										22
680	Lines, cart	do		1	1									1	
681	Lines, lead	do		9	9									8	35
682	Locomotives	do	6		6						4				2
683	Lines, tape	do		197	197		21	10	6			1		111	57
684	Levels, spirit	do		88	88		1	4	1			5		6	99
685	Lines, chalk	do		1, 141	1, 141		6	220				11		267	2, 076
686	Lanterns	do		91	91									3	120
687	Lanterns, bull's-eye	do		131	131	93	6	12	5					99	40
688	Lamps, oil	do		9	9										18
689	Lamps, cab	do		12	12									23	

Report showing the disposition of United States military railroad property in the military division of the Tennessee, &c.—Continued.

Running number.	Articles.	Captured property on hand May 1, 1865.	Property purchased by the United States on hand May 1, 1865.	Total amount of property on hand May 1, 1865.	Property sold on credit to railroad companies under the Executive Orders of August 8 and October 14, 1865.				Captured property returned to owners.		Sold to the Southwestern Iron Company.	Sold at public auction for cash.	Lost or expended in public service.	Transferred to officers.
					Western and Atlantic Railroad Company.	East Tennessee and Virginia Railroad Company.	East Tennessee and Georgia Railroad Company.	Wills Valley Railroad Company.	Western and Atlantic Railroad Company.	East Tennessee and Virginia Railroad Company.				
690	Lamps, coal-oil ... number		84	84	2	4	10				10		85	36
691	Lead, sheet ... pounds												270	
692	Lights, blue ... number												2	6
693	Levers, wrought and columns ... do		6	6							6			
694	Lights, head ... do		10	10	16	7	8	4			1		15	43
695	Lights, red ... do		725	725	61	34	78	12			2		226	675
696	Lights, white ... do		1,579	1,579	108	115	116	12			28		898	781
697	Lathes, small ... do		3	3							1		2	
698	Lathes, roller ... do		1	1							1			
699	Lathes, engine ... do		9	9									9	
700	Lathes, turning ... do		4	4									2	2
701	Lead, pig ... pounds		302	302		30							2,657	570
702	Lead, white ... do		696	696		250	800						3,044	27
703	Lead, red ... do		25	25		21		50					125	110
704	Links, coupling ... number		542	542									1,072	185
705	Leaf, gold ... papers		½	½									½	
706	Leather, harness ... pounds		84	84									400	173
707	Lime ... bushels		275	275								125	75	1,150
708	Litharge ... pounds		19	19				6					55	45
709	Levers, tank ... number		12	12									12	
710	Locks, pad ... do		111	111	33	16	28				15		451	225
711	Lumber, pine ... feet		½	½									102,087	8,709
712	Lye, concentrated ... boxes		15	15		1							15	
713	Lampblack ... pounds				4								97	48
714	Ledgers ... number												5	
715	Ledgers, engine ... do												3	
716	Leather, lace ... sides				3	1	8	2					37	2
717	Letters ... sets						1						1	
718	Locks, switch ... number				3		12						3	45
719	Locks, chest ... do						2						280	95
720	Locks, desk drawer ... do					5	1						264	66
721	Lines ... do										24			

722	Lamps, car	do						2	5						10
723	Lumber, oak	feet				15,177									
724	Leaf, gold	books					29					1			
725	Links, straight	number				87	20								34
726	Lead, sugar of	pounds					3								
727	Lead	do													16
728	Leather, bridle	do												18	
729	Locks, iron drawer	number												30	
730	Locks, rim door	do												97	2
731	Lines, crotch	do												15	
732	Locks, car brass	do												254	74
733	Lumber, yellow pine	feet													10,804
734	Lamps, hanging	number					2							2	11
735	Lumber, oak	feet													400
736	Lumber, assorted	do				2,328,334	29,857	80,273							4,000
737	Lead, black	pounds													1,400
738	Links, crooked	number													49
739	Levers, switch	do													10
740	Lake, madder	pounds												5	
741	Mucilage	bottles		40	40				1					76	
742	Mules	number		142	142									73	270
743	Machines, boring	do		20	20										23
744	Mallets	do		211	211									1	381
745	Mauls, carpenters'	do		194	194			1	1			3		172	22
746	Mandrils	do		1	1			1							
747	Mandrils, wrought	do		2	2							2			
748	Machinery, lots of	do		1	1							1			
749	Machines, planing	do		1	1										1
750	Machines, boring, and bits	do		21	21				6					8	27
751	Machines, colter and key seat drill	do		1	1			1							
752	Machines, iron planing	do		1	1										6
753	Machines, punching and shaping	do		1	1							1			
754	Machines, shaping	do		2	2							1			1
755	Machines, boring	do													3
756	Machines, setting-down	do		1	1			1							
757	Machines, screw-cut	do		1	1										2
758	Machines, swedging	do		1	1									1	
759	Machines, travelling and h'd shaping	do		1	1										2
760	Machines, double-seaming	do		1	1										1
761	Machines, large turning	do		1	1			1							
762	Machines, small turning	do		1	1			1							
763	Machines, guttering	do		1	1										1
764	Mauls, railroad spike	do		488	488	100	25	90	12			20		92	1,275
765	Measures	do		28	28	1								24	3
766	Measures, dry	sets		1	1										1
767	Mills, coffee	number		155	155		1	2	1			10		7	295
768	Moulds, candle	do		1	1									1	
769	Marlin, tarred	feet		338	338		26	40						33	366
770	Metal, babbit	pounds		393	393	90	48	500						710	53
771	Matches	gross					1	6	1					3	69
772	Mauls, bridge	number										1			38
773	Mills, saw, incomplete	do											1		

Report showing the disposition of United States military railroad property in the military division of the Tennessee, &c.—Continued.

Running number.	Articles.	Captured property on hand May 1, 1865.	Property purchased by the United States on hand May 1, 1865.	Total amount of property on hand May 1, 1865.	Property sold on credit to railroad companies under the Executive Orders of August 8 and October 14, 1865.				Captured property returned to owners.		Sold to the Southwestern Iron Company.	Sold at public auction for cash.	Lost or expended in public service.	Transferred to officers.
					Western and Atlantic Railroad Company.	East Tennessee and Virginia Railroad Company.	East Tennessee and Georgia Railroad Company.	Wills Valley Railroad Company.	Western and Atlantic Railroad Company.	East Tennessee and Virginia Railroad Company.				
774	Mills, saw, complete .... number..											2		
775	Mills, paint .... do...													3
776	Measures, tin .... do...					3	1				2			25
777	Machines, bolt-cut .... do...					1					1			1
778	Machines, folding .... do...													3
779	Machines, beadding .... do...						1							3
780	Machines, screw-cut lathe .... do...													2
781	Machines, grooving .... do...						1							
782	Machines, burring, large .... do...						1							
783	Mauls, iron .... do...													2
784	Moulds, cast .... do...													4
785	Measures, tape .... do...												20	
786	Nippers, wire-cut .... do...		6	6							1		2	4
787	Nails, assorted .... pounds..		2, 434	2, 434									26, 317	200
788	Nails, clinch .... do...		800	800									100	
789	Nipples, shoulder .... number..		156	156							156			
790	Nipples, gas-pipe .... do...		11	11									11	
791	Nuts, hexagon .... pounds..		950	950	720	996	430						1, 350	
792	Nuts, wrought .... number..		4	4							4			
793	Netting, wire .... feet...		68	68			270						82	165
794	Nails, horseshoe .... pounds..												225	212
795	Nails, mule-shoe .... do...												25	
796	Nails, clout .... do...												50	49
797	Nails, cut .... kegs...				3		205	4					5	2
798	Nuts, assorted .... pounds..					2, 907	867	1, 055					5, 840	5, 989
799	Nails, finishing .... do...					168								
800	Nalls, finishing .... kegs...						5							
801	Nails, finishing .... papers..				68	63	27							103
802	Nails, cut, assorted .... pounds..				392	4, 692								
803	Nails, clinch .... kegs...				39									
804	Nails, brass, round head .... gross...												3	
805	Oats .... pounds..		1, 000	1, 000							5, 000		115, 700	3, 450

806	Oxen .... number		12	12										12
807	Oilers .... do		191	191										381
808	Oilers, engine .... do		99	99	28		28	6			11		5	21
809	Oilers, S. B. .... do		91	91		6	33	6			13		33	
810	Oilers, tin .... do		263	263										318
811	Oil, coal .... gallons		12	12		19	25						515	8
812	Ochre, yellow .... pounds					238	65						623	30
813	Offices, small .... number											1		
814	Oil, lard .... gallons		615	615	17	412	303						11, 157	94
815	Oil, raw linseed .... do		95	95		6¼	57						133	2
816	Oil, kerosene .... do												44	
817	Oil, boiled linseed .... do					22	55	25					251	
818	Oil, lubricating .... do												1, 205	
819	Oakum .... pounds												11	14
820	Oil, neat's-foot .... gallons												5	30
821	Ovens, camp .... number				268	21								17
822	Ochre, French .... pounds					15								
823	Paper, cap .... quires					20	294	120					10	1, 200
824	Paper, letter .... do		74	74	10	20	8	20					215	
825	Paper, note .... do		480	480		5	40						600	
826	Paper, abstract .... do		15	15									7	8
827	Paper, blotting .... sheets		122	122		26	27	40					547	104
828	Pencils, lead .... number		348	348			144						976	
829	Pens, ruling .... do		6	6		1							7	1
830	Presses, letter .... do		12	12		2	1	1			1			9
831	Pots, tar .... do		138	138									133	78
832	Pincers .... do		1	1									1	
833	Planes, match .... do		3	3		3	1						1	42
834	Planes, assorted .... do		84	84									84	
835	Planes, arm match .... do		34	34									28	6
836	Pens, steel .... do						288						14, 460	12
837	Pink, rose .... pounds					1½							58	16
838	Planes, match screw .... number		6	6										6
839	Planes, bead .... do		418	418			26	2			5		29	532
840	Planes, jack .... do		84	84			2						7	159
841	Planes, jointer .... do		371	371			12	2			7		265	101
842	Planes, pannel plough .... do		3	3									20	21
843	Planes, plough and bits .... do		10	10			7				1		1	2
844	Planes, rabbet .... do		76	76		4	18				3		24	197
845	Planes, smooth .... do		337	337			12	2			7		101	492
846	Planes, sash .... do		4	4										4
847	Planes, wood .... do		3	3									4	
848	Plumb and level .... do		1	1									1	
849	Plumb and lead .... do		1	1										1
850	Pans, dish .... do		431	431		3	9				36		31	364
851	Pans, drip .... do		154	154							6			431
852	Pans, fry .... do		186	186		3					2		32	475
853	Pans, mess .... do		118	118							9		24	167
854	Pans, wash .... do		194	194									6	201
855	Paulins .... do		6	6									2	17
856	Pencils, scrawling .... do		36	36									36	
857	Peels .... pounds		772	772							772			

Report showing the disposition of United States military railroad property in the military division of the Tennessee, &c.—Continued.

Running number.	Articles.	Captured property on hand May 1, 1865.	Property purchased by the United States on hand May 1, 1865.	Total amount of property on hand May 1, 1865.	Property sold on credit to railroad companies under the Executive Orders of August 8 and October 14, 1865.				Captured property returned to owners.		Sold to the Southwestern Iron Company.	Sold at public auction for cash.	Lost or expended in public service.	Transferred to officers.
					Western and Atlantic Railroad Company.	East Tennessee and Virginia Railroad Company.	East Tennessee and Georgia Railroad Company.	Wills Valley Railroad Company.	Western and Atlantic Railroad Company.	East Tennessee and Virginia Railroad Company.				
858	Plaster of Paris ... pounds												171	146
859	Picks ... number		1, 399	1, 399	168	101	139				52		640	299
860	Picks, tamping ... do		91	91	320	40	48	24			2			837
861	Pins, turn, lignumvitæ ... do		2	2										2
862	Pipe former, stove ... do		1	1			1							
863	Pipe former, tin ... do		1	1										2
864	Planers ... do		1	1									1	
865	Planers, complete ... do		1	1									1	
866	Plates, tin ... do		5, 699	5, 699		24	123				323		1, 488	6, 634
867	Plates, bed for saw stand ... do		2	2							2			
868	Plates, cast ... do		4	4							4			
869	Plates, curving ... do		2	2							2			
870	Plates, wrought ... do		6	6							6			
871	Plates, straightening ... do		2	2							2			
872	Pots, coffee ... do		217	217		2	3				59		45	230
873	Pots, coffee, small ... do		49	49										49
874	Pots, coffee, three-quart ... do		185	185										280
875	Pots, coffee, three-gallon ... do		156	156										156
876	Pots, glue ... do		13	13		1	3	1			2		2	28
877	Pots, solder ... do		3	3										3
878	Pieces, distance, cast ... do		16	16							16			
879	Pencils, slate ... box		1	1									1	
880	Paint, mineral ... barrels						140						6	
881	Presses, boring ... number		1	1										1
882	Presses, drill ... do		3	3							1		1	5
883	Presses, screw ... do		1	1										1
884	Pumps, oil ... do		1	1										1
885	Pumps, complete ... do		9	9										31
886	Pulleys ... pounds		856	856									856	
887	Pulleys ... number		5	5							20		46	
888	Pulleys, 12-inch ... do		2	2										2
889	Pulleys, 2½-feet ... do		1	1									1	

890	Pulleys, friction	do		1	1									1	
891	Punches, spring	do		2	2									4	
892	Punches, hydraulic	do		1	1									1	
893	Punches, turners'	do		10	10			8							10
894	Punches and chisels, solid	do		2	2									4	
895	Plyers, flat-nose	do		6	6			6						8	36
896	Packing, rubber	pounds		75½	75½									318	200
897	Pencils, carpenters'	number		144	144									144	
898	Putty	pounds		800	800	480	198	260	200						833
899	Pipe, gas	feet		2, 227 1-12	2, 227 1-12	7, 341	300						2, 480	1, 394	7, 388
900	Powder	kegs		12	12									38	32
901	Points, glaziers'	number					6							46	50
902	Plyers	do												4	
903	Pipe, water	feet		3, 120	3, 120									3, 120	
904	Pumps, force	number		22	22	21			2						8
905	Paper, sand	quires		6	6		29¼		20					46	14
906	Plugs, assorted	number		468	468							468			
907	Pipe, wrought	feet		512 9-12	512 9-12									512 9-12	
908	Paper, hardware	quires												2	
909	Paper, envelope	do					10	80	40					2	40
910	Packing, hemp	pounds				699	125	127	30					1, 015	390
911	Paper, emery	quires				160	52½	40	10					40	8
912	Planers, compound	number										1			
913	Paint, mixed	pounds					400							350	
914	Pins, coupling	number													103
915	Pipes, blast, wood	do					280								
916	Pans, bake	do					1								
917	Pots, tea	do						1							
918	Plates, number engine	do						8							
919	Points, steel frog	do					249	307							
920	Plates, steel frog	do					939	997							
921	Paper, oil	sheets						6							
922	Packing, gum	pounds				155	15¾	116	130						468
923	Pots, fire	number							1						8
924	Remers and drills	do													175
925	Pipe, tin, assorted	feet													475
926	Pipe, lead	pounds													1, 330
927	Pumps, tin	number													4
928	Potash	pounds													12
929	Pincers, blacksmiths'	do													8
930	Pincers, carpenters'	do												11	8
931	Pans, ash	do													4
932	Pipes, nozzle and hose	do													1
933	Pipe, stove	joints					63	90	25						1, 416
934	Planes, fore	number												5	375
935	Pans, tin	do					2	9	3			64		41	1, 456
936	Packing, steam	pounds				43		79						339	1, 098
937	Pink, Dutch	do												6	
938	Points, cast frog	number						140	40					12	
939	Paper, folio post	quires													50
940	Planes, dadoes	number												4	16
941	Picks, earth	do												78	1, 570

Report showing the disposition of United States military railroad property in the military division of the Tennessee, &c.—Continued.

Running number.	Articles.	Captured property on hand May 1, 1865.	Property purchased by the United States on hand May 1, 1865.	Total amount of property on hand May 1, 1865.	Property sold on credit to railroad companies under the Executive Orders of August 8 and October 14, 1865. — Western and Atlantic Railroad Company.	Property sold on credit … — East Tennessee and Virginia Railroad Company.	Property sold on credit … — East Tennessee and Georgia Railroad Company.	Property sold on credit … — Wills Valley Railroad Company.	Captured property returned to owners. — Western and Atlantic Railroad Company.	Captured property returned to owners. — East Tennessee and Virginia Railroad Company.	Sold to the Southwestern Iron Company.	Sold at public auction for cash.	Lost or expended in public service.	Transferred to officers.
942	Protractors ..... sheets												10	
943	Pencils, artists' ..... number												144	
944	Pipe, water ..... pounds													1,255
945	Pots, marking ..... number													4
946	Pots, watering ..... do													17
947	Pots, iron stove ..... do													178
948	Pencils, C. H ..... do													28
949	Planes, jack, rabbet ..... do													17
950	Pumps, hand-lifting ..... do													1
951	Powers, horse-tread ..... do													2
952	Pike poles ..... do													48
953	Punchers, tank-hook ..... do													3
954	Punchers, screw ..... do													1
955	Punchers, track ..... do													4
956	Planes, hollow ..... do												9	
957	Planes, moulding ..... do					27								16
958	Planes, filister ..... do					1								7
959	Pulley and shafts ..... do				2									
960	Platforms, railroad ..... do				3									
961	Pieces, standard ..... do										4			
962	Pumps, steam, 14-inch cylinder ..... do										1			
963	Pumps, Worthington ..... do										1			2
964	Pivots, tin ..... do										1			
965	Racks, pen ..... do		88	88		2	4				4		55	90
966	Rules, office ..... do		12	12										38
967	Rules, rubber ..... do		70	70		1	1				2		58	21
968	Rules, wood ..... do		36	36				1			2		22	11
969	Ropes, pack-saddle ..... do		6	6									6	
970	Rasps, horse ..... do		39	39							5		23	14
971	Reels, chalk-line ..... do		7	7									21	77
972	Rules, box-wood ..... do		108	108									155	
973	Rules, 2-foot ..... do		98	98				12			12		94	328

No.	Article	Unit													
974	Riddles	do		2	2							1		20	29
975	Rollers, cast	do		14	14							14			
976	Rivets, iron	do												18,000	127
977	Ropes, switch	do				2		3						2	53
978	Rollers, plain grove	do		4	4							5			
979	Rolls for rolling-mill	do		1	1							1			
980	Rags	pounds		939	939	1,230	1,606	810						24,150	794
981	Resin	do		270	270		3	230						402	40
982	Rings, flush	number		108	108			13						108	25
983	Rivets, copper	pounds		2	2			4						58	4
984	Rivets, tinner's	do		499	499									6,499	17,000
985	Rivets, smoke-stack	do		24	24		61	175						24	190
986	Rods, extra	number		3	3										5
987	Rope, assorted	pounds		8,173	8,173	465	1,035	2,718	1,559					4,693	28,965
988	Red, India	do					11¼	15						106	5
989	Red, Venetian	do					6¾	95						93	65
990	Rasps, wood	number												10	2
991	Rolls, turn	sets										1			
992	Rivets, assorted	pounds					15½								1,161
993	Rings, brass racking	number						2	4						8
994	Rods, brake	do						206							
995	Rivets, boiler	do					38	200							
996	Rivets, black	pounds					8								
997	Rivets, tank	do					118	200							325
998	Rooms, store	number					1								
999	Reamers, steel	pounds					17½								
1000	Rivets, stove-pipe	do						10							
1001	Rivets and burr, copper	number					7		11						
1002	Rings, brass cylinder	do													6
1003	Roofing, patent	pounds													160
1004	Rods, switch	number													5
1005	Rests, lathe	do													1
1006	Range, cook, and fixtures	do													1
1007	Reflectors, h'd light	do													10
1008	Rules, parallel	do													1
1009	Slates, office	do													7
1010	Safes, field	do		2	2										3
1011	Safes, iron	do		6	6			1				1			6
1012	Shears, office	do		3	3									3	
1013	Sheets, oil	do		19	19									13	6
1014	Saddles, riding	do		9	9									9	14
1015	Saddles, wagon	do		77	77									63	51
1016	Saddles, pack	do		6	6									6	
1017	Solder, spelter	pounds					20	55							
1018	Singletrees	number		60	60									41	201
1019	Sticks, jockey	do		135	135									128	39
1020	Spreaders	do		20	20									43	23
1021	Stirrups, wood	do		9	9									9	
1022	Straps, coupling	do		87	87									161	1
1023	Straps, halter	do		9	9									2	4
1024	Straps, neck	do		379	379									373	18
1025	Straps, stirrup	do		12	12									12	

Report showing the disposition of United States military railroad property in the military division of the Tennessee, &c.—Continued.

Running number.	Articles.	Captured property on hand May 1, 1865.	Property purchased by the United States on hand May 1, 1865.	Total amount of property on hand May 1, 1865.	Property sold on credit to railroad companies under the Executive Orders of August 8 and October 14, 1865.				Captured property returned to owners.		Sold to the Southwestern Iron Company.	Sold at public auction for cash.	Lost or expended in public service.	Transferred to officers.
					Western and Atlantic Railroad Company.	East Tennessee and Virginia Railroad Company.	East Tennessee and Georgia Railroad Company.	Wills Valley Railroad Company.	Western and Atlantic Railroad Company.	East Tennessee and Virginia Railroad Company.				
1026	Stretchers .... number		71	71									71	
1027	Skins, sheep .... do		5	5									8	
1028	Sledges, blacksmiths' .... do		50	50			2				22		5	105
1029	Stocks and dies .... do		27	27			4	2			12		3	6
1030	Saws .... do		22	22									22	
1031	Saws, back .... do		98	98			8				1		106	38
1032	Saws, circular .... do		29	29		1	1	2			10			20
1033	Saws, compass .... do		53	53			12						19	92
1034	Saws, cross-cut .... do		111	111	24	4	5	8			1		6	141
1035	Saws, hand .... do		978	978		7	53	2					230	1, 144
1036	Saws, gig .... do		6	6		5							16	5
1037	Saws, mulay .... do		1	1									7	
1038	Spikes, bridge .... kegs				5	10	17	18					205	571½
1039	Straw .... pounds												680	
1040	Saws, rip .... number		233	233			12	1					24	406
1041	Saws, tenon .... do		3	3									9	130
1042	Saw gummers .... do		1	1	1									1
1043	Saw sets .... do		75	75			14				2		12	49
1044	Screws, bench .... do		26	26		12	5							11
1045	Screws, hand-bench .... do		25	25			8	6			9		2	173
1046	Slicks .... do		43	43									43	
1047	Shaves, spoke .... do		50	50			7				3		6	34
1048	Squares, steel .... do		296	296		3	30	2			14		126	425
1049	Squares, try .... do		175	175			22				5		85	223
1050	Stones, oil .... do		303	303			8				7		42	244
1051	Stones, oil .... pounds		130	130									319	
1052	Saws, mill .... number		11	11										18
1053	Sacks, gunny .... do		3, 540	3, 540									7, 495	2, 756
1054	Singes .... do		6	6									6	
1055	Safes, match .... do		1	1									2	
1056	Saws, buck .... do		15	15									12	3
1057	Saws, hack .... do		1	1			1						1	12

1058	Saw mills, portable ....do..		1	1								1		
1059	Spouts, tank ....do..												12	
1060	Stocks and dies, gas-pipe ....do..						1							3
1061	Screws, iron bench ....do..		30	30									19	11
1062	Screws, for pulleys ....do..		2	2									2	
1063	Scales, platform ....do..		15	15		1	4	1			1		3	8
1064	Shafts, wrought ....do..		4	4							6		4	
1065	Shears, tinner's bench ....do..		2	2			1							3
1066	Shafts, wrought ....pounds..		264	264									264	
1067	Shears, lamp ....pairs..		63	63		2	2				2		110	7
1068	Shears, sheep ....do..		1	1									1	
1069	Scoops ....number..		1	1									18	22
1070	Scythes, brier, and snaths ....do..		2	2									1	1
1071	Seamers, double-roofing ....do..		1	1										2
1072	Shades, lamp ....do..		27	27		4					3		20	7
1073	Shovels ....do..		1, 936	1, 936	283	252	467	60			121		168	1, 826
1074	Saddlers' tools ....sets..		2	2									2	
1075	Sets, rivet ....number..		3	3			2	2					3	
1076	Sets, screw ....do..		4	4									4	
1077	Sieves, wire ....do..		10	10							6		5	2
1078	Smoothers ....do..		239	239							239			
1079	Snips, circular ....do..		2	2									2	
1080	Shoes, horse ....pounds..												500	356
1081	Shoes, mule ....do..												1, 000	625
1082	Snips, straight ....number..		5	5										5
1083	Slates, double ....do..		1	1									1	
1084	Sockets ....do..		66	66							66			
1085	Sockets, reducing ....do..		8	8							8			
1086	Sockets, for blast boxes ....do..		6	6							6			
1087	Spoons, basting ....do..		260	260		3					17		35	324
1088	Spoons, table ....do..		254	254		11	66				218		95	2, 452
1089	Spoons, tea ....do..		2, 803	2, 803		16	50				278		797	1, 924
1090	Sprinklers ....do..		24	24									21	3
1091	Stakes ....do..		10	10									7	3
1092	Stakes, hatchet ....do..		2	2			1						1	
1093	Stakes, square ....do..		3	3			2	1						2
1094	Stands, beader ....do..		2	2									2	
1095	Stands, cast, for rollers ....do..		4	4							4			
1096	Sticks, double ....do..		1	1									1	
1097	Shears, hand, tinners' ....do..		9	9									9	
1098	Stocks, cut-off ....do..		2	2							2			
1099	Stocks, screw ....do..		2	2							2			
1100	Stones, grind, and fixtures ....do..		78	78		2	3	2			4		12	61
1101	Stems, wrought ....do..		6	6							6			
1102	Stands, cast, and caps ....do..		1, 934	1, 934							1, 934			
1103	Sinks, counter ....do..												1	
1104	Scales, box, 12-inch ....do..												1	
1105	Stones, half-dressed ....do..											17		
1106	Stones, dressed ....do..											50		
1107	Stones, dressed ....perch..											105		
1108	Stones, rough ....do..											300		
1109	Stables, small ....number..											1		

Report showing the disposition of United States military railroad property in the military division of the Tennessee, &c.—Continued.

Running number.	Articles.	Captured property on hand May 1, 1865.	Property purchased by the United States on hand May 1, 1865.	Total amount of property on hand May 1, 1865.	Property sold on credit to railroad companies under the Executive Orders of August 8 and October 14, 1865.				Captured property returned to owners.		Sold to the Southwestern Iron Company.	Sold at public auction for cash.	Lost or expended in public service.	Transferred to officers.
					Western and Atlantic Railroad Company.	East Tennessee and Virginia Railroad Company.	East Tennessee and Georgia Railroad Company.	Wills Valley Railroad Company.	Western and Atlantic Railroad Company.	East Tennessee and Virginia Railroad Company.				
1110	Sleeves, water-pipe .... number													22
1111	Spatulas .... do													8
1112	Shaves, spoke .... do												3	7
1113	Saws, felloe .... do													2
1114	Swages, B. S .... do													11
1115	Stands, head-light .... do													1
1116	Shafts, counter and 4-pulley .... do													1
1117	Screws, large and 4-nut .... do													2
1118	Sash .... pieces												170	106
1119	Switches, monkey .... number										3		16	18
1120	Strainers, tin .... do												6	13
1121	Squares, bevel .... do												5	2
1122	Stoves, coal .... do					4	6							39
1123	Stoves, Sibley .... do													33
1124	Stoves, sheet-iron .... do													14
1125	Screws, brass .... gross												4	18
1126	Screws, iron .... number												20	
1127	Steel, spring .... pounds					2,125	4,120						1,540	6,031
1128	Spokes, wagon .... number												400	
1129	Strings, hame .... do												24	
1130	Saws, web .... do													14
1131	Slicks, carpenters' .... do						3						13	55
1132	Squares, iron .... do													97
1133	Springs, large D .... pounds						298							
1134	Springs, small D .... do						156							
1135	Screws, hand, assorted .... number						18							
1136	Springs, steel tender .... pounds						1,320							47
1137	Steel, blister .... do						70							
1138	Stakes, blow-horn .... number						1							
1139	Stakes, beak-horn .... do						1							
1140	Stakes, double-seaming .... do						1							1
1141	Stakes, needle-case .... do						1							

1142	Stakes, candle-mould .... do						1							
1143	Strainers, pump .... do					2								20
1144	Smoke stack .... do					1								
1145	Saddles, smoke-stack .... do					2								
1146	Stools, office .... do					1								4
1147	Stands, letter-press .... do					2								3
1148	Screws, hand, iron .... do					15							10	
1149	Springs, spiral patent .... do					40								
1150	Shears, cold, and fixtures, complete .. pairs										1			
1151	Sets, screw, for housing .... number										8			
1152	Scales, beam .... do										1			
1153	Shovels, scoop .... do										5			
1154	Shears, iron .... do													32
1155	Skins, chamois .... do										2			
1156	Studs and nuts .... do										20			
1157	Screws for saws .... do										2			
1158	Shops, machine .... do										1			
1159	Sheds, corral .... do										1	1		
1160	Shops, paint .... do										1			
1161	Shops, carpenter .... do										1			
1162	Shops, blacksmith .... do										1	1		
1163	Sheds, engine .... do										1			
1164	Stands, wash .... do													4
1165	Switch stands and targets .... do				7	6		6						31
1166	Spades .... do													16
1167	Sinks, stove .... do													96
1168	Steelyards .... do													1
1169	Steel, scrap .... pounds													5,510
1170	Springs, gum car .... do													359
1171	Stands, drawing .... number													4
1172	Shafting .... pounds													550
1173	Skillets .... number							1					10	
1174	Shafting, assorted .... feet										169			
1175	Scales, counter, small .... number				1			2						3
1176	Steel, cast .... pounds				515	1,579¾		220						
1177	Shingles .... number				121,000		117,750							
1178	Sheds, open .... do				1						1			
1179	Snips, tinner's .... do						2	1						
1180	Stoves, cook .... do		151	151		4	3	3			10		5	178
1181	Stoves, camp .... do		23	23									23	
1182	Stoves, centre platform .... do		1	1										1
1183	Stoves, box heating .... do		31	31		15	20	2			7			94
1184	Stoves, imperial cook and boiler .... do		2	2										2
1185	Studs and nuts .... do		20	20									20	
1186	Screws .... gross		124	124									124	
1187	Screws, assorted .... do		270	270		375	91						150	60
1189	Screws, lag, assorted .... number		350	350	128		53	130					372	593
1190	Screws, brass, round head .... gross		46	46		18	24						28	1
1191	Sal ammonia .... pounds		49	49		12	83							33
1192	Solder .... do		265	265				40					98	497
1193	Steel, frog .... do		1,590	1,590									5,933	1,972
1194	Steel, assorted .... do		433	433			3,820						9,465	4,493

Report showing the disposition of United States military railroad property in the military division of the Tennessee, &c.—Continued.

Running number.	Articles.	Captured property on hand May 1, 1865.	Property purchased by the United States on hand May 1, 1865.	Total amount of property on hand May 1, 1865.	Property sold on credit to railroad companies under the Executive Orders of August 8 and October 14, 1865.				Captured property returned to owners.		Sold to the Southwestern Iron Company.	Sold at public auction for cash.	Lost or expended in public service.	Transferred to officers.
					Western and Atlantic Railroad Company.	East Tennessee and Virginia Railroad Company.	East Tennessee and Georgia Railroad Company.	Wills Valley Railroad Company.	Western and Atlantic Railroad Company.	East Tennessee and Virginia Railroad Company.				
1195	Stones, pumice .... number..		10	10		5							96	39
1196	Sulphur .... pounds..		199	199									117	490
1197	Sienna, burnt .... do...		18	18		13	15						38	45
1198	Sienna, raw .... do...		14	14		13	30						24	39
1199	Soap, castile .... do...		359	359									359	
1200	Spikes, railroad .... kegs...		727	725	25	25	100						2,624	
1201	Shoes, brake .... number..													4
1202	Staffs, flag .... do...		76	76			30						46	
1203	Sponge, common .... pounds..					½							20	81
1204	Tools, heading .... number..												4	
1205	Tables .... do...		2	2		4								46
1206	Tables, camp .... do...		1	1									1	
1207	Tools, metallic fastener .... sets...		1	1										1
1208	Taps and dies .... number..		1	1			2				13			2
1209	Tongs, blacksmiths' .... do...		56	56			1				50			628
1210	Tools, blacksmiths' .... sets...		15	15			1	2					9	55
1211	Tools, shoeing .... do...		1	1										2
1212	Tools, carpenters' .... do...		2	2										5
1213	Tools, sash .... do...		26	26		9					7		10	
1214	Trowels, masons' .... number..		33	33							10		47	20
1215	Trowels, brick .... do...		50	50										94
1216	Taps .... do...		4	4										144
1217	Timber rollers .... do...		24	24									24	
1218	Tongs, rail .... do...		78	78							6		5	82
1219	Tongs, gas pipe .... do...		18	18	2		2				17		3	30
1220	Tongs, roofing .... do...		1	1										4
1221	Tongs, rolling mill .... pounds..		138	138							138			
1222	Trucks .... number..		5	5									5	
1223	Trucks, warehouse .... do...		6	6			8	2			1			2
1224	Tacks .... papers..		117	117	15	40	48						216	195
1225	Tape .... spools..		45	45									45	
1226	Tanks, water .... number..		12	12				4						8

1227	Tallow ....pounds..		915	915	840	2,173							15,000	
1228	Tees, gas pipe ....number..		18	18									19	7
1229	Tees, assorted ....do....		150	150							150			
1230	Ties, cross ....do....		49,500	49,500	12,720								125,748	
1231	Tin, block ....pounds..		604	604		24							1,025	
1232	Twine ....do....		30	30	2¼		1¼						54	
1233	Turpentine ....gallons..		79	79		5	43						138	
1234	Tube, assorted ....feet...		3,725 1-6	3,725 1-6							3,725 1-6			
1235	Tar............barrels..												5	
1236	Tin, assorted............boxes...					8	6						24	
1237	Tripods ....number..													105
1238	Tools, blacksmiths'............pounds..													28
1239	Tables, office............number..													9
1240	Tables, field and desk............do....													9
1241	Tools, steel lathe............pounds..													317
1242	Tools, turning............do....													300
1243	Tools, steel............number..													200
1244	Tools, graining............do....													7
1245	Tin boxes............do....				59	3								
1246	Timber, hewn and sawed ....feet...				259,428		5,491							
1247	Tables, turn ....number..				1									
1248	Timber turn tables............do....				12									
1249	Tables, turn frames............do....				1									
1250	Tanks and frames ....do....				21						2			
1251	Thimbles, flue............do....				200	279								70
1252	Tools, planer and lathe............pounds..					400								
1253	Taps, steel ....number..					8								
1254	Tacks, small head............papers..					24								
1255	Trucks, car ....number..					5								
1256	Tackle, triple com............do....					2								
1257	Tire, engine wheel ....pounds..						1,312							1,525
1258	Umber, burnt ....do....						20						50	9
1259	Umber, raw............do....					6	42						29	63
1260	Tools ....do....											1,479		
1261	Thread, shoe ....pounds..													1
1262	Targets, switch............number..													27
1263	Trucks, engine............do....													2
1264	Tongs, engine............do....													21
1265	Tongues, wagon............do....													20
1266	Tubing, copper ....pounds..													670
1267	Timber............sticks...											15		
1268	Unions, mal ....number..		33	33							33			
1269	Vermillion, American ....pounds..						26						39	1
1270	Vices ....number..		41	41		7	3	2			6			91
1271	Vices, parallel............do....							2					5	19
1272	Valves, body flange............do....		88	88							88			
1273	Valves, check, 2-inch............do....		2	2							2			
1274	Valves, globe, 2-inch............do....		2	2							2			
1275	Valves, tank............do....		9	9			6	4			2			15
1276	Valves, brass ....do....		216	216							216			
1277	Varnish, Japan ....gallons..		31½	31½		27¼	34						31½	50
1278	Varnish, coach ....barrels..					12							5	

Report showing the disposition of United States military railroad property in the military division of the Tennessee, &c.—Continued.

Running number.	Articles.	Captured property on hand May 1, 1865.	Property purchased by the United States on hand May 1, 1865.	Total amount of property on hand May 1, 1865.	Property sold on credit to railroad companies under the Executive Orders of August 8 and October 14, 1865.				Captured property returned to owners.		Sold to the Southwestern Iron Company.	Sold at public auction for cash.	Lost or expended in public service.	Transferred to officers.
					Western and Atlantic Railroad Company.	East Tennessee and Virginia Railroad Company.	East Tennessee and Georgia Railroad Company.	Wills Valley Railroad Company.	Western and Atlantic Railroad Company.	East Tennessee and Virginia Railroad Company.				
1279	Varnish, coach .... gallons													26
1280	Varnish, copal .... do						24							
1281	Varnish, brown .... do					5								
1282	Varnish, Demar .... do					19								
1283	Varnish, white .... do					19								
1284	Wood .... cords		1,000	1,000	5,100								31,904	108
1285	Weights, paper .... number		60	60							1		7	52
1286	Wagons, army .... do		138	138									11	180
1287	Whips, wagon .... do		164	164									173	28
1288	Wrenches, monkey .... do		390	390	123	29	18	3			25		40	589
1289	Whistles, steam .... do		1	1							1		1	1
1290	Wheelbarrows .... do		99	99	5	12					27		20	343
1291	Wheels, buggy cart .... do		4	4							4			
1292	Wheels, bevel plate, and brackets .... do		1	1									1	
1293	Wheels, gear box .... do		1	1									1	
1294	Wheels, mitre bevel .... do		1	1									1	
1295	Wrenches, assorted .... do		275	275				3					156	105
1296	Wrenches, pipe .... do		2	2									2	
1297	Wrenches, tap .... do		1	1							1			49
1298	Waste .... pounds		938	938	105	715	50						5,543	
1299	Washers .... do		177	177		900	815						2,000	13,069
1300	Wicks, coal oil .... number		2	2									2	
1301	Wicks, lamp, flat .... do					24	96						147	24
1302	Wire, iron .... pounds					113	510				1,526		3,802	1,815
1303	Wire, copper .... do						13						21	4
1304	Whiting .... do												319	1,444
1305	Wire, brass .... coil												1	
1306	Wicks, lamp .... pounds												2	2¼
1307	Wire, broom .... do												12	
1308	Wrenches, lathe .... number													21
1309	Wrenches, locket .... do													10
1310	Wheels and frames, water .... do				1									

1311	Wheels, truck .... do					4								6
1312	Wheels, tender .... do					10								
1313	Wheels, car .... do					22	5							
1314	Wrenches, gas pipe .... do					1							1	
1315	Wicking, ball .... do						53¼							
1316	Webbing, car .... yards					130								
1317	Wheels, spur .... number										1			
1318	Well and building and ventilator .... do										1			
1319	Wheels, hand car .... do													2
1320	Wrenches, iron, assorted .... do													358
1321	Wagons, wood .... do											3		
1322	Yokes, ox .... do		290	290				2					12	445
1323	Zinc, pig .... pounds		500	500		274	880						1,126	375
1324	Zinc, sheet .... do		195	195		37	250	42					711	3

[Enclosure No. 3.]

Report showing the disposition of United States military railroad property in the military division of the Tennessee, for which Captain S. R. Hamill, A. Q. M., is responsible.

Running number.	Articles.	Captured property on hand.	Property purchased by the United States on hand.	Cost to the United States of property purchased.	Total amount of property on hand.	Property sold on credit to railroad companies under Executive Orders of August 8 and October 14, 1865.								
						Macon and Brunswick railroad.	Muscogee railroad.	Montgomery and W. P. railroad.	Wills Valley railroad.	Macon and Western railroad.	Edgefield and Kentucky railroad.	Memphis and Charleston railroad.	Nashville and N. W. railroad.	Nashville and Chattanooga railroad.
1	Coal ... bushels		44, 269		44, 269							275		2, 426
2	Coke ... do		3, 975		3, 975									250
3	Charcoal ... do		648		648									
4	Charcoal ... barrels		2		2									
5	Wood ... cords		14, 663⅛		14, 663⅛						4, 811	1, 899	23, 002¼	29, 053
6	Corn ... pounds		874, 397		874, 397									
7	Hay ... do		1, 346, 737		1, 346, 737									
8	Oats ... do		208, 336		208, 336									
9	Sacks, grain ... number		12, 025		12, 025									
10	Straw ... pounds		3, 150		3, 150									
11	Blanks		15		15								5	10
12	Blanks, quartermasters' ... quires		1, 172		1, 172									
13	Blanks, way freight		500		500									
14	Books, blank, 1½-quire		38		38									
15	Books, blank, 2-quire		55	$66 00	55							6	9	18
16	Books, blank, 3-quire		196	270 48	196							8	28	49
17	Books, blank, 4-quire		204	301 92	204							3	23	44
18	Books, blank, 6-quire		27	97 20	27									1
19	Books, blank, 8-quire		11		11									
20	Books, blank, assorted		1, 022		1, 022								72	239
21	Books, ration return		10		10									
22	Books, time		11, 428		11, 428							25	16	106
23	Books, order		35		35									
24	Books, memorandum		229	114 50	229							6		41
25	Books, abstract		3		3								10	
26	Books, indorsement		5		5									
27	Books, way-bill copying		15		15								4	7
28	Books, record		26		26									14

29	Books, copying		20		20								1	1
30	Books, stub													
31	Books, letter		1		1									
32	Books, requisition		6		6									
33	Books, discharge		72		72									
34	Books, general order		1		1									
35	Books, clothing order		6		6									
36	Books, receipt		1		1									
37	Bands, rubber		204	6 12	204								10	21
38	Boards, file		24		24									
39	Cutters, paper		73		73							2	4	17
40	Clips, letter		181	33 93	181								5	12
41	Clips, paper		26		26									6
42	Clips, board		79		79							11	13	32
43	Clips, letter board		8		8									
44	Clips, metal		7		7									
45	Erasers		13		13									
46	Erasers, steel		38	35 62	38								1	7
47	Erasers, rubber		30	1 87	30								5	9
48	Envelopes		2, 750		2, 750									
49	Envelopes, letter		76, 210	495 36	76, 210							950	3, 000	5, 000
50	Envelopes, official		75, 360	508 68	75, 360							500	1, 166	1, 734
51	Files, paper		124		124							2	4	85
52	Files, adhesive		14		14									
53	Folders, paper		1		1							1		1
54	Fasteners, paper ....papers		25½		25½									25
55	Holders, pen		2, 959	308 20	2, 959							43	96	416
56	Holders, paper		4		4									
57	Ink, (quart) ....bottles		540	810 00	540								1	1
58	Ink, copying ....do		459	918 00	459							26	2	4
59	Ink, carmine ....do		1, 078	134 75	1, 078							12	81	162
60	Ink, blue ....do		16		16							13	2	4
61	Journals		1		1									1
62	Ledgers		1		1									1
63	Mucilage ....bottles		556	113 98	556							13	35	69
64	Paper, letter, assorted ....quires		6, 671	2, 251 12	6, 671								63	127
65	Paper, flat letter ....do		1, 965	884 25	1, 965							50		
66	Paper, note ....do		1, 265	347 82	1, 265								37	73
67	Paper, cap ....do		2, 698	1, 133 16	2, 698								73	167
68	Paper, flat cap ....do		2, 554	1, 072 68	2, 554							230		
69	Paper, oil ....sheets		195	48 75	195							4	25	51
70	Paper, blotting ....do		1, 079	101 25	1, 079								50	95
71	Paper, cross section ....do		120		120									120
72	Paper, envelope ....quires		121	72 00	121								4	26
73	Paper, folio post ....do													
74	Paper, news ....do													
75	Paper, colored ....do		40		40									
76	Paper, printing ....bundles													
77	Paper, P. O ....quires		37½	21 00	37½									
78	Paper, heavy yellow ....lots		1		1									
79	Paper, heavy yellow ....do		1		1									
80	Paper, white demi ....quires		1, 890		1, 890									

Report showing the disposition of United States military railroad property in the military division of the Tennessee, &c.—Continued.

Running number.	Articles.	Captured property on hand.	Property purchased by the United States on hand.	Cost to the United States of property purchased.	Total amount of property on hand.	Property sold on credit to railroad companies under Executive Orders of August 8 and October 14, 1865. Macon and Brunswick railroad.	Muscogee railroad.	Montgomery and W. P. railroad.	Wills Valley railroad.	Macon and Western railroad.	Edgefield and Kentucky railroad.	Memphis and Charleston railroad.	Nashville and N. W. railroad.	Nashville and Chattanooga railroad.
81	Pencils, lead		2,779	$347 37	2,779								180	352
82	Pencils, slate		8,443	63 32¼	8,443							72	250	550
83	Pens, steel ......gross		140½	98 35	140½								9	17
84	Pens, steel		624		624									
85	Pens, ruling		1,000	500 00	1,000									1
86	Pens, extension ......boxes		¼		¼									
87	Rulers, rubber		22	16 94	22								3	17
88	Rulers, wood													
89	Rulers, rosewood		11		11									
90	Rulers, boxwood		15	18 75	15									2
91	Rulers, mahogany		13	1 08	13									
92	Rulers, ebony		7	2 19	7							2		3
93	Rulers, assorted		95		95									7
94	Racks, pen		251	125 50	251							9	7	57
95	Rings, elastic		24		24									
96	Stands, ink		349	174 50	349							19	13	114
97	Tearers, paper													
98	Tape ......spools		39		39							2	3	5
99	Weights, paper		304	114 00	304							5	16	74
100	Wax, sealing ......pounds		23		23									
101	Buckets, tin, assorted		168	63 00	168									11
102	Buckets, mess		22	11 88	22									
103	Buckets, slop		6		6									
104	Buckets													
105	Basins, wash		1,145	767 15	1,145							18	11	38
106	Basins, tin wash		172		172									
107	Basins, tin		39		39									
108	Boilers, coffee		1,065		1,065									
109	Boilers, assorted		740		740							13		5
110	Boilers, wash		208		208									
111	Boilers, meat		7		7									
112	Boilers, tin		14		14									

113	Boilers, iron		2		2									
114	Boilers with cocks		18		18									
115	Boilers, copper range		9		9									
116	Boilers, tin wash													
117	Boilers, tin wash, with cocks													
118	Brooms, hickory		123	34 44	123								16	31
119	Brooms, splint		85	23 80	85									
120	Brooms, corn		1, 832	572 75	1, 832							15	93	160
121	Brooms, ratan		1		1									
122	Brooms		488	152 50	488	1			1	1	1	2	5	19
123	Brushes, copying		29		29							1		1
124	Brushes, window		1		1									
125	Brushes, counter		225	70 31	225					48			21	46
126	Brushes, dust		19		19									
127	Brushes, assorted													
128	Boxes, P. O		15	30 00	15							3	2	15
129	Boxes, letter		1		1									
130	Boxes, paper		1		1									
131	Boxes, dredge		369		369							1		
132	Boxes, twine		10	5 00	10								1	1
133	Boxes, tin		2		2									
134	Boxes, spice		1		1									
135	Boxes, ice		7		7									1
136	Boxes, sugar		3		3									
137	Boxes, salt		15		15									
138	Boxes, pepper		2, 202	110 10	2, 202							4		14
139	Boxes, mess		22		22								1	3
140	Boxes, bill-head		3		3									1
141	Boxes, black walnut													
142	Boxes, cash													
143	Benches, assorted		230		230									
144	Baskets, paper		13		13									8
145	Bells, office		2		2									1
146	Balances, letter		1		1									1
147	Boards, wash		14		14									
148	Boards, black		7		7									
149	Boards, diagram		5		5									4
150	Boards, paper		4		4									
151	Boards, pressing													
152	Boards, card ... sheets		3, 300		3, 300									
153	Boards, binders'													
154	Boards, Bristol		132		132									
155	Bowls, sugar		6		6									6
156	Bowls, wash		2		2									
157	Bowls, feet wash		135		135									
158	Bowls, assorted		166	401 17	166									
159	Bunks		399		399									2
160	Bunks, single		1		1								1	1
161	Bureaus		2		2									
162	Bedsteads		54		54									
163	Bins, flour		2		2									
164	Blocks, meat		2		2									

Report showing the disposition of United States military railroad property in the military division of the Tennessee, &c.—Continued.

Running number.	Articles.	Captured property on hand.	Property purchased by the United States on hand.	Cost to the United States of property purchased.	Total amount of property on hand.	Property sold on credit to railroad companies under Executive Orders of August 8 and October 14, 1865.								
						Macon and Brunswick railroad.	Muscogee railroad.	Montgomery and W. P. railroad.	Wills Valley railroad.	Macon and Western railroad.	Edgefield and Kentucky railroad.	Memphis and Charleston railroad.	Nashville and N. W. railroad.	Nashville and Chattanooga railroad.
165	Cups		155	$16 25	155									
166	Cups, palette		2		2									
167	Cups, tin, assorted		7,276	757 91	7,276							220	56	719
168	Cups, sponge		4		4									3
169	Cups, copying		1		1									
170	Cups, molasses		335	67 00	335							5		
171	Cans, milk, (covered)													
172	Cans, molasses		150		150									
173	Cans, watering		22		22									2
174	Covers, bucket		3,482	348 20	3,482									
175	Covers, coffee-pot		4,248	169 92	4,248									
176	Covers, oven													
177	Covers, tallow can		690	172 50	690									
178	Cleavers, meat		50	100 00	50									1
179	Casters		10	17 50	10									
180	Canisters, tea		33		33									
181	Cots		45		45									10
182	Chests, mess		30		30									
183	Chests, field													
184	Chests, assorted		6		6									
185	Clocks		56	840 00	56							2	3	33
186	Cupboards		102		102									6
187	Cupboards, pigeon-hole													8
188	Counters		4		4									
189	Chambers		9		9									
190	Chairs, assorted		553		553							20	40	140
191	Chairs, office		356	652 66	356									
192	Chairs, split bottom		6		6									
193	Coolers, water		18	117 00	18									4
194	Cases, tin		3		3									
195	Cases, post-office		3		3									
196	Cases, blank		3		3									1

197	Cases, shelves, and drawers		2		2									2
198	Cases, assorted		10		10									1
199	Cases, book													
200	Cases, pillow													
201	Cases, pigeon-hole		33		33								1	
202	Closets, picket		22		22								1	
203	Cleaners, stove		104		104									
204	Cullenders		6		6									
205	Cushions		130		130							2	4	11
206	Curtains, window		2		2									
207	Charts, time		1		1									
208	Calendars		59	44 25	59							1	2	19
209	Cellars, salt		4	40	4									4
210	Cutters, cake		23		23									
211	Carvers		4		4									
212	Carvers and forks		1	90	1									
213	Caps, stove pipe		90	45 00	90									19
214	Counterpanes													
215	Carpet, Brussels ... yards		25		25									25
216	Coverlets													
217	Desks, assorted		173		173							8	6	54
218	Dusters		2		2								1	
219	Dusters, feather		90	247 50	90							3	6	19
220	Dippers		111	51 06	111									
221	Dippers, tin		641	294 86	641							1	34	4
222	Drums, stove		3		3									4
223	Drums, sheet-iron		15		15									
224	Dishes, tin		15	2 82	15									
225	Dishes, soup		10	3 50	10									
226	Dishes, fruit		7		7									
227	Dishes, vegetable		4		4									
228	Dishes, meat		2		2									
229	Dishes, sauce		9	1 12	9									
230	Dishes, large		1		1									
231	Dishes, small		2		2									
232	Dishes, assorted		59	209 65	59									
233	Demijohns		3		3									
234	Drawers		1		1									
236	Elbows		91		91									25
237	Elbows, stove-pipe		1,001	1,001 00	1,001							20	2	109
238	Fixtures, cook-stove ... sets		21		21									10
239	Forks		156		156							165	16	10
240	Forks, iron		4		4							4		
241	Forks, flesh		908		908									
242	Forks, table		1,682		1,682									207
243	Forks, carving		2		2									
244	Forks, large		4		4									
245	Funnels, assorted		101		101								1	39
246	Funnels, tin, assorted		292		292							4		2
247	Fillers, lamp		309		309						6		45	82
248	Feeders, lamp		83		83									
249	Furniture, cherry ... lots													

Report showing the disposition of United States military railroad property in the military division of the Tennessee, &c.—Continued.

Running number.	Articles.	Captured property on hand.	Property purchased by the United States on hand.	Cost to the United States of property purchased.	Total amount of property on hand.	Property sold on credit to railroad companies under Executive Orders of August 8 and October 14, 1865.								
						Macon and Brunswick railroad.	Muscogee railroad.	Montgomery and W. P. railroad.	Wills Valley railroad.	Macon and Western railroad.	Edgefield and Kentucky railroad.	Memphis and Charleston railroad.	Nashville and N. W. railroad.	Nashville and Chattanooga railroad.
250	Firkins		1		1									
251	Grates		126		126									
252	Grates, nutmeg		374	$26 18	374									
253	Gridirons		77		77							15		
254	Gates, molasses		35	28 80	35								2	16
255	Griddles, stove		246		246									
256	Glasses, looking		6		6									
257	Globes, lamp		7		7									
258	Grates		15		15									
259	Hods, coal		20		20								10	26
260	Horns, tin		1		1									
261	Hooks, clothes		3		3									3
262	Hooks, meat		11		11									
263	Jugs													
264	Jars, earthen													
265	Kettles, camp		541		541									
266	Kettles, iron		75		75									
267	Kettles, tea		147		147									
268	Kettles, mess		5		5									
269	Kettles		11		11							21		40
270	Knives		323		323									10
271	Knives, table		2,338		2,338							153	16	256
272	Knives, butcher		1,572	955 20	1,572							4		6
273	Knives and forks ... sets		1	90	1									
274	Knives and forks		2,691	592 05	2,691									
275	Knives, carving		74	74 00	74									
276	Knives, cook		84		84									
277	Knives, chopping		6		6									
278	Lamps, office		98	134 75	98							9	1	
279	Lamps, coal-oil		135	185 62	135								3	24
280	Lamps		87		87									
281	Ladles, soup		27	17 55	27									

282	Larders		12		12									
283	Lids		9		9									
284	Matting, floor ... feet		144		144									129
285	Mortars		2		2							1		
286	Mills, coffee		354	354 00	354							10		10
287	Mattresses		17		17									
288	Mops, floor		2		2									
289	Mashers, potato		4		4									
290	Nests, pigeon-hole		5		5								1	3
291	Ovens, Dutch		71		71									9
292	Ovens, bake		2	5 00	2									
293	Punches, paper													
294	Presses, letter		33	1,980 00	33								2	12
295	Presses, letter, with stamp		5		5									
296	Presses and stands, (letter)											2		8
297	Pipe, stove ... feet		1,736		1,736									
298	Pipe, stove ... joints		2,537	2,410 15	2,537			50			13	279	26	461
299	Pipe, stove, assorted ... pounds		925		925									945
300	Pipes, connecting, for range		1		1									
301	Pans, fry		1,610	939 16	1,610							1		2
302	Pans, try													
303	Pans, mess, assorted		1,586		1,586							46		72
304	Pans, dish		312		312							11	1	1
305	Pans, baking		24	30 00	24									3
306	Pans, dripping		87		87							25		16
307	Pans, tin sauce		8		8								3	6
308	Pans, dust		14		14									
309	Pans, stew		13		13									
310	Pans, assorted		2,780		2,780									
311	Pans, tin, assorted		935		935									
312	Pans, ash		29		29									11
313	Pans, tin ... sets		10		10									
314	Pans, pie													
315	Pans, wash													
316	Pans, cake													
317	Pails, tin		13		13									
318	Pails		2		2									
319	Plates, tin		8,914	802 26	8,914							222	18	322
320	Plates, soup		147	55 12	147									
321	Plates, sauce		48		48									
322	Plates, dinner		12	2 50	12									
323	Plates		330		330									
324	Plates, pie													
325	Plates, meat													
326	Pots, assorted		1		1									
327	Pots, mess		5		5									
328	Pots, tea		23		23									
329	Pots, coffee		1,025	2,050 00	1,025							28	1	9
330	Pots, fire		3		3									
331	Pots, sprinkling		158		158							1	3	23
332	Pots, iron		249		249							20		
333	Pots, tin		6		6									

Report showing the disposition of United States military railroad property in the military division of the Tennessee, &c.—Continued.

Running number.	Articles.	Captured property on hand.	Property purchased by the United States on hand.	Cost to the United States of property purchased.	Total amount of property on hand.	Property sold on credit to railroad companies under Executive Orders of August 8 and October 14, 1865.								
						Macon and Brunswick railroad.	Muscogee railroad.	Montgomery and W. P. railroad.	Wills Valley railroad.	Macon and Western railroad.	Edgefield and Kentucky railroad.	Memphis and Charleston railroad.	Nashville and N. W. railroad.	Nashville and Chattanooga railroad.
334	Pots, tin stew		10		10									
335	Pots, water													
336	Pitchers		2		2									
337	Pitchers, stone		22		22									
338	Pitchers, water		2		2									
339	Pillows		8		8									
340	Pokers, assorted		82		82									3
341	Peels, bakers'		4		4									
342	Pins, time		12		12									
343	Pins, rolling													
344	Plugs, basin		5		5									
345	Quilts													
346	Racks, letter		26		26							2		
347	Racks and desk, card		1		1									
348	Racks, towel													
349	Ranges and fixtures, cooking		7		7									1
350	Ranges, cooking		13	$5, 200 00	13									
351	Ranges, patent													
352	Railing, office ... pieces		22		22								2	7
353	Railing, hand, with banisters ... feet	50			50									
354	Refrigerators		1		1									
355	Safes, iron		3		3									
356	Safes, office		29		29							1	1	9
357	Safes, fire-proof		2	310 00	2									
358	Safes, paymasters'		3		3									
359	Safes, field													
360	Safes, match		160	20 00	160								17	37
361	Safes, twine		56		56									
362	Safes, S. P.		34		34									
363	Scissors ... pairs													1
364	Shears ... do		2		2									
365	Shears, lamp ... do		20	6 60	20								4	6

366	Shears, banker's ....do		21	52 50	21								2	8
367	Slates, assorted		372		372						6	9	19	66
368	Shovels, fire		86	50 16	86									4
369	Shovels, baker's		6		6									
370	Sieves		72		72							1		
371	Sieves, flour		16	88 00	16									8
372	Sieves, meal		13		13									1
373	Sieves, fine		1		1									
374	Scuttles, coal		16		16									6
375	Scoops		117	205 00	117								8	27
376	Scoops, flour		13		13									
377	Spittoons		117		117								1	7
378	Spittoons, wooden		79		79									1
379	Shades		3		3									
380	Shades, lamp		82	20 50	82								1	28
381	Shades, lamp, (tin)		4		4									
382	Shades and clasps		36		36									
383	Spiders		16		16							1		
384	Spoons, table		14, 956		14, 956							116	12	61
385	Spoons, tea		7, 314	329 13	7, 314							39	1	42
386	Spoons, basting		1, 626		1, 626									2
387	Spoons, assorted		3, 143		3, 143									166
388	Skimmers		57	8 88	57									
389	Steamers		168		168									1
390	Steamers, tin		102		102							10		
391	Skillets		142	76 00	142							14		
392	Skillets, stove		96		96									
393	Stoves, box		434	3 906 00	434			12		6	6	8	3	84
394	Stoves, sheet-iron		113	1, 356 00	113									
395	Stoves, cast-iron		116		116									
396	Stoves, coal		70	2, 100 00	70								1	14
397	Stoves, open coal		2		2									
398	Stoves, tent		98		98									
399	Stoves, camp													
400	Stoves, cooking		121	3, 630 00	121							16		8
401	Stoves, cooking, and pipe		1		1									
402	Stoves, cooking, and fixtures		155		155								10	7
403	Stoves, cooking, complete		19		19									
404	Stoves, parlor		5		5									1
405	Stoves and pipe		2		2									
406	Stoves, glue		3		3									2
407	Stoves, heating		10		10									
408	Stoves, assorted		125		125								1	19
409	Stoves, office		1		2									
410	Stoves, shop		7		7									
411	Stoves, cylinder		7		7									
412	Stoves, old ....tons		25		25									
413	Stands		25		25									2
414	Stands, wash		80		80							2	2	19
415	Stands, letter-press		1		1									1
416	Stands, light, and hose		1		1									1
417	Stands and lamp globe		1		1									

Report showing the disposition of United States military railroad property in the military division of the Tennessee, &c.—Continued.

Running number.	Articles.	Captured property on hand.	Property purchased by the United States on hand.	Cost to the United States of property purchased.	Total amount of property on hand.	Property sold on credit to railroad companies under Executive Orders of August 8 and October 14, 1865.								
						Macon and Brunswick railroad.	Muscogee railroad.	Montgomery and W. P. railroad.	Wills Valley railroad.	Macon and Western railroad.	Edgefield and Kentucky railroad.	Memphis and Charleston railroad.	Nashville and N. W. railroad.	Nashville and Chattanooga railroad.
418	Stands, light													
419	Stands, bed													
420	Snuffers ....pairs		1		1									
421	Snuffers, candle ....do		7		7									
422	Stools		220		220							2	5	12
423	Stools, bench		3		3									3
424	Spouts, funnel		60		60									
425	Shelves and brackets ....sets		1		1									
426	Sticks, candle		1, 025	$85 41	1, 025							8		8
427	Steels, carving		8		8									
428	Saucers, tin		522		522									
429	Saucers													
430	Sinks		7		7									1
431	Sheets													
432	Screens		4		4								4	
433	Settees		7		7									
434	Strainers, coffee		1		1									
435	Sprinklers													
436	Sprinklers, copper													
437	Sacks, bed													
438	Scales, letter													
439	Tables, field													
440	Tables, camp													
441	Tables, office		21		21									9
442	Tables, round		8		8									
443	Tables, centre		1		1									
444	Tables, dining		1		1									
445	Tables, draughting		1		1									
446	Tables, assorted											2	5	29
447	Tables, time		26		26									
448	Trimmers, lamp		3		3								1	
449	Tumblers		15		15									

450	Thimbles, stovepipe		74		74									
451	Toasters		1		1									
452	Tubs, wash		1		1									
453	Tubs, bathing		2		2									
454	Ticks, bed													
455	Troughs, bread		2		2									
456	Urinals													
457	Wardrobes		54		54									
458	Waiters		3		3								1	8
459	Ambulances		6		6									
460	Axles, ambulance		2		2									
461	Blankets, saddle		532		532									
462	Bits, mullen		36	6 00	36									
463	Bridles, riding		103		103									
464	Bridles, blind		363		363									
465	Buckets, U. S. horse		324		324									
466	Bows, wagon		337		337									
467	Bows, ox		404	333 30	404									
468	Bows, ambulance		56		56									
469	Brushes, horse		1,155	635 25	1,155								2	3
470	Boxes, feed		83		83									
471	Boxes, wagon		48		48									
472	Boxes, cutting		1		1									
473	Boxes, ambulance pipe		12		12									
474	Boards, foot		12		12									
475	Bolsters, extra log wagon												5	11
476	Bolsters, army wagon		26		26									
477	Bolts, king		29		29									
478	Bolts, king .... pounds		1,270		1,270							345		900
479	Bolts, tongue		20		20									
480	Bodies, wagon		40		40									
481	Bodies, cart		1		1									
482	Breeching, cart		81		81									
482½	Bits, bridle		251		251									
483	Beds, axle		6											
484	Carts		65		65									
485	Chains, halter		499		499									
486	Chains, trace		38		38									
487	Chains, fifth		102		102									
488	Chains, bearing		69		69									
489	Chains, breast		382		382									
490	Chains, spreader		195		195									
491	Chains, stretcher		190		190									
492	Chains, stretcher, and S. S		24		24									
493	Chains, ox		2		2									
494	Collars, horse		240		240									
495	Collars, mule		395		395									
496	Covers, wagon		32		32									
497	Combs, curry		1,332	279 72	1,332									

Report showing the disposition of United States military railroad property in the military division of the Tennessee, &c.—Continued.

Running number.	Articles.	Captured property on hand.	Property purchased by the United States on hand.	Cost to the United States of property purchased.	Total amount of property on hand.	Property sold on credit to railroad companies under Executive Orders of August 8 and October 14, 1865.								
						Macon and Brunswick railroad.	Muscogee railroad.	Montgomery and W. P. railroad.	Wills Valley railroad.	Macon and Western railroad.	Edgefield and Kentucky railroad.	Memphis and Charleston railroad.	Nashville and N. W. railroad.	Nashville and Chattanooga railroad.
498	Cruppers		41		41									
499	Drays		12		12									
500	Felloes, wagon		3, 553		3, 553									
501	Gears, running		26		36									
502	Gearings, hind													
503	Gearings, front													
504	Gates, end		139		139									
505	Horses		262		262									7
506	Harness ... sets		2		2									2
507	Harness, S. S. ambulance		9		9									
508	Harness, S. S. wheel		546		546									
509	Harness, S. S. lead		674		674									
510	Harness, S. S. wheel-horse		12		12									
511	Harness, S. S. wheel-mule		10		10									
512	Harness, S. S. lead-mule		80		80									
513	Harness, cart		114		114									
514	Harness, dray		2		2									
515	Hames, horse ... pairs		132		132									
516	Hames ... do		6		6									
517	Halters, rope		28		28									
518	Halters, head		572		572									
519	Halters, head, and strap		12		12									
520	Halters and chains		124		124									
521	Hounds, front, army wagon		577		577									
522	Hounds, hind, army wagon		571		571									
523	Hammers, wagon		1		1									
524	Jacks, wagon		1		1									
525	Kegs, ambulance		4		4									
526	Lines, cart		45		45									
527	Lines, check		94		94									
528	Lines, lead		238		238									
529	Lines, 2-horse		33		33									

530	Leathers, sweat		126		126									
531	Links, open		10		10									
532	Mules		976		976									1
533	Martingales		4		4									
534	Oxen		53		53									
535	Poles, ridge		29		29									
536	Poles, coupling		29		29									
537	Rakes, stable													
538	Rims, bent ambulance		42		42									
539	Rims, ox-yoke bow		3		3									
540	Rings, open		838		838									
541	Rails, body		271		271									
542	Stretchers		245		245									
543	Spreaders		72		72									
544	Saddles, riding		57		57									
545	Saddles, wagon		455		455									
546	Saddles, cart		76		76									
547	Saddles		1		1									
548	Sticks, jockey		306		306									
549	Sticks, cart-dumping		4		4									
550	Springs, ambulance		6		6									
551	Sprinklers, wagon		1		1									
552	Sprinklers, cart													
553	Straps, neck		808		808									
554	Straps, coupling		75		75									
555	Straps, neck and chain		27		27									
556	Straps, back													
557	Straps, choke													
558	Straps, halter		26		26									
559	Straps, stirrup													
560	Straps, yoke		12		12									
561	Spokes, wagon		102		102									
562	Spokes		2,000		2,000									
563	Spokes, army wagon		1,246		1,246									
564	Spokes, 2-horse wagon		220		220									
565	Spokes, ambulance		187		187									
566	Stirrups, wooden		51		51									
567	Stirrups, leather		388		388									
568	Shafts, cart		46		46									
569	Shafts													
570	Strings, tie		200		200									
571	Stocks, whip		8		8									
572	Trees, single		1,313		1,313									
573	Trees, double		373		373									
574	Trees, saddle		17		17									
575	Tongues, wagon		413		413									
576	Tongues, rough		86		86									
577	Troughs, feed		109		109									
578	Tires, wagon		75		75									
579	Wheels, hind		25		25									
580	Wheels, front		25		25									
581	Wheels, wagon		113		113									

Report showing the disposition of United States military railroad property in the military division of the Tennessee, &c.—Continued.

Running number.	Articles.	Captured property on hand.	Property purchased by the United States on hand.	Cost to the United States of property purchased.	Total amount of property on hand.	Property sold on credit to railroad companies under Executive Orders of August 8 and October 14, 1865.								
						Macon and Brunswick railroad.	Musogee railroad.	Montgomery and W. P. railroad.	Wills Valley railroad.	Macon and Western railroad.	Edgefield and Kentucky railroad.	Memphis and Charleston railroad.	Nashville and N. W. railroad.	Nashville and Chattanooga railroad.
582	Wagons, lumber		47		47									
583	Wagons, army		226		226									
584	Wagons, spring		1		1									
585	Wagons, log		76		76									
586	Wagons, 2-horse		14		14									
587	Wagons, ox		1		1									
588	Wagons, wood		15		15									
589	Wagons, water		2		2									
590	Wagons, box		12		12									
591	Wagons													
592	Whips, wagon		549		549									
593	Yokes, ox		305	$4,740 00	305									
594	Yokes and bows, ox		387		387									
595	Axes, chopping		21,047	42,094 00	21,047	1		120	1	120	14	131	177	198
596	Axes, chopping, and handles													
597	Axes, felling		20		20									
598	Axes, felling, and handles		143		143									
599	Axes, hand		176	264 00	176						12	4	34	89
600	Axes, pick		38		38									
601	Axes, broad		1,746	6,984 00	1,746			12		6		11	17	36
602	Axes, narrow		580		580									
603	Axes, assorted		495		495									
604	Augers ... sets		1		1									
605	Augers		6,095	5,485 50	6,095							54	60	143
606	Augers, long, assorted		25		25									
607	Augers, hollow ... sets		2		2									
608	Augers, gas-fitting		1	3 00	1									
609	Augers, bridge		123		123									
610	Augers, pump ... sets		6	300 00	6									
611	Augers, boring machine		24		24									
612	Augers, machine ... sets		47		47							3		
613	Augers, machine		37		37									

614	Augers and handles													
615	Augers and handles, ¼-inch													
616	Augers and handles, 1½-inch													
617	Augers, spike		4		4									
618	Augers, convex		38		38									
619	Augers, wheelwright		26		26									
620	Augers, nut		132		132									
621	Anvils, assorted		174		174									
622	Anvils, cast		6		6					4	2	12		52
623	Anvils, wrought		4		4									
624	Anvils, block		3		3									
625	Anvils, wrought ... pounds													
626	Anvils, blacksmiths'													
627	Awls, scratch		485	48 50	485									
628	Awls, brad		1,008	46 20	1,008							12		1
629	Awls, belt											4		
630	Awls, scribe		6		6									
631	Awls and tacks, shoe		6		6									
632	Awls, scratch, and handles													
633	Awls, peg, and handles													
634	Adzes		412		412									
635	Adzes and handles													40
636	Adzes, railroad		1,001	3,503 50	1,001									
637	Adzes, foot or carpenters'		664	1,992 00	664			6		48	6		117	33
638	Axles, car ... pounds		285,139	35,642 37	285,139							61	4	72
639	Axles, car		18		18					33,574	13,990			
639½	Arbors, circular saw		2		2									
640	Axles, car and tender		251		251									
641	Axles, truck ... pounds		24,351		24,351									
642	Axles, engine-driving		31		31									
643	Axles, engine truck ... pounds													6
644	Axles, tender									2,120	6,308			
645	Axles, truck		5		5									
646	Axles, tender truck		1		1									
647	Axles, timber buggy		59		59									
648	Anchors		1		1									
649	Acid, oxalic ... pounds		59½	47 60	59½									
650	Acid, muriatic ... do		250	65 00	250									
651	Acid ... do		6		6							6	5	10
652	Aqua ammonia ... do		7		7									
653	Aloes ... do		10		10									
654	Alum ... do		292	20 44	292									
655	Antimony ... do		2,657	584 54	2,657									
656	Alcohol ... gallons		567½	2,468 62	567½					200				761
657	Ammoniac, sal ... pounds		185	74 00	185							3	22	64
658	Arms, hand-car		4		4								8	17
659	Arms, engine pump		6		6									4
660	Arms, seat, cast ... pounds		139		139									4
661	Apparatus, automatic ... sets													
662	Asphaltum ... gallons		30		30									
663	Bellows, blacksmiths'	1	117	5,850 00	118									
664	Bellows, assorted		31		31						1	4	2	11

Report showing the disposition of United States military railroad property in the military division of the Tennessee, &c.—Continued.

Running number.	Articles.	Captured property on hand.	Property purchased by the United States on hand.	Cost to the United States of property purchased.	Total amount of property on hand.	Property sold on credit to railroad companies under the Executive Orders of August 8 and October 14, 1865.								
						Macon and Brunswick railroad.	Muscogee railroad.	Montgomery and W. P. railroad.	Wills Valley railroad.	Macon and Western railroad.	Edgefield and Kentucky railroad.	Memphis and Charleston railroad.	Nashville and N. W. railroad.	Nashville and Chattanooga railroad.
665	Bellows, hand		9	$72 00	9									9
666	Bellows, 48-inch		1	50 00	1									
667	Bars, switch		119		119									
668	Bars, switch ....sets		1		1									
669	Bars, lining		632		632							60	152	84
670	Bars, raising													
671	Bars, iron													
672	Bars, pinch		333		333	1			1	2	15	7	66	128
673	Bars, pinch ....pounds		813		813									
674	Bars, grate ....do		86		86									
675	Bars, draw		12		12									
676	Bars, assorted											88		6
677	Bars, timber		299		299								2	
678	Bars, grate		15		15									
679	Bars, pinch steel		1		1									
680	Bars, wrought iron pinch ....pounds		453		453									
681	Bars, switch ....do		294		294									
682	Bars, grate ....sets													
683	Bars, carpenters'		54		54									
684	Bars, pry and pinch		130											
685	Bars, pry		1											
686	Bars, fish ....pounds		19,374											
687	Bars, tamping		270								36	3	275	300
688	Bars, crow	12	428											
689	Bars, claw		507	4,056 00				24			12	32	98	149
690	Bars, wrench		3											
691	Bars, engine coupling													
692	Bars, boring	1	12											3
693	Bars, cylinder boring		1											
694	Bars, long		25											
695	Bars, short		96											
696	Bars, steel		13											10

697	Bars, assorted .... pounds		7,889									236		7,653
698	Bars, pins, and bolts .... do		1,090											1,090
699	Brushes, varnish, assorted		400							11		9	46	94
700	Brushes, C. H		92	53 00						4			7	15
701	Brushes, W. W		271	223 57								2	2	16
702	Brushes, scrub		485	161 66								5	20	40
703	Brushes, painters' dust		52											
704	Brushes, paint, assorted		1,160	1,933 00						3		24	36	133
705	Brushes, flat		29	17 40										
706	Brushes, oval		4											
707	Brushes, marking		203	25 38						49				2
708	Brushes, striping		24											
709	Brushes, car window		31	72 33									10	21
710	Brushes, artists'		108											
711	Brushes, artists' red sable		108	14 00						73				
712	Brushes, glue		5									1		
713	Brushes, sash		6											
714	Brushes, whitewash .... lots		1											
715	Brushes, machinists'													
716	Braces		103											
717	Braces, iron		79									4		3
718	Braces, wood		31											
719	Braces and bits .... sets		136											
720	Braces and bits		26											
721	Braces and bits, car .... sets		4											
722	Braces, hand		1											
723	Braces, joiner													
724	Braces, switch		6											
725	Braces, pedestal		2											
726	Braces, ratchet .... sets		2											
727	Braces, truck .... pounds		42,480											
728	Braces, engine		1											
729	Braces, engine bar		1											
730	Blenders, painters'		13	67 00									4	7
731	Blenders, painters'		7											
732	Bits .... sets											6		
733	Bits, brace .... do		5											
734	Bits, auger, assorted .... do		176	1,056 00										
735	Bits, auger, assorted		483											
736	Bits, gimlet		941	141 15										
737	Bits, gimlet .... sets		1											
738	Bits, plough plane		20											
739	Bits, plough plane .... sets		45									1		
740	Bits, double plane		18											
741	Bits, car		399											
742	Bits, car .... sets		306	4,437 00								4	5	10
743	Bits, centre													
744	Bits, rose	25	45		70									56
745	Bits, (sets of six each)		26											
746	Bits, gummer		24											
747	Bits, ratchet drill		229	366 40										
748	Bits, assorted		562											

Report showing the disposition of United States military railroad property in the military division of the Tennessee, &c.—Continued.

Running number.	Articles.	Captured property on hand.	Property purchased by the United States on hand.	Cost to the United States of property purchased.	Total amount of property on hand.	Property sold on credit to railroad companies under Executive Orders of August 8 and October 14, 1865. Macon and Brunswick railroad.	Muscogee railroad.	Montgomery and W. P. railroad.	Wills Valley railroad.	Macon and Western railroad.	Edgefield and Kentucky railroad.	Memphis and Charleston railroad.	Nashville and N. W. railroad.	Nashville and Chattanooga railroad.
749	Bits, centre .... sets		3											
750	Bits, planer													
751	Bits, double-cut													
752	Bits, brace													
753	Buts, assorted .... pairs		1,251½							168	18	447	531	2,564
754	Buts, brass, assorted		4,071	$1,696 00										
755	Buts, brass, assorted .... pairs		3,195											
756	Buts													
757	Buts, loose joint		303	50 50										
758	Buts, wrought, assorted		1,593	318 60										
759	Buts, cast-iron .... pairs		2,054	513 50										
760	Buts, assorted		12											
761	Buts, wrought .... pairs		45											
762	Buts, fast		24											
763	Buts, cast		805											
764	Buts, rivet		100											
765	Buts, flat		258											
766	Buts, wrought-iron .... pairs		61											
767	Buts, patent .... do		48											
768	Buts, cast, loose joint .... do		18											
769	Buts, wrought, common joint		30											
770	Buts, cast, loose joint													
771	Buts, wrought-iron													
772	Bolts, tank hoop													
773	Bolts, iron hexagon-head .... pounds		75											
774	Bolts, fish-bar .... do		55,485											
775	Bolts		13,246							200		959	334	12,825
776	Bolts, carriage .... pounds		490											
777	Bolts, carriage		22,405											
778	Bolts, iron bar													
779	Bolts, brass, assorted		12	6 00										
780	Bolts, barrel		16	2 00										

781	Bolts, brass flush		36	2 10										
782	Bolts, fire		800											
783	Bolts, long $\frac{3}{4}$-inch .... pounds		500											
784	Bolts, ring		16											
785	Bolts, chain door		135											
786	Bolts, tower		84											
787	Bolts, square head .... pounds		5,098											
788	Bolts, bridge .... do		9,439	849 51										
789	Bolts, wrought .... do		95											
790	Bolts, wrought-iron		30											
791	Bolts and nuts		145											
792	Bolts and buts		159											
793	Bolts, brass knob		305											
794	Bolts, wagon		49											
795	Bolts, steel-spring square		62											
796	Bolts, pulley		40											
797	Bolts, coupling		15											
798	Bolts and keys		72											
799	Bolts .... pounds		422,637							1,765		16	1,584	6,520
800	Bolts, door		16	1 87										
801	Bolts, bridge		289											
802	Bolts and nuts .... pounds		2,565									2,565		
803	Blocks, punch	1	1		2									
804	Blocks, swedge	5	28		33									
805	Blocks, die .... pounds		126								1			6
806	Blocks, iron pulley													
807	Blocks, iron		12											
808	Blocks, purchase		2											
809	Blocks, notch		39											
810	Blocks, snatch		223	4,460 00										
811	Blocks, head, with truck		1									5		18
812	Blocks, upsetting		4											
813	Blocks, patent		2											
814	Blocks, tackle .... sets		13											
815	Blocks, tackle		361								6		15	7
816	Blocks and tackle .... sets	1			1						2	30	4	
817	Blocks and tackle		37									1		
818	Blocks, assorted		177											41
819	Blocks, double-tackle										1			46
820	Blocks, head	2	13		15									
821	Blocks, triple		5	90 00								1		
822	Blocks, assorted .... pounds		12,096									96		1,200
823	Blocks, assorted .... pairs		9											
824	Blocks, cast-iron swedge .... pounds		380									380		
825	Blocks, cast-iron swedge													
826	Blocks, pillow .... pounds		600											
827	Blocks, single		2											
828	Blocks, double		17	187 00										
829	Blocks, head .... sets		2											
830	Blocks, double-head .... do		1											
831	Blocks, cast-iron swedge and tackle .... do		1											
832	Blocks, gum .... pounds		$147\frac{1}{2}$											

Report showing the disposition of United States military railroad property in the military division of the Tennessee, &c.—Continued.

Running number.	Articles.	Captured property on hand.	Property purchased by the United States on hand.	Cost to the United States of property purchased.	Total amount of property on hand.	Property sold on credit to railroad companies under Executive Orders of August 8 and October 14, 1865.								
						Macon and Brunswick railroad.	Muscogee railroad.	Montgomery and W. P. railroad.	Wills Valley railroad.	Macon and Western railroad.	Edgefield and Kentucky railroad.	Memphis and Charleston railroad.	Nashville and N. W. railroad.	Nashville and Chattanooga railroad.
833	Blocks, single													
834	Blocks, tackle ....pairs													
835	Buckets, assorted										12	99	177	641
836	Buckets, water		2, 213											
837	Buckets, fire		102											
838	Buckets, wood		541	$367 88										
839	Buckets		26											
840	Buckets, engine		152								2	8	46	87
841	Buckets, iron		163											
842	Buckets, coal		9											
843	Buckets, varnish		20											20
844	Buckets, tar		92											
845	Buckets, paint		20									14		
846	Buckets, rubber		5											
847	Buckets, sand		8											
848	Buckets, swing		44											
849	Buckets, stiff		9											
850	Buckets, well		1											
851	Buckets, mortar		2											
852	Buckets, leather		1											
853	Boilers, steam													6
854	Boilers, tin-flue		7											
855	Boilers, small-flue		1											
856	Boilers, double-flue		4											
857	Boilers, 14 feet long, 40 inches diameter		2											
858	Boilers, tubular, 12 feet long, 42 inches diameter		1											
859	Boilers, steam, 2 flues, 21 ft. long, 34 inches diameter													
860	Boilers, steam, 4 flues, 24 ft. long, 39 inches diameter													3
861	Boilers, stationary													
862	Boilers, iron-punch	1			1									
863	Boilers, iron-flue, 26 feet x 44 inches	1			1									
864	Brass, old ....pounds	200	3, 241		3, 441									

865	Brass, sheet ... do.		5,014½	2,858 16						61		105	429	872
866	Brass ... do.		1,653									98	71	140
867	Brass, scrap ... do.		25											
868	Brass, wrought ... do.		414											
869	Brass turnings ... do.		9,535											
870	Brasses ... do.		7,959											1,823
871	Brasses, truck ... do.		505											417
872	Bricks, common		32,500									10		2,000
873	Bricks, setting, for boilers		1											1
874	Bricks, fire		19,302	9,071 44										
875	Bricks, soap-fire		2,000											
876	Bricks, split-fire		3,000											
877	Bricks, key		1,000											
878	Burlaps ... yards		3,845	1,826 37									376	1,323
879	Buttons, assorted ... gross		120										100⅓	232⅜
880	Buttons, upholsterers' ... do.		719⅜	1,079 50										
881	Buttons, hand ... sets		8											
882	Buttons, brass, on plates		26											
883	Buttons, brass ... gross		1											
884	Buttons, brass		136											
885	Brown, Vandyke ... pounds		153	22 18									20	38
886	Brown, Spanish ... do.		2,541	254 10									28	56
887	Brown, Vandyke ... tubes		12	1 75										
888	Black, India ... pounds		166	83 00									10	20
889	Black, lamp ... do.		682¼	68 20								16¾	136	284
890	Black, lamp ... tubes		12	1 35									4	8
891	Black, Japan ... barrels		1											
892	Black, ivory ... tubes		12	1 35										
893	Blue, ultramarine ... pounds		320	160 00								12	19	37½
894	Blue, Prussian ... do.		119¼	178 87								20	½	1
895	Black, blue ... do.		100	35 00										
896	Black, drop ... do.		241⅜	60 43								48	23	46½
897	Blue, cobalt ... tubes		3	1 25										
898	Blacking, stove ... papers		335										48	96
899	Bronze, gold ... do.		45	33 75									2	4
900	Brilliant, American ... tubes		12											
901	Bells, gong, hanging		3											
902	Bells, engine		2	200 00									1	1
903	Bells, engine, alarm		81			1		8			3	4	11	22
904	Bells, engine, gong		17											
905	Bells, alarm		7											
906	Bells, engine and frame													
907	Bells, cast-steel	1			1									
908	Bells, cab		1											
909	Balances, spring		31	62 00						1			1	
910	Balances, locomotive spring		121	3,630 00				18			1		7	13
911	Balances, iron beam		24											
912	Balances, beam shive		26											
913	Balances, steam													
914	Balances, elliptic spring													
915	Balances, counter													
916	Bushings, brass		168											72

Report showing the disposition of United States military railroad property in the military division of the Tennessee, &c.—Continued.

Running number.	Articles.	Captured property on hand.	Property purchased by the United States on hand.	Cost to the United States of property purchased.	Total amount of property on hand.	Property sold on credit to railroad companies under Executive Orders of August 8 and October 14, 1865.								
						Macon and Brunswick railroad.	Muscogee railroad.	Montgomery and W. P. railroad.	Wills Valley railroad.	Macon and Western railroad.	Edgefield and Kentucky railroad.	Memphis and Charleston railroad.	Nashville and N. W. railroad.	Nashville and Chattanooga railroad.
917	Bushings, gas-pipe		815											
918	Bushings, bell cord													
919	Bushings, brass gland		105											
920	Bushings, silver-plated		11											
921	Brads, patent, assorted ... papers		2,753	$110 12										89
922	Bunting, assorted ... yards		427	288 22		2			2			23½	36	177½
923	Bunting, red, assorted ... do		386	260 55										
924	Burners, common		720	72 00										
925	Burners, patent		140	35 00										
926	Burners, eureka		123											
927	Burners, screw		24											
928	Brakes		289											
929	Brakes, lever ... pounds		45									45		
930	Brakes, car													159
931	Bevels, assorted		240									1		1
932	Bevels, square		30											
933	Bevels, T		643	482 00								2		
934	Boards, guttering		1											
935	Boards, bulletin		7										1	4
936	Boards, tally		4											
937	Boards, draft		10											8
938	Boards, running													
939	Boards, straw ... pounds		200											
940	Boards, pressing		10											
941	Boards, binders'		125											
942	Boards, sign		3											
943	Brooms, hair		2											
944	Brooms, stable		62											
945	Bottoms, composition ... pounds		68											
946	Bottoms, copper ... do		759	645 15										
947	Bottoms, dipper		625											
948	Bottoms, bolt head		1											1

949	Boxes, emery		230	77 05									24	46
950	Boxes, rivet		59	14 75										
951	Boxes, wood		2											
952	Boxes, tinder		179			2			2	4		13	2	33
953	Boxes, engine ... pounds		1,308											
954	Boxes, engine ... do		97			2			2				2	18
955	Boxes, tool		148							2		12	1	25
956	Boxes, packing		6											2
957	Boxes, tinder		1											
958	Boxes, axle													
959	Boxes, lamp		34											42
960	Boxes, link													
961	Boxes, oil		6									1		
962	Boxes, hand car ... pounds		922											922
963	Boxes, car, (Wood's patent) ... do		2,294									2,294		
964	Boxes, assorted		2											2
965	Boxes, engine truck ... pounds		1,313											
966	Boxes, roller		4											
967	Boxes, iron		5											
968	Boxes, screw, blind		1											
969	Boxes, signal-light		10											
970	Boxes, shoeing		9											
971	Boxes, cutting		1											
972	Boxes, drawing-paper		10											
973	Boxes, cast													
974	Boxes, journal		144											
975	Belting leather, assorted ... feet		23,560 7-12				282	700		356	116	89¼	97	9,427
976	Belting, gum ... do	470	3,122½		3,592½							17	13	209
977	Belting, rubber ... do		231											
978	Belting, assorted ... do											86		
979	Bottoms, tin lamp													
980	Bottoms, car lamp													
981	Blades, hack-saw		46										2	2
982	Brackets ... pounds		816											510
983	Brackets		14											
984	Brackets, swing		5	18 75										
985	Buggies, timber		47	1,175 00										
986	Borers, cylinder													
987	Borers, cylinder, portable	1			1									
988	Borers, tap		10											
989	Borers, hand		23											
990	Barrels		34									17		
991	Bodkins		6											
992	Barrows, wheel	8	383	1,436 25	391							1	9	19
993	Bridges, truss ... feet													
994	Bridges, arch truss, McCallum's pat. inflexible. do													
995	Borax ... pounds		604	271 80								45	34	46
996	Benches, stationery ... feet		1,162											1,024
997	Benches, work		181									4	5	16
998	Benches, vice		1											
999	Bearings, centre ... pounds		1,965											555
1000	Buildings	6	366		372							2	14	53

Report showing the disposition of United States military railroad property in the military division of the Tennessee, &c.—Continued.

Running number.	Articles.	Captured property on hand.	Property purchased by the United States on hand.	Cost to the United States of property purchased.	Total amount of property on hand.	Property sold on credit to railroad companies under Executive Orders of August 8 and October 14, 1865. Macon and Brunswick railroad.	Muscogee railroad.	Montgomery and W. P. railroad.	Wills Valley railroad.	Macon and Western railroad.	Edgefield and Kentucky railroad.	Memphis and Charleston railroad.	Nashville and N. W. railroad.	Nashville and Chattanooga railroad.
1001	Building and water tank	1												
1002	Burrs ... pounds		31½					2			2			14½
1003	Burrs, copper ... do		47											
1004	Bumpers ... do		432											432
1005	Buttresses		26											
1006	Bumpers		2											
1007	Bodies, box car		3											
1008	Breeching ... pounds		50											
1009	Bibbs, finished, S. S. and S		90											
1010	Buckles, assorted		316											
1011	Buckles, harness ... gross		18											
1012	Buckles, roller, assorted ... do		24 29-36											
1013	Buckles, assorted ... do		15											
1014	Blocks, railroad splice, Trimble's wooden		2, 014											
1015	Backs, car-seat		8											
1016	Bands, spring ... pounds		600											
1017	Bands, gum ... do													
1018	Blinds, window		1											
1019	Boats, flat		2											
1020	Baskets, medicine		1											
1021	Benzine ... gallons		5											
1022	Burgois No. 8, 3 "D" ... pounds		13½											
1023	Buckles, round, log ruled ... gross		2											
1024	Bolts, stay		36											
1025	Braces, tank		12											
1026	Barges											1		
1027	Burners, gas													
1027¼	Chisels and handles	150	9		9									
1027½	Chisels, cold		2, 258		2, 406	2			1	2	4	97	126	895
1027¾	Chisels, hand cold		1	$1 25	1									
1028	Chisels, chipping		332	332 00	332									
1029	Chisels, hand chipping		100		100									

1030	Chisels, firmer		307		307							19	48	204
1031	Chisels, firmer ..... sets		66	264 00	66									
1032	Chisels, socket firmer ..... do		45	270 00	45							1	5	
1033	Chisels, socket		1,116		1,116									
1034	Chisels, framing ..... sets		5		5									
1035	Chisels, framing		1,870		1,870							19	30	68
1036	Chisels, track		1,466		1,466						12	15	69	144
1037	Chisels, cold track		2		2									
1038	Chisels, masons'		79		79									
1039	Chisels, corner		12		12									
1040	Chisels, bolt		16		16									
1041	Chisels, splitting		10		10									
1042	Chisels, coppersmiths'		7		7									
1043	Chisels, tamping		11		11									
1044	Chisels, B. S		74		74						24			
1045	Chisels, cape		38		38									
1046	Chisels, assorted		621		621							50	2	118
1047	Chisels, carpenters'		3		3									
1048	Chisels, gouging		46		46									
1049	Chisels, socket ..... sets		20		20									
1050	Chisels, socket framing		418		418									
1051	Chisels, socket, and handles		6		6									
1052	Chisels, oval back		6		6									
1053	Chisels, mortise		13		13									
1054	Chisels, tinners' ..... sets		1		1									
1055	Chills, frog		11		11									
1056	Calipers, assorted ..... pairs		57	28 50	57							2	4	40
1057	Calipers, spring ..... do		69		69									
1058	Compasses, assorted		561	275 50	551							3	17	42
1059	Compasses, wing ..... do		31	26 66	31									
1060	Cups, oil		135	202 50	135									
1061	Cups, oil, spring bottom		7	731 25	7									
1062	Cups, tallow		117		117								31	61
1063	Cups, tin paint		85	8 85	85									29
1064	Cups, tin striping		20		20									
1065	Cups, brass		2		2									
1066	Cups, steam chest oil		12	75 00	12							12		
1067	Cups, valve oil		39		39									
1068	Cups, brass oil		3		3									
1069	Cups, varnish		21		21									
1070	Cans, powder		24		24									
1071	Cans, engine oil		21		21									
1072	Cans, oil, spring-bottom		98		98							3		
1073	Cans, tallow		52	65 00	52									
1074	Cans, assorted		2,027		2,027	2			2	6	28	165	138	409
1075	Cans, oil, assorted	3	594		597									
1076	Cans, tin, assorted		118		118									
1077	Cans, emery		12		12									
1078	Cans, bench oil		5		5									
1079	Couplings, tender ..... pounds		90		90									
1080	Couplings, 3-link		115		115								2	12
1081	Couplings, 3-link ..... pounds		1,038		1,038									

Report showing the disposition of United States military railroad property in the military division of the Tennessee, &c.—Continued.

Running number.	Articles.	Captured property on hand.	Property purchased by the United States on hand.	Cost to the United States of property purchased.	Total amount of property on hand.	Property sold on credit to railroad companies under Executive Orders of August 8 and October 14, 1865.								
						Macon and Brunswick railroad.	Muscogee railroad.	Montgomery and W. P. railroad.	Wills Valley railroad.	Macon and Western railroad.	Edgefield and Kentucky railroad.	Memphis and Charleston railroad.	Nashville and N. W. railroad.	Nashville and Chattanooga railroad.
1082	Couplings, straight		469		469						3		98	269
1083	Couplings, crooked		218		218								47	76
1084	Couplings, brass union, assorted ... pairs		250		250									
1085	Couplings, clamp and screw		1		1									
1086	Couplings, hose		30		30								4	7
1087	Couplings, chain ... pounds													
1088	Couplings ... do		2, 549		2, 549									
1089	Couplings, brass hose ... do		212		212									
1090	Couplings, hose													
1091	Couplings, assorted													
1092	Chains, engine		13		13									
1093	Chains, assorted		17		17	1								
1094	Chains, log		205	$1, 640 00	205								1	2
1095	Chains, switch		78		78						16	3	39	49
1096	Chains, Powers' endless		4		4									
1097	Chains, brake ... pounds													100
1098	Chains, large		1		1									
1099	Chains, small		1		1									
1100	Chains, civil engineers'		1	15 00	1								1	1
1101	Chains, surveyors', (100 feet)													
1102	Chains, switch ... pounds											370		
1103	Chains, log ... do													
1104	Chain, assorted ... feet		1, 064		1, 064									
1105	Chain, assorted ... pounds		1, 376		1, 376							2, 285		3, 435
1106	Chain, cable ... do		500		500									
1107	Chain, cable ... feet													
1108	Chain, German ... do		45		45									
1109	Chain, German coil ... do		1, 475	221 25	1, 475								36	134
1110	Chain, coil, proved, ⅜-inch ... pounds		1, 103		1, 103									
1111	Chain, coil, assorted ... do		31, 050½	4, 554 57	31, 050½							46	1, 200	2, 550
1112	Castings, assorted ... do		334, 672		334, 672							23, 226		152, 908
1113	Castings, iron ... do		357, 869	30, 418 86	357, 869									

1114	Castings, pump ....do		508		508									
1115	Castings, brass ....do		56,449½		56,449½						4,614	1,604½	2,342	9,458
1116	Castings, grate bar ....do		9,291		9,291									
1117	Castings, old stove ....lot		1		1									
1118	Castings, car ....pounds													
1119	Castings, tender ....do		22		22									
1120	Caps, double		3		3									
1121	Caps, gas pipe		776		776									
1122	Clamps, iron ....pairs													11
1123	Clamps, steel		8		8									
1124	Clamps, cabinet-makers'		4		4									
1125	Clamps, saddlers'		6		6									3
1126	Clamps, switch													
1127	Clamps, belt		6		6									1
1128	Clamps, spring		2		2									
1129	Clamps, block ....sets		1		1									
1130	Clamps, horseshoe		26		26									
1131	Clamps ....pairs		3		3									2
1132	Clamps ....pounds		1,642		1,642									175
1133	Clamps, iron horse		63		63									
1134	Clamps, iron		55		55									
1135	Clamps, iron, for tender		10		10									
1136	Clamps, iron boiler		17		17									
1137	Clamps, chimney		2		2									
1138	Clamps, saw-set		3		3									
1139	Clamps, wood bench		28		28									
1140	Clamps, screw	10	25		35									
1141	Cars, box	45	1,628		1,673	8		32	4	37	24	116	99	358
1142	Cars, box freight		71		71									
1143	Cars, flat	47	491		538	8			8	15	24	44	25	100
1144	Cars, wrecking		2		2							1		1
1145	Cars, passenger	8	34		42							3	2	7
1146	Cars, hand		62		62							20	20	41
1147	Cars, truck		55		55							9	16	47
1148	Cars, caboose													
1149	Cars, coal	2			2									
1150	Cars, stock	1			1									
1151	Cars, push or dump	5			5									
1152	Cutters, card		3		3									1
1153	Cutters, lead		1		1									
1153½	Cutters, cast-steel		16		16									
1154	Cutters, boring		20		20									
1155	Cutters, iron		13		13									
1156	Covers, cylinder head													
1157	Covers, flag		116		116									25
1158	Covers, box		27		27									
1159	Covers, hand-car ....pounds		465		465									
1160	Covers, axle-box ....do		224		224							224		
1161	Covers, cushion		12		12									
1162	Covers, enamelled		2		2									
1163	Covers, plush		5		5									
1164	Covers, sand box		623		623									

Report showing the disposition of United States military railroad property in the military division of the Tennessee, &c.—Continued.

Running number.	Articles.	Captured property on hand.	Property purchased by the United States on hand.	Cost to the United States of property purchased.	Total amount of property on hand.	Property sold on credit to railroad companies under the Executive Orders of August 8 and October 14, 1865.								
						Macon and Brunswick railroad.	Muscogee railroad.	Montgomery and W. P. railroad.	Wills Valley railroad.	Macon and Western railroad.	Edgefield and Kentucky railroad.	Memphis and Charleston railroad.	Nashville and N. W. railroad.	Nashville and Chattanooga railroad.
1165	Covers, dome		819		819									
1166	Covers, smoke-stack		83		83									
1167	Covers, smoke-stack hand hole		16		16									
1168	Crucibles		125		125								8	16
1169	Cylinders, steam engine		2		2									
1170	Cylinders, locomotive		1		1									
1171	Cylinders, 5 feet long, 12-inch bore													
1172	Chairs, guard rail		64		64									
1173	Chairs, railroad, assorted		21,572		21,572	810						2,870		1,000
1174	Chairs, railroad ... pounds		398	34 82	398							398		
1175	Chairs, frog		6		6									
1176	Chairs, head ... sets		3		3							3		
1177	Chairs, step		27		27									
1178	Chairs, assorted		346		346									
1179	Chairs, railroad guard		13		13									
1180	Cocks, waste		33		33							9		
1181	Cocks, miss gauge		125		125					12				
1182	Cocks, lock		8		8									
1183	Cocks, stop		636		636									
1184	Cocks, blow-off		22		22							3	3	4
1185	Cocks, bibb		232		232						6		8	42
1186	Cocks, bibb, brass		232		232									
1187	Cocks, pet		70	175 00	70								11	21
1188	Cocks, gauge		169	507 00	169			36			11	46	16	42
1189	Cocks, racking		131	196 50	131									
1190	Cocks, heater and cylinder		83		83							55	10	
1191	Cocks, steam, assorted		226		226									
1192	Cocks, brass		14		14									
1193	Cocks, cylinder		145	507 50	145									6
1194	Cocks, heater		121		121									11
1195	Cocks, water		2	4 50	2									
1196	Cocks, lever		2		2									

1197	Cocks, rough		64	320 00	64									
1198	Cocks, air		1	1 08	1									
1199	Cocks, basin		1		1									
1200	Cocks, gas		9		9									
1201	Cocks, steam-gauge		39		39									
1202	Cocks, steam-stop		54		54									
1203	Chimneys, assorted		651		651									
1204	Chimneys, head-light		1,164	242 50	1,164									
1205	Chimneys, flint		1,259		1,259									
1206	Chimneys, stationary smoke-stack		1		1									1
1207	Chimneys, lamp, assorted		291		291	1			1			68	173	425
1208	Chimneys, coal-oil lamp		211	17 60	211									
1209	Cases, drawing		9		9									1
1210	Cases, engine tool box-key		1		1									
1211	Cases, tin stencil		2		2									1
1212	Cases, medicine		1		1									
1213	Cases, turning paper		2		2									
1214	Cupolas		2		2									2
1215	Copper, bar ... pounds		257		257									97,193
1216	Copper, assorted ... do		8,585		8,585							20		
1217	Copper, sheet ... do		35,355	24,571 72	35,355					1,608	100	4,246	2,669	5,614
1218	Copper, ingot ... do		25,219	9,457 12	25,219							480	1,333⅓	7,675⅔
1219	Copper, scrap ... do													
1220	Copper, tinned ... do													
1221	Copper, pig ... do		435		435									
1222	Cloth, emery ... quires		1,985⅓		1,985⅓							5		20
1223	Cloth, emery ... gross		100		100									
1224	Cloth, gum ... pounds		159		159									
1225	Cloth, enamelled ... yards		566	1,698 00	566									
1226	Cloth, enamelled ... pieces		17		17									
1227	Cloth, tracing ... rolls		1		1									
1228	Cloth, tracing ... yards		60	87 00	60									
1229	Crayons ... gross		1¾	87	1¾									1¾
1230	Chalk, white ... pounds		4,962	123 29	4,962					228		15	68	141
1231	Chalk, red ... do		201½	20 15	201½							18	17	33
1232	Chalk ... do		15		15									
1233	Chalk, prepared ... do		1 1-6		1 1-6									
1234	Cranes, blacksmiths'	1	7		8									2
1235	Cranes, iron													
1236	Cranes, assorted ... pounds		3,295		3,295									3,295
1237	Cranes, tank		20		20									
1238	Cranes, water		1		1									
1239	Cuffs, hand ... pairs		6		6									2
1240	Chests, tool		13		13									
1241	Chests, carpenters' tool	5	5		10									
1242	Chests, pin													
1243	Chests, saddlers'		4		4									
1244	Cupboards, tool		19		19									14
1245	Cupboards, oil		1		1									1
1246	Combs, graining ... lots		3		3									
1247	Combs, graining ... sets		1		1									
1248	Chucks, assorted		9		9							2		2

Report showing the disposition of United States military railroad property in the military division of the Tennessee, &c.—Continued.

Running number.	Articles.	Captured property on hand.	Property purchased by the United States on hand.	Cost to the United States of property purchased.	Total amount of property on hand.	Property sold on credit to railroad companies under Executive Orders of August 8 and October 14, 1865.								
						Macon and Brunswick railroad.	Muscogee railroad.	Montgomery and W. P. railroad.	Wills Valley railroad.	Macon and Western railroad.	Edgefield and Kentucky railroad.	Memphis and Charleston railroad.	Nashville and N. W. railroad.	Nashville and Chattanooga railroad.
1249	Chucks, screw		4	$280 00	4			2		1	1			
1250	Chucks, drill		4		4									
1251	Chucks, brass		38		38								13	25
1252	Chucks, planer		5		5									
1253	Chucks, universal		13	1,625 00	13					1	1			6
1254	Chucks, universal lathe													
1255	Chucks, tap and nut		49		49									
1256	Chucks, lathe													
1257	Chases, assorted		42		42								5	9
1258	Cranks, hand-car ... pounds		81		81									
1259	Cranks, iron													
1260	Chasers, screw		170		170									110
1261	Catches, cupboard		710		710									
1262	Catches, brake		11		11									
1263	Catches, window		10		10									
1264	Chrome, yellow ... pounds		1,679¾		1,679¾							48	214½	435
1265	Chrome, orange, American ... tubes		12		12									
1266	Chrome, orange, dry ... pounds		30		30									
1267	Chrome, green ... do		39		39									
1268	Colors ... tubes		1,252		1,252								238	780
1269	Colors ... boxes													
1270	Candles, car ... pounds		1,246	386 26	1,246								124	361
1271	Candles, star ... do		802		802									30
1272	Copperas ... do		4,249		4,249									
1273	Cord, hemp bell ... do		2,189½	875 80	2,189½	2				39		2¾	354⅓	669⅔
1274	Cords, bell		2		2									
1275	Cement, composition ... cans		46		46									
1276	Cement ... barrels													
1277	Connexions, meter													
1278	Cobs, loco		78		78									5
1279	Circulars, switch		27		27									
1280	Centres, lathe		8		8								3	5

1281	Carriages, iron lathe		41		41									41
1282	Carriages, iron .... sections		1		1									
1283	Clasps, hand		24		24							24		
1284	Crabs, drilling		1		1									1
1285	Chamber, engine pump		7		7									7
1286	Corrals		1		1									
1287	Casings, cylinder head		18		18									
1288	Cantharides, tincture .... pounds		1		1									
1289	Camphor, gum .... do		2		2									
1290	Calomel .... do		2		2									
1291	Cochineal .... pounds		23		23									
1292	Composition, chemical .... cans		32		32									
1293	Carriers		22		22									
1294	Crosses, gas-pipe		65		65									
1295	Collars, gas-bracket		67		67									
1296	Circles, iron		18		18									
1297	Coffins		3		3									
1298	Casks		12		12									
1299	Cones, blacksmiths'		1		1									
1300	Drills, iron pipe		10		10									
1301	Drills, breast		1		1									
1302	Drills, stone		12		12									
1303	Drills, ratchet, assorted		167	3, 331 65	167			2		3	3	4	13	36
1304	Drills, ratchet, brace, steel		20		20									
1305	Drills, stock and clamp		1		1									1
1306	Drills, blacksmiths'		1		1									
1307	Drills, assorted		559		559							52	17	96
1308	Drills, pin		21		21									
1309	Drills, lathe, steel		2		2									
1310	Drills, counter, steel		12		12									
1311	Drills, cast steel .... pounds		230		230									183
1312	Drills, cast steel		84		84									88
1313	Drills, vertical, 36-inch		2		2		1							
1314	Drills, vertical, 45-inch, compound table		2		2									
1315	Drills, vertical, 45-inch, plain table		1		1									
1316	Drills, prop, iron table, complete		1		1									
1317	Drills, churn		89	1, 068 00	89									
1318	Drills, upright		1		1									
1319	Drills, drill press	25			25									
1320	Drills, steel standard		1		1									
1321	Drills, upright, ungeared, press and counter shafts		1											
1323	Drills, assorted .... sets		1											
1324	Drills, quarry		2											
1325	Drills, ratchets and bits		3											
1326	Drills, black enamelled .... yards		1, 448½									108	122	360½
1327	Dividers .... pairs		53									4		
1328	Dividers, spring .... do		36											
1329	Drifts		22											4
1330	Drifts, steel		25											
1331	Dogs	2			2									
1332	Dogs, lathe		25									4		3
1333	Dogs, ratchet .... pounds		39									39		

Report showing the disposition of United States military railroad property in the military division of the Tennessee, &c.—Continued.

Running number.	Articles.	Captured property on hand.	Property purchased by the United States on hand.	Cost to the United States of property purchased.	Total amount of property on hand.	Property sold on credit to railroad companies under Executive Orders of August 8 and October 14, 1865.								
						Macon and Brunswick railroad.	Muscogee railroad.	Montgomery and W. P. railroad.	Wills Valley railroad.	Macon and Western railroad.	Edgefield and Kentucky railroad.	Memphis and Charleston railroad.	Nashville and N. W. railroad.	Nashville and Chattanooga railroad.
1334	Dogs, planer		4											4
1335	Dogs, saw		2											
1336	Dusters, counter		6	$4 50										
1337	Dusters, painters'		171	114 00									11	22
1338	Duck ... yards		289										1	193
1339	Duck, car		105											
1340	Dippers, oil		31											
1341	Dippers, lye		57											
1342	Drippers, oil												3	5
1343	Diamonds, glaziers'		9	45 00	9							1		
1344	Dadoes		41		41							6		
1345	Doors, fire, and frames													
1346	Doors, unfinished		48		48									
1347	Doors, panel	7			7									
1348	Doors, furnace		3		3									
1349	Doors, glass		2		2									
1350	Doors, glazed ... pieces		2		2									
1351	Doors, assorted		17		17									
1552	Doors, car		27		27									
1353	Dryer, patent ... pounds		284	71 00	284							28	18	58
1354	Dryer, sand		4		4									
1355	Drums for lathe, (W. I.) ... pounds		6		6									
1356	Derricks		1		1									
1357	Derrick blocks, falls and dies		2		2									
1358	Derricks, crab		2		2									
1359	Drivers, iron lathe ... pounds		44		44									
1360	Drivers, screw ... lots													
1361	Dies and plates													
1362	Dies, pipe, and stocks ... sets		1									1		
1363	Dies, hand ... pounds		8½											8½
1364	Dies, assorted		21									5		16
1365	Dies, gas pipe		8									8		

1366	Dies and plates ....sets		10											
1367	Dies ....do		170											
1368	Dies and hubs ....pounds		21											
1369	Dies, forge		49											
1370	Die stocks ....sets	3	165		168					2		6		4
1371	Drivers, screw		1, 033									6		30
1372	Drums, stove		1		1									
1373	Drawers, moulders'		23		23									
1374	Dust, bone ....pounds		933		933									
1375	Engines, stationary		1		1									1
1376	Engines, pumping, No. 3		2		2									
1377	Engines and boilers, dummy		2		2									
1378	Engines, dummy													
1379	Engines and boilers, stationary	1	1		2									1
1380	Engines, steam fire		2		2									2
1381	Engines, single, steam													
1382	Engines, rotary fire, (Holley's patent)													
1383	Engines, caloric													2
1384	Engines, rotary													
1385	Engines, pilot													
1386	Engines, portable	2			2									
1387	Engines, locomotive													
1388	Engine, locomotive, No. 212	1			1									
1389	Engines, locomotive, and tenders	48	139		187	1			1	2	2	3	15	34
1390	Engine, double stationary, 11¼-inch bore, 24-inch stroke, Ellis & More's patent.													1
1391	Engines, stationary, 2 boilers 24 feet long, 40 inches diameter.		1		1									
1392	Engine, double stationary, pulley and counter shaft		1		1									1
1393	Engines, pumping													2
1393½	Engine and boiler, 5-inch cylinder, 12-inch stroke, (complete.)													1
1394	Engine and boiler, (complete)													1
1395	Engines, steam	1			1				1					
1396	Engine, 12-inch bore, 36-inch stroke	1			1									
1397	Engines, hoisting, complete		1		1									
1398	Engines and boilers, stationary, (complete)													
1399	Eyes, brass screw		372	5 50	372								40	80
1400	Eyes, bell cord		775	135 00	775								60	715
1401	Eyes, iron ....gross		5		5									
1402	Eyes, screw ....do		6		6									
1403	Ears, tin kettle ....do		91½	343 12	91½									
1404	Ears, kettle		5, 950	82 70	5, 950							24	480	960
1405	Ears, bucket		31, 529		31, 529							288		
1406	Ears, C. C. saw		248		248									
1407	Elbows, reducing		6		6									
1408	Elbows, drop		6		6									
1409	Elbows gas-pipe		687		687									
1410	Elbows, water-pipe													
1411	Elbows, goose-neck		67		67									
1412	Emery, assorted ....pounds		2, 028	405 60	2, 028						75	10¼	16	34
1413	Emery flour ....do		160	11 00	100									

Report showing the disposition of United States military railroad property in the military division of the Tennessee, &c.—Continued.

Running number.	Articles.	Captured property on hand.	Property purchased by the United States on hand.	Cost to the United States of property purchased.	Total amount of property on hand.	Property sold on credit to railroad companies under Executive Orders of August 8 and October 14, 1865.								
						Macon and Brunswick railroad.	Muscogee railroad.	Montgomery and W. P. railroad.	Wills Valley railroad.	Macon and Western railroad.	Edgefield and Kentucky railroad.	Memphis and Charleston railroad.	Nashville and N. W. railroad.	Nashville and Chattanooga railroad.
1414	Edges, iron		1		1									
1415	Edges, steel, straight		27	$20 25	27								5	17
1416	Ends, draw bar		10		10									10
1417	Ends, equalizer		4		4									4
1418	Easels		1		1									1
1419	Escutcheons		54		54									
1420	Easers		1		1									
1421	Forges, blacksmiths'		64		64						1			25
1422	Forges and bellows		4		4									
1423	Forges, portable		17	637 50	17			1				1		1
1424	Forges, blacksmiths' portable													
1425	Forges, cast-iron		2		2									24
1426	Forges		19		19									
1427	Furnaces, bolt		2		2									
1428	Furnaces, plumbers'		3		3									
1429	Furnaces, tinners'		15		15									
1430	Furnaces, charcoal		5		5									
1431	Frogs, cast		30		30									
1432	Frogs, patent portable		24	3, 600 00	24									
1433	Frogs, assorted .... pounds		287, 271		287, 271						4, 512	17, 612	2, 136	48, 006
1434	Frogs, chilled		15	750 00	15									
1435	Frogs, plated		16		16									
1436	Frogs, assorted		16		16									
1437	Frogs, T		4		4									
1438	Fittings, gas .... pounds		3, 158		3, 158									
1439	Fittings, gas pipe .... do		1, 445		1, 445					355				
1440	Fittings, gas		568		568									
1441	Fittings, brass cock and valve	75			75									
1442	Fasteners, car window		409	130 88	409								125	250
1443	Fasteners, sash		98		98									
1444	Fixtures, grindstone .... sets		207	276 00	207							4		12
1445	Fixtures, lathe .... pounds		306		306									

1446	Frames, saw		13		13							3		
1447	Frames, engine truck		18		18									
1448	Frames, truck, iron pounds		1,764		1,764							1,764		
1449	Frames, brake, beam		87		87									
1450	Frames and slides, car window		5		5									
1451	Frames, tank		8		8									8
1452	Frames, truck													
1453	Frames, wreck	3			3									
1454	Frames, bell pounds		96		96									
1455	Frames, bell		96		96									
1456	Frames, hack-saw		1		1									
1457	Frames, saw, railroad cut-off		1		1									
1458	Frames, bolt		1		1									
1459	Frames, circular-saw		2	150 00	2									
1460	Frames, bellows		11		11									
1461	Frames, door		1		1									
1462	Frames, window		39		39									
1463	Frames, lock		18		18									
1464	Frames, grindstone		3		3									
1465	Frames, for buildings		1		1									
1466	Frames and hammers, pile-driving													
1467	Frames		4		4									
1468	Flatters		175		175							14		122
1469	Fullers		404		404						11	14		185
1470	Flasks pounds		9,599		9,599									7,230
1471	Flasks		291		291									
1472	Flasks and tools pounds		11,972		11,972									
1473	Flasks, iron sets													1
1474	Flannel, Canton yards		322¼	193 65	322¼							3	18	51
1475	Flannel, red do		25		25									
1476	Faucets		86		86							8		1
1477	Faucets, brass		5	1 25	5									
1478	Fitches, assorted		343	57 12	343					4		14	18	36
1479	Flags, red		314		314					2		3	42	25
1480	Fans, blowing		7	4,550 00	7									2
1481	Fans, foundry		1		1									
1482	Fans, snail-shell		1		1									
1483	Flanges		15		15									
1484	Followers pounds		22,531		22,531							748		16,416
1485	Followers, piston		31		31									
1486	Figures sets		6		6							1		1
1487	Figures		20		20									
1488	Figures pounds		6		6									
1489	Froes		2		2									
1490	Forks, "T" rail		2		2									
1491	Forks, manure		7		7									
1492	Forks, railroad													
1493	Forks, pitch													
1494	Fuze, safety feet		6,100	43 92	6,100								333	1,167
1495	Feeders, oil		26		26									
1496	Formers, tin													
1497	Formers, stove-pipe		1		1									

Report showing the disposition of United States military railroad property in the military division of the Tennessee, &c.—Continued.

Running number.	Articles.	Captured property on hand.	Property purchased by the United States on hand.	Cost to the United States of property purchased.	Total amount of property on hand.	Property sold on credit to railroad companies under Executive Orders of August 8 and October 14, 1865.								
						Macon and Brunswick railroad.	Muscogee railroad.	Montgomery and W. P. railroad.	Wills Valley railroad.	Macon and Western railroad.	Edgefield and Kentucky railroad.	Memphis and Charleston railroad.	Nashville and N. W. railroad.	Nashville and Chattanooga railroad.
1498	Formers, tin gutter		1		1									
1499	Facings, coal ... barrels		25		25									
1500	Facings, sea coal ... do													
1501	Folders, tinners'		1		1									
1502	Folders, iron		3		3									
1503	Ferrules ... pounds		75		75									75
1504	Fences		3		3									
1505	Files, assorted		54, 246		54, 246					522	240	241	1, 025	3, 333
1506	Files, flat, assorted		495		495									
1507	Files, half-round bastard, assorted		4, 962		4, 962			60		192	132	70	402	1, 484
1508	Files, flat bastard, assorted	204	8, 154		8, 358			120				135	375	2, 040
1509	Files, saw, assorted		648		648									
1510	Files, flat, second-cut, assorted		3, 230		3, 230					192			120	240
1511	Files, taper, second-cut, assorted		24		24									
1512	Files, hand, second-cut, assorted		623		623									
1513	Files, round, second-cut, assorted		1, 054		1, 054									
1514	Files, half-round, second-cut, assorted		1, 585		1, 585								96	192
1515	Files, coulter, second-cut, assorted		41		41									
1516	Files, square, smooth, assorted		132		132							24		15
1517	Files, flat, smooth, assorted		3, 170		3, 170					192		62	264	863
1518	Files, round, smooth, assorted		1, 192		1, 192						24	23	151	395
1519	Files, hand dead, smooth, assorted		460		460									
1520	Files, flat dead, smooth, asorted		1, 261		1, 261					48		9	128	
1521	Files, hand, bastard, assorted		4, 130		4, 130					12	234		164	329
1522	Files, square, bastard, assorted		4, 362		4, 362					192	72	68	272	791
1523	Files, coulter, bastard, assorted		140		140									
1524	Files, three-square, bastard, assorted		264		264									
1525	Files, round parallel, bastard, assorted		150		150								48	96
1526	Files, square parallel, bastard, assorted		356		356									
1527	Files, dead, smooth, assorted		66		66									
1528	Files, three-square, assorted		312		312							29		
1529	Files, smooth, bastard, assorted		108		108									

1530	Files, wire		103		103								3	7
1531	Files, bastard		452		452									
1532	Files, hand-saw, assorted		9,779		9,779							116	220	620
1533	Files, mill-saw, assorted		12,169		12,169							8	334	715
1534	Files, pit-saw		24		24									
1535	Files, patent													
1536	Files, round, bastard		3,285		3,285									
1537	Files, half-round, smooth		2,388		2,388									
1538	Files, half-round	1,002			1,002									
1539	Files, hand, smooth		996		996									
1540	Files, taper		6,831		6,831									
1541	Files, round		9		9									
1542	Files, bastard, second-cut		174		174									
1543	Files, smooth		101		101									
1544	Files, switch		36		36									
1545	Files, second-cut		366		366									
1546	Files, parallel		24		24									
1547	Files, square-cut		84		84									
1548	Files, square taper		12		12									
1549	Files, equalizing		84		84									
1550	Files, cut, bastard		36		36									
1551	Files, taper, bastard		354		354									
1552	Files, parallel, bastard		36		36									
1553	Flues, copper .... pounds		668		668									
1554	Flues, copper .... feet		38		38									
1555	Fixings, forge .... pounds		334		334									
1556	Fronts to boilers		1		1									
1557	Funnels, sand-box		5		5									
1558	Flaxseed .... pounds		30		30									
1559	Flaxseed, ground .... do													
1560	Gauges, assorted		71											
1561	Gauges, panel		49										4	2
1562	Gauges, mortise		350	$315 00										
1563	Gauges, wire		22	148 50										2
1564	Gauges, marking		162	135 00									2	
1565	Gauges, thumb		237	27 37								13		
1566	Gauges, single		53											
1567	Gauges, double		6											
1568	Gauges, cutting		1											
1569	Gauges, wheel		15											
1570	Gauges, track		312									12	17	45
1571	Gauges, tinners'		1											
1572	Gauges, barrel		5											
1573	Gauges, screw		3	10 00									1	
1574	Gauges, steam		221	7,956 00						2	5	18	20	28
1575	Gauges, quarter-circle		1											
1576	Gauges, cocks and syphon steam		28											
1577	Gouges		75									1		
1578	Gouges, firmer		82									10	1	
1579	Gouges, paring		38											
1580	Gouges, paring, and handles		8											
1581	Gouges, patent marking		15											

Report showing the disposition of United States military railroad property in the military division of the Tennessee, &c.—Continued.

Running number.	Articles.	Captured property on hand.	Property purchased by the United States on hand.	Cost to the United States of property purchased.	Total amount of property on hand.	Property sold on credit to railroad companies under Executive Orders of August 8 and October 14, 1865.								
						Macon and Brunswick railroad.	Muscogee railroad.	Montgomery and W. P. railroad.	Wills Valley railroad.	Macon and Western railroad.	Edgefield and Kentucky railroad.	Memphis and Charleston railroad.	Nashville and N. W. railroad.	Nashville and Chattanooga railroad.
1582	Gouges, flat sweep		1											
1583	Gouges and handles, firmer ... sets		41									3	13	
1584	Gouges, ¼-inch		2											
1585	Gouges, firmer ... sets		7	$52 50										26
1586	Gouges, flat ... do		1	15 00										
1587	Gouges, paring ... do		14											
1588	Gouges, neck		37											
1589	Gimlets		577	15 00								4	24	48
1590	Gummers, saw		1	40 00										
1591	Gummers, assorted		12											3
1592	Greasers		1											
1593	Grooves, hand, steel		3									3		
1594	Grainers, top		2											
1595	Galleys, single-column brass-lined		2											
1596	Galleys, double-column brass-lined		4											
1597	Galleys, double-column brass-lined		2											
1598	Galleys, slice		1											
1599	Galleys, improved folio slice		1											
1600	Glass, assorted ... boxes		703 1-20									23 3-10		131¾
1601	Glass, tail, light		51										12	24
1602	Glass, window, assorted ... lights	486	88										21	104
1603	Glass, double-thick ... feet		1,900										637	1,263
1604	Glass, head-light ... boxes		2											
1605	Glasses, head-light		37											
1606	Glasses, cab, light		212											
1607	Grooves, hand		6											
1608	Grooves, tinners'		1											
1609	Gauze, brass ... feet													
1610	Gauze, brass ... coils		3											
1611	Gauze, iron ... do		1											
1612	Greene, chrome ... pounds		117	52 65								64	264	527
1613	Green, Hibernian ... do		206	72 10									106	212

1614	Green, German emerald ... do		662¼									20	11	22
1615	Green, Paris ... do		184										17	33
1616	Green, silk ... do		88	132 00								54	3	5
1617	Green, Quaker ... do		229										12	24
1618	Green, emerald ... do		64	38 40										
1619	Green, American chrome ... tubes		12											
1620	Grease, car ... pounds		3,755											
1621	Grease, car ... gallons		514½	694 57									30	293¼
1622	Grease, car ... barrels		4											
1623	Grease, wagon ... pounds													
1624	Grease, axle ... boxes		35											
1625	Glue ... pounds		1,935½	367 74								30¼	151	301
1626	Gates, switch ... do		110											
1627	Gates, molasses													
1628	Gates, switch		4									4		
1629	Gates, pine		1											
1630	Gibbs, bridge		13											13
1631	Gibbs, cross-head ... pounds		39											
1632	Gibbs, cross-head		8											
1633	Gibbs, bridge ... pounds		822											
1634	Governors		4											1
1635	Glands, snuffing-box ... pounds		88											
1636	Gongs, locomotive, 8-inch		36											
1637	Gongs and fixtures		1											
1638	Gongs, alarm		4											
1639	Globes, ruby		2											
1640	Gutters, tin ... feet		24											
1641	Gutters ... lots		1											
1642	Grease, wagon ... gallons		18											
1643	Hammers, blacksmiths'		201	552 75	201						12	118		25
1644	Hammers, blacksmiths' hand											10		
1645	Hammers, chipping		389	622 40	389								8	16
1646	Hammers, shoe		4		4									
1647	Hammers, set		14		14									
1648	Hammers, hand		479		479						3		1	
1649	Hammers, sledge		182		182									
1650	Hammers, claw		1,698	2,334 75	1,698							5		
1651	Hammers, tack		100		100									1
1652	Hammers, engine		974	2,435 00	974	1			1	6	2	4	49	91
1653	Hammers, tinners'		36		36									
1654	Hammers, saddlers'		2		2									
1655	Hammers, stone		152		152						12	5		
1656	Hammers, clasp and punch		1		1									
1657	Hammers, ballast		425		425								37	179
1858	Hammers, shoeing													
1659	Hammers, masons'		79	177 75	79									20
1660	Hammers, spike		209		209			3						80
1661	Hammers, backing		36		36									
1662	Hammers, jack													
1663	Hammers, copper		1		1									1
1664	Hammers, assorted		319		319						18	32	6	172
1665	Hammers, trip		1		1									1

Report showing the disposition of United States military railroad property in the military division of the Tennessee, &c.—Continued.

Running number.	Articles.	Captured property on hand.	Property purchased by the United States on hand.	Cost to the United States of property purchased.	Total amount of property on hand.	Property sold on credit to railroad companies under Executive Orders of August 8 and October 14, 1865.								
						Macon and Brunswick railroad.	Muscogee railroad.	Montgomery and W. P. railroad.	Wills Valley railroad.	Macon and Western railroad.	Edgefield and Kentucky railroad.	Memphis and Charleston railrord.	Nashville and N. W. railroad.	Nashville and Chattanooga railroad.
1666	Hammers, steam engine, trip, complete													
1667	Hammers, steam, assorted		3	$9, 750 00	3							1		1
1668	Hammers, machine	24			24									
1669	Hammers, boiler-makers'													
1670	Hammers, riveting		58	33 06	58									
1671	Hammers, soft		4		4									
1672	Hammers, steel		100		100									
1673	Hammers, raising		1	4 50	1									
1674	Hammers, pointing													
1675	Hammers, wagon													
1676	Hammers, saw													
1677	Hatchets		234		234							40	1	3
1678	Hatchets and handles		460		460									
1679	Hatchets, shingling		493	517 65	493								10	24
1680	Hatchets, broad		1, 299	2, 403 15	1, 299							4	4	
1681	Hatchets, soldering		12		12									
1682	Handles, firmer chisel, assorted		441		441									
1683	Handles, socket firmer chisel, assorted		3		3									
1684	Handles, socket chisel		79	6 58	79									
1685	Handles, chisel		376	35 25	376						144	14		
1686	Handles, auger, assorted		1, 639	54 68	1, 639							19	20	37
1687	Handles, adze		1, 306	380 91	1, 306							37	192	179
1688	Handles, foot or carpenters' adze		15		15									
1689	Handles, railroad adze		1		1									
1690	Handles, broadaxe		694	187 38	694							5		
1691	Handles, hatchet		746	60 30	746							1	1	
1692	Handles, broad hatchet		50		50									
1693	Handles, hammer		882	88 20	882						24	70		
1694	Handles, stone hammer		103		103									
1695	Handles, spike, maul		7, 771	621 68	7, 771							11	257	12
1696	Handles, maul		24	1 92	24									
1697	Handles, pick		13, 940	1, 672 80	13, 940							120	247	125

1698	Handles, awl		390		390							2		
1699	Handles, sledge		229		229						24	20	46	93
1700	Handles, brad awl		564		564									
1701	Handles, firmer gouge		2		2									
1702	Handles, jackplane		36	1 50	36									
1703	Handles, handsaw		38	5 54	38									
1704	Handles, handsaw, polished		12		12									
1705	Handles, file	200	3, 329		3, 529					144	144	92	307	773
1706	Handles, cross-cut saw		150	93 75	150							22		
1707	Handles, cant hook		47		47									
1708	Handles, axe		2, 328	582 00	2, 328							39	225	228
1709	Handles, chopping axe		730	182 50	730									
1710	Handles, hand axe		17		17									1
1711	Handles, saucepan		905		905									
1712	Handles, chest		770		770									9
1713	Handles, assorted		33		33									
1714	Handles, front end door		26		26									
1715	Handles, machinists'													
1716	Handles, chest, japanned, Paris ... pairs		38		38									
1717	Handles, flush drawer		16		16									
1718	Handles, chest ... pairs		415		415									
1719	Handles, mallet		4		4									
1720	Handles, door		3		3									
1721	Handles, stretcher		72		72									
1722	Handles, mop		1		1									
1723	Handles, couch		4		4									
1724	Hangers, post		127		127									
1725	Hangers, drop, belt		100		100									100
1726	Hangers, spring		36		36									16
1727	Hangers, step		8		8									8
1728	Hangers, shafting ... pounds		15, 206		15, 206									9, 696
1729	Hangers, step ... do		1, 660		1, 660									
1730	Hangers and boxes ... do		2, 354		2, 354									2, 354
1731	Hangers, truck		4		4									
1732	Hangers ... pounds		11, 470		11, 470									
1733	Hangers, drop		13		13									
1734	Hangers and fasteners, window blind ... sets		26		26									
1735	Hangers, cast-iron ... pounds													
1736	Hangers, door		55		55									
1737	Heads, cylinder		16		16									1
1738	Heads, square		1		1									1
1739	Heads, coppersmith		8		8									8
1740	Heads, brake ... pounds		12, 654		12, 654							4, 225		6, 478
1741	Heads, brake, frame		285		285							140		
1742	Heads, draw													
1743	Heads, draw ... pounds		51, 684		51, 684									
1744	Heads, cross, engine	1			1									
1745	Heads, stake													
1746	Heads and beams, brake		8		8									
1747	Heads, piston		13		13									
1748	Heads, bull, small		2, 000		2, 000									
1749	Heads, bull, large		3, 000		3, 000									

Report showing the disposition of United States military railroad property in the military division of the Tennessee, &c.—Continued.

Running number.	Articles.	Captured property on hand.	Property purchased by the United States on hand.	Cost to the United States of property purchased.	Total amount of property on hand	Property sold on credit to railroad companies under the Executive Orders of August 8 and October 14, 1865.								
						Macon and Brunswick railroad.	Muscogee railroad.	Montgomery and W. P. railroad.	Wills Valley railroad.	Macon and Western railroad.	Edgefield and Kentucky railroad.	Memphis and Charleston railroad.	Nashville and N. W. railroad.	Nashville and Chattanooga railroad.
1750	Heads, draw, cash ... pounds													
1751	Heads, cross		14		14									
1752	Hooks, cant		405		405							8	2	4
1753	Hooks, belt, assorted		8,965	$26 89	8,965			500					251	499
1754	Hooks, horn, beak		1		1									
1755	Hooks, packing		104		104	1						1	8	2
1756	Hooks, tackle ... pounds													
1757	Hooks and links, switch rope													
1758	Hooks, safety chair ... pounds		66		66							66		
1759	Hooks, assorted		60		60									
1760	Hooks and staples		147		147									
1761	Hooks, gas pipe		321		321									
1762	Hooks and eyes, brass ... gross		1		1									
1763	Hooks, safety chain		23		23									
1764	Hooks, curling		4		4									
1765	Hooks, iron ... pounds													263
1766	Hooks, packing, and spools		36		36									
1767	Hooks, curving		7		7									
1768	Hooks, switch rope ... pounds		100		100									
1769	Hooks and thimbles, switch rope		250		250									
1770	Hooks, cotton		8		8									
1771	Hook and chain gate		1		1									
1772	Hooks, ice		3		3									
1773	Hooks, hay		17		17									
1774	Hooks, timber		2		2									
1775	Hooks and chains		21		21									
1776	Hooks, iron		80		80									
1777	Hooks and stands ... pounds		32		32									
1778	Hooks, car hat		7		7									
1779	Heaters, iron		119		119									1
1780	Heaters, pipe		1		1									
1781	Hoes		3	3 00	3									

1782	Hoes, handled		27	27 00	27									
1783	Hoes, boat		11	11 00	11									
1784	Hoes, garden		1	100	1									
1785	Hoes, stable													
1786	Hose, assorted ... feet		16, 299		16, 299		100	450			229½	570	763	464
1787	Hose, gum ... do		2, 896		2, 896									
1788	Hubs and collars ... sets		1	150 00	1									
1789	Hubs for dies		34		34									
1790	Hinges, strap, assorted		2, 407	541 60	2, 407					120		186	8	16
1791	Hinges, blind, patent		68		68									48
1792	Hinges, T ... pairs		186	47 74	186								19	38
1793	Hinges, table, assorted ... do		116		116									
1794	Hinges, window ... do		40		40									
1795	Hinges, brass ... do		24		24									
1796	Hinges and fasteners, blind ... sets		12		12									
1797	Hinges, strap, assorted ... pairs		368½		368½									
1798	Hinges, brass		6		6									
1799	Hinges ... pounds		180		180									
1800	Hinges, unfinished		121		121									
1801	Hinges, butt, brass ... pairs		48		48									
1802	Hinges, butt, brass ... do		1, 155		1, 155									
1803	Hinges, back, flat		24		24									
1804	Hinges, butt, cast ... pairs		36		36									
1805	Hinges, blind ... do		18	22 50	18									
1806	Hasps, hinges and staples, assorted		637		637									17
1807	Hasps and staples		1, 246	259 16	1, 246							6		
1808	Hasps, hinge		100		100					48			8	
1809	Hasps		112		112									
1810	Hasps and hooks		36		36									
1811	Hair, plasterers' ... bushels		23	6 90	23									
1812	Hair, curled ... pounds		702	561 60	702								49	99
1813	Hair, plasterers' ... do		7		7									
1814	Hair, plasterers' ... lots													
1815	Holders, mandrel		2		2									2
1816	Hoods, forge		5		5									2
1817	Hoods, smoke-stack													
1818	Horses, wrought-iron		5		5									
1819	Horses, cast-iron		2		2									2
1820	Horses, wooden		5		5									1
1821	Horses, carpenter, saw		2		2									
1822	Horses, drawing		10		10									
1823	Horses, nail		1		1									
1824	Horses, blacksmiths'													
1825	Hoops, tank ... pounds		563		563									
1826	Hoops, truss		12		12									
1827	Housing for cupola	1			1									
1828	Hods, mortar		10		10									
1829	Hardies		8		8									
1830	Hubs, ambulance		8		8									
1831	Hubs, wagon		2		2									
1832	Headings, blacksmiths'													
1833	Hydrants													

Report showing the disposition of United States military railroad property in the military division of the Tennessee, &c.—Continued.

Running number.	Articles.	Captured property on hand.	Property purchased by the United States on hand.	Cost to the United States of property purchased.	Total amount of property on hand.	Property sold on credit to railroad companies under the Executive Orders of August 8 and October 14, 1865.								
						Macon and Brunswick railroad.	Musogee railroad.	Montgomery and W. P. railroad.	Wills Valley railroad.	Macon and Western railroad.	Edgefield and Kentucky railroad.	Memphis and Charleston railroad.	Nashville and N. W. railroad.	Nashville and Chattanooga railroad.
1834	Heads, cylinder .... pounds..	......	236	....	236	......	......	......	......	......	......	......	......	......
1835	Handles, ballast hammer	......	....	....	....	......	......	......	......	......	......	......	......	......
1836	Hickory for handles .... pieces..	......	38	....	38	......	......	......	......	......	......	......	......	......
1836½	Hinges	......	26	....	26	......	......	......	......	......	......	......	......	......
1837	Iron, angle .... pounds..	......	3, 904	....	3, 904	......	......	......	......	......	......	371	......	......
1838	Iron, railroad .... bars...	......	70, 417	$1,760,425 00	70, 417	3, 985	......	......	......	......	......	3	10, 790	8, 061
1839	Iron, railroad .... pounds..	22, 400	698, 720	....	721, 120	......	......	......	......	......	......	......	......	......
1840	Iron, round, assorted .... do...	......	736, 143	....	736, 143	......	......	......	......	23, 847	......	32, 907	......	179, 159
1841	Iron, bar, assorted .... do...	......	2, 654, 000	....	2, 654, 000	......	......	......	......	3, 790	10, 995	14, 760	......	215, 125
1842	Iron, flat, assorted .... do...	......	....	....	....	......	......	......	......	......	......	......	......	......
1843	Iron, galvanized .... do...	......	8, 809	2, 466 52	8, 809	......	......	......	......	......	......	......	225	450
1844	Iron, Russia .... do...	......	16, 033	4, 809 90	16, 033	......	......	......	......	......	487	915	1, 293⅓	3, 407⅜
1845	Iron, assorted .... do...	......	196, 036½	....	196, 036½	......	......	......	......	1, 010	2, 375	6, 771	53	111, 343
1846	Iron, boiler .... do...	......	82, 262	12, 339 30	82, 262	......	......	......	......	4, 403	......	621	......	21, 321
1847	Iron, tank .... do...	......	2, 934	351 48	2, 934	......	......	......	......	4, 067	1, 912	1, 376	......	14, 705
1848	Iron, oval and ½-oval .... do...	......	7, 038	....	7, 038	......	......	......	......	......	......	......	......	......
1849	Iron, hoop .... do...	......	13, 933	....	13, 923	......	......	......	......	......	......	......	......	......
1850	Iron, tire .... do...	......	49, 515	....	49, 515	......	......	......	......	......	......	......	......	......
1851	Iron, ½-round .... do...	......	19, 945	....	19, 945	......	......	......	......	......	......	......	......	......
1852	Iron, square .... do...	......	699, 038	....	699, 038	......	......	......	......	4, 516	5, 598	12, 447	......	26, 337
1853	Iron, plough slab .... do...	......	4, 950	....	4, 950	......	......	......	......	......	......	......	......	......
1854	Iron, nail rod .... do...	......	4, 536	....	4, 536	......	......	......	......	......	......	......	......	750
1855	Iron, pig .... do...	......	153, 200	4, 441 66	153, 200	......	......	......	......	......	......	......	......	......
1856	Iron, round bridge .... do...	......	150, 000	....	150, 000	......	......	......	......	......	......	......	......	......
1857	Iron, flat bridge .... do...	......	64, 158	....	64, 158	......	......	......	......	......	......	......	......	......
1858	Iron, scrap .... do...	3, 993	1, 279, 975⅓	....	1, 283, 968⅓	......	......	......	......	......	......	7, 924	......	16, 405
1859	Iron, sheet .... do...	......	71, 305	....	71, 305	......	......	......	......	......	......	......	......	......
1860	Iron, tire .... do...	......	160	....	160	......	......	......	......	......	......	......	......	......
1861	Iron, scrap, 1st class .... do...	......	20, 000	....	20, 000	......	......	......	......	......	......	......	......	......
1862	Iron, scrap, blacksmiths' 1st class .... do...	......	200, 000	....	200, 000	......	......	......	......	......	......	......	......	......
1863	Iron, scrap, blacksmiths' common .... do...	......	300, 000	....	300, 000	......	......	......	......	......	......	......	......	......
1864	Iron, tank and fire box scrap .... do...	......	99, 000	....	99, 000	......	......	......	......	......	......	......	......	......

1865	Iron, light sheet scrap ... do		50,000		50,000									
1866	Iron, sheet, galvanized ... do		71,720		71,720									
1867	Iron, band, assorted ... do		528		528									
1868	Iron, smoke-stack ... do		8,997		8,997									
1869	Iron, scrap, rings and staples ... do		584		584									
1870	Iron, round and square ... do		3,460		3,460									
1871	Iron, old ... do		40,543		40,543									
1872	Iron, wrought ... do													
1873	Iron, perforated ... sheets		47		47									
1874	Irons, platform		3		3									
1875	Irons, clinch		4		4									
1876	Irons, and		1		1									
1877	Irons, solid		2		2									
1878	Irons, double plough		2		2									
1879	Irons, heading		1		1									
1880	Irons, branding		6		6									
1881	Irons, angle, 25 feet each													
1882	Irons, switch		51		51									
1883	Irons, twyre		191		191									
1884	Irons, plane		27		27									
1885	Irons, double-plane		73	83 95	73									
1886	Irons, soldering		68	255 00	68						6	4	5	19
1887	Irons, large, for drawing, (on wheels)													
1888	Irons, guide ... pounds													7,880
1889	Irons, dog ... pairs													
1890	Irons, roofing, double seaming													
1891	Irons, step ... pounds		38		38							38		
1892	Irons, blacksmiths' ... do		2,125		2,125									2,125
1893	Irons, chafing ... do		2,790		2,790							555		4.430
1894	Iron, brake ... do		753		753							32		
1895	Instruments, veterinary ... sets		1		1									
1896	Instruments, levelling		4		4									
1897	Instruments, mathematical ... sets		1		1									
1898	Instruments, transit		1		1									
1899	Injectors, engine		46		46								2	6
1900	Injectors, assorted		38		38									
1901	Injectors, steam		3		3									
1902	Indicators, steam		3		3									
1903	Ipecac ... pounds		2		2									
1904	Ink, printing ... cases		11		11									
1904½	Irons, hand-grooving		9,880		9,880									
1905	Jacks, ratchet		101		101									
1906	Jacks, screw and lever		23		23	2			2	4	9	27	44	80
1907	Jacks, hydraulic, assorted		125		125			2		2	4	21	4	28
1908	Jacks, hydraulic, 7-ton		2		2									
1909	Jacks, hydraulic, 10-ton		4	500 00	4									
1910	Jacks, hydraulic, 15-ton		13	1,950 00	13									
1911	Jacks, timber		133		133									
1912	Jacks, lever		227	5,107 50	227			12		2	1	26	6	22
1913	Jacks, screw	6	260	7,800 00	266									
1914	Jacks, pump, 15-ton		9		9									
1915	Jacks, pump, 10-ton		2		2									

Report showing the disposition of United States military railroad property in the military division of the Tennessee, &c.—Continued.

Running number.	Articles.	Captured property on hand.	Property purchased by the United States on hand.	Cost to the United States of property purchased.	Total amount of property on hand.	Property sold on credit to railroad companies under Executive Orders of August 8 and October 14, 1865. Macon and Brunswick railroad.	Muscogee railroad.	Montgomery and W. P. railroad.	Wills Valley railroad.	Macon and Western railroad.	Edgefield and Kentucky railroad.	Memphis and Charleston railroad.	Nashville and N. W. railroad.	Nashville and Chattanooga railroad.
1916	Jacks, pump													
1917	Journals, brass	8			8									
1918	Japan ... gallons		153		153									
1919	Jaws, switch-lever		49		49									
1920	Knives, farriers'		24		24									
1921	Knives, drawing		1,806		1,806							13	8	16
1922	Knives, frog													
1923	Knives, bench		2		2									
1924	Knives, paring		3		3									
1925	Knives, round		1		1									
1926	Knives, pallet		62	$69 75	62							2	10	20
1927	Knives, putty		148	74 00	148							2	10	20
1928	Knives, shoe		9		9								1	3
1929	Knives, packing		4		4								4	
1930	Knives, C. S. Daniel's planer													
1931	Knives, brush		3		3									
1932	Kettles, soldering		21		21									
1933	Kettles, glue		19		19									
1934	Kettles, spring ... pounds		13,825		13,825									
1935	Keys, car		2,510		2,510			100				24	9	52
1936	Keys, assorted		30		30									30
1937	Keys, assorted ... pounds		522		522									522
1938	Keys, draw-head		170		170						170			
1939	Keys, split ... pounds													
1940	Keys, padlock		16		16									
1941	Keys, connecting-rod		3		3									
1942	Keys		1		1									
1943	Knobs, mahogany		1,118	19 00	1,118								48	102
1944	Knobs, mineral		330	110 00	330							30		14
1945	Knobs, drawer		1,613		1,613									
1946	Knobs, door													
1947	Knobs, desk, wood, assorted		144		144									

1948	Knobs, tin-kettle		720		720									
1949	Knobs, tea-pot ..... gross		6		6									
1950	Kings, American ..... tubes		12		12									
1951	Knees, tender		4		4									
1952	Kasses, switch		2		2									
1953														
1954	Lights, white		5,881	10,216 50	5,881	1		48		48	19	263	364	655
1955	Lights, red		2,521	7,563 00	2,521			24	2	26	8	188	122	216
1956	Lights, blue		57		57							28		
1957	Lights, cab		161		161	1					2	3	5	102
1958	Lights, head	19	211	23,210 00	230	1		4	1	2	4	15	26	50
1959	Lights, pail		75	1,500 00	75							11	18	40
1960	Lamps, Dutch		458		458							28		55
1961	Lamps, bull's-eye		155	193 75	155					24	1	4	30	30
1962	Lamps, bracket		28	140 00	28								2	6
1963	Lamps, railroad		8		8									
1964	Lamps, hand		1		1									
1965	Lamps, green		12		12			12						
1966	Lamps, signal		106		106								28	57
1967	Lamps, torch		21		21									
1968	Lamps, coach		33		33									
1969	Lamps, brass car		55		55									
1970	Lamps, car, candle		11	42 35	11									
1971	Lamps, hanging		16	40 00	16									
1972	Lamps, spring		6		6									
1973	Lanterns		410		410									
1974	Lanterns, railroad, globe		12		12									
1975	Lanterns, dark		17		17									
1976	Lanterns, square		6		6									
1977	Lantern bottoms, (W. L., old)		11		11									
1978	Locks, pad, assorted		1,593		1,593	2			2			51	43	161
1979	Locks, mortise		87		87								17	34
1980	Locks, door, with mineral knobs, complete		600		600									6
1981	Locks, assorted		1,392		1,392							2	71	398
1982	Locks, switch		64		64									
1983	Locks, car		4,540	7,559 10	4,540							4		1
1984	Locks car, seat-back		310		310									310
1985	Locks, door		294	72 50	294							35		
1986	Locks, chest		339	271 20	339									
1987	Locks, spring-chest		156		156									
1988	Locks, drawer		74	37 00	74									
1989	Locks, rim		630		630									
1990	Locks, iron drawer		30		30									
1991	Locks, desk and drawer		361		361									
1992	Locks, Japan-covered		120	15 00	120									
1993	Locks, wardrobe		12		12									
1994	Locks and chains		1		1									
1995	Lines, sea-grass		25		25					24				
1996	Lines, tape, assorted		502		502							5	12	42
1997	Lines, plough		30		30									
1998	Lines, chalk		1,603	199 50	1,603					24		29	26	48
1999	Lines, chalk and reel		17		17									

Report showing the disposition of United States military railroad property in the military division of the Tennessee, &c.—Continued

Running number.	Articles.	Captured property on hand.	Property purchased by the United States on hand.	Cost to the United States of property purchased.	Total amount of property on hand.	Property sold on credit to railroad companies under Executive Orders of August 8 and October 14, 1865.								
						Macon and Brunswick railroad.	Muscogee railroad.	Montgomery and W. P. railroad.	Wills Valley railroad.	Macon and Western railroad.	Edgefield and Kentucky railroad.	Memphis and Charleston railroad.	Nashville and N. W. railroad.	Nashville and Chattanooga railroad.
2000	Line, chalk .... feet		2,000		2,000									
2001	Lime .... bushels		601		601							6		
2002	Lime .... pounds												83	167
2003	Lumber, pine .... feet		780,118		780,118							14,126		137,394
2004	Lumber, oak and poplar, assorted .... do		150,000		150,000							36,212		215,378
2005	Lumber, B. W .... do		42,214		42,214									
2006	Lumber, assorted .... do		3,442,255		3,442,255							3,800		211,332
2007	Lumber, old .... lots		2		2									
2008	Lumber, oak .... feet		920,746		920,746									
2009	Lumber, poplar .... do		29,358		29,358									
2010	Lumber, walnut .... do		7,504		7,504									
2011	Lead, pig .... pounds		2,460	$418 20	2,460							250	17	
2012	Lead, white, assorted .... do		5,362	750 68	5,362						51	1,250	369	1,874
2013	Lead, black .... do		333		333								43	87
2014	Lead, sugar of .... do		60	45 00	60								4	8
2015	Lead, sheet .... do		1,726	517 80	1,726					350			103	204
2016	Lead, red, in oil and dry .... do		3,113		3,113						50	75	92	183
2017	Lead, bar and pig .... do													980
2018	Lead, red .... do		599	143 76	599									
2019	Lead, scrap .... do		187		187									
2020	Litharge .... do		75¼	10 90	75¼							10¼	6	18
2021	Lathes, screw-cutting		3		3	1	1	2						2
2022	Lathes, complete, 7 feet bed, 9-inch swing		2		2									
2023	Lathes, shear, and head		2		2									
2024	Lathes, engine	1	10	29,000 00	11						1	3		9
2025	Lathes, hand		1		1									
2026	Lathes, axle		2	2,800 00	2									2
2027	Lathes, wood, turning													1
2028	Lathes, iron, turning													
2029	Lathes, dog, wrought, No. 20													
2030	Lathes, screw-cutting machine, 8 feet chain, feed, with chuck													

2031	Lathes, screw-cutting machine, 10 feet bed, 23-inch swing													
2032	Lathes, screw-cutting machine, with pulleys and shafts													
2033	Lathes, with chuck		1		1									
2034	Lathes, 24-inch, universal chuck		1		1									
2035	Lathes, 24-inch, White's patent		1		1									1
2036	Lathes, driving wheel		1		1									
2037	Lathes, turning													
2038	Lathes													
2039	Lathes, double-head, 20 feet long, 26-inch swing, with counter shafts, tools, and fixtures	1			1									
2040	Lathes, screw-cutting, with counter shafts	1			1									
2041	Lathes, small counter shaft	1			1									
2041½	Lathes, No. 8	1			1									
2042	Lathes, double-head, wood	1			1									
2043	Lathes, iron	1			1									
2044	Lathes, screw-cutting, 16 feet bed, 15-inch swing		1		1									
2045	Lathes, shear and head, 10 feet bed, 12-inch swing		2		2									
2046	Lathes, small, with screw, gear, and four extra rods		1		1									
2047	Lathes, 30-inch		2		2									
2048	Ladders, mounting		24		24									
2049	Ladders, shop and step	2	28		30									2
2050	Letters ... sets		6		6									9
2051	Letters		6		6							1		2
2052	Letters and figures, incomplete ... sets		3		3									
2053	Links, crooked													
2054	Links, chain		1		1									
2055	Links, coupling ... pounds		1,045		1,045									
2056	Links, straight ... do		202		202									
2057	Links, crooked ... do		556		556									
2058	Links, coupling													
2059	Ladles		61		61									
2060	Ladles, tin		235		235							1		1
2061	Ladles, perforated		70		70									
2062	Ladles, melting		15		15									
2063	Ladles, iron		4		4									3
2064	Ladles, iron ... pounds		1,700		1,700									
2065	Lifts, window		813		813									1,700
2066	Lifts, brass, sash		72		72									144
2067	Links, switch rope ... pounds		1,753		1,753									
2068	Links, straight		1,079		1,079									
2069	Links and pins, coupling ... pounds		1,010		1,010									
2070	Leather, sole ... do		423¼	254 25	423¼							1,010		
2071	Leather, lace ... sides		188	564 00	188							73¾	19	47
2072	Leather, harness ... pounds		1,797	934 44	1,797							13	7	18
2073	Leather, bridle ... do		225		225							3¼		
2074	Leather, russet ... sides		8		8									
2075	Leather, burnt ... pounds		12¾		12¾									
2076	Leather, sole ... sides		3		3									
2077	Leather, assorted ... pounds													
2078	Leather, blue, title ... dozen		1		1									

Report showing the disposition of United States military railroad property in the military division of the Tennessee, &c.—Continued.

Running number.	Articles.	Captured property on hand.	Property purchased by the United States on hand.	Cost to the United States of property purchased.	Total amount of property on hand.	Property sold on credit to railroad companies under Executive Orders of August 8 and October 14, 1865.								
						Macon and Brunswick railroad.	Muscogee railroad.	Montgomery and W. P. railroad.	Wills Valley railroad.	Macon and Western railroad.	Edgefield and Kentucky railroad.	Memphis and Charleston railroad.	Nashville and N. W. railroad.	Nashville and Chattanooga railroad.
2079	Levels, spirit		256		256							9	10	20
2080	Levels, pocket		20		20									
2081	Levels, machinists'		4	$7 50	4									
2082	Levels		1		1									
2083	Levers, hand-car		2		2									
2084	Levers and rods, tank		74		74									
2085	Levers, switch		7		7									
2086	Levers, wrought											4		
2087	Levers													
2088	Levers, brake		33		33									
2089	Levers, track		1		1									
2090	Levers, whistle		6		6									
2091	Levers, blacksmith		16		16									
2092	Leaves, steel, for fender springs ... pounds													
2093	Leaf, gold ... packages		59 2-5	712 80	59 2-5								2 1-	$4\frac{1}{8}$
2094	Ley, concentrated ... cans		253		253								27	40
2095	Ley, concentrated ... boxes		2		2									
2096	Lead, bar ... pounds												81	
2097	Lead, white ... kegs													
2098	Lugs, water tank		10		10									
2099	Lugs, water tank ... pounds		847		847									
2100	Laths, pine		10, 200		10, 200									
2101	Lake, madder ... tubes		17	6 37	17									
2102	Laudanum ... pounds		1		1									
2103	Logs, B. W ... feet		1, 745, 646		1, 745, 646									
2104	Lifters, rail		4		4									
2105	Legs, table		58		58									
2106	Litters													
2107	Machines, small engine		1		1									
2108	Machines, double engine		1		1									
2109	Machines, hoisting engine													
2110	Machines, straightening		1		1									1

2111	Machines, drill press		1		1		1	1						
2112	Machines, wheel press		1		1									
2113	Machines, press boring, cylinder													
2114	Machines, press drilling, vertical, Nos. 62 and 63													1
2115	Machines, manifest, suspension													
2116	Machines, pipe-cutting		2		2									2
2117	Machines, stove-pipe former		1		1									1
2118	Machines, wooden former		3		3									
2119	Machines, burring		4		4							2		2
2120	Machines, pinning down		1		1									
2121	Machines, setting down		1		1									1
2122	Machines, swedging		1		1							1		
2123	Machines, scanning		1		1									
2124	Machines, scanning, double		1		1									
2125	Machines, bolt header		1		1					1				
2126	Machines, screw cutting	1	6	6, 106 80	7							1		4
2127	Machines, beading		2	60 00	2									1
2128	Machines, twyring		2		2									
2129	Machines, tenoning		2		2									1
2130	Machines, wiring		2		2							7		1
2131	Machines, squaring		1		1									1
2132	Machines, grooving	1	1		2							1		1
2133	Machines, folding		3		3							1		3
2134	Machines, planing, common		1		1									
2135	Machines, planing	2	13		15							1		1
2136	Machines, quartering wheel		1		1									
2137	Machines, quartering wheel, double-headed		1		1									1
2138	Machines, flooring	1			1									
2139	Machines, striker		1		1									
2140	Machines, scroll moulding		1		1									
2141	Machines, boring, assorted		138		138			6				2		2
2142	Machines, boring and auger													
2143	Machines, boring and drilling, Bement & Dougherty		1		1									
2144	Machines and bits, boring		1		1									
2145	Machines, boring, No. 32, Bement & Dougherty													1
2146	Machines, sawing		3		3									3
2147	Machines, skiving		1		1									
2148	Machines, mortising	1	1		2									
2149	Machines, mortising and boring, car		1		1									1
2150	Machines, mortising, and chisels, foot, portable		2		2									1
2151	Machines, thick edge		1		1									
2152	Machines, rolling		2		2									1
2153	Machines, slotting		3	9, 000 00	3									1
2154	Machines, milling		1		1									1
2155	Machines, gear cutting		1		1									
2156	Machines, bolt cutting, taps and dies		2		2									1
2157	Machines, small vertical drill		1		1									1
2158	Machines, key cutting		1		1									1
2159	Machines, key seat drill, No. 12, complete													
2160	Machines, large vertical drill, intermediate shafts, pulleys and hangers.		1		1									1
2161	Machines, nut tapping	2			2									

Report showing the disposition of United States military railroad property in the military division of the Tennessee, &c.—Continued.

Running number.	Articles.	Captured property on hand.	Property purchased by the United States on hand.	Cost to the United States of property purchased.	Total amount of property on hand.	Property sold on credit to railroad companies under Executive Orders of August 8 and October 14, 1865.								
						Macon and Brunswick railroad.	Muscogee railroad.	Montgomery and W. P. railroad.	Wills Valley railroad.	Macon and Western railroad.	Edgefield and Kentucky railroad.	Memphis and Charleston railroad.	Nashville and N. W. railroad.	Nashville and Chattanooga railroad.
2162	Machines, moulding		3		3									
2163	Machines, railroad cut-off sawing		1		1									
2164	Machines, stove pipe breaking		1		1									1
2165	Machines, binders' board cutting		1		1									
2166	Machines, shaping		2	$2,600 00	2									
2167	Mrchines, shaping, 12-inch, No. 20													
2168	Machines, drilling		2		2									1
2169	Machines, portable, drilling													
2170	Machines, guttering													
2171	Machines, bolt, with taps and dyes		1	800 00	1									
2172	Machines, car trimming, common		1		1									
2173	Machines, car, wood turning		1		1									
2174	Machines, turning, large													1
2175	Machines, beading, and extra rolls													1
2176	Machines, hoisting		20		20			5		2		1		1
2177	Machines, shingle		1		1									
2178	Machines, copper pipe breaking		1		1									
2179	Machines, spring setting		1		1									1
2180	Machines, flue drawing		1		1									1
2181	Machines, slide lathe		18		18									1
2182	Machines, wood lathe		5		5									2
2183	Machines, hand lathe		2		2									
2184	Machines, eyelet		1		1									
2185	Machines, double seaming													
2186	Machines, boring and turning		1		1									
2187	Machines, laying off													
2188	Machines, bolt cutting, large, with 7 sets taps and dies, plugs for repairing dies, counter shafts, pulleys and hangers.		1		1									
2189	Machines, bolt cutting, with 13 sets taps and dies, counter shafts, pulleys and hangers.		1		1									
190	Machines, mortising, with bits, Rogers's patent													1

2191	Machines, planing, compound													
2192	Machines, car planing and matching, complete													3
2193	Machines, bolt head, and fixtures													
2194	Machines, planing, 12 feet, with counter shafting, wrenches, tools, &c.	1			1									1
2195	Machines, tongue-grooving	1			1									
2196	Machines, planer, (Daniels's patent)	1			1									
2197	Machines, circular rip-saw, No. 6	1			1									
2198	Machines, circular rip-saw, No. 5	1			1									
2199	Machines, board planer, No. 2	1			1									
2200	Machines, babbiting, No. 5	1			1									
2201	Machines, wheel, burring lath	1			1									
2202	Machines, surface planing, No. 2	1			1									
2203	Machines, ruling		1		1									
2204	Machines, paper cutting		2		2									
2205	Machines, gumming		2		2									
2206	Machines, bolt cutting							1						1
2207	Machines, car planing													
2208	Machines, wood													
2209	Machines, cylinder boring	1	4		5									3
2210	Mills, shingle		3		3									1
2211	Mills, saw, with engine boiler complete		2		2									
2212	Mills, saw, (O. S. and D. patent)		2		2									
2213	Mills, saw, (Clemens's patent)		1		1									
2214	Mills, saw, circular, (Clemens's patent)		2		2									
2215	Mills, saw, circular, (Lea & Leavitt's)		4		4									
2216	Mills, saw, (H. & Co.'s patent, "A," 2 boilers complete.)		1		1									
2217	Mills, saw, (H. & Co.'s patent, "D," complete)		1		1									
2218	Mills, saw, stationery, L and D patent, incomplete		1		1									
2219	Mills, saw, A. B. H. & Co.'s patent, incomplete		1		1									
2220	Mills, saw													
2221	Mills, steam saw, portable													
2222	Mills, paint, assorted		35	380 00	35					1		1		3
2223	Mills, borax		1		1									1
2224	Mills, corn		4		4									
2225	Mills, boring, counter, shafts, pulleys, and hangers		2		2									
2226	Mandrels		12		12									
2227	Mandrels, saw		2		2						1	5		52
2228	Mandrels, S. P		3		3									
2229	Mandrels, iron, assorted		195		195									1
2230	Mandrels, steel-nut		36		36									
2231	Mandrels, steel		411		411									
2232	Mandrels, cast-steel		7		7									151
2233	Mandrels, cast		2		2									
2234	Mandrels, lathe, steel		16		16									
2235	Mallets, assorted		1,337		1,337									
2236	Mallets, carpenters'		958	479 00	958							3	16	34
2237	Mallets, lignumvitæ		305	343 12	305							11		8
2238	Mallets, caulking		22		22									
2239	Mallets, iron-ring		2		2									
2240	Mallets, stonecutters'		19	23 75	19									

Report showing the disposition of United States military railroad property in the military division of the Tennessee, &c.—Continued.

Running number.	Articles.	Captured property on hand.	Property purchased by the United States on hand.	Cost to the United States of property purchased.	Total amount of property on hand.	Property sold on credit to railroad companies under Executive Orders of August 8 and October 14, 1865.								
						Macon and Brunswick railroad.	Muscogee railroad.	Montgomery and W. P. railroad.	Wills Valley railroad.	Macon and Western railroad.	Edgefield and Kentucky railroad.	Memphis and Charleston railroad.	Nashville and N. W. railroad.	Nashville and Chattanooga railroad.
2241	Mallets, tinners'		1		1									
2242	Mauls		11		11							17		
2243	Mauls, spike		430		430									
2244	Mauls, carpenters'		38		38									
2245	Mauls, carpenters' top		120		120									
2246	Mauls, carpenters' spike		404	$808 00	404							5	4	
2247	Mauls, railroad spike		1,850	5,550 00	1,850							44	351	201
2248	Mauls, wooden		12		12									
2249	Mauls, iron													
2250	Mauls, bridge		13		13									
2251	Mauls, dirt		2		2									
2252	Measures, assorted		360		360									55
2253	Measures, tin, assorted		52		52							6	12	3
2254	Measures, tin ... sets		1		1									
2255	Measures, oil ... do		1		1									
2256	Measures, pint		4		4									
2257	Measures, dry ... sets		1	1 75	1									
2258	Mullers		4	30 00	4									
2259	Moulds, soldering		1		1									
2260	Moulds, cast													
2261	Magazines, powder		2		2									
2262	Marline, tarred ... pounds		515½	180 42	515½							13½	57	192
2263	Matches ... gross		481¾	843 06	481¾							3¼	2	4
2264	Meter, gas													
2265	Metal, Babbitt ... pounds		1,686½	455 35	1,686½						103½	364	111	244½
2266	Molasses ... gallons		10		10									
2267	Moulens, wooden-wreath		1		1									
2268	Machinery, saw-mill ... box		1		1									
2269	Machinery, rolling-mill ... pounds		26,500		26,500									
2270	Nippers		35		35									
2271	Nippers, cutting		44	52 25	44							4		
2272	Needles, assorted		28		28									

2273	Needles, tufting		59		59									
2274	Needles, upholsterers'		24	9 60	24								8	31
2275	Needles, harness .... papers		11		11									
2276	Nozzles		19		19									
2277	Nozzles, brass		6		6									
2278	Nozzles, pipe		4		4									
2279	Nozzles, hose		12		12			1						7
2280	Nozzles .... pounds		30		30									
2281	Nuts, assorted .... do		44, 692		44, 692			1, 286		1, 726	3, 171	3, 729	3, 629	20, 808
2282	Nuts, brass .... do		17		17									17
2283	Nuts, square .... do		28, 349	3, 968 86	28, 349									
2284	Nuts, hexagon .... do		30, 085	4, 813 60	30, 085									
2285	Nuts and washers .... do		672		672									
2286	Nuts and bolts .... do		11, 430		11, 430									
2287	Nuts, keeper, and rods		10		10							10		
2288	Nuts, iron		12		12									
2289	Nails, assorted .... kegs		1, 117¼		1, 117¼									
2290	Nails, finishing, assorted .... papers		3, 069	429 66	3, 069					84		94	528	1, 338
2291	Nails, clout .... do		583	81 62	583									
2292	Nails, tufting		3, 112	12 90	3, 112									
2293	Nails, clinch .... pounds		14, 536		14, 536							205	852	2, 169
2294	Nails, horseshoe .... do		1, 850	952 75	1, 850									
2295	Nails, enamelled .... gross		455		455								38	272
2296	Nails, lining .... papers		24	14 40	24							24		
2297	Nails, assorted .... pounds		48, 492		48, 492					9, 000		6, 746	11, 679⅛	28, 522
2298	Nails, plush .... gross		40	64 00	40								5	12
2299	Nails, finishing .... kegs		31	325 50	31									
2300	Nails, cut .... do		1, 200	9, 000 00	1, 200									
2301	Nails, finishing .... pounds		254		254									
2302	Nails, round-head brass .... gross		3		3									
2303	Nails, cut .... pounds		1, 199		1, 199									
2304	Nails, copper .... do		22¼		22¼									
2305	Nails, tin .... papers		28		28									
2306	Nails, lining, blued .... gross		50		50									
2307	Nails, lining, silver .... do													
2308	Numbers, key .... lots		1		1									
2309	Numbers .... sets		1		1									
2310	Netting, wire .... feet		3, 059	1, 376 55	3, 059							250	201	403
2311	Oilers		273		273									29
2312	Oilers, engine, assorted		355		355	2			1		12	25	19	42
2313	Oilers, spring		96		96									
2314	Oilers, spring-top		72		72									
2315	Oilers, spring-bottom		515	150 50	515					48	6		16	67
2316	Oilers, machine		447		447								33	67
2317	Oilers, small		7		7									
2318	Oilers, tin		91		91									
2319	Oil, lard .... gallons		9, 942½	15, 908 00	9, 942½							482	306	733½
2320	Oil, coal .... do		1, 157⅓	1, 018 60	1, 157⅓							99¾	27	59
2321	Oil, lubricating .... do		2, 171	3, 473 60	2, 171								380	761
2322	Oil, linseed, raw .... do		63	97 65	63							121	109	293
2323	Oil, linseed, boiled .... do		1, 514 7-10	2, 574 99	1, 514 7-10									
2324	Oil, linseed .... do		82		82									

Report showing the disposition of United States military railroad property in the military division of the Tennessee, &c—Continued.

Running number.	Articles.	Captured property on hand.	Property purchased by the United States on hand.	Cost to the United States of property purchased.	Total amount of property on hand.	Property sold on credit to railroad companies under Executive Orders of August 8 and October 14, 1865.								
						Macon and Brunswick railroad.	Muscogee railroad.	Montgomery and W. P. railroad.	Wills Valley railroad.	Macon and Western railroad.	Edgefield and Kentucky railroad.	Memphis and Charleston railroad.	Nashville and N. W. railroad.	Nashville and Chattanooga railroad.
2325	Oil ... gallons		295		295								125	70
2326	Oil, head-light ... do		129½	$271 95	129½									
2327	Oil, neat's-foot ... do		119	184 45	119									
2328	Oil, castor ... bottles		2½		2½									
2329	Ochre, French, yellow ... pounds		1,377		1,377								92	185
2330	Oakum ... do		2,425	424 37	2,425									
2331	Ornaments, brass		13		13							13		
2332	Planes, rounding		2		2									
2333	Planes, double-smooth		31		31									
2334	Planes, fore		1,435	3,157 00	1,435						2	12	5	10
2335	Planes, jack		1,129	1,806 40	1,129						2	7	9	10
2336	Planes, joiner		42	92 40	42								5	10
2337	Planes, joint		9		9									
2338	Planes, rabbet, assorted		867	1,083 65	867						6	9		
2339	Planes, jack, rabbet													
2340	Planes, bead, assorted		400	400 00	400						2	5		1
2341	Planes, bench ... sets		6		6									
2342	Planes, long-jointer		168		168						2			
2343	Planes, moulding		1		1									
2344	Planes, smooth		501	626 25	501						2	11	5	10
2345	Planes, sash		18	30 24	18							1		
2346	Planes, match		243		243									
2347	Planes, match ... pairs		5	9 80	5							3		
2348	Planes, screw-arm match													
2349	Planes, panel-plough		10		10							1		
2350	Planes, plough		67		67							7		
2351	Planes and bits, plough		65		65						1			
2352	Planes, floor ... sets													
2353	Planes, assorted		152		152									21
2354	Planes, double-iron													
2355	Planes, grooving ... pairs											5		
2356	Planes and set bits		6		6									

2357	Planes, joiners' short													
2358	Planes, panel plough and bits													
2359	Planes .... sets													
2360	Planers		3		3						1			
2361	Planers .... sets													
2362	Planers, rabbet													
2363	Planers, car, complete		1		1									
2364	Planers, compound adjustment head		2		2									
2365	Planers and matcher with counter shafts		1		1									
2366	Planers, iron, to plane 16 ft., 4 ft. square, complete		1		1									
2367	Planers, iron													1
2368	Planers, 48-inch		1	5,650 00	1									
2369	Planers, iron, 36 x 36 inches, 28-feet bed, 18-feet platform, (Seller's patent.)													
2370	Planers, 5-feet													
2371	Planers, 36 x 36 inches, No. 124, (Seller's patent)						1							
2372	Planers, 36 x 36 inches, No. 125, (Seller's patent)													
2373	Planers, (Seller's patent)													
2374	Planers, compound, (Bement & Dougherty)						1							
2375	Planers, compound		1		1			1				1		
2376	Planers, compound, chuck, No. 14, double, (Bement & Dougherty.)													
2377	Planers, 36 x 36 inches													
2378	Planers, link and link-block		1	175 00	1									
2379	Planers, cast-iron link													1
2380	Pulleys, assorted	7	665		672									306
2381	Pulleys, complete, assorted		32		32									
2382	Pulleys, upright		30		30									
2383	Pulleys for main shafts, common		11		11									
2384	Pulleys, two-ton		1		1									
2385	Pulleys for paint mill		1		1									
2386	Pulleys and shafts													
2387	Pulleys and chain, 2-ton		1		1									
2388	Pulleys, iron, 2 feet 10 inches face		5		5									
2389	Pulleys, iron, 2 feet 4 inches face		1		1									
2390	Pulleys, cast iron, assorted .... pounds													
2391	Pulleys, drawer, No. 10		1		1									
2392	Pulleys and hangers	22			22									
2393	Pulleys .... pounds		573		573									
2394	Pulleys, turned for ⅞, 10 by 12, with sets of screws		10		10									
2395	Pulleys, cast-iron		396		396									
2396	Ploughs and grooves .... sets		1		1									
2397	Ploughs													
2398	Pincers, carpenters' .... pairs		1		1									
2399	Pincers, blacksmiths' .... do		15		15									
2400	Pincers, upholsterers' .... do		18	29 16	18									
2401	Pincers, shoeing .... do		3		3									
2402	Pincers, assorted .... do		76		76								2	4
2403	Pincers, boiler-makers' .... do													
2404	Pencils, carpenters'		84	2 62	84									
2405	Pencils, coloring		54		54									
2406	Pencils, C. H		194		194								22	65

Report showing the disposition of United States military railroad property in the military division of the Tennessee, &c.—Continued.

Running number.	Articles.	Captured property on hand.	Property purchased by the United States on hand.	Cost to the United States of property purchased.	Total amount of property on hand.	Property sold on credit to railroad companies under Executive Orders of August 8 and October 14, 1865.								
						Macon and Brunswick railroad.	Muscogee railroad.	Montgomery and W. P. railroad.	Wills Valley railroad.	Macon and Western railroad.	Edgefield and Kentucky railroad.	Memphis and Charleston railroad.	Nashville and N. W. railroad.	Nashville and Chattanooga railroad.
2407	Pencils, artists' red sable		155		155								12	24
2408	Pencils, striping		42	$1 26	42								18	37
2409	Pencils, marking		24	72	24								8	16
2410	Pencils, lettering		29	87	29									
2411	Punches		227		227						7			155
2412	Punches, belt		228	71 25	228					12			4	12
2413	Punches, screws and dies		2		2									
2414	Punches, screw		3		3									
2415	Punches, hollow		5		5									18
2416	Punches, hydraulic		1		1									
2417	Punches, centre		42		42									1
2418	Punches, steel		287		287									9
2419	Punches, lever		2		2									2
2420	Punches, coppersmiths'		4		4									
2421	Punches, harness		3		3									
2422	Punches, spring		3		3									1
2423	Punches, conductors'		15	45 00	15									
2424	Punches, track		16		16							1		
2425	Punches, blacksmiths'		97		97									
2426	Punches, tinners'													
2427	Punches, tank hoop													
2428	Punches, clamp		1		1									
2429	Punches boiler-makers'		1		1									
2430	Punches, iron track ... sets		1		1									
2431	Punches, short		4		4									
2432	Punches, hound		113		113									
2433	Presses, drill	1	3		4						1	1		
2434	Presses, upright drill													1
2435	Presses, upright drill, &c													
2436	Presses, hydraulic, with shaft and pulleys		2		2									
2437	Presses, wheel	2			2									2
2438	Presses, hand wheel	1			1									

2439	Presses, upright drill, and counter shafts	2			2								
2440	Presses, medium "Franklin"		1		1								
2441	Presses, ½-medium "Franklin"		1		1								
2442	Presses, binders' hand		1		1								
2443	Presses, manifest		1		1								
2444	Presses, drill, and bits		1		1								
2445	Plyers ... pairs		62	18 60	62								2
2446	Plyers, cutting ... do		4		4								
2447	Plyers, common ... do		25		25								3
2448	Plyers, upholsterers' ... do		3		3								
2449	Plyers, flat nose ... do		2		2								
2450	Pots, glue		63	173 25	63						5	1	9
2451	Pots, marking		82		82							21	43
2452	Pots, wood paint		8		8								
2453	Pots, tin soldering		9		9								
2454	Pots, tinners' fire												
2455	Pots, paste		1		1								
2456	Pots, paint ... lot		1		1								
2457	Pots, cast		33		33								
2458	Pots, tallow		20		20						3		5
2459	Pots, rosin		1		1								
2460	Pots, melting												
2461	Pots, soldering												
2462	Pots, paint		69		69								
2463	Pots, iron		4		4								
2464	Pumps, steam												
2465	Pumps, steam, Woodland		1		1								
2466	Pumps, cylinder		1		1								
2467	Pumps, force, McGowan's	5	4		9					4		7	19
2467½	Pumps												
2468	Pumps, McGowan, with engine complete		1		1								
2469	Pumps, force		141		141					6			
2470	Pumps, Worthington		4	2, 400 00	4			1					
2471	Pumps, oil		9		9						1	1	2
2472	Pumps, oil, copper		4		4								1
2473	Pumps, engine		15		15							2	11
2474	Pumps, rotary fire		4		4								1
2475	Pumps, donkey		2	500 00	2								
2476	Pumps, cistern		3		3								
2477	Pumps, proving		1		1								
2478	Pumps, Harris		1		1								
2479	Pump, engine, and boiler, complete												
2480	Pumps, incomplete												
2481	Pumps, steam, with engine, Worthington												1
2482	Pumps, test and gauge	1			1								
2483	Pumps, force, with gearing and shafting	1			1								
2484	Pumps and fixtures, McGowan		1		1								
2485	Picks, earth, and handles		7		7								
2486	Picks		2, 594	3, 891 00	2, 594					24	189	314	418
2487	Picks, tamping		1, 596	2, 657 34	1, 596						240	270	349
2488	Picks, railroad		24		24								
2489	Picks, stone		6		6								4

Report showing the disposition of United States military railroad property in the military division of the Tennessee, &c.—Continued.

Running number.	Articles.	Captured property on hand.	Property purchased by the United States on hand.	Cost to the United States of property purchased.	Total amount of property on hand.	Property sold on credit to railroad companies under Executive Orders of August 8 and October 14, 1865.								
						Macon and Brunswick railroad.	Muscogee railroad.	Montgomery and W. P. railroad.	Wills Valley railroad.	Macon and Western railroad.	Edgefield and Kentucky railroad.	Memphis and Charleston railroad.	Nashville and N. W. railroad.	Nashville and Chattanooga railroad.
2490	Pins, wooden ... barrels		3		3									
2491	Pins, coupling ... pounds		281		281									
2492	Pins, coupling		459		459								78	142
2493	Pins, turned L. V													
2494	Pins, switch											20		
2495	Pipes, blast		8		8									
2496	Pipe, blast ... feet		220		220									
2497	Pipes, copper, with coupling		1		1									
2498	Pipe, copper ... pounds		301		301									
2499	Pipe, round		1		1									
2500	Pipe, sheet iron ... pounds		606		606									
2501	Pipe, wrought ... feet		22		22									
2502	Pipe, iron, galvanized ... do		35	$17 50	35									
2503	Pipe, galvanized ... pieces		4		4									
2504	Pipes, copper hose		3		3									
2505	Pipes, rubber hose		2		2									
2506	Pipe, iron ... pounds													
2507	Plugs, assorted		35		35									
2508	Plugs, gas pipe		615	153 75	615									
2509	Plugs, for repairing, dies		7		7									
2510	Plugs, flue		6		6									
2511	Plugs, assorted ... pounds													25
2512	Plugs and feathers													
2513	Plates, wrought scrap fish bar ... pounds													
2514	Plates, engine window													
2515	Plates, blacksmiths'													
2516	Plates, chuck		17		17									
2517	Plates, head ... pounds		11,814		11,814									1,316
2518	Plates, face ... do		12,395		12,395						150			
2519	Plates, face		10		10						2			5
2520	Plates, gas-fitters' screw		9		9									
2521	Plates, screw cutter		4		4									

2522	Plates, screw		18		18							1		
2523	Plates, screws and dies													
2524	Plates, angle		14		14							2		7
2525	Plates, surface		2		2									1
2526	Plates, turntable ....sets													
2527	Plates and rolls ....do													
2528	Plates, bolster ....pounds		6, 219		6, 219							384		5, 835
2529	Plates, assorted ....do		16, 202		16, 202							595		15, 607
2530	Plates, die													
2531	Points, glaziers' ....papers													
2532	Points, glaziers' ....pounds		112	44 80	112								4	8
2533	Points, frog, steel ....do													
2534	Patterns, tin													
2535	Patterns, moulders'													
2536	Patterns, wheelwrights'													
2537	Patterns, sheet iron ....sets													
2538	Patterns, assorted		499		499									1, 970
2539	Patterns, tin ....sets		1		1									
2540	Patterns, sheet iron ....pounds		810		810									
2541	Patterns ....lots													1
2542	Pikes													
2543	Piping, assorted ....feet		17		17									
2544	Putty ....pounds		2, 408	204 68	2, 408								328	660
2545	Pilots, loco													12
2546	Pilots, loco, wood		13		13									
2547	Paulins		47		47									
2548	Potash, prussiate ....pounds		1, 429	885 98	1, 429					25		5		
2549	Potash ....do		8		8									
2550	Pipe, for cistern pump ....feet		14		14									
2551	Pipe, water, assorted ....do	6, 576	3, 370		9, 946									1, 392
2552	Pipe, water ....pounds		1, 387		1, 387									
2553	Pipe, gum hose fire		2		2									
2554	Pipe, gas ....feet		52, 659 5-6		52, 659 5-6					705	420¼	1, 059		1, 445
2555	Pipe, lead ....pounds		1, 952		1, 952								82	163
2556	Pipe, brass ....feet		1, 791		791									
2557	Pipe, nozzle and hose													
2558	Pipe, inside, and netting for engine, No. 30													
2559	Pipe, outside, for engine, No. 30													
2560	Pipe, inside, for smoke stack		2		2									
2561	Pipe, copper ....feet		49		49								26	51
2562	Pipe, tin ....do		119		119									
2563	Pipe, iron ....bundles		4		4									
2564	Pipe, iron ....pieces		5		5									
2565	Pipe, escape		1		1									
2566	Paper, drawing ....quires		41 5-12		41 5-12									
2567	Paper, tracing ....rolls		15¼		15¼									
2568	Paper, waste ....pounds		5, 049		5, 049									
2569	Paper, antiquarian ....sheets		6		6									
2570	Paper, sand ....quires		136 3-12	33 32	136 3-12						10	20	120	270
2571	Paper, emery ....do		817 1-12	43 00	817 1-12						10		26⅜	73⅛
2572	Paper, wrapping ....do		320	197 92	320								5	10
2573	Paper, white drawing ....yards													

Report showing the disposition of United States military railroad property in the military division of the Tennessee, &c.—Continued.

Running number.	Articles.	Captured property on hand.	Property purchased by the United States on hand.	Cost to the United States of property purchased.	Total amount of property on hand.	Property sold on credit to railroad companies under Executive Orders of August 8 and October 14, 1865.								
						Macon and Brunswick railroad.	Muscogee railroad.	Montgomery and W. P. railroad.	Wills Valley railroad.	Macon and Western railroad.	Edgefield and Kentucky railroad.	Memphis and Charleston railroad.	Nashville and N. W. railroad.	Nashville and Chattanooga railroad.
2574	Paper, marble .... reams		1		1									
2575	Paper, brown drawing .... pounds		200	$60 00	200									
2576	Paper, white drawing .... do		273	212 94	273									
2577	Paper, printing .... do		38		38								13	25
2578	Pickets		19		19									
2579	Paint, black .... pounds		119		119									
2580	Paint, chrome yellow .... do		146		146									
2581	Pint, pink Dutch .... do		372		372								6	11
2582	Paint, mineral .... do		3,072	220 40	3,072								53	525
2583	Paint, assorted .... do													70
2584	Paint, mineral .... barrels													
2585	Paint, mixed .... pounds		1,393		1,393									
2586	Polish, stove .... papers		130		130									
2587	Powder, blasting .... pounds		2		2									
2588	Powder .... kegs		59	501 50	59								1⅛	2⅜
2589	Powder, blue .... pounds		1		1									
2590	Plungers, brass pump		1		1									
2591	Pans, oil		12		12									
2592	Packing, hemp .... pounds		10,389½	4,259 69	10,389½			560		407	270	75		
2593	Packing, gum .... do	210	5,811½	5,462 81	6,021½					48	100	350	181	139
2594	Packing, steam .... do		105		105									
2595	Pendants, gas-pipe		27		27									
2496	Poles, pipe		122		122							3		
2597	Pedestals .... pounds													6,970
2598	Pedestals		167		167									
2599	Powers, horse		3	450 00	3									4
2600	Platforms, railroad car													
2601	Paris, plaster .... pounds		280	28 00	280							6	4	97
2602	Pockets, iron		900		900									900
2603	Pits, transfer and masonry		1		1									1
2604	Pink, rose .... pounds		326½		326½							86	142	284
2605	Pinions, feed		9		9									

2606	Patterns, for brass castings		840		840									
2607	Patterns, for iron castings		1, 131		1, 131									
2608	Plank, oak .... feet		6, 000		6, 000									
2609	Pistons, C. I.		4		4									
2610	Paste, blue .... pots		1		1									
2610½	Ploughs													
2611	Quods, hollow .... pounds		25		25									
2612	Quods, pica, corner .... sets		4		4									
2613	Rules, steel		1		1									1
2614	Rules, foot		52		52									
2615	Rules, 2-foot		1		1								1	
2616	Rules, pocket		1	25	1									
2617	Rules, board		52	39 00	52									
2618	Rules, boxwood		87		87							6		3
2619	Rules, assorted		47		47								1	1
2620	Rods, guttering		1		1									
2621	Rods, pipe ram		4		4									
2622	Rods, brake .... pounds		14, 164		14, 164									
2623	Rods, brass .... do		2, 873		2, 873							2, 735		
2624	Rods, switch		7		7									11
2625	Rods, switch .... sets		29		29									17
2626	Rods, switch .... pounds		1, 532		1, 532							332	1, 200	
2627	Rods, levelling		5		5									
2628	Rods, tank .... sets		8		8									
2629	Rods, copper .... pounds		3, 320		3, 320							80		666
2630	Rods, connecting .... do		876		876							141		
2631	Rods, piston, wrought iron		2		2									2
2632	Rods, nuts, and bolts .... pounds		189		189							189		
2633	Rods, iron, for cars .... do		300		300							300		
2634	Rods, brake		22		22									
2635	Rods, brake, and wheel		1		1									
2636	Rods, piston		11		11									
2637	Rods, tank		81		81									
2638	Rods and levers, tank .... sets		2		2									
2639	Rods and bolts, wrought .... pounds		5, 056		5, 056									
2640	Rods, bridge .... do		102, 869		102, 869									
2641	Rollers .... pairs		3		3									1
2642	Rollers, door		34		34									
2643	Rollers, boiler-makers' .... sets		1		1							1		
2644	Rollers, timber		143		143									
2645	Rollers, large .... sets	1			1									
2646	Rollers, small, stove-pipe	1			1									
2647	Rollers, iron													
2648	Ratchets	2	33		35						1			10
2649	Ratchets and dogs .... pounds		730		730									730
2650	Ratchets and stands													
2651	Reamers		131		131							44	2	66
2652	Reamers and burrs, steel		24		24									
2653	Reamers and drills .... pounds													
2654	Reamers, C. S. .... do		30		30									
2655	Reamers and drills	175			175									
2656	Reamers, globe		1		1									

Report showing the disposition of United States military railroad property in the military division of the Tennessee, &c.—Continued.

Running number.	Articles.	Captured property on hand.	Property purchased by the United States on hand.	Cost to the United States of property purchased.	Total amount of property on hand.	Property sold on credit to railroad companies under the Executive Orders of August 8 and October 14, 1865.								
						Macon and Brunswick railroad.	Muscogee railroad.	Montgomery and W. P. railroad.	Wills Valley railroad.	Macon and Western railroad.	Edgefield and Kentucky railroad.	Memphis and Charleston railroad.	Nashville and N. W. railroad.	Nashville and Chattanooga railroad.
2657	Reamers, tap		2		2									
2658	Rivets, assorted		1,312,000		1,312,000			22,000			5,000			4,179
2659	Rivets, assorted ... pounds		37,758		37,758			315			1,226	1,207	2,178	
2660	Rivets, boiler ... do		9,925	$1,439 12	9,925			402					2,154	4,154
2661	Rivets, tinned		106,000		106,000							23		
2662	Rivets, black and tinned ... pounds		8,968		8,968								31⅓	61½
2663	Rivets, seat-back ... do		759	1,024 65	759								8	47½
2664	Rivets, tank ... do		5	1 10	5									
2665	Rivets, smokestack ... do													
2666	Rivets, copper ... do		287	200 90	287			8		4	8		6	14
2667	Rivets, brass ... do		65		65								2	3
2668	Rivets, tinned ... papers													22
2669	Rivets, iron ... pounds		2,180		2,180									
2670	Rivets, car seat, and burrs, brass													
2671	Rivets, iron													
2672	Rivets, iron ... papers		303	303 00	303									
2673	Rivets ... sets		2		2									
2674	Rivets, tinned ... pounds													
2675	Rivets, brass seat-back													
2676	Rope, assorted ... pounds		45,029½		45,029½					25	420	2,199	15	2,487
2677	Rope, manilla ... do		28,431	7,960 68	28,431			683				1,901	604	1,136½
2678	Rope, 1-inch ... feet		100		100									100
2679	Rope, 1½-inch ... coils		1		1									
2680	Rope ... do		½		½									
2681	Rope ... feet		160		160									
2682	Rope, bell ... pounds		10		10									
2683	Rope, old ... do													
2684	Ropes, small		5		5									
2685	Ropes, guy		4		4									
2686	Ropes, fall		2		2									
2687	Ropes, switch		57		57						2	3	17⅛	14⅜
2688	Ropes, wire ... coils		3		3									

2689	Rounds and hollows		37		37						2	3		
2690	Rounds and hollows ...sets		1		1									
2691	Rounds and hollows ...pairs		26		26									
2692	Rounds, chair		85		85									
2693	Rounds, timber, buggy		112		112									
2694	Riddles		64	128 00	64									5
2695	Regulators, upholsterers'		18		18									1
2696	Reels, chalk-line		96		96									
2697	Resin ...pounds		1, 462	116 96	1, 462							150	87	173
2698	Rubber, block ...do		60		60								11	21
2699	Rammers		37		37									
7000	Rams, battering		2		2									1
2701	Riving froe		1		1									
2702	Rings, flush, brass		1, 500	15 62	1, 500									
2703	Rings, brass, packing ...pounds		1, 814		1, 814								491	981
2704	Rings, packing													
2705	Rings, brass, cylinder													
2706	Rings, water tank		5		5							2		
2707	Rings, piston, for water works ...pounds		110		110									
2708	Rings, old brass		86		86									
2709	Rings, brass packing		288		288									
2710	Rings, Japan mall ...gross		4		4									
2711	Rings, Japan harness ...do		11½		11½									
2712	Rings breeching		5		5									
2713	Rings muffin		12		12									
2714	Rings harness ...gross		4		4									
2715	Red, American India ...tubes		14		14								4	8
2716	Red, India, in oil ...pounds		736		736									
2717	Red, vermilion ...do		20		20									
2718	Red, India ...do		830	415 00	830							96	93	198
2719	Red, Venetian ...do		1, 063	85 04	1, 063								35	70
2720	Red, Italian ...do		206		206									
2721	Rags ...do		25, 041	4, 757 79	25, 041							1, 259	726	3, 110
2722	Reservoir		1		1									1
2723	Racks, assorted		20		20							3		12
2724	Racks, forge, iron ...pounds		70		70									
2725	Racks, form													
2726	Rasps, assorted		345		345							289		12
2727	Rasps, wood		513		513									
2728	Rasps, horse		204	289 00	204									
2729	Rails, T		1, 493		1, 493						111			
2730	Rolls, steel, for turn-table ...sets		2	629 84	2									
2731	Rests, steady for lathe		4		4									
2732	Rests, tank, lever		46		46									
2733	Rests, iron		1		1									
2734	Rests, arm		1		1									
2735	Rakes, stable		7		7									
2736	Rakes, iron													
2737	Reflectors, head-light		19		19									
2738	Registers, conductors'		2		2									
2739	Rigging for steam balance		1		1									
2740	Roofing, patent ...pounds		130		130									

Report showing the disposition of United States military railroad property in the military division of the Tennessee, &c.—Continued.

Running number.	Articles.	Captured property on hand.	Property purchased by the United States on hand.	Cost to the United States of property purchased.	Total amount of property on hand.	Property sold on credit to railroad companies under the Executive Orders of August 8 and October 14, 1865.								
						Macon and Brunswick railroad.	Muscogee railroad.	Montgomery and W. P. railroad.	Wills Valley railroad.	Macon and Western railroad.	Edgefield and Kentucky railroad.	Memphis and Charleston railroad.	Nashville and N. W. railroad.	Nashville and Chattanooga railroad.
2741	Saws, hand		2, 833	$10, 856 00	2, 833				1		2	24	140	134
2742	Saws, tenon		23		23							3	3	4
2743	Saws, hack		71		71								3	14
2744	Saws, compass, assorted		219	229 95	219							8		
2745	Saws, back		1, 327	3, 207 00	1, 327							2	11	25
2746	Saws, rip		477	1, 908 00	477							7		
2747	Saws, buck		12		12									5
2748	Saws, web		1		1									
2749	Saws, cross-cut, assorted		1, 246		1, 246			21				18	4	8
2750	Saws, cross-cut, 5-foot													
2751	Saws, cross-cut, large		6		6									
2752	Saws, cross-cut, hand		106		106							3		
2753	Saws, cross-cut, tenon		2		2									
2754	Saws, jig		179		179									
2755	Saws, scroll		20		20									1
2756	Saws, circular, 48-inch													
2757	Saws, circular and arbor	2	1		3									1
2758	Saws, brass back		55		55									
2759	Saws, blue back		123		123									
2760	Saws, mill		29		29									
2761	Saws, muley		22		22									
2762	Saws, meat		26		26									1
2763	Saws, drag		8		8									
2764	Saws, keyhole		8	7 68	8									
2765	Saws, wood		43	53 75	43									
2766	Saws and frames, wood		27		27									
2767	Saws, wooden frame		50		50									
2768	Saws, pit		33		33									
2769	Saws, fine		40		40									
2770	Saws, whip		35		35									
2771	Saws, cut-off, 32-inch		2		2									
2772	Saws, shingle, 36-inch		1		1									

2773	Saws, assorted		170		170	1								
2774	Saws, bright back		25		25									
2775	Saws, panel		86		86									
2776	Saws, cut-off		3		3									1
2777	Squares, steel		1, 043	1, 715 73	1, 043						2	19	17	51
2778	Squares, try, assorted		1, 248		1, 248						2	11		4
2779	Squares, iron		4		4									
2780	Squares, centre		13		13									
2781	Squares, framing		75		75							2		
2782	Squares, bevel		6		6									
2783	Squares, lumber													
2784	Squares		3		3							1		
2785	Squares, head		2		2							2		
2786	Stands, head-light		583		583									
2787	Stands, switch		14		14						5	32		1
2788	Stands, flag		25		25									
2789	Stands for machines		3		3									3
2790	Stands, monkey switch		17		17									
2791	Stands, target switch		24		24									
2792	Stands, wood switch		8		8									
2793	Stands, iron													
2794	Stamps, U. S. M. R. R.		3		3									3
2795	Stands, brass lamp		2		2									
2796	Stands, locomotive lamp ... pounds		583		583									
2797	Stands, sand box ... do		719		719									
2798	Stands, Califor: ia, double		2		2									
2799	Stands, California, single		3		3									
2800	Stands, lead		1		1									
2801	Stands, type		3		3									
2802	Stands, chain, cast ... pounds											72		
2803	Stands, gauge lamp											1		
2804	Stands, flag ... pounds		25		25									
2805	Stamps, U. S.		7		7									
2806	Stones, grind, assorted		105		105		1				6	2	5	13
2807	Stones, grind, assorted ... pounds		6, 154	123 08	6, 154									
2808	Stones, grind, and fixtures ... sets		4		4									7
2809	Stones, grind, 4 feet diameter, cast iron frame													
2810	Stones, paint and muller		4	8 00	4									2
2811	Stones, paint		4		4									
2812	Stones, oil		268		268					24		9		1
2813	Stones, oil, assorted ... pounds		2, 394		2, 394								19	38
2814	Stones, whet		12		12									
2815	Stone ... lot		1		1									
2816	Stones, grind, frame, hangers complete		1		1									
2817	Stones, mill, and fixtures ... pairs		1		1									
2818	Stones, imposing		1		1									
2819	Stones, grind, frames and pulleys		1		1									
2820	Stones, grind, and fixtures		24		24									
2821	Stone, blue ... pounds		35		35									
2822	Stone, rotten ... do		554	55 40	554								4	7
2823	Stone, pumice ... do		1, 225	110 25	1, 225								17	363
2824	Stone, setting for engine													1

Report showing the disposition of United States military railroad property in the military division of the Tennessee, &c.—Continued.

Running number.	Articles.	Captured property on hand.	Property purchased by the United States on hand.	Cost to the United States of property purchased.	Total amount of property on hand.	Property sold on credit to railroad companies under Executive Orders of August 8 and October 14, 1865.								
						Macon and Brunswick railroad.	Muscogee railroad.	Montgomery and W. P. railroad.	Wills Valley railroad.	Macon and Western railroad.	Edgefield and Kentucky railroad.	Memphis and Charleston railroad.	Nashville and N. W. railroad.	Nashville and Chattanooga railroad.
2825	Snips ... pairs		4		4									1
2826	Snips, circular ... do		3		3								1	2
2827	Snips, tinners', assorted ... do		28		28								4	9
2828	Snips, straight ... do													
2829	Shaves, spoke		111		111							2		
2830	Shaves, spoke, wood		246	$123 00	246									
2831	Shaves, spoke, iron		233	116 50	233									
2832	Sets, saw		90		90							1		19
2833	Swedges, creasing		2		2									
2834	Swedges, bottom		395		395									
2835	Swedges, top		11		11									
2836	Swedges and chisels													
2837	Screws, assorted ... gross		3, 067		3, 067					131	6	159	396	970
2838	Screws, round head, brass ... do		107		107									
2839	Screws, brass, assorted ... do		$575\frac{1}{2}$		$575\frac{1}{2}$								35	86
2840	Screws, brass cap ... do		190		190					12				23
2841	Screws, round head, blued ... do		1, 119		1, 119					26				
2842	Screws, blued ... do		$347\frac{1}{2}$		$347\frac{1}{2}$									
2843	Screws, hand, assorted		152		152							12	24	47
2844	Screws, bench		130		130									
2845	Screws, wood bench		164		164							16	4	8
2846	Screws, iron bench		176		176							2	4	8
2847	Screws, bed		272		272									
2848	Screws, lag, assorted		6, 030		6, 030							396		1, 496
2849	Screws, lag ... pounds		3, 619		3, 619								$388\frac{3}{8}$	$778\frac{1}{8}$
2850	Screws, top		5		5									
2851	Screws, fore		1		1									
2852	Screws, hydraulic jack		6		6									
2853	Screws, small steel ... sets		8		8									
2854	Screws, clamp													
2855	Screws, large, and 4-inch nuts													
2856	Screws for shaft		1		1									

2857	Screws, auger .... gross		64		64									
2858	Screws, turn-table		1		1									
2859	Screws, gimblet, brass .... gross		7		7									
2860	Screws, tank		12		12									
2861	Screws		2		2									
2862	Screws, iron wood .... gross		89½		89½									
2863	Screws, head .... sets		9		9									
2864	Screws, lathe		1		1									
2865	Screws, tire .... sets													
2866	Screws, hand .... pairs		191		191									
2867	Screws, jack		16		16									
2868	Screws, wood .... pounds		84		84									
2869	Screws, gimlet .... gross		1,718		1,718									
2870	Sticks, creasing		3		3							1		2
2871	Sticks, yard		80	30 00	80									
2872	Sticks, composing		8		8									
2873	Sinks, counter		5		5									
2874	Sinks, drifts, and calking tools .... pounds		20		20									20
2875	Slicks, carpenters'		96		96							2		
2876	Slicks, large framing		2		2									
2877	Slicks, glass		3	3 00	3									
2878	Scrapers, plumbers'		17		17									
2879	Scrapers, box		5	3 75	5									
2880	Scrapers		176		176	1			1	2	2	2	3	13
2881	Scrapers, iron		133		133									
2882	Scrapers, drill		62		62									
2883	Scrapers, stone		1		1									
2884	Scrapers, carriage		1		1									
2885	Scrapers, stove		7		7									
2886	Scrapers, ash-pan		1		1									
2887	Straighteners, axle		1		1									
2888	Sockets, top		2		2									1
2889	Sockets, chisel		133		133									
2890	Sockets, gas-pipe		740		740									
2891	Shafts and pulleys		1		1									
2892	Shafts		10		10									
2893	Shafts, saw mandril counter		1		1									
2894	Shafting and pulleys .... pounds													
2895	Shafts with pulleys, counter, shafting, &c ... feet		96		96									
2896	Shafting, assorted .... do	368	997		1,365									1,032
2897	Shafting, iron, 2-inch .... pounds													
2898	Shafting .... do		2,163		2,163									1,758
2899	Shafting, 3¼-inch, with pulleys and hangers, complete .... feet													158
2900	Shafting, 3-inch .... feet													
2901	Shafting, 3¼-inch, tinned, 12 feet 6 inches long, with couplings and bolts, complete .... sections		12		12									
2902	Shafts, counter, with pulleys	1			1									
2903	Shafts, counter	1			1									
2904	Strainers		4		4							1		3
2905	Strainers, paint		2		2									
2906	Strainers, pump		311		311									

Report showing the disposition of United States military railroad property in the military division of the Tennessee, &c.—Continued.

Running number.	Articles.	Captured property on hand.	Property purchased by the United States on hand.	Cost to the United States of property purchased.	Total amount of property on hand.	Property sold on credit to railroad companies under Executive Orders of August 8 and October 14, 1865.								
						Macon and Brunswick railroad.	Muscogee railroad.	Montgomery and W. P. railroad.	Wills Valley railroad.	Macon and Western railroad.	Edgefield and Kentucky railroad.	Memphis and Charleston railroad.	Nashville and N. W. railroad.	Nashville and Chattanooga railroad.
2907	Strainers, copper		270	$405 00	270								70	142
2908	Strainers, feed-pipe													
2909	Skins, chamois		69	57 50	69							6		
2910	Skins, sheep		31		31									
2911	Skins, bark ... dozen		6		6									
2912	Shellac, gum ... pounds		408	510 00	408					20		36	63	127
2913	Saltpetre ... do		68		68									
2914	Spouts, bent		5, 194		5, 194								360	720
2915	Spouts, tank		21		21									
2916	Spouts, sheet-iron													
2917	Shafts, counter, and 4 pulleys													
2918	Spouts, fluid can		762		762									
2919	Spouts, tin		151		151									
2920	Spouts, funnel		56		56									
2921	Staffs, flag		1, 700		1, 700					2	4	8	61	128
2922	Staffs, brake		14		14							14		
2923	Steel, assorted ... pounds		11, 430		11, 430		253			202	2, 974			
2924	Steel, scrap ... do		40, 791		40, 791								1, 083	
2925	Steel, cast ... do		24, 855	11, 681 85	24, 855							3, 964		19, 350
2926	Steel, spring, assorted ... do		37, 389	9, 721 14	37, 389						1, 789	995		19, 167
2927	Steel, square ... do		92, 056¾	43, 266 67	92, 056¾						835	1, 216		1, 947
2928	Steel, octagon ... do		14, 594	6, 859 18	14, 594						1, 171	77		585
2929	Steel, frog ... do		22, 174	5, 543 50	22, 174							48		892
2930	Steel, blister ... do		3, 593		3, 593									
2931	Stocks, screw		9		9									
2932	Stocks, iron													3
2933	Stocks, drill		6		6									4
2934	Stocks, iron ... pairs		3		3									
2935	Stocks, roller		21		21									
2936	Saddles, smoke-stack ... pounds		1, 529		1, 529							100		
2937	Saddles for cylinder ... pairs		1		1									
2938	Stacks, smoke, locomotive		1		1									1

2939	Stacks, smoke, stationary, 31 feet x 22 inches		2		2									
2940	Stacks, smoke, sheet-iron, boiler frame		1		1									1
2941	Stacks, smoke and cap ....pounds		2,434		2,434									
2942	Scraps, forge ....do		1,278		1,278									
2943	Stacks, smoke, sheet-iron		1		1									
2944	Stacks, smoke		31		31							1		7
2945	Stacks, smoke ....feet		301		301									
2946	Sieves, sand		56		56									1
2947	Sieves, moulders'		51		51									
2948	Strips, parallel		98		98							50		48
2949	Strips, parallel ....pounds		61		61									
2950	Strips, copper-flue ....do		1,594		1,594									
2951	Spikes, bridge ....do		21,869		21,869									
2952	Spikes, railroad ....kegs		1,986¼		1,986¼	50						1505-150	2626-150	51 52-150
2953	Spikes, marlin		21	17 50	21									
2954	Spikes, bridge and cut ....kegs		203		203									
2955	Spikes, railroad		100		100									
2956	Spikes, railroad ....pounds		280,152	14,707 98	280,152									
2957	Spikes, cut, assorted ....kegs		3	27 00	3									
2958	Spikes, assorted ....pounds		1,000		1,000					500	600	3,195		6,600
2959	Spikes ....kegs	3			3									
2960	Scales, spring balance		8		8									5
2961	Scales, platform, assorted		40	4,680 00	40						1		2	16
2962	Scales, counter		18	360 00	18						1		1	2
2963	Scales and weights		1		1									1
2964	Scales, warehouse													
2965	Scales, brass scoop		1		1									
2966	Scales, set		3		3									
2967	Scales, beam		1		1							1		
2968	Scales		2		2									
2969	Scales, track		1		1									1
2970	Scales, safety-valve		7		7							3		
2971	Scales, stone		1		1									
2972	Scales, spring		3		3									
2973	Scales, platform counter		9	121 05	9									
2974	Stretchers, iron		52		52									1
2975	Stretchers, car		10		10									
2976	Snatches, gate		1		1									
2977	Springs, assorted ....pounds		1,414		1,414									
2978	Springs, rubber car ....do		1,200		1,200									
2979	Springs, car		1		1									
2980	Springs, packing		84		84									
2981	Springs, rubber ....pounds		70		70									
2982	Springs, gum		2		2									
2983	Springs, engine tender ....pounds		21,690		21,690									
2984	Springs, spiral ....do		8,467		8,467									
2985	Springs, assorted		4		4									
2986	Springs, gum ....pounds		40,267	49,125 74	40,267							981	571¼	4,652
2987	Springs, car ....do		28,257		28,257						959	858		
2988	Springs, tender													8
2989	Springs, engine		21		21									43
2990	Springs, engine ....pounds		18,187		18,187									2,545

Report showing the disposition of United States military railroad property in the military division of the Tennessee, &c.—Continued.

Running number.	Articles.	Captured property on hand.	Property purchased by the United States on hand.	Cost to the United States of property purchased.	Total amount of property on hand.	Property sold on credit to railroad companies under Executive Orders of August 8 and October 14, 1865.								
						Macon and Brunswick railroad.	Muscogee railroad.	Montgomery and W. P. railroad.	Wills Valley railroad.	Macon and Western railroad.	Edgefield and Kentucky railroad.	Memphis and Charleston railroad.	Nashville and N. W. railroad.	Nashville and Chattanooga railroad.
2991	Springs, window		256	$95 14	256									
2992	Springs, large D		4		4									
2993	Springs, small D		16		16									
2994	Springs, packing ... pounds		120¾		120¾									129¾
2995	Shovels	12	4,017	7,029 75	4,029	1				1	38	344	355	585
2996	Shovels, railroad		75		75									
2997	Shovels, scoop		4	7 20	4									
2998	Shovels, coal		1	58	1									
2999	Shovels, moulder, steel		62	89 90	62									62
3000	Shovels and scrapers													
3001	Spades	12	383		395							54	17	31
3002	Screens, sand		2		2									
3003	Screens, cloth		6		6									
3004	Screens, zinc		1		1									
3005	Screens, coal		1		1									
3006	Screens, wire													
3007	Spools, chalk line		40		40									
3008	Soap ... pounds		183		183									
3009	Soap, castile ... do		40		40									
3010	Soap ... bars		15		15									
3011	Spanners		3		3									
3012	Sienna, assorted ... pounds		420½		420½							96	61	120
3013	Sienna, burnt ... do		63	28 35	63									
3014	Sienna, raw Italian ... do		254	50 80	254									
3015	Sienna, raw, in oil ... do		60		60									
3016	Sienna, raw ... do		10	4 50	10									
3017	Springs, brass													
3018	Sledges, (12-pound)		3		3									
3019	Springs, patent		40		40									
3020	Stirrups, log ... pairs		4		4									
3021	Stencils, copper		28		28									11
3022	Scythes, snath		35		35									

3023	Scythes, grass		13		13									
3024	Scythes, brier		14		14									
3025	Sponge, common .... pounds		607½		607½									
3026	Sponge, fine .... do		21¾	65 25	21¾							5	19	38
3027	Sponge .... do		33		33								¼	¼
3028	Sulphur .... do		675½	67 55	675½							2½	83	167
3029	Sulphur flowers .... do		423		423									
3030	Sash, assorted .... lights		1,298		1,298									
3031	Sash, ... pieces		1,117		1,117									
3032	Sash .... lots		1		1								9	119
3033	Sash, wire		5		5									
3034	Sash, sky-light		21		21									
3035	Switches, monkey		27		27									
3036	Slides, switch .... sets		119		119									
3037	Slides, track .... pounds		3,745		3,745									2,528
3038	Signals, fog .... gross		10		10									
3039	Stools, saddlers'		2		2									
3040	Spaces, pica quod .... pounds		23¼		23¼									
3041	Staples, iron .... do		110		110									
3042	Staples, iron		189		189									
3043	Straps, seat, back		742	5 05	742								144	144
3044	Straps, connecting, and brasses	4			4									
3045	Skivers		17		17									
3046	Skivers, white		24		24									
3047	Skids, loading		9		9							3	1	2
3048	Sizing, gold .... pounds		3		3									
3049	Shoes, mule .... do		1,155		1,155									
3050	Shoes, mule		1,200		1,200									
3051	Sellars, rod .... pounds		75		75									
3052	Straps, eccentric .... do		158		158									
3053	Stems, check valve		189		189									
3054	Settings, masonry, with iron chimney													1
3055	Scrapers, hoe		3		3									
3056	Sprinklers, fire		1		1									
3057	Squares, plated		6		6									
3058	Shingles		717,850		717,850									
3059	Saucers, stove		3		3									
3060	Shackles, engine .... pounds		177		177							177		
3061	Salt .... do		575		575									200
3062	Salts, epsom .... do		10		10									
3063	Sublimate, corr .... do		1		1									
3064	Staves, tank .... lots		1		1									
3065	Staves, tank .... pieces		4		4									
3066	Staples, back harness		28		28									
3067	Settings, masonry		4		4									
3068	Seamers, double roofing													
3069	Solder .... pounds		1,318½		1,318½						28	75½	167	379
3070	Soda, sal .... do		2½		2½							2½		
3071	Swivels		1		1									
3072	Seats, coach		4		4									
3073	Seats		7		7									
3074	Shelving .... lots		2		2									

Report showing the disposition of United States military railroad property in the military division of the Tennessee, &c.—Continued.

Running number.	Articles.	Captured property on hand.	Property purchased by the United States on hand.	Cost to the United States of property purchased.	Total amount of property on hand.	Property sold on credit to railroad companies under Executive Orders of August 8 and October 14, 1865.								
						Macon and Brunswick railroad.	Muscogee railroad.	Montgomery and W. P. railroad.	Wills Valley railroad.	Macon and Western railroad.	Edgefield and Kentucky railroad.	Memphis and Charleston railroad.	Nashville and N. W. railroad.	Nashville and Chattanooga railroad.
3075	Shelves, wooden		1		1									
3076	Syphons and cocks		1		1									
3077	Spoons, packing		7		7									
3078	Signs, tin													
3079	Signs		22		22									
3080	Signs, loco		68		68									
3081	Shutters, window		24		24									
3082	Steps, engine		1		1									
3083	Slides, switch													
3084	Staves, tank ... cases													
3085	Shimmers, paint		2		2									
3086	Shoes, horse ... pounds		622		622							2,841		12,825
3087	Shoes, brake											1		
3088	Sets, hand-saw		34	$7 10	34									
3089	Sets, cross-cut saw		19		19									
3090	Sets, mill-saw		5	3 12	5									
3091	Sets, lever-saw		13		13									
3092	Sets, blacksmiths' cold		6		6							2		14
3093	Sets, rivet		25		25									26
3094	Sets, iron button		26		26									
3095	Sets, spring		1		1							7	38	96
3096	Sledges, assorted		65		65									
3097	Sledges and handles		80		80						24	21	1	63
3098	Sledges, blacksmiths'		360		360									
3099	Sledges, heavy		2		2									
3100	Sledges, stone		313		313							3		1
3102	Shears, hand ... pairs		7		7							5		
3103	Shears, tinners' ... do		12		12									2
3104	Shears, sheet ... do		24		24									1
3105	Shears, circular ... do		2		2								1	1
3106	Shears, lever ... do		3		3									5
3107	Shears, bench ... do		5	20 00	5									

3108	Shears, squaring ..... do		2		2									1
3109	Shears and punch combined ..... do		1		1					5				
3110	Shears, rotary ..... do		2		2									
3111	Shears, table, trimmers' ..... do		1		1									
3112	Shears, table, gauge ..... do		1		1									
3113	Shears ..... do													
3114	Shives, iron													
3115	Stakes, square, Weddell		14		14									
3116	Stakes, funnel		2		2									
3117	Stakes, bench		4		4									
3118	Stakes, tinners'		1		1							2		11
3119	Stakes, needle		2		2									1
3120	Stakes, double seaming		1		1							1		1
3121	Stakes, oval-head		1		1									
3122	Stakes, head		6		6									
3123	Stakes, pointing		1		1									
3124	Stakes, beak-horn													
3125	Stakes, hatchet		4	22 00	4									
3126	Stakes, square-head		1		1									
3127	Stakes, horn-blow		1		1									
3128	Stakes, round-head													
3129	Swedges, assorted		298		298						18	38		553
3130	Swedges, square ..... pairs		1		1									1
3131	Swedges, C. S ..... pounds		325		325									
3132	Swedges, W. I ..... do		629		629									160
3133	Swedges, B. S		353		353									
3134	Swedges and fullers		19		19									
3135	Swedges and chisels ..... sets		597		597									350
3136	Sleeves, water pipe													
3137	Sheives ..... pairs		1		1									
3138	Stacks, smoke, stationary													7
3139	Shafts, steam, wheel		1		1									
3139¼	Saws, circular, assorted		198		198							3	8	24
3139½	Slicks		104		104									
3139¾	Sellar's engine truck		321		321									
3140	Tools, plumbers' ..... sets													
3141	Tools, blacksmiths', assorted ..... do	3	35	5,250 00	38							3		2
3142	Tools, blacksmiths' ..... pounds													
3143	Tools, shoeing ..... sets		10		10									
3144	Tools, carpenters' ..... do		2		2									
3145	Tools, carpenters' ..... chests		1		1									
3146	Tools, turning, assorted	225	412		637									152
3147	Tools, wheelwright ..... sets		9		9									
3148	Tools, wheelwright, and chest, (incomplete)													
3149	Tools, grooving		3		3									
3150	Tools, sash, assorted		365		365					58		6	21	42
3151	Tools, French sash, assorted		156	19 50	156									
3152	Tools, hand		108		108									
3153	Tools, planing, steel		492		492									67
3154	Tools, boring		44		44									
3155	Tools, boring, steel		5		5									26
3156	Tools, lathe, steel ..... pounds		1,129		1,129		35½							60

Report showing the disposition of United States military railroad property in the military division of the Tennessee, &c.—Continued.

Running number.	Articles.	Captured property on hand.	Property purchased by the United States on hand.	Cost to the United States of property purchased.	Total amount of property on hand.	Property sold on credit to railroad companies under Executive Orders of August 8 and October 14, 1865.								
						Macon and Brunswick railroad.	Muscogee railroad.	Montgomery and W. P. railroad.	Wills Valley railroad.	Macon and Western railroad.	Edgefield and Kentucky railroad.	Memphis and Charleston railroad.	Nashville and N. W. railroad.	Nashville and Chattanooga railroad.
3157	Tools, lathe		165		165							128	7	14
3158	Tools, steel, for turning rolls ... pounds	200			200									
3159	Tools, saddlers' ... chests		2		2									
3160	Tools, saddlers' ... sets		6	$78 00	6									
3161	Tools, tinners' ... do		2	780 00	2									
3162	Tools, tinners' ... pounds		68		68									
3163	Tools, C. S. ... do		455		455							68		
3164	Tools, coppersmith ... sets		1	310 00	1							311		189
3165	Tools, graining ... do		7	21 00	7								1	1
3166	Tools, cupping		19		19									
3167	Tools, heading		137		137									
3168	Tools, slotting		19		19									18
2169	Tools, rotary-cutting		20		20									20
3170	Tools, spring ... sets		1		1									
3171	Tools, calking		8		8									
3172	Tools, flat paint, assorted		6		6									
3173	Tools and chains, W. I ... pounds		700		700									700
3174	Tools, iron		40		40									40
3175	Tools, turning ... boxes		1		1									
3176	Tools, lathe and planer		16		16			365						
3177	Trams ... pairs		5		5									4
3178	Taps and dies ... sets	1	9		10									
3179	Taps and dies	31	53		84									60
3180	Taps, steel ... pounds		83		83									
3181	Taps, steel		422		422							19		137
3182	Taps, C. S. ... pounds													
3183	Taps, machine		62		62							23		12
3184	Taps		134		134									40
3185	Tips, C. S.		40		40							46		
3186	Tanks, oil, assorted		3		3									5
3187	Tanks, engine		6		6									
3188	Tanks, water	24	57		81						5		9	23

3189	Tanks, locomotive	1			1									
3190	Tanks, oil, (45 galls)		1		1									
3191	Tanks, oil, (50 galls)		1		1									
3192	Tanks, oil, (75 galls)		1		1									
3193	Tanks, oil, (80 galls)		1		1									
3194	Tanks, tin water, (parts) ... lots		1		1									
3195	Tongs, roofing ... pairs		4		4									2
3196	Tongs, G. P. ... do		281	1,854 60	281							111	12	43
3197	Tongs, ice ... do		2		2									
3198	Tongs, B. S ... do		1,189	832 30	1,189						19	2		852
3199	Tongs, tinners' ... sets		1		1									
3200	Tongs, grainers' ... do		1		1									
3201	Tongs, engine ... pairs		30		30	1			1	2	4	4	7	18
3202	Tongs, R. R ... do		13		13									
3203	Tongs, tools, and pokers ... pounds		318		318									318
3204	Tongs, assorted ... pairs		311		311									17
3205	Tongs, B. S. and R. R		446		446									
3206	Tin, sheet ... boxes		690½		690½					100		47	42	97½
3207	Tin, perforated ... sheets		22	5 17	22									
3208	Tin, block ... pounds		2,391	1,123 77	2,391							154		600
3209	Tin, sheet ... sheets		368		368									
3210	Tin, sheet, and screws ... pounds		300		300									
3211	Timber ... feet		3,500		3,500								122,787	
3212	Timber, oak ... do		553,974		553,974									
3213	Timber, square, assorted ... do		100,700		100,700									
3214	Timber, bridge ... do		545,857		545,857									
3215	Timber, B. M., assorted ... do		412,921		412,921									
3216	Timber, framed ... lots		1		1									
3217	Ties, cross		89,879		89,879						14,107	10,110	11,015	13,931
3218	Tallow ... pounds		18,382½	3,125 02	18,382½							1,330	2,410½	4,211½
3219	Tallow ... barrels		26½		26½									
3220	Thimbles		7		7									
3221	Thimbles, flue, iron ... pounds		238		238									
3222	Thimbles, cast ... do		228		228									
3223	Thermometers		2		2									
3224	Tarpaulins		13		13									
3225	Tripods		260		260									
3226	T's, gas-pipe		513		513									
3227	T's, water-pipe		4		4									
3228	T's, cast iron		6		6									
3229	Tubes, blast		19		19									
3230	Tubing, copper ... pounds		972		972								214	428
3231	Trucks, timber	1	6		7							3		
3232	Trucks, warehouse		22		22							1	13	41
3233	Trucks, engine													
3234	Trucks ... pairs		3		3									
3235	Trucks, car	19	66		85									
3236	Trucks, car ... pairs		1		1									
3237	Trucks, tender and locomotive ... pounds		5,336		5,336									
3238	Trucks, engine ... pairs		3		3									
3239	Trucks, machine ... do		5		5									
3240	Tires, wrought iron ... pounds		169		169									1,110

Report showing the disposition of United States military railroad property in the military division of the Tennessee, &c.—Continued.

Running number.	Articles.	Captured property on hand.	Property purchased by the United States on hand.	Cost to the United States of property purchased.	Total amount of property on hand	Property sold on credit to railroad companies under the Executive Orders of August 8 and October 14, 1865.								
						Macon and Brunswick railroad.	Muscogee railroad.	Montgomery and W. P. railroad.	Wills Valley railroad.	Macon and Western railroad.	Edgefield and Kentucky railroad.	Memphis and Charleston railroad.	Nashville and N. W. railroad.	Nashville and Chattanooga railroad.
3241	Tires, cast iron		33		33									
3242	Tires, locomotive		80		80			21						8
3243	Tires, locomotive flange ... pounds		146, 700		146, 700				7, 560	3, 360				25, 970
3244	Tires, flange cast iron ... do													
3245	Tires, old ... do		270		270									
3246	Tires, wrought iron													
3247	Trowels, masons'		18	$36 00	18									2
3248	Trowels, plasterers'		15	22 50	15									4
3249	Tables, circular saw		9		9									2
3250	Tables, turn		1	2, 783 00	1									1
3251	Tables, turn and foundation	1			1									
3252	Tables, binders' sewing		1		1									
3253	Torches, gas		5		5									
3254	Troughs, flock		34		34									1
3255	Troughs, guttering		2		2									
3256	Troughs, forge													
3257	Tops and screws, lamp		253		253									
3258	Tops, chimney		7		7									
3259	Tops, turn-table		2		2									
3260	Tops, car-lamp		22		22									
3261	Tops, screw ... gross		9½	52 25	9½			1					4⅜	9
3262	Tops, tallow, can		48		48								48	
3263	Tops and bottoms, can		1, 109		1, 109									
3264	Tops and bottoms, car-lamp		2		2									
3265	Tops and bottoms for turn-table		2		2									
3266	Type ... founts		138		138									
3267	Type ... pounds		971 35-48		971 35-48									
3268	Tapes, measuring, assorted		60		60									
3269	Tripoli ... pounds		213		213							112		
3270	Tripoli ... papers		185	10 80	185									
3271	Tacks, assorted ... do		15, 958		15, 958					130		81	717	3, 374
3272	Tacks, gimp ... do		1, 112	1, 556 80	1, 112								120	240

3273	Tacks, upholsterers' ......do		2,466	567 18	2,466									
3274	Tacks, blued ......do		12	1 60	12									
3275	Targets		26		26									
3276	Tickts, mess													
3277	Tickets		132,750		132,750									70,750
3278	Tar, coal ......gallons		50		50							35		
3279	Tar, coal ......barrels		4½		4½									
3280	Thread, black ......pounds		28	63 00	28								7	21
3281	Thread, black ......bundles		6		6									
3282	Thread, shoe ......pounds		15		15									
3283	Thread, saddlers' ......do		4½		4½									
3284	Thread, linen ......do		24		24									
3285	Thread, black ......skeins		20		20									
3286	Twine, hemp ......pounds		46½	46 50	46½								4	7½
3287	Twine, tufting ......do		35¾	67 92	35¾					2¾			5½	26½
3288	Twine, wrapping ......do		22½		22½									
3289	Twine ......balls		8		8									
3290	Turpentine ......gallons		380¼	1,425 94	380¼							3¾	18	40
3291	Trestles		180		180							20		49
3292	Trusses, iron		3		3						2			
3293	Torpedoes		1,440		1,440								480	960
3294	Tongues, frog ......pounds		120		120									120
3295	Templets, switch ......sets		1		1									1
3296	Templets		36		36									
3297	Transits		4		4									
3298	Tenders, locomotive		1		1									
3299	Tincture, iodine ......pounds		1½		1½									
3300	Transoms, wrought ......do		8,824		8,824									
3301	Testers, gas-pipe		1		1									
3302	Tiles, fire		38		38									
3303	Traps, rat		2		2									
3304	Tighteners, belt		1		1									
3305	Triangles		2		2									
3306	Tubs, tool		1		1									
3307	Tags, shipping ......lots		1		1									
3308	Unions, brass, assorted		502	1,480 90	502									
3309	Umber, raw, in oil ......pounds		95	17 57	95							25	16	23
3310	Umber, raw ......do		167	30 90	167							36	7	13
3311	Umber, burnt ......do		67¼	13 10	67¼								10	21
3312	Umber, burnt ......tubes		3	43	3									
3313	Umber, burnt, in oil ......pounds		114		114									
3314	Vices, assorted	5	332		337								6	69
3315	Vices, parallel		95	855 00	95			2				14		1
3316	Vices, bench		2		2							1		1
3317	Vices, B. S.		36		36						2			
3318	Vices, solid box	1	5		6									
3319	Vices, hand		490		490									
3320	Vices, solid ......pounds		1,344	537 60	1,344									
3321	Ventilators		18		18									
3322	Ventilators, tin		12		12									
3323	Ventilators, car		59		59									9
3324	Ventilators, car, lamp		9		9									

Report showing the disposition of United States military railroad property in the military division of the Tennessee, &c.—Continued.

Running number.	Articles.	Captured property on hand.	Property purchased by the United States on hand.	Cost to the United States of property purchased.	Total amount of property on hand.	Property sold on credit to railroad companies under Executive Orders of August 8 and October 14, 1865.								
						Macon and Brunswick railroad.	Muscogee railroad.	Montgomery and W. P. railroad.	Wills Valley railroad.	Macon and Western railroad.	Edgefield and Kentucky railroad.	Memphis and Charleston railroad.	Nashville and N. W. railroad.	Nashville and Chattanooga railroad.
3325	Valves, globe, assorted		532	$12,236 00	532					8				
3326	Valves, tank		7		7									
3327	Valves, water, assorted		7	332 50	7									
3328	Valves, angle		14	280 00	14									9
3329	Valves, check		3		3							1		
3330	Valves, engine		51		51									
3331	Valves, brass, pump													2
3332	Valves, safety, complete													
3333	Valves, brass, pump ... pounds		128		128									
3334	Valves, brass, check ... do		85		85									
3335	Valves, brass, steam ... do		12		12									
3336	Valves, governor		3		3									
3337	Valves, engine ... pounds		51		51									
3338	Valves, safety ... do		8		8									
3339	Vermilion, English "D" ... do		225	416 25	225							54	24	48
3340	Vermilion, American extra ... do		6	2 22	6								70	
3341	Vermilion, German ... do		212		212									140
3342	Vermilion, Chinese ... do		83	153 55	83								10	43
3343	Vermilion, Chinese ... tubes		12	2 00	12									
3344	Vermilion, scarlet ... pounds		12		12									
3345	Vermilion, chrome ... do		½		½									
3346	Vermilion ... do													
3347	Varnish, copal ... gallons		178	694 20	178									
3348	Varnish, coach body ... do		711½	3,130 60	711½							41½	55	211
3349	Varnish, shellac		53		53									
3350	Varnish, Japan		445	2,047 00	445							65	10	49
3351	Varnish, damar ... do		187	748 00	187								10	61
3352	Varnish, asphaltum ... do		23		23									
3353	Varnish, white ... pounds		84		84									
3354	Varnish, white ... gallons		100		100									
3355	Verdigriss ... pounds		50	62 50	50								4	8
3356	Vitriol ... do		30	1 95	30									

3357	Wrenches, assorted		2,365		2,365	12			11	16	36	118	209	425
3358	Wrenches, monkey, assorted	12	2,002	5,005 00	2,014	1		24	1	14	16	113	143	333
3359	Wrenches, blast pipe		1		1									
3360	Wrenches, tap, assorted	15	51		66									9
3361	Wrenches, ratchet		1		1									
3362	Wrenches, straight		1		1									
3363	Wrenches, screw		72		72									32
3364	Wrenches, bridge		18		18									6
3365	Wrenches, wheel		5		5							1		
3366	Wrenches, key		9	90 00	9							1		
3367	Wrenches, hose		1		1									
3368	Wrenches, long bar		1		1									
3369	Wrenches, lathe	20			20									
3370	Wrenches, socket	10	151		161									
3371	Wrenches, spanner		184		184									
3372	Wrenches, hand		16		16									
3373	Wrenches, iron tap ... pounds		42		42									
3374	Wrenches, "S"		4		4									
3375	Wrenches, pipe		57		57									
3376	Wrenches, follower		5		5									
3377	Wrenches, iron		498		498									
3378	Wrenches, packing		2		2									
3379	Wrenches, post		3		3									
3380	Wedges, stonemasons'													10
3381	Wedges ... pounds		2,456		2,456							150		2,946
3382	Wedges, iron		59		59							7		1
3383	Wedges, steel		10		10									
3384	Wedges		60		60									
3385	Wedges, blacksmiths'		27		27									
3386	Wedges and feathers		158		158									
3387	Whistles, locomotive		16	1,200 00	16							3	1	3
3388	Whistles, steam													
3389	Windlass, quaker		2		2									1
3390	Windlass, hand		1		1									
3391	Wheels, tender, and truck, on axles ... pairs		110		110							6		51
3392	Wheels, car, with axles		12		12									
3393	Wheels, car, on axles ... pairs		225	19,860 75	225							30		71
3394	Wheels and axles ... pounds		43,470		43,470									
3395	Wheels, driving, on axles ... pairs		5		5									
3396	Wheels, turn-table ... pounds		1,084		1,084									
3397	Wheels, press gear ... do		1,536		1,536									
3398	Wheels, car		196		196									4
3399	Wheels, car ... pounds		1,634		1,634									8,400
3400	Wheels, water		1		1									1
3401	Wheels, hand car ... pounds													
3402	Wheels, hand car		22		22									22
3403	Wheels, cog, hand car		7		7							7		
3404	Wheels, car and tender		407		407							8		1
3405	Wheels, driving		9		9									
3406	Wheels, engine truck		197		197									191
3407	Wheels, truck ... pairs													
3408	Wheels, iron pulley		3		3									

Report showing the disposition of United States military railroad property in the military division of the Tennessee, &c.—Continued.

Running number.	Articles.	Captured property on hand.	Property purchased by the United States on hand.	Cost to the United States of property purchased.	Total amount of property on hand.	Property sold on credit to railroad companies under Executive Orders of August 8 and October 14, 1865.								
						Macon and Brunswick railroad.	Muscogee railroad.	Montgomery and W. P. railroad.	Wills Valley railroad.	Macon and Western railroad.	Edgefield and Kentucky railroad.	Memphis and Charleston railroad.	Nashville and N. W. railroad.	Nashville and Chattanooga railroad.
3409	Wheels, brake ... pounds		2,000		2,000									2,000
3410	Wheels, brake		20		20							14		
3411	Wheels, engine													
3412	Wheels, engine and tender, on axles ... pairs													
3413	Wheels, for counter shaft		2		2									
3414	Wheels and axles, hand car ... pairs													
3415	Wheels, car ... do	85			85									
3416	Wheels and axles ... sets		8		8									
3417	Wheels, engine truck, on axles ... pairs	5			5									
3418	Wheels, bevel	2	2		4									
3419	Wheels, fly, ten feet	1	1		2									
3420	Wheels, press gear		1,168		1,168									
3421	Wheels, spur		11		11									
3422	Wheels, truck		18		18									
3423	Wheels, car, 24-inch, pattern No. 25		50		50									
3424	Wheels, car, 26-inch, pattern No. 27		50		50									
3425	Wheels, freight car		158		158									
3426	Wheels, balance		5		5									
3427	Wheels, hand car ... pairs		241		241									
3428	Wheels, hand car, on axles ... pounds													
3429	Wheels, ratchet		37		37									
3430	Wicks, flat		11,867	$206 00	11,867							72	114	4,405
3431	Wicks, lamp ... pounds		53¾	63 95	53¾							½	12½	7½
3432	Wicks, lamp ... gross													
3433	Wicking ... balls		72		72									
3434	Wire, brass ... pounds		385	265 65	385					55			50	100
3435	Wire, telegraph ... do		2,204		2,204									
3436	Wire, copper ... do		984	777 36	984						76	16½	50	100
3436½	Wire, iron ... do		5,160	1,032 00	5,160					85	99	272	150	347
3437	Wire, assorted ... do		292		292								24	
3438	Wire, tin ... do		83		83									
3439	Wire ... bundles		8		8									

3440	Washers, assorted .... pounds		46,719		46,719			900		1,639	3,661	76½	199	5,251
3441	Washers, cast .... do		28,308	9,058 56	28,308									
3442	Webbing .... yards		170½		170½								257	1,161
3443	White, China .... pounds		496	223 20	496								42	84
3444	White, flake, assorted .... do		462½	208 12	462½							20	30	75
3445	White, flake .... tubes		6		6									
3446	Whiting .... pounds		1,076	48 42	1,076							10	35	381
3447	Whiting, Spanish .... do		765		765									
3448	Wax, bees .... do		279	209 25	279							2	17	33
3449	Winches, crane		2		2									
3450	Waste, cotton .... pounds		3,282	1,345 62	3,282							385	85	380
3451	Waste, tow .... do		507		507									
3452	Waste .... do		1,215		1,215									
3453	Weights .... do		7,600		7,600									7,600
3454	Weights		1		1									
3455	Weights, sash		24		24									
3456	Walks, plank		1		1									
3457	Webbing .... bolts		21		21									
3458	Wrenches, square		1		1									
3459	Yarn, lubricating, packing .... pounds		8,429		8,429								2,174	5,576
3460	Yellow, canary .... do		72	32 40	72								10	20
3461	Yarn, packing .... reels		3½		3½									
3462	Yawls		1		1									
3463	Zinc, slab .... pounds		581	98 77	581					455				
3464	Zinc, sheet .... do		3,163	442 82	3,163								446	1,183
3465	Zinc, sheet .... pieces													

Report showing the disposition of United States military railroad property in the military division of the Tennessee, &c.—Continued

Running number.	Articles.	Property sold on credit to railroad companies under Executive Orders of August 8 and October 14, 1865.													
		Alabama and Florida railroad.	East Tennessee and Georgia railroad.	Mobile and Great Northern railroad.	Tennessee and Alabama railroad.	East Tennessee and Virginia railroad.	Mobile and Ohio railroad.	Tennessee and Alabama Central railroad.	Central Southern railroad.	New Orleans and Ohio railroad.	Rome railroad.	Memphis and Ohio railroad.	Southwestern railroad.	Georgia Railroad and Banking Company.	New Orleans, Jackson, and Great Northern railroad.
1	Coal .... bushels														
2	Coke .... do														
3	Charcoal .... do														
4	Charcoal .... barrels														
5	Wood .... cords		5, 042		4, 196	6, 108		3, 542	3, 026						
6	Corn .... pounds														
7	Hay .... do														
8	Oats .... do														
9	Sacks, grain .... number														
10	Straw .... pounds														
11	Blanks														
12	Blanks, quartermasters' .... quires														
13	Blanks, way freight														
14	Books, blank, 1½-quire														
15	Books, blank, 2-quire														
16	Books, blank, 3-quire														
17	Books, blank, 4-quire		24												
18	Books, blank, 6-quire														
19	Books, blank, 8-quire														
20	Books, blank, assorted														
21	Books, ration return														
22	Books, time														
23	Books, order									48					
24	Books, memorandum														
25	Books, abstract														
26	Books, indorsement														
27	Books, way-bill, copying														
28	Books, record														
29	Books, copying														
30	Books, stub														
31	Books, letter														
32	Books, requisition														

No.	Article	Unit														
33	Books, discharge															
34	Books, general order															
35	Books, clothing order															
36	Books, receipt															
37	Bands, rubber															
38	Boards, file															
39	Cutters, paper															
40	Clips, letter															
41	Clips, paper															
42	Clips, board					4										
43	Clips, letter board															
44	Clips, metal															
45	Erasers															
46	Erasers, steel															
47	Erasers, rubber															
48	Envelopes															
49	Envelopes, letter															
50	Envelopes, official															
51	Files, paper															
52	Files, adhesive															
53	Folders, paper															
54	Fasteners, paper	papers														
55	Holders, pen															
56	Holders, paper															
57	Ink, (quart)	bottles														
58	Ink, copying	do														
59	Ink, carmine	do														
60	Ink, blue	do														
61	Journals															
62	Ledgers															
63	Mucilage	bottles		24												
64	Paper, letter, assorted	quires														
65	Paper, flat letter	do														
66	Paper, note	do														
67	Paper, cap	do														
68	Paper, flat cap	do														
69	Paper, oil	sheets														
70	Paper, blotting	do														
71	Paper, cross section	do														
72	Paper, envelope	quires														
73	Paper, folio post	do														
74	Paper, news	do														
75	Paper, colored	do														
76	Paper, printing	bundles														
77	Paper, P. O	quires														
78	Paper, heavy yellow	lots														
79	Paper, heavy	do														
80	Paper, white demi	quires														
81	Pencils, lead															
82	Pencils, slate															
83	Pens, steel	gross														
84	Pens, steel															

Report showing the disposition of United States military railroad property in the military division of the Tennessee, &c.—Continued.

Running number.	Articles.	Property sold on credit to railroad companies under Executive Orders of August 8 and October 14, 1865.													
		Alabama and Florida railroad.	East Tennessee and Georgia railroad.	Mobile and Great Northern railroad.	Tennessee and Alabama railroad.	East Tennessee and Virginia railroad.	Mobile and Ohio railroad.	Tennessee and Alabama Central railroad.	Central Southern railroad.	New Orleans and Ohio railroad.	Rome railroad.	Memphis and Ohio railroad.	Southwestern railroad.	Georgia Railroad and Banking Company.	New Orleans, Jackson, and Great Northern railroad.
85	Pens, ruling														
86	Pens, extension ... boxes														
87	Rulers, rubber														
88	Rulers, wood														
89	Rulers, rosewood														
90	Rulers, boxwood														
91	Rulers, mahogany														
92	Rulers, ebony														
93	Rulers, assorted														
94	Racks, pen														
95	Rings, elastic														
96	Stands, ink														
97	Tearers, paper														
98	Tape ... spools														
99	Weights, paper														
100	Wax, sealing ... pounds														
101	Buckets, tin, assorted														
102	Buckets, mess														
103	Buckets, slop														
104	Buckets														
105	Basins, wash														6
106	Basins, tin wash														
107	Basins, tin														
108	Boilers, coffee														
109	Boilers, assorted														
110	Boilers, wash														
111	Boilers, meat														
112	Boilers, tin														
113	Boilers, iron														
114	Boilers with cocks														
115	Boilers, copper range														
116	Boilers, tin wash														

117	Boilers, tin wash, with cocks														
118	Brooms, hickory														
119	Brooms, splint														
120	Brooms, corn														
121	Brooms, ratan														
122	Brooms	2	5			5	8	2	1		1				1
123	Brushes, copying														
124	Brushes, window														
125	Brushes, counter														
126	Brushes, dust														
127	Brushes, assorted														
128	Boxes, P. O														
129	Boxes, letter														
130	Boxes, paper														
131	Boxes, dredge														
132	Boxes, twine														
133	Boxes, tin														
134	Boxes, spice														
135	Boxes, ice														
136	Boxes, sugar														
137	Boxes, salt														
138	Boxes, pepper														
139	Boxes, mess														
140	Boxes, bill-head														
141	Boxes, black walnut														
142	Boxes, cash														
143	Benches, assorted														
144	Baskets, paper														
145	Bells, office														
146	Balances, letter														
147	Boards, wash														
148	Boards, black														
149	Boards, diagram														
150	Boards, paper														
151	Boards, pressing														
152	Boards, card ....sheets														
153	Boards, binders'														
154	Boards, Bristol														
155	Bowls, sugar														
156	Bowls, wash														
157	Bowls, feet wash														
158	Bowls, assorted														
159	Bunks														3
160	Bunks, single														
161	Bureaus														
162	Bedsteads														
163	Bins, flour														
164	Blocks, meat														
165	Cups														
166	Cups, palette														
167	Cups, tin, assorted														36
168	Cups, sponge														

Report showing the disposition of United States military railroad property in the military division of the Tennessee, &c.—Continued.

Running number.	Articles.	Property sold on credit to railroad companies under Executive Orders of August 8 and October 14, 1865.													
		Alabama and Florida railroad.	East Tennessee and Georgia railroad.	Mobile and Great Northern railroad.	Tennessee and Alabama railroad.	East Tennessee and Virginia railroad.	Mobile and Ohio railroad.	Tennessee and Alabama Central railroad.	Central Southern railroad.	New Orleans and Ohio railroad.	Rome railroad.	Memphis and Ohio railroad.	Southwestern railroad.	Georgia Railroad and Banking Company.	New Orleans, Jackson, and Great Northern railroad.
169	Cups, copying														
170	Cups, molasses														
171	Cans, milk, (covered)														
172	Cans, molasses														
173	Cans, watering														
174	Covers, bucket														
175	Covers, coffee-pot														
176	Covers, oven														
177	Covers, tallow can														
178	Cleavers, meat														
179	Casters														
180	Canisters, tea														
181	Cots														
182	Chests, mess														
183	Chests, field														
184	Chests, assorted														
185	Clocks														
186	Cupboards														
187	Cupboards, pigeon-hole														
188	Counters														
189	Chambers														
190	Chairs, assorted														
191	Chairs, office														
192	Chairs, split bottom														
193	Coolers, water														
194	Cases, tin														
195	Cases, post-office														
196	Cases, blank														
197	Cases, shelves, and drawers														
198	Cases, assorted														
199	Cases, book														
200	Cases, pillow														

No.	Article	Unit														
201	Cases, pigeon-hole															
202	Closets, picket															
203	Cleaners, stove															
204	Cullenders															
205	Cushions			4		5		6	4	4						2
206	Curtains, window															
207	Charts, time															
208	Calendars															
209	Cellars, salt															
210	Cutters, cake															
211	Carvers															
212	Carvers and forks															
213	Caps, stove pipe															
214	Counterpanes															
215	Carpet, Brussels	yards														
216	Coverlets															
217	Desks, assorted															
218	Dusters															
219	Dusters, feather															3
220	Dippers															3
221	Dippers, tin															
222	Drums, stove															
223	Drums, sheet-iron															
224	Dishes, tin															
225	Dishes, soup															
226	Dishes, fruit															
227	Dishes, vegetable															
228	Dishes, meat															
229	Dishes, sauce															
230	Dishes, large															
231	Dishes, small															
232	Dishes, assorted															
233	Demijohns															
234	Drawers															
236	Elbows															
237	Elbows, stove-pipe															
238	Fixtures, cook-stove	sets														
239	Forks															
240	Forks, iron															
241	Forks, flesh															
242	Forks, table															36
243	Forks, carving															
244	Forks, large															
245	Funnels, assorted															
246	Funnels, tin, assorted															
247	Fillers, lamp					1										3
248	Feeders, lamp															
249	Furniture, cherry	lots														
250	Firkins															
251	Grates															
252	Grates, nutmeg															
253	Gridirons															

Report showing the disposition of United States military railroad property in the military division of the Tennessee, &c.—Continued.

Running number.	Articles.	Property sold on credit to railroad companies under Executive Orders of August 8 and October 14, 1865.													
		Alabama and Florida railroad.	East Tennessee and Georgia railroad.	Mobile and Great Northern railroad.	Tennessee and Alabama railroad.	East Tennessee and Virginia railroad.	Mobile and Ohio railroad.	Tennessee and Alabama Central railroad.	Central Southern railroad.	New Orleans and Ohio railroad.	Rome railroad.	Memphis and Ohio railroad.	Southwestern railroad.	Georgia Railroad and Banking Company.	New Orleans, Jackson, and Great Northern railroad.
254	Gates, molasses														
255	Griddles, stove														
256	Glasses, looking														
257	Globes, lamp														
258	Grates														
259	Hods, coal														
260	Horns, tin														
261	Hooks, clothes														
262	Hooks, meat														
263	Jugs														
264	Jars, earthen														
265	Kettles, camp														
266	Kettles, iron														
267	Kettles, tea														
268	Kettles, mess														
269	Kettles														
270	Knives														
271	Knives, table														36
272	Knives, butcher														3
273	Knives and forks ... sets														
274	Knives and forks														
275	Knives, carving														
276	Knives, cook														
277	Knives, chopping														
278	Lamps, office														
279	Lamps, coal-oil														
280	Lamps														
281	Ladles, soup														
282	Larders														
283	Lids														
284	Matting, floor ... feet														
285	Mortars														

286	Mills, coffee														3
287	Mattresses														
288	Mops, floor														
289	Mashers, potato														
290	Nests, pigeon-hole														
291	Ovens, Dutch														
292	Ovens, bake														
293	Punches, paper														
294	Presses, letter				2										
295	Presses, letter, with stamp														
296	Presses and stands, (letter)				1										
297	Pipe, stove ... feet														
298	Pipe, stove ... joints														
299	Pipe, stove, assorted ... pounds														12
300	Pipes, connecting, for range														
301	Pans, fry														
302	Pans, try														
303	Pans, mess, assorted														18
304	Pans, dish														3
305	Pans, baking														
306	Pans, dripping														
307	Pans, tin sauce														
308	Pans, dust														
309	Pans, stew														
310	Pans, assorted														
311	Pans, tin, assorted														
312	Pans, ash														
313	Pans, tin ... sets														
314	Pans, pie														
315	Pans, wash														
316	Pans, cake														
317	Pails, tin														
318	Pails														
319	Plates, tin														36
320	Plates, soup														
321	Plates, sauce														
322	Plates, dinner														
323	Plates														
324	Plates, pie														
325	Plates, meat														
326	Pots, assorted														
327	Pots, mess														
328	Pots, tea														
329	Pots, coffee														
330	Pots, fire														
331	Pots, sprinkling														
332	Pots, iron														
333	Pots, tin														
334	Pots, tin stew														
335	Pots, water														
336	Pitchers														
337	Pitchers, stone														

Report showing the disposition of United States military railroad property in the military division of the Tennessee, &c.—Continued.

Running number.	Articles.	Property sold on credit to railroad companies under Executive orders of August 8 and October 14, 1865.													
		Alabama and Florida railroad.	East Tennessee and Georgia railroad.	Mobile and Great Northern railroad.	Tennessee and Alabama railroad.	East Tennessee and Virginia railroad.	Mobile and Ohio railroad.	Tennessee and Alabama Central railroad.	Central Southern railroad.	New Orleans and Ohio railroad.	Rome railroad.	Memphis and Ohio railroad.	Southwestern railroad.	Georgia Railroad and Banking Company.	New Orleans, Jackson, and Great Northern railroad.
338	Pitchers, water														
339	Pillows														
340	Pokers, assorted														
341	Peels, bakers'														
342	Pins, time														
343	Pins, rolling														
344	Plugs, basin														
345	Quilts														
346	Racks, letter														
347	Racks and desk, card														
348	Racks, towel														
349	Ranges and fixtures, cooking														
350	Ranges, cooking														
351	Ranges, patent														
352	Railing, office ... pieces														
353	Railing, hand, with banisters ... feet														
354	Refrigerators														
355	Safes, iron														
356	Safes, office				1										
357	Safes, fire-proof														
358	Safes, paymasters'		1												
359	Safes, field														
360	Safes, match														
361	Safes, twine														2
362	Safes, S. P.														
363	Scissors ... pairs														
364	Shears ... do														
365	Shears, lamp ... do														
366	Shears, banker's ... do														
367	Slates, assorted						12								
368	Shovels, fire														
369	Shovels, baker's														

370	Sieves														
371	Sieves, flour														
372	Sieves, meal														
373	Sieves, fine														
374	Scuttles, coal														
375	Scoops														
376	Scoops, flour														
377	Spittoons														
378	Spittoons, wooden														
379	Shades														
380	Shades, lamp														
381	Shades, lamp, (tin)														
382	Shades and clasps														
383	Spiders														
384	Spoons, table														
385	Spoons, tea														
386	Spoons, basting														
387	Spoons, assorted														
388	Skimmers														
389	Steamers														
390	Steamers, tin														
391	Skillets														
392	Skillets, stove														
393	Stoves, box														
394	Stoves, sheet-iron														
395	Stoves, cast-iron														
396	Stoves, coal		3												
397	Stoves, open coal														
398	Stoves, tent														
399	Stoves, camp														
400	Stoves, cooking														
401	Stoves, cooking, and pipe														
402	Stoves, cooking, and fixtures														3
403	Stoves, cooking, complete														
404	Stoves, parlor														
405	Stoves and pipe														
406	Stoves, glue														
407	Stoves, heating														
408	Stoves, assorted														
409	Stoves, office														
410	Stoves, shop														
411	Stoves, cylinder														
412	Stoves, old ... tons														
413	Stands														
414	Stands, wash														
415	Stands, letter-press														
416	Stands, light, and hose														
417	Stands, lamp and globe														
418	Stands, light														
419	Stands, bed														
420	Snuffers ... pairs														
421	Snuffers, candle ... do														

Report showing the disposition of United States military railroad property in the military division of the Tennessee, &c.—Continued.

Running number.	Articles.	Property sold on credit to railroad companies under Executive Orders of August 8 and October 14, 1865.													
		Alabama and Florida railroad.	East Tennessee and Georgia railroad.	Mobile and Great Northern railroad.	Tennessee and Alabama railroad.	East Tennessee and Virginia railroad.	Mobile and Ohio railroad.	Tennessee and Alabama Central railroad.	Central Southern railroad.	New Orleans and Ohio railroad.	Rome railroad.	Memphis and Ohio railroad.	Southwestern railroad.	Georgia Railroad and Banking Company.	New Orleans, Jackson, and Great Northern railroad.
422	Stools														
423	Stools, bench														
424	Spouts, funnel														
425	Shelves and brackets ... sets														
426	Sticks, candle														
427	Steels, carving														
428	Saucers, tin														
429	Saucers														
430	Sinks														
431	Sheets														
432	Screens														
433	Settees														
434	Strainers, coffee														
435	Sprinklers														
436	Sprinklers, copper														
437	Sacks, bed														
438	Scales, letter														
439	Tables, field														
440	Tables, camp														
441	Tables, office														
442	Tables, round														
443	Tables, centre														
444	Tables, dining														
445	Tables, draughting														
446	Tables, assorted														
447	Tables, time														
448	Trimmers, lamp														
449	Tumblers														
450	Thimbles, stovepipe														
451	Toasters														
452	Tubs, wash														
453	Tubs, bathing														

454	Ticks, bed														
455	Troughs, bread														
456	Urinals														
457	Wardrobes														
458	Waiters														
459	Ambulances														
460	Axles, ambulance														
461	Blankets, saddle														
462	Bits, mullen														
463	Bridles, riding														
464	Bridles, blind														
465	Buckets, U. S. horse														
466	Bows, wagon														
467	Bows, ox														
468	Bows, ambulance														
469	Brushes, horse														
470	Boxes, feed														
471	Boxes, wagon														
472	Boxes, cutting														
473	Boxes, ambulance pipe														
474	Boards, foot														
475	Bolsters, extra log wagon														
476	Bolsters, army wagon														
477	Bolts, king														
478	Bolts, king ... pounds														
479	Bolts, tongue														
480	Bodies, wagon														
481	Bodies, cart														
482	Breeching, cart														
482½	Bits, bridle														
483	Beds, axle														
484	Carts														
485	Chains, halter														
486	Chains, trace														
487	Chains, fifth														
488	Chains, bearing														
489	Chains, breast														
490	Chains, spreader														
491	Chains, stretcher														
492	Chains, stretcher, and S. S														
493	Chains, ox														
494	Collars, horse														
495	Collars, mule														
496	Covers, wagon														
497	Combs, curry														
498	Cruppers														
499	Drays														
500	Felloes, wagon														
501	Gears, running														
502	Gearings, hind														
503	Gearings, front														

Report showing the disposition of United States military railroad property in the military division of the Tennessee, &c.—Continued.

Running number.	Articles.	Property sold on credit to railroad companies under Executive Orders of August 8 and October 14, 1865.													
		Alabama and Florida railroad.	East Tennessee and Georgia railroad.	Mobile and Great Northern railroad.	Tennessee and Alabama railroad.	East Tennessee and Virginia railroad.	Mobile and Ohio railroad.	Tennessee and Alabama Central railroad.	Central Southern railroad.	New Orleans and Ohio railroad.	Rome railroad.	Memphis and Ohio railroad.	Southwestern railroad.	Georgia Railroad and Banking Company.	New Orleans, Jackson, and Great Northern railroad.
504	Gates, end														
505	Horses														
506	Harness ... sets														
507	Harness, S. S. ambulance														
508	Harness, S. S. wheel														
509	Harness, S. S. lead														
510	Harness, S. S. wheel-horse														
511	Harness, S. S. wheel-mule														
512	Harness, S. S. lead-mule														
513	Harness, cart														
514	Harness, dray														
515	Hames, horse ... pairs														
516	Hames ... do														
517	Halters, rope														
518	Halters, head														
519	Halters, head, and strap														
520	Halters and chains														
521	Hounds, front, army wagon														
522	Hounds, hind, army wagon														
523	Hammers, wagon														
524	Jacks, wagon														
525	Kegs, ambulance														
526	Lines, cart														
527	Lines, check														
528	Lines, lead														
529	Lines, 2-horse														
530	Leathers, sweat														
531	Links, open														
532	Mules														
533	Martingales														
534	Oxen														
535	Poles, ridge														

No.	Article														
536	Poles, coupling														
537	Rakes, stable														
538	Rims, bent ambulance														
539	Rims, ox-yoke bow														
540	Rings, open														
541	Rails, body														
542	Stretchers														
543	Spreaders														
544	Saddles, riding														
545	Saddles, wagon														
546	Saddles, cart														
547	Saddles														
548	Sticks, jockey														
549	Sticks, cart-dumping														
550	Springs, ambulance														
551	Sprinklers, wagon														
552	Sprinklers, cart														
553	Straps, neck														
554	Straps, coupling														
555	Straps, neck and chain														
556	Straps, back														
557	Straps, choke														
558	Straps, halter														
559	Straps, stirrup														
560	Straps, yoke														
561	Spokes, wagon														
562	Spokes														
563	Spokes, army wagon														
564	Spokes, 2-horse wagon														
565	Spokes, ambulance														
566	Stirrups, wooden														
567	Stirrups, leather														
568	Shafts, cart														
569	Shafts														
570	Strings, tie														
571	Stocks, whip														
572	Trees, single														
573	Trees, double														
574	Trees, saddle														
575	Tongues, wagon														
576	Tongues, rough														
577	Troughs, feed														
578	Tires, wagon														
579	Wheels, hind														
580	Wheels, front														
581	Wheels, wagon														
582	Wagons, lumber														
583	Wagons, army														
584	Wagons, spring														
585	Wagons, log														
586	Wagons, 2-horse														
587	Wagons, ox														

Report showing the disposition of United States military railroad property in the military division of the Tennessee, &c.—Continued.

Running number.	Articles.	Property sold on credit to railroad companies under Executive Orders of August 8 and October 14, 1865.													
		Alabama and Florida railroad.	East Tennessee and Georgia railroad.	Mobile and Great Northern railroad.	Tennessee and Alabama railroad.	East Tennessee and Virginia railroad.	Mobile and Ohio railroad.	Tennessee and Alabama Central railroad.	Central Southern railroad.	New Orleans and Ohio railroad.	Rome railroad.	Memphis and Ohio railroad.	Southwestern railroad.	Georgia railroad and Banking Company.	New Orleans, Jackson, and Great Northern railroad.
588	Wagons, wood														
589	Wagons, water														
590	Wagons, box														
591	Wagons														
592	Whips, wagon														
593	Yokes, ox														
594	Yokes and bows, ox														
595	Axes, chopping	2	6	4	1	5	362		2				120	24	
596	Axes, chopping, and handles														
597	Axes, felling														
598	Axes, felling, and handles														
599	Axes, hand														
600	Axes, pick														
601	Axes, broad			1			24						6		
602	Axes, narrow														
603	Axes, assorted														
604	Augers ... sets														
605	Augers						84						60	12	
606	Augers, long, assorted														
607	Augers, hollow ... sets														
608	Augers, gas-fitting														
609	Augers, bridge														
610	Augers, pump ... sets														
611	Augers, boring machine														
612	Augers, machine ... sets														
613	Augers, machine														
614	Augers and handles														
615	Augers and handles, $\frac{1}{4}$-inch														
616	Augers and handles, $1\frac{1}{2}$-inch														
617	Augers, spike														
618	Augers, convex														
619	Augers, wheelwright														

620	Augers, nut														
621	Anvils, assorted			2			12					2	3	3	
622	Anvils, cast														
623	Anvils, wrought														
624	Anvils, block														
625	Anvils, wrought ... pounds														
626	Anvils, blacksmiths'														
627	Awls, scratch														
628	Awls, brad														
629	Awls, belt														
630	Awls, scribe														
631	Awls and tacks, shoe														
632	Awls, scratch, and handles														
633	Awls, peg, and handles														
634	Adzes														
635	Adzes and handles														
636	Adzes, railroad			12			72						4		
637	Adzes, foot or carpenters'														
638	Axles, car ... pounds												3,344		
639	Axles, car		100												
639½	Arbors, circular saw														
640	Axles, car and tender														
641	Axles, truck ... pounds														
642	Axles, engine-driving					6								2	
643	Axles, engine truck ... pounds													2,847	
644	Axles, tender												12		
645	Axles, truck														
646	Axles, tender truck														
647	Axles, timber buggy														
648	Anchors														
649	Acid, oxalic ... pounds														
650	Acid, muriatic ... do														
651	Acid ... do														
652	Aqua ammonia ... do														
653	Aloes ... do														
654	Alum ... do														
655	Antimony ... do														
656	Alcohol ... gallons														
657	Ammoniac, sal ... pounds														
658	Arms, hand-car														
659	Arms, engine pump														
660	Arms, seat, cast ... pounds		139												
661	Apparatus, automatic ... sets														
662	Asphaltum ... gallons														
663	Bellows, blacksmiths'														
664	Bellows, assorted														
665	Bellows, hand														
666	Bellows, 48-inch														
667	Bars, switch														
668	Bars, switch ... sets														
669	Bars, lining														
670	Bars, raising														

Report showing the disposition of United States military railroad property in the military division of the Tennessee, &c.—Continued.

Running number.	Articles.	Property sold on credit to railroad companies under Executive Orders of August 8 and October 14, 1865.													
		Alabama and Florida railroad.	East Tennessee and Georgia railroad.	Mobile and Great Northern railroad.	Tennessee and Alabama railroad.	East Tennessee and Virginia railroad.	Mobile and Ohio railroad.	Tennessee and Alabama Central railroad.	Central Southern railroad.	New Orleans and Ohio railroad.	Rome railroad.	Memphis and Ohio railroad.	Southwestern railroad.	Georgia Railroad and Banking Company.	New Orleans, Jackson, and Great Northern railroad.
671	Bars, iron														
672	Bars, pinch	2	7			5	11		2	2	1	13			
673	Bars, pinch ... pounds														
674	Bars, grate ... do														
675	Bars, draw														
676	Bars, assorted														
677	Bars, timber						100								
678	Bars, grate														
679	Bars, pinch steel														
680	Bars, wrought iron pinch ... pounds														
681	Bars, switch ... do														
682	Bars, grate ... sets														
683	Bars, carpenters'														
684	Bars, pry and pinch														
685	Bars, pry														
686	Bars, fish ... pounds														
687	Bars, tamping											24			
688	Bars, crow														
689	Bars, claw														
690	Bars, wrench														
691	Bars, engine coupling														
692	Bars, boring														
693	Bars, cylinder boring														
694	Bars, long														
695	Bars, short														
696	Bars, steel		1												
697	Bars, assorted ... pounds														
698	Bars, pins, and bolts ... do														
699	Brushes, varnish, assorted						27						19		
700	Brushes C. H						24						2		
701	Brushes, W. W														
702	Brushes, scrub														

No.	Article	Unit	1	2	3	4	5	6	7	8	9	10	11	12	13	14
703	Brushes, painters' dust															
704	Brushes, paint, assorted							72						48		
705	Brushes, flat															
706	Brushes, oval															
707	Brushes, marking															
708	Brushes, striping															
709	Brushes, car window															
710	Brushes, artists'															
711	Brushes, artists' red sable															
712	Brushes, glue															
713	Brushes, sash															
714	Brushes, whitewash	lots														
715	Brushes, machinists'															
716	Braces															
717	Braces, iron															
718	Braces, wood															
719	Braces and bits	sets														
720	Braces and bits															
721	Braces and bits, car	sets														
722	Braces, hand															
723	Braces, joiner															
724	Braces, switch															
725	Braces, pedestal															
726	Braces, ratchet	sets														
727	Braces, truck	pounds														
728	Braces, engine															
729	Braces, engine bar															
730	Blenders, painters'															
731	Blenders, painters'															
732	Bits, brace	sets														
733	Bits	do														
734	Bits, auger, assorted	do						1								
735	Bits, auger, assorted															
736	Bits, gimlet															
737	Bits, gimlet	sets														
738	Bits, plough plane															
739	Bits, plough plane	sets														
740	Bits, double plane															
741	Bits, car															
742	Bits, car	sets						1								
743	Bits, centre															
744	Bits, rose															
745	Bits, (sets of six each)															
746	Bits, gummer															
747	Bits, ratchet drill															
748	Bits, assorted															
749	Bits, centre	sets														
750	Bits, planer															
751	Bits, double-cut															
752	Bits, brace															
753	Buts, assorted	pairs						546								
754	Buts, brass, assorted															

Report showing the disposition of United States military railroad property in the military division of the Tennessee, &c.—Continued.

Running number.	Articles.	Property sold on credit to railroad companies under Executive Orders of August 8 and October 14, 1865.													
		Alabama and Florida railroad.	East Tennessee and Georgia railroad.	Mobile and Great Northern railroad.	Tennessee and Alabama railroad.	East Tennessee and Virginia railroad.	Mobile and Ohio railroad.	Tennessee and Alabama Central railroad.	Central Southern railroad.	New Orleans and Ohio railroad.	Rome railroad.	Memphis and Ohio railroad.	Southwestern railroad.	Georgia Railroad and Banking Company.	New Orleans, Jackson, and Great Northern railroad.
755	Buts, brass, assorted ... pairs														
756	Buts														
757	Buts, loose joint														
758	Buts, wrought, assorted														
759	Buts. cast-iron ... pairs														
760	Buts, assorted														
761	Buts, wrought ... pairs														
762	Buts, fast														
763	Buts, cast														
764	Buts, rivet														
765	Buts, flat														
766	Buts, wrought-iron ... pairs														
767	Buts, patent ... do														
768	Buts, cast, loose joint ... do														
769	Buts, wrought, common joint														
770	Buts, cast, loose joint														
771	Buts, wrought-iron														
772	Bolts, tank hoop														
773	Bolts, iron hexagon-head ... pounds														
774	Bolts, fish-bar ... do														
775	Bolts														
776	Bolts, carriage ... pounds														
777	Bolts, carriage														
778	Bolts, iron bar														
779	Bolts, brass, assorted														
780	Bolts, barrel														
781	Bolts, brass flush														
782	Bolts, fire														
783	Bolts, long $\frac{3}{8}$-inch ... pounds														
784	Bolts, ring														
785	Bolts, chain door														
786	Bolts, tower														

No.	Article														
787	Bolts, square head ....pounds														
788	Bolts, bridge ....do														
789	Bolts, wrought ....do														
790	Bolts, wrought-iron														
791	Bolts and nuts														
792	Bolts and butts														
793	Bolts, brass knob														
794	Bolts, wagon														
795	Bolts, steel-spring square														
796	Bolts, pulley														
797	Bolts, coupling														
798	Bolts and keys														
799	Bolts ....pounds												1,850		
800	Bolts, door														
801	Bolts, bridge														
802	Bolts and nuts ....pounds														
803	Blocks, punch														
804	Blocks, swedge											2			
805	Blocks, die ....pounds														
806	Blocks, iron pulley														
807	Blocks, iron														
808	Blocks, purchase														
809	Blocks, notch														
810	Blocks, snatch						2					2			
811	Blocks, head, with truck														
812	Blocks, upsetting														
813	Blocks, patent														
814	Blocks, tackle ....sets														
815	Blocks, tackle											4			
816	Blocks and tackle ....sets														
817	Blocks and tackle						5								
818	Blocks, assorted														
819	Blocks, double-tackle														
820	Blocks, head														
821	Blocks, triple														
822	Blocks, assorted ....pounds														
823	Blocks, assorted ....pairs														
824	Blocks, cast-iron swedge ....pounds														
825	Blocks, cast-iron swedge														
826	Blocks, pillow ....pounds														
827	Blocks, single														
828	Blocks, double														
829	Blocks, head ....sets														
830	Blocks, double-head ....do														
831	Blocks, cast-iron swedge and tackle ....do														
832	Blocks, gum ....pounds														
833	Blocks, single														
834	Blocks, tackle ....pairs														
835	Buckets, assorted		1		1						1				6
836	Buckets, water														
837	Buckets, fire														
838	Buckets, wood														

Report showing the disposition of United States military railroad property in the military division of the Tennessee, &c.—Continued.

Running number.	Articles.	Property sold on credit to railroad companies under Executive Orders of August 8 and October 14, 1865.													
		Alabama and Florida railroad.	East Tennessee and Georgia railroad.	Mobile and Great Northern railroad.	Tennessee and Alabama railroad.	East Tennessee and Virginia railroad.	Mobile and Ohio railroad.	Tennessee and Alabama Central railroad.	Central Southern railroad.	New Orleans and Ohio railroad.	Rome railroad.	Memphis and Ohio railroad.	Southwestern railroad.	Georgia railroad and Banking Company.	New Orleans, Jackson, and Great Northern railroad.
839	Buckets														
840	Buckets, engine		3		1	1	9	2	1	2					3
841	Buckets, iron														
842	Buckets, coal														
843	Buckets, varnish														
844	Buckets, tar														
845	Buckets, paint														
846	Buckets, rubber														
847	Buckets, sand														
848	Buckets, swing														
849	Buckets, stiff														
850	Buckets, well														
851	Buckets, mortar														
852	Buckets, leather														
853	Boilers, steam														
854	Boilers, tin-flue														
855	Boilers, small-flue														
856	Boilers, double-flue														
857	Boilers, 14 feet long, 40 inches diameter														
858	Boilers, tubular, 12 feet long, 42 inches diameter														
859	Boilers, steam, 2 flues, 21 ft. long, 34 inches diameter														
860	Boilers, steam, 4 flues, 24 ft. long, 39 inches diameter														
861	Boilers, stationary														
862	Boilers, iron-punch														
863	Boilers, iron-flue, 26 feet x 44 inches														
864	Brass, old ... pounds														
865	Brass, sheet ... do			60			194					180		54	
866	Brass ... do														
867	Brass, scrap ... do														
868	Brass, wrought ... do														
869	Brass turnings ... do														
870	Brasses ... do														

871	Brasses, truck ... do														
872	Bricks, common														
873	Bricks, setting, for boilers														
874	Bricks, fire														
875	Bricks, soap, fire														
876	Bricks, split, fire														
877	Bricks, key														
878	Burlaps ... yards													365	
879	Buttons, assorted ... gross													$1\frac{2}{8}$	
880	Buttons, upholsterers' ... do														
881	Buttons, hand ... sets														
882	Buttons, brass, on plates														
883	Buttons, brass ... gross														
884	Buttons, brass														
885	Brown, Vandyke ... pounds						6								
886	Brown, Spanish ... do														
887	Brown, Vandyke ... tubes														
888	Black, India ... pounds														
889	Black, lamp ... do														
890	Black, lamp ... tubes														
891	Black, Japan ... barrels														
892	Black, ivory ... tubes														
893	Blue, ultramarine ... pounds														
894	Blue, Prussian ... do														
895	Black, blue ... do														
896	Black, drop ... do														
897	Blue, cobalt ... tubes														
898	Blacking, stove ... papers														
899	Bronze, gold ... do														
900	Brilliant, American ... tubes														
901	Bells, gong, hanging														
902	Bells, engine														
903	Bells, engine, alarm	2	4	2	2	5	6	1	2		1	2			1
904	Bells, engine, gong														
905	Bells, alarm														
906	Bells, engine and frame														
907	Bells, cast-steel														
908	Bells, cab														
909	Balances, spring						7								
910	Balances, locomotive spring						8					2			
911	Balances, iron beam														
912	Balances, beam shive														
913	Balances, steam														
914	Balances, elliptic spring														
915	Balances, counter														
916	Bushings, brass														
917	Bushings, gas-pipe														
918	Bushings, bell cord														
919	Bushings, brass gland														
920	Bushings, silver-plated														
921	Brads, patent, assorted ... papers						1,043								
922	Bunting, assorted ... yards	4	6			10	2								

Report showing the disposition of United States military railroad property in the military division of the Tennessee, &c.—Continued.

Running number.	Articles.	Property sold on credit to railroad companies under the Executive Orders of August 8 and October 14, 1865.													
		Alabama and Florida railroad.	East Tennessee and Georgia railroad.	Mobile and Great Northern railroad.	Tennessee and Alabama railroad.	East Tennessee and Virginia railroad.	Mobile and Ohio railroad.	Tennessee and Alabama Central railroad.	Central Southern railroad.	New Orleans and Ohio railroad.	Rome railroad.	Memphis and Ohio railroad.	Southwestern railroad.	Georgia Railroad and Banking Company.	New Orleans, Jackson, and Great Northern railroad.
923	Bunting, red, assorted .... yards														
924	Burners, common														
925	Burners, patent														
926	Burners, eureka														
927	Burners, screw														
928	Brakes														
929	Brakes, lever .... pounds														
930	Brakes, car														
931	Bevels, assorted														
932	Bevels, square														
933	Bevels, T														
934	Boards, guttering														
935	Boards, bulletin														
936	Boards, tally														
937	Boards, draft														
938	Boards, running														
939	Boards, straw .... pounds														
940	Boards, pressing														
941	Boards, binders'														
942	Boards, sign														
943	Brooms, hair														
944	Brooms, stable														
945	Bottoms, composition .... pounds														
946	Bottoms, copper .... do														
947	Bottoms, dipper														
948	Bottoms, bolt head														
949	Boxes, emery														
950	Boxes, rivet														
951	Boxes, wood														
952	Boxes, tinder	4	10		6	10	19	4	4	4		2			2
953	Boxes, engine .... pounds														
954	Boxes, engine	4	10			10	2								

955	Boxes, tool					6		13	4	4	4		2			2
956	Boxes, packing															
957	Boxes, tinder															
958	Boxes, axle															
959	Boxes, lamp															
960	Boxes, link															
961	Boxes, oil			1		1		1					1			
962	Boxes, hand car	pounds														
963	Boxes, car, (Wood's patent)	do														
964	Boxes, assorted															
965	Boxes, engine truck	pounds														
966	Boxes, roller															
967	Boxes, iron															
968	Boxes, screw, blued															
969	Boxes, signal-light															
970	Boxes, shoeing															
971	Boxes, cutting															
972	Boxes, drawing-paper															
973	Boxes, cast															
974	Boxes, journal															
975	Belting leather, assorted	feet		1,017 5-6	100			50				63		110		
976	Belting, gum	do			66			946								
977	Belting, rubber	do														
978	Belting, assorted	do														
979	Bottoms, tin lamp															
980	Bottoms, car lamp															
981	Blades, hack-saw															
982	Brackets	pounds														
983	Brackets															
984	Brackets, swing															
985	Buggies, timber															
986	Borers, cylinder															
987	Borers, cylinder, portable															
988	Borers, tap															
989	Borers, hand															
990	Barrels															
991	Bodkins															
992	Barrows, wheel															
993	Bridges, truss	feet														
994	Bridges, arch truss, McCallum's pat. inflexible	do														
995	Borax	pounds														
996	Benches, stationery	feet														
997	Benches, work			38												
998	Benches, vice															
999	Bearings, centre	pounds														
1000	Buildings			4		6				2						
1001	Buildings and water tank															
1002	Burrs	pounds						3								
1003	Burrs, copper	do														
1004	Bumpers	do														
1005	Buttresses															
1006	Bumpers															

Report showing the disposition of United States military railroad property in the military division of the Tennessee, &c.—Continued.

Running number.	Articles.	Property sold on credit to railroad companies under Executive Orders of August 8 and October 14, 1865.													
		Alabama and Florida railroad.	East Tennessee and Georgia railroad.	Mobile and Great Northern railroad.	Tennessee and Alabama railroad.	East Tennessee and Virginia railroad.	Mobile and Ohio railroad.	Tennessee and Alabama Central railroad.	Central Southern railroad.	New Orleans and Ohio railroad.	Rome railroad.	Memphis and Ohio railroad.	Southwestern railroad.	Georgia Railroad and Banking Company.	New Orleans, Jackson, and Great Northern railroad.
1007	Bodies, box car														
1008	Breeching ... pounds														
1009	Bibbs, finished, S. S. and S														
1010	Buckles, assorted														
1011	Buckles, harness ... gross														
1012	Buckles, roller, assorted ... do														
1013	Buckles, assorted ... do														
1014	Blocks, railroad splice, Trimble's wooden														
1015	Backs, car-seat														
1016	Bands, spring ... pounds														
1017	Bands, gum ... do														
1018	Blinds, window														
1019	Boats, flat														
1020	Baskets, medicine														
1021	Benzine ... gallons														
1022	Burgois No. 8, 3 "D" ... pounds														
1023	Buckles, round leg, ruled ... gross														
1024	Bolts, stay														
1025	Braces, tank														
1026	Barges														
1027	Burners, gas														
1027¼	Chisels and handles														
1027½	Chisels, cold	4	13		2	10	24	5	6	2	1	1			7
1027¾	Chisels, hand cold														
1028	Chisels, chipping														
1029	Chisels, hand chipping														
1030	Chisels, firmer														
1031	Chisels, firmer ... sets														
1032	Chisels, socket firmer ... do														
1033	Chisels, socket														
1034	Chisels, framing ... sets														
1035	Chisels, framing						360								

1036	Chisels, track														
1037	Chisels, cold track														
1038	Chisels, masons'														
1039	Chisels, corner														
1040	Chisels, bolt														
1041	Chisels, splitting														
1042	Chisels, coppersmiths'														
1043	Chisels, tamping														
1044	Chisels, B. S														
1045	Chisels, cape														
1046	Chisels, assorted														
1047	Chisels, carpenters'														
1048	Chisels, gouging														
1049	Chisels, socket ....sets														
1050	Chisels, socket framing														
1051	Chisels, socket, and handles														
1052	Chisels, oval back														
1053	Chisels, mortise														
1054	Chisels, tinners' ....sets														
1055	Chills, frog														
1056	Calipers, assorted ....pairs														
1057	Calipers, spring ....do														
1058	Compasses, assorted ....do														
1059	Compasses, wing ....do														
1060	Cups, oil														
1061	Cups, oil, spring bottom														
1062	Cups, tallow														
1063	Cups, tin paint														
1064	Cups, tin striping														
1065	Cups, brass														
1066	Cups, steam chest oil										6				
1067	Cups, valve oil														
1068	Cups, brass oil														
1069	Cups, varnish														
1070	Cans, powder														
1071	Cans, engine oil														
1072	Cans, oil, spring-bottom														
1073	Cans, tallow														1
1074	Cans, assorted	4	24		8	13	43	2	4	6	3	3			13
1075	Cans, oil, assorted														2
1076	Cans, tin, assorted														
1077	Cans, emery														
1078	Cans, bench oil														
1079	Couplings, tender ....pounds														
1080	Couplings, 3-link											6			
1081	Couplings, 3-link ....pounds														
1082	Couplings, straight											12			
1083	Couplings, crooked						120					24			
1084	Couplings, brass union, assorted ....pairs														
1085	Couplings, clamp and screw														
1086	Couplings, hose														
1087	Couplings, chain ....pounds														

Report showing the disposition of United States military railroad property in the military division of the Tennessee, &c.—Continued.

Running number.	Articles.	Alabama and Florida railroad.	East Tennessee and Georgia railroad.	Mobile and Great Northern railroad.	Tennessee and Alabama railroad.	East Tennessee and Virginia railroad.	Mobile and Ohio railroad.	Tennessee and Alabama Central railroad.	Central Southern railroad.	New Orleans and Ohio railroad	Rome railroad.	Memphis and Ohio railroad.	Southwestern railroad.	Georgia Railroad and Banking Company.	New Orleans, Jackson, and Great Northern railroad.
		Property sold on credit to railroad companies under Executive Orders of August 8 and October 14, 1865.													
1088	Couplings ..... pounds..														
1089	Couplings, brass hose ..... do....														
1090	Couplings, hose														
1091	Couplings, assorted														
1092	Chains, engine														
1093	Chains, assorted														
1094	Chains, log													34	
1095	Chains, switch	2	5			2	2					2			3
1096	Chains, Powers' endless														
1097	Chains, brake ..... pounds..														
1098	Chains, large														
1099	Chains, small														
1100	Chains, civil engineers'														
1101	Chains, surveyors', (100 feet)														
1102	Chains, switch ..... pounds..														
1103	Chains, log ..... do....														
1104	Chain, assorted ..... feet..														
1105	Chain, assorted ..... pounds..														
1106	Chain, cable ..... do....														
1107	Chain, cable ..... feet..														
1108	Chain, German ..... do....														
1109	Chain, German coil ..... do....														
1110	Chain, coil, proved, $\frac{3}{8}$-inch ..... pounds..														
1111	Chain, coil, assorted ..... do....						1,586								
1112	Castings, assorted ..... do....		7,700												
1113	Castings, iron ..... do....														
1114	Castings, pump ..... do....														
1115	Castings, brass ..... do....														97
1116	Castings, grate bar ..... do....														
1117	Castings, old stove ..... lots....														
1118	Castings, car ..... pounds..														
1119	Castings, tender ..... do....														

No.	Article														
1120	Caps, double														
1121	Caps, gas pipe														
1122	Clamps, iron ... pairs		1												
1123	Clamps, steel														
1124	Clamps, cabinet-makers'														
1125	Clamps, saddlers'														
1126	Clamps, switch														
1127	Clamps, belt														
1128	Clamps, spring														
1129	Clamps, block ... sets														
1130	Clamps, horseshoe														
1131	Clamps ... pairs														
1132	Clamps ... pounds														
1133	Clamps, iron horse														
1134	Clamps, iron														
1135	Clamps, iron, for tender														
1136	Clamps, iron boiler														
1137	Clamps, chimney														
1138	Clamps, saw-set														
1139	Clamps, wood bench														
1140	Clamps, screw														
1141	Cars, box	21	122	4	34	102	110	17	24	10	5	46	32		101
1142	Cars, box freight														
1143	Cars, flat	1	39	6	14	13		11	11		1	20	15		27
1144	Cars, wrecking		1												
1145	Cars, passenger		5		1	3		1	1			1			
1146	Cars, hand														
1147	Cars, truck														
1148	Cars, caboose														
1149	Cars, coal														
1150	Cars, stock														
1151	Cars, push or dump														
1152	Cutters, card														
1153	Cutters, lead														
1153½	Cutters, cast-steel														
1154	Cutters, boring														
1155	Cutters, iron														
1156	Covers, cylinder head														
1157	Covers, flag				4		2	2	4						
1158	Covers, box														
1159	Covers, hand-car ... pounds														
1160	Covers, axle-box ... do														
1161	Covers, cushion														
1162	Covers, enamelled														
1163	Covers, plush														
1164	Covers, sand box														
1165	Covers, dome														
1166	Covers, smoke-stack														
1167	Covers, smoke-stack hand hole														
1168	Crucibles		13										19		
1169	Cylinders, steam engine														
1170	Cylinders, locomotive														

Report showing the disposition of United States military railroad property in the military division of the Tennessee, &c.—Continued.

Running number.	Articles.	Property sold on credit to railroad companies under Executive Orders of August 8 and October 14, 1865.													
		Alabama and Florida railroad.	East Tennessee and Georgia railroad.	Mobile and Great Northern railroad.	Tennessee and Alabama railroad.	East Tennessee and Virginia railroad.	Mobile and Ohio railroad.	Tennessee and Alabama Central railroad.	Central Southern railroad.	New Orleans and Ohio railroad.	Rome railroad.	Memphis and Ohio railroad.	Southwestern railroad.	Georgia Railroad and Banking Company.	New Orleans, Jackson, and Great Northern railroad.
1171	Cylinders, 5 feet long, 12-inch bore														
1172	Chairs, guard rail														
1173	Chairs, railroad, assorted														
1174	Chairs, railroad ... pounds														
1175	Chairs, frog														
1176	Chairs, head ... sets														
1177	Chairs, step														
1178	Chairs, assorted														
1179	Chairs, railroad guard														
1180	Cocks, waste														
1181	Cocks, miss gauge											6			
1182	Cocks, lock														
1183	Cocks, stop														
1184	Cocks, blow-off														
1185	Cocks, bibb												6		
1186	Cocks, bibb, brass														
1187	Cocks, pet														
1188	Cocks, gauge			12											
1189	Cocks, racking														
1190	Cocks, heater and cylinder														
1191	Cocks, steam, assorted														
1192	Cocks, brass														
1193	Cocks, cylinder			4											
1194	Cocks, heater														
1195	Cocks, water														
1196	Cocks, lever														
1197	Cocks, rough														
1198	Cocks, air														
1199	Cocks, basin														
1200	Cocks, gas														
1201	Cocks, steam-gauge														
1202	Cocks, steam-stop														

No.	Article	Unit														
1203	Chimneys, assorted															
1204	Chimneys, head-light															
1205	Chimneys, flint															
1206	Chimneys, stationary smoke-stack															
1207	Chimneys, lamp, assorted		2	7			5	1								
1208	Chimneys, coal-oil lamp															
1209	Cases, drawing															
1210	Cases, engine tool-box key															
1211	Cases, tin stencil															
1212	Cases, medicine															
1213	Cases, turning paper															
1214	Cupolas															
1215	Copper, bar	pounds														
1216	Copper, assorted	do														
1217	Copper, sheet	do		175	160			1,577					55		520	
1218	Copper, ingot	do		2,949												
1219	Copper, scrap	do														
1220	Copper, tinned	do														
1221	Copper, pig	do														
1222	Cloth, emery	quires						280					40			
1223	Cloth, emery	gross														
1224	Cloth, gum	pounds														
1225	Cloth, enamelled	yards														
1226	Cloth, enamelled	pieces														
1227	Cloth, tracing	rolls														
1228	Cloth, tracing	yards														
1229	Crayons	gross														
1230	Chalk, white	pounds													390	
1231	Chalk, red	do														
1232	Chalk	do														
1233	Chalk, prepared	do														
1234	Cranes, blacksmiths'															
1235	Cranes, iron															
1236	Cranes, assorted	pounds														
1237	Cranes, tank															
1238	Cranes, water															
1239	Cuffs, hand	pairs														
1240	Chests, tool															
1241	Chests, carpenters' tool															
1242	Chests, tin															
1243	Chests, saddlers'															
1244	Cupboards, tool															
1245	Cupboards, oil															
1246	Combs, graining	lots														
1247	Combs, graining	sets														
1248	Chucks, assorted															
1249	Chucks, screw															
1250	Chucks, drill															
1251	Chucks, brass															
1252	Chucks, planer															
1253	Chucks, universal			2												
1254	Chucks, universal lathe															

Report showing the disposition of United States military railroad property in the military division of the Tennessee, &c.—Continued.

Running number.	Articles.	Property sold on credit to railroad companies under Executive Orders of August 8 and October 14, 1865.													
		Alabama and Florida railroad.	East Tennessee and Georgia railroad.	Mobile and Great Northern railroad.	Tennessee and Alabama railroad.	East Tennessee and Virginia railroad.	Mobile and Ohio railroad.	Tennessee and Alabama Central railroad.	Central Southern railroad.	New Orleans and Ohio railroad.	Rome railroad.	Memphis and Ohio railroad.	Southwestern railroad.	Georgia Railroad and Banking Company.	New Orleans, Jackson, and Great Northern railroad.
1255	Chucks, tap and nuts														
1256	Chucks, lathe														
1257	Chases, assorted		10												
1258	Cranks, hand-car ... pounds														
1259	Cranks, iron														
1260	Chasers, screw														
1261	Catches, cupboard														
1262	Catches, brake														
1263	Catches, window														
1264	Chrome, yellow ... pounds						48							18	
1265	Chrome, orange, American ... tubes														
1266	Chrome, orange, dry ... pounds														
1267	Chrome, green ... do														
1268	Colors ... tubes														
1269	Colors ... boxes														
1270	Candles, car ... pounds												37		
1271	Candles, star ... do														
1272	Copperas ... do														
1273	Cord, hemp bell ... do	4	60			10	2				2		57		
1274	Cords, bell														
1275	Cement, composition ... cans														
1276	Cement ... barrels														
1277	Connexions, meter														
1278	Cabs, loco														
1279	Circulars, switch														
1280	Centres, lathe														
1281	Carriages, iron lathe														
1282	Carriages, iron ... sections														
1283	Clasps, hand														
1284	Crabs, drilling														
1285	Chamber, engine pump														
1286	Corrals														

1287	Casings, cylinder head														
1288	Cantharides, tincture ... pounds														
1289	Camphor, gum ... do														
1290	Calomel ... do														
1291	Cochineal ... do														
1292	Composition, chemical ... cans														
1293	Carriers														
1294	Crosses, gas-pipe														
1295	Collars, gas-bracket														
1296	Circles, iron														
1297	Coffins														
1298	Casks														
1299	Cones, blacksmiths'														
1300	Drills, iron pipe														
1301	Drills, breast														
1302	Drills, stone														
1303	Drills, ratchet, assorted						12					2	3		
1304	Drills, ratchet, brace, steel														
1305	Drills, stock and clamp														
1306	Drills, blacksmiths'														
1307	Drills, assorted														
1308	Drills, pin														
1309	Drills, lathe, steel														
1310	Drills, counter, steel														
1311	Drills, cast steel ... pounds		22												
1312	Drills, steel														
1313	Drills, vertical, 36-inch														
1314	Drills, vertical, 45-inch, compound table														
1315	Drills, vertical, 45-inch, plain table														
1316	Drills, prop, iron table, complete														
1317	Drills, churn														
1318	Drills, upright														
1319	Drills, drill press														
1320	Drills, steel standard														
1321	Drills, upright, ungeared, press and counter shafts														
1323	Drills, assorted ... sets														
1324	Drills, quarry														
1325	Drills, ratchets and bits														
1326	Drills, black enamelled ... yards			60											
1327	Dividers ... pairs														
1328	Dividers, spring ... do														
1329	Drifts														
1330	Drifts, steel														
1331	Dogs														
1332	Dogs, lathe														
1333	Dogs, ratchet ... pounds														
1334	Dogs, planer														
1335	Dogs, saw														
1336	Dusters, counter														
1337	Dusters, painters'														
1338	Duck ... yards														
1339	Duck, car ... do														

Report showing the disposition of United States military railroad property in the military division of the Tennessee, &c.—Continued.

Running number.	Articles.	Property sold on credit to railroad companies under Executive Orders of August 8 and October 14, 1865.													
		Alabama and Florida railroad.	East Tennessee and Georgia railroad.	Mobile and Great Northern railroad.	Tennessee and Alabama railroad.	East Tennessee and Virginia railroad.	Mobile and Ohio railroad.	Tennessee and Alabama Central railroad.	Central Southern railroad.	New Orleans and Ohio railroad.	Rome railroad.	Memphis and Ohio railroad.	Southwestern railroad.	Georgia railroad and Banking Company.	New Orleans, Jackson, and Great Northern railroad.
1340	Dippers, oil														
1341	Dippers, lye														
1342	Drippers, oil														
1343	Diamonds, glaziers'														
1344	Dadoes														
1345	Doors, fire, and frames														
1346	Doors, unfinished														
1347	Doors, panel														
1348	Doors, furnace														
1349	Doors, glass														
1350	Doors, glazed ... pieces														
1351	Doors, assorted														
1552	Doors, car														
1353	Dryer, patent ... pounds														
1354	Dryer, sand														
1355	Drums for lathe, (W. I.) ... pounds		6												
1356	Derricks														
1357	Derrick blocks falls and dies														
1358	Derricks, crab														
1359	Drivers, iron lathe, round ... pounds														
1360	Drivers, screw ... lots														
1361	Dies and plates														
1362	Dies, pipe, and stocks ... sets														
1363	Dies, hand ... pounds														
1364	Dies, assorted														
1365	Dies, gas pipe														
1366	Dies and plates ... sets											2			
1367	Dies ... do														
1368	Dies and hubs ... pounds														
1369	Dies, forge														
1370	Die stocks ... sets						6								
1371	Drivers, screw														

No.	Article														
1372	Drums, stove														
1373	Drawers, moulders'														
1374	Dust, bone ... pounds														
1375	Engines, stationary														
1376	Engines, pumping, No. 3														
1377	Engines and boilers, dummy														
1378	Engines, dummy														
1379	Engines and boilers, stationary														
1380	Engines, steam fire														
1381	Engines, single, steam														
1382	Engines, rotary fire, (Holley's patent)														
1383	Engines, caloric														
1384	Engines, rotary														
1385	Engines, pilot														
1386	Engines, portable														
1387	Engines, locomotive														
1388	Engine, locomotive, No. 212														
1389	Engines, locomotive, and tenders	2	7		3	7	15	3	2	2	1				5
1390	Engine, double stationary, 11¼-inch bore, 24-inch stroke, Ellis & Moore's patent														
1391	Engines, stationary, 2 boilers 24 feet long, 40 inches diameter														
1392	Engine, double stationary, pulley and counter shaft														
1393	Engines, pumping														
1393½	Engine and boiler, 5-inch cylinder, 12-inch stroke, (complete)														
1394	Engine and boiler, (complete)														
1395	Engines, steam														
1396	Engine, 12-inch bore, 36-inch stroke														
1397	Engines, hoisting, complete														
1398	Engines and boilers, stationary, (complete)														
1399	Eyes, brass screw														
1400	Eyes, bell cord														
1401	Eyes, iron ... gross														
1402	Eyes, screw ... do														
1403	Ears, tin kettle ... do						720								
1404	Ears, kettle														
1405	Ears, bucket														
1406	Ears, C. C. saw														
1407	Elbows, reducing														
1408	Elbows, drop														
1409	Elbows gas-pipe														
1410	Elbows, water-pipe														
1411	Elbows, goose-neck														
1412	Emery, assorted ... pounds						38								
1413	Emery flour ... do														
1414	Edges, iron														
1415	Edges, steel, straight														
1416	Ends, draw bar														
1417	Ends, equalizer														
1418	Easels														
1419	Escutcheons														

Report showing the disposition of United States military railroad property in the military division of the Tennessee, &c.—Continued.

Running number.	Articles.	Property sold on credit to railroad companies under Executive Orders of August 8 and October 14, 1865.													
		Alabama and Florida railroad.	East Tennessee and Georgia railroad.	Mobile and Great Northern railroad.	Tennessee and Alabama railroad.	East Tennessee and Virginia railroad.	Mobile and Ohio railroad.	Tennessee and Alabama Central railroad.	Central Southern railroad.	New Orleans and Ohio railroad.	Rome railroad.	Memphis and Ohio railroad.	Southwestern railroad.	Georgia railroad and Banking Company.	New Orleans, Jackson, and Great Northern railroad.
1420	Easers														
1421	Forges, blacksmiths'											2			
1422	Forges and bellows														
1423	Forges, portable			1			2								
1424	Forges, blacksmiths' portable														
1425	Forges, cast-iron														
1426	Forges														
1427	Furnaces, bolt		2												
1428	Furnaces, plumbers'														
1429	Furnaces, tinners'														
1430	Furnaces, charcoal														
1431	Frogs, cast														
1432	Frogs, patent portable						2								
1433	Frogs, assorted ... pounds		4,810									1,504			
1434	Frogs, chilled														
1435	Frogs, plated														
1436	Frogs, assorted														
1437	Frogs, T														
1438	Fittings, gas ... pounds														
1439	Fittings, gas pipe ... do												410		
1440	Fittings, gas														
1441	Fittings, brass cock and valve														
1442	Fasteners, car window														
1443	Fasteners, sash														
1444	Fixtures, grindstone ... sets						36								
1445	Fixtures, lathe ... do														
1446	Frames, saw						6								
1447	Frames, engine truck														
1448	Frames, truck, iron ... pounds														
1449	Frames, brake, beam														
1450	Frames and slides, car window														
1451	Frames, tank														

1452	Frames, truck															
1453	Frames, wreck															
1454	Frames, bell	pounds														
1455	Frames, bell															
1456	Frames, hack-saw															
1457	Frames, saw, railroad cut-off															
1458	Frames, bolt															
1459	Frames, circular-saw															
1460	Frames, bellows															
1461	Frames, door															
1462	Frames, window															
1463	Frames, lock															
1464	Frames, grindstones															
1465	Frames, for buildings															
1466	Frames and hammers, pile-driving															
1467	Frames															
1468	Flatters															
1469	Fullers															
1470	Flasks	pounds														
1471	Flasks															
1472	Flasks and tools	pounds														
1473	Flasks, iron	sets														
1474	Flannel, Canton	yards														
1475	Flannel, red	do														
1476	Faucets															
1477	Faucets, brass															
1478	Fitches, assorted															
1479	Flags, red						1					1				
1480	Fans, blowing			1												
1481	Fans, foundry															
1482	Fans, snail-shell															
1483	Flanges															
1484	Followers	pounds														
1485	Followers, piston															
1486	Figures	sets			1										1	
1487	Figures															
1488	Figures	pounds														
1489	Froes															
1490	Forks, "T" rail															
1491	Forks, manure															
1492	Forks, railroad															
1493	Forks, pitch															
1494	Fuze, safety	feet														
1495	Feeders, oil															
1496	Formers, tin															
1497	Formers, stove-pipe															
1498	Formers, tin gutter															
1499	Facings, coal	barrels														
1500	Facings, sea coal	do														
1501	Folders, tinners'															
1502	Folders, iron															
1503	Ferrules	pounds														

Report showing the disposition of United States military railroad property in the military division of the Tennessee, &c.—Continued.

Running number.	Articles.	Property sold on credit to railroad companies under Executive Orders of August 8 and October 14, 1865.													
		Alabama and Florida railroad.	East Tennessee and Georgia railroad.	Mobile and Great Northern railroad.	Tennessee and Alabama railroad.	East Tennessee and Virginia railroad.	Mobile and Ohio railroad.	Tennessee and Alabama Central railroad.	Central Southern railroad.	New Orleans and Ohio railroad.	Rome railroad.	Memphis and Ohio railroad.	Southwestern railroad.	Georgia Railroad and Banking Company.	New Orleans, Jackson, and Great Northern railroad.
1504	Fences														
1505	Files, assorted						294								
1506	Files, flat, assorted														
1507	Files, half-round bastard, assorted			60			228								
1508	Files, flat bastard, assorted			60			288								
1509	Files, saw, assorted														
1510	Files, flat, second-cut, assorted														
1511	Files, taper, second-cut, assorted														
1512	Files, hand, second-cut, assorted														
1513	Files, round, second-cut, assorted														
1514	Files, half-round, second-cut, assorted														
1515	Files, coulter, second-cut, assorted														
1516	Files, square, smooth, assorted														
1517	Files, flat, smooth, assorted						306								
1518	Files, round, smooth, assorted														
1519	Files, hand dead, smooth, assorted														
1520	Files, flat dead, smooth, asorted														
1521	Files, hand, bastard, assorted						48								
1522	Files, square, bastard, assorted						96								
1523	Files, coulter, bastard, assorted														
1524	Files, three-square, bastard, assorted														
1525	Files, round parallel, bastard, assorted														
1526	Files, square parallel, bastard, assorted														
1527	Files, dead, smooth, assorted														
1528	Files, three-square, assorted														
1529	Files, smooth, bastard, assorted														
1530	Files, wire														
1531	Files, bastard														
1532	Files, hand-saw, assorted						192								
1533	Files, mill-saw, assorted						60							120	
1534	Files, pit-saw														
1535	Files, patent														

1536	Files, round, bastard														
1537	Files, half-round, smooth														
1538	Files, half-round														
1539	Files, hand, smooth														
1540	Files, taper														
1541	Files, round														
1542	Files, bastard, second-cut														
1543	Files, smooth														
1544	Files, switch														
1545	Files, second-cut														
1546	Files, parallel														
1547	Files, square-cut														
1548	Files, square taper														
1549	Files, equalizing														
1550	Files, cut, bastard														
1551	Files, taper, bastard														
1552	Files, parallel, bastard														
1553	Flues, copper ... pounds														
1554	Flues ... feet														
1555	Fixings, forge ... pounds														
1556	Fronts to boilers														
1557	Funnels, sand-box														
1558	Flaxseed ... pounds														
1559	Flaxseed, ground ... do														
1560	Gauges, assorted														
1561	Gauges, panel														
1562	Gauges, mortise														
1563	Gauges, wire														
1564	Gauges, marking														
1565	Gauges, thumb														
1566	Gauges, single														
1567	Gauges, double														
1568	Gauges, cutting														
1569	Gauges, wheel														
1570	Gauges, track														
1571	Gauges, tinners'														
1572	Gauges, barrel														
1573	Gauges, screw														
1574	Gauges, steam		2	4	5		16	3	3	2	1	1			5
1575	Gauges, quarter-circle														
1576	Gauges, cocks and syphon steam														
1577	Gouges														
1578	Gouges, firmer														
1579	Gouges, paring														
1580	Gouges, paring, and handles														
1581	Gouges, patent marking														
1582	Gouges, flat sweep														
1583	Gouges and handles, firmer ... sets														
1584	Gouges, $\frac{1}{4}$-inch														
1585	Gouges, firmer ... sets														
1586	Gouges, flat ... do														
1587	Gouges, paring ... do														

Report showing the disposition of United States military railroad property in the military division of the Tennessee, &c.—Continued.

Running number.	Articles.	Property sold on credit to railroad companies under Executive Orders of August 8 and October 14, 1865.													
		Alabama and Florida railroad.	East Tennessee and Georgia railroad.	Mobile and Great Northern railroad.	Tennessee and Alabama railroad.	East Tennessee and Virginia railroad.	Mobile and Ohio railroad.	Tennessee and Alabama Central railroad.	Central Southern railroad.	New Orleans and Ohio railroad.	Rome railroad.	Memphis and Ohio railroad.	Southwestern railroad.	Georgia Railroad and Banking Company.	New Orleans, Jackson, and Great Northern railroad.
1588	Gouges, neck														
1589	Gimlets														
1590	Gummers, saw													1	
1591	Gummers, assorted														
1592	Greasers														
1593	Grooves, hand, steel														
1594	Grainers, top														
1595	Galleys, single-column brass-lined														
1596	Galleys, double-column brass-lined														
1597	Galleys, double-column brass-lined														
1598	Galleys, slice														
1599	Galleys, improved folio slice														
1600	Glass, assorted ... boxes		10												
1601	Glass, tail, light														
1602	Glass, window, assorted ... lights														
1603	Glass, double-thick ... feet														
1604	Glass, head-light ... boxes														
1605	Glasses, head-light														
1606	Glasses, cab, light														
1607	Grooves, hand														
1608	Grooves, tinners'														
1609	Gauze, brass ... feet						50								
1610	Gauze, brass ... coils														
1611	Gauze, iron ... do														
1612	Greene, chrome ... pounds						12								
1613	Green, Hibernian ... do														
1614	Green, German emerald ... do														
1615	Green, Paris ... do														
1616	Green, silk ... do														
1617	Green, Quaker ... do														
1618	Green, emerald ... do														
1619	Green, American chrome ... tubes														

No.	Article	Unit														
1620	Grease, car	pounds														
1621	Grease, car	gallons														
1622	Grease, car	barrels														
1623	Grease, wagon	pounds														
1624	Grease, axle	boxes														
1625	Glue	pounds						24							185	
1626	Gates, switch	do														
1627	Gates, molasses															
1628	Gates, switch															
1629	Gates, pine															
1630	Gibbs, bridge															
1631	Gibbs, cross-head	pounds														
1632	Gibbs, cross-head															
1633	Gibbs, bridge	pounds														
1634	Governors															
1635	Glands, snuffing-box	pounds														
1636	Gongs, locomotive, 8-inch															
1637	Gongs and fixtures															
1638	Gongs, alarm															
1639	Globes, ruby															
1640	Gutters, tin	feet														
1641	Gutters	lots														
1642	Grease, wagon	gallons														
1643	Hammers, blacksmiths'															
1644	Hammers, blacksmiths' hand															
1645	Hammers, chipping															
1646	Hammers, shoe															
1647	Hammers, set															
1648	Hammers, hand					2										
1649	Hammers, sledge															
1650	Hammers, claw															
1651	Hammers, tack															
1652	Hammers, engine		2	7		5	6	69	3	1	2	1	7	12		4
1653	Hammers, tinners'															
1654	Hammers, saddlers'															
1655	Hammers, stone															
1656	Hammers, clasp and punch															
1657	Hammers, ballast															
1658	Hammers, shoeing															
1659	Hammers, masons'															
1660	Hammers, spike															
1661	Hammers, backing															
1662	Hammers, jack															
1663	Hammers, copper															
1664	Hammers, assorted							90	1	5			15			
1665	Hammers, trip															
1666	Hammers, steam engine, trip, complete															
1667	Hammers, steam, assorted															
1668	Hammers, machine															
1669	Hammers, boiler-makers'															
1670	Hammers, riveting															
1671	Hammers, soft															

Report showing the disposition of United States military railroad property in the military division of the Tennessee, &c.—Continued.

Running number.	Articles.	Property sold on credit to railroad companies under Executive Orders of August 8 and October 14, 1865.													
		Alabama and Florida railroad.	East Tennessee and Georgia railroad.	Mobile and Great Northern railroad.	Tennessee and Alabama railroad.	East Tennessee and Virginia railroad.	Mobile and Ohio railroad.	Tennessee and Alabama Central railroad.	Central Southern railroad.	New Orleans and Ohio railroad.	Rome railroad.	Memphis and Ohio railroad.	Southwestern railroad.	Georgia Railroad and Banking Company.	New Orleans, Jackson, and Great Northern railroad.
1672	Hammers, steel														
1673	Hammers, raising														
1674	Hammers, pointing														
1675	Hammers, wagon														
1676	Hammers, saw														
1677	Hatchets						36								
1678	Hatchets and handles														
1679	Hatchets, shingling														
1680	Hatchets, broad												48	24	3
1681	Hatchets, soldering														
1682	Handles, firmer chisel, assorted														
1683	Handles, socket firmer chisel, assorted														
1684	Handles, socket chisel														
1685	Handles, chisel														
1686	Handles, auger, assorted														
1687	Handles, adze														
1688	Handles, foot or carpenters' adze														
1689	Handles, railroad adze														
1690	Handles, broadaxe														
1691	Handles, hatchet														
1692	Handles, broad hatchet														
1693	Handles, hammer														
1694	Handles, stone hammer														
1695	Handles, spike, maul														
1696	Handles, maul														
1697	Handles, pick														
1698	Handles, awl														
1699	Handles, sledge														
1700	Handles, brad awl														
1701	Handles, firmer gouge														
1702	Handles, jackplane														
1703	Handles, handsaw														

No.	Article	Unit														
1704	Handles, handsaw, polished															
1705	Handles, file															
1706	Handles, cross-cut saw															
1707	Handles, cant hook															
1708	Handles, axe							132								
1709	Handles, chopping axe															
1710	Handles, hand axe															
1711	Handles, saucepan															
1712	Handles, chest															
1713	Handles, assorted														3	
1714	Handles, front end door															
1715	Handles, machinists'															
1716	Handles, chest, japanned, Paris	pairs														
1717	Handles, flush drawer															
1718	Handles, chest	pairs														
1719	Handles, mallet															
1720	Handles, door															
1721	Handles, stretcher															
1722	Handles, mop															
1723	Handles, couch															
1724	Hangers, post															
1725	Hangers, drop, belt															
1726	Hangers, spring															
1727	Hangers, step															
1728	Hangers, shafting	pounds		1,000												
1729	Hangers, step	do														
1730	Hangers and boxes	do														
1731	Hangers, truck															
1732	Hangers	pounds														
1733	Hangers, drop															
1734	Hangers and fasteners, window blind	sets														
1735	Hangers, cast-iron	pounds														
1736	Hangers, door															
1737	Heads, cylinder															
1738	Heads, square															
1739	Heads, coppersmith															
1740	Heads, brake	pounds														
1741	Heads, brake, frame															
1742	Heads, draw															
1743	Heads, draw	pounds														
1744	Heads, cross, engine															
1745	Heads, stake															
1746	Heads and beams, brake															
1747	Heads, piston															
1748	Heads, bull, small															
1749	Heads, bull, large															
1750	Heads, draw, cash	pounds														
1751	Heads, cross															
1752	Hooks, cant															
1753	Hooks, belt, assorted															
1754	Hooks, horn, beak															
1755	Hooks, packing		2	1			5									1

Report showing the disposition of United States military railroad property in the military division of the Tennessee, &c.—Continued

Running number.	Articles.		Property sold on credit to railroad companies under Executive Orders of August 8 and October 14, 1865.													
			Alabama and Florida railroad.	East Tennessee and Georgia railroad.	Mobile and Great Northern railroad.	Tennessee and Alabama railroad.	East Tennessee and Virginia railroad.	Mobile and Ohio railroad.	Tennessee and Alabama Central railroad.	Central Southern railroad.	New Orleans and Ohio railroad.	Rome railroad.	Memphis and Ohio railroad.	Southwestern railroad.	Georgia Railroad and Banking Company.	New Orleans, Jackson, and Great Northern railroad.
1756	Hooks, tackle	pounds														
1757	Hooks and links, switch rope															
1758	Hooks, safety chair	pounds											4			6
1759	Hooks, assorted															
1760	Hooks and staples							60								
1761	Hooks, gas pipe							48								
1762	Hooks and eyes, brass	gross														
1763	Hooks, safety chain															
1764	Hooks, curling															
1765	Hooks, iron	pounds														
1766	Hooks, packing, and spools															
1767	Hooks, curving															
1768	Hooks, switch rope	pounds														
1769	Hooks and thimbles, switch rope	do														
1770	Hooks, cotton															
1771	Hook and chain gate															
1772	Hooks, ice															
1773	Hooks, hay															
1774	Hooks, timber															
1775	Hooks and chains															
1776	Hooks, iron															
1777	Hooks and stands	pounds														
1778	Hooks, car hat															
1779	Heaters, iron															
1780	Heaters, pipe															
1781	Hoes															
1782	Hoes, handled															
1783	Hoes, boat															
1784	Hoes, garden															
1785	Hoes, stable															
1786	Hose, assorted	feet		150	200	56		340	8	48						
1787	Hose, gum	do												300	600	

No.	Article														
1788	Hubs and collars .... sets														
1789	Hubs for dies														
1790	Hinges, strap, assorted						432					48			
1791	Hinges, blind, patent														
1792	Hinges, T .... pairs											60			
1793	Hinges, table, assorted .... do														
1794	Hinges, window .... do														
1795	Hinges, brass .... do														
1796	Hinges and fasteners, blind .... sets														
1797	Hinges, strap, assorted .... pairs														
1798	Hinges, brass														
1799	Hinges .... pounds														
1800	Hinges, unfinished														
1801	Hinges, butt, brass .... pairs														
1802	Hinges, butt, brass .... do														
1803	Hinges, back, flat														
1804	Hinges, butt, cast .... pairs														
1805	Hinges, blind .... do														
1806	Hasps, hinges and staples, assorted														
1807	Hasps and staples														
1808	Hasps, hinge											24	72		
1809	Hasps														
1810	Hasps and hooks														
1811	Hair, plasterers' .... bushels														
1812	Hair, curled .... pounds														
1813	Hair, plasterers' .... do														
1814	Hair, plasterers' .... lots														
1815	Holders, mandrel														
1816	Hoods, forge		2												
1817	Hoods, smoke-stack											2			
1818	Horses, wrought-iron														
1819	Horses, cast-iron														
1820	Horses, wooden														
1821	Horses, carpenter, saw														
1822	Horses, drawing														
1823	Horses, nail														
1824	Horses, blacksmiths'														
1825	Hoops, tank .... pounds														
1826	Hoops, truss														
1827	Housing for cupola														
1828	Hods, mortar														
1829	Hardies														
1830	Hubs, ambulance														
1831	Hubs, wagon														
1832	Headings, blacksmiths'														
1833	Hydrants														
1834	Heads, cylinder .... pounds														
1835	Handles, ballast hammer														
1836	Hickory for handles .... pieces														
1836½	Hinges														
1837	Iron, angle .... pounds												112		
1838	Iron, railroad .... bars														

Report showing the disposition of United States military railroad property in the military division of the Tennessee, &c.—Continued.

Running number.	Articles.	Property sold on credit to railroad companies under Executive Orders of August 8 and October 14, 1865. Alabama and Florida railroad.	East Tennessee and Georgia railroad.	Mobile and Great Northern railroad.	Tennessee and Alabama railroad.	East Tennessee and Virginia railroad.	Mobile and Ohio railroad.	Tennessee and Alabama Central railroad.	Central Southern railroad.	New Orleans and Ohio railroad.	Rome railroad.	Memphis and Ohio railroad.	Southwestern railroad.	Georgia Railroad and Banking Company.	New Orleans, Jackson, and Great Northern railroad.
1839	Iron, railroad ... pounds														
1840	Iron, round, assorted ... do		3,680	4,071			16,952						586	2,044	
1841	Iron, bar, assorted ... do		385	10,374									9,068		
1842	Iron, flat, assorted ... do														
1843	Iron, galvanized ... do														
1844	Iron, Russia ... do		1,353				250							764	
1845	Iron, assorted ... do			490			21,177						3,682	1,890	
1846	Iron, boiler ... do		1,589	1,125			10,236						7,220	2,047	
1847	Iron, tank ... do		3,380	1,050			3,940						2,286		
1848	Iron, oval and ½-oval ... do														
1849	Iron, hoop ... do														
1850	Iron, tire ... do														
1851	Iron, ½-round ... do														
1852	Iron, square ... do			4,053											
1853	Iron, plough slab ... do														
1854	Iron, nail rod ... do														
1855	Iron, pig ... do													66,000	
1856	Iron, round bridge ... do														
1857	Iron, flat bridge ... do														
1858	Iron, scrap ... do														
1859	Iron, sheet ... do														
1860	Iron, tuyere ... do														
1861	Iron, scrap, 1st class ... do														
1862	Iron, scrap, blacksmiths' 1st class ... do														
1863	Iron, scrap, blacksmiths' common ... do														
1864	Iron, tank and fire box scrap ... do														
1865	Iron, light sheet scrap ... do														
1866	Iron, sheet, galvanized ... do														
1867	Iron, band, assorted ... do														
1868	Iron, smoke-stack ... do														
1869	Iron, scrap, rings and staples ... do														
1870	Iron, round and square ... do														

No.	Article	Unit														
1871	Iron, old	do.														
1872	Iron, wrought	do.														
1873	Iron, perforated	sheets.														
1874	Irons, platform															
1875	Irons, clinch															
1876	Irons, and															
1877	Irons, solid															
1878	Irons, double plough															
1879	Irons, heading															
1880	Irons, branding															
1881	Irons, angle, 25 feet each															
1882	Irons, switch															
1883	Irons, twyre															
1884	Irons, plane															
1885	Irons, double-plane															
1886	Irons, soldering															
1887	Irons, large, for drawing, (on wheels)															
1888	Irons, guide	pounds.														
1889	Irons, dog	pairs.														
1890	Irons, roofing, double seaming															
1891	Irons, step	pounds.														
1892	Irons, blacksmiths'	do.														
1893	Irons, chafing	do.														
1894	Iron, brake	do.														
1895	Instruments, veterinary	sets.														
1896	Instruments, levelling															
1897	Instruments, mathematical	sets.														
1898	Instruments, transit															
1899	Injectors, engine															
1900	Injectors, assorted															
1901	Injectors, steam															
1902	Indicators, steam															
1903	Ipecac	pounds.														
1904	Ink, printing	cases.														
1904½	Irons, hand-grooving															
1905	Jacks, ratchet															
1906	Jacks, screw and lever		4	13	1	6	13	34	4	8	4	2	4			4
1907	Jacks, hydraulic, assorted				4	2		2	1					4	4	14
1908	Jacks, hydraulic, 7-ton															
1909	Jacks, hydraulic, 10-ton															
1910	Jacks, hydraulic, 15-ton															
1911	Jacks, timber			1												
1912	Jacks, lever				10		1	8					4		12	
1913	Jacks, screw															
1914	Jacks, pump, 15-ton															
1915	Jacks, pump, 10-ton															
1916	Jacks, pump															
1917	Journals, brass															
1918	Japan	gallons.														
1919	Jaws, switch-lever															
1920	Knives, farriers'							36						36		
1921	Knives, drawing															

Report showing the disposition of United States military railroad property in the military division of the Tennessee, &c.—Continued.

Running number.	Articles.	Property sold on credit to railroad companies under Executive orders of August 8 and October 14, 1865.													
		Alabama and Florida railroad.	East Tennessee and Georgia railroad.	Mobile and Great Northern railroad.	Tennessee and Alabama railroad.	East Tennessee and Virginia railroad.	Mobile and Ohio railroad.	Tennessee and Alabama Central railroad.	Central Southern railroad.	New Orleans and Ohio railroad.	Rome railroad.	Memphis and Ohio railroad.	Southwestern railroad.	Georgia Railroad and Banking Company.	New Orleans, Jackson, and Great Northern railroad.
1922	Knives, frog														
1923	Knives, bench														
1924	Knives, paring														
1925	Knives, round														
1926	Knives, pallet														
1927	Knives, putty						12								
1928	Knives, shoe														
1929	Knives, packing														
1930	Knives, C. S. Daniel's planer		30												
1931	Knives, brush														
1932	Kettles, soldering														
1933	Kettles, glue														
1934	Kettles, spring ... pounds														
1935	Keys, car														24
1936	Keys, assorted														
1937	Keys, assorted ... pounds														
1938	Keys, draw-head														
1939	Keys, split ... pounds														
1940	Keys, padlock														
1941	Keys, connecting-rods														
1942	Keys														
1943	Knobs, mahogany														
1944	Knobs, mineral														
1945	Knobs, drawer														
1946	Knobs, door														
1947	Knobs, desk, wood, assorted														
1948	Knobs, tin-kettle														
1949	Knobs, tea-pot ... gross														
1950	Kings, American ... tubes														
1951	Knees, tender														
1952	Kasses, switch														
1953															

1954	Lights, white	2	6	48		5	146						48		12
1955	Lights, red		6	24			104			2			24		11
1956	Lights, blue														
1957	Lights, cab	2	3		3	5	7	2	2						1
1958	Lights, head	2	6		5	5	17	3	3	2	1	1			5
1959	Lights, tail														4
1960	Lamps, Dutch														
1961	Lamps, bull's-eye		4		4		10	6	6				12		1
1962	Lamps, bracket														
1963	Lamps, railroad														
1964	Lamps, hand														
1965	Lamps, green														
1966	Lamps, signal														
1967	Lamps, torch														
1968	Lamps, coach														
1969	Lamps, brass car														
1970	Lamps, car, candle														
1971	Lamps, hanging														
1972	Lamps, spring														
1973	Lanterns														
1974	Lanterns, railroad, globe														
1975	Lanterns, dark														
1976	Lanterns, square														
1977	Lantern bottoms, (W. L., old)														
1978	Locks, pad, assorted	4	10			10	2								
1979	Locks, mortise														
1980	Locks, door, with mineral knobs, complete														
1981	Locks, assorted		2												
1982	Locks, switch														
1983	Locks, car														
1984	Locks car, seat-back														
1985	Locks, door														
1986	Locks, chest														
1987	Locks, spring-chest														
1988	Locks, drawer														
1989	Locks, rim														
1990	Locks, iron drawer														
1991	Locks, desk and drawer														
1992	Locks, Japan-covered														
1993	Locks, wardrobe														
1994	Locks and chains														
1995	Lines, sea-grass														
1996	Lines, tape, assorted														
1997	Lines, plough														
1998	Lines, chalk														
1999	Lines, chalk and reel														
2000	Line, chalk ... feet														
2001	Lime ... bushels														
2002	Lime ... pounds														
2003	Lumber, pine ... feet		39,691		1,606										
2004	Lumber, oak and poplar, assorted ... do														
2005	Lumber, B. M ... do														

Report showing the disposition of United States military railroad property in the military division of the Tennessee, &c.—Continued.

Running number.	Articles.	Property sold on credit to railroad companies under Executive Orders of August 8 and October 14, 1865.													
		Alabama and Florida railroad.	East Tennessee and Georgia railroad.	Mobile and Great Northern railroad.	Tennessee and Alabama railroad.	East Tennessee and Virginia railroad.	Mobile and Ohio railroad.	Tennessee and Alabama Central railroad.	Central Southern railroad.	New Orleans and Ohio railroad.	Rome railroad.	Memphis and Ohio railroad.	Southwestern railroad.	Georgia Railroad and Banking Company.	New Orleans, Jackson, and Great Northern railroad.
2006	Lumber, assorted ... feet.		6, 032												
2007	Lumber, old ... lots.														
2008	Lumber, oak ... feet.		20, 861		1, 273										
2009	Lumber, poplar ... do.				6, 502										
2010	Lumber, walnut ... do.														
2011	Lead, pig ... pounds.														
2012	Lead, white, assorted ... do.														
2013	Lead, black ... do.														
2014	Lead, sugar of ... do.						353								
2015	Lead, sheet ... do.		167											857	
2016	Lead, red, in oil and dry ... do.						200							300	
2017	Lead, bar and pig ... do.														
2018	Lead, red ... do.														
2019	Lead, scrap ... do.														
2020	Litharge ... do.														
2021	Lathes, screw-cutting		2												
2022	Lathes, complete, 7 feet bed, 9-inch swing														
2023	Lathes, shear, and head														
2024	Lathes, engine	1													
2025	Lathes, hand														
2026	Lathes, axle														
2027	Lathes, wood, turning														
2028	Lathes, iron, turning														
2029	Lathes, dog, wrought, No. 20														
2030	Lathes, screw-cutting machine, 8 feet chain, feed, with chuck														
2031	Lathes, screw-cutting machine, 10 feet bed, 23-inch swing										1				
2032	Lathes, screw-cutting machine, with pulleys and shafts														
2033	Lathes, with chuck		1												
2034	Lathes, 24-inch, universal chuck														

No.	Article														
2035	Lathes, 24-inch, White's patent														
2036	Lathes, driving wheel		1												
2037	Lathes, turning														
2038	Lathes														
2039	Lathes, double-head, 20 feet long, 26-inch swing, with counter shafts, tools, and fixtures														
2040	Lathes, screw-cutting, with counter shafts														
2041	Lathes, small counter shaft														
2041½	Lathes, No. 8														
2042	Lathes, double-head, wood														
2043	Lathes, iron														
2044	Lathes, screw-cutting, 16 feet bed, 15-inch swing														
2045	Lathes, shear and head, 10 feet bed, 12-inch swing														
2046	Lathes, small, with screw, gear, and four extra rods														
2047	Lathes, 30-inch														
2048	Ladders, mounting														
2049	Ladders, shop and step														
2050	Letters .... sets			1										1	
2051	Letters														
2052	Letters and figures, incomplete .... sets														
2053	Links, crooked														
2054	Links, chain														
2055	Links, coupling .... pounds														
2056	Links, straight .... do														
2057	Links, crooked .... do														
2058	Links, coupling														
2059	Ladles														
2060	Ladles, tin														
2061	Ladles, perforated														
2062	Ladles, melting														
2063	Ladles, iron														
2064	Ladles, iron .... pounds														
2065	Lifts, window													435	
2066	Lifts, brass, sash														
2067	Links, switch rope .... pounds														
2068	Links, straight														
2069	Links and pins, coupling .... pounds														
2070	Leather, sole .... do		36												
2071	Leather, lace .... sides												6		
2072	Leather, harness .... pounds														
2073	Leather, bridle .... do														
2074	Leather, russet .... sides														
2075	Leather, burnt .... pounds														
2076	Leather, sole .... sides														
2077	Leather, assorted .... pounds														
2078	Leather, blue, title .... dozen														
2079	Levels, spirit														
2080	Levels, pocket														
2081	Levels, machinists'														
2082	Levels														
2083	Levers, hand-car														
2084	Levers and rods, tank														

Report showing the disposition of United States military railroad property in the military division of the Tennessee, &c.—Continued.

Running number.	Articles.	Property sold on credit to railroad companies under Executive Orders of August 8 and October 14, 1865.													
		Alabama and Florida railroad.	East Tennessee and Georgia railroad.	Mobile and Great Northern railroad.	Tennessee and Alabama railroad.	East Tennessee and Virginia railroad.	Mobile and Ohio railroad.	Tennessee and Alabama Central railroad.	Central Southern railroad.	New Orleans and Ohio railroad.	Rome railroad.	Memphis and Ohio railroad.	Southwestern railroad.	Georgia Railroad and Banking Company.	New Orleans, Jackson, and Great Northern railroad.
2085	Levers, switch														
2086	Levers, wrought														
2087	Levers							2							
2088	Levers, brake														
2089	Levers, track														
2090	Levers, whistle														
2091	Levers, blacksmith														
2092	Leaves, steel, for tender springs ... pounds														
2093	Leaf, gold ... packages														
2094	Ley, concentrated ... cans														
2095	Ley, concentrated ... boxes														
2096	Lead, bar ... pounds														
2097	Lead, white ... kegs														
2098	Lugs, water tank														
2099	Lugs, water tank ... pounds														
2100	Laths, pine														
2101	Lake, madder ... tubes														
2102	Laudanum ... pounds														
2103	Logs, B. M ... feet														
2104	Lifters, rail														
2105	Legs, table														
2106	Litters														
2107	Machines, small engine														
2108	Machines, double engine														
2109	Machines, hoisting engine														
2110	Machines, straightening														
2111	Machines, drill press														
2112	Machines, wheel press														
2113	Machines, press boring, cylinder														
2114	Machines, press drilling, vertical, Nos. 62 and 63		1												
2115	Machines, manifest, suspension														
2116	Machines, pipe-cutting														

No.	Article														
2117	Machines, stove pipe former														
2118	Machines, wooden former														
2119	Machines, burring														
2120	Machines, pinning down														
2121	Machines, setting down														
2122	Machines, swedging														
2123	Machines, scanning														
2124	Machines, scanning, double														
2125	Machines, bolt header														
2126	Machines, screw cutting														
2127	Machines, beading														
2128	Machines, twyring														
2129	Machines, tenoning														
2130	Machines, wiring														
2131	Machines, squaring														
2132	Machines, grooving														
2133	Machines, folding														
2134	Machines, planing, common														
2135	Machines, planing														
2136	Machines, quartering wheel														
2137	Machines, quartering wheel, double-headed														
2138	Machines, flooring														
2139	Machines, striker														
2140	Machines, scroll-moulding														
2141	Machines, boring, assorted														
2142	Machines, boring and auger														
2143	Machines, boring and drilling, Bement & Dougherty										1				
2144	Machines and bits, boring														
2145	Machines, boring, No. 32, Bement & Dougherty														
2146	Machines, sawing														
2147	Machines, skiving														
2148	Machines, mortising														
2149	Machines, mortising and boring, car														
2150	Machines, mortising, and chisels, foot, portable		1												
2151	Machines, thick edge														
2152	Machines, rolling		1												
2153	Machines, slotting														
2154	Machines, milling														
2155	Machines, gear cutting														
2156	Machines, bolt cutting, taps and dies														
2157	Machines, small vertical drill														
2158	Machines, key cutting														
2159	Machines, key seat drill, No. 12, complete														
2160	Machines, large vertical drill, intermediate shafts, pulleys and hangers														
2161	Machines, nut tapping		1												
2162	Machines, moulding														
2163	Machines, railroad cut-off sawing														
2164	Machines, stove pipe breaking														
2165	Machines, binders' board cutting														
2166	Machines, shaping														
2167	Machines, shaping, 12-inch, No. 20														

Report showing the disposition of United States military railroad property in the military division of the Tennessee, &c.—Continued.

Running number.	Articles.	Property sold on credit to railroad companies under Executive Orders of August 8 and October 14, 1865.													
		Alabama and Florida railroad.	East Tennessee and Georgia railroad.	Mobile and Great Northern railroad.	Tennessee and Alabama railroad.	East Tennessee and Virginia railroad.	Mobile and Ohio railroad.	Tennessee and Alabama Central railroad.	Central Southern railroad.	New Orleans and Ohio railroad.	Rome railroad.	Memphis and Ohio railroad.	Southwestern railroad.	Georgia Railroad and Banking Company.	New Orleans, Jackson, and Great Northern railroad.
2168	Machines, drilling														
2169	Machines, portable, drilling														
2170	Machines, guttering														
2171	Machines, bolt, with taps and dyes														
2172	Machines, car trimming, common														
2173	Machines, car, wood turning														
2174	Machines, turning, large														
2175	Machines, beading, and extra rolls														
2176	Machines, hoisting												1	4	
2177	Machines, shingle														
2178	Machines, copper pipe breaking														
2179	Machines, spring setting														
2180	Machines, flue drawing														
2181	Machines, slide lathe														
2182	Machines, wood lathe														
2183	Machines, hand lathe														
2184	Machines, eyelet														
2185	Machines, double seaming														
2186	Machines, boring and turning		1												
2187	Machines, laying off														
2188	Machines, bolt cutting, large, with 7 sets taps and dies, plugs for repairing dies, counter shafts, pulleys and hangers														
2189	Machines, bolt cutting, with 13 sets taps and dies, counter shafts, pulleys and hangers														
2190	Machines, mortising, with bits, Rogers's patent														
2191	Machines, planing, compound														
2192	Machines, car planing and matching, complete														
2193	Machines, bolt head, and fixtures														
2194	Machines, planing, 12 feet, with counter shafting, wrenches, tools, &c														
2195	Machines, tongue-grooving														

2196	Machines, planer, (Daniels's patent)														
2197	Machines, circular rip-saw, No. 6														
2198	Machines, circular rip-saw, No. 5														
2199	Machines, board planer, No. 2														
2200	Machines, rabbiting, No. 5														
2201	Machines, wheel, burring lath														
2202	Machines, surface planing, No. 2														
2203	Machines, ruling														
2204	Machines, paper cutting														
2205	Machines, gumming														
2206	Machines, bolt cutting		1												
2207	Machines, car planing		1												
2208	Machines, wood														
2209	Machines, cylinder boring														
2210	Mills, shingle														
2211	Mills, saw, with engine boiler complete														
2212	Mills, saw, (O. S. and D. patent)														
2213	Mills, saw, (Clemens's patent)														
2214	Mills, saw, circular, (Clemens's patent)														
2215	Mills, saw, circular, (Lea & Leavitt's)														
2216	Mills, saw, (H. & Co.'s patent, "A," 2 boilers complete.)														
2217	Mills, saw, (H. & Co.'s patent, "D," complete)														
2218	Mills, saw, stationery, L and D patent, incomplete														
2219	Mills, saw, A. B. H. & Co.'s patent, incomplete														
2220	Mills, saw														
2221	Mills, steam saw, portable														
2222	Mills, paint, assorted												1		
2223	Mills, borax														
2224	Mills, corn														
2225	Mills, boring, counter, shafts, pulleys, and hangers														
2226	Mandrels														
2227	Mandrels, saw														
2228	Mandrels, S. P														
2229	Mandrels, iron, assorted														
2230	Mandrels, steel-nut														
2231	Mandrels, steel														
2232	Mandrels, cast-steel														
2233	Mandrels, cast														
2234	Mandrels, lathe, steel														
2235	Mallets, assorted														
2236	Mallets. carpenters'														
2237	Mallets, lignumvitæ														
2238	Mallets, caulking														
2239	Mallets, iron-ring														
2240	Mallets, stonecutters'														
2241	Mallets, tinners'														
2242	Mauls														
2243	Mauls, spike														
2244	Mauls, carpenters'														
2245	Mauls, carpenters' top														
2246	Mauls, carpenters' spike			12			48								

Report showing the disposition of United States military railroad property in the military division of the Tennessee, &c.—Continued.

Running number.	Articles.	Property sold on credit to railroad companies under Executive Orders of August 8 and October 14, 1865.													
		Alabama and Florida railroad.	East Tennessee and Georgia railroad.	Mobile and Great Northern railroad.	Tennessee and Alabama railroad.	East Tennessee and Virginia railroad.	Mobile and Ohio railroad.	Tennessee and Alabama Central railroad.	Central Southern railroad.	New Orleans and Ohio railroad.	Rome railroad.	Memphis and Ohio railroad.	Southwestern railroad.	Georgia Railroad and Banking Company.	New Orleans, Jackson, and Great Northern railroad.
2247	Mauls, railroad spike														
2248	Mauls, wooden														
2249	Mauls, iron														
2250	Mauls, bridge														
2251	Mauls, dirt														
2252	Measures, assorted														
2253	Measures, tin, assorted														
2254	Measures, tin ... sets														
2255	Measures, oil ... do														
2256	Measures, pint														
2257	Measures, dry ... sets														
2258	Mullers														
2259	Moulds, soldering														
2260	Moulds, cast														
2261	Magazines, powder														
2262	Marline, tarred ... pounds														
2263	Matches ... gross														
2264	Meter, gas														
2265	Metal, Babbitt ... pounds														
2266	Molasses ... gallons														
2267	Moulens, wooden-wreath														
2268	Machinery, saw-mill ... box														
2269	Machinery, rolling-mill ... pounds														
2270	Nippers														
2271	Nippers, cutting														
2272	Needles, assorted														
2273	Needles, tufting														
2274	Needles, upholsterers'														
2275	Needles, harness ... papers														
2276	Nozzles														
2277	Nozzles, brass													1	
2278	Nozzles, pipe														

No.	Article	Unit														
2279	Nozzles, hose															
2280	Nozzles	pounds														
2281	Nuts, assorted	do			945			7,999						2,101	910	
2282	Nuts, brass	do														
2283	Nuts, square	do														
2284	Nuts, hexagon	do														
2285	Nuts and washers	do														
2286	Nuts and bolts	do														
2287	Nuts, keeper, and rods															
2288	Nuts, iron															
2289	Nails, assorted	kegs														
2290	Nails, finishing, assorted	papers												62	50	
2291	Nails, clout	do						29								
2292	Nails, tufting															
2293	Nails, clinch	pounds						1,320								
2294	Nails, horseshoe	do														
2295	Nails, enamelled	gross														
2296	Nails, lining	papers														
2297	Nails, assorted	pounds			2,500	369	19,000									
2298	Nails, plush	gross														
2299	Nails, finishing	kegs														
2300	Nails, cut	do														
2301	Nails, finishing	pounds														
2302	Nails, round-head brass	gross														
2303	Nails, cut	pounds														
2304	Nails, copper	do														
2305	Nails, tin	papers														
2306	Nails, lining, blued	gross														
2307	Nails, lining, silver	do														
2308	Numbers, key	lots														
2309	Numbers	sets														
2310	Netting, wire	feet						100					110			
2311	Oilers															
2312	Oilers, engine, assorted		4	9			10	1								
2313	Oilers, spring															
2314	Oilers, spring-top															
2315	Oilers, spring-bottom				12									48		
2316	Oilers, machine															
2317	Oilers, small															
2318	Oilers, tin															
2319	Oil, lard	gallons														
2320	Oil, coal	do														
2321	Oil, lubricating	do														
2322	Oil, linseed, raw	do														
2323	Oil, linseed, boiled	do														
2324	Oil, linseed	do														
2325	Oil	do														
2326	Oil, head-light	do														
2327	Oil, neat's-foot	do														
2328	Oil, castor	bottles														
2329	Ochre, French, yellow	pounds														
2330	Oakum	do														

Report showing the disposition of United States military railroad property in the military division of the Tennessee, &c.—Continued.

Running number.	Articles.	Property sold on credit to railroad companies under Executive Orders of August 8 and October 14, 1865.													
		Alabama and Florida railroad.	East Tennessee and Georgia railroad.	Mobile and Great Northern railroad.	Tennessee and Alabama railroad.	East Tennessee and Virginia railroad.	Mobile and Ohio railroad.	Tennessee and Alabama Central railroad.	Central Southern railroad.	New Orleans and Ohio railroad.	Rome railroad.	Memphis and Ohio railroad.	Southwestern railroad.	Georgia Railroad and Banking Company.	New Orleans, Jackson, and Great Northern railroad.
2331	Ornaments, brass														
2332	Planes, rounding														
2333	Planes, double-smooth														
2334	Planes, fore														
2335	Planes, jack														
2336	Planes jointer														
2337	Planes, joint														
2338	Planes, rabbet, assorted														
2339	Planes, jack, rabbet														
2340	Planes, bead, assorted														
2341	Planes, bench ... sets														
2342	Planes, long-jointer														
2343	Planes, moulding														
2344	Planes, smooth														
2345	Planes, sash														
2346	Planes, match														
2347	Planes, match ... pairs														
2348	Planes, screw-arm match														
2349	Planes, panel-plough														
2350	Planes, plough														
2351	Planes and bits, plough														
2352	Planes, floor ... sets														
2353	Planes, assorted														
2354	Planes, double-iron														
2355	Planes, grooving ... pairs														
2356	Planes and set bits														
2357	Planes, joiners' short														
2358	Planes, panel plough and bits														
2359	Planes ... sets														
2360	Planers														
2361	Planers ... sets														
2362	Planers, rabbet														

2363	Planers, car, complete														
2364	Planers, compound adjustment head														
2365	Planers and matcher with counter shafts														
2366	Planers, iron, to plane 16 ft., 4 ft. square, complete														
2367	Planers, iron														
2368	Planers, 48-inch														
2369	Planers, iron, 36 x 36 inches, 28-feet bed, 18-feet platform, (Seller's patent.)										1				
2370	Planers, 5-feet														
2371	Planers, 36 x 36 inches, No. 124, (Seller's patent)														
2372	Planers, 36 x 36 inches, No. 125, (Seller's patent)														
2373	Planers, (Seller's patent)														
2374	Planers, compound, (Bement & Dougherty)														
2375	Planers, compound														
2376	Planers, compound, chuck, No. 14, double, (Bement & Dougherty.)		1												
2377	Planers, 36 x 36 inches		1												
2378	Planers, link and link-block														
2379	Planers, cast-iron link														
2380	Pulleys, assorted														
2381	Pulleys, complete, assorted														
2382	Pulleys, upright														
2383	Pulleys for main shafts, common														
2384	Pulleys, two-ton														
2385	Pulleys for paint mill														
2386	Pulleys and shafts														
2387	Pulleys and chain, 2-ton														
2388	Pulleys, iron, 2 feet 10 inches face														
2389	Pulleys, iron, 2 feet 4 inches face														
2390	Pulleys, cast iron, assorted ... pounds														
2391	Pulleys, drawer, No. 10														
2392	Pulleys and hangers														
2393	Pulleys ... pounds														
2394	Pulleys, turned for ¾, 10 by 12, with sets of screws														
2395	Pulleys, cast-iron														
2396	Ploughs and grooves ... sets														
2397	Ploughs														
2398	Pincers, carpenters' ... pairs														
2399	Pincers, blacksmiths' ... do														
2400	Pincers, upholsterers' ... do														
2401	Pincers, shoeing ... do														
2402	Pincers, assorted ... do														
2403	Pincers, boiler-makers' ... do														
2404	Pencils, carpenters'														
2405	Pencils, coloring														
2406	Pencils, C. H														
2407	Pencils, artists' red sable						72								
2408	Pencils, striping														
2409	Pencils, marking						48								
2410	Pencils, lettering														
2411	Punches														
2412	Punches, belt						6						12		

Report showing the disposition of United States military railroad property in the military division of the Tennessee, &c.—Continued.

Running number.	Articles.	Property sold on credit to railroad companies under Executive Orders of August 8 and October 14, 1865.													
		Alabama and Florida railroad.	East Tennessee and Georgia railroad.	Mobile and Great Northern railroad.	Tennessee and Alabama railroad.	East Tennessee and Virginia railroad.	Mobile and Ohio railroad.	Tennessee and Alabama Central railroad.	Central Southern railroad.	New Orleans and Ohio railroad.	Rome railroad.	Memphis and Ohio railroad.	Southwestern railroad.	Georgia Railroad and Banking Company.	New Orleans, Jackson, and Great Northern railroad.
2413	Punches, screws and dies														
2414	Punches, screw														
2415	Punches, hollow														
2416	Punches, hydraulic														
2417	Punches, centre														
2418	Punches, steel														
2419	Punches, lever														
2420	Punches, coppersmiths'														
2421	Punches, harness														
2422	Punches, spring														
2423	Punches, conductors'														
2424	Punches, track														
2425	Punches, blacksmiths'														
2426	Punches, tinners'														
2427	Punches, tank hoop														
2428	Punches, clamp														
2429	Punches, boiler-makers'														
2430	Punches, iron track ... sets														
2431	Punches, short														
2432	Punches, hound														
2433	Presses, drill														
2434	Presses, upright drill														
2435	Presses, upright drill, &c														
2436	Presses, hydraulic, with shafts and pulleys														
2437	Presses, wheel														
2438	Presses, hand wheel														
2439	Presses, upright drill, and counter shafts														
2440	Presses, medium "Franklin"														
2441	Presses, ½-medium "Franklin"														
2442	Presses, binders' hand														
2443	Presses, manifest														
2444	Presses, drill, and bits														

No.	Article	Unit														
2445	Plyers	pairs														
2446	Plyers, cutting	do														
2447	Plyers, common	do														
2448	Plyers, upholsterers'	do														
2449	Plyers, flat nose	do														
2450	Pots, glue															
2451	Pots, marking															
2452	Pots, wood paint															
2453	Pots, tin soldering															
2454	Pots, tinners' fire															
2455	Pots, paste															
2456	Pots, paint	lot														
2457	Pots, cast					1		1		1						
2458	Pots, tallow															
2459	Pots, rosin															
2460	Pots, melting															
2461	Pots, soldering															
2462	Pots, paint															
2463	Pots, iron															
2464	Pumps, steam															
2465	Pumps, steam, Woodland															
2466	Pumps, cylinder				2	7				8			3			
2467	Pumps, force, McGowan's															
2467½	Pumps															
2468	Pumps, McGowan, with engine complete															
2469	Pumps, force															
2470	Pumps, Worthington															
2471	Pumps, oil															
2472	Pumps, oil, copper															
2473	Pumps, engine															
2474	Pumps, rotary fire															
2475	Pumps, donkey															
2476	Pumps, cistern															
2477	Pumps, proving															
2478	Pumps, Harris															
2479	Pumps, engine, and boiler, complete															
2480	Pumps, incomplete															
2481	Pumps, steam, with engine, Worthington															
2482	Pumps, test and gauge															
2483	Pumps, force, with gearing and shafting															
2484	Pumps and fixtures, McGowan															
2485	Picks, earth, and handles															
2486	Picks															
2487	Picks, tamping															
2488	Picks, railroad															
2489	Picks, stone															
2490	Pins, wooden	barrels														
2491	Pins, coupling	pounds														
2492	Pins, coupling															
2493	Pins, turned L. V															
2494	Pins, switch															
2495	Pipes, blast															

Report showing the disposition of United States military railroad property in the military division of the Tennessee, &c.—Continued.

Running number.	Articles.	Property sold on credit to railroad companies under Executive Orders of August 8 and October 14, 1865.													
		Alabama and Florida railroad.	East Tennessee and Georgia railroad.	Mobile and Great Northern railroad.	Tennessee and Alabama railroad.	East Tennessee and Virginia railroad.	Mobile and Ohio railroad.	Tennessee and Alabama Central railroad.	Central Southern railroad.	New Orleans and Ohio railroad.	Rome railroad.	Memphis and Ohio railroad.	Southwestern railroad.	Georgia Railroad and Banking Company.	New Orleans, Jackson, and Great Northern railroad.
2496	Pipe, blast ... feet														
2497	Pipes, copper, with couplings														
2498	Pipe, copper ... pounds														
2499	Pipe, round														
2500	Pipe, sheet iron ... pounds														
2501	Pipe, wrought ... feet														
2502	Pipe, iron, galvanized ... do														
2503	Pipe, galvanized ... pieces														
2504	Pipes, copper hose														
2505	Pipes, rubber hose														
2506	Pipe, iron ... pounds														
2507	Plugs, assorted														
2508	Plugs, gas pipe														
2509	Plugs, for repairing, dies														
2510	Plugs, flue														
2511	Plugs, assorted ... pounds														
2512	Plugs and feathers														
2513	Plates, wrought scrap fish bar ... pounds														
2514	Plates, engine window														
2515	Plates, blacksmiths'														
2516	Plates, chuck														
2517	Plates, head ... pounds														
2518	Plates, face ... do														
2519	Plates, face														
2520	Plates, gas-fitters' screw														
2521	Plates, screw cutter														
2522	Plates, screw		1												
2523	Plates, screws and dies														
2524	Plates, angle														
2525	Plates, surface														
2526	Plates, turntable ... sets														
2527	Plates and rolls ... do														

2528	Plates, bolster .... pounds														
2529	Plates, assorted .... do														
2530	Plates, die														
2531	Points, glaziers' .... papers														
2532	Points, glaziers' .... pounds														
2533	Points, frog, steel .... do														
2534	Patterns, tin														
2535	Patterns, moulders'														
2536	Patterns, wheelwrights'														
2537	Patterns, sheet iron .... sets														
2538	Patterns, assorted		150												
2539	Patterns, tin .... sets														
2540	Patterns, sheet iron .... pounds														
2541	Patterns .... lots														
2542	Pikes														
2543	Piping, assorted .... feet														
2544	Putty .... pounds														
2545	Pilots, loco														
2546	Pilots, loco, wood														
2547	Paulins														
2548	Potash, prussiate .... pounds														
2549	Potash .... do														
2550	Pipe, for cistern pump .... feet														
2551	Pipe, water, assorted .... do				358			233	444						
2552	Pipe, water .... pounds														
2553	Pipe, gum hose fire														
2554	Pipe, gas .... feet													1	
2555	Pipe, lead .... pounds						996½					202 11-12	803	418⅛	
2556	Pipe, brass .... feet														
2557	Pipe, nozzle and hose														
2558	Pipe, inside, and netting for engine, No. 30														
2559	Pipe, outside, for engine, No. 30														
2560	Pipe, inside, for smoke stack														
2561	Pipe, copper .... feet						267								
2562	Pipe, tin .... do														
2563	Pipe, iron .... bundles														
2564	Pipe, iron .... pieces														
2565	Pipe, escape														
2566	Paper, drawing .... quires														
2567	Paper, tracing .... rolls														
2568	Paper, waste .... pounds														
2569	Paper, antiquarian .... sheets														
2570	Paper, sand .... quires														
2571	Paper, emery .... do														
2572	Paper, wrapping .... do												60		
2573	Paper, white drawing .... yards														
2574	Paper, marble .... reams														
2575	Paper, brown drawing .... pounds														
2576	Paper, white drawing .... do														
2577	Paper, printing .... do														
2578	Pickets														
2579	Paint, black .... pounds						1							1	

Report showing the disposition of United States military railroad property in the military division of the Tennessee, &c.—Continued.

Running number.	Articles	Property sold on credit to railroad companies under Executive Orders of August 8 and October 14, 1865.													
		Alabama and Florida railroad.	East Tennessee and Georgia railroad.	Mobile and Great Northern railroad.	Tennessee and Alabama railroad.	East Tennessee and Virginia railroad.	Mobile and Ohio railroad.	Tennessee and Alabama Central railroad.	Central Southern railroad.	New Orleans and Ohio railroad.	Rome railroad.	Memphis and Ohio railroad.	Southwestern railroad.	Georgia Railroad and Banking Company.	New Orleans, Jackson, and Great Northern railroad.
2580	Paint, chrome yellow ... pounds														
2581	Piaut, pink Dutch ... do														
2582	Paint, mineral ... do														
2583	Paint, assorted ... do														
2584	Paint, mineral ... barrels														
2585	Paint, mixed ... pounds														
2586	Polish, stove ... papers														
2587	Powder, blasting ... pounds														
2588	Powder ... kegs														
2589	Powder, blue ... pounds														
2590	Plungers, brass pump														
2591	Pans, oil														
2592	Packing, hemp ... pounds			501			1,025						390	1,556	
2593	Packing, gum ... do						297						10		
2594	Packing, steam ... do														
2595	Pendants, gas-pipe														
2596	Poles, pipe														
2597	Pedestals ... pounds														
2598	Pedestals														
2599	Powers, horse														
2600	Platforms, railroad car														
2601	Paris, plaster ... pounds														
2602	Pockets, iron														
2603	Pits, transfer and masonry														
2604	Pink, rose ... pounds														
2605	Pinions, feed														
2606	Patterns, for brass castings														
2607	Patterns, for iron castings														
2608	Plank, oak ... feet														
2609	Pistons, C. I														
2610	Paste, blue ... pots														
2610¼	Ploughs														

2611	Quods, hollow . . . pounds														
2612	Quods, pica, corner . . . sets														
2613	Rules, steel														
2614	Rules, foot														
2615	Rules, 2-foot														
2616	Rules, pocket														
2617	Rules, board														
2618	Rules, boxwood														
2619	Rules, assorted														
2620	Rods, guttering														
2621	Rods, pipe ram														
2622	Rods, brake . . . pounds														
2623	Rods, brass . . . do														
2624	Rods, switch														
2625	Rods, switch . . . sets														
2626	Rods, switch . . . pounds														
2627	Rods, levelling														
2628	Rods, tank . . . sets														
2629	Rods, copper . . . pounds														
2630	Rods, connecting . . . do														
2631	Rods, piston, wrought iron														
2632	Rods, nuts, and bolts . . . pounds														
2633	Rods, iron, for cars . . . do														
2634	Rods, brake														
2635	Rods, brake, and wheel														
2636	Rods, piston														
2637	Rods, tank														
2638	Rods and levers, tank . . . sets														
2639	Rods and bolts, wrought . . . pounds														
2640	Rods, bridge . . . do														
2641	Rollers . . . pairs														
2642	Rollers, door														
2643	Rollers, boiler-makers' . . . sets														
2644	Rollers, timber														
2645	Rollers, large . . . sets														
2646	Rollers, small, stove-pipe														
2647	Rollers, iron														
2648	Ratchets				1										
2649	Ratchets and dogs . . . pounds														
2650	Ratchets and stands														
2651	Reamers														
2652	Reamers and burrs, steel														
2653	Reamers and drills . . . pounds														
2654	Reamers, C. S . . . do			168											
2655	Reamers and drills														
2656	Reamers, globe														
2657	Reamers, tap														
2658	Rivets, assorted			6,000			146,000						6,000	12,004	
2659	Rivets, assorted . . . pounds			200			8,610						636		
2660	Rivets, boiler . . . do			200										825	
2661	Rivets, tinned														
2662	Rivets, black and tinned . . . pounds														

Report showing the disposition of United States military railroad property in the military division of the Tennessee, &c.—Continued.

Running number.	Articles.	Property sold on credit to railroad companies under Executive Orders of August 8 and October 14, 1865.													
		Alabama and Florida railroad.	East Tennessee and Georgia railroad.	Mobile and Great Northern railroad.	Tennessee and Alabama railroad.	East Tennessee and Virginia railroad.	Mobile and Ohio railroad.	Tennessee and Alabama Central railroad.	Central Southern railroad.	New Orleans and Ohio railroad.	Rome railroad.	Memphis and Ohio railroad.	Southwestern railroad.	Georgia railroad and Banking Company.	New Orleans, Jackson, and Great Northern railroad.
2663	Rivets, seat-back ... pounds														
2664	Rivets, tank ... do														
2665	Rivets, smokestack ... do														
2666	Rivets, copper ... do						440								
2667	Rivets, brass ... do														
2668	Rivets, tinned ... papers														
2669	Rivets, iron ... pounds														
2670	Rivets, car seat, and burrs, brass														
2671	Rivets, iron														
2672	Rivets, iron ... papers														
2673	Rivets ... sets														
2674	Rivets, tinned ... pounds														
2675	Rivets, brass seat-back														
2676	Rope, assorted ... pounds			607			2, 067								
2677	Rope, Manilla ... do														114
2678	Rope, 1-inch ... feet														
2679	Rope, 1½-inch ... coils												46	348	
2680	Rope ... do														
2681	Rope ... feet														
2682	Rope, bell ... pounds														
2683	Rope, old ... do														
2684	Ropes, small														
2685	Ropes, guy														
2686	Ropes, fall														
2687	Ropes, switch														
2688	Ropes, wire ... coils														
2689	Rounds and hollows														
2690	Rounds and hollows ... sets														
2691	Rounds and hollows ... pairs														
2692	Rounds, chair														
2693	Rounds, timber, buggy														
2694	Riddles														

2695	Regulators, upholsterers'														
2696	Reels, chalk-line														
2697	Resin .... pounds														
2698	Rubber, block .... do														
2699	Rammers														
2700	Rams, battering														
2701	Riving froe														
2702	Rings, flush, brass														
2703	Rings, brass, packing .... pounds														
2704	Rings, packing														
2705	Rings, brass, cylinder														
2706	Rings, water tank		3												
2707	Rings, piston, for water works .... pounds														
2708	Rings, old brass														
2709	Rings, brass packing														
2710	Rings, Japan mall .... gross														
2711	Rings, Japan harness .... do														
2712	Rings, breeching														
2713	Rings, muffin														
2714	Rings, harness .... gross														
2715	Red, American India .... tubes														
2716	Red, India, in oil .... pounds														
2717	Red, vermilion .... do														
2718	Red, India .... do		120												
2719	Red, Venetian .... do													574	
2720	Red, Italian .... do														
2721	Rags .... do														
2722	Reservoirs														
2723	Racks, assorted														
2724	Racks, forge, iron .... pounds														
2725	Racks, form														
2726	Rasps, assorted						12								
2727	Rasps, wood														
2728	Rasps, horse														
2729	Rails, T														
2730	Rolls, steel, for turn-table .... sets														
2731	Rests, steady for lathe														
2732	Rests, tank, lever														
2733	Rests, iron														
2734	Rests, arm														
2735	Rakes, stable														
2736	Rakes, iron														
2737	Reflectors, head-light														
2738	Registers, conductors'														
2739	Rigging for steam balance														
2740	Roofing, patent .... pounds														
2741	Saws, hand	2	4	1	1	5	49								4
2742	Saws, tenon														
2743	Saws, hack						6								
2744	Saws, compass, assorted														
2745	Saws, back														
2746	Saws, rip														

Report showing the disposition of United States military railroad property in the military division of the Tennessee, &c.—Continued.

Running number.	Articles.	Property sold on credit to railroad companies under Executive Orders of August 8 and October 14, 1865.													
		Alabama and Florida railroad.	East Tennessee and Georgia railroad.	Mobile and Great Northern railroad.	Tennessee and Alabama railroad.	East Tennessee and Virginia railroad.	Mobile and Ohio railroad.	Tennessee and Alabama Central railroad.	Central Southern railroad.	New Orleans and Ohio railroad.	Rome railroad.	Memphis and Ohio railroad.	Southwestern railroad.	Georgia railroad and Banking Company.	New Orleans, Jackson, and Great Northern railroad.
2747	Saws, buck														
2748	Saws, web														
2749	Saws, cross-cut, assorted			18			12						30	12	
2750	Saws, cross-cut, 5-foot														
2751	Saws, cross-cut, large														
2752	Saws, cross-cut, hand														
2753	Saws, cross-cut, tenon														
2754	Saws, jig														
2755	Saws, scroll														
2756	Saws, circular, 48-inch														
2757	Saws, circular and arbor														
2758	Saws, brass back														
2759	Saws, blue back														
2760	Saws, mill														
2761	Saws, muley														
2762	Saws, meat														
2763	Saws, drag														
2764	Saws, keyhole														
2765	Saws, wood														
2766	Saws and frames, wood														
2767	Saws, wooden frame														
2768	Saws, pit														
2769	Saws, fine														
2770	Saws, whip														
2771	Saws, cut-off, 32-inch														
2772	Saws, shingle, 36-inch														
2773	Saws, assorted														
2774	Saws, bright back														
2775	Saws, panel														
2776	Saws, cut-off														
2777	Squares, steel						24								
2778	Squares, try, assorted														

7279	Squares, iron														
2780	Squares, centre														
2781	Squares, framing														
2782	Squares, bevel														
2783	Squares, lumber														
2784	Squares														
2785	Squares, head														
2786	Stands, head-light														
2787	Stands, switch														
2788	Stands, flag						2								
2789	Stands for machines														
2790	Stands, monkey switch														
2791	Stands, target switch														
2792	Stands, wood switch														
2793	Stands, iron														
2794	Stamps, U. S. M. R. R.														
2795	Stands, brass lamp														
2796	Stands, locomotive lamp ... pounds														
2797	Stands, sand box ... do														
2798	Stands, California, double														
2799	Stands, California, single														
2800	Stands, lead														
2801	Stands, type														
2802	Stands, chain, cast ... pounds														
2803	Stands, gauge lamp														
2804	Stands, flag ... pounds														
2805	Stamps, U. S.														
2806	Stones, grind, assorted						37								
2807	Stones, grind, assorted ... pounds														2, 000
2808	Stones, grind, and fixtures ... sets														
2809	Stones, grind, 4 feet diameter, cast iron frame														
2810	Stones, paint and muller														
2811	Stones, paint														
2812	Stones, oil											24			
2813	Stones, oil, assorted ... pounds														
2814	Stones, whet														
2815	Stone ... lot														
2816	Stones, grind, frame, hangers complete		1												
2817	Stones, mill, and fixtures ... pairs														
2818	Stones, imposing														
2819	Stones, grind, frames and pulleys														
2820	Stones, grind, and fixtures														
2821	Stone, blue ... pounds														
2822	Stone, rotten ... do														
2823	Stone, pumice ... do														
2824	Stone, setting for engine														
2825	Snips ... pairs														
2826	Snips, circular ... do														
2827	Snips, tinners', assorted ... do														
2828	Snips, straight ... do														
2829	Shaves, spoke														
2830	Shaves, spoke, wood														

Report showing the disposition of United States military railroad property in the military division of the Tennessee, &c.—Continued.

Running number.	Articles.	Property sold on credit to railroad companies under Executive Orders of August 8 and October 14, 1865.													
		Alabama and Florida railroad.	East Tennessee and Georgia railroad.	Mobile and Great Northern railroad.	Tennessee and Alabama railroad.	East Tennessee and Virginia railroad.	Mobile and Ohio railroad.	Tennessee and Alabama Central railroad.	Central Southern railroad.	New Orleans and Ohio railroad.	Rome railroad.	Memphis and Ohio railroad.	Southwestern railroad.	Georgia Railroad and Banking Company.	New Orleans, Jackson, and Great Northern railroad.
2831	Shaves, spoke, iron														
2832	Sets, saw														
2833	Swedges, creasing														
2834	Swedges, bottom														
2835	Swedges, top														
2836	Swedges and chisels														
2837	Screws, assorted ... gross						488						143	92	
2838	Screws, round head, brass ... do														
2839	Screws, brass, assorted ... do						214								
2840	Screws, brass cap ... do														
2841	Screws, round head, blued ... do												18		
2842	Screws, blued ... do														
2843	Screws, hand, assorted						9						4		
2844	Screws, bench														
2845	Screws, wood bench														
2846	Screws, iron bench														
2847	Screws, bed														
2848	Screws, lag, assorted														
2849	Screws, lag ... pounds														
2850	Screws, top														
2851	Screws, fore														
2852	Screws, hydraulic jack														
2853	Screws, small steel ... sets														
2854	Screws, clamp														
2855	Screws, large, and 4-inch nuts														
2856	Screws for shaft														
2857	Screws, auger ... gross														
2858	Screws, turn-table														
2859	Screws, gimblet, brass ... gross														
2860	Screws, tank														
2861	Screws														
2862	Screws, iron wood ... gross														

2863	Screws, head ....sets														
2864	Screws, lathe														
2865	Screws, tire ....sets		1												
2866	Screws, hand ....pairs														
2867	Screws, jack														
2868	Screws, wood ....pounds														
2869	Screws, gimlet ....gross														
2870	Sticks, creasing														
2871	Sticks, yard														
2872	Sticks, composing														
2873	Sinks, counter														
2874	Sinks, drifts, and calking tools ....pounds														
2875	Slicks, carpenters'						6								
2876	Slicks, large framing														
2877	Slicks, glass														
2878	Scrapers, plumbers'														
2879	Scrapers, box														
2880	Scrapers	2	5		1	5	6	1	2	2	1				2
2881	Scrapers, iron														
2882	Scrapers, drill														
2883	Scrapers, stone														
2884	Scrapers, carriage														
2885	Scrapers, stove														
2886	Scrapers, ash-pan														1
2887	Straighteners, axle														
2888	Sockets, top														
2889	Sockets, chisel														
2890	Sockets, gas-pipe														
2891	Shafts and pulleys														
2892	Shafts														
2893	Shafts, saw mandril counter														
2894	Shafting and pulleys ....pounds														
2895	Shafts with pulleys, counter, shafting, &c ....feet														
2896	Shafting, assorted ....do		109												
2897	Shafting, iron, 2-inch ....pounds														
2898	Shafting ....do														
2899	Shafting, 3½-inch, with pulleys and hangers, complete ....feet														
2900	Shafting, 3-inch ....feet														
2901	Shafting, 3½-inch, tinned, 12 feet 6 inches long, with couplings and bolts, complete ....sections														
2902	Shafts, counter, with pulleys														
2903	Shafts, counter														
2904	Strainers				2		3								
2905	Strainers, paint														
2906	Strainers, pump														
2907	Strainers, copper														
2908	Strainers, feed-pipe														
2909	Skins, chamois														
2910	Skins, sheep														
2911	Skins, bark ....dozen														
2912	Shellac, gum ....pounds												20		

Report showing the disposition of United States military railroad property in the military division of the Tennessee, &c.—Continued.

Running number.	Articles.	Property sold on credit to railroad companies under Executive Orders of August 8 and October 14, 1865.													
		Alabama and Florida railroad.	East Tennessee and Georgia railroad.	Mobile and Great Northern railroad.	Tennessee and Alabama railroad.	East Tennessee and Virginia railroad.	Mobile and Ohio railroad.	Tennessee and Alabama Central railroad.	Central Southern railroad.	New Orleans and Ohio railroad.	Rome railroad.	Memphis and Ohio railroad.	Southwestern railroad.	Georgia Railroad and Banking Company.	New Orleans, Jackson, and Great Northern railroad.
2913	Saltpetre ... pounds														
2914	Spouts, bent						864								
2915	Spouts, tank														
2916	Spouts, sheet-iron														
2917	Shafts, counter, and 4 pulleys														
2918	Spouts, fluid can														
2919	Spouts, tin														
2920	Spouts, funnel														
2921	Staffs, flag		4		5		13	4	6		1				2
2922	Staffs, brake														
2923	Steel, assorted ... pounds		270				795						1,980	564	
2924	Steel, scrap ... do														
2925	Steel, cast ... do		110												
2926	Steel, spring, assorted ... do		440											2,389	
2927	Steel, square ... do			114			1,135							730	
2928	Steel, octagon ... do			39			684							65	
2929	Steel, frog ... do														
2930	Steel, blister ... do														
2931	Stocks, screw														
2932	Stocks, iron														
2933	Stocks, drill														
2934	Stocks, iron ... pairs														
2935	Stocks, roller														
2936	Saddles, smoke-stack ... pounds														
2937	Saddles for cylinder ... pairs														
2938	Stacks, smoke, locomotive														
2939	Stacks, smoke, stationary, 31 feet x 22 inches														
2940	Stacks, smoke, sheet-iron, boiler frame														
2941	Stacks, smoke and cap ... pounds														
2942	Scraps, forge ... do														
2943	Stacks, smoke, sheet-iron														
2944	Stacks, smoke														

No.	Article	Unit														
2945	Stacks, smoke	feet														
2946	Sieves, sand															
2947	Sieves, moulders'															
2948	Strips, parallel															
2949	Strips, parallel	pounds														
2950	Strips, copper-flue	do														
2951	Spikes, bridge	do														
2952	Spikes, railroad	kegs														
2953	Spikes, marlin															
2954	Spikes, bridge and cut	kegs														
2955	Spikes, railroad															
2956	Spikes, railroad	pounds														
2957	Spikes, cut, assorted	kegs														
2958	Spikes, assorted	pounds						3,000					2,400			
2959	Spikes	kegs														
2960	Scales, spring balance															
2961	Scales, platform, assorted															
2962	Scales, counter							3								
2963	Scales and weights															
2964	Scales, warehouse															
2965	Scales, brass scoop															
2966	Scales, set															
2967	Scales, beam															
2968	Scales															
2969	Scales, track															
2970	Scales, safety-valve															
2971	Scales, stone															
2972	Scales, spring															
2973	Scales, platform counter															
2974	Stretchers, iron															
2975	Stretchers, car															
2976	Snatches, gate															
2977	Springs, assorted	pounds														
2978	Springs, rubber car	do														
2979	Springs, car															
2980	Springs, packing															
2981	Springs, rubber	pounds														
2982	Springs, gum															
2983	Springs, engine tender	pounds														
2984	Springs, spiral	do														
2985	Springs, assorted															
2986	Springs, gum	pounds			1,098			5,836					2,086			
2987	Springs, car	do														
2988	Springs, tender															
2989	Springs, engine															
2990	Springs, engine	pounds														
2991	Springs, window															
2992	Springs, large D															
2993	Springs, small D															
2994	Springs, packing	pounds														
2995	Shovels		2	5		2	5	45	2	2		1				4
2996	Shovels, railroad															

Report showing the disposition of United States military railroad property in the military division of the Tennessee, &c.—Continued.

Running number.	Articles.	Property sold on credit to railroad companies under Executive Orders of August 8 and October 14, 1865.													
		Alabama and Florida railroad.	East Tennessee and Georgia railroad.	Mobile and Great Northern railroad.	Tennessee and Alabama railroad.	East Tennessee and Virginia railroad.	Mobile and Ohio railroad.	Tennessee and Alabama Central railroad.	Central Southern railroad.	New Orleans and Ohio railroad	Rome railroad.	Memphis and Ohio railroad.	Southwestern railroad.	Georgia Railroad and Banking Company.	New Orleans, Jackson, and Great Northern railroad.
2997	Shovels, scoop														
2998	Shovels, coal														
2999	Shovels, moulder, steel														
3000	Shovels and scrapers														
3001	Spades						102								
3002	Screens, sand														
3003	Screens, cloth														
3004	Screens, zinc														
3005	Screens, coal														
3006	Screens, wire														
3007	Spools, chalk line														
3008	Soap ... pounds														
3009	Soap, castile ... do														
3010	Soap ... bars														
3011	Spanners														
3012	Sienna, assorted ... pounds						12							20	
3013	Sienna, burnt ... do														
3014	Sienna, raw Italian ... do														
3015	Sienna, raw, in oil ... do														
3016	Sienna, raw ... do														
3017	Springs, brass														
3018	Sledges, (12-pound)														
3019	Springs, patent														
3020	Stirrups, log ... pairs														
3021	Stencils, copper														
3022	Scythes, snath														
3023	Scythes, grass														
3024	Scythes, brier														
3025	Sponge, common ... pounds														
3026	Sponge, fine ... do														
3027	Sponge ... do														
3028	Sulphur ... do														

3029	Sulphur flowers ... do														
3030	Sash, assorted ... lights														
3031	Sash, ... pieces														
3032	Sash ... lots														
3033	Sash, wire														
3034	Sash, sky-light														
3035	Switches, monkey														
3036	Slides, switch ... sets														
3037	Slides, track ... pounds														
3038	Signals, fog ... gross														
3039	Stools, saddlers'														
3040	Spaces, pica quod ... pounds														
3041	Staples, iron ... do														
3042	Staples, iron														
3043	Straps, seat, back														
3044	Straps, connecting, and brasses													200	
3045	Skivers														
3046	Skivers, white														
3047	Skids, loading														
3048	Sizing, gold ... pounds														
3049	Shoes, mule ... do														
3050	Shoes, mule														
3051	Sellars, rod ... pounds														
3052	Straps, eccentric ... do														
3053	Stems, check valve														
3054	Settings, masonry, with iron chimney														
3055	Scrapers, hoe														
3056	Sprinklers, fire														
3057	Squares, plated														
3058	Shingles		104, 050												
3059	Saucers, stove														
3060	Shackles, engine ... pounds														
3061	Salt ... do														
3062	Salts, epsom ... do														
3063	Sublimate, corr ... do														
3064	Staves, tank ... lots														
3065	Staves, tank ... pieces														
3066	Staples, back harness														
3067	Settings, masonry														
3068	Seamers, double roofing														
3069	Solder ... pounds														
3070	Soda, sal ... do														
3071	Swivels														
3072	Seats, coach														
3073	Seats														
3074	Shelving ... lots														
3075	Shelves, wooden														
3076	Syphons and cocks														
3077	Spoons, packing														
3078	Signs, tin														
3079	Signs														
3080	Signs, loco														

Report showing the disposition of United States military railroad property in the military division of the Tennessee, &c.—Continued.

Running number.	Articles.	Property sold on credit to railroad companies under Executive Orders of August 8 and October 14, 1865.													
		Alabama and Florida railroad.	East Tennessee and Georgia railroad.	Mobile and Great Northern railroad.	Tennessee and Alabama railroad.	East Tennessee and Virginia railroad.	Mobile and Ohio railroad.	Tennessee and Alabama Central railroad.	Central Southern railroad.	New Orleans and Ohio railroad.	Rome railroad.	Memphis and Ohio railroad.	Southwestern railroad.	Georgia railroad and Banking Company.	New Orleans, Jackson, and Great Northern railroad.
3081	Shutters, window														
3082	Steps, engine														
3083	Slides, switch														
3084	Staves, tank ... cases														
3085	Shimmers, paint														
3086	Shoes, horse ... pounds														
3087	Shoes, brake														
3088	Sets, hand-saw														
3089	Sets, cross-cut saw														
3090	Sets, mill-saw														
3091	Sets, lever-saw														
3092	Sets, blacksmiths' cold														
3093	Sets, rivet														
3094	Sets, iron button														
3095	Sets, spring														
3096	Sledges, assorted														
3097	Sledges and handles											6			
3098	Sledges, blacksmiths'														
3099	Sledges, heavy														
3100	Sledges, stone														
3102	Shears, hand ... pairs														
3103	Shears, tinners' ... do														
3104	Shears, sheet ... do														
3105	Shears, circular ... do														
3106	Shears, lever ... do														
3107	Shears, bench ... do														
3108	Shears, squaring ... do														
3109	Shears and punch combined ... do														
3110	Shears, rotary ... do														
3111	Shears, table, trimmers' ... do														
3112	Shears, table, gauge ... do														
3113	Shears ... do														

3114	Shives, iron														
3115	Stakes, square, Weddell														
3116	Stakes, funnel														
3117	Stakes, bench														
3118	Stakes, tinners'														
3119	Stakes, needle														
3120	Stakes, double seaming														
3121	Stakes, oval-head														
3122	Stakes, head														
3123	Stakes, pointing														
3124	Stakes, beak-horn														
3125	Stakes, hatchet														
3126	Stakes, square-head														
3127	Stakes, horn-blow														
3128	Stakes, round-head														
3129	Swedges, assorted														
3130	Swedges, square ... pairs														
3131	Swedges, C. S ... pounds														
3132	Swedges, W. I ... do														
3133	Swedges, B. S														
3134	Swedges and fullers														
3135	Swedges and chisels ... sets														
3136	Sleeves, water pipe														
3137	Sheives ... pairs	1													
3138	Stacks, smoke, stationary		2												
3139	Shafts, steam, wheel														
3139¼	Saws, circular, assorted		2				4								
3139½	Slicks														
3139¾	Sellar's engine truck														
3140	Tools, plumbers' ... sets														
3141	Tools, blacksmiths', assorted ... do														
3142	Tools, blacksmiths' ... pounds														
3143	Tools, shoeing ... sets														
3144	Tools, carpenters' ... do														
3145	Tools, carpenters' ... chests														
3146	Tools, turning, assorted														
3147	Tools, wheelwright ... sets														
3148	Tools, wheelwright, and chest, (incomplete)														
3149	Tools, grooving														
3150	Tools, sash, assorted						24						48		
3151	Tools, French sash, assorted														
3152	Tools, hand														
3153	Tools, planing, steel														
3154	Tools, boring														
3155	Tools, boring, steel														
3156	Tools, lathe, steel ... pounds		160	178											
3157	Tools, lathe														
3158	Tools, steel, for turning rolls ... pounds														
3159	Tools, saddlers' ... chests														
3160	Tools, saddlers' ... sets														
3161	Tools, tinners' ... do														
3162	Tools, tinners' ... pounds														

Report showing the disposition of United States military railroad property in the military division of the Tennessee, &c.—Continued.

Running number.	Articles.	Property sold on credit to railroad companies under Executive Orders of August 8 and October 14, 1865.													
		Alabama and Florida railroad.	East Tennessee and Georgia railroad.	Mobile and Great Northern railroad.	Tennessee and Alabama railroad.	East Tennessee and Virginia railroad.	Mobile and Ohio railroad.	Tennessee and Alabama Central railroad.	Central Southern railroad.	New Orleans and Ohio railroad.	Rome railroad.	Memphis and Ohio railroad.	Southwestern railroad.	Georgia Railroad and Banking Company.	New Orleans, Jackson, and Great Northern railroad.
3163	Tools, C. S. ... pounds		50												
3164	Tools, coppersmith ... sets														
3165	Tools, graining ... do														
3166	Tools, cupping														
3167	Tools, heading														
3168	Tools, slotting														
3169	Tools, rotary-cutting														
3170	Tools, spring ... sets														
3171	Tools, calking														
3172	Tools, flat paint, assorted														
3173	Tools and chains, W. I ... pounds														
3174	Tools, iron														
3175	Tools, turning ... boxes														
3176	Tools, lathe and planer														
3177	Trams ... pairs														
3178	Taps and dies ... sets														
3179	Taps and dies														
3180	Taps, steel ... pounds														
3181	Taps, steel														
3182	Taps, C. S. ... pounds		3												
3183	Taps, machine														
3184	Taps														
3185	Tips, C. S														
3186	Tanks, oil, assorted														
3187	Tanks, engine														
3188	Tanks, water				7			2	7						
3189	Tanks, locomotive														
3190	Tanks, oil, (45 galls)														
3191	Tanks, oil, (50 galls)														
3192	Tanks, oil, (75 galls)														
3193	Tanks, oil, (80 galls)														
3194	Tanks, tin water, (parts) ... lots														

3195	Tongs, roofing	pairs														
3196	Tongs, G. P	do														
3197	Tongs, ice	do														
3198	Tongs, B. S	do														
3199	Tongs, tinners'	sets														
3200	Tongs, grainers'	do														
3201	Tongs, engine	pairs	2	5		1	5	11		1	2	1	1			4
3202	Tongs, R. R	do														
3203	Tongs, tools, and pokers	pounds														
3204	Tongs, assorted	pairs														
3205	Tongs, B. S. and R. R															
3206	Tin, sheet	boxes		42												
3207	Tin, perforated	sheets														
3208	Tin, block	pounds														
3209	Tin, sheet	sheets														
3210	Tin, sheet, and screws	pounds														
3211	Timber	feet		20, 437			2, 053			10, 783						
3212	Timber, oak	do								40, 150						
3213	Timber, square, assorted	do														
3214	Timber, bridge	do														
3215	Timber, B. M., assorted	do														
3216	Timber, framed	lots														
3217	Ties, cross			24, 013			2, 401			4, 600						
3218	Tallow	pounds														
3219	Tallow	barrels														
3220	Thimbles															
3221	Thimbles, flue, iron	pounds														
3222	Thimbles, cast	do														
3223	Thermometers															
3224	Tarpaulins															
3225	Tripods															
3226	T's, gas-pipe															
3227	T's, water-pipe															
3228	T's, cast iron															
3229	Tubes, blast															
3230	Tubing, copper	pounds														
3231	Trucks, timber															
3232	Trucks, warehouse															
3233	Trucks, engine															
3234	Trucks	pairs														1
3235	Trucks, car															
3236	Trucks, car	pairs														
3237	Trucks, tender and locomotive	pounds														
3238	Trucks, engine	pairs														
3239	Trucks, machine	do														
3240	Tires, wrought iron	pounds														
3241	Tires, cast iron															
3242	Tires, locomotive				12										4	
3243	Tires, locomotive flange	pounds		23, 520				19, 280						7, 200	11, 551	
3244	Tires, flange cast iron	do														
3245	Tires, old	do														
3246	Tires, wrought iron															

Report showing the disposition of United States military railroad property in the military division of the Tennessee, &c.—Continued.

Running number.	Articles.	Property sold on credit to railroad companies under Executive Orders of August 8 and October 14, 1865.													
		Alabama and Florida railroad.	East Tennessee and Georgia railroad.	Mobile and Great Northern railroad.	Tennessee and Alabama railroad.	East Tennessee and Virginia railroad.	Mobile and Ohio railroad.	Tennessee and Alabama Central railroad.	Central Southern railroad.	New Orleans and Ohio railroad.	Rome railroad.	Memphis and Ohio railroad.	Southwestern railroad.	Georgia Railroad and Banking Company.	New Orleans, Jackson, and Great Northern railroad.
3247	Trowels, masons'														
3248	Trowels, plasterers'														
3249	Tables, circular saw		1												
3250	Tables, turn														
3251	Tables, turn and foundation														
3252	Tables, binders' sewing														
3253	Torches, gas														
3254	Troughs, flock														
3255	Troughs, guttering														
3256	Troughs, forge														
3257	Tops and screws, lamp														
3258	Tops, chimney														
3259	Tops, turn-table														
3260	Tops, car-lamp														
3261	Tops, screw ... gross			1											
3262	Tops, tallow, can														
3263	Tops and bottoms, can														
3264	Tops and bottoms, car-lamp														
3265	Tops and bottoms for turn-table														
3266	Type ... founts														
3267	Type ... pounds														
3268	Tapes, measuring, assorted						6								
3269	Tripoli ... pounds														
3270	Tripoli ... papers														
3271	Tacks, assorted ... do												10,468	720	
3272	Tacks, gimp ... do														
3273	Tacks, upholsterers' ... do						1,284								
3274	Tacks, blued ... do														
3275	Targets														
3276	Tickets, mess														
3277	Tickets														
3278	Tar, coal ... gallons														

3279	Tar, coal	barrels														
3280	Thread, black	pounds														
3281	Thread, black	bundles														
3282	Thread, shoe	pounds														
3283	Thread, saddlers'	do														
3284	Thread, linen	do														
3285	Thread, black	skeins														
3286	Twine, hemp	pounds														
3287	Twine, tufting	do														
3288	Twine, wrapping	do														
3289	Twine	balls														
3290	Turpentine	gallons														
3291	Trestles															
3292	Trusses, iron															
3293	Torpedoes															
3294	Tongues, frog	pounds														
3295	Templets, switch	sets														
3296	Templets															
3297	Transits															
3298	Tenders, locomotive															
3299	Tincture, iodine	pounds														
3300	Transoms, wrought	do														
3301	Testers, gas-pipe															
3302	Tiles, fire															
3303	Traps, rat															
3304	Tighteners, belt															
3305	Triangles															
3306	Tubs, tool															
3307	Tags, shipping	lots														
3308	Unions, brass, assorted															
3309	Umber, raw, in oil	pounds													21	
3310	Umber, raw	do					8									
3311	Umber, burnt	do														
3312	Umber, burnt	tubes														
3313	Umber, burnt, in oil	pounds														
3314	Vices, assorted				2			2							4	
3315	Vices, parallel							4								
3316	Vices, bench															
3317	Vices, B. S			8												
3318	Vices, solid box															
3319	Vices, hand															
3320	Vices, solid	pounds														
3321	Ventilators															
3322	Ventilators, tin															
3323	Ventilators, car															
3324	Ventilators, car, lamp															
3325	Valves, globe, assorted															
3326	Valves, tank											2				
3327	Valves, water, assorted															
3328	Valves, angle															
3329	Valves, check															
3330	Valves, engine															

Report showing the disposition of United States military railroad property in the military division of the Tennessee, &c.—Continued.

Running number.	Articles.	Property sold on credit to railroad companies under Executive Orders of August 8 and October 14, 1865.													
		Alabama and Florida railroad.	East Tennessee and Georgia railroad.	Mobile and Great Northern railroad.	Tennessee and Alabama railroad.	East Tennessee and Virginia railroad.	Mobile and Ohio railroad.	Tennessee and Alabama Central railroad.	Central Southern railroad.	New Orleans and Ohio railroad.	Rome railroad.	Memphis and Ohio railroad.	Southwestern railroad.	Georgia railroad and Banking Company.	New Orleans, Jackson, and Great Northern railroad.
3331	Valves, brass, pump														
3332	Valves, safety, complete														
3333	Valves, brass, pump ... pounds														
3334	Valves, brass, check ... do														
3335	Valves, brass, steam ... do														
3336	Valves, governor														
3337	Valves, engine ... pounds														
3338	Valves, safety ... do														
3339	Vermilion, English "D" ... do														
3340	Vermilion, American extra ... do														
3341	Vermilion, German ... do														
3342	Vermilion, Chinese ... do														
3343	Vermilion, Chinese ... tubes														
3344	Vermilion, scarlet ... pounds														
3345	Vermilion, chrome ... do														
3346	Vermilion ... do														
3347	Varnish, copal ... gallons														
3348	Varnish, coach body ... do						83¼								
3349	Varnish, shellac ... do														
3350	Varnish, Japan ... do														
3351	Varnish, demar ... do														
3352	Varnish, asphaltum ... do														
3353	Varnish, white ... pounds														
3354	Varnish, white ... gallons														
3355	Verdigriss ... pounds														
3356	Vitriol ... do														
3357	Wrenches, assorted	24	63		63	66	180	50	50	17	14	9			39
3358	Wrenches, monkey, assorted	2	9	24	4	6	51	7	4	2	1	1	12	12	10
3359	Wrenches, blast pipe														
3360	Wrenches, tap, assorted														
3361	Wrenches, ratchet														
3362	Wrenches, straight														

3363	Wrenches, screw					2				2					1
3364	Wrenches, bridge														
3365	Wrenches, wheel														
3366	Wrenches, key														
3367	Wrenches, hose														
3368	Wrenches, long bar														
3369	Wrenches, lathe														
3370	Wrenches, socket														1
3371	Wrenches, spanner														
3372	Wrenches, hand														
3373	Wrenches, iron tap ... pounds														
3374	Wrenches, "S"														
3375	Wrenches, pipe														
3376	Wrenches, follower														
3377	Wrenches, iron														
3378	Wrenches, packing														
3379	Wrenches, post														
3380	Wedges, stonemasons'														
3381	Wedges ... pounds														
3382	Wedges, iron														
3383	Wedges, steel														
3384	Wedges														
3385	Wedges, blacksmiths'														
3386	Wedges and feathers														
3387	Whistles, locomotive														
3388	Whistles, steam														
3389	Windlass, quaker														
3390	Windlass, hand														
3391	Wheels, tender, and truck, on axles ... pairs														
3392	Wheels, car, with axles														
3393	Wheels, car, on axles ... pairs		25												
3394	Wheels and axles ... pounds														
3395	Wheels, driving, on axles ... pairs														
3396	Wheels, turn-table ... pounds														
3397	Wheels, press gear ... do														
3398	Wheels, car														
3399	Wheels, car ... pounds														
3400	Wheels, water														
3401	Wheels, hand car ... pounds														
3402	Wheels, hand car														
3403	Wheels, cog, hand car														
3404	Wheels, car and tender														
3405	Wheels, driving														
3406	Wheels, engine truck						6								
3407	Wheels, truck ... pairs														
3408	Wheels, iron pulley														
3409	Wheels, brake ... pounds														
3410	Wheels, brake														
3411	Wheels, engine														
3412	Wheels, engine and tender, on axles ... pairs														
3413	Wheels, for counter shaft														
3414	Wheels and axles, hand car ... pairs														

Report showing the disposition of United States military railroad property in the military division of the Tennessee, &c.—Continued.

Running number.	Articles.	Property sold on credit to railroad companies under Executive orders of August 8 and October 14, 1865.													
		Alabama and Florida railroad.	East Tennessee and Georgia railroad.	Mobile and Great Northern railroad.	Tennessee and Alabama railroad.	East Tennessee and Virginia railroad.	Mobile and Ohio railroad.	Tennessee and Alabama Central railroad.	Central Southern railroad.	New Orleans and Ohio railroad.	Rome railroad.	Memphis and Ohio railroad.	Southwestern railroad.	Georgia Railroad and Banking Company.	New Orleans, Jackson, and Great Northern railroad.
3415	Wheels, car .... pairs														
3416	Wheels and axles .... sets														
3417	Wheels, engine truck, on axles .... pairs														
3418	Wheels, bevel														
3419	Wheels, fly, ten feet														
3420	Wheels, press gear														
3421	Wheels, spur														
3422	Wheels, truck														
3423	Wheels, car, 24-inch, pattern No. 25														
3424	Wheels, car, 26-inch, pattern No. 27														
3425	Wheels, freight car														
3426	Wheels, balance														
3427	Wheels, hand car .... pairs														
3428	Wheels, hand car, on axles .... pounds														
3429	Wheels, ratchet														
3430	Wicks, flat														
3431	Wicks, lamp .... pounds														
3432	Wicks, lamp .... gross														
3433	Wicking .... balls														
3434	Wire, brass .... pounds														
3435	Wire, telegraph .... do														
3436	Wire, copper .... do														
3436½	Wire, iron .... do						190						107		
3437	Wire, assorted .... do														
3438	Wire, tin .... do														
3439	Wire .... bundles														
3440	Washers, assorted .... pounds			439			1,349						1,336		
3441	Washers, cast .... do														
3442	Webbing .... yards														
3443	White, China .... pounds														
3444	White, flake, assorted .... do														
3445	White, flake .... tubes														

3446	Whiting ... pounds													332	
3447	Whiting, Spanish ... do														
3448	Wax, bees ... do														
3449	Winches, crane														
3450	Waste, cotton ... pounds														
3451	Waste, tow ... do														
3452	Waste ... do														
3453	Weights ... do														
3454	Weights														
3455	Weights, sash														
3456	Walks, plank														
3457	Webbing ... bolts														
3458	Wrenches, square														
3459	Yarn, lubricating, packing ... pounds														262
3460	Yellow, canary ... do														
3461	Yarn, packing ... reels														
3462	Yawls														
3463	Zinc, slab ... pounds												455		
3464	Zinc, sheet ... do		70												
3465	Zinc, sheet ... pieces														

Report showing the disposition of United States military railroad property in the military division of the Tennessee, &c.—Continued.

Running number.	Articles.	Property sold on credit to railroad companies under Executive Orders of August 8 and October 14, 1865.										Sold at public auction to railroad companies on credit on same terms as authorized by Executive Orders of August 8 and October 14, 1865.			
		Mississippi Central railroad.	Mississippi, Gainesville, and Tuscaloosa railroad.	Alabama and Tennessee River railroad.	Mississippi and Tennessee railroad.	Memphis, Clarksville, and Louisville railroad.	Western and Atlantic railroad.	Southwestern Iron Company.	Selma and Meridian railroad.	Nashville and Decatur railroad.	Virginia and Tennessee raiload.	McMinnville and Manchester railroad.	Mobile and Ohio railroad.	Edgefield and Kentucky railroad.	South Carolina railroad.
1	Coal .... bushels						560	25, 000							
2	Coke .... do														
3	Charcoal .... do														
4	Charcoal .... barrels														
5	Wood .... cords					3, 969¼									
6	Corn .... pounds														
7	Hay .... do														
8	Oats .... do														
9	Sacks, grain .... number														
10	Straw .... pounds														
11	Blanks														
12	Blanks, quartermasters' .... quires														
13	Blanks, way freight														
14	Books, blank, 1½-quire														
15	Books, blank, 2-quire														
16	Books, blank, 3-quire						1								
17	Books, blank, 4-quire						1								
18	Books, blank, 6-quire						2								
19	Books, blank, 8-quire														
20	Books, blank, assorted														
21	Books, ration return														
22	Books, time						8, 001								
23	Books, order														
24	Books, memorandum														
25	Books, abstract														
26	Books, indorsement														
27	Books, way-bill, copying														
28	Books, record														
29	Books, copying														
30	Books, stub									12					
31	Books, letter														

32	Books, requisition														
33	Books, discharge														
34	Books, general order														
35	Books, clothing order														
36	Books, receipt														
37	Bands, rubber														
38	Boards, file														
39	Cutters, paper														
40	Clips, letter														
41	Clips, paper														
42	Clips, board									6					
43	Clips, letter board														
44	Clips, metal														
45	Erasers														
46	Erasers, steel														
47	Erasers, rubber														
48	Envelopes														
49	Envelopes, letter									2,000					
50	Envelopes, official									2,000					
51	Files, paper									37					
52	Files, adhesive														
53	Folders, paper														
54	Fasteners, paper ... papers														
55	Holders, pen									144					
56	Holders, paper														
57	Ink, (quart) ... bottles					24				16					
58	Ink, copying ... do					24				12					
59	Ink, carmine ... do									36					
60	Ink, blue ... do														
61	Journals														
62	Ledgers														
63	Mucilage ... bottles					12				24					
64	Paper, letter, assorted ... quires						20			40					
65	Paper, flat letter ... do														
66	Paper, note ... do									40					
67	Paper, cap ... do						10			40					
68	Paper, flat cap ... do														
69	Paper, oil ... sheets									24					
70	Paper, blotting ... do									36					
71	Paper, cross section ... do														
72	Paper, envelope ... quires														
73	Paper, folio post ... do														
74	Paper, news ... do														
75	Paper, colored ... do														
76	Paper, printing ... bundles														
77	Paper, P. O ... quires														
78	Paper, heavy yellow ... lots														
79	Paper, heavy ... do														
80	Paper, white demi ... quires														
81	Pencils, lead									288					
82	Pencils, slate					100				100					
83	Pens, steel ... gross														

Report showing the disposition of United States military railroad property in the military division of the Tennessee, &c.—Continued.

Running number.	Articles.	Property sold on credit to railroad companies under Executive Orders of August 8 and October 14, 1865.										Sold at public auction to railroad companies on credit on same terms as authorized by Executive Orders of August 8 and October 14, 1865.			
		Mississippi Central railroad.	Mississippi, Gainesville, and Tuscaloosa railroad.	Alabama and Tennessee River railroad.	Mississippi and Tennessee railroad.	Memphis, Clarksville, and Louisville railroad.	Western and Atlantic railroad.	Southwestern Iron Company.	Selma and Meridian railroad.	Nashville and Decatur railroad.	Virginia and Tennessee railroad.	McMinnville and Manchester railroad.	Mobile and Ohio railroad.	Edgefield and Kentucky railroad.	South Carolina railroad.
84	Pens, steel														
85	Pens, ruling														
86	Pens, extension ... boxes														
87	Rulers, rubber									8					
88	Rulers, wood														
89	Rulers, rosewood														
90	Rulers, boxwood														
91	Rulers, mahogany														
92	Rulers, ebony														
93	Rulers, assorted														
94	Racks, pen						2			1					
95	Rings, elastic														
96	Stands, ink					2	2			20					
97	Tearers, paper														
98	Tape ... spools														
99	Weights, paper									6					
100	Wax, sealing ... pounds														
101	Buckets, tin, assorted					12									
102	Buckets, mess														
103	Buckets, slop														
104	Buckets														
105	Basins, wash					3	2			2					
106	Basins, tin wash														
107	Basins, tin														
108	Boilers, coffee									6					
109	Boilers, assorted									3					
110	Boilers, wash														
111	Boilers, meat														
112	Boilers, tin														
113	Boilers, iron														
114	Boilers with cocks														

115	Boilers, copper range														
116	Boilers, tin wash														
117	Boilers, tin wash, with cocks														
118	Brooms, hickory														
119	Brooms, splint														
120	Brooms, corn									73					1
121	Brooms, ratan														
122	Brooms			8	2		6		6						
123	Brushes, copying														
124	Brushes, window														
125	Brushes, counter									10					
126	Brushes, dust														
127	Brushes, assorted														
128	Boxes, P. O														
129	Boxes, letter														
130	Boxes, paper														
131	Boxes, dredge														
132	Boxes, twine														
133	Boxes, tin														
134	Boxes, spice														
135	Boxes, ice														
136	Boxes, sugar														
137	Boxes, salt														
138	Boxes, pepper														
139	Boxes, mess														
140	Boxes, bill-head														
141	Boxes, black walnut														
142	Boxes, cash														
143	Benches, assorted														
144	Baskets, paper														
145	Bells, office														
146	Balances, letter														
147	Boards, wash														
148	Boards, black														
149	Boards, diagram														
150	Boards, paper														
151	Boards, pressing														
152	Boards, card ... sheets														
153	Boards, binders'														
154	Boards, Bristol														
155	Bowls, sugar														
156	Bowls, wash														
157	Bowls, feet wash														
158	Bowls, assorted														
159	Bunks														
160	Bunks, single														
161	Bureaus														
162	Bedsteads														
163	Bins, flour														
164	Blocks, meat														
165	Cups														
166	Cups, palette														

Report showing the disposition of United States military railroad property in the military division of the Tennessee, &c.—Continued.

Running number.	Articles.	Property sold on credit to railroad companies under Executive Orders of August 8 and October 14, 1865.										Sold at public auction to railroad companies on credit on same terms as authorized by Executive Orders of August 8 and October 14, 1865.			
		Mississippi Central railroad.	Mississippi, Gainesville, and Tuscaloosa railroad.	Alabama and Tennesse River railroad.	Mississippi and Tennessee railroad.	Memphis, Clarksville, and Louisville railroad.	Western and Atlantic railroad.	Southwestern Iron Company.	Selma and Meridian railroad.	Nashville and Decatur railroad.	Virginia and Tennessee railroad.	McMinnville and Manchester railroad.	Mobile and Ohio railroad.	Edgefield and Kentucky railroad.	South Carolina railroad.
167	Cups, tin, assorted						2			12					
168	Cups, sponge														
169	Cups, copying														
170	Cups, molasses														
171	Cans, milk, (covered)														
172	Cans, molasses														
173	Cans, watering														
174	Covers, bucket														
175	Covers, coffee-pot														
176	Covers, oven														
177	Covers, tallow can														
178	Cleavers, meat														
179	Casters														
180	Canisters, tea														
181	Cots					2									
182	Chests, mess	3													1
183	Chests, field														
184	Chests, assorted														
185	Clocks						1			1					
186	Cupboards														
187	Cupboards, pigeon-hole														
188	Counters														
189	Chambers														
190	Chairs, assorted					11	2			20					8
191	Chairs, office														
192	Chairs, split bottom														
193	Coolers, water														1
194	Cases, tin														
195	Cases, post-office									1					
196	Cases, blank														
197	Cases, shelves, and drawers														

198	Cases, assorted					1									
199	Cases, book														
200	Cases, pillow														
201	Cases, pigeon-hole									3					
202	Closets, p.cket									5					
203	Cleaners, stove														
204	Cullenders														
205	Cushions														
206	Curtains, window														
207	Charts, time														
208	Calendars														
209	Cellars, salt														
210	Cutters, cake														
211	Carvers														
212	Carvers and forks														
213	Caps, stove pipe														
214	Counterpanes														
215	Carpet, Brussels ... yards														
216	Coverlets														
217	Desks, assorted					6	2			5					
218	Dusters														
219	Dusters, feather									1					
220	Dippers									12					
221	Dippers, tin														
222	Drums, stove														
223	Drums, sheet-iron														
224	Dishes, tin														
225	Dishes, soup														
226	Dishes, fruit														
227	Dishes, vegetable														
228	Dishes, meat														
229	Dishes, sauce														
230	Dishes, large														
231	Dishes, small														
232	Dishes, assorted														
233	Demijohns														
234	Drawers														
236	Elbows									35					
237	Elbows, stove-pipe									3					
238	Fixtures, cook-stove ... sets														
239	Forks														
240	Forks, iron														
241	Forks, flesh														
242	Forks, table									12					
243	Forks, carving														
244	Forks, large														
245	Funnels, assorted						1			12					
246	Funnels, tin, assorted														
247	Fillers, lamp					12			24	25					
248	Feeders, lamp														
249	Furniture, cherry ... lots														
250	Firkins														

Report showing the disposition of United States military railroad property in the military division of the Tennessee, &c.—Continued.

Running number.	Articles.	Property sold on credit to railroad companies under Executive Orders of August 8 and October 14, 1865.										Sold at public auction to railroad companies on credit on same terms as authorized by Executive Orders of August 8 and October 14, 1865.			
		Mississippi Central railroad.	Mississippi, Gainesville, and Tuscaloosa railroad.	Alabama and Tennessee River railroad.	Mississippi and Tennessee railroad.	Memphis, Clarksville, and Louisville railroad.	Western and Atlantic railroad.	Southwestern Iron Company.	Selma and Meridian railroad.	Nashville and Decatur railroad.	Virginia and Tennessee railroad.	McMinnville and Manchester railroad.	Mobile and Ohio railroad.	Edgefield and Kentucky railroad.	South Carolina railroad.
251	Grates														
252	Grates, nutmeg														
253	Gridirons														1
254	Gates, molasses									5					
255	Griddles, stove									9					
256	Glasses, looking														
257	Globes, lamp														
258	Grates									3					
259	Hods, coal									4					
260	Horns, tin														
261	Hooks, clothes														
262	Hooks, meat														
263	Jugs														
264	Jars, earthen														
265	Kettles, camp									6					
266	Kettles, iron														
267	Kettles, tea									6					1
268	Kettles, mess														
269	Kettles														
270	Knives														
271	Knives, table									12					
272	Knives, butcher														
273	Knives and forks ..... sets														
274	Knives and forks														3
275	Knives, carving														
276	Knives, cook														
277	Knives, chopping														
278	Lamps, office														
279	Lamps, coal-oil						3								
280	Lamps														
281	Ladles, soup														

282	Larders														
283	Lids														
284	Matting, floor ... feet														
285	Mortars														
286	Mills, coffee									3					
287	Mattresses														
288	Mops, floor														
289	Mashers, potato														
290	Nests, pigeon-hole														
291	Ovens, Dutch														
292	Ovens, bake														
293	Punches, paper														
294	Presses, letter									1					
295	Presses, letter, with stamp														
296	Presses and stands, (letter)					1									
297	Pipe, stove ... feet														
298	Pipe, stove ... joints					200	21		48	320					24
299	Pipe, stove, assorted ... pounds														
300	Pipes, connecting, for range														
301	Pans, fry														
302	Pans, try														
303	Pans, mess, assorted									2					
304	Pans, dish									3					
305	Pans, baking														2
306	Pans, dripping									16					
307	Pans, tin sauce														
308	Pans, dust														
309	Pans, stew														
310	Pans, assorted														
311	Pans, tin, assorted														
312	Pans, ash														
313	Pans, tin ... sets														
314	Pans, pie														
315	Pans, wash														
316	Pans, cake														
317	Pails, tin														
318	Pails														
319	Plates, tin									12					
320	Plates, soup														
321	Plates, sauce														
322	Plates, dinner														
323	Plates														
324	Plates, pie														
325	Plates, meat														
326	Pots, assorted									11					
327	Pots, mess														
328	Pots, tea														
329	Pots, coffee									2					
330	Pots, fire														
331	Pots, sprinkling						1			1					
332	Pots, iron														2
333	Pots, tin														

Report showing the disposition of United States military railroad property in the military division of the Tennessee, &c.—Continued.

Running number.	Articles.	Property sold on credit to railroad companies under Executive Orders of August 8 and October 14, 1865.										Sold at public auction to railroad companies on credit on same terms as authorized by Executive Orders of August 8 and October 14, 1865.			
		Mississippi Central railroad.	Mississippi, Gainesville, and Tuscaloosa railroad.	Alabama and Tennessee River railroad.	Mississippi and Tennessee railroad.	Memphis, Clarksville, and Louisville railroad.	Western and Atlantic railroad.	Southwestern Iron Company.	Selma and Meridian railroad.	Nashville and Decatur railroad.	Virginia and Tennessee railroad.	McMinnville and Manchester railroad.	Mobile and Ohio railroad.	Edgefield and Kentucky railroad.	South Carolina railroad.
334	Pots, tin stew														
335	Pots, water														
336	Pitchers														
337	Pitchers, stone														
338	Pitchers, water														
339	Pillows														
340	Pokers, assorted						26								
341	Peels, bakers'														
342	Pins, time														
343	Pins, rolling														
344	Plugs, basin														
345	Quilts														
346	Racks, letter														
347	Racks and desk, card														
348	Racks, towel														
349	Ranges and fixtures, cooking					1									
350	Ranges, cooking														
351	Ranges, patent														
352	Railing, office ... pieces														
353	Railing, hand, with banisters ... feet														
354	Refrigerators														
355	Safes, iron														
356	Safes, office														
357	Safes, fire-proof														
358	Safes, paymasters'														
359	Safes, field														
360	Safes, match														
361	Safes, twine														
362	Safes, S. P.				4		4								
363	Scissors ... pairs														
364	Shears ... do														

365	Shears, lamp .... do														
366	Shears, banker's .... do									1					
367	Slates, assorted					6				14					
368	Shovels, fire						26								
369	Shovels, baker's														
370	Sieves					6									
371	Sieves, flour									6					
372	Sieves, meal														
373	Sieves, fine														
374	Scuttles, coal														
375	Scoops														
376	Scoops, flour														
377	Spittoons														
378	Spittoons, wooden														
379	Shades														
380	Shades, lamp														
381	Shades, lamp, (tin)														
382	Shades and clasps														
383	Spiders									2					
384	Spoons, table									12					
385	Spoons, tea														
386	Spoons, basting														
387	Spoons, assorted														
388	Skimmers														
389	Steamers														
390	Steamers, tin														
391	Skillets									10					
392	Skillets, stove														
393	Stoves, box					10			12	11					
394	Stoves, sheet-iron					1				1					
395	Stoves, cast-iron														
396	Stoves, coal					2	2								
397	Stoves, open coal														
398	Stoves, tent														
399	Stoves, camp														
400	Stoves, cooking									7					
401	Stoves, cooking, and pipe														
402	Stoves, cooking, and fixtures					5				5					
403	Stoves, cooking, complete														
404	Stoves, parlor														
405	Stoves and pipe														
406	Stoves, glue														
407	Stoves, heating														
408	Stoves, assorted									8					
409	Stoves, office														
410	Stoves, shop														
411	Stoves, cylinder														
412	Stoves, old .... tons														
413	Stands														
414	Stands, wash						1								
415	Stands, letter-press														
416	Stands, light, and hose														

Report showing the disposition of United States military railroad property in the military division of the Tennessee, &c.—Continued.

Running number.	Articles.	Property sold on credit to railroad companies under Executive Orders of August 8 and October 14, 1865.										Sold at public auction to railroad companies on credit on same terms as authorized by Executive Orders of August 8 and October 14, 1865.			
		Mississippi Central railroad.	Mississippi, Gainesville, and Tuscaloosa railroad.	Alabama and Tennessee River railroad.	Mississippi and Tennessee railroad.	Memphis, Clarksville, and Louisville railroad.	Western and Atlantic railroad.	Southwestern Iron Company.	Selma and Meridian railroad.	Nashville and Decatur railroad.	Virginia and Tennessee railroad.	McMinnville and Manchester railroad.	Mobile and Ohio railroad.	Edgefield and Kentucky railroad.	South Carolina railroad.
417	Stands, andlamp globe														
418	Stands, light														
419	Stands, bed														
420	Snuffers ... pairs														
421	Snuffers, candle ... do														
422	Stools						2			5					
423	Stools, bench														
424	Spouts, funnel														
425	Shelves and brackets ... sets														
426	Sticks, candle					36									
427	Steels, carving														
428	Saucers, tin														
429	Saucers														
430	Sinks														
431	Sheets														
432	Screens														
433	Settees														
434	Strainers, coffee														
435	Sprinklers														
436	Sprinklers, copper														
437	Sacks, bed														
438	Scales, letter														
439	Tables, field														
440	Tables, camp														
441	Tables, office														
442	Tables, round														
443	Tables, centre														
444	Tables, dining														
445	Tables, draughting														
446	Tables, assorted					1				1					
447	Tables, time														

448	Trimmers, lamp														
449	Tumblers														
450	Thimbles, stovepipe														
451	Toasters														
452	Tubs, wash														
453	Tubs, bathing														
454	Ticks, bed														
455	Troughs, bread														
456	Urinals														
457	Wardrobes														1
458	Waiters														
459	Ambulances														
460	Axles, ambu ance														
461	Blankets, saddle														
462	Bits, mullen														
463	Bridles, riding														
464	Bridles, blind														
465	Buckets, U. S. horse														
466	Bows, wagon														
467	Bows, ox														
468	Bows, ambulance														
469	Brushes, horse														
470	Boxes, feed														
471	Boxes, wagon														
472	Boxes, cutting														
473	Boxes, ambulance pipe														
474	Boards, foot														
475	Bolsters, extra log wagon														
476	Bolsters, army wagon														
477	Bolts, king														
478	Bolts, king ... pounds														
479	Bolts, tongue														
480	Bodies, wagon														
481	Bodies, cart														
482	Breeching, cart														
482½	Bits, bridle														
483	Beds, axle														
484	Carts														
485	Chains, halter														
486	Chains, trace														
487	Chains, fifth														
488	Chains, bearing														
489	Chains, breast														
490	Chains, spreader														
491	Chains, stretcher														
492	Chains, stretcher, and S. S														
493	Chains, ox														
494	Collars, horse														
495	Collars, mule														
496	Covers, wagon														
497	Combs, curry														

Report showing the disposition of United States military railroad property in the military division of the Tennessee, &c.—Continued.

Running number.	Articles.	Property sold on credit to railroad companies under Executive Orders of August 8 and Ootober 14, 1865.										Sold at public auction to railroad companies on credit on same terms as authorized by Executive Orders of August 8 and October 14, 1865.			
		Mississippi Central railroad.	Mississippi, Gainesville, and Tuscaloosa railroad.	Alabama and Tennessee River railroad.	Mississippi and Tennessee railroad.	Memphis, Clarksville, and Louisville railroad.	Western and Atlantic railroad.	Southwestern Iron Company.	Selma and Meridian railroad.	Nashville and Decatur railroad.	Virginia and Tennessee railroad.	McMinnville and Manchester railroad.	Mobile and Ohio railroad.	Edgefield and Kentucky railroad.	South Carolina railroad.
498	Cruppers														
499	Drays														
500	Felloes, wagon														
501	Gears, running														
502	Gearings, hind														
503	Gearings, front														
504	Gates, end														
505	Horses														
506	Harness ..... sets														
507	Harness, S. S. ambulance														
508	Harness, S. S. wheel														
509	Harness, S. S. lead														
510	Harness, S. S. wheel-horse														
511	Harness, S. S. wheel-mule														
512	Harness, S. S. lead-mule														
513	Harness, cart														
514	Harness, dray														
515	Hames, horse ..... pairs														
516	Hames ..... do														
517	Halters, rope														
518	Halters, head														
519	Halters, head, and strap														
520	Halters and chains														
521	Hounds, front, army wagon														
522	Hounds, hind, army wagon														
523	Hammers, wagon														
524	Jacks, wagon														
525	Kegs, ambulance														
526	Lines, cart														
527	Lines, check														
528	Lines, lead														

529	Lines, 2-horse														
530	Leathers, sweat														
531	Links, open														
532	Mules														
533	Martingales														
534	Oxen														
535	Poles, ridge														
536	Poles, coupling														
537	Rakes, stable														
538	Rims, bent ambulance														
539	Rims, ox-yoke bow														
540	Rings, open														
541	Rails, body														
542	Stretchers														
543	Spreaders														
544	Saddles, riding														
545	Saddles, wagon														
546	Saddles, cart														
547	Saddles														
548	Sticks, jockey														
549	Sticks, cart-dumping														
550	Springs, ambulance														
551	Sprinklers, wagon														
552	Sprinklers, cart														
553	Straps, neck														
554	Straps, coupling														
555	Straps, neck and chain														
556	Straps, back														
557	Straps, choke														
558	Straps, halter														
559	Straps, stirrup														
560	Straps, yoke														
561	Spokes, wagon														
562	Spokes														
563	Spokes, army wagon														
564	Spokes, 2-horse wagon														
565	Spokes, ambulance														
566	Stirrups, wooden														
567	Stirrups, leather														
568	Shafts, cart														
569	Shafts														
570	Strings, tie														
571	Stocks, whip														
572	Trees, single														
573	Trees, double														
574	Trees, saddle														
575	Tongues, wagon														
576	Tongues, rough														
577	Troughs, feed														
578	Tires, wagon														
579	Wheels, hind														
580	Wheels, front														

Report showing the disposition of United States military railroad property in the military division of the Tennessee, &c.—Continued.

Running number.	Articles.	Property sold on credit to railroad companies under Executive Orders of August 8 and October 14, 1865.										Sold at public auction to railroad companies on credit on same terms as authorized by Executive Orders of August 8 and October 14, 1865.			
		Mississippi Central railroad.	Mississippi, Gainesville, and Tuscaloosa railroad.	Alabama and Tennessee River railroad.	Mississippi and Tennessee railroad.	Memphis, Clarksville, and Louisville railroad.	Western and Atlantic railroad.	Southwestern Iron Company.	Selma and Meridian railroad.	Nashville and Decatur railroad.	Virginia and Tennessee railroad.	McMinnville and Manchester railroad.	Mobile and Ohio railroad.	Edgefield and Kentucky railroad.	South Carolina railroad.
581	Wheels, wagon														
582	Wagons, lumber														
583	Wagons, army														
584	Wagons, spring														
585	Wagons, log														
586	Wagons, 2-horse														
587	Wagons, ox														
588	Wagons, wood														
589	Wagons, water														
590	Wagons, box														
591	Wagons														
592	Whips, wagon														
593	Yokes, ox														
594	Yokes and bows, ox														
595	Axes, chopping														
596	Axes, chopping, and handles														
597	Axes, felling														
598	Axes, felling, and handles														
599	Axes, hand														
600	Axes, pick														
601	Axes, broad														
602	Axes, narrow														
603	Axes, assorted														
604	Augers ... sets														
605	Augers														
606	Augers, long, assorted														
607	Augers, hollow ... sets														
608	Augers, gas-fitting														
609	Augers, bridge														
610	Augers, pump ... sets														
611	Augers, boring machine														

612	Augers, machine	sets														
613	Augers, machine															
614	Augers and handles															
615	Augers and handles, ¼-inch															
616	Augers and handles, 1½-inch															
617	Augers, spike															
618	Augers, convex															
619	Augers, wheelwright															
620	Augers, nut															
621	Anvils, assorted															
622	Anvils, cast															
623	Anvils, wrought															
624	Anvils, block															
625	Anvils, wrought	pounds														
626	Anvils, blacksmiths'															
627	Awls, scratch															
628	Awls, brad															
629	Awls, b-lt															
630	Awls, scribe															
631	Awls and tacks, shoe															
632	Awls, scratch, and handles															
633	Awls, peg, and handles															
634	Adzes															
635	Adzes and handles															
636	Adzes, railroad															
637	Adzes, foot or carpenters'															
638	Axles, car	pounds														
639	Axles, car															
639½	Arbors, circular saw															
640	Axles, car and tender															
641	Axles, truck	pounds														
642	Axles, engine-driving															
643	Axles, engine truck	pounds														
644	Axles, tender															
645	Axles, truck										14					
646	Axles, tender truck															
647	Axles, timber buggy															
648	Anchors															
649	Acid, oxalic	pounds														
650	Acid, muriatic	do														
651	Acid	do														
652	Aqua ammonia	do														
653	Aloes	do														
654	Alum	do														
655	Antimony	do														
656	Alcohol	gallons														
657	Ammoniac, sal	pounds														
658	Arms, hand-car															
659	Arms, engine pump															
660	Arms, seat, cast	pounds														
661	Apparatus, automatic	sets														
662	Asphaltum	gallons														

Report showing the disposition of United States military railroad property in the military division of the Tennessee, &c.—Continued.

Running number.	Articles.	Property sold on credit to railroad companies under Executive Orders of August 8 and October 14, 1865.										Sold at public auction to railroad companies on credit on same terms as authorized by Executive Orders of August 8 and October 14, 1865.			
		Mississippi Central railroad.	Mississippi, Gainesville, and Tuscaloosa railroad.	Alabama and Tennessee River railroad.	Mississippi and Tennessee railroad.	Memphis, Clarksville, and Louisville railroad.	Western and Atlantic railroad.	Southwestern Iron Company.	Selma and Meridian railroad.	Nashville and Decatur railroad.	Virginia and Tennessee railroad.	McMinnville and Manchester railroad.	Mobile and Ohio railroad.	Edgefield and Kentucky railroad.	South Carolina railroad.
663	Bellows, blacksmiths'		1			4	1			3					
664	Bellows, assorted														
665	Bellows, hand									1					
666	Bellows, 48-inch														
667	Bars, switch														
668	Bars, switch ... sets														
669	Bars, lining									2					
670	Bars, raising														
671	Bars, iron	1	2	9	2	77	8	1	6	10					
672	Bars, pinch														
673	Bars, pinch ... pounds														
674	Bars, grate ... do					8,455				86					
675	Bars, draw									24					
676	Bars, assorted														
677	Bars, timber									8					
678	Bars, grate														
679	Bars, pinch steel														
680	Bars, wrought iron pinch ... pounds														
681	Bars, switch ... do														
682	Bars, grate ... sets														
683	Bars, carpenters'														
684	Bars, pry and pinch														
685	Bars, pry														
686	Bars, fish ... pounds														
687	Bars, tamping					30				27					
688	Bars, crow									42					
689	Bars, claw					25			24	40					
690	Bars, wrench														
691	Bars, engine coupling														
692	Bars, boring									5					
693	Bars, cylinder boring														

694	Bars, long														
695	Bars, short														
696	Bars, steel														
697	Bars, assorted ... pounds									1					
698	Bars, pins, and bolts ... do														
699	Brushes, varnish, assorted														
700	Brushes, C. H.									12					
701	Brushes, W. W.						34								
702	Brushes, scrub					12	1								
703	Brushes, painters' dust					36	1			24					
704	Brushes, paint, assorted														
705	Brushes, flat					96	144			60					
706	Brushes, oval														
707	Brushes, marking														
708	Brushes, striping														
709	Brushes, car window														
710	Brushes, artists'									6					
711	Brushes, artists' red sable														
712	Brushes, glue														
713	Brushes, sash														
714	Brushes, whitewash ... lots														
715	Brushes, machinists'														
716	Braces														
717	Braces, iron														
718	Braces, wood									4					
719	Braces and bits ... sets														
720	Braces and bits					3			6						
721	Braces and bits, car ... sets														
722	Braces, hand														
723	Braces, joiner														
724	Braces, switch														
725	Braces, pedestal									6					
726	Braces, ratchet ... sets									2					
727	Braces, truck ... pounds														
728	Braces, engine														
729	Braces, engine bar														
730	Blenders, painters'														
731	Blenders, painters'														
732	Bits, brace ... sets														
733	Bits ... do														
734	Bits, auger, assorted ... do														
735	Bits, auger, assorted								31	3					
736	Bits, gimlet														
737	Bits, gimlet ... sets														
738	Bits, plough plane														
739	Bits, plough plane ... sets														
740	Bits, double plane														
741	Bits, car														
742	Bits, car ... sets														
743	Bits, centre								6	1					
744	Bits, rose														
745	Bits, (sets of six each)									21					

Report showing the disposition of United States military railroad property in the military division of the Tennessee, &c.—Continued.

Running number.	Articles.	Property sold on credit to railroad companies under Executive Orders of August 8 and October 14, 1865.										Sold at public auction to railroad companies on credit on same terms as authorized by Executive Orders of August 8 and October 14, 1865.			
		Mississippi Central railroad.	Mississippi, Gainesville, and Tuscaloosa railroad.	Alabama and Tennessee River railroad.	Mississippi and Tennessee railroad.	Memphis, Clarksville, and Louisville railroad.	Western and Atlantic railroad.	Southwestern Iron Company.	Selma and Meridian railroad.	Nashville and Decatur railroad.	Virginia and Tennessee railroad.	McMinnville and Manchester railroad.	Mobile and Ohio railroad.	Edgefield and Kentucky railroad.	South Carolina railroad.
746	Bits, gummer														
717	Bits, ratchet drill		6												
748	Bits, assorted														
749	Bits, centre ... sets														
750	Bits, planer														
751	Bits, double-cut														
752	Bits, brace														
753	Buts, assorted ... pairs					234				288					
754	Buts, brass, assorted														
755	Buts, brass, assorted ... pairs														
756	Buts														
757	Buts, loose joint														
758	Buts, wrought, assorted														
759	Buts, cast-iron ... pairs														
760	Buts, assorted														
761	Buts, wrought ... pairs														
762	Buts, fast														
763	Buts, cast														
764	Buts, rivet														
765	Buts, flat														
766	Buts, wrought-iron ... pairs														
767	Buts, patent ... do														
768	Buts, cast, loose joint ... do														
769	Buts, wrought, common joint														
770	Buts, cast, loose joint														
771	Buts, wrought-iron														
772	Bolts, tank hoop														
773	Bolts, iron hexagon-head ... pounds														
774	Bolts, fish-bar ... do									1,940					
775	Bolts					481	6,435								
776	Bolts, carriage ... pounds														

777	Bolts, carriage									500					
778	Bolts, iron bar									12					
779	Bolts, brass, assorted														
780	Bolts, barrel														
781	Bolts, brass flush														
782	Bolts, fire														
783	Bolts, long ¾-inch ... pounds														
784	Bolts, ring														
785	Bolts, chain door														
786	Bolts, tower														
787	Bolts, square head ... pounds														
788	Bolts, bridge ... do														
789	Bolts, wrought ... do														
790	Bolts, wrought-iron														
791	Bolts and nuts														
792	Bolts and butts														
793	Bolts, brass knob														
794	Bolts, wagon														
795	Bolts, steel-spring square														
796	Bolts, pulley														
797	Bolts, coupling														
798	Bolts and keys														
799	Bolts ... pounds					1, 324									
800	Bolts, door														
801	Bolts, bridge														
802	Bolts and nuts ... pounds														
803	Blocks, punch														
804	Blocks, swedge					1	1			1					
805	Blocks, die ... pounds														
806	Blocks, iron pulley														
807	Blocks, iron														
808	Blocks, purchase														
809	Blocks, notch														
810	Blocks, snatch					4				7					
811	Blocks, head, with truck														
812	Blocks, upsetting														
813	Blocks, patent														
814	Blocks, tackle ... sets														
815	Blocks, tackle		2			8			2						
816	Blocks and tackle ... sets														
817	Blocks and tackle														
818	Blocks, assorted														
819	Blocks, double-tackle									15					
820	Blocks, head														
821	Blocks, triple									7					
822	Blocks, assorted ... pounds														
823	Blocks, assorted ... pairs														
824	Blocks, cast-iron swedge ... pounds														
825	Blocks, cast-iron swedge														
826	Blocks, pillow ... pounds														
827	Blocks, single														
828	Blocks, double														

Report showing the disposition of United States military railroad property in the military division of the Tennessee, &c.—Continued.

Running number.	Articles.	Property sold on credit to railroad companies under Executive Orders of August 8 and October 14, 1865.										Sold at public auction to railroad companies on credit on same terms as authorized by Executive Orders of August 8 and October 14, 1865.			
		Mississippi Central railroad.	Mississippi, Gainesville, and Tuscaloosa railroad.	Alabama and Tennessee River railroad.	Mississippi and Tennessee railroad.	Memphis, Clarksville, and Louisville railroad.	Western and Atlantic railroad.	Southwestern Iron Company.	Selma and Meridian railroad.	Nashville and Decatur railroad.	Virginia and Tennessee railroad.	McMinnville and Manchester railroad.	Mobile and Ohio railroad.	Edgefield and Kentucky railroad.	South Carolina railroad.
829	Blocks, head .... sets														
830	Blocks, double-head .... do														
831	Blocks, cast-iron swedge and tackle .... do														
832	Blocks, gum .... pounds														
833	Blocks, single														
834	Blocks, tackle .... pairs														
835	Buckets, assorted					36	51								
836	Buckets, water														1
837	Buckets, fire														
838	Buckets, wood									74					
839	Buckets														
840	Buckets, engine		1			13	2	1		6					
841	Buckets, iron														
842	Buckets, coal														
843	Buckets, varnish														
844	Buckets, tar														
845	Buckets, paint						27								
846	Buckets, rubber														
847	Buckets, sand														
848	Buckets, swing														
849	Buckets, stiff														
850	Buckets, well														
851	Buckets, mortar														
852	Buckets, leather														
853	Boilers, steam						1								
854	Boilers, tin-flue														
855	Boilers, small-flue														
856	Boilers, double-flue														
857	Boilers, 14 feet long, 40 inches diameter														
858	Boilers, tubular, 12 feet long, 42 inches diameter														
859	Boilers, steam, 2 flues, 21 ft. long, 34 inches diameter														

860	Boilers, steam, 4 flues, 24 ft. long, 39 inches diameter														
861	Boilers, stationary														
862	Boilers, iron-punch														
863	Boilers, iron-flue, 26 feet x 44 inches														
864	Brass, old ... pounds														
865	Brass, sheet ... do								137½						
866	Brass ... do				1,309										
867	Brass, scrap ... do														
868	Brass, wrought ... do														
869	Brass turnings ... do														
870	Brasses ... do														
871	Brasses, truck ... do		178							2,972					
872	Bricks, common							9,000							
873	Bricks, setting, for boilers														
874	Bricks, fire														
875	Bricks, soap, fire														
876	Bricks, split, fire														
877	Bricks, key														
878	Burlaps ... yards				470				329	360					
879	Buttons, assorted ... gross						4								
880	Buttons, upholsterers' ... do														
881	Buttons, hand ... sets														
882	Buttons, brass, on plates									36					
883	Buttons, brass ... gross														
884	Buttons, brass														
885	Brown, Vandyke ... pounds														
886	Brown, Spanish ... do					865									
887	Brown, Vandyke ... tubes														
888	Black, India ... pounds														
889	Black, lamp ... do					30				4					
890	Black, lamp ... tubes														
891	Black, Japan ... barrels														
892	Black, ivory ... tubes														
893	Blue, ultramarine ... pounds														
894	Blue, Prussian ... do						17								
895	Black, blue ... do														
896	Black, drop ... do					1½									
897	Blue, cobalt ... tubes														
898	Blacking, stove ... papers														
899	Bronze, gold ... do														
900	Brilliant, American ... tubes														
901	Bells, gong, hanging														
902	Bells, engine														
903	Bells, engine, alarm			8	1	3	7		6	12					
904	Bells, engine, gong										2				
905	Bells, alarm														
906	Bells, engine and frame									1					
907	Bells, cast-steel														
908	Bells, cab														
909	Balances, spring			3			1		4						
910	Balances, locomotive spring					12				15					
911	Balances, iron beam														

Report showing the disposition of United States military railroad property in the military division of the Tennessee, &c.—Continued.

Running number.	Articles.	Property sold on credit to railroad companies under Executive Orders of August 8 and October 14, 1865.										Sold at public auction to railroad companies on credit on same terms as authorized by Executive Orders of August 8 and October 14, 1865.			
		Mississippi Central railroad.	Mississippi, Gainesville, and Tuscaloosa railroad.	Alabama and Tennessee River railroad.	Mississippi and Tennessee railroad.	Memphis, Clarksville, and Louisville railroad.	Western and Atlantic railroad.	Southwestern Iron Company.	Selma and Meridian railroad.	Nashville and Decatur railroad.	Virginia and Tennessee railroad.	McMinnville and Manchester railroad.	Mobile and Ohio railroad.	Edgefield and Kentucky railroad.	South Carolina railroad.
912	Balances, beam shive														
913	Balances, steam														
914	Balances, elliptic spring														
915	Balances, counter														
916	Bushings, brass														
917	Bushings, gas-pipe														
918	Bushings, bell cord									32					
919	Bushings, brass gland														
920	Bushings, silver-plated														
921	Brads, patent, assorted ... papers														
922	Bunting, assorted ... yards			16	2	82	14	2	52½	40½					
923	Bunting, red, assorted ... do														
924	Burners, common														
925	Burners, patent														
926	Burners, eureka														
927	Burners, screw														
928	Brakes														
929	Brakes, lever ... pounds														
930	Brakes, car														
931	Bevels, assorted														
932	Bevels, square														
933	Bevels, T					3									
934	Boards, guttering														
935	Boards, bulletin														
936	Boards, tally														
937	Boards, draft									2					
938	Boards, running														
939	Boards, straw ... pounds														
940	Boards, pressing														
941	Boards, binders'														
942	Boards, sign														

943	Brooms, hair														
944	Brooms, stable														
945	Bottoms, composition ... pounds														
946	Bottoms, copper ... do														
947	Bottoms, dipper														
948	Bottoms, bolt head														
949	Boxes, emery														
950	Boxes, rivet														
951	Boxes, wood														
952	Boxes, tinder	1		16	6	16	16	2	12		7		5	3	
953	Boxes, engine ... pounds														
954	Boxes, engine			16	4		13	2	12						
955	Boxes, tool	1				12				9	7		6	1	
956	Boxes, packing														
957	Boxes, tinder														
958	Boxes, axle														
959	Boxes, lamp														
960	Boxes, link														
961	Boxes, oil							1							
962	Boxes, hand car ... pounds														
963	Boxes, car, (Wood's patent) ... do														
964	Boxes, assorted														
965	Boxes, engine truck ... pounds														
966	Boxes, roller														
967	Boxes, iron														
968	Boxes, screw, blued														
969	Boxes, signal-light														
970	Boxes, shoeing														
971	Boxes, cutting														
972	Boxes, drawing-paper														
973	Boxes, cast														
974	Boxes, journal														
975	Belting leather, assorted ... feet			497	50	703½	1,693		108	3,104					
976	Belting, gum ... do				25										
977	Belting, rubber ... do														
978	Belting, assorted ... do														
979	Bottoms, tin lamp														
980	Bottoms, car lamp														
981	Blades, hack-saw														
982	Brackets ... pounds														
983	Brackets														
984	Brackets, swing														
985	Buggies, timber					12				4					
986	Borers, cylinder														
987	Borers, cylinder, portable														
988	Borers, tap														
989	Borers, hand														
990	Barrels														
991	Bodkins														
992	Barrows, wheel		12			79	1								
993	Bridges, truss ... feet														
994	Bridges, arch truss, McCallum's pat. inflexible ... do														

Report showing the disposition of United States military railroad property in the military division of the Tennessee, &c.—Continued.

Running number.	Articles.	Property sold on credit to railroad companies under Executive Orders of August 8 and October 14, 1865.										Sold at public auction to railroad companies on credit on same terms as authorized by Executive Orders of August 8 and October 14, 1865.			
		Mississippi Central railroad.	Mississippi, Gainesville, and Tuscaloosa railroad.	Alabama and Tennessee River railroad.	Mississippi and Tennessee railroad.	Memphis, Clarksville, and Louisville railroad.	Western and Atlantic railroad.	Southwestern Iron Company.	Selma and Meridian railroad.	Nashville and Decatur railroad.	Virginia and Tennessee railroad.	McMinnville and Manchester railroad.	Mobile and Ohio railroad.	Edgefield and Kentucky railroad.	South Carolina railroad.
995	Borax .... pounds						5			10					
996	Benches, stationery .... feet						100								
997	Benches, work						20			2					
998	Benches, vice														
999	Bearings, centre .... pounds														
1000	Buildings						2								
1001	Buildings and water tank														
1002	Burrs .... pounds														
1003	Burrs, copper .... do									10					
1004	Bumpers .... do														
1005	Buttresses														
1006	Bumpers														
1007	Bodies, box car														
1008	Breeching .... pounds														
1009	Bibbs, finished, S. S. and S														
1010	Buckles, assorted														
1011	Buckles, harness .... gross														
1012	Buckles, roller, assorted .... do														
1013	Buckles, assorted .... do														
1014	Blocks, railroad splice, Trimble's wooden														
1015	Backs, car-seat														
1016	Bands, spring .... pounds														
1017	Bands, gum .... do														
1018	Blinds, window														
1019	Boats, flat														
1020	Baskets, medicine														
1021	Benzine .... gallons														
1022	Burgois No. 8, 3 "D" .... pounds														
1023	Buckles, round leg, ruled .... gross														
1024	Bolts, stay									36					
1025	Braces, tank														

1026	Barges														
1027	Burners, gas														
1027¼	Chisels and handles														
1027½	Chisels, cold	1	16	16	3	309	14	2	12	207					
1027¾	Chisels, hand cold														
1028	Chisels, chipping														
1029	Chisels, hand chipping														
1030	Chisels, firmer														
1031	Chisels, firmer ... sets														
1032	Chisels, socket firmer ... do														
1033	Chisels, socket														
1034	Chisels, framing ... sets														
1035	Chisels, framing				24	21				49					
1036	Chisels, track									24					
1037	Chisels, cold track														
1038	Chisels, masons'														
1039	Chisels, corner														
1040	Chisels, bolt														
1041	Chisels, splitting														
1042	Chisels, coppersmiths'														
1043	Chisels, tamping														
1044	Chisels, B. S						27								
1045	Chisels, cape														
1046	Chisels, assorted														
1047	Chisels, carpenters'														
1048	Chisels, gouging									9					
1049	Chisels, socket ... sets														
1050	Chisels, socket framing														
1051	Chisels, socket, and handles														
1052	Chisels, oval back														
1053	Chisels, mortise														
1054	Chisels, tinners' ... sets														
1055	Chills, frog														
1056	Calipers, assorted ... pairs					6				20					
1057	Calipers, spring ... do														
1058	Compasses, assorted ... do														
1059	Compasses, wing ... do														
1060	Cups, oil				16	36									
1061	Cups, oil, spring bottom														
1062	Cups, tallow									12					
1063	Cups, tin paint														
1064	Cups, tin striping														
1065	Cups, brass														
1066	Cups, steam chest oil				4	12									
1067	Cups, valve oil														
1068	Cups, brass oil														
1069	Cups, varnish														
1070	Cans, powder														
1071	Cans, engine oil														
1072	Cans, oil, spring-bottom									12					
1073	Cans, tallow	1								2	3				
1074	Cans, assorted		8	16	6	53	21	2	18	69	8				

Report showing the disposition of United States military railroad property in the military division of the Tennessee, &c.—Continued.

Running number.	Articles.	Property sold on credit to railroad companies under Executive Orders of August 8 and October 14, 1865.										Sold at public auction to railroad companies on credit on same terms as authorized by Executive Orders of August 8 and October 14, 1865.			
		Mississippi Central railroad.	Mississippi, Gainesville, and Tuscaloosa railroad.	Alabama and Tennessee River railroad.	Mississippi and Tennessee railroad.	Memphis, Clarksville, and Louisville railroad.	Western and Atlantic railroad.	Southwestern Iron Company.	Selma and Meridian railroad.	Nashville and Decatur railroad.	Virginia and Tennessee railroad.	McMinnville and Manchester railroad.	Mobile and Ohio railroad.	Edgefield and Kentucky railroad.	South Carolina railroad.
1075	Cans, oil, assorted	2													
1076	Cans, tin, assorted														1
1077	Cans, emery									12					
1078	Cans, bench oil														
1079	Couplings, tender ...pounds														
1080	Couplings, 3-link			12		89									
1081	Couplings, 3-link ...pounds														
1082	Couplings, straight			50											
1083	Couplings, crooked			42		66									
1084	Couplings, brass union, assorted ...pairs														
1085	Couplings, clamp and screw														
1086	Couplings, hose														
1087	Couplings, chain ...pounds									980					
1088	Couplings ...do									1,888					
1089	Couplings, brass hose ...do														
1090	Couplings, hose														
1091	Couplings, assorted														
1092	Chains, engine										3				
1093	Chains, assorted														
1094	Chains, log														
1095	Chains, switch			8	1		6	1	12	12					
1096	Chains, Powers' endless					4									
1097	Chains, brake ...pounds														
1098	Chains, large														
1099	Chains, small														
1100	Chains, civil engineers'														
1101	Chains, surveyors', (100 feet)														
1102	Chains, switch ...pounds														
1103	Chains, log ...do														
1104	Chain, assorted ...feet														
1105	Chain, assorted ...pounds									905					

No.	Article	Unit														
1106	Chain, cable	do														
1107	Chain, cable	feet														
1108	Chain, German	do														
1109	Chain, German coil	do									100					
1110	Chain, coil, proved, ⅝-inch	pounds														
1111	Chain, coil, assorted	do					386	359								
1112	Castings, assorted	do					12,236	15,611			36,068					
1113	Castings, iron	do														
1114	Castings, pump	do														
1115	Castings, brass	do					2,285				5,743					
1116	Castings, grate bar	do														
1117	Castings, old stove	lots														
1118	Castings, car	pounds														
1119	Castings, tender	do														
1120	Caps, double															
1121	Caps, gas pipe															
1122	Clamps, iron	pairs					4									
1123	Clamps, steel										9					
1124	Clamps, cabinet-makers'															
1125	Clamps, saddlers'															
1126	Clamps, switch															
1127	Clamps, belt						2									
1128	Clamps, spring															
1129	Clamps, block	sets														
1130	Clamps, horseshoe										5					
1131	Clamps	pairs														
1132	Clamps	pounds														
1133	Clamps, iron horse										63					
1134	Clamps, iron										5					
1135	Clamps, iron, for tender										10					
1136	Clamps, boiler															
1137	Clamps, chimney															
1138	Clamps, saw-set															
1139	Clamps, wood bench															
1140	Clamps, screw															
1141	Cars, box		30	4	36	28	74	155		40	8	42	12			
1142	Cars, box freight															
1143	Cars, flat		16	6	23	20	40	56	17	10	1	12	9			7
1144	Cars, wrecking							1								
1145	Cars, passenger						3	3								1
1146	Cars, hand			1							14					
1147	Cars, truck						3				15					
1148	Cars, caboose															1
1149	Cars, coal															
1150	Cars, stock															
1151	Cars, push or dump															
1152	Cutters, card															
1153	Cutters, lead															
1153½	Cutters, cast-steel															
1154	Cutters, boring										6					
1155	Cutters, iron															
1156	Covers, cylinder head															

Report showing the disposition of United States military railroad property in the military division of the Tennessee, &c.—Continued.

Running number.	Articles.	Property sold on credit to railroad companies under Executive Orders of August 8 and October 14, 1865.										Sold at public auction to railroad companies on credit on same terms as authorized by Executive Orders of August 8 and October 14, 1865.			
		Mississippi Central railroad.	Mississippi, Gainesville, and Tuscaloosa railroad.	Alabama and Tennessee River railroad.	Mississippi and Tennessee railroad.	Memphis, Clarksville, and Louisville railroad.	Western and Atlantic railroad.	Southwestern Iron Company.	Selma and Meridian railroad.	Nashville and Decatur railroad.	Virginia and Tennessee railroad.	McMinnville and Manchester railroad.	Mobile and Ohio railroad.	Edgefield and Kentucky railroad.	South Carolina railroad.
1157	Covers, flag					1				12					
1158	Covers, box														
1159	Covers, hand-car ... pounds														
1160	Covers, axle-box ... do														
1161	Covers, cushion														
1162	Covers, enamelled														
1163	Covers, plush														
1164	Covers, sand box														
1165	Covers, dome														
1166	Covers, smoke-stack														
1167	Covers, smoke-stack hand hole														
1168	Crucibles														
1169	Cylinders, steam engine									24					
1170	Cylinders, locomotive														
1171	Cylinders, 5 feet long, 12-inch bore														
1172	Chairs, guard rail														
1173	Chairs, railroad, assorted														
1174	Chairs, railroad ... pounds														
1175	Chairs, frog														
1176	Chairs, head ... sets														
1177	Chairs, step														
1178	Chairs, assorted														
1179	Chairs, railroad guard														
1180	Cocks, waste														
1181	Cocks, miss gauge														
1182	Cocks, lock														
1183	Cocks, stop														
1184	Cocks, blow-off					6									
1185	Cocks, bibb									12					
1186	Cocks, bibb, brass									12					
1187	Cocks, pet														

1188	Cocks, gauge			12	24		24								
1189	Cocks, racking														
1190	Cocks, heater and cylinder														
1191	Cocks, steam, assorted														
1192	Cocks, brass														
1193	Cocks, cylinder				4	4				24					
1194	Cocks, h ater														
1195	Cocks, water														
1196	Cocks, lever														
1197	Cocks, rough														
1198	Cocks, air														
1199	Cocks, basin														
1200	Cocks, gas														
1201	Cocks, steam-gauge														
1202	Cocks, steam-stop														
1203	Chimneys, assorted														
1204	Chimneys, head-light									108					
1205	Chimneys, flint														
1206	Chimneys, stationary smoke-stack														
1207	Chimneys, lamp, assorted		6	8	1		13	1	6						
1208	Chimneys, coal-oil lamp														
1209	Cases, drawing														
1210	Cases, engine tool-box key														
1211	Cases, tin stencil														
1212	Cases, medicine														
1213	Cases, turning paper														
1214	Cupolas														
1215	Copper, bar .... pounds														
1216	Copper, assorted .... do														
1217	Copper, sheet .... do		137		293	1, 020	957			3, 472					
1218	Copper, ingot .... do														
1219	Copper, scrap .... do														
1220	Copper, tinned .... do														
1221	Copper, pig .... do									3, 010					
1222	Cloth, emery .... quires				20	40				40					
1223	Cloth, emery .... gross														
1224	Cloth, gum .... pounds														
1225	Cloth, enamelled .... yards														
1226	Cloth, enamelled .... pieces														
1227	Cloth, tracing .... rolls														
1228	Cloth, tracing .... yards														
1229	Crayons .... gross														
1230	Chalk, white .... pounds					25				10					
1231	Chalk, red .... do					20									
1232	Chalk .... do														
1233	Chalk, prepared .... do														
1234	Cranes, blacksmiths'									1					
1235	Cranes, iron														
1236	Cranes, assorted .... pounds														
1237	Cranes, tank														
1238	Cranes, water														
1239	Cuffs, hand .... pairs														

Report showing the disposition of United States military railroad property in the military division of the Tennessee, &c.—Continued.

Running number.	Articles.	Property sold on credit to railroad companies under Executive Orders of August 8 and October 14, 1865.										Sold at public auction to railroad companies on credit on same terms as authorized by Executive Orders of August 8 and October 14, 1865.			
		Mississippi Central railroad.	Mississippi, Gainesville, and Tuscaloosa railroad.	Alabama and Tennessee River railroad.	Mississippi and Tennessee railroad.	Memphis, Clarksville, and Louisville railroad.	Western and Atlantic railroad.	Southwestern Iron Company.	Selma and Meridian railroad.	Nashville and Decatur railroad.	Virginia and Tennessee railroad.	McMinnville and Manchester railroad.	Mobile and Ohio railroad.	Edgefield and Kentucky railroad.	South Carolina railroad.
1240	Chests, tool														
1241	Chests, carpenters' tool														
1242	Chests, tin														
1243	Chests, saddlers'														
1244	Cupboards, tool									2					
1245	Cupboards, oil														
1246	Combs, graining ... lots														
1247	Combs, graining ... sets														
1248	Chucks, assorted														
1249	Chucks, screw									2					
1250	Chucks, drill														
1251	Chucks, brass														
1252	Chucks, planer									1					
1253	Chucks, universal									1					
1254	Chucks, universal lathe														
1255	Chucks, tap and nuts														
1256	Chucks, lathe														
1257	Chases, assorted									44					
1258	Cranks, hand-car ... pounds														
1259	Cranks, iron														
1260	Chasers, screw														
1261	Catches, cupboard														
1262	Catches, brake									11					
1263	Catches, window														
1264	Chrome, yellow ... pounds					102				6					
1265	Chrome, orange, American ... tubes														
1266	Chrome, orange, dry ... pounds														
1267	Chrome, green ... do														
1268	Colors ... tubes						108								
1269	Colors ... boxes														
1270	Candles, car ... pounds														

1271	Candles, star .... do					375									
1272	Copperas .... do														
1273	Cord, hemp bell .... do			16	2	6	16		12	137					
1274	Cords, bell	1									1				
1275	Cement, composition .... cans														
1276	Cement .... barrels														
1277	Connexions, meter														
1278	Cabs, loco														
1279	Circulars, switch		4												
1280	Centres, lathe														
1281	Carriages, iron lathe														
1282	Carriages, iron .... sections														
1283	Clasps, hand														
1284	Crabs, drilling														
1285	Chamber, engine pump														
1286	Corrals														
1287	Casings, cylinder head														
1288	Cantharides, tincture .... pounds														
1289	Camphor, gum .... do														
1290	Calomel .... do														
1291	Cochineal .... do														
1292	Composition, chemical .... cans														
1293	Carriers														
1294	Crosses, gas-pipe														
1295	Collars, gas-bracket														
1296	Circles, iron														
1297	Coffins														
1298	Casks														
1299	Cones, blacksmiths'														
1300	Drills, iron pipe														
1301	Drills, breast														
1302	Drills, stone														
1303	Drills, ratchet, assorted		1		3	4				6					
1304	Drills, ratchet, brace, steel														
1305	Drills, stock and clamp														
1306	Drills, blacksmiths'														
1307	Drills, assorted														
1308	Drills, pin														
1309	Drills, lathe, steel														
1310	Drills, counter, steel														
1311	Drills, cast steel .... pounds						25								
1312	Drills, steel									192					
1313	Drills, vertical, 36-inch														
1314	Drills, vertical, 45-inch, compound table														
1315	Drills, vertical, 45-inch, plain table														
1316	Drills, prop, iron table, complete														
1317	Drills, churn														
1318	Drills, upright														
1319	Drills, drill press														
1320	Drills, steel standard									1					
1321	Drills, upright, ungeared, press and counter shafts														
1323	Drills, assorted .... sets														

Report showing the disposition of United States military railroad property in the military division of the Tennessee, &c.—Continued.

Running number.	Articles.	Property sold on credit to railroad companies under Executive Orders of August 8 and October 14, 1865.										Sold at public auction to railroad companies on credit on same terms as authorized by Executive Orders of August 8 and October 14, 1865.			
		Mississippi Central railroad.	Mississippi, Gainesville, and Tuscaloosa railroad.	Alabama and Tennessee River railroad.	Mississippi and Tennessee railroad.	Memphis, Clarksville, and Louisville railroad.	Western and Atlantic railroad.	Southwestern Iron Company.	Selma and Meridian railroad.	Nashville and Decatur railroad.	Virginia and Tennessee railroad.	McMinnville and Manchester railroad.	Mobile and Ohio railroad.	Edgefield and Kentucky railroad.	South Carolina railroad.
1324	Drills, quarry														
1325	Drills, ratchets and bits														
1326	Drills, black enamelled ... yards						672		20						
1327	Dividers ... pairs					3				9					
1328	Dividers, spring ... do														
1329	Drifts														
1330	Drifts, steel														
1331	Dogs														
1332	Dogs, lathe									20					
1333	Dogs, ratchet ... pounds														
1334	Dogs, planer														
1335	Dogs, saw														
1336	Dusters, counter														
1337	Dusters, painters'														
1338	Duck ... yards														
1339	Duck, car ... do														
1340	Dippers, oil														
1341	Dippers, lye														
1342	Drippers, oil														
1343	Diamonds, glaziers'					1									
1344	Dadoes														
1345	Doors, fire, and frames														
1346	Doors, unfinished					48									
1347	Doors, panel														
1348	Doors, furnace														
1349	Doors, glass														
1350	Doors, glazed ... pieces														
1351	Doors, assorted														
1352	Doors, car														
1353	Dryer, patent ... pounds									1					
1354	Dryer, sand					1									

1355	Drums for lathe, (W. I.) ... pounds														
1356	Derricks														
1357	Derrick blocks falls and dies														
1358	Derricks, crab														
1359	Drivers, iron lathe, round ... pounds														
1360	Drivers, screw ... lots														
1361	Dies and plates														
1362	Dies, pipe, and stocks ... sets														
1363	Dies, hand ... pounds														
1364	Dies, assorted														
1365	Dies, gas pipe														
1366	Dies and plates ... sets		1		1	6									
1367	Dies ... do														
1368	Dies and hubs ... pounds														
1369	Dies, forge														
1370	Die stocks ... sets									5					
1371	Drivers, screw					24				12					
1372	Drums, stove														
1373	Drawers, moulders'														
1374	Dust, bone ... pounds														
1375	Engines, stationary														
1376	Engines, pumping, No. 3														
1377	Engines and boilers, dummy														
1378	Engines, dummy														
1379	Engines and boilers, stationary														
1380	Engines, steam fire														
1381	Engines, single, steam														
1382	Engines, rotary fire, (Holley's patent)														
1383	Engines, caloric														
1384	Engines, rotary														
1385	Engines, pilot														
1386	Engines, portable														
1387	Engines, locomotive														
1388	Engine, locomotive, No. 212														
1389	Engines, locomotive, and tenders		2	8	2	12	8	1	6		4	2	3	1	2
1390	Engine, double stationary, 11¼-inch bore, 24-inch stroke, Ellis & Moore's patent														
1391	Engines, stationary, 2 boilers 24 feet long, 40 inches diameter						1								
1392	Engine, double stationary, pulley and counter shaft														
1393	Engines, pumping														
1393½	Engine and boiler, 5-inch cylinder, 12-inch stroke, (complete)														
1394	Engine and boiler, (complete)														
1395	Engines, steam														
1396	Engine, 12-inch bore, 36-inch stroke														
1397	Engines, hoisting, complete														
1398	Engines and boilers, stationary, (complete)														
1399	Eyes, brass screw														
1400	Eyes, bell cord														
1401	Eyes, iron ... gross														
1402	Eyes, screw ... do														

Report showing the disposition of United States military railroad property in the military division of the Tennessee, &c.—Continued.

Running number.	Articles.	Property sold on credit to railroad companies under Executive Orders of August 8 and October 14, 1865.										Sold at public auction to railroad companies on credit on same terms as authorized by Executive Orders of August 8 and October 14, 1865.			
		Mississippi Central railroad.	Mississippi, Gainesville, and Tuscaloosa railroad.	Alabama and Tennessee River railroad.	Mississippi and Tennessee railroad.	Memphis, Clarksville, and Louisville railroad.	Western and Atlantic railroad.	Southwestern Iron Company.	Selma and Meridian railroad.	Nashville and Decatur railroad.	Virginia and Tennessee railroad.	McMinnville and Manchester railroad.	Mobile and Ohio railroad.	Edgefield and Kentucky railroad.	South Carolina railroad.
1403	Ears, tin kettle ... gross														
1404	Ears, kettle									72					
1405	Ears, bucket														
1406	Ears, C. C. saw														
1407	Elbows, reducing														
1408	Elbows, drop														
1409	Elbows gas-pipe					96				10					
1410	Elbows, water-pipe														
1411	Elbows, goose-neck														
1412	Emery, assorted ... pounds		10			$94\frac{3}{4}$	75			44					
1413	Emery flour ... do														
1414	Edges, iron														
1415	Edges, steel, straight									5					
1416	Ends, draw bar														
1417	Ends, equalizer														
1418	Easels														
1419	Escutcheons														
1420	Easers														
1421	Forges, blacksmiths'														
1422	Forges and bellows														
1423	Forges, portable					2									
1424	Forges, blacksmiths' portable														
1425	Forges, cast-iron														
1426	Forges					4	8								
1427	Furnaces, bolt														
1428	Furnaces, plumbers'														
1429	Furnaces, tinners'														
1430	Furnaces, charcoal														
1431	Frogs, cast														
1432	Frogs, patent portable														
1433	Frogs, assorted ... pounds														

No.	Article														
1434	Frogs, chilled														
1435	Frogs, plated														
1436	Frogs, assorted														
1437	Frogs, T														
1438	Fittings, gas ... pounds														
1439	Fittings, gas pipe ... do														
1440	Fittings, gas														
1441	Fittings, brass cock and valve														
1442	Fasteners, car window														
1443	Fasteners, sash														
1444	Fixtures, grindstone ... sets									8					
1445	Fixtures, lathe ... pounds														
1446	Frames, saw					1									
1447	Frames, engine truck														
1448	Frames, truck, iron ... pounds														
1449	Frames, brake, beam														
1450	Frames and slides, car window						5								
1451	Frames, tank														
1452	Frames, truck									1					
1453	Frames, wreck														
1454	Frames, bell ... pounds														
1455	Frames, bell														
1456	Frames, hack-saw														
1457	Frames, saw, railroad cut-off														
1458	Frames, bolt														
1459	Frames, circular-saw														
1460	Frames, bellows														
1461	Frames, door														
1462	Frames, window														
1463	Frames, lock														
1464	Frames, grindstones														
1465	Frames, for buildings														
1466	Frames and hammers, pile-driving														
1467	Frames														
1468	Flatters						10			24					
1469	Fullers						15								
1470	Flasks ... pounds														
1471	Flasks														
1472	Flasks and tools ... pounds														
1473	Flasks, iron ... sets														
1474	Flannel, Canton ... yards									10					
1475	Flannel, red ... do														
1476	Faucets														
1477	Faucets, brass														
1478	Fitches, assorted														
1479	Flags, red	1	4		2	4				15	6				1
1480	Fans, blowing					1	1								
1481	Fans, foundry														
1482	Fans, snail-shell														
1483	Flanges														
1484	Followers ... pounds														
1485	Followers, piston														

Report showing the disposition of United States military railroad property in the military division of the Tennessee, &c.—Continued.

Running number.	Articles.	Property sold on credit to railroad companies under Executive Orders of August 8 and October 14, 1865.										Sold at public auction to railroad companies on credit on same terms as authorized by Executive Orders of August 8 and October 14, 1865.			
		Mississippi Central railroad.	Mississippi, Gainesville, and Tuscaloosa railroad.	Alabama and Tennessee River railroad.	Mississippi and Tennessee railroad.	Memphis, Clarksville, and Louisville railroad.	Western and Atlantic railroad.	Southwestern Iron Company.	Selma and Meridian railroad.	Nashville and Decatur railroad.	Virginia and Tennessee railroad.	McMinnville and Manchester railroad.	Mobile and Ohio railroad.	Edgefield and Kentucky railroad.	South Carolina railroad.
1486	Figures ... sets				1		1								
1487	Figures									20					
1488	Figures ... pounds														
1489	Froes														
1490	Forks, "T" rail														
1491	Forks, manure														
1492	Forks, railroad														
1493	Forks, pitch														
1494	Fuze, safety ... feet														
1495	Feeders, oil														
1496	Formers, tin														
1497	Formers, stove-pipe														
1498	Formers, tin gutter														
1499	Facings, coal ... barrels														
1500	Facings, sea coal ... do														
1501	Folders, tinners'														
1502	Folders, iron														
1503	Ferrules ... pounds														
1504	Fences														
1505	Files, assorted					252	102								
1506	Files, flat, assorted														
1507	Files, half-round bastard, assorted		12		72		114			96					
1508	Files, flat bastard, assorted		12		108	96	168			396					
1509	Files, saw, assorted														
1510	Files, flat, second-cut, assorted									24					
1511	Files, taper, second-cut, assorted														
1512	Files, hand, second-cut, assorted														
1513	Files, round, second-cut, assorted									18					
1514	Files, half-round, second-cut, assorted		12			36									
1515	Files, coulter, second-cut, assorted														
1516	Files, square, smooth, assorted														

1517	Files, flat, smooth, assorted						60			18					
1518	Files, round, smooth, assorted									12					
1519	Files, hand dead, smooth, assorted					36									
1520	Files, flat dead, smooth, asorted					12				24					
1521	Files, hand, bastard, assorted					120				48					
1522	Files, square, bastard, assorted					24				54					
1523	Files, coulter, bastard, assorted									54					
1524	Files, three-square, bastard, assorted														
1525	Files, round parallel, bastard, assorted														
1526	Files, square parallel, bastard, assorted														
1527	Files, dead, smooth, assorted														
1528	Files, three-square, assorted														
1529	Files, smooth, bastard, assorted														
1530	Files, wire														
1531	Files, bastard														
1532	Files, hand-saw, assorted						72			216					
1533	Files, mill-saw, assorted		12							36					
1534	Files, pit-saw														
1535	Files, patent														
1536	Files, round, bastard									54					
1537	Files, half-round, smooth									60					
1538	Files, half-round														
1539	Files, hand, smooth														
1540	Files, taper														
1541	Files, round														
1542	Files, bastard, second-cut														
1543	Files, smooth														
1544	Files, switch														
1545	Files, second-cut														
1546	Files, parallel														
1547	Files, square-cut														
1548	Files, square taper														
1549	Files, equalizing														
1550	Files, cut, bastard														
1551	Files, taper, bastard														
1552	Files, parallel, bastard														
1553	Flues, copper ... pounds														
1554	Flues ... feet														
1555	Fixings, forge ... pounds														
1556	Fronts to boilers														
1557	Funnels, sand-box														
1558	Flaxseed ... pounds														
1559	Flaxseed, ground ... do														
1560	Gauges, assorted														
1561	Gauges, panel					3									
1562	Gauges, mortise					3									
1563	Gauges, wire									1					
1564	Gauges, marking					3									
1565	Gauges, thumb														
1566	Gauges, single														
1567	Gauges, double														
1568	Gauges, cutting														

Report showing the disposition of United States military railroad property in the military division of the Tennessee, &c.—Continued.

Running number.	Articles.	Property sold on credit to railroad companies under Executive Orders of August 8 and October 14, 1865.										Sold at public auction to railroad companies on credit on same terms as authorized by Executive Orders of August 8 and October 14, 1865.			
		Mississippi Central railroad.	Mississippi, Gainesville, and Tuscaloosa railroad.	Alabama and Tennessee River railroad.	Mississippi and Tennessee railroad.	Memphis, Clarksville, and Louisville railroad.	Western and Atlantic railroad.	Southwestern Iron Company.	Selma and Meridian railroad.	Nashville and Decatur railroad.	Virginia and Tennessee railroad.	McMinnville and Manchester railroad.	Mobile and Ohio railroad.	Edgefield and Kentucky railroad.	South Carolina railroad.
1569	Gauges, wheel														
1570	Gauges, track					6				22					
1571	Gauges, tinners'														
1572	Gauges, barrel														
1573	Gauges, screw														
1574	Gauges, steam	1	2	3	1	14	6		4	6	4		3	1	
1575	Gauges, quarter-circle														
1576	Gauges, cocks and syphon steam														
1577	Gouges														
1578	Gouges, firmer														
1579	Gouges, paring														
1580	Gouges, paring, and handles														
1581	Gouges, patent marking														
1582	Gouges, flat sweep ... sets														
1583	Gouges and handles, firmer ... do														
1584	Gouges, ¼-inch														
1585	Gouges, firmer ... sets														
1586	Gouges, flat ... do														
1587	Gouges, paring ... do														
1588	Gouges, neck														
1589	Gimlets														
1590	Gummers, saw														
1591	Gummers, assorted														
1592	Greasers														
1593	Grooves, hand, steel														
1594	Grainers, top														
1595	Galleys, single-column brass-lined														
1596	Galleys, double-column brass-lined														
1597	Galleys, double-column brass-lined														
1598	Galleys, slice														
1599	Galleys, improved folio slice														

1600	Glass, assorted	boxes					37				13					
1601	Glass, tail, light															
1602	Glass, window, assorted	lights					120									
1603	Glass, double-thick	feet														
1604	Glass, head-light	boxes														
1605	Glasses, head-light															
1606	Glasses, cab, light															
1607	Grooves, hand															
1608	Grooves, tinners'															
1609	Gauze, brass	feet														
1610	Gauze, brass	coils														
1611	Gauze, iron	do														
1612	Greene, chrome	pounds					6									
1613	Green, Hibernian	do														
1614	Green, German emerald	do														
1615	Green, Paris	do									53					
1616	Green, silk	do														
1617	Green, Quaker	do														
1618	Green, emerald	do														
1619	Green, American chrome	tubes														
1620	Grease, car	pounds														
1621	Grease, car	gallons						126								
1622	Grease, car	barrels														
1623	Grease, wagon	pounds														
1624	Grease, axle	boxes														
1625	Glue	pounds					40				15					
1626	Gates, switch	do														
1627	Gates, molasses															
1628	Gates, switch															
1629	Gates, pine															
1630	Gibbs, bridge															
1631	Gibbs, cross-head	pounds														
1632	Gibbs, cross-head															
1633	Gibbs, bridge	pounds														
1634	Governors															
1635	Glands, snuffing-box	pounds														
1636	Gongs, locomotive, 8-inch															
1637	Gongs and fixtures															
1638	Gongs, alarm															
1639	Globes, ruby															
1640	Gutters, tin	feet														
1641	Gutters	lots														
1642	Grease, wagon	gallons														
1643	Hammers, blacksmiths'							10								
1644	Hammers, blacksmiths' hand															
1645	Hammers, chipping															
1646	Hammers, shoe															
1647	Hammers, set															
1648	Hammers, hand							7			7					
1649	Hammers, sledge										6					
1650	Hammers, claw						48				24					
1651	Hammers, tack															

Report showing the disposition of United States military railroad property in the military division of the Tennessee, &c.—Continued.

Running number.	Articles.	Property sold on credit to railroad companies under Executive Orders of August 8 and October 14, 1865.										Sold at public auction to railroad companies on credit on same terms as authorized by Executive Orders of August 8 and October 14, 1865.			
		Mississippi Central railroad.	Mississippi, Gainesville, and Tuscaloosa railroad.	Alabama and Tennessee River railroad.	Mississippi and Tennessee railroad.	Memphis, Clarksville, and Louisville railroad.	Western and Atlantic railroad.	Southwestern Iron Company.	Selma and Meridian railroad.	Nashville and Decatur railroad.	Virginia and Tennessee railroad.	McMinnville and Manchester railroad.	Mobile and Ohio railroad.	Edgefield and Kentucky railroad.	South Carolina railroad.
1652	Hammers, engine	1	1	8	2	34	8	1	6		4				
1653	Hammers, tinners'			2											
1654	Hammers, saddlers'														
1655	Hammers, stone									12					
1656	Hammers, clasp and punch														
1657	Hammers, ballast														
1658	Hammers, shoeing														
1659	Hammers, masons'														
1660	Hammers, spike														
1661	Hammers, backing														
1662	Hammers, jack														
1663	Hammers, copper														
1664	Hammers, assorted									27					
1665	Hammers, trip														
1666	Hammers, steam engine, trip, complete														
1667	Hammers, steam, assorted														
1668	Hammers, machine									36					
1669	Hammers, boiler-makers'									6					
1670	Hammers, riveting														
1671	Hammers, soft														
1672	Hammers, steel														
1673	Hammers, raising														
1674	Hammers, pointing														
1675	Hammers, wagon														
1676	Hammers, saw														
1677	Hatchets									6					
1678	Hatchets and handles														
1679	Hatchets, shingling					39				6					
1680	Hatchets, broad				12	39									
1681	Hatchets, soldering														
1682	Handles, firmer chisel, assorted														

1683	Handles, socket firmer chisel, assorted														
1684	Handles, socket chisel														
1685	Handles, chisel														
1686	Handles, auger, assorted														
1687	Handles, adze									28					
1688	Handles, foot or carpenters' adze														
1689	Handles, railroad adze														
1690	Handles, broadaxe														
1691	Handles, hatchet														
1692	Handles, brad hatchet														
1693	Handles, hammer									2					
1694	Handles, stone hammer														
1695	Handles, spike, maul														
1696	Handles, maul														
1697	Handles, pick					324									
1698	Handles, awl														
1699	Handles, sledge														
1700	Handles, brad awl														
1701	Handles, firmer gouge														
1702	Handles, jackplane														
1703	Handles, handsaw														
1704	Handles, handsaw, polished														
1705	Handles, file					96				222					
1706	Handles, cross-cut saw														
1707	Handles, cant hook									2					
1708	Handles, axe									46					
1709	Handles, chopping axe														
1710	Handles, hand axe														
1711	Handles, saucepan														
1712	Handles, chest														
1713	Handles, assorted					288									
1714	Handles, front end door									26					
1715	Handles, machinists'														
1716	Handles, chest, japanned, Paris ....pairs														
1717	Handles, flush drawer														
1718	Handles, chest ....pairs														
1719	Handles, mallet														
1720	Handles, door														
1721	Handles, stretcher														
1722	Handles, mop														
1723	Handles, couch														
1724	Hangers, post									16					
1725	Hangers, drop, belt														
1726	Hangers, spring														
1727	Hangers, step														
1728	Hangers, shafting ....pounds						3,680								
1729	Hangers, step ....do						1,660								
1730	Hangers and boxes ....do														
1731	Hangers, truck									4					
1732	Hangers ....pounds														
1733	Hangers, drop														
1734	Hangers and fasteners, window blind ....sets														

Report showing the disposition of United States military railroad property in the military division of the Tennessee, &c.—Continued.

Running number.	Articles.	Property sold on credit to railroad companies under Executive Orders of August 8 and October 14, 1865.										Sold at public auction to railroad companies on credit on same terms as authorized by Executive Orders of August 8 and October 14, 1865.			
		Mississippi Central railroad.	Mississippi, Gainesville, and Tuscaloosa railroad.	Alabama and Tennessee River railroad.	Mississippi and Tennessee railroad.	Memphis, Clarksville, and Louisville railroad.	Western and Atlantic railroad.	Southwestern Iron Company.	Selma and Meridian railroad.	Nashville and Decatur railroad.	Virginia and Tennessee railroad.	McMinnville and Manchester railroad.	Mobile and Ohio railroad.	Edgefield and Kentucky railroad.	South Carolina railroad.
1735	Hangers, cast-iron .... pounds..														
1736	Hangers, door														
1737	Heads, cylinder					2									
1738	Heads, square														
1739	Heads, coppersmith														
1740	Heads, brake .... pounds..														
1741	Heads, brake, frame														
1742	Heads, draw														
1743	Heads, draw .... pounds..														
1744	Heads, cross, engine					1									
1745	Heads, stake														
1746	Heads and beams, brake														
1747	Heads, piston														
1748	Heads, bull, small														
1749	Heads, bull, large														
1750	Heads, draw, cash .... pounds..														
1751	Heads, cross														
1752	Hooks, cant					12				2					
1753	Hooks, belt, assorted						240								
1754	Hooks, horn, beak														
1755	Hooks, packing			7	2		6	1	6	41					
1756	Hooks, tackle .... pounds..														
1757	Hooks and links, switch rope					30									
1758	Hooks, safety chair .... pounds..														
1759	Hooks, assorted														
1760	Hooks and staples														
1761	Hooks, gas pipe														
1762	Hooks and eyes, brass .... gross..														
1763	Hooks, safety chain									23					
1764	Hooks, curling									1					
1765	Hooks, iron .... pounds..														

No.	Article														
1766	Hooks, packing, and spools														
1767	Hooks, curving														
1768	Hooks, switch rope ... pounds														
1769	Hooks and thimbles, switch rope ... do														
1770	Hooks, cotton														
1771	Hook and chain gate														
1772	Hooks, ice														
1773	Hooks, hay														
1774	Hooks, timber														
1775	Hooks and chains														
1776	Hooks, iron														
1777	Hooks and stands ... pounds														
1778	Hooks, car hat														
1779	Heaters, iron									4					
1780	Heaters, pipe														
1781	Hoes														
1782	Hoes, handled														
1783	Hoes, boat														
1784	Hoes, garden														
1785	Hoes, stable														
1786	Hose, assorted ... feet		50	260	100	1,000			200	332					
1787	Hose, gum ... do														
1788	Hubs and collars ... sets														
1789	Hubs for dies														
1790	Hinges, strap, assorted					96				60					
1791	Hinges, blind, patent														
1792	Hinges, T ... pairs			1											
1793	Hinges, table, assorted ... do														
1794	Hinges, window ... do														
1795	Hinges, brass ... do														
1796	Hinges and fasteners, blind ... sets									12					
1797	Hinges, strap, assorted ... pairs														
1798	Hinges, brass														
1799	Hinges ... pounds														
1800	Hinges, unfinished														
1801	Hinges, butt, brass ... pairs														
1802	Hinges, butt, brass ... do														
1803	Hinges, back, flat														
1804	Hinges, butt, cast ... pairs														
1805	Hinges, blind ... do														
1806	Hasps, hinges and staples, assorted														
1807	Hasps and staples														
1808	Hasps, hinge					24									
1809	Hasps														
1810	Hasps and hooks														
1811	Hair, plasterers' ... bushels														
1812	Hair, curled ... pounds														
1813	Hair, plasterers' ... do														
1814	Hair, plasterers' ... lots														
1815	Holders, mandrel														
1816	Hoods, forge														
1817	Hoods, smoke-stack					4	8								

Report showing the disposition of United States military railroad property in the military division of the Tennessee, &c.—Continued.

Running number.	Articles.	Property sold on credit to railroad companies under Executive Orders of August 8 and October 14, 1865.										Sold at public auction to railroad companies on credit on same terms as authorized by Executive Orders of August 8 and October 14, 1865.			
		Mississippi Central railroad.	Mississippi, Gainesville, and Tuscaloosa railroad.	Alabama and Tennessee River railroad.	Mississippi and Tennessee railroad.	Memphis, Clarksville, and Louisville railroad.	Western and Atlantic railroad.	Southwestern Iron Company.	Selma and Meridian railroad.	Nashville and Decatur railroad.	Virginia and Tennessee railroad.	McMinnville and Manchester railroad.	Mobile and Ohio railroad.	Edgefield and Kentucky railroad.	South Carolina railroad.
1818	Horses, wrought-iron														
1819	Horses, cast-iron									1					
1820	Horses, wooden									4					
1821	Horses, carpenter, saw														
1822	Horses, drawing														
1823	Horses, nail														
1824	Horses, blacksmiths'														
1825	Hoops, tank ... pounds														
1826	Hoops, truss														
1827	Housing for cupola														
1828	Hods, mortar														
1829	Hardies														
1830	Hubs, ambulance														
1831	Hubs, wagon														
1832	Headings, blacksmiths'														
1833	Hydrants														
1834	Heads, cylinder ... pounds														
1835	Handles, ballast hammer														
1836	Hickory for handles ... pieces														
1836½	Hinges														
1837	Iron, angle ... pounds									252					
1838	Iron, railroad ... bars														
1839	Iron, railroad ... pounds														
1840	Iron, round, assorted ... do		962	4 946		27, 642	15, 570		4, 916	16, 415					
1841	Iron, bar, assorted ... do						14, 056								
1842	Iron, flat, assorted ... do														
1843	Iron, galvanized ... do					1, 014									
1844	Iron, Russia ... do					253	578			498					
1845	Iron, assorted ... do		1, 080			30, 472	6, 903			11, 328					
1846	Iron, boiler ... do					10, 680	9, 151			3, 333					
1847	Iron, tank ... do					2, 070	12, 015			2, 668					

1848	Iron, oval and ½-oval ... do														
1849	Iron, hoop ... do														
1850	Iron, tire ... do														
1851	Iron, ½-round ... do					1,072									
1852	Iron, square ... do		130			10,167	7,833			6,723					
1853	Iron, plough slab ... do														
1854	Iron, nail rod ... do														
1855	Iron, pig ... do														
1856	Iron, round bridge ... do														
1857	Iron, flat bridge ... do														
1858	Iron, scrap ... do						15,937½								
1859	Iron, sheet ... do									645					
1860	Iron, tuyere ... do														
1861	Iron, scrap, 1st class ... do														
1862	Iron, scrap, blacksmiths' 1st class ... do														
1863	Iron, scrap, blacksmiths' common ... do														
1864	Iron, tank and fire box scrap ... do														
1865	Iron, light sheet scrap ... do														
1866	Iron, sheet, galvanized ... do														
1867	Iron, band, assorted ... do														
1868	Iron, smoke-stack ... do														
1869	Iron, scrap, rings and staples ... do														
1870	Iron, round and square ... do														
1871	Iron, old ... do														
1872	Iron, wrought ... do														
1873	Iron, perforated ... sheets														
1874	Irons, platform														
1875	Irons, clinch														
1876	Irons, and														
1877	Irons, solid														
1878	Irons, double plough														
1879	Irons, heading														
1880	Irons, branding														
1881	Irons, angle, 25 feet each														
1882	Irons, switch		16												
1883	Irons, twyre														
1884	Irons, plane														
1885	Irons, double-plane														
1886	Irons, soldering		1	6						6					
1887	Irons, large, for drawing, (on wheels)														
1888	Irons, guide ... pounds														
1889	Irons, dog ... pairs														
1890	Irons, roofing, double seaming														
1891	Irons, step ... pounds														
1892	Irons, blacksmiths' ... do														
1893	Irons, chafing ... do														
1894	Iron, brake ... do														
1895	Instruments, veterinary ... sets	2													
1896	Instruments, levelling														
1897	Instruments, mathematical ... sets														
1898	Instruments, transit														
1899	Injectors, engine					3									

Report showing the disposition of United States military railroad property in the military division of the Tennessee, &c.—Continued.

Running number.	Articles.	Property sold on credit to railroad companies under Executive Orders of August 8 and October 14, 1865.										Sold at public auction to railroad companies on credit on same terms as authorized by Executive Orders of August 8 and October 14, 1865.			
		Mississippi Central railroad.	Mississippi, Gainesville, and Tuscaloosa railroad.	Alabama and Tennessee River railroad.	Mississippi and Tennessee railroad.	Memphis, Clarksville, and Louisville railroad.	Western and Atlantic railroad.	Southwestern Iron Company.	Selma and Meridian railroad.	Nashville and Decatur railroad.	Virginia and Tennessee railroad.	McMinnville and Manchester railroad.	Mobile and Ohio railroad.	Edgefield and Kentucky railroad.	South Carolina railroad.
1900	Injectors, assorted									6					
1901	Injectors, steam														
1902	Indicators, steam														
1903	Ipecac ... pounds														
1904	Ink, printing ... cases														
1904½	Irons, hand-grooving														
1905	Jacks, ratchet														
1906	Jacks, screw and lever		6	16	4	48	16	2	12						
1907	Jacks, hydraulic, assorted			2	4	1			2						
1908	Jacks, hydraulic, 7-ton														
1909	Jacks, hydraulic, 10-ton									5					
1910	Jacks, hydraulic, 15-ton									7					
1911	Jacks, timber														
1912	Jacks, lever					4			4	31					
1913	Jacks, screw									6					
1914	Jacks, pump, 15-ton														
1915	Jacks, pump, 10-ton														
1916	Jacks, pump														
1917	Journals, brass														
1918	Japan ... gallons														
1919	Jaws, switch-lever														
1920	Knives, farriers'														
1921	Knives, drawing					3				24					
1922	Knives, frog														
1923	Knives, bench														
1924	Knives, paring														
1925	Knives, round														
1926	Knives, pallet									2					
1927	Knives, putty														
1928	Knives, shoe														
1929	Knives, packing														

No.	Article														
1930	Knives, C. S. Daniels's planer														
1931	Knives, brush														
1932	Kettles, soldering														
1933	Kettles, glue									1					
1934	Kettles, spring ... pounds														
1935	Keys, car		6						2	144					
1936	Keys, assorted														
1937	Keys, assorted ... pounds														
1938	Keys, draw-head														
1939	Keys, split ... pounds									18					
1940	Keys, padlock														
1941	Keys, connecting-rods														
1942	Kegs														
1943	Knobs, mahogany									48					
1944	Knobs, mineral														
1945	Knobs, drawer														
1946	Knobs, door														
1947	Knobs, desk, wood, assorted														
1948	Knobs, tin-kettle														
1949	Knobs, tea-pot ... gross														
1950	Kings, American ... tubes														
1951	Knees, tender														
1952	Kasses, switch														
1953															
1954	Lights, white		6	56	1	72	54		54	273					
1955	Lights, red	1		12	26	37	26	2		287	4				
1956	Lights, blue														
1957	Lights, cab		1	8	2		6		6		4				
1958	Lights, head	1	2	8	5	16	8	1	6	8			2	1	18
1959	Lights, tail														
1960	Lamps, Dutch									12					
1961	Lamps, bull's-eye				1			1		12					
1962	Lamps, bracket					19									
1963	Lamps, railroad														
1964	Lamps, hand														
1965	Lamps, green														
1966	Lamps, signal														
1967	Lamps, torch														
1968	Lamps, coach														
1969	Lamps, brass car					6									1
1970	Lamps, car, candle														
1971	Lamps, hanging														
1972	Lamps, spring														
1973	Lanterns														3
1974	Lanterns, railroad globe														
1975	Lanterns, dark														
1976	Lanterns, square														
1977	Lantern bottoms, (W. L., old)														
1978	Locks, pad, assorted			16	2	30	12		12	58					
1979	Locks, mortise														
1980	Locks, door, with mineral knobs, complete					6									
1981	Locks, assorted					30				30					

Report showing the disposition of United States military railroad property in the military division of the Tennessee, &c.—Continued.

Running number.	Articles.	Property sold on credit to railroad companies under Executive Orders of August 8 and October 14, 1865.										Sold at public auction to railroad companies on credit on same terms as authorized by Executive Orders of August 8 and October 14, 1865.			
		Mississippi Central railroad.	Mississippi, Gainesville, and Tuscaloosa railroad.	Alabama and Tennessee River railroad.	Mississippi and Tennessee railroad.	Memphis, Clarksville, and Louisville railroad.	Western and Atlantic railroad.	Southwestern Iron Company.	Selma and Meridian railroad.	Nashville and Decatur railroad.	Virginia and Tennessee railroad.	McMinnville and Manchester railroad.	Mobile and Ohio railroad.	Edgefield and Kentucky railroad.	South Carolina railroad.
1982	Locks, switch									42					
1983	Locks, car		4							144					
1984	Locks, car, seat-back														
1985	Locks, door									9					
1986	Locks, chest														
1987	Locks, spring-chest														
1988	Locks, drawer														
1989	Locks, rim														
1990	Locks, iron drawer														
1991	Locks, desk and drawer														
1992	Locks, Japan-covered														
1993	Locks, wardrobe														
1994	Locks and chains														
1995	Lines, sea-grass														
1996	Lines, tape, assorted														
1997	Lines, plough														
1998	Lines, chalk					96									
1999	Lines, chalk and reel														
2000	Line, chalk ... feet														
2001	Lime ... bushels														
2002	Lime ... pounds														
2003	Lumber, pine ... feet					134, 297	11, 051								
2004	Lumber, oak and poplar, assorted ... do					219, 537	53, 941	2, 000							
2005	Lumber, B. M. ... do														
2006	Lumber assorted ... do					45, 000	6, 068								
2007	Lumber, old ... lots														
2008	Lumber, oak ... feet														
2009	Lumber, poplar ... do														
2010	Lumber walnut ... do														
2011	Lead, pig ... pounds														
2012	Lead, white, assorted ... do					15				215					

2013	Lead, black ... do						40								
2014	Lead, sugar of ... do														
2015	Lead, sheet ... do														
2016	Lead, red, in oil and dry ... do					500				114					
2017	Lead, bar and pig ... do														
2018	Lead, red ... do														
2019	Lead, scrap ... do														
2020	Litharge ... do														
2021	Lathes, screw-cutting									1					
2022	Lathes, complete, 7 feet bed, 9-inch swing														
2023	Lathes, shear and head														
2024	Lathes, engine				1	2			1						
2025	Lathes, hand														
2026	Lathes, axle														
2027	Lathes, wood turning			1						1					
2028	Lathes, iron turning														
2029	Lathes, dog, wrought, No. 20														
2030	Lathes, screw-cutting machine, 8 feet chain, feed, with chuck														
2031	Lathes, screw-cutting machine, 10 feet bed, 23-inch swing														
2032	Lathes, screw-cutting machine, with pulleys and shafts														
2033	Lathes, with chuck														
2034	Lathes, 24-inch, universal chuck														
2035	Lathes, 24-inch, White's patent			1											
2036	Lathes, driving wheel														
2037	Lathes, turning									1					
2038	Lathes									3					
2039	Lathes, double-head, 20 feet long, 26-inch swing, with counter shafts, tools, and fixtures														
2040	Lathes, screw-cutting, with counter shafts														
2041	Lathes, small counter shaft														
2041½	Lathes, No. 8														
2042	Lathes, double-head, wood														
2043	Lathes, iron														
2044	Lathes, screw-cutting, 16 feet bed, 15-inch swing														
2045	Lathes, shear and head, 10 feet bed, 12-inch swing														
2046	Lathes, small, with screw, gear, and four extra rods														
2047	Lathes, 30-inch														
2048	Ladders, mounting						4								
2049	Ladders, shop and step														
2050	Letters ... sets				1										
2051	Letters									30					
2052	Letters and figures, incomplete ... sets														
2053	Links, crooked									2					
2054	Links, chain									1					
2055	Links, coupling ... pounds														
2056	Links, straight ... do														
2057	Links, crooked ... do														
2058	Links, coupling														
2059	Ladles														

Report showing the disposition of United States military railroad property in the military division of the Tennessee, &c.—Continued.

Running number.	Articles.	Property sold on credit to railroad companies under Executive Orders of August 8 and October 14, 1865.										Sold at public auction to railroad companies on credit on same terms as authorized by Executive Orders of August 8 and October 14, 1865.			
		Mississippi Central railroad.	Mississippi, Gainesville, and Tuscaloosa railroad.	Alabama and Tennessee River railroad.	Mississippi and Tennessee railroad.	Memphis, Clarksville, and Louisville railroad.	Western and Atlantic railroad.	Southwestern Iron Company.	Selma and Meridian railroad.	Nashville and Decatur railroad.	Virginia and Tennessee railroad.	McMinnville and Manchester railroad.	Mobile and Ohio railroad.	Edgefield and Kentucky railroad.	South Carolina railroad.
2060	Ladles, tin														
2061	Ladles, perforated														
2062	Ladles, melting														
2063	Ladles, iron														
2064	Ladles, iron ... pounds														
2065	Lifts, window									72					
2066	Lifts, brass sash														
2067	Links, switch rope ... pounds														
2068	Links, straight									41					
2069	Links and pins, coupling ... pounds														
2070	Leather, sole ... do														
2071	Leather, lace ... sides			12					12	8					
2072	Leather, harness ... pounds														
2073	Leather, bridle ... do														
2074	Leather, russet ... sides														
2075	Leather, burnt ... pounds														
2076	Leather, sole ... sides														
2077	Leather, assorted ... pounds														
2078	Leather, blue, title ... dozen														
2079	Levels, spirit				6	4				6					
2080	Levels, pocket														
2081	Levels, machinists'														
2082	Levels														
2083	Levers, hand-car														
2084	Levers and rods, tank														
2085	Levers, switch														
2086	Levers, wrought														
2087	Levers														
2088	Levers, brake									14					
2089	Levers, track														
2090	Levers, whistle														

2091	Levers, blacksmith														
2092	Leaves, steel, for tender springs ... pounds														
2093	Leaf, gold ... packages						9-10								
2094	Ley, concentrated ... cans														
2095	Ley, concentrated ... boxes														
2096	Lead, bar ... pounds														
2097	Lead, white ... kegs														
2098	Lugs, water tank														
2099	Lugs, water tank ... pounds									10					
2100	Laths, pine														
2101	Lake madder ... tubes														
2102	Laudanum ... pounds														
2103	Logs, B. M ... feet														
2104	Lifters, rail														
2105	Legs, table														
2106	Litters														
2107	Machines, small engine														
2108	Machines, double engine														
2109	Machines, hoisting engine														
2110	Machines, straightening														
2111	Machines, drill press			1											
2112	Machines, wheel press														
2113	Machines, press boring, cylinder														
2114	Machines, press drilling, vertical, Nos. 62 and 63														
2115	Machines, manifest, suspension														
2116	Machines, pipe-cutting														
2117	Machines, stove pipe former														
2118	Machines, wooden former														
2119	Machines, burring														
2120	Machines, pinning down														
2121	Machines, setting down														
2122	Machines, swedging														
2123	Machines, scanning														
2124	Machines, scanning, double														
2125	Machines, bolt header														
2126	Machines, screw cutting					1	1								
2127	Machines, beading														
2128	Machines, twyring														
2129	Machines, tenoning					1									
2130	Machines, wiring														
2131	Machines, squaring														
2132	Machines, grooving														
2133	Machines, folding														
2134	Machines, planing, common														
2135	Machines, planing						1								
2136	Machines, quartering wheel														
2137	Machines, quartering wheel, double-headed														
2138	Machines, flooring														
2139	Machines, striker														
2140	Machines, scroll moulding														
2141	Machines, boring, assorted														
2142	Machines, boring, and augers														

Report showing the disposition of United States military railroad property in the military division of the Tennessee, &c.—Continued.

Running number.	Articles.	Property sold on credit to railroad companies under Executive Orders of August 8 and October 14, 1865.										Sold at public auction to railroad companies on credit on same terms as authorized by Executive Orders of August 8 and October 14, 1865.			
		Mississippi Central railroad.	Mississippi, Gainesville, and Tuscaloosa railroad.	Alabama and Tennessee River railroad.	Mississippi and Tennessee railroad.	Memphis, Clarksville, and Louisville railroad.	Western and Atlantic railroad.	Southwestern Iron Company.	Selma and Meridian railroad.	Nashville and Decatur railroad.	Virginia and Tennessee railroad.	McMinnville and Manchester railroad.	Mobile and Ohio railroad.	Edgefield and Kentucky railroad.	South Carolina railroad.
2143	Machines, boring and drilling, Bement & Dougherty														
2144	Machines and bits, boring									1					
2145	Machines, boring, No. 32, Bement & Dougherty														
2146	Machines, sawing														
2147	Machines, skiving														
2148	Machines, mortising						1								
2149	Machines, mortising and boring, car														
2150	Machines, mortising, and chisels, foot, portable														
2151	Machines, thick edge														
2152	Machines, rolling														
2153	Machines, slotting														
2154	Machines, milling			4											
2155	Machines, gear cutting														
2156	Machines, bolt cutting, taps and dies														
2157	Machines, small vertical drill														
2158	Machines, key cutting														
2159	Machines, key seat drill, No. 12, complete														
2160	Machines, large vertical drill, intermediate shafts, pulleys and hangers														
2161	Machines, nut tapping														
2162	Machines, moulding														
2163	Machines, railroad cut-off sawing														
2164	Machines, stove pipe breaking														
2165	Machines, binders' board cutting														
2166	Machines, shaping														
2167	Machines, shaping, 12-inch, No. 20														
2168	Machines, drilling														
2169	Machines, portable, drilling														
2170	Machines, guttering														
2171	Machines, bolt, with taps and dyes														
2172	Machines, car trimming, common														

2173	Machines, car, wood turning														
2174	Machines, turning, large														
2175	Machines, beading, and extra rolls														
2176	Machines, hoisting						2			1					
2177	Machines, shingle														
2178	Machines, copper pipe breaking														
2179	Machines, spring setting														
2180	Machines, flue drawing														
2181	Machines, slide lathe														
2182	Machines, wood lathe														
2183	Machines, hand lathe														
2184	Machines, eyelet														
2185	Machines, double seaming														
2186	Machines, boring and turning														
2187	Machines, laying off														
2188	Machines, bolt cutting, large, with 7 sets taps and dies, plugs for repairing dies, counter shafts, pulleys and hangers														
2189	Machines, bolt cutting, with 13 sets taps and dies, counter shafts, pulleys and hangers														
2190	Machines, mortising, with bits, Rogers's patent														
2191	Machines, planing, compound														
2192	Machines, car planing and matching, complete														
2193	Machines, bolt head, and fixtures									1					
2194	Machines, planing, 12 feet, with counter shafting, wrenches, tools, &c														
2195	Machines, tongue-grooving														
2196	Machines, planer, (Daniels's patent)														
2197	Machines, circular rip-saw, No. 6														
2198	Machines, circular rip-saw, No. 5														
2199	Machines, board planer, No. 2														
2200	Machines, rabbiting, No. 5														
2201	Machines, wheel burring lath														
2202	Machines, surface planing, No. 2														
2203	Machines, ruling														
2204	Machines, paper cutting														
2205	Machines, gumming														
2206	Machines, bolt cutting														
2207	Machines, car planing														
2208	Machines, wood														
2209	Machines, cylinder boring														
2210	Mills, shingle														
2211	Mills, saw, with engine boiler complete														
2212	Mills, saw, (O. S. and D. patent)														
2213	Mills, saw, (Clemens's patent)														
2214	Mills, saw, circular, (Clemens's patent)														
2215	Mills, saw, circular, (Lea & Leavitt's patent)														
2216	Mills, saw, (H. & Co.'s patent, "A," 2 boilers complete)														
2217	Mills, saw, (H. & Co.'s patent, "D," complete)														
2218	Mills, saw, stationary, L and D patent, incomplete														
2219	Mills, saw, A. B. H. & Co.'s patent, incomplete														

Report showing the disposition of United States military railroad property in the military division of the Tennessee, &c.—Continued.

Running number.	Articles.	Property sold on credit to railroad companies under Executive Orders of August 8 and October 14, 1865.										Sold at public auction to railroad companies on credit on same terms as authorized by Executive Orders of August 8 and October 14, 1865.			
		Mississippi Central railroad.	Mississippi, Gainesville, and Tuscaloosa railroad.	Alabama and Tennessee River railroad.	Mississippi and Tennessee railroad.	Memphis, Clarksville, and Louisville railroad.	Western and Atlantic railroad.	Southwestern Iron Company.	Selma and Meridian railroad.	Nashville and Decatur railroad.	Virginia and Tennessee railroad.	McMinnville and Manchester railroad.	Mobile and Ohio railroad.	Edgefield and Kentucky railroad.	South Carolina railroad.
2220	Mills, saw														
2221	Mills, steam saw, portable														
2222	Mills, paint, assorted					1	1			1					
2223	Mills, borax														
2224	Mills, corn														
2225	Mills, boring, counter shafts, pulleys, and hangers														
2226	Mandrels														
2227	Mandrels, saw														
2228	Mandrels, S. P														
2229	Mandrels, iron, assorted									1					
2230	Mandrels, steel-nut														
2231	Mandrels, steel									12					
2232	Mandrels, cast-steel														
2233	Mandrels, cast														
2234	Mandrels, lathe, steel														
2235	Mallets, assorted														
2236	Mallets, carpenters'									24					
2237	Mallets, lignumvitæ					3									
2238	Mallets, caulking														
2239	Mallets, iron-ring														
2240	Mallets, stonecutters'														
2241	Mallets, tinners'														
2242	Mauls														
2243	Mauls, spike									39					
2244	Mauls, carpenters'														
2245	Mauls, carpenters' top														
2246	Mauls, carpenters' spike								6						
2247	Mauls, railroad spike					48									
2248	Mauls, wooden														
2249	Mauls, iron														
2250	Mauls, bridge														

No.	Article	Unit														
2251	Mauls, dirt															
2252	Measures, assorted						6	1			72					
2253	Measures, tin, assorted															
2254	Measures, tin	sets														
2255	Measures, oil	do														
2256	Measures, pint															
2257	Measures, dry	sets														
2258	Mullers										1					
2259	Moulds, soldering															
2260	Moulds, cast															
2261	Magazines, powder															
2262	Marline, tarred	pounds					69				58					
2263	Matches	gross					20									
2264	Meter, gas															
2265	Metal, Babbitt	pounds		47												
2266	Molasses	gallons														
2267	Moulens, wooden-wreath															
2268	Machinery, saw-mill	box														
2269	Machinery, rolling-mill	pounds														
2270	Nippers															
2271	Nippers, cutting															
2272	Needles, assorted															
2273	Needles, tufting															
2274	Needles, upholsterers'															
2275	Needles, harness	papers														
2276	Nozzles															
2277	Nozzles, brass															
2278	Nozzles, pipe															
2279	Nozzles, hose			2							1					
2280	Nozzles	pounds														
2281	Nuts, assorted	do		50		893	4, 184	5, 825			3, 766					
2282	Nuts, brass	do														
2283	Nuts, square	do														
2284	Nuts, hexagon	do														
2285	Nuts and washers	do														
2286	Nuts and bolts	do														
2287	Nuts, keeper, and rods															
2288	Nuts, iron															
2289	Nails, assorted	kegs														
2290	Nails, finishing, assorted	papers						20			324					
2291	Nails, clout	do														
2292	Nails, tufting															
2293	Nails, clinch	pounds														
2294	Nails, horseshoe	do														
2295	Nails, enamelled	gross														
2296	Nails, lining	papers														
2297	Nails, assorted	pounds			7, 900	1, 000	20, 000	30, 000		8, 000	286					
2298	Nails, plush	gross														
2299	Nails, finishing	kegs									20					
2300	Nails, cut	do														
2301	Nails, finishing	pounds														
2302	Nails, round-head brass	gross														

Report showing the disposition of United States military railroad property in the military division of the Tennessee, &c.—Continued.

Running number.	Articles.	Property sold on credit to railroad companies under Executive Orders of August 8 and October 14, 1865.										Sold at public auction to railroad companies on credit on same terms as authorized by Executive Orders of August 8 and October 14, 1865.			
		Mississippi Central railroad.	Mississippi, Gainesville, and Tuscaloosa railroad.	Alabama and Tennessee River railroad.	Mississippi and Tennessee railroad.	Memphis, Clarksville, and Louisville railroad.	Western and Atlantic railroad.	Southwestern Iron Company.	Selma and Meridian railroad.	Nashville and Decatur railroad.	Virginia and Tennessee railroad.	McMinnville and Manchester railroad.	Mobile and Ohio railroad.	Edgefield and Kentucky railroad.	South Carolina railroad.
2303	Nails, cut ... pounds														
2304	Nails, copper ... do														
2305	Nails, tin ... papers														
2306	Nails, lining, blued ... gross														
2307	Nails, lining, silver ... do														
2308	Numbers, key ... lots														
2309	Numbers ... sets														
2310	Netting, wire ... feet			51			100			531					
2311	Oilers														1
2312	Oilers, engine, assorted			16	2	13	14	1	12	68					
2313	Oilers, spring														
2314	Oilers, spring-top				6	3									
2315	Oilers, spring-bottom				6					2					
2316	Oilers, machine									2					
2317	Oilers, small														
2318	Oilers, tin														
2319	Oil, lard ... gallons									3					
2320	Oil, coal ... do														
2321	Oil, lubricating ... do														
2322	Oil, linseed, raw ... do														
2323	Oil, linseed, boiled ... do									42					
2324	Oil, linseed ... do					84									
2325	Oil ... do														
2326	Oil, head-light ... do														
2327	Oil, neat's-foot ... do														
2328	Oil, castor ... bottles														
2329	Ochre, French, yellow ... pounds														
2330	Oakum ... do														
2331	Ornaments, brass														
2332	Planes, rounding														
2333	Planes, double-smooth														

2334	Planes, fore					3				2					
2335	Planes, jack					3				2					
2336	Planes jointer					3									
2337	Planes, joint														
2338	Planes, rabbet, assorted					6									
2339	Planes, jack, rabbet									2					
2340	Planes, bead, assorted					3									
2341	Planes, bench ... sets														
2342	Planes, long-jointer														
2343	Planes, moulding														
2344	Planes, smooth					3				2					
2345	Planes, sash														
2346	Planes, match														
2347	Planes, match ... pairs					3									
2348	Planes, screw-arm match														
2349	Planes, panel-plough														
2350	Planes, plough														
2351	Planes and bits, plough					3									
2352	Planes, floor ... sets														
2353	Planes, assorted														
2354	Planes, double-iron														
2355	Planes, grooving ... pairs														
2356	Planes and set bits														
2357	Planes, joiners' short														
2358	Planes, panel plough and bits														
2359	Planes ... sets														
2360	Planers									2					
2361	Planers ... sets														
2362	Planers, rabbet														
2363	Planers, car, complete														
2364	Planers, compound adjustment head														
2365	Planers and matcher with counter shafts														
2366	Planers, iron, to plane 16 ft., 4 ft. square, complete														
2367	Planers, iron														
2368	Planers, 48-inch														
2369	Planers, iron, 36 x 36 inches, 28-feet bed, 18-feet platform, (Seller's patent)														
2370	Planers, 5-feet														
2371	Planers, 36 x 36 inches, No. 124, (Seller's patent)														
2372	Planers, 36 x 36 inches, No. 125, (Seller's patent)														
2373	Planers, (Seller's patent)														
2374	Planers, compound, (Bement & Dougherty)														
2375	Planers, compound						1			1					
2376	Planers, compound, chuck, No. 14, double, (Bement & Dougherty)														
2377	Planers, 36 x 36 inches														
2378	Planers, link and link-block														
2379	Planers, cast-iron link														
2380	Pulleys, assorted						25			47					
2381	Pulleys, complete, assorted														
2382	Pulleys, upright														
2383	Pulleys for main shafts, common														

Report showing the disposition of United States military railroad property in the military division of the Tennessee, &c.—Continued.

Running number.	Articles.	Property sold on credit to railroad companies under Executive Orders of August 8 and October 14, 1865.										Sold at public auction to railroad companies on credit on same terms as authorized by Executive Orders of August 8 and October 14, 1865.			
		Mississippi Central railroad.	Mississippi, Gainesville, and Tuscaloosa railroad.	Alabama and Tennessee River railroad.	Mississippi and Tennessee railroad.	Memphis, Clarksville, and Louisville railroad.	Western and Atlantic railroad.	Southwestern Iron Company.	Selma and Meridian railroad.	Nashville and Decatur railroad.	Virginia and Tennessee railroad.	McMinnville and Manchester railroad.	Mobile and Ohio railroad.	Edgefield and Kentucky railroad.	South Carolina railroad.
2384	Pulleys, two-ton														
2385	Pulleys for paint mill														
2386	Pulleys and shafts														
2387	Pulleys and chain, 2-ton														
2388	Pulleys, iron, 2 feet 10 inches face														
2389	Pulleys, iron, 2 feet 4 inches face														
2390	Pulleys, cast iron, assorted ... pounds									200					
2391	Pulleys, drawer, No. 10														
2392	Pulleys and hangers														
2393	Pulleys ... pounds														
2394	Pulleys, turned for $\frac{3}{4}$, 10 by 12, with set screws														
2395	Pulleys, cast-iron														
2396	Ploughs and grooves ... sets														
2397	Ploughs														
2398	Pincers, carpenters' ... pairs														
2399	Pincers, blacksmiths' ... do														
2400	Pincers, upholsterers' ... do														
2401	Pincers, shoeing ... do														
2402	Pincers, assorted ... do			1						12					
2403	Pincers, boiler-makers' ... do					3									
2404	Pencils, carpenters'														
2405	Pencils, coloring														
2406	Pencils, C. H														
2407	Pencils, artists' red sable														
2408	Pencils, striping														
2409	Pencils, marking														
2410	Pencils, lettering														
2411	Punches									35					
2412	Punches, belt									1					
2413	Punches, screws and dies														
2414	Punches, screw														

2415	Punches, hollow														
2416	Punches, hydraulic														
2417	Punches, centre														
2418	Punches, steel						43								
2419	Punches, lever														
2420	Punches, coppersmiths'														
2421	Punches, harness														
2422	Punches, spring														
2423	Punches, conductors'														
2424	Punches, track														
2425	Punches, blacksmiths'														
2426	Punches, tinners'														
2427	Punches, tank hoop														
2428	Punches, clamp									1					
2429	Punches, boiler-makers'														
2430	Punches, iron track ... sets														
2431	Punches, short														
2432	Punches, hound														
2433	Presses, drill				1		1			1					
2434	Presses, upright drill														
2435	Presses, upright drill, &c														
2436	Presses, hydraulic, with shafts and pulleys														
2437	Presses, wheel						1								
2438	Presses, hand wheel														
2439	Presses, upright drill, and counter shafts														
2440	Presses, medium "Franklin"														
2441	Presses, ½-medium "Franklin"														
2442	Presses, binders' hand														
2443	Presses, manifest														
2444	Presses, drill, and bits														
2445	Plyers ... pairs														
2446	Plyers, cutting ... do														
2447	Plyers, common ... do														
2448	Plyers, upholsterers' ... do														
2449	Plyers, flat nose ... do														
2450	Pots, glue					2									
2451	Pots, marking														
2452	Pots, wood paint														
2453	Pots, tin soldering														
2454	Pots, tinners' fire														
2455	Pots, paste														
2456	Pots, paint ... lot														
2457	Pots, cast														
2458	Pots, tallow														
2459	Pots, rosin														
2460	Pots, melting														
2461	Pots, soldering														
2462	Pots, paint														
2463	Pots, iron														
2464	Pumps, steam														
2465	Pumps, steam, Woodland														
2466	Pumps, cylinder														

Report showing the disposition of United States military railroad property in the military division of the Tennessee, &c.—Continued.

Running number.	Articles.	Property sold on credit to railroad companies under Executive Orders of August 8 and October 14, 1865.										Sold at public auction to railroad companies on credit on same terms as authorized by Executive Orders of August 8 and October 14, 1865.			
		Mississippi Central railroad.	Mississippi, Gainesville, and Tuscaloosa railroad.	Alabama and Tennessee River railroad.	Mississippi and Tennessee railroad.	Memphis, Clarksville, and Louisville railroad.	Western and Atlantic railroad.	Southwestern Iron Company.	Selma and Meridian railroad.	Nashville and Decatur railroad.	Virginia and Tennessee railroad.	McMinnville and Manchester railroad.	Mobile and Ohio railroad.	Edgefield and Kentucky railroad.	South Carolina railroad.
2467	Pumps, force, McGowan's		1	4	3	9	1		6	4					
2467½	Pumps														
2468	Pumps, McGowan, with engine complete														
2469	Pumps, force														
2470	Pumps, Worthington														
2471	Pumps, oil														
2472	Pumps, oil, copper														
2473	Pumps, engine														
2474	Pumps, rotary fire														
2475	Pumps, donkey														
2476	Pumps, cistern						2								
2477	Pumps, proving														
2478	Pumps, Harris														
2479	Pumps, engine, and boiler, complete														
2480	Pumps, incomplete					1									
2481	Pumps, steam, with engine, Worthington														
2482	Pumps, test and gauge														
2483	Pumps, force, with gearing and shafting														
2484	Pumps and fixtures, McGowan														
2485	Picks, earth, and handles														
2486	Picks					8				9					
2487	Picks, tamping					84				73					
2488	Picks, railroad														
2489	Picks, stone														
2490	Pins, wooden ....barrels														
2491	Pins, coupling ....pounds														
2492	Pins, coupling									222					
2493	Pins, turned L. V														
2494	Pins, switch														
2495	Pipes, blast														
2496	Pipe, blast ....feet														

2497	Pipes, copper, with couplings														
2498	Pipe, copper ... pounds														
2499	Pipe, round														
2500	Pipe, sheet iron ... pounds														
2501	Pipe, wrought ... feet														
2502	Pipe, iron, galvanized ... do														
2503	Pipe, galvanized ... pieces														
2504	Pipes, copper hose														
2505	Pipes, rubber hose														
2506	Pipe, iron ... pounds														
2507	Plugs, assorted														
2508	Plugs, gas pipe					33									
2509	Plugs, for repairing, dies														
2510	Plugs, flue														
2511	Plugs, assorted ... pounds														
2512	Plugs and feathers														
2513	Plates, wrought scrap fish bar ... pounds														
2514	Plates, engine window														
2515	Plates, blacksmiths'														
2516	Plates, chuck														
2517	Plates, head ... pounds					1,956									
2518	Plates, face ... do														
2519	Plates, face					2				5					
2520	Plates, gas-fitters' screw														
2521	Plates, screw cutter														
2522	Plates, screw														
2523	Plates, screws and dies						5								
2524	Plates, angle														
2525	Plates, surface														
2526	Plates, turntable ... sets					1									
2527	Plates and rolls ... do														
2528	Plates, bolster ... pounds														
2529	Plates, assorted ... do														
2530	Plates, die									1					
2531	Points, glaziers' ... papers														
2532	Points, glaziers' ... pounds														
2533	Points, frog, steel ... do														
2534	Patterns, tin														
2535	Patterns, moulders'														
2536	Patterns, wheelwrights'														
2537	Patterns, sheet iron ... sets														
2538	Patterns, assorted														
2539	Patterns, tin ... sets														
2540	Patterns, sheet iron ... pounds														
2541	Patterns ... lots														
2542	Pikes														
2543	Piping, assorted ... feet														
2544	Putty ... pounds									300					
2545	Pilots, locomotive														
2546	Pilots, locomotive, wood														
2547	Paulins								12						
2548	Potash, prussiate ... pounds					100									

Report showing the disposition of United States military railroad property in the military division of the Tennessee, &c.—Continued.

Running number.	Articles.	Property sold on credit to railroad companies under Executive Orders of August 8 and October 14, 1865.										Sold at public auction to railroad companies on credit on same terms as authorized by Executive Orders of August 8 and October 14, 1865.			
		Mississippi Central railroad.	Mississippi, Gainesville, and Tuscaloosa railroad.	Alabama and Tennessee River railroad.	Mississippi and Tennessee railroad.	Memphis, Clarksville, and Louisville railroad.	Western and Atlantic railroad.	Southwestern Iron Company.	Selma and Meridian railroad.	Nashville and Decatur railroad.	Virginia and Tennessee railroad.	McMinnville and Manchester railroad.	Mobile and Ohio railroad.	Edgefield and Kentucky railroad.	South Carolina railroad.
2549	Potash ... pounds														
2550	Pipe, for cistern pump ... feet														
2551	Pipe, water, assorted ... do						216½								
2552	Pipe, water ... pounds														
2553	Pipe, gum hose fire														
2554	Pipe, gas ... feet		40			5,495				$329\frac{2}{8}$					
2555	Pipe, lead ... pounds									257					
2556	Pipe, brass ... feet					100	52								
2557	Pipe, nozzle and hose														
2558	Pipe, inside, and netting for engine, No. 30														
2559	Pipe, outside, for engine, No. 30														
2560	Pipe, inside, for smoke stack					2									
2561	Pipe, copper ... feet					500									
2562	Pipe, tin ... do						12								
2563	Pipe, iron ... bundles														
2564	Pipe, iron ... pieces														
2565	Pipe, escape														
2566	Paper, drawing ... quires														
2567	Paper, tracing ... rolls														
2568	Paper, waste ... pounds														
2569	Paper, antiquarian ... sheets														
2570	Paper, sand ... quires			60					80	40					
2571	Paper, emery ... do			80					80	241¾					
2572	Paper, wrapping ... do														
2573	Paper, white drawing ... yards														
2574	Paper, marble ... reams														
2575	Paper, brown drawing ... pounds														
2576	Paper, white drawing ... do														
2577	Paper, printing ... do														
2578	Pickets														
2579	Paint, black ... pounds														

2580	Paint, chrome yellow ....pounds..														
2581	Paint, pink Dutch ....do...														
2582	Paint, mineral ....do...														
2583	Paint, assorted ....do...						375								
2584	Paint, mineral ....barrels..														
2585	Paint, mixed ....pounds..														
2586	Polish, stove ....papers..														
2587	Powder, blasting ....pounds..														
2588	Powder ....kegs..														
2589	Powder, blue ....pounds..														
2590	Plungers, brass pump														
2591	Pans, oil														
2592	Packing, hemp ....pounds..		156		380	525				1, 653½					
2593	Packing, gum ....do...		47	27	63	152	152		80	500					
2594	Packing, steam ....do...														
2595	Pendants, gas-pipe														
2596	Poles, pipe														
2597	Pedestals ....pounds..														
2598	Pedestals														
2599	Powers, horse					2									
2600	Platforms, railroad car														
2601	Paris, plaster ....pounds..														
2602	Pockets, iron														
2603	Pits, transfer and masonry														
2604	Pink, rose ....pounds..					12				12½					
2605	Pinions, feed														
2606	Patterns, for brass castings														
2607	Patterns, for iron castings														
2608	Plank, oak ....feet..														
2609	Pistons, C. I.														
2610	Paste, blue ....pots..														
2610½	Ploughs														
2611	Quods, hollow ....pounds..														
2612	Quods, pica, corner ....sets..														
2613	Rules, steel														
2614	Rules, foot														
2615	Rules, 2-foot														
2616	Rules, pocket														
2617	Rules, board														
2618	Rules, boxwood					3									
2619	Rules, assorted														
2620	Rods, guttering														
2621	Rods, pipe ram														
2622	Rods, brake ....pounds..						2, 626								
2623	Rods, brass ....do...														
2624	Rods, switch		4												
2625	Rods, switch ....sets..														
2626	Rods, switch ....pounds..														
2627	Rods, levelling														
2628	Rods, tank ....sets..					8									
2629	Rods, copper ....pounds..														
2630	Rods, connecting ....do...														

Report showing the disposition of United States military railroad property in the military division of the Tennessee, &c.—Continued.

Running number.	Articles.	Property sold on credit to railroad companies under Executive Orders of August 8 and October 14, 1865.										Sold at public auction to railroad companies on credit on same terms as authorized by Executive Orders of August 8 and October 14, 1865.			
		Mississippi Central railroad.	Mississippi, Gainesville, and Tuscaloosa railroad.	Alabama and Tennessee River railroad.	Mississippi and Tennessee railroad.	Memphis, Clarksville, and Louisville railroad.	Western and Atlantic railroad.	Southwestern Iron Company.	Selma and Meridian railroad.	Nashville and Decatur railroad.	Virginia and Tennessee railroad.	McMinnville and Manchester railroad.	Mobile and Ohio railroad.	Edgefield and Kentucky railroad.	South Carolina railroad.
2631	Rods, piston, wrought iron														
2632	Rods, nuts, and bolts ... pounds														
2633	Rods, iron, for cars ... do														
2634	Rods, brake									22					
2635	Rods, brake, and wheel														
2636	Rods, piston														
2637	Rods, tank														
2638	Rods and levers, tank ... sets														
2639	Rods and bolts, wrought ... pounds														
2640	Rods, bridge ... do														
2641	Rollers ... pairs									1					
2642	Rollers, door														
2643	Rollers, boiler-makers' ... sets														
2644	Rollers, timber					12				4					
2645	Rollers, large ... sets														
2646	Rollers, small, stove-pipe														
2647	Rollers, iron														
2648	Ratchets														
2649	Ratchets and dogs ... pounds														
2650	Ratchets and stands														
2651	Reamers									4					
2652	Reamers and burrs, steel									25					
2653	Reamers and drills ... pounds														
2654	Reamers, C. S ... do														
2655	Reamers and drills														
2656	Reamers, globe														
2657	Reamers, tap														
2658	Rivets, assorted				11,000	165,000									
2659	Rivets, assorted ... pounds					4,337	2,885								
2660	Rivets, boiler ... do									462					
2661	Rivets, tinned									18,000					

2662	Rivets, black and tinned....pounds														
2663	Rivets, seat-back....pounds														
2664	Rivets, tank....do									312					
2665	Rivets, smokestack....do														
2666	Rivets, copper....do						1			73					
2667	Rivets, brass....do														
2668	Rivets, tinned....papers				9	12									
2669	Rivets, iron....pounds									114					
2670	Rivets, car seat, and burrs, brass									72					
2671	Rivets, iron									56, 000					
2672	Rivets, iron....papers														
2673	Rivets....sets														
2674	Rivets, tinned....pounds														
2675	Rivets, brass seat-back														
2676	Rope, assorted....pounds		87		310	808	678			1, 136					
2677	Rope, Manilla....do				47				706½						
2678	Rope, 1-inch....feet														
2679	Rope, 1½-inch....coils														
2680	Rope....do														
2681	Rope....feet														
2682	Rope, bell....pounds														
2683	Rope, old....do														
2684	Ropes, small														
2685	Ropes, guy														
2686	Ropes, fall														
2687	Ropes, switch									9					
2688	Ropes, wire....coils														
2689	Rounds and hollows														
2690	Rounds and hollows....sets														
2691	Rounds and hollows....pairs														
2692	Rounds, chair														
2693	Rounds, timber, buggy														
2694	Riddles														
2695	Regulators, upholsterers'														
2696	Reels, chalk-line														
2697	Resin....pounds														
2698	Rubber, block....do														
2699	Rammers														
2700	Rams, battering									1					
2701	Riving froe														
2702	Rings, flush, brass														
2703	Rings, brass, packing....pounds					77	677			255					
2704	Rings, packing														
2705	Rings, brass, cylinder														
2706	Rings, water tank														
2707	Rings, piston, for water works....pounds														
2708	Rings, old brass														
2709	Rings, brass packing														
2710	Rings, Japan mall....gross														
2711	Rings, Japan harness....do														
2712	Rings, breeching														
2713	Rings, muffin														

Report showing the disposition of United States military railroad property in the military division of the Tennessee, &c.—Continued.

Running number.	Articles.	Property sold on credit to railroad companies under Executive Orders of August 8 and October 14, 1865.										Sold at public auction to railroad companies on credit on same terms as authorized by Executive Orders of August 8 and October 14, 1865.			
		Mississippi Central railroad.	Mississippi, Gainesville, and Tuscaloosa railroad.	Alabama and Tennessee River railroad.	Mississippi and Tennessee railroad.	Memphis, Clarksville, and Louisville railroad.	Western and Atlantic railroad.	Southwestern Iron Company.	Selma and Meridian railroad.	Nashville and Decatur railroad.	Virginia and Tennessee railroad.	McMinnville and Manchester railroad.	Mobile and Ohio railroad.	Edgefield and Kentucky railroad.	South Carolina railroad.
2714	Rings, harness ....gross..														
2715	Red, American India........tubes..														
2716	Red, India, in oil........pounds..														
2717	Red, vermilion........do....														
2718	Red, India........do....					78				5					
2719	Red, Venetian........do....														
2720	Red, Italian........do....														
2721	Rags........do....														
2722	Reservoirs														
2723	Racks, assorted														
2724	Racks, forge, iron........pounds..														
2725	Racks, form														
2726	Rasps, assorted														
2727	Rasps, wood														
2728	Rasps, horse														
2729	Rails, T														
2730	Rolls, steel, for turn-table........sets..														
2731	Rests, steady for lathe														
2732	Rests, tank, lever														
2733	Rests, iron														
2734	Rests, arm														
2735	Rakes, stable														
2736	Rakes, iron														
2737	Reflectors, head-light														
2738	Registers, conductors'														
2739	Rigging for steam balance														
2740	Roofing, patent........pounds..														
2741	Saws, hand		1	8	13	3	6	1	6	26					
2742	Saws, tenon									1					
2743	Saws, hack					1									
2744	Saws, compass, assorted				6	3									

2745	Saws, back				6	6				12					
2746	Saws, rip					3				5					
2747	Saws, buck														
2748	Saws, web														
2749	Saws, cross-cut, assorted		1			10				6					
2750	Saws, cross-cut, 5-foot														
2751	Saws, cross-cut, large														
2752	Saws, cross-cut, hand														
2753	Saws, cross-cut, tenon														
2754	Saws, jig														
2755	Saws, scroll														
2756	Saws, circular, 48-inch														
2757	Saws, circular and arbor														
2758	Saws, brass back														
2759	Saws, blue back														
2760	Saws, mill														
2761	Saws, muley														
2762	Saws, meat														
2763	Saws, drag														
2764	Saws, keyhole														
2765	Saws, wood														
2766	Saws and frames, wood														
2767	Saws, wooden frame														
2768	Saws, pit														
2769	Saws, fine														
2770	Saws, whip														
2771	Saws, cut-off, 32-inch														
2772	Saws, shingle, 36-inch														
2773	Saws, assorted														
2774	Saws, bright back														
2775	Saws, panel														
2776	Saws, cut-off														
2777	Squares, steel					3									
2778	Squares, try, assorted					9				12					
7279	Squares, iron														
2780	Squares, centre														
2781	Squares, framing														
2782	Squares, bevel														
2783	Squares, lumber														
2784	Squares														
2785	Squares, head														
2786	Stands, head-light														
2787	Stands, switch														
2788	Stands, flag														
2789	Stands for machines														
2790	Stands, monkey switch														
2791	Stands, target switch														
2792	Stands, wood switch														
2793	Stands, iron														
2794	Stamps, U. S. M. R. R.														
2795	Stands, brass lamp														
2796	Stands, locomotive lamp ... pounds														

Report showing the disposition of United States military railroad property in the military division of the Tennessee, &c.—Continued.

Running number.	Articles.	Property sold on credit to railroad companies under Executive Orders of August 8 and October 14, 1865.										Sold at public auction to railroad companies on credit on same terms as authorized by Executive Orders of August 8 and October 14, 1865.			
		Mississippi Central railroad.	Mississippi, Gainesville, and Tuscaloosa railroad.	Alabama and Tennessee River railroad.	Mississippi and Tennessee railroad.	Memphis, Clarksville, and Louisville railroad.	Western and Atlantic railroad.	Southwestern Iron Company.	Selma and Meridian railroad.	Nashville and Decatur railroad.	Virginia and Tennessee railroad.	McMinnville and Manchester railroad.	Mobile and Ohio railroad.	Edgefield and Kentucky railroad.	South Carolina railroad.
2797	Stands, sand box ... pounds														
2798	Stands, California, double														
2799	Stands, California, single														
2800	Stands, lead														
2801	Stands, type														
2802	Stands, chain, cast ... pounds														
2803	Stands, gauge lamp														
2804	Stands, flag ... pounds														
2805	Stamps, U. S.														
2806	Stones, grind, assorted									9					
2807	Stones, grind, assorted ... pounds			3, 000		3, 012									
2808	Stones, grind, and fixtures ... sets						1								
2809	Stones, grind, 4 feet diameter, cast iron frame														
2810	Stones, paint and muller					1	1								
2811	Stones, paint									1					
2812	Stones, oil					21				10					
2813	Stones, oil, assorted ... pounds														
2814	Stones, whet														
2815	Stone ... lot														
2816	Stones, grind, frame, hangers complete														
2817	Stones, mill, and fixtures ... pairs														
2818	Stones, imposing														
2819	Stones, grind, frames and pulleys														
2820	Stones, grind, and fixtures														
2821	Stone, blue ... pounds														
2822	Stone, rotten ... do														
2823	Stone, pumice ... do					15	15								
2824	Stone, setting for engine														
2825	Snips ... pairs			3						1					
2826	Snips, circular ... do														
2827	Snips, tinners', assorted ... do					2									

2828	Snips, straight ... do														
2829	Shaves, spoke														
2830	Shaves, spoke, wood														
2831	Shaves, spoke, iron														
2832	Sets, saw														
2833	Swedges, creasing														
2834	Swedges, bottom														
2835	Swedges, top														
2836	Swedges and chisels														
2837	Screws, assorted ... gross					12	46			114					
2838	Screws, round head, brass ... do														
2839	Screws, brass, assorted ... do					12				22					
2840	Screws, brass cap ... do														
2841	Screws, round head, blued ... do														
2842	Screws, blued ... do														
2843	Screws, hand, assorted					12				18					
2844	Screws, bench														
2845	Screws, wood bench					15				24					
2846	Screws, iron bench				6					6					
2847	Screws, bed														
2848	Screws, lag, assorted				200	500									
2849	Screws, lag ... pounds														
2850	Screws, top						5								
2851	Screws, fore														
2852	Screws, hydraulic jack														
2853	Screws, small steel ... sets														
2854	Screws, clamp														
2855	Screws, large, and 4-inch nuts														
2856	Screws for shaft														
2857	Screws, auger ... gross														
2858	Screws, turn-table														
2859	Screws, gimblet, brass ... gross														
2860	Screws, tank														
2861	Screws														
2862	Screws, iron wood ... gross														
2863	Screws, head ... sets														
2864	Screws, lathe														
2865	Screws, tire ... sets														
2866	Screws, hand ... pairs														
2867	Screws, jack														
2868	Screws, wood ... pounds														
2869	Screws, gimlet ... gross														
2870	Sticks, creasing														
2871	Sticks, yard														
2872	Sticks, composing														
2873	Sinks, counter														
2874	Sinks, drifts, and calking tools ... pounds														
2875	Slicks, carpenters'					3									
2876	Slicks, large framing														
2877	Slicks, glass														
2878	Scrapers, plumbers'														
2879	Scrapers, box														

Report showing the disposition of United States military railroad property in the military division of the Tennessee, &c.—Continued.

Running number.	Articles.	Property sold on credit to railroad companies under Executive Orders of August 8 and October 14, 1865.										Sold at public auction to railroad companies on credit on same terms as authorized by Executive Orders of August 8 and October 14, 1865.			
		Mississippi Central railroad.	Mississippi, Gainesville, and Tuscaloosa railroad.	Alabama and Tennessee River railroad.	Mississippi and Tennessee railroad.	Memphis, Clarksville, and Louisville railroad.	Western and Atlantic railroad.	Southwestern Iron Company.	Selma and Meridian railroad.	Nashville and Decatur railroad.	Virginia and Tennessee railroad.	McMinnville and Manchester railroad.	Mobile and Ohio railroad.	Edgefield and Kentucky railroad.	South Carolina railroad.
2880	Scrapers			8	2	5	8		6						
2881	Scrapers, iron														
2882	Scrapers, drill														
2883	Scrapers, stone														
2884	Scrapers, carriage														
2885	Scrapers, stove														
2886	Scrapers, ash-pan														
2887	Straighteners, axle														
2888	Sockets, top														
2889	Sockets, chisel														
2890	Sockets, gas-pipe														
2891	Shafts and pulleys														
2892	Shafts														
2893	Shafts, saw mandril counter														
2894	Shafting and pulleys .... pounds														
2895	Shafts with pulleys, counter, shafting, &c .... feet														
2896	Shafting, assorted .... do						133½			128					
2897	Shafting, iron, 2-inch .... pounds														
2898	Shafting .... do														
2899	Shafting, 3¼-inch, with pulleys and hangers, complete .... feet														
2900	Shafting, 3-inch .... feet														
2901	Shafting, 3¼-inch, tinned, 12 feet 6 inches long, with couplings and bolts, complete .... sections														
2902	Shafts, counter, with pulleys														
2903	Shafts, counter														
2904	Strainers														
2905	Strainers, paint														
2906	Strainers, pump														
2907	Strainers, copper					48									
2908	Strainers, feed-pipe									144					

2909	Skins, chamois						1			2					
2910	Skins, sheep														
2911	Skins, bark .... dozen														
2912	Shellac, gum .... pounds														
2913	Saltpetre .... pounds														
2914	Spouts, bent									24					
2915	Spouts, tank														
2916	Spouts, sheet-iron														
2917	Shafts, counter, and 4 pulleys														
2918	Spouts, fluid can														
2919	Spouts, tin														
2920	Spouts, funnel														
2921	Staffs, flag	1	4		2	5					6				
2922	Staffs, brake														
2923	Steel, assorted .... pounds						189			45					
2924	Steel, scrap .... do									892					
2925	Steel, cast .... do		260			5, 433	1, 352			1, 378					
2926	Steel, spring, assorted .... do														
2927	Steel, square .... do					2, 103	1, 517			1, 359					
2928	Steel, octagon .... do					1, 591	417			666					
2929	Steel, frog .... do					1, 004									
2930	Steel, blister .... do									368					
2931	Stocks, screw														
2932	Stocks, iron														
2933	Stocks, drill														
2934	Stocks, iron .... pairs														
2935	Stocks, roller														
2936	Saddles, smoke-stack .... pounds					1, 205									
2937	Saddles for cylinder .... pairs														
2938	Stacks, smoke, locomotive														
2939	Stacks, smoke, stationary, 31 feet x 22 inches														
2940	Stacks, smoke, sheet-iron, boiler frame														
2941	Stacks, smoke and cap .... pounds						2, 434								
2942	Scraps, forge .... do														
2943	Stacks, smoke, sheet-iron														
2944	Stacks, smoke														
2945	Stacks, smoke .... feet														
2946	Sieves, sand														
2947	Sieves, moulders'														
2948	Strips, parallel														
2949	Strips, parallel .... pounds									61					
2950	Strips, copper-flue .... do									743					
2951	Spikes, bridge .... do									9, 000					
2952	Spikes, railroad .... kegs									11½					
2953	Spikes, marlin						2								
2954	Spikes, bridge and cut .... kegs														
2955	Spikes, railroad														
2956	Spikes, railroad .... pounds														
2957	Spikes, cut, assorted .... kegs														
2958	Spikes, assorted .... pounds		200	400	43, 750	10, 000		2, 500							
2959	Spikes .... kegs														
2960	Scales, spring balance														

Report showing the disposition of United States military railroad property in the military division of the Tennessee, &c.—Continued.

Running number.	Articles.	Property sold on credit to railroad companies under Executive Orders of August 8 and October 14, 1865.										Sold at public auction to railroad companies on credit on same terms as authorized by Executive Orders of August 8 and October 14, 1865.			
		Mississippi Central railroad.	Mississippi, Gainesville, and Tuscaloosa railroad.	Alabama and Tennessee River railroad.	Mississippi and Tennessee railroad.	Memphis, Clarksville, and Louisville railroad.	Western and Atlantic railroad.	Southwestern Iron Company.	Selma and Meridian railroad.	Nashville and Decatur railroad.	Virginia and Tennessee railroad.	McMinnville and Manchester railroad.	Mobile and Ohio railroad.	Edgefield and Kentucky railroad.	South Carolina railroad.
2961	Scales, platform, assorted					1	1			1					
2962	Scales, counter					1	1		6	2					
2963	Scales and weights														
2964	Scales, warehouse														
2965	Scales, brass scoop														
2966	Scales, set														
2967	Scales, beam														
2968	Scales														
2969	Scales, track														
2970	Scales, safety-valve														
2971	Scales, stone														
2972	Scales, spring														
2973	Scales, platform counter														
2974	Stretchers, iron														
2975	Stretchers, car														
2976	Snatches, gate														
2977	Springs, assorted ... pounds														
2978	Springs, rubber car ... do														
2979	Springs, car														
2980	Springs, packing									76					
2981	Springs, rubber ... pounds														
2982	Springs, gum														
2983	Springs, engine tender ... pounds														
2984	Springs, spiral ... do														
2985	Springs, assorted						4								
2986	Springs, gum ... pounds					3,958	3,816			1,234					
2987	Springs, car ... do						337		1,446						
2988	Springs, tender														
2989	Springs, engine														
2990	Springs, engine ... pounds														
2991	Springs, window														

2992	Springs, large D																
2993	Springs, small D																
2994	Springs, packing	pounds															
2995	Shovels			14	8	2	205	20	1	150	110						
2996	Shovels, railroad																
2997	Shovels, scoop																
2998	Shovels, coal																
2999	Shovels, moulder, steel																
3000	Shovels and scrapers										14						
3001	Spades			12													
3002	Screens, sand																
3003	Screens, cloth																
3004	Screens, zinc																
3005	Screens, coal																
3006	Screens, wire																
3007	Spools, chalk line																
3008	Soap	pounds															
3009	Soap, castile	do															
3010	Soap	bars															
3011	Spanners																
3012	Sienna, assorted	pounds					34										
3013	Sienna, burnt	do															
3014	Sienna, raw Italian	do															
3015	Sienna, raw, in oil	do															
3016	Sienna, raw	do															
3017	Springs, brass																
3018	Sledges, (12-pound)																
3019	Springs, patent																
3020	Stirrups, log	pairs															
3021	Stencils, copper																
3022	Scythes, snath																
3023	Scythes, grass																
3024	Scythes, brier																
3025	Sponge, common	pounds					50				15						
3026	Sponge, fine	do															
3027	Sponge	do															
3028	Sulphur	do		25			239				25						
3029	Sulphur flowers	do															
3030	Sash, assorted	lights															
3031	Sash,	pieces					160										
3032	Sash	lots															
3033	Sash, wire																
3034	Sash, sky-light																
3035	Switches, monkey																
3036	Slides, switch	sets															
3037	Slides, track	pounds															
3038	Signals, fog	gross															
3039	Stools, saddlers'																
3040	Spaces, pica quod	pounds															
3041	Staples, iron	do									110						
3042	Staples, iron																
3043	Straps, seat, back										72						

Report showing the disposition of United States military railroad property in the military division of the Tennessee, &c.—Continued.

Running number.	Articles.	Property sold on credit to railroad companies under Executive Orders of August 8 and October 14, 1865.										Sold at public auction to railroad companies on credit on same terms as authorized by Executive Orders of August 8 and October 14, 1865.			
		Mississippi Central railroad.	Mississippi, Gainesville, and Tuscaloosa railroad.	Alabama and Tennessee River railroad.	Mississippi and Tennessee railroad.	Memphis, Clarksville, and Louisville railroad.	Western and Atlantic railroad.	Southwestern Iron Company.	Selma and Meridian railroad.	Nashville and Decatur railroad.	Virginia and Tennessee railroad.	McMinnville and Manchester railroad.	Mobile and Ohio railroad.	Edgefield and Kentucky railroad.	South Carolina railroad.
3044	Straps, connecting, and brasses														
3045	Skivers														
3046	Skivers, white														
3047	Skids, loading														
3048	Sizing, gold ... pounds														
3049	Shoes, mule ... do														
3050	Shoes, mule														
3051	Sellars, rod ... pounds														
3052	Straps, eccentric ... do														
3053	Stems, check valve														
3054	Settings, masonry, with iron chimney														
3055	Scrapers, hoe									3					
3056	Sprinklers, fire									1					
3057	Squares, plated														
3058	Shingles														
3059	Saucers, stove														
3060	Shackles, engine ... pounds														
3061	Salt ... do														
3062	Salts, epsom ... do														
3063	Sublimate, corr ... do														
3064	Staves, tank ... lots														
3065	Staves, tank ... pieces														
3066	Staples, back harness														
3067	Settings, masonry						2								
3068	Seamers, double roofing														
3069	Solder ... pounds		10			57									
3070	Soda, sal ... do														
3071	Swivels														
3072	Seats, coach														
3073	Seats														
3074	Shelving ... lots														

3075	Shelves, wooden														
3076	Syphons and cocks														
3077	Spoons, packing														
3078	Signs, tin														
3079	Signs														
3080	Signs, loco														
3081	Shutters, window														
3082	Steps, engine														
3083	Slides, switch														
3084	Staves, tank ... cases														
3085	Shimmers, paint														
3086	Shoes, horse ... pounds														
3087	Shoes, brake														
3088	Sets, hand-saw					4									
3089	Sets, cross-cut saw														
3090	Sets, mill-saw					5									
3091	Sets, lever-saw														
3092	Sets, blacksmiths' cold														
3093	Sets, rivet														
3094	Sets, iron button														
3095	Sets, spring														
3096	Sledges, assorted														
3097	Sledges and handles														
3098	Sledges, blacksmiths'						9			10					
3099	Sledges, heavy														
3100	Sledges, stone														
3102	Shears, hand ... pairs														
3103	Shears, tinners' ... do														
3104	Shears, sheet ... do					1									
3105	Shears, circular ... do														
3106	Shears, lever ... do														
3107	Shears, bench ... do			1						3					
3108	Shears, squaring ... do														
3109	Shears and punch combined ... do														
3110	Shears, rotary ... do														
3111	Shears, table, trimmers' ... do														
3112	Shears, table, gauge ... do														
3113	Shears ... do														
3114	Shives, iron														
3115	Stakes, square, Weddell														
3116	Stakes, funnel														
3117	Stakes, bench														
3118	Stakes, tinners'														
3119	Stakes, needle														
3120	Stakes, double seaming														
3121	Stakes, oval-head														
3122	Stakes, head														
3123	Stakes, pointing														
3124	Stakes, beak-horn														
3125	Stakes, hatchet														
3126	Stakes, square-head														
3127	Stakes, horn-blow														

Report showing the disposition of United States military railroad property in the military division of the Tennessee, &c.—Continued.

Running number.	Articles.	Property sold on credit to railroad companies under Executive Orders of August 8 and October 14, 1865.										Sold at public auction to railroad companies on credit on same terms as authorized by Executive Orders of August 8 and October 14, 1865.			
		Mississippi Central railroad.	Mississippi, Gainesville, and Tuscaloosa railroad.	Alabama and Tennesse River railroad.	Mississippi and Tennessee railroad.	Memphis, Clarksville, and Louisville railroad.	Western and Atlantic railroad.	Southwestern Iron Company.	Selma and Meridian railroad.	Nashville and Decatur railroad.	Virginia and Tennessee railroad.	McMinnville and Manchester railroad.	Mobile and Ohio railroad.	Edgefield and Kentucky railroad.	South Carolina railroad.
3128	Stakes, round-head														
3129	Swedges, assorted						60			418					
3130	Swedges, square ... pairs														
3131	Swedges, C. S ... pounds									64					
3132	Swedges, W. I ... do														
3133	Swedges, B. S														
3134	Swedges and fullers														
3135	Swedges and chisels ... sets														
3136	Sleeves, water pipe														
3137	Sheives ... pairs														
3138	Stacks, smoke, stationary.														
3139	Shafts, steam, wheel														
$3139\frac{1}{4}$	Saws, circular, assorted					13	21			16					
$3139\frac{1}{2}$	Slicks									2					
$3139\frac{3}{4}$	Sellar's engine truck														
3140	Tools, plumbers' ... sets														
3141	Tools, blacksmiths', assorted ... do					4									
3142	Tools, blacksmiths' ... pounds														
3143	Tools, shoeing ... sets														
3144	Tools, carpenters' ... do														
3145	Tools, carpenters' ... chests														
3146	Tools, turning, assorted														
3147	Tools, wheelwright ... sets														
3148	Tools, wheelwright, and chest, (incomplete)														
3149	Tools, grooving														
3150	Tools, sash, assorted					12				12					
3151	Tools, French sash, assorted														
3152	Tools, hand														
3153	Tools, planing, steel									30					
3154	Tools, boring														
3155	Tools, boring, steel														

No.	Article														
3156	Tools, lathe, steel ... pounds									16					
3157	Tools, lathe														
3158	Tools, steel, for turning rolls ... pounds														
3159	Tools, saddlers' ... chests														
3160	Tools, saddlers' ... sets														
3161	Tools, tinners' ... do														
3162	Tools, tinners' ... pounds														
3163	Tools, C. S ... pounds														
3164	Tools, coppersmith ... sets			1											
3165	Tools, graining ... do						2								
3166	Tools, cupping						13			6					
3167	Tools, heading														
3168	Tools, slotting														
3169	Tools, rotary-cutting														
3170	Tools, spring ... sets														
3171	Tools, calking														
3172	Tools, flat paint, assorted														
3173	Tools and chains, W. I ... pounds														
3174	Tools, iron														
3175	Tools, turning ... boxes														
3176	Tools, lathe and planer									1					
3177	Trams ... pairs														
3178	Taps and dies ... sets									13					
3179	Taps and dies														
3180	Taps, steel ... pounds									72					
3181	Taps, steel														
3182	Taps, C. S ... pounds														
3183	Taps, machine						5								
3184	Taps														
3185	Tips, C. S														
3186	Tanks, oil, assorted														
3187	Tanks, engine					8									
3188	Tanks, water														
3189	Tanks, locomotive														
3190	Tanks, oil, (45 galls)														
3191	Tanks, oil, (5) galls)														
3192	Tanks, oil, (75 galls)														
3193	Tanks, oil, (80 galls)														
3194	Tanks, tin water, (parts) ... lots														
3195	Tongs, roofing ... pairs														
3196	Tongs, G. P ... do					6				6					
3197	Tongs, ice ... do						76			79					
3198	Tongs, B. S ... do														
3199	Tongs, tinners' ... sets														
3200	Tongs, grainers' ... do														
3201	Tongs, engine ... pairs	1	2	8	2	9	8	1	6	16	3				
3202	Tongs, R. R ... do														
3203	Tongs, tools, and pokers ... pounds														
3204	Tongs, assorted ... pairs														
3205	Tongs, B. S. and R. R					5	125			35					
3206	Tin, sheet ... boxes														
3207	Tin, perforated ... sheets														

Report showing the disposition of United States military railroad property in the military division of the Tennessee, &c.—Continued.

Running number.	Articles.	Property sold on credit to railroad companies under Executive Orders of August 8 and October 14, 1865.										Sold at public auction to railroad companies on credit on same terms as authorized by Executive Orders of August 8 and October 14, 1865.			
		Mississippi Central railroad.	Mississippi, Gainesville, and Tuscaloosa railroad.	Alabama and Tennessee River railroad.	Mississippi and Tennessee railroad.	Memphis Clarksville, and Louisville railroad.	Western and Atlantic railroad.	Southwestern Iron Company.	Selma and Meridian railroad.	Nashville and Decatur railroad.	Virginia and Tennessee railroad.	McMinnville and Manchester railroad.	Mobile and Ohio railroad.	Edgefield and Kentucky railroad.	South Carolina railroad.
3208	Tin, block .... pounds														
3209	Tin, sheet .... sheets														
3210	Tin, sheet, and screws .... pounds														
3211	Timber .... feet														
3212	Timber, oak .... do					10,000									
3213	Timber, square, assorted .... do														
3214	Timber, bridge .... do														
3215	Timber, B. M., assorted .... do														
3216	Timber, framed .... lots														
3217	Ties, cross														
3218	Tallow .... pounds														
3219	Tallow .... barrels														
3220	Thimbles														
3221	Thimbles, flue, iron .... pounds														
3222	Thimbles, cast .... do														
3223	Thermometers														
3224	Tarpaulins														
3225	Tripods														
3226	T's, gas-pipe					26				5					
3227	T's, water-pipe														
3228	T's, cast iron														
3229	Tubes, blast														
3230	Tubing, copper .... pounds					1,000									
3231	Trucks, timber														
3232	Trucks, warehouse									2					1
3233	Trucks, engine														
3234	Trucks .... pairs														
3235	Trucks, car						4			6					
3236	Trucks, car .... pairs														
3237	Trucks, tender and locomotive .... pounds														
3238	Trucks, engine .... pairs														

No.	Article	Unit														
3239	Trucks, machine	do														
3240	Tires, wrought iron	pounds														
3241	Tires, cast iron															
3242	Tires, locomotive				8						21					
3243	Tires, locomotive flange	pounds					4, 060	23, 040								
3244	Tires, flange cast iron	do														
3245	Tires, old	do														
3246	Tires, wrought iron															
3247	Trowels, masons'															
3248	Trowels, plasterers'															
3249	Tables, circular saw						6									
3250	Tables, turn															
3251	Tables, turn and foundation															
3252	Tables, binders' sewing															
3253	Torches, gas															
3254	Troughs, flock															
3255	Troughs, guttering															
3256	Troughs, forge															
3257	Tops and screws, lamp															
3258	Tops, chimney															
3259	Tops, turn-table															
3260	Tops, car-lamp															
3261	Tops, screw	gross														
3262	Tops, tallow, can															
3263	Tops and bottoms, can															
3264	Tops and bottoms, car-lamp															
3265	Tops and bottoms for turn-table															
3266	Type	founts														
3267	Type	pounds														
3268	Tapes, measuring, assorted						6				12					
3269	Tripoli	pounds														
3270	Tripoli	papers														
3271	Tacks, assorted	do				240					84					
3272	Tacks, gimp	do														
3273	Tacks, upholsterers'	do														
3274	Tacks, blued	do														
3275	Targets		4								6					
3276	Tickets, mess															
3277	Tickets										62, 000					
3278	Tar, coal	gallons														
3279	Tar, coal	barrels														
3280	Thread, black	pounds														
3281	Thread, black	bundles														
3282	Thread, shoe	pounds														
3283	Thread, saddlers'	do														
3284	Thread, linen	do														
3285	Thread, black	skeins														
3286	Twine, hemp	pounds									8½					
3287	Twine, tufting	do									1					
3288	Twine, wrapping	do														
3289	Twine	balls														
3290	Turpentine	gallons														

Report showing the disposition of United States military railroad property in the military division of the Tennessee, &c.—Continued.

Running number.	Articles.	Property sold on credit to railroad companies under Executive Orders of August 8 and October 14, 1865.										Sold at public auction to railroad companies on credit on same terms as authorized by Executive Orders of August 8 and October 14, 1865.			
		Mississippi Central railroad.	Mississippi, Gainesville, and Tuscaloosa railroad.	Alabama and Tennessee River railroad.	Mississippi and Tennessee railroad.	Memphis, Clarksville, and Louisville railroad.	Western and Atlantic railroad.	Southwestern Iron Company.	Selma and Meridian railroad.	Nashville and Decatur railroad.	Virginia and Tennessee railroad.	McMinnville and Manchester railroad.	Mobile and Ohio railroad.	Edgefield and Kentucky railroad.	South Carolina railroad.
3291	Trestles						10								
3292	Trusses, iron														
3293	Torpedoes														
3294	Tongues, frog ... pounds														
3295	Templets, switch ... sets														
3296	Templets														
3297	Transits														
3298	Tenders, locomotive														1
3299	Tincture, iodine ... pounds														
3300	Transoms, wrought ... do														
3301	Testers, gas-pipe														
3302	Tiles, fire														
3303	Traps, rat														
3304	Tighteners, belt														
3305	Triangles														
3306	Tubs, tool														
3307	Tags, shipping ... lots														
3308	Unions, brass, assorted														
3309	Umber, raw, in oil ... pounds														
3310	Umber, raw ... do					15									
3311	Umber, burnt ... do									5¼					
3312	Umber, burnt ... tubes														
3313	Umber, burnt, in oil ... pounds														
3314	Vices, assorted		1	6		6	6		6	12					
3315	Vices, parallel					1									
3316	Vices, bench														
3317	Vices, B. S														
3318	Vices, solid box														
3319	Vices, hand														
3320	Vices, solid ... pounds														
3321	Ventilators														

3322	Ventilators, tin															
3323	Ventilators, car															
3324	Ventilators, car, lamp															
3325	Valves, globe, assorted						24	18		6	24					
3326	Valves, tank															
3327	Valves, water, assorted															
3328	Valves, angle															
3329	Valves, check															
3330	Valves, engine															
3331	Valves, brass, pump															
3332	Valves, safety, complete															
3333	Valves, brass, pump	pounds														
3334	Valves, brass, check	do														
3335	Valves, brass, steam	do														
3336	Valves, governor															
3337	Valves, engine	pounds														
3338	Valves, safety	do														
3339	Vermilion, English "D"	do														
3340	Vermilion, American extra	do														
3341	Vermilion, German	do														
3342	Vermilion, Chinese	do						2								
3343	Vermilion, Chinese	tubes														
3344	Vermilion, scarlet	pounds														
3345	Vermilion, chrome	do														
3346	Vermilion	do														
3347	Varnish, copal	gallons														
3348	Varnish, coach body	do									40½					
3349	Varnish, shellac	do														
3350	Varnish, Japan	do														
3351	Varnish, demar	do														
3352	Varnish, asphaltum	do														
3353	Varnish, white	pounds														
3354	Varnish, white	gallons														
3355	Verdigriss	pounds														
3356	Vitriol	do														
3357	Wrenches, assorted		4	23	77	20	187	95	21	72	18	24				
3358	Wrenches, monkey, assorted		1	3	8	14	59	8	1	6	88	4				
3359	Wrenches, blast pipe															
3360	Wrenches, tap, assorted										8					
3361	Wrenches, ratchet															
3362	Wrenches, straight															
3363	Wrenches, screw															
3364	Wrenches, bridge															
3365	Wrenches, wheel										1					
3366	Wrenches, key															
3367	Wrenches, hose															
3368	Wrenches, long bar															
3369	Wrenches, lathe															
3370	Wrenches, socket										53					
3371	Wrenches, spanner										5					
3372	Wrenches, hand										16					
3373	Wrenches, iron tap	pounds														

Report showing the disposition of United States military railroad property in the military division of the Tennessee, &c.—Continued.

Running number.	Articles.	Property sold on credit to railroad companies under Executive Orders of August 8 and October 14, 1865.										Sold at public auction to railroad companies on credit on same terms as authorized by Executive Orders of August 8 and October 14, 1865.			
		Mississippi Central railroad.	Mississippi, Gainesville, and Tuscaloosa railroad.	Alabama and Tennessee River railroad.	Mississippi and Tennessee railroad.	Memphis, Clarksville, and Louisville railroad.	Western and Atlantic railroad.	Southwestern Iron Company.	Selma and Meridian railroad.	Nashville and Decatur railroad.	Virginia and Tennessee railroad.	McMinnville and Manchester railroad.	Mobile and Ohio railroad.	Edgefield and Kentucky railroad.	South Carolina railroad.
3374	Wrenches, "S"														
3375	Wrenches, pipe														
3376	Wrenches, follower														
3377	Wrenches, iron														
3378	Wrenches, packing														
3379	Wrenches, post														
3380	Wedges, stonemasons'														
3381	Wedges ... pounds														
3382	Wedges, iron														
3383	Wedges, steel														
3384	Wedges														
3385	Wedges, blacksmiths'														
3386	Wedges and feathers														
3387	Whistles, locomotive					1				2					
3388	Whistles, steam														
3389	Windlass, quaker														
3390	Windlass, hand									1					
3391	Wheels, tender, and truck, on axles ... pairs						5								
3392	Wheels, car, with axles														
3393	Wheels, car, on axles ... pairs		6							64					
3394	Wheels and axles ... pounds														
3395	Wheels, driving, on axles ... pairs														
3396	Wheels, turn-table ... pounds														
3397	Wheels, press gear ... do														
3398	Wheels, car														
3399	Wheels, car ... pounds														
3400	Wheels, water														
3401	Wheels, hand car ... pounds														
3402	Wheels, hand car														
3403	Wheels, cog, hand car														
3404	Wheels, car and tender									59					

3405	Wheels, driving														
3406	Wheels, engine truck														
3407	Wheels, truck ... pairs														
3408	Wheels, iron pulley														
3409	Wheels, brake ... pounds														
3410	Wheels, brake														
3411	Wheels, engine									28					
3412	Wheels, engine and tender, on axles ... pairs									12					
3413	Wheels, for counter shaft									2					
3414	Wheels and axles, hand car ... pairs														
3415	Wheels, car ... do														
3416	Wheels and axles ... sets														
3417	Wheels, engine truck, on axles ... pairs														
3418	Wheels, bevel														
3419	Wheels, fly, ten feet														
3420	Wheels, press gear														
3421	Wheels, spur														
3422	Wheels, truck														
3423	Wheels, car, 24-inch, pattern No. 25														
3424	Wheels, car, 26-inch, pattern No. 27														
3425	Wheels, freight car														
3426	Wheels, balance														
3427	Wheels, hand car ... pairs														
3428	Wheels, hand car, on axles ... pounds														
3429	Wheels, ratchet														
3430	Wicks, flat									612					
3431	Wicks, lamp ... pounds									18					
3432	Wicks, lamp ... gross									24					
3433	Wicking ... balls														
3434	Wire, brass ... pounds									118					
3435	Wire, telegraph ... do														
3436	Wire, copper ... do		4½							127¼					
3436½	Wire, iron ... do					178				644					
3437	Wire, assorted ... do					268									
3438	Wire, tin ... do														
3439	Wire ... bundles														
3440	Washers, assorted ... pounds		43		280	2,559	1,774½			948					
3441	Washers, cast ... do														
3442	Webbing ... yards						420		200						
3443	White, China ... pounds														
3444	White, flake, assorted ... do														
3445	White, flake ... tubes														
3446	Whiting ... pounds					160	60								
3447	Whiting, Spanish ... do														
3448	Wax, bees ... do									15					
3449	Winches, crane														
3450	Waste, cotton ... pounds		25				60								
3451	Waste, tow ... do														
3452	Waste ... do														
3453	Weights ... do														
3454	Weights														
3455	Weights, sash														

Report showing the disposition of United States military railroad property in the military division of the Tennessee, &c.—Continued.

Running number.	Articles.	Property sold on credit to railroad companies under Executive Orders of August 8 and October 14, 1865.										Sold at public auction to railroad companies on credit on same terms as authorized by Executive Orders of August 8 and October 14, 1865.			
		Mississippi Central railroad.	Mississippi, Gainesville, and Tuscaloosa railroad.	Alabama and Tennessee River railroad.	Mississippi and Tennessee railroad.	Memphis, Clarksville, and Louisville railroad.	Western and Atlantic railroad.	Southwestern Iron Company.	Selma and Meridian railroad.	Nashville and Decatur railroad.	Virginia and Tennessee railroad.	McMinnville and Manchester railroad.	Mobile and Ohio railroad.	Edgefield and Kentucky railroad.	South Carolina railroad.
3456	Walks, plank														
3457	Webbing ... bolts														
3458	Wrenches, square														
3459	Yarn, lubricating, packing ... pounds														
3460	Yellow, canary ... do														
3461	Yarn, packing ... reels														
3462	Yawls														
3463	Zinc, slab ... pounds														
3464	Zinc, sheet ... do									321					
3465	Zinc, sheet ... pieces														

Report showing the disposition of United States military railroad property in the military division of the Tennessee, &c.—Continued.

Running number.	Articles.	Sold at public auction to railroad companies on credit on same terms as authorized by Executive Orders of August 8 and October 14, 1865.						Sold at auction for cash.	Transferred to officers.	Lost or expended in the public service.	Captured property returned to railroad companies.	Captured property returned to individuals.	Balance on hand June 1, 1866.
		Nashville and Northwestern railroad.	Selma and Meridian railroad.	Nashville and Decatur railroad.	New Orleans, Jackson, and Great Northern railroad.	Mississippi and Tennessee railroad.	Mississippi Central railroad.						
1	Coal ... bushels							10,749	220	31,019			
2	Coke ... do							1,662		2,123			
3	Charcoal ... do							565		83			
4	Charcoal ... barrels							2					
5	Wood ... cords												
6	Corn ... pounds							5,794	15,503	1,055,553			
7	Hay ... do								44,056	1,963,962			
8	Oats ... do							11,295		395,007			
9	Sacks, grain ... number								11,527				498
10	Straw ... pounds							3,150					
11	Blanks												
12	Blanks, quartermasters' ... quires								296	576			300
13	Blanks, way freight								500				
14	Books, blank, 1½-quire									38			
15	Books, blank, 2-quire									30			
16	Books, blank, 3-quire									110			
17	Books, blank, 4-quire								36	75			
18	Books, blank, 6-quire									23			1
19	Books, blank, 8-quire									11			
20	Books, blank, assorted							18	6	605			82
21	Books, ration return									10			
22	Books, time							2,118	120	1,002			
23	Books, order									27			
24	Books, memorandum								26	206			
25	Books, abstract									3			
26	Books, indorsement									5			
27	Books, way-bill, copying								2	13			
28	Books, record									12			
29	Books, copying								3	13			2
30	Books, stub												
31	Books, letter								1				

Report showing the disposition of United States military railroad property in the military division of the Tennessee, &c.—Continued.

Running number.	Articles.	Sold at public auction to railroad companies on credit on same terms as authorized by Executive Orders of August 8 and October 14, 1865.						Sold at auction for cash.	Transferred to officers.	Lost or expended in the public service.	Captured property returned to railroad companies.	Captured property returned to individuals.	Balance on hand June 1, 1866.
		Nashville and Northwestern railroad.	Selma and Meridian railroad.	Nashville and Decatur railroad.	New Orleans, Jackson, and Great Northern railroad.	Mississippi and Tennessee railroad.	Mississippi Central railroad.						
32	Books, requisition								3	3			
33	Books, discharge								72				
34	Books, general order												1
35	Books, clothing order									6			
36	Books, receipt									1			
37	Bands, rubber								2	123			48
38	Boards, file												24
39	Cutters, paper							28					22
40	Clips, letter							126					38
41	Clips, paper												20
42	Clips, board							1	6				6
43	Clips, letter board												8
44	Clips, metal												7
45	Erasers												13
46	Erasers, steel												30
47	Erasers, rubber									30			
48	Envelopes									2,750			
49	Envelopes, letter								20,125	48,200			
50	Envelopes, official								12,185	53,275			4,500
51	Files, paper							78					
52	Files, adhesive												14
53	Folders, paper												
54	Fasteners, paper ... papers												
55	Holders, pen							576	228	1,035½			421
56	Holders, paper												4
57	Ink, (quart) ... bottles							586	49	170			
58	Ink, copying ... do							28	22	83			258
59	Ink, carmine ... do							48	123	364			252
60	Ink, blue ... do								2	8			
61	Journals												
62	Ledgers												

63	Mucilage .... bottles							96	83	276			
64	Paper, letter, assorted .... quires								3,781 5-6	3,076 1-6			
65	Paper, flat letter .... do									1,980			
66	Paper, note .... do								515	1,090			
67	Paper, cap .... do								491	2,377			
68	Paper, flat cap .... do							880	1,720	214			
69	Paper, oil .... sheets								10	81			
70	Paper, blotting .... do								500	435			
71	Paper, cross section .... do												
72	Paper, envelope .... quires								63	58			
73	Paper, folio post .... do									25			
74	Paper, news .... do								20	12			
75	Paper, colored .... do								40				
76	Paper, printing .... bundles								3				
77	Paper, P. O .... quires								20	17½			
78	Paper, heavy yellow .... lots								1				
79	Paper, heavy .... do								1				
80	Paper, white demi .... quires							1,000	1,290	600			
81	Pencils, lead								1,156	2,214			
82	Pencils, slate							7,900	150	617			
83	Pens, steel .... gross								81	58½			
84	Pens, steel									624			
85	Pens, ruling								1,000				
86	Pens, extension .... boxes									¼			
87	Rulers, rubber							2	1				
88	Rulers, wood												
89	Rulers, rosewood												11
90	Rulers, boxwood												13
91	Rulers, mahogany												13
92	Rulers, ebony							18	3				
93	Rulers, assorted							28					60
94	Racks, pen							114	9				52
95	Rings, elastic									24			
96	Stands, ink							195	43				
97	Tearers, paper												
98	Tape .... spools								2	39			
99	Weights, paper							71	12				120
100	Wax, sealing .... pounds							17	3	3			
101	Buckets, tin, assorted							131		9			5
102	Buckets, mess							41					
103	Buckets, slop							6					
104	Buckets												
105	Basins, wash							241	38	104			682
106	Basins, tin wash							188					
107	Basins, tin							19					20
108	Boilers, coffee							623	8	428			
109	Boilers, assorted							608	15	153			
110	Boilers, wash							29	2	8			169
111	Boilers, meat												7
112	Boilers, tin							6		6			2
113	Boilers, iron												2
114	Boilers with cocks							18					

Report showing the disposition of United States military railroad property in the military division of the Tennessee, &c.—Continued.

Running number.	Articles.	Sold at public auction to railroad companies on credit on same terms as authorized by Executive Orders of August 8 and October 14, 1865.						Sold at auction for cash.	Transferred to officers.	Lost or expended in the public service.	Captured property returned to railroad companies.	Captured property returned to individuals.	Balance on hand June 1, 1866.
		Nashville and North-western railroad.	Selma and Meridian railroad.	Nashville and Decatur railroad.	New Orleans, Jackson, and Great Northern railroad.	Mississippi and Tennessee railroad.	Mississippi Central railroad.						
115	Boilers, copper range							9					
116	Boilers, tin wash							135		13			
117	Boilers, tin wash, with cocks							1					
118	Brooms, hickory							93	18	10			
119	Brooms, splint							533	86				
120	Brooms, corn							758	270	183			299
121	Brooms, ratan							2					
122	Brooms							36	7	98			270
123	Brushes, copying								1				26
124	Brushes, window												1
125	Brushes, counter							116		1			
126	Brushes, dust							45	1				
127	Brushes, assorted							10					
128	Boxes, P. O							12					
129	Boxes, letter							2					
130	Boxes, paper							500					
131	Boxes, dredge							348		11			9
132	Boxes, twine							1					7
133	Boxes, tin												2
134	Boxes, spice												1
135	Boxes, ice							6					
136	Boxes, sugar												3
137	Boxes, salt							3					12
138	Boxes, pepper								22	76			2,086
139	Boxes, mess							1					17
140	Boxes, bill-head												2
141	Boxes, black walnut							1					
142	Boxes, cash							1					
143	Benches, assorted							316					
144	Baskets, paper												5
145	Bells, office												1

146	Balances, letter												
147	Boards, wash												14
148	Boards, black							1					6
149	Boards, diagram												1
150	Boards, paper								4				
151	Boards, pressing								10				
152	Boards, card ..... sheets								3,300				
153	Boards, binders'								125				
154	Boards, Bristol								132				
155	Bowls, sugar												
156	Bowls, wash							61					
157	Bowls, feet wash							4					131
158	Bowls, assorted							2	4				160
159	Bunks							34	1	344			15
160	Bunks, single								1				
161	Bureaus							1					1
162	Bedsteads							42					12
163	Bins, flour							2					
164	Blocks, meat							2					
165	Cups								3				152
166	Cups, palette												2
167	Cups, tin, assorted							5,348	233	1,393			
168	Cups, sponge												1
169	Cups, copying												1
170	Cups, molasses							329					1
171	Cans, milk, (covered)							2					
172	Cans, molasses							150	1				
173	Cans, watering							62					
174	Covers, bucket									534			3,348
175	Covers, coffee-pot							4,847		424			
176	Covers, oven							7					
177	Covers, tallow can							690					
178	Cleavers, meat							49					
179	Casters									3			7
180	Canisters, tea							32					1
181	Cots							35	2				
182	Chests, mess							4	1				21
183	Chests, field							1					
184	Chests, assorted							3					3
185	Clocks							28	2				
186	Cupboards							46					50
187	Cupboards, pigeon-hole												
188	Counters							3					1
189	Chambers							2					7
190	Chairs, assorted							391	10	3			
191	Chairs, office								18				338
192	Chairs, split bottom									6			
193	Coolers, water							13	3				
194	Cases, tin							1					2
195	Cases, post-office							1					1
196	Cases, blank							3					
197	Cases, shelves, and drawers												

Report showing the disposition of United States military railroad property in the military division of the Tennessee, &c.—Continued.

Running number.	Articles.	Sold at public auction to railroad companies on credit on same terms as authorized by Executive Orders of August 8 and October 14, 1865.						Sold at auction for cash.	Transferred to officers.	Lost or expended in the public service.	Captured property returned to railroad companies.	Captured property returned to individuals.	Balance on hand June 1, 1866.
		Nashville and Northwestern railroad.	Selma and Meridian railroad.	Nashville and Decatur railroad.	New Orleans, Jackson, and Great Northern railroad.	Mississippi and Tennessee railroad.	Mississippi Central railroad.						
198	Cases, assorted							9					
199	Cases, book							1					
200	Cases, pillow							5					
201	Cases, pigeon-hole							33					
202	Closets, picket												16
203	Cleaners, stove												104
204	Cullenders							1		6			
205	Cushions							29		59			
206	Curtains, window												
207	Charts, time												
208	Calendars												37
209	Cellars, salt												
210	Cutters, cake							23					
211	Carvers												4
212	Carvers and forks												1
213	Caps, stove pipe							62	6	3			
214	Counterpanes							5					
215	Carpet, Brussels ... yards												
216	Coverlets							1					
217	Desks, assorted							101	9				
218	Dusters							1					
219	Dusters, feather							7	1	2			48
220	Dippers							258		36			
221	Dippers, tin							163	11	147			281
222	Drums, stove							6					
223	Drums, sheet-iron							1					14
224	Dishes, tin							4					11
225	Dishes, soup												10
226	Dishes, fruit												7
227	Dishes, vegetable												4
228	Dishes, meat												2

229	Dishes, sauce												9
230	Dishes, large												1
231	Dishes, small												2
232	Dishes, assorted							36					23
233	Demijohns							1					2
234	Drawers							1					
236	Elbows							25	9	6			
237	Elbows, stove-pipe							674	8	192			
238	Fixtures, cook-stove ... sets								1	10			
239	Forks							136	31	60			
240	Forks, iron												
241	Forks, flesh							967	8	10			
242	Forks, table							3,934	173	1,618			
243	Forks, carving												2
244	Forks, large												4
245	Funnels, assorted							270		1			
246	Funnels, tin, assorted							62	4				220
247	Fillers, lamp							86	9	125			
248	Feeders, lamp												83
249	Furniture, cherry ... lots								1				
250	Firkins							1					
251	Grater							401					
252	Grater, nutmeg							99					248
253	Gridirons							62	1				
254	Gates, molasses												12
255	Griddles, stove							218	12				7
256	Glasses, looking							6					
257	Globes, lamp							7					
258	Grates							15					
259	Hods, coal							24		7			
260	Horns, tin							1					
261	Hooks, clothes												
262	Hooks, meat							11					
263	Jugs							2					
264	Jars, earthen												
265	Kettles, camp							859	51	74			
266	Kettles, iron							34	2				39
267	Kettles, tea							143	8	22			
268	Kettles, mess												5
269	Kettles							3	1				
270	Knives							209	74	60			
271	Knives, table							3,652	258	1,542			
272	Knives, butcher							1,635	27	6			
273	Knives and forks ... sets							1					
274	Knives and forks								224				1,464
275	Knives, carving							38		36			
276	Knives, cook							54					30
277	Knives, chopping							4	1	1			
278	Lamps, office									3			85
279	Lamps, coal-oil							49	24	3			29
280	Lamps							3					84
281	Ladles, soup							12		3			12

Report showing the disposition of United States military railroad property in the military division of the Tennessee, &c.—Continued.

Running number.	Articles.	Sold at public auction to railroad companies on credit on same terms as authorized by Executive Orders of August 8 and October 14 1865.						Sold at auction for cash.	Transferred to officers.	Lost or expended in the public service.	Captured property returned to railroad companies.	Captured property returned to individuals.	Balance on hand June 1, 1866.
		Nashville and North-western railroad.	Selma and Meridian railroad.	Nashville and Decatur railroad.	New Orleans, Jackson, and Great Northern railroad.	Mississippi and Tennessee railroad.	Mississippi Central railroad.						
282	Larders												12
283	Lids							9					
284	Matting, floor ... feet												15
285	Mortars								1				
286	Mills, coffee							218	13	206			
287	Mattresses							18					
288	Mops, floor									4			
289	Mashers, potato							4					
290	Nests, pigeon-hole												1
291	Ovens, Dutch							60		2			
292	Ovens, bake							3					
293	Punches, paper												
294	Presses, letter							5	4				7
295	Presses, letter, with stamp												5
296	Presses and stands, (letter)							1	1				
297	Pipe, stove ... feet								600				1, 136
298	Pipe, stove ... joints							4, 599	256	1, 653			
299	Pipe, stove, assorted ... pounds												
300	Pipes, connecting, for range							1					
301	Pans, fry								9	56			1, 542
302	Pans, try							1, 720					
303	Pans, mess, assorted							3, 285	41	352			
304	Pans, dish							612	48	283			
305	Pans, baking							334	10	43			
306	Pans, dripping							491	27	154			
307	Pans, tin sauce							1		4			
308	Pans, dust							7		2			5
309	Pans, stew							27		10			
310	Pans, assorted							30					2, 750
311	Pans, tin, assorted							963	4	97			
312	Pans, ash							8		12			

313	Pans, tin ......sets												
314	Pans, pie							41					
315	Pans, wash							754					
316	Pans, cake							203					
317	Pails, tin							1					12
318	Pails								77				
319	Plates, tin							8,378	962	1,499			
320	Plates, soup							6					141
321	Plates, sauce												48
322	Plates, dinner							4					8
323	Plates							330					
324	Plates, pie							161					
325	Plates, meat												
326	Pots, assorted							247	13				
327	Pots, mess												5
328	Pots, tea							6		3			14
329	Pots, coffee							454	20	120			391
330	Pots, fire									2			1
331	Pots, sprinkling							559	2	6			
332	Pots, iron							124		8			95
333	Pots, tin							6					
334	Pots, tin stew							15					
335	Pots, water							16					
336	Pitchers							7					
337	Pitchers, stone												22
338	Pitchers, water												2
339	Pillows							26					
340	Pokers, assorted							54					
341	Peels, bakers'							4					
342	Pins, time							12					
343	Pins, rolling							6					
344	Plugs, basin							5					
345	Quilts							2					
346	Racks, letter												24
347	Racks and desk, card												1
348	Racks, towel							1					
349	Ranges and fixtures, cooking							2		3			
350	Ranges, cooking							12					1
351	Ranges, patent							2					
352	Railing, office ......pieces							13					
353	Railing, hand, with banisters ......feet											50	
354	Refrigerators							1					
355	Safes, iron							3					
356	Safes, office								3				14
357	Safes, fire-proof								1				1
358	Safes, paymasters'							1					1
359	Safes, field												
360	Safes, match							106					
361	Safes, twine												56
362	Safes, S. P							50					
363	Scissors ......pairs												
364	Shears ......do												2

Report showing the disposition of United States military railroad property in the military division of the Tennessee, &c.—Continued.

Running number.	Articles.	Sold at public auction to railroad companies on credit on same terms as authorized by Executive Orders of August 8 and October 14, 1865.						Sold at auction for cash.	Transferred to officers.	Lost or expended in the public service.	Captured property returned to railroad companies.	Captured property returned to individuals.	Balance on hand June 1, 1866.
		Nashville and North-western railroad.	Selma and Meridian railroad.	Nashville and Decatur railroad.	New Orleans, Jackson, and Great Northern railroad.	Mississippi and Tennessee railroad.	Mississippi Central railroad.						
365	Shears, lamp ....pairs								12				
366	Shears, banker's ....do								1				9
367	Slates, assorted							245	1				
368	Shovels, fire							56	1				
369	Shovels, baker's							6					
370	Sieves							16	2	1			46
371	Sieves, flour							37	4				
372	Sieves, meal												12
373	Sieves, fine												1
374	Scuttles, coal							3	3				4
375	Scoops							86	2	1			
376	Scoops, flour								3	3			7
377	Spittoons							103	4				2
378	Spittoons, wooden							78					
379	Shades												3
380	Shades, lamp							31					22
381	Shades, lamp, (tin)							4					
382	Shades and clasps												36
383	Spiders							7	4				2
384	Spoons, table							22, 503	234	521			
385	Spoons, tea							6, 293	280	390			269
386	Spoons, basting							1, 630	7	10			
387	Spoons, assorted							3					2, 974
388	Skimmers							2		13			42
389	Steamers							96		87			
390	Steamers, tin							56	10	17			9
391	Skillets							124	8	1			
392	Skillets, stove							96					
393	Stoves, box							325		22			
394	Stoves, sheet-iron							90	13	44			
395	Stoves, cast-iron							105					11

396	Stoves, coal							43	8				
397	Stoves, open coal							2					
398	Stoves, tent							97					1
399	Stoves, camp							1					
400	Stoves, cooking							271	9				
401	Stoves, cooking, and pipe												1
402	Stoves, cooking, and fixtures							13	8				104
403	Stoves, cooking, complete												19
404	Stoves, parlor							15					
405	Stoves and pipe												2
406	Stoves, glue												
407	Stoves, heating							1					9
408	Stoves, assorted							39	3				55
409	Stoves, office								2				
410	Stoves, shop								7				
411	Stoves, cylinder												7
412	Stoves, old ... tons												25
413	Stands							10	1				12
414	Stands, wash							57	1				
415	Stands, letter-press							5					
416	Stands, light, and hose												
417	Stands, and lamp globe												1
418	Stands, light												
419	Stands, bed												
420	Snuffers ... pairs												1
421	Snuffers, candle ... do												7
422	Stools							246	3				
423	Stools, bench												
424	Spouts, funnel												60
425	Shelves and brackets ... sets												1
426	Sticks, candle							925		90			
427	Steels, carving												8
428	Saucers, tin							102					420
429	Saucers							11					
430	Sinks							5	1				
431	Sheets							4					
432	Screens												
433	Settees												7
434	Strainers, coffee												1
435	Sprinklers												
436	Sprinklers, copper							1					
437	Sacks, bed												
438	Scales, letter							7					
439	Tables, field							1					
440	Tables, camp								2				
441	Tables, office							20					
442	Tables, round							9					
443	Tables, centre												1
444	Tables, dining												1
445	Tables, draughting												1
446	Tables, assorted							319	4				
447	Tables, time												26

Report showing the disposition of United States military railroad property in the military division of the Tennessee, &c.—Continued.

Running number.	Articles.	Sold at public auction to railroad companies on credit on same terms as authorized by Executive Orders of August 8 and October 14, 1865.						Sold at auction for cash.	Transferred to officers.	Lost or expended in the public service.	Captured property returned to railroad companies.	Captured property returned to individuals.	Balance on hand June 1, 1865.
		Nashville and North-western railroad.	Selma and Meridian railroad.	Nashville and Decatur railroad.	New Orleans, Jackson, and Great Northern railroad.	Mississippi and Tennessee railroad.	Mississippi Central railroad.						
448	Trimmers, lamp								1				1
449	Tumblers												15
450	Thimbles, stovepipe							74					
451	Toasters												1
452	Tubs, wash							1					
453	Tubs, bathing							2					
454	Ticks, bed							33					
455	Troughs, bread							2					
456	Urinals							1					
457	Wardrobes								46				
458	Waiters												3
459	Ambulances							8					
460	Axles, ambulance												
461	Blankets, saddle							2	351	189			
462	Bits, mullen									163			
463	Bridles, riding								101	2			
464	Bridles, blind								405	11			
465	Buckets, U. S. horse												324
466	Bows, wagon							138	199				
467	Bows, ox							1	21	292			91
468	Bows, ambulance									150			
469	Brushes, horse							260	386	504			
470	Boxes, feed								97				
471	Boxes, wagon								26	8			14
472	Boxes, cutting									1			
473	Boxes, ambulance pipe									12			
474	Boards, foot												
475	Bolsters, extra log wagon												
476	Bolsters, army wagon								32				
477	Bolts, king							5	43				

478	Bolts, king .... pounds							25					
479	Bolts, tongue								2	18			
480	Bodies, wagon								50				
481	Bodies, cart								9				
482	Breeching, cart								81				
482½	Bits, bridle							10		213			28
483	Beds, axle								6				
484	Carts								65				
485	Chains, halter								499				
486	Chains, trace								13				25
487	Chains, fifth							2	100				
488	Chains, bearing								62				7
489	Chains, breast								398	1			
490	Chains, spreader								285				
491	Chains, stretcher							24	100				
492	Chains, stretcher, and S. S								24				
493	Chains, ox								2				
494	Collars, horse								189	3			48
495	Collars, mule								319	238			
496	Covers, wagon								27				5
497	Combs, curry							252	567	513			
498	Cruppers								41				
499	Drays								12				
500	Felloes, wagon								1,777	1,776			
501	Gears, running								26				
502	Gearings, hind								17				
503	Gearings, front								9				
504	Gates, end								39				100
505	Horses								283	1			
506	Harness .... sets												
507	Harness, S. S. ambulance								1				8
508	Harness, S. S. wheel								315	22			209
509	Harness, S. S. lead								247	4			423
510	Harness, S. S. wheel-horse								101				
511	Harness, S. S. wheel-mule								299				
512	Harness, S. S. lead-mule								439	50			
513	Harness, cart								34	89			
514	Harness, dray												2
515	Hames, horse .... pairs								33				99
516	Hames .... do								99	164			
517	Halters, rope								14	14			
518	Halters, head								463	114			
519	Halters, head, and strap												12
520	Halters and chains								124				
521	Hounds, front, army wagon								249	358			
522	Hounds, hind, army wagon								271	300			
523	Hammers, wagon									1			
524	Jacks, wagon								1				
525	Kegs, ambulance								4				
526	Lines, cart												45
527	Lines, check								13				81
528	Lines, lead								127	8			103

Report showing the disposition of United States military railroad property in the military division of the Tennessee, &c.—Continued.

Running number.	Articles.	Sold at public auction to railroad companies on credit on same terms as authorized by Executive Orders of August 8 and October 14, 1865.						Sold at auction for cash.	Transferred to officers.	Lost or expended in the public service.	Captured property returned to railroad companies.	Captured property returned to individuals.	Balance on hand June 1, 1866.
		Nashville and Northwestern railroad.	Selma and Meridian railroad.	Nashville and Decatur railroad.	New Orleans, Jackson, and Great Northern railroad.	Mississippi and Tennessee railroad.	Mississippi Central railroad.						
529	Lines, 2-horse								300				
530	Leathers, sweat							74					52
531	Links, open							10					
532	Mules								955	42			
533	Martingales								4				
534	Oxen								25	28			
535	Poles, ridge								29				
536	Poles, coupling								29				
537	Rakes, stable								2				
538	Rims, bent ambulance								42				
539	Rims, ox-yoke bow							3					
540	Rings, open								838				
541	Rails, body								171	100			
542	Stretchers							214					30
543	Spreaders								30	73			
544	Saddles, riding								34	23			
545	Saddles, wagon								386	67			2
546	Saddles, cart								78	7			
547	Saddles							1	1	1			
548	Sticks, jockey								204	102			
549	Sticks, cart-dumping							4					
550	Springs, ambulance									3			3
551	Sprinklers, wagon												1
552	Sprinklers, cart												
553	Straps, neck								634	134			40
554	Straps, coupling												75
555	Straps, neck and chain								27				
556	Straps, back							32	53				
557	Straps, choke								12				
558	Straps, halter								40				
559	Straps, stirrup												

560	Straps, yoke												12
561	Spokes, wagon							102					
562	Spokes								200	2,150			
563	Spokes, army wagon								483	413			350
564	Spokes, 2-horse wagon								20	200			
565	Spokes, ambulance								187				
566	Stirrups, wooden							7	12	24			8
567	Stirrups, leather							388					
568	Shafts, cart								55				
569	Shafts							10					
570	Strings, tie							200					
571	Stocks, whip							8					
572	Trees, single							48	265				1,000
573	Trees, double							24	349				
574	Trees, saddle							7					10
575	Tongues, wagon								284	229			
576	Tongues, rough								43	43			
577	Troughs, feed							8	98	11			
578	Tires, wagon							75					
579	Wheels, hind								26				
580	Wheels, front								22				3
581	Wheels, wagon								126	40			
582	Wagons, lumber								47				
583	Wagons, army								234	1			
584	Wagons, spring								1				
585	Wagons, log								85				
586	Wagons, 2-horse								22				
587	Wagons, ox								1				
588	Wagons, wood								15				
589	Wagons, water								2				
590	Wagons, box												12
591	Wagons								1				
592	Whips, wagon								234	315			
593	Yokes, ox							18	109				178
594	Yokes and bows, ox							344		53			
595	Axes, chopping							11,592	103				8,064
596	Axes, chopping, and handles							879	2				
597	Axes, felling							8					12
598	Axes, felling, and handles												143
599	Axes, hand							65	8				
600	Axes, pick							1					37
601	Axes, broad							910	8				715
602	Axes, narrow												580
603	Axes, assorted							9,081	107			12	
604	Augers .... sets							5					
605	Augers							6,060	83	12			473
606	Augers, long, assorted												25
607	Augers, hollow .... sets												2
608	Augers, gas-fitting												1
609	Augers, bridge							123					
610	Augers, pump .... sets							6					
611	Augers, boring machine							26					

Report showing the disposition of United States military railroad property in the military division of the Tennessee, &c.—Continued.

Running number.	Articles.	Sold at public auction to railroad companies on credit on same terms as authorized by Executive Orders of August 8 and October 14, 1865.						Sold at auction for cash.	Transferred to officers.	Lost or expended in the public service.	Captured property returned to railroad companies.	Captured property returned to individuals.	Balance on hand June 1, 1866.
		Nashville and Northwestern railroad.	Selma and Meridian railroad.	Nashville and Decatur railroad.	New Orleans, Jackson, and Great Northern railroad.	Mississippi and Tennessee railroad.	Mississippi Central railroad.						
612	Augers, machine ... sets							19		1			24
613	Augers, machine							37					
614	Augers and handles												
615	Augers and handles, ¼-inch												
616	Augers and handles, 1½-inch												
617	Augers, spike							4					
618	Augers, convex							381					
619	Augers, wheelwright							26					
620	Augers, nut							132					
621	Anvils, assorted							7, 383	5				
622	Anvils, cast							2	3				1
623	Anvils, wrought							31	2				
624	Anvils, block												3
625	Anvils, wrought ... pounds							500					
626	Anvils, blacksmiths'							1					
627	Awls, scratch							194	13	45			220
628	Awls, brad							560	76				368
629	Awls, belt												
630	Awls, scribe								6				
631	Awls and tacks, shoe								6				
632	Awls, scratch, and handles							24					
633	Awls, peg, and handles							120					
634	Adzes							311	3	15			43
635	Adzes and handles												
636	Adzes, railroad							457	24				222
637	Adzes, foot or carpenters'							939	5				
638	Axles, car ... pounds							256, 119		8			
639	Axles, car							12					
639½	Arbors, circular saw							2					
640	Axles, car and tender							33		8			210
641	Axles, truck ... pounds									6, 613			17, 738

642	Axles, engine-driving							14					3
643	Axles, engine truck ... pounds												
644	Axles, tender												
645	Axles, truck								3,643	5			
646	Axles, tender truck									1			
647	Axles, timber buggy							59					
648	Anchors							1					
649	Acid, oxalic ... pounds							19½	40				
650	Acid, muriatic ... do							109		105			15
651	Acid ... do									6			
652	Aqua ammonia ... do									7			
653	Aloes ... do									10			
654	Alum ... do							204		88			
655	Antimony ... do							1,360		250			86
656	Alcohol ... gallons							161	118½	199			
657	Ammoniac, sal ... pounds							160					
658	Arms, hand-car												
659	Arms, engine pump												2
660	Arms, seat, cast ... pounds												
661	Apparatus, automatic ... sets								9				
662	Asphaltum ... gallons								2	28			
663	Bellows, blacksmiths'							106	6	24		1	
664	Bellows, assorted							1	1				29
665	Bellows, hand							2					
666	Bellows, 48-inch								1				
667	Bars, switch							131					
668	Bars, switch ... sets												1
669	Bars, lining							410					
670	Bars, raising												
671	Bars, iron							165					
672	Bars, pinch							75	80	3			
673	Bars, pinch ... pounds												813
674	Bars, grate ... do												
675	Bars, draw							1					
676	Bars, assorted												
677	Bars, timber							5					184
678	Bars, grate									15			
679	Bars, pinch steel												1
680	Bars, wrought iron pinch ... pounds								453				
681	Bars, switch ... do								294				
682	Bars, grate ... sets								1				
683	Bars, carpenters'							54					
684	Bars, pry and pinch							130					
685	Bars, pry							1					
686	Bars, fish ... pounds							19,374					
687	Bars, tamping							873	24				
688	Bars, crow							62	29			12	295
689	Bars, claw							683	10				
690	Bars, wrench							14					
691	Bars, engine coupling												
692	Bars, boring										1		4
693	Bars, cylinder boring												1

Report showing the disposition of United States military railroad property in the military division of the Tennessee, &c.—Continued.

Running number.	Articles.	Sold at public auction to railroad companies on credit on same terms as authorized by Executive Orders of August 8 and October 14, 1865.						Sold at auction for cash.	Transferred to officers.	Lost or expended in the public service.	Captured property returned to railroad companies.	Captured property returned to individuals.	Balance on hand June 1, 1866.
		Nashville and Northwestern railroad.	Selma and Meridian railroad.	Nashville and Decatur railroad.	New Orleans, Jackson, and Great Northern railroad.	Mississippi and Tennessee railroad.	Mississippi Central railroad.						
694	Bars, long												
695	Bars, short												25
696	Bars, steel												96
697	Bars, assorted ... pounds							2					
698	Bars, pins, and bolts ... do												
699	Brushes, varnish, assorted												
700	Brushes, C. H.							30	49				103
701	Brushes, W. W.							30	6	2			
702	Brushes, scrub							89	6	143			
703	Brushes, painters' dust							148	89	31			91
704	Brushes, paint, assorted												52
705	Brushes, flat							441	62	24			17
706	Brushes, oval									8			21
707	Brushes, marking												4
708	Brushes, striping								6				146
709	Brushes, car window												24
710	Brushes, artists'							34					
711	Brushes, artists' red sable												108
712	Brushes, glue												35
713	Brushes, sash									5			
714	Brushes, whitewash ... lots								18				
715	Brushes, machinists'							1					
716	Braces							10					
717	Braces, iron							7					96
718	Braces, wood							63	4				1
719	Braces and bits ... sets							9		2			20
720	Braces and bits							64	2				61
721	Braces and bits, car ... sets							11					15
722	Braces, hand							6	2				
723	Braces, joiner												1
724	Braces, switch								4				

725	Braces, pedestal												
726	Braces, ratchet ... sets								2				
727	Braces, truck ... pounds							42, 480					
728	Braces, engine							1					
729	Braces, engine bar							1					
730	Blenders, painters'							9					
731	Blenders, painters'												7
732	Bits, brace ... sets							1					
733	Bits ... do							11¼	1				
734	Bits, auger, assorted ... do							152	3				
735	Bits, auger, assorted							341	38	15			89
736	Bits, gimlet							1					940
737	Bits, gimlet ... sets												1
738	Bits, plough plane												20
739	Bits, plough plane ... sets								1				43
740	Bits, double plane												18
741	Bits, car							168	38				193
742	Bits, car ... sets							279	28 5-6				
743	Bits, centre												
744	Bits, rose											25	
745	Bits, (sets of six each)								9				17
746	Bits, gummer							20		20			
747	Bits, ratchet drill							421					
748	Bits, assorted							70					492
749	Bits, centre ... sets												3
750	Bits, planer							3					
751	Bits, double-cut							50					
752	Bits, brace							63					
753	Buts, assorted ... pairs								49				
754	Buts, brass, assorted							1, 059		1, 648			1, 364
755	Buts, brass, assorted ... pairs							932		269			1, 994
756	Buts												
757	Buts, loose joint							30		180			93
758	Buts, wrought, assorted							269	96	558			670
759	Buts, cast-iron ... pairs							394	5	1, 092			563
760	Buts, assorted							12					
761	Buts, wrought ... pairs							45					
762	Buts, fast							24					
763	Buts, cast							805					
764	Buts, rivet							100					
765	Buts, flat							258					
766	Buts, wrought-iron ... pairs												61
767	Buts, patent ... do							48					
768	Buts, cast, loose joint ... do							18					
769	Buts, wrought, common joint							30					
770	Buts, cast, loose joint							12					
771	Buts, wrought-iron												
772	Bolts, tank hoop												
773	Bolts, iron hexagon-head ... pounds												75
774	Bolts, fish-bar ... do							17, 611		14, 700			21, 234
775	Bolts							300	1, 400				
776	Bolts, carriage ... pounds									490			

Report showing the disposition of United States military railroad property in the military division of the Tennessee, &c.—Continued.

Running number.	Articles.	Sold at public auction to railroad companies on credit on same terms as authorized by Executive Orders of August 8 and October 14, 1865.						Sold at auction for cash.	Transferred to officers.	Lost or expended in the public service.	Captured property returned to railroad companies.	Captured property returned to individuals.	Balance on hand June 1, 1866.
		Nashville and North-western railroad.	Selma and Meridian railroad.	Nashville and Decatur railroad.	New Orleans, Jackson, and Great Northern railroad.	Mississippi and Tennessee railroad.	Mississippi Central railroad.						
777	Bolts, carriage							10,357	1,598	9,950			
778	Bolts, iron bar												
779	Bolts, brass, assorted									12			
780	Bolts, barrel							12		4			
781	Bolts, brass flush									36			
782	Bolts, fire									800			
783	Bolts, long ¾-inch ... pounds									500			
784	Bolts, ring							15		1			
785	Bolts, chain door							10		12			113
786	Bolts, tower							84					
787	Bolts, square head ... pounds							4,098					1,000
788	Bolts, bridge ... do							9,439					
789	Bolts, wrought ... do							95					
790	Bolts, wrought-iron							30					
791	Bolts and nuts							145					
792	Bolts and butts							159					
793	Bolts, brass knob							305					
794	Bolts, wagon							49					
795	Bolts, steel-spring square							62					
796	Bolts, pulley							40					
797	Bolts, coupling							15					
798	Bolts and keys							72					
799	Bolts ... pounds							421,312					
800	Bolts, door							12	4				
801	Bolts, bridge									289			
802	Bolts and nuts ... pounds												
803	Blocks, punch								1		1		
804	Blocks, swedge							13	10		5		
805	Blocks, die ... pounds								63				64
806	Blocks, iron pulley												
807	Blocks, iron												12

808	Blocks, purchase												2
809	Blocks, notch												39
810	Blocks, snatch							286	30	4			
811	Blocks, head, with truck												1
812	Blocks, upsetting												4
813	Blocks, patent												2
814	Blocks, tackle ... sets							2					
815	Blocks, tackle							261	8	18			26
816	Blocks and tackle ... sets											1	
817	Blocks and tackle								1				
818	Blocks, assorted							22	13				95
819	Blocks, double-tackle												
820	Blocks, head									15		2	
821	Blocks, triple								1				
822	Blocks, assorted ... pounds								5				
823	Blocks, assorted ... pairs												9
824	Blocks, cast-iron swedge ... pounds												
825	Blocks, cast-iron swedge							2	1				
826	Blocks, pillow ... pounds								600				
827	Blocks, single								2				
828	Blocks, double							89	1				
829	Blocks, head ... sets									2			
830	Blocks, double-head ... do									1			
831	Blocks, cast-iron swedge and tackle ... do												1
832	Blocks, gum ... pounds									147½			
833	Blocks, single												
834	Blocks, tackle ... pairs							87					
835	Buckets, assorted							165		25			
836	Buckets, water							840	91	659			622
837	Buckets, fire							62					40
838	Buckets, wood								224				297
839	Buckets								122				
840	Buckets, engine							24					
841	Buckets, iron							99					64
842	Buckets, coal												9
843	Buckets, varnish												
844	Buckets, tar									92			
845	Buckets, paint												
846	Buckets, rubber							5					
847	Buckets, sand							4					4
848	Buckets, swing							79					
849	Buckets, stiff							9					
850	Buckets, well							1					
851	Buckets, mortar							2					
852	Buckets, leather							1					
853	Boilers, steam							7					
854	Boilers, tin-flue												7
855	Boilers, small-flue												1
856	Boilers, double-flue												4
857	Boilers, 14 feet long, 40 inches diameter												2
858	Boilers, tubular, 12 feet long, 42 inches diameter												1
859	Boilers, steam, 2 flues, 21 ft. long, 34 inches diameter												

Report showing the disposition of United States military railroad property in the military division of the Tennessee, &c.—Continued.

Running number.	Articles.	Sold at public auction to railroad companies on credit on same terms as authorized by Executive Orders of August 8 and October 14, 1865.						Sold at auction for cash.	Transferred to officers.	Lost or expended in the public service.	Captured property returned to railroad companies.	Captured property returned to individuals.	Balance on hand June 1, 1866.
		Nashville and Northwestern railroad.	Selma and Meridian railroad.	Nashville and Decatur railroad.	New Orleans, Jackson, and Great Northern railroad.	Mississippi and Tennessee railroad.	Mississippi Central railroad.						
860	Boilers, steam, 4 flues, 24 ft. long, 39 inches diameter												
861	Boilers, stationary												
862	Boilers, iron-punch										1		
863	Boilers, iron-flue, 26 feet x 44 inches											1	
864	Brass, old ... pounds							100	1,795	904		200	442
865	Brass, sheet ... do							1,058	504	1,403			
866	Brass ... do									35			
867	Brass, scrap ... do							740					
868	Brass, wrought ... do							414					
869	Brass turnings ... do							9,535					
870	Brasses ... do								2,569				3,567
871	Brasses, truck ... do									505			
872	Bricks, common									6,185			15,305
873	Bricks, setting, for boilers												
874	Bricks, fire								18,752	550			
875	Bricks, soap, fire								2,000				
876	Bricks, split, fire								3,000				
877	Bricks, key								1,000				
878	Burlaps ... yards							50		572			
879	Buttons, assorted ... gross												
880	Buttons, upholsterers' ... do							404		97			$218\frac{2}{3}$
881	Buttons, hand ... sets									8			
882	Buttons, brass, on plates												
883	Buttons, brass ... gross									1			
884	Buttons, brass									136			
885	Brown, Vandyke ... pounds							83		6			
886	Brown, Spanish ... do							20		1,572			
887	Brown, Vandyke ... tubes									12			
888	Black, India ... pounds							84	12	40			
889	Black, lamp ... do							$7\frac{1}{2}$		216			
890	Black, lamp ... tubes												

891	Black, Japan	barrels									1			
892	Black, ivory	tubes									12			
893	Blue, ultramarine	pounds							117½	47	87			
894	Blue, Prussian	do							47¼	13½	20			
895	Black, blue	do							54		46			
896	Black, drop	do							2¾		120			
897	Blue, cobalt	tubes							3					
898	Blacking, stove	papers							206		115			
899	Bronze, gold	do							16	12	11			
900	Brilliant, American	tubes									12			
901	Bells, gong, hanging										3			
902	Bells, engine								7					
903	Bells, engine, alarm								2					
904	Bells, engine, gong								12					3
905	Bells, alarm													7
906	Bells, engine and frame								15					
907	Bells, cast-steel												1	
908	Bells, cab								1					
909	Balances, spring								3	3				8
910	Balances, locomotive spring								43	12	12			
911	Balances, iron beam													24
912	Balances, beam shive													26
913	Balances, steam								7					
914	Balances, elliptic spring								3					
915	Balances, counter								2					
916	Bushings, brass								9		94			
917	Bushings, gas-pipe										150			665
918	Bushings, bell cord													
919	Bushings, brass gland								60		45			
920	Bushings, silver-plated										11			
921	Brads, patent, assorted	papers							826	125	205			465
922	Bunting, assorted	yards							35	93	78			
923	Bunting, red, assorted	do									179			207
924	Burners, common										300			420
925	Burners, patent								96					44
926	Burners, eureka										123			
927	Burners, screw										24			
928	Brakes									57				232
929	Brakes, lever	pounds												
930	Brakes, car													
931	Bevels, assorted								821	2	16			
932	Bevels, square													30
933	Bevels, T									2	10			626
934	Boards, guttering													1
935	Boards, bulletin								6					
936	Boards, tally													4
937	Boards, draft								35					
938	Boards, running													
939	Boards, straw	pounds												200
940	Boards, pressing													10
941	Boards, binders'													125
942	Boards, sign								3					

Report showing the disposition of United States military railroad property in the military division of the Tennessee, &c.—Continued.

Running number.	Articles.	Sold at public auction to railroad companies on credit on same terms as authorized by Executive Orders of August 8 and October 14, 1865.						Sold at auction for cash.	Transferred to officers.	Lost or expended in the public service.	Captured property returned to railroad companies.	Captured property returned to individuals.	Balance on hand June 1, 1866.
		Nashville and Northwestern railroad.	Selma and Meridian railroad.	Nashville and Decatur railroad.	New Orleans, Jackson, and Great Northern railroad.	Mississippi and Tennessee railroad.	Mississippi Central railroad.						
943	Brooms, hair												2
944	Brooms, stable									17			45
945	Bottoms, composition ... pounds												68
946	Bottoms, copper ... do							829		100			30
947	Bottoms, dipper									30			595
948	Bottoms, bolt head												
949	Boxes, emery							85		17			58
950	Boxes, rivet							59					
951	Boxes, wood							2					
952	Boxes, tender							8					
953	Boxes, engine ... pounds							2		1,005			301
954	Boxes, engine												
955	Boxes, tool							330	2	4			
956	Boxes, packing							54					
957	Boxes, tinder												1
958	Boxes, axle							23					
959	Boxes, lamp												
960	Boxes, link												
961	Boxes, oil												
962	Boxes, hand car ... pounds												
963	Boxes, car, (Wood's patent) ... do												
964	Boxes, assorted							13	13				
965	Boxes, engine truck ... pounds								1,313				
966	Boxes, roller								4				
967	Boxes, iron							5					
968	Boxes, screw, blued							1					
969	Boxes, signal-light							10					
970	Boxes, shoeing							9					
971	Boxes, cutting							1					1
972	Boxes, drawing-paper							10					10
973	Boxes, cast							4					

974	Boxes, journal									144			
975	Belting leather, assorted ... feet							7,670		403			
976	Belting, gum ... do							2,953	213	920¾		470	
977	Belting, rubber ... do												231
978	Belting, assorted ... do							64					
979	Bottoms, tin lamp							128					
980	Bottoms, car lamp							6					
981	Blades, hack-saw												42
982	Brackets ... pounds								10				296
983	Brackets							3					11
984	Brackets, swing												5
985	Buggies, timber							47					
986	Borers, cylinder												
987	Borers, cylinder, portable										1		
988	Borers, tap							12					
989	Borers, hand							23					
990	Barrels							1					16
991	Bodkins								3				3
992	Barrows, wheel							224	9	56		8	
993	Bridges, truss ... feet												
994	Bridges, arch truss, McCallum's pat. inflexible ... do							850					
995	Borax ... pounds								13	251			200
996	Benches, stationery ... feet												38
997	Benches, work							113	10	19			
998	Benches, vice							1					
999	Bearings, centre ... pounds								1,410				
1000	Buildings							276	23		6		
1001	Buildings and water tank										1		
1002	Burrs ... pounds												10
1003	Burrs, copper ... do									32			5
1004	Bumpers ... do												
1005	Buttresses							19		7			
1006	Bumpers							2					
1007	Bodies, box car										3		
1008	Breeching ... pounds								50				
1009	Bibbs, finished, S. S. and S												90
1010	Buckles, assorted							28					288
1011	Buckles, harness ... gross							4		18			
1012	Buckles, roller, assorted ... do							16 29-36		6			2
1013	Buckles, assorted ... do							13		2			
1014	Blocks, railroad splice, Trimble's wooden									2,014			
1015	Backs, car-seat							8					
1016	Bands, spring ... pounds							600					
1017	Bands, gum ... do							505					
1018	Blinds, window							1					
1019	Boats, flat							2					
1020	Baskets, medicine							1					
1021	Benzine ... gallons							5					
1022	Bourgeois No. 8, 3 "D" ... pounds									13½			
1023	Buckles, round leg, ruled ... gross							2					
1024	Bolts, stay												
1025	Braces, tank							12					

Report showing the disposition of United States military railroad property in the military division of the Tennessee, &c.—Continued.

Running number.	Articles.	Sold at public auction to railroad companies on credit on same terms as authorized by Executive Orders of August 8 and October 14, 1865. Nashville and Northwestern railroad.	Selma and Meridian railroad.	Nashville and Decatur railroad.	New Orleans, Jackson, and Great Northern railroad.	Mississippi and Tennessee railroad.	Mississippi Central railroad.	Sold at auction for cash.	Transferred to officers.	Lost or expended in the public service.	Captured property returned to railroad companies.	Captured property returned to individuals.	Balance on hand June 1, 1866.
1026	Barges												
1027	Burners, gas												
1027¼	Chisels and handles												9
1027½	Chisels, cold							296	85			150	95
1027¾	Chisels, hand cold												1
1028	Chisels, chipping							1, 791	83				
1029	Chisels, hand chipping												100
1030	Chisels, firmer							158					
1031	Chisels, firmer ... sets							52					14
1032	Chisels, socket firmer ... do							12	25				2
1033	Chisels, socket							1, 116					
1034	Chisels, framing ... sets							3	2				
1035	Chisels, framing							294	85	3			917
1036	Chisels, track							1, 959	12				
1037	Chisels, cold track												2
1038	Chisels, masons'							67					12
1039	Chisels, corner							8					4
1040	Chisels, bolt												16
1041	Chisels, splitting												10
1042	Chisels, coppersmiths'												7
1043	Chisels, tamping								5				6
1044	Chisels, B. S							60					
1045	Chisels, cape							1					37
1046	Chisels, assorted							614		5			
1047	Chisels, carpenters'								1				2
1048	Chisels, gouging							37					
1049	Chisels, socket ... sets							20					
1050	Chisels, socket framing							418					
1051	Chisels, socket, and handles							6					
1052	Chisels, oval back							6					
1053	Chisels, mortise							13					

1054	Chisels, tinners' .... sets							1					
1055	Chills, frog												11
1056	Calipers, assorted .... pairs							46	2				
1057	Calipers, spring .... do								10				59
1058	Compasses, assorted .... do							508	12				
1059	Compasses, wing .... do												31
1060	Cups, oil							83					
1061	Cups, oil, spring bottom												7
1062	Cups, tallow								13				
1063	Cups, tin paint							52	24				
1064	Cups, tin striping												20
1065	Cups, brass												2
1066	Cups, steam chest oil								6				
1067	Cups, valve oil												39
1068	Cups, brass oil							23					
1069	Cups, varnish							18	3				
1070	Cans, powder							24					
1071	Cans, engine oil							174					
1072	Cans, oil, spring-bottom							30					53
1073	Cans, tallow								51				
1074	Cans, assorted							312	48	38			555
1075	Cans, oil, assorted							1, 183	80	114		3	
1076	Cans, tin, assorted								7				110
1077	Cans, emery												
1078	Cans, bench oil								5				
1079	Couplings, tender .... pounds												90
1080	Couplings, 3-link							1, 073					
1081	Couplings, 3-link .... pounds							5, 220					
1082	Couplings, straight							161		71			
1083	Couplings, crooked												
1084	Couplings, brass union, assorted .... pairs												250
1085	Couplings, clamp and screw												1
1086	Couplings, hose							30					
1087	Couplings, chain .... pounds												
1088	Couplings .... do								2, 549				
1089	Couplings, brass hose .... do							106	106				106
1090	Couplings, hose												
1091	Couplings, assorted												
1092	Chains, engine												10
1093	Chains, assorted							1		5			10
1094	Chains, log							69	136				
1095	Chains, switch							131	19	33			
1096	Chains, Powers' endless												
1097	Chains, brake .... pounds												
1098	Chains, large												1
1099	Chains, small												1
1100	Chains, civil engineers'							2					
1101	Chains, surveyors', (100 feet)												
1102	Chains, switch .... pounds												
1103	Chains, log .... do							356					
1104	Chain, assorted .... feet								222	50			792
1105	Chain, assorted .... pounds							34		236			

Report showing the disposition of United States military railroad property in the military division of the Tennessee, &c.—Continued.

Running number.	Articles.	Sold at public auction to railroad companies on credit on same terms as authorized by Executive Orders of August 8 and October 14, 1865.						Sold at auction for cash.	Transferred to officers.	Lost or expended in the public service.	Captured property returned to railroad companies.	Captured property returned to individuals.	Balance on hand June 1, 1866.
		Nashville and Northwestern railroad.	Selma and Meridian railroad.	Nashville and Decatur railroad.	New Orleans, Jackson, and Great Northern railroad.	Mississippi and Tennessee railroad.	Mississippi Central railroad.						
1106	Chain, cable ... pounds								203				297
1107	Chain, cable ... feet												
1108	Chain, German ... do												45
1109	Chain, German coil ... do							800		75			330
1110	Chain, coil, proved, ⅝-inch ... pounds												1,103
1111	Chain, coil, assorted ... do							24,723					206¼
1112	Castings, assorted ... do							284,622	45,828	22,167			
1113	Castings, iron ... do									105,787			252,082
1114	Castings, pump ... do									164			344
1115	Castings, brass ... do							20,374	1,212	9,657			
1116	Castings, grate bar ... do									2,336			6,955
1117	Castings, old stove ... lots							1					
1118	Castings, car ... pounds							109,634					
1119	Castings, tender ... do							22					
1120	Caps, double												3
1121	Caps, gas pipe												776
1122	Clamps, iron ... pairs												
1123	Clamps, steel												
1124	Clamps, cabinet-makers'							3					1
1125	Clamps, saddlers'							3					
1126	Clamps, switch												
1127	Clamps, belt												3
1128	Clamps, spring												2
1129	Clamps, block ... sets												1
1130	Clamps, horseshoe							18					3
1131	Clamps ... pairs							140					
1132	Clamps ... pounds												1,467
1133	Clamps, iron horse												
1134	Clamps, iron												50
1135	Clamps, iron, for tender												
1136	Clamps, boiler							17					

1137	Clamps, chimney							2					
1138	Clamps, saw-set							3					
1139	Clamps, wood bench							28					
1140	Clamps, screw							36				10	
1141	Cars, box	10	3	73	6	18	36	253			45		
1142	Cars, box freight								13				58
1143	Cars, flat	3			6		6	81	27		47		
1144	Cars, wrecking												
1145	Cars, passenger							1	3		8		
1146	Cars, hand			12				12	3				
1147	Cars, truck							18					
1148	Cars, caboose							1					
1149	Cars, coal	1									2		
1150	Cars, stock											1	
1151	Cars, push or dump							1				5	
1152	Cutters, card								2				
1153	Cutters, lead												1
1153½	Cutters, cast-steel												16
1154	Cutters, boring												4
1155	Cutters, iron							43	7				
1156	Covers, cylinder head												
1157	Covers, flag							38					28
1158	Covers, box												27
1159	Covers, hand-car ... pounds												465
1160	Covers, axle-box ... do												
1161	Covers, cushion							12					
1162	Covers, enamelled							2					
1163	Covers, plush							5					
1164	Covers, sand box								623				
1165	Covers, dome								819				
1166	Covers, smoke-stack								83				
1167	Covers, smoke-stack hand hole								16				
1168	Crucibles							52	6				
1169	Cylinders, steam engine												2
1170	Cylinders, locomotive												1
1171	Cylinders, 5 feet long, 12-inch bore												
1172	Chairs, guard rail												64
1173	Chairs, railroad, assorted							3,779	5,904	7,625			
1174	Chairs, railroad ... pounds												
1175	Chairs, frog												6
1176	Chairs, head ... sets												
1177	Chairs, step							27					
1178	Chairs, assorted												346
1179	Chairs, railroad guard							13					
1180	Cocks, waste									20			4
1181	Cocks, miss gauge							61	2	44			
1182	Cocks, lock							2					6
1183	Cocks, stop							455	104	72			
1184	Cocks, blow-off									10			
1185	Cocks, bibb							34		196			
1186	Cocks, bibb, brass							199	3	48			
1187	Cocks, pet							5		33			

Report showing the disposition of United States military railroad property in the military division of the Tennessee, &c.—Continued.

Running number.	Articles.	Sold at public auction to railroad companies on credit on same terms as authorized by Executive Orders of August 8 and October 14, 1865.						Sold at auction for cash.	Transferred to officers.	Lost or expended in the public service.	Captured property returned to railroad companies.	Captured property returned to individuals.	Balance on hand June 1, 1866.
		Nashville and Northwestern railroad.	Selma and Meridian railroad.	Nashville and Decatur railroad.	New Orleans, Jackson, and Great Northern railroad.	Mississippi and Tennessee railroad.	Mississippi Central railroad.						
1188	Cocks, gauge							40		106			
1189	Cocks, racking							46		7			78
1190	Cocks, heater and cylinder												18
1191	Cocks, steam, assorted							1		101			124
1192	Cocks, brass							16	1				
1193	Cocks, cylinder							91	123				
1194	Cocks, heater							77		41			
1195	Cocks, water									2			
1196	Cocks, lever									2			
1197	Cocks, rough							64					
1198	Cocks, air							1					
1199	Cocks, basin							1					
1200	Cocks, gas							9					
1201	Cocks, steam-gauge							39					
1202	Cocks, steam-stop							178					
1203	Chimneys, assorted							41	25	728			
1204	Chimneys, head-light							40	210	506			300
1205	Chimneys, flint									569			690
1206	Chimneys, stationary smoke-stack												
1207	Chimneys, lamp, assorted							3	132	159			
1208	Chimneys, coal-oil lamp								150				61
1209	Cases, drawing							1					7
1210	Cases, engine tool-box key												1
1211	Cases, tin stencil												1
1212	Cases, medicine							1					
1213	Cases, turning paper							2					
1214	Cupolas												
1215	Copper, bar ... pounds									96			
1216	Copper, assorted ... do									1, 175			7, 390
1217	Copper, sheet ... do							602	1, 387	3, 547			7, 721
1218	Copper, ingot ... do								2, 000	2, 029			

1219	Copper, scrap ... do							1,181					
1220	Copper, tinned ... do							134					
1221	Copper, pig ... do							435					
1222	Cloth, emery ... quires							1,530⅛	40	110			
1223	Cloth, emery ... gross							100					
1224	Cloth, gum ... pounds												159
1225	Cloth, enamelled ... yards							57	504				5
1226	Cloth, enamelled ... pieces							17					
1227	Cloth, tracing ... rolls								1				
1228	Cloth, tracing ... yards							64					
1229	Crayons ... gross												
1230	Chalk, white ... pounds							2,610	17½	454½			3
1231	Chalk, red ... do							88		25½			
1232	Chalk ... do							3		15			
1233	Chalk, prepared ... do							1 1-6					
1234	Cranes, blacksmiths'							2				1	2
1235	Cranes, iron												
1236	Cranes, assorted ... pounds												
1237	Cranes, tank							27					
1238	Cranes, water							1					
1239	Cuffs, hand ... pairs							6					
1240	Chests, tool							4	5				4
1241	Chests, carpenters' tool												10
1242	Chests, tin												
1243	Chests, saddlers'							4					
1244	Cupboards, tool												3
1245	Cupboards, oil												
1246	Combs, graining ... lots							1					2
1247	Combs, graining ... sets												1
1248	Chucks, assorted												5
1249	Chucks, screw							7					
1250	Chucks, drill												4
1251	Chucks, brass												
1252	Chucks, planer												4
1253	Chucks, universal							1					1
1254	Chucks, universal lathe												
1255	Chucks, tap and nuts												49
1256	Chucks, lathe												
1257	Chases, assorted								18				
1258	Cranks, hand-car ... pounds												81
1259	Cranks, iron												
1260	Chasers, screw												60
1261	Catches, cupboard							552		158			
1262	Catches, brake												
1263	Catches, window							10					
1264	Chrome, yellow ... pounds							148½	255¼	314			90
1265	Chrome, orange, American ... tubes							12					
1266	Chrome, orange, dry ... pounds							120					
1267	Chrome, green ... do												39
1268	Colors ... tubes							102					24
1269	Colors ... boxes							2					
1270	Candles, car ... pounds								85	639			

Report showing the disposition of United States military railroad property in the military division of the Tennessee, &c.—Continued.

Running number.	Articles.	Sold at public auction to railroad companies on credit on same terms as authorized by Executive Orders of August 8 and October 14, 1865.						Sold at auction for cash.	Transferred to officers.	Lost or expended in the public service.	Captured property returned to railroad companies.	Captured property returned to individuals.	Balance on hand June 1, 1866.
		Nashville and Northwestern railroad.	Selma and Meridian railroad.	Nashville and Decatur railroad.	New Orleans, Jackson, and Great Northern railroad.	Mississippi and Tennessee railroad.	Mississippi Central railroad.						
1271	Candles, star ... pounds								2	395			
1272	Copperas ... do							3,862		387			
1273	Cord, hemp bell ... do								653	561			
1274	Cords, bell												
1275	Cement, composition ... cans									30			16
1276	Cement ... barrels							5	3				
1277	Connexions, meter												
1278	Cabs, locomotive												73
1279	Circulars, switch							23					
1280	Centres. lathe												
1281	Carriages, iron lathe												
1282	Carriages, iron ... sections							1					
1283	Clasps, hand												
1284	Crabs, drilling												
1285	Chamber, engine pump												
1286	Corrals							1					
1287	Casings, cylinder head							18					
1288	Cantharides, tincture ... pounds							1					
1289	Camphor, gum ... do							2					
1290	Calomel ... do							2					
1291	Cochineal ... do							23					
1292	Composition, chemical ... cans							48					
1293	Carriers							22					
1294	Crosses, gas-pipe							65					
1295	Collars, gas-bracket							67					
1296	Circles, iron							18					
1297	Coffins							3					
1298	Casks							12					
1299	Cones, blacksmiths'							1					
1300	Drills, iron pipe												10
1301	Drills, breast							1					

1302	Drills, stone							55					
1303	Drills, ratchet, assorted							129	17				
1304	Drills, ratchet, brace, steel												20
1305	Drills, stock and clamp												
1306	Drills, blacksmiths'												1
1307	Drills, assorted							22	11				361
1308	Drills, pin												21
1309	Drills, lathe, steel							21					
1310	Drills, counter, steel												12
1311	Drills, cast steel ... pounds												
1312	Drills, steel												
1313	Drills, vertical, 36-inch												1
1314	Drills, vertical, 45-inch, compound table												2
1315	Drills, vertical, 45-inch, plain table												1
1316	Drills, prop, iron table, complete												1
1317	Drills, churn							252					
1318	Drills, upright								1				
1319	Drills, drill press											25	
1320	Drills, steel standard												
1321	Drills, upright, ungeared, press and counter shafts								1				
1323	Drills, assorted ... sets								1				
1324	Drills, quarry							2					
1325	Drills, ratchets and bits							8					
1326	Drills, black enamelled ... yards								11	95			
1327	Dividers ... pairs							72		1			
1328	Dividers, spring ... do												36
1329	Drifts							43					
1330	Drifts, steel												25
1331	Dogs											2	
1332	Dogs, lathe												
1333	Dogs, ratchet ... pounds												
1334	Dogs, planer												
1335	Dogs, saw							22					
1336	Dusters, counter												6
1337	Dusters, painters'							140	6				
1338	Duck ... yards								105	95			
1339	Duck, car ... do												105
1340	Dippers, oil							1	4				26
1341	Dippers, lye							1					56
1342	Drippers, oil												
1343	Diamonds, glaziers'							3	2				2
1344	Dadoes							27					8
1345	Doors, fire, and frames												
1346	Doors, unfinished												
1347	Doors, panel										7		
1348	Doors, furnace							3		2			
1349	Doors, glass							2					
1350	Doors, glazed ... pieces							2					
1351	Doors, assorted							37					
1352	Doors, car							27					
1353	Dryer, patent ... pounds							81	3	96			
1354	Dryer, sand							2					1

Report showing the disposition of United States military railroad property in the military division of the Tennessee, &c.—Continued.

Running number.	Articles.	Sold at public auction to railroad companies on credit on same terms as authorized by Executive Orders of August 8 and October 14, 1865.						Sold at auction for cash.	Transferred to officers.	Lost or expended in the public service.	Captured property returned to railroad companies.	Captured property returned to individuals.	Balance on hand June 1, 1866.
		Nashville and Northwestern railroad.	Selma and Meridian railroad.	Nashville and Decatur railroad.	New Orleans, Jackson, and Great Northern railroad.	Mississippi and Tennessee railroad.	Mississippi Central railroad.						
1355	Drums for lathe, (W. I.) ... pounds												
1356	Derricks							1					
1357	Derrick blocks falls and dies							2					
1358	Derricks, crab							2					
1359	Drivers, iron lathe, round ... pounds									44			
1360	Drivers, screw ... lots							1					
1361	Dies and plates								4				
1362	Dies, pipe, and stocks ... sets							31					
1363	Dies, hand ... pounds												
1364	Dies, assorted							12					
1365	Dies, gas pipe												
1366	Dies and plates ... sets												
1367	Dies ... do							106					64
1368	Dies and hubs ... pounds												21
1369	Dies, forge												49
1370	Die stocks ... sets								166			3	
1371	Drivers, screw							888	22	7			44
1372	Drums, stove							6		1			
1373	Drawers, moulders'							3					20
1374	Dust, bone ... pounds							933					
1375	Engines, stationary												
1376	Engines, pumping, No. 3												2
1377	Engines and boilers, dummy							2					
1378	Engines, dummy												
1379	Engines and boilers, stationary								1		1		
1380	Engines, steam fire								1				
1381	Engines, single, steam												
1382	Engines, rotary fire, (Holley's patent)												
1383	Engines, caloric												
1384	Engines, rotary												
1385	Engines, pilot												

1386	Engines, portable										1	1	
1387	Engines, locomotive												
1388	Engine, locomotive, No. 212										1		
1389	Engines, locomotive, and tenders			5		2	1	27			46	2	
1390	Engine, double stationary, 11¼-inch bore, 24-inch stroke, Ellis & Moore's patent												
1391	Engines, stationary, 2 boilers 24 feet long, 40 inches diameter												
1392	Engine, double stationary, pulley and counter shaft												
1393	Engines, pumping												
1393½	Engine and boiler, 5-inch cylinder, 12-inch stroke, (complete)												
1394	Engine and boiler, (complete)												
1395	Engines, steam											1	
1396	Engine, 12-inch bore, 36-inch stroke											1	
1397	Engines, hoisting, complete								1				
1398	Engines and boilers, stationary, (complete)								1				
1399	Eyes, brass screw							108		144			
1400	Eyes, bell cord												
1401	Eyes, iron ... gross							2					3
1402	Eyes, screw ... do							6					
1403	Ears, tin kettle ... do							85		5			
1404	Ears, kettle							4, 646		950			
1405	Ears, bucket							3, 121		540			27, 580
1406	Ears, C. C. saw							248					
1407	Elbows, reducing												6
1408	Elbows, drop												6
1409	Elbows gas-pipe							275	3	76			227
1410	Elbows, water-pipe												
1411	Elbows, goose-neck							67					
1412	Emery, assorted ... pounds							1, 292	179	477			
1413	Emery flour ... do								50	50			
1414	Edges, iron												1
1415	Edges, steel, straight												
1416	Ends, draw bar												
1417	Ends, equalizer												
1418	Easels												
1419	Escutcheons							54		24			
1420	Easers												1
1421	Forges, blacksmiths'							17	2				17
1422	Forges and bellows												4
1423	Forges, portable							8		1			
1424	Forges, blacksmiths' portable												
1425	Forges, cast-iron								1				1
1426	Forges							18					
1427	Furnaces, bolt												
1428	Furnaces, plumbers'												3
1429	Furnaces, tinners'							17					
1430	Furnaces, charcoal							6	1	1			
1431	Frogs, cast									30			
1432	Frogs, patent portable							12	6				4
1433	Frogs, assorted ... pounds							169, 967		38, 715			9

Report showing the disposition of United States military railroad property in the military division of the Tennessee, &c.—Continued.

Running number.	Articles.	Sold at public auction to railroad companies on credit on same terms as authorized by Executive Orders of August 8 and October 14, 1865.						Sold at auction for cash.	Transferred to officers.	Lost or expended in the public service.	Captured property returned to railroad companies.	Captured property returned to individuals.	Balance on hand June 1, 1866.
		Nashville and Northwestern railroad.	Selma and Meridian railroad.	Nashville and Decatur railroad.	New Orleans, Jackson, and Great Northern railroad.	Mississippi and Tennessee railroad.	Mississippi Central railroad.						
1434	Frogs, chilled							44		4			
1435	Frogs, plated									16			
1436	Frogs, assorted									16			
1437	Frogs, T							6					
1438	Fittings, gas ... pounds							4, 270		36			
1439	Fittings, gas pipe ... do												680
1440	Fittings, gas									100			468
1441	Fittings, brass cock and valve											75	
1442	Fasteners, car window							93		310			
1443	Fasteners, sash							52		46			
1444	Fixtures, grindstone ... sets							161	1				5
1445	Fixtures, lathe ... pounds								306				
1446	Frames, saw							3					
1447	Frames, engine truck												18
1448	Frames, truck, iron ... pounds												
1449	Frames, brake, beam								87				
1450	Frames and slides, car window												
1451	Frames, tank												
1452	Frames, truck			5				7					
1453	Frames, wreck										3		
1454	Frames, bell ... pounds								96				
1455	Frames, bell									96			
1456	Frames, hack-saw								1				
1457	Frames, saw, railroad cut-off							1					
1458	Frames, bolt							1					
1459	Frames, circular-saw							4					
1460	Frames, bellows							11					
1461	Frames, door							1					
1462	Frames, window							39					
1463	Frames, lock							18					
1464	Frames, grindstones							3					

1465	Frames, for buildings							1					
1466	Frames and hammers, pile-driving							1					
1467	Frames							4					
1468	Flatters								5				
1469	Fullers							13					166
1470	Flasks ... pounds							363					2, 006
1471	Flasks												291
1472	Flasks and tools ... pounds												11, 972
1473	Flasks, iron ... sets												
1474	Flannel, Canton ... yards								176¾	80			
1475	Flannel, red ... do									25			
1476	Faucets							82					
1477	Faucets, brass												5
1478	Fitches, assorted							4		12			255
1479	Flags, red							208	1				
1480	Fans, blowing							2					
1481	Fans, foundry											1	
1482	Fans, snail-shell								1		1		
1483	Flanges									1			14
1484	Followers ... pounds									5, 367			
1485	Followers, piston									15			16
1486	Figures ... sets							1					
1487	Figures												
1488	Figures ... pounds							6					
1489	Froes							2					
1490	Forks, "T" rail												
1491	Forks, manure							8	11				
1492	Forks, railroad							58					
1493	Forks, pitch							3					
1494	Fuze, safety ... feet							1, 850	900	1, 850			
1495	Feeders, oil												26
1496	Formers, tin							2					
1497	Formers, stove-pipe							1					
1498	Formers, tin gutter												1
1499	Facings, coal ... barrels							4	1	20			
1500	Facings, sea coal ... do												
1501	Folders, tinners'								1				
1502	Folders, iron							3					
1503	Ferrules ... pounds												
1504	Fences							3					
1505	Files, assorted							60, 539	580				
1506	Files, flat, assorted							101	11				383
1507	Files, half-round bastard, assorted							1, 849	227				
1508	Files, flat bastard, assorted							4, 820	319			204	
1509	Files, saw, assorted							2	531				115
1510	Files, flat, second-cut, assorted							3, 004	8				
1511	Files, taper, second-cut, assorted												24
1512	Files, hand, second-cut, assorted							180					443
1513	Files, round, second-cut, assorted							928					108
1514	Files, half-round, second-cut, assorted							1, 271					
1515	Files, coulter, second-cut, assorted												41
1516	Files, square, smooth, assorted							93					

Report showing the disposition of United States military railroad property in the military division of the Tennessee, &c.—Continued.

Running number.	Articles.	Sold at public auction to railroad companies on credit on same terms as authorized by Executive Orders of August 8 and October 14, 1865.						Sold at auction for cash.	Transferred to officers.	Lost or expended in the public service.	Captured property returned to railroad companies.	Captured property returned to individuals.	Balance on hand June 1, 1866.
		Nashville and Northwestern railroad.	Selma and Meridian railroad.	Nashville and Decatur railroad.	New Orleans, Jackson, and Great Northern railroad.	Mississippi and Tennessee railroad.	Mississippi Central railroad.						
1517	Files, flat, smooth, assorted							2,261	144				
1518	Files, round, smooth, assorted							587					
1519	Files, hand dead, smooth, assorted							226					198
1520	Files, flat dead, smooth, asorted							736					304
1521	Files, hand, bastard, assorted							3,063	124				
1522	Files, square, bastard, assorted							2,895	72				
1523	Files, coulter, bastard, assorted												86
1524	Files, three-square, bastard, assorted												264
1525	Files, round parallel, bastard, assorted												10
1526	Files, square parallel, bastard, assorted							96					260
1527	Files, dead, smooth, assorted							59	12				
1528	Files, three-square, assorted							132					151
1529	Files, smooth, bastard, assorted							36					72
1530	Files, wire												93
1531	Files, bastard							452					
1532	Files, hand-saw, assorted							113	1,181				7,049
1533	Files, mill-saw, assorted							10,668	225				
1534	Files, pit-saw												24
1535	Files, patent												
1536	Files, round, bastard							1,827	168				1,236
1537	Files, half-round, smooth							647	73				1,608
1538	Files, half-round							36	13			1,002	
1539	Files, hand, smooth							372	49				575
1540	Files, taper							6,585	1				245
1541	Files, round												9
1542	Files, bastard, second-cut							174					
1543	Files, smooth							108					
1544	Files, switch							36					
1545	Files, second-cut							339					27
1546	Files, parallel							24					
1547	Files, square-cut							84					

1548	Files, square taper							12					
1549	Files, equalizing							84					
1550	Files, cut, bastard							36					
1551	Files, taper, bastard							354					
1552	Files, parallel, bastard							36					
1553	Flues, copper ... pounds							668					
1554	Flues ... feet							38					
1555	Fixings, forge ... pounds							334					
1556	Fronts to boilers							1					
1557	Funnels, sand-box							5					
1558	Flaxseed ... pounds									30			
1559	Flaxseed, ground ... do												
1560	Gauges, assorted							18	1	29			23
1561	Gauges, panel							38	2	3			
1562	Gauges, mortise							273	3	2			69
1563	Gauges, wire								1				18
1564	Gauges, marking							453	8				
1565	Gauges, thumb							25	31	26			142
1566	Gauges, single									2			51
1567	Gauges, double												6
1568	Gauges, cutting								1				
1569	Gauges, wheel												15
1570	Gauges, track							435		5			
1571	Gauges, tinners'												1
1572	Gauges, barrel							11					
1573	Gauges, screw												2
1574	Gauges, steam					2		56	7	7			
1575	Gauges, quarter-circle								1				
1576	Gauges, cocks and syphon steam							28					
1577	Gouges							92					
1578	Gouges, firmer							59					12
1579	Gouges, paring							33					5
1580	Gouges, paring, and handles												8
1581	Gouges, patent marking							12					3
1582	Gouges, flat sweep ... sets												1
1583	Gouges and handles, firmer ... do												25
1584	Gouges, ½-inch								1				1
1585	Gouges, firmer ... sets							7					
1586	Gouges, flat ... do								1				
1587	Gouges, paring ... do							14					
1588	Gouges, neck							37					
1589	Gimlets							462	1				38
1590	Gummers, saw												
1591	Gummers, assorted							11					
1592	Greasers												1
1593	Grooves, hand, steel												
1594	Grainers, top												2
1595	Galleys, single-column brass-lined												2
1596	Galleys, double-column brass-lined												4
1597	Galleys, double-column brass												2
1598	Galleys, slice												1
1599	Galleys, improved folio slice												1

Report showing the disposition of United States military railroad property in the military division of the Tennessee, &c.—Continued.

Running number.	Articles.	Sold at public auction to railroad companies on credit on same terms as authorized by Executive Orders of August 8 and October 14, 1865.						Sold at auction for cash.	Transferred to officers.	Lost or expended in the public service.	Captured property returned to railroad companies.	Captured property returned to individuals.	Balance on hand June 1, 1866.
		Nashville and Northwestern railroad.	Selma and Meridian railroad.	Nashville and Decatur railroad.	New Orleans, Jackson, and Great Northern railroad.	Mississippi and Tennessee railroad.	Mississippi Central railroad.						
1600	Glass, assorted ... boxes							343	104	41			
1601	Glass, tail, light							15					
1602	Glass, window, assorted ... lights									339	486		
1603	Glass, double-thick ... feet												
1604	Glass, head-light ... boxes												2
1605	Glasses, head-light								21	15			1
1606	Glasses, cab, light									212			
1607	Grooves, hand							6					
1608	Grooves, tinners'							1					
1609	Gauze, brass ... feet												
1610	Gauze, brass ... coils												3
1611	Gauze iron ... do									1			
1612	Green, chrome ... pounds							12	102	129			
1613	Green, Hibernian ... do							350		10			
1614	Green, German emerald ... do									70			539¼
1615	Green, Paris ... do							50	31				
1616	Green, silk ... do							18					8
1617	Green, Quaker ... do							193					
1618	Green, emerald ... do								539¼	64			
1619	Green, American chrome ... tubes									12			
1620	Grease, car ... pounds							535	2,740				500
1621	Grease, car ... gallons							65					
1622	Grease, car ... barrels								9				
1623	Grease, wagon ... pounds								480	650			
1624	Grease, axle ... boxes							35					
1625	Glue ... pounds							141	286	762			
1626	Gates, switch ... do								70	40			
1627	Gates, molasses							5	12				
1628	Gates, switch												
1629	Gates, pine							1					
1630	Gibbs, bridge												

1631	Gibbs, cross-head .... pounds								39				
1632	Gibbs, cross-head							8					
1633	Gibbs, bridge .... pounds							822					
1634	Governors							3					
1635	Glands, snuffing-box .... pounds								88				
1636	Gongs, locomotive, 8-inch									4			32
1637	Gongs and fixtures												1
1638	Gongs, alarm												4
1639	Globes, ruby							2					
1640	Gutters, tin .... feet							24					
1641	Gutters .... lots							1					1
1642	Grease, wagon .... gallons							18					
1643	Hammers, blacksmiths'							378					
1644	Hammers, blacksmiths' hand												
1645	Hammers, chipping							319	17				29
1646	Hammers, shoe								1				3
1647	Hammers, set							10		3			1
1648	Hammers, hand							29	28				402
1649	Hammers, sledge							16	3				157
1650	Hammers, claw							1,802	33	1			
1651	Hammers, tack							90	10				
1652	Hammers, engine							779	55				
1653	Hammers, tinners'							19	1				14
1654	Hammers, saddlers'												2
1655	Hammers, stone							515					
1656	Hammers, clasp and punch							52					
1657	Hammers, ballast							153					56
1658	Hammers, shoeing							6					
1659	Hammers, masons'							99					
1660	Hammers, spike							9					117
1661	Hammers, backing												36
1662	Hammers, jack												
1663	Hammers, copper							2					
1664	Hammers, assorted							16	16	1			
1665	Hammers, trip							1					
1666	Hammers, steam engine, trip, complete							1					
1667	Hammers, steam, assorted							2					
1668	Hammers, machine								1			24	
1669	Hammers, boiler-makers'							191					
1670	Hammers, riveting							100					
1671	Hammers, soft							4					
1672	Hammers, steel												100
1673	Hammers, raising												1
1674	Hammers, pointing							1					
1675	Hammers, wagon							9					
1676	Hammers, saw							1					
1677	Hatchets							683	31	2			
1678	Hatchets and handles												460
1679	Hatchets, shingling							909	6				
1680	Hatchets, broad							924	4				240
1681	Hatchets, soldering							12					
1682	Handles, firmer chisel, assorted												441

Report showing the disposition of United States military railroad property in the military division of the Tennessee, &c.—Continued.

Running number.	Articles.	Sold at public auction to railroad companies on credit on same terms as authorized by Executive Orders of August 8 and October 14, 1865.						Sold at auction for cash.	Transferred to officers.	Lost or expended in the public service.	Captured property returned to railroad companies.	Captured property returned to individuals.	Balance on hand June 1, 1866.
		Nashville and Northwestern railroad.	Selma and Meridian railroad.	Nashville and Decatur railroad.	New Orleans, Jackson, and Great Northern railroad.	Mississippi and Tennessee railroad.	Mississippi Central railroad.						
1683	Handles, socket firmer chisel, assorted												3
1684	Handles, socket chisel												79
1685	Handles, chisel							794	237				
1686	Handles, auger, assorted							1, 535	39	171			
1687	Handles, adze							848		70			
1688	Handles, foot or carpenters' adze												15
1689	Handles, railroad adze												1
1690	Handles, broadaxe							656	2	31			590
1691	Handles, hatchet							585		160			
1692	Handles, brad hatchet							50					
1693	Handles, hammer							334	80	412			
1694	Handles, stone hammer							261		17			
1695	Handles, spike, maul							7, 041	319	94			37
1696	Handles, maul							2		98			
1697	Handles, pick							13, 404	10	372			
1698	Handles, awl							734		18			
1699	Handles, sledge							3	34	21			
1700	Handles, brad awl									200			364
1701	Handles, firmer gouge												2
1702	Handles, jack plane							18					18
1703	Handles, handsaw							32					6
1704	Handles, handsaw, polished												12
1705	Handles, file							2, 598	72	289		200	
1706	Handles, cross-cut saw							128					
1707	Handles, cant hook							49					
1708	Handles, axe							391	65	1, 060			142
1709	Handles, chopping axe												730
1710	Handles, hand axe							7		9			
1711	Handles, saucepan							750		155			
1712	Handles, chest							102					659
1713	Handles, assorted							245	24				

1714	Handles, front end door												
1715	Handles, machinists'												
1716	Handles, chest, japanned, Paris ... pairs								3				35
1717	Handles, flush drawer							18		16			
1718	Handles, chest ... pairs							415		35			
1719	Handles, mallet							4					
1720	Handles, door							3					
1721	Handles, stretcher							72					
1722	Handles, mop							1					1
1723	Handles, couch							4					
1724	Hangers, post									27			84
1725	Hangers, drop, belt												
1726	Hangers, spring												20
1727	Hangers, step												
1728	Hangers, shafting ... pounds								415	415			
1729	Hangers, step ... do												
1730	Hangers and boxes ... do												
1731	Hangers, truck												
1732	Hangers ... pounds							180	11, 470				
1733	Hangers, drop								13				
1734	Hangers and fasteners, window blind ... sets							26					
1735	Hangers, cast-iron ... pounds							2, 252					
1736	Hangers, door							54		1			
1737	Heads, cylinder									7			6
1738	Heads, square												
1739	Heads, coppersmith												
1740	Heads, brake ... pounds								1, 857	94			
1741	Heads, brake, frame								145				
1742	Heads, draw							6, 240					
1743	Heads, draw ... pounds							35, 474					1, 620
1744	Heads, cross, engine									1		1	
1745	Heads, stake												
1746	Heads and beams, brake								8				
1747	Heads, piston									13			
1748	Heads, bull, small									2, 000			
1749	Heads, bull, large									3, 000			
1750	Heads, draw, cast ... pounds							9, 970					
1751	Heads, cross									14			
1752	Hooks, cant							442					
1753	Hooks, belt, assorted							6, 545		930			
1754	Hooks, horn, beak												1
1755	Hooks, packing							29					
1756	Hooks, tackle ... pounds												
1757	Hooks and links, switch rope												
1758	Hooks, safety chair ... pounds												
1759	Hooks, assorted												
1760	Hooks and staples							99					
1761	Hooks, gas pipe							69		252			
1762	Hooks and eyes, brass ... gross									1			
1763	Hooks, safety chain												
1764	Hooks, curling									4			
1765	Hooks, iron ... pounds							142					

Report showing the disposition of United States military railroad property in the military division of the Tennessee, &c.—Continued.

Running number.	Articles.	Sold at public auction to railroad companies on credit on same terms as authorized by Executive Orders of August 8 and October 14, 1865.						Sold at auction for cash.	Transferred to officers.	Lost or expended in the public service.	Captured property returned to railroad companies.	Captured property returned to individuals.	Balance on hand June 1, 1866.
		Nashville and Northwestern railroad.	Selma and Meridian railroad.	Nashville and Decatur railroad.	New Orleans, Jackson, and Great Northern railroad.	Mississippi and Tennessee railroad.	Mississippi Central railroad.						
1766	Hooks, packing, and spools							36					
1767	Hooks, curving							6					1
1768	Hooks, switch rope ... pounds							100					
1769	Hooks and thimbles, switch rope ... do							2, 511					
1770	Hooks, cotton							8					
1771	Hook and chain gate							1					
1772	Hooks, ice							3					
1773	Hooks, hay							17					
1774	Hooks, timber							2					
1775	Hooks and chains							21					
1776	Hooks, iron							200		80			
1777	Hooks and stands ... pounds									32			
1778	Hooks, car hat									7			
1779	Heaters, iron							95	9	10			
1780	Heaters, pipe							1					
1781	Hoes							7					
1782	Hoes, handled							28		10			
1783	Hoes, boat												11
1784	Hoes, garden												1
1785	Hoes, stable							13					
1786	Hose, assorted ... feet							8, 974 7-12	45				
1787	Hose, gum ... do								279	162			2, 455
1788	Hubs and collars ... sets												1
1789	Hubs for dies												34
1790	Hinges, strap, assorted							114	156	1, 159			12
1791	Hinges, blind, patent									20			
1792	Hinges, T ... pairs							93	25	176			
1793	Hinges, table, assorted ... do							79	18	20			
1794	Hinges, window ... do								40				
1795	Hinges, brass ... do								24				
1796	Hinges and fasteners, blind ... sets												

1797	Hinges, strap, assorted	pairs							309½					59
1798	Hinges, brass													6
1799	Hinges	pounds												180
1800	Hinges, unfinished								121					
1801	Hinges, butt, brass	pairs							48					
1802	Hinges, butt, brass	do							1, 155					
1803	Hinges, back, flat								24					
1804	Hinges, butt, cast	pairs									36			
1805	Hinges, blind	do							6		18			
1806	Hasps, hinges and staples, assorted								210		229			181
1807	Hasps and staples								1, 068		172			
1808	Hasps, hinge								105					
1809	Hasps									4	108			
1810	Hasps and hooks								36					
1811	Hair, plasterers'	bushels							2		17			4
1812	Hair, curled	pounds							29	232	283			10
1813	Hair, plasterers'	do							7					
1814	Hair, plasterers'	lots							1					
1815	Holders, mandrel													
1816	Hoods, forge													
1817	Hoods, smoke-stack													
1818	Horses, wrought-iron													5
1819	Horses, cast-iron													
1820	Horses, wooden													
1821	Horses, carpenter, saw								2					
1822	Horses, drawing								10					
1823	Horses, nail								1					
1824	Horses, blacksmiths'													
1825	Hoops, tank	pounds							1, 120					
1826	Hoops, truss								12					
1827	Housing for cupola											1		
1828	Hods, mortar								10					
1829	Hardies								8					
1830	Hubs, ambulance								8					
1831	Hubs, wagon								2					
1832	Headings, blacksmiths'								55					
1833	Hydrants								1					
1834	Heads, cylinder	pounds								118	118			
1835	Handles, ballast hammer										12			
1836	Hickory for handles	pieces												38
1836½	Hinges								26					
1837	Iron, angle	pounds							2, 429					7, 412
1838	Iron, railroad	bars							1, 529	1, 250				44, 799
1839	Iron, railroad	pounds							721, 120			22, 400		
1840	Iron, round, assorted	do							316, 625	5, 853				79, 968
1841	Iron, bar, assorted	do							1, 348, 782					1, 026, 665
1842	Iron, flat, assorted	do												
1843	Iron, galvanized	do							7, 538					
1844	Iron, Russia	do							225					6, 009
1845	Iron, assorted	do							295, 462	49, 484				
1846	Iron, boiler	do							62, 872					
1847	Iron, tank	do							106					

Report showing the disposition of United States military railroad property in the military division of the Tennessee, &c.—Continued.

Running number.	Articles.	Sold at public auction to railroad companies on credit on same terms as authorized by Executive Orders of August 8 and October 14, 1865.						Sold at auction for cash.	Transferred to officers.	Lost or expended in the public service.	Captured property returned to railroad companies.	Captured property returned to individuals.	Balance on hand June 1, 1866.
		Nashville and North-western railroad.	Selma and Meridian railroad.	Nashville and Decatur railroad.	New Orleans, Jackson, and Great Northern railroad.	Mississippi and Tennessee railroad.	Mississippi Central railroad.						
1848	Iron, oval and ½-oval .... pounds..							6, 138					900
1849	Iron, hoop .... do...							6, 471	1, 515				5, 937
1850	Iron, tire .... do...							29, 727	160				19, 628
1851	Iron, ½-round .... do...							14, 508					4, 365
1852	Iron, square .... do...							411, 178					210, 356
1853	Iron, plough slab .... do...							4, 325					625
1854	Iron, nail rod .... do...							24, 148					
1855	Iron, pig .... do...												87, 200
1856	Iron, round bridge .... do...												150, 000
1857	Iron, flat bridge .... do...							46, 723					17, 435
1858	Iron, scrap .... do...							2, 353, 320			3, 993		
1859	Iron, sheet .... do...							32, 998					37, 662
1860	Iron, tuyere .... do...												160
1861	Iron, scrap, 1st class .... do...							20, 000					
1862	Iron, scrap, blacksmiths' 1st class .... do...							200, 000					
1863	Iron, scrap, blacksmiths' common .... do...							300, 000					
1864	Iron, tank and fire box scrap .... do...							96, 210					3, 290
1865	Iron, light sheet scrap .... do...							50, 000					
1866	Iron, sheet, galvanized .... do...												71, 720
1867	Iron, band, assorted .... do...												528
1868	Iron, smoke-stack .... do...							8, 997					
1869	Iron, scrap, rings and staples .... do...							584					
1870	Iron, round and square .... do...							3, 460					
1871	Iron, old .... do...							40, 543					
1872	Iron, wrought .... do...							21, 297					
1873	Iron, perforated .... sheets..							47					
1874	Irons, platform												3
1875	Irons, clinch							4					
1876	Irons, and							1					
1877	Irons, solid							2					
1878	Irons, double plough							2					

1879	Irons, heading							1					
1880	Irons, branding							6					
1881	Irons, angle, 25 feet each												
1882	Irons, switch							35					
1883	Irons, twyre							44					147
1884	Irons, plane							27					
1885	Irons, double-plane							35					38
1886	Irons, soldering							12	2				7
1887	Irons, large, for drawing, (on wheels)												
1888	Irons, guide ... pounds												
1889	Irons, dog ... pairs							8					
1890	Irons, roofing, double seaming												
1891	Irons, step ... pounds												
1892	Irons, blacksmiths' ... do												
1893	Irons, chafing ... do												
1894	Iron, brake ... do												721
1895	Instruments, veterinary ... sets								1				
1896	Instruments, levelling							5					
1897	Instruments, mathematical ... sets							1					
1898	Instruments, transit							2					
1899	Injectors, engine												35
1900	Injectors, assorted							4					28
1901	Injectors, steam							60					
1902	Indicators, steam							3					
1903	Ipecac ... pounds												2
1904	Ink, printing ... cases								11				
1904½	Irons, hand-grooving							3	1				9,876
1905	Jacks, ratchet							7	15				75
1906	Jacks, screw and lever							14	32				
1907	Jacks, hydraulic, assorted							7	16				15
1908	Jacks, hydraulic, 7-ton												2
1909	Jacks, hydraulic, 10-ton							3					
1910	Jacks, hydraulic, 15-ton							4					2
1911	Jacks, timber												132
1912	Jacks, lever							53	4				27
1913	Jacks, screw							82	10		4	2	162
1914	Jacks, pump, 15-ton								9				
1915	Jacks, pump, 10-ton								2				
1916	Jacks, pump												
1917	Journals, brass											8	
1918	Japan ... gallons							57	21	89			
1919	Jaws, switch-lever							49					
1920	Knives, farriers'							16		12			
1921	Knives, drawing							1,535	28	10			97
1922	Knives, frog												
1923	Knives, bench								1				1
1924	Knives, paring							11					
1925	Knives, round												1
1926	Knives, pallet							28	7				
1927	Knives, putty							59	42	4			
1928	Knives, shoe							1		1			3
1929	Knives, packing												

Report showing the disposition of United States military railroad property in the military division of the Tennessee, &c.—Continued.

Running number.	Articles.	Sold at public auction to railroad companies on credit on same terms as authorized by Executive Orders of August 8 and October 14, 1865.						Sold at auction for cash.	Transferred to officers.	Lost or expended in the public service.	Captured property returned to railroad companies.	Captured property returned to individuals.	Balance on hand June 1, 1866.
		Nashville and Northwestern railroad.	Selma and Meridian railroad.	Nashville and Decatur railroad.	New Orleans, Jackson, and Great Northern railroad.	Mississippi and Tennessee railroad.	Mississippi Central railroad.						
1930	Knives, C. S. Daniels's planer												
1931	Knives, brush									3			
1932	Kettles, soldering								2				19
1933	Kettles, glue									*1			17
1934	Kettles, spring ..... pounds							13, 825					
1935	Keys, car							1, 430	174	495			50
1936	Keys, assorted							262					
1937	Keys, assorted ..... pounds												
1938	Keys, draw-head												
1939	Keys, split ..... pounds												
1940	Keys, padlock							1		16			
1941	Keys, connecting-rods							3					
1942	Kegs							1					
1943	Knobs, mahogany									706			214
1944	Knobs, mineral							228		166			
1945	Knobs, drawer							2, 767					
1946	Knobs, door												
1947	Knobs, desk, wood, assorted									144			
1948	Knobs, tin-kettle							720					
1949	Knobs, tea-pot ..... gross							6					
1950	Kings, American ..... tubes									12			
1951	Knees, tender							4					
1952	Kasses, switch							2					
1953													
1954	Lights, white							2, 828	768	87			17
1955	Lights, red							1, 749	138	6			
1956	Lights, blue							32	1				
1957	Lights, cab												
1958	Lights, head					2		113	7	9	19		
1959	Lights, tail							2					
1960	Lamps, Dutch							168					195

1961	Lamps, bull's-eye							24		4			
1962	Lamps, bracket							1					
1963	Lamps, railroad							3					5
1964	Lamps, hand												1
1965	Lamps, green												
1966	Lamps, signal												21
1967	Lamps, torch												21
1968	Lamps, coach								7	12			14
1969	Lamps, brass car							26	23	10			
1970	Lamps, car, candle							28					
1971	Lamps, hanging							17					
1972	Lamps, spring							5					1
1973	Lanterns							24		129			254
1974	Lanterns, railroad globe							1					11
1975	Lanterns, dark												17
1976	Lanterns, square												6
1977	Lantern bottoms, (W. L., old)												11
1978	Locks, pad, assorted							383	263	536			
1979	Locks, mortise									36			
1980	Locks, door, with mineral knobs, complete								43	267			278
1981	Locks, assorted							481		244			134
1982	Locks, switch							38		25			
1983	Locks, car							1, 916	371	2, 179			
1984	Locks, car, seat-back												
1985	Locks, door							482	32	15			
1986	Locks, chest								147	192			
1987	Locks, spring-chest								48	108			
1988	Locks, drawer								74				
1989	Locks, rim								120	510			
1990	Locks, iron drawer								30				
1991	Locks, desk and drawer									361			
1992	Locks, Japan-covered									120			
1993	Locks, wardrobe									12			
1994	Locks and chains												1
1995	Lines, sea-grass									1			
1996	Lines, tape, assorted							47	9	20			367
1997	Lines, plough									18			12
1998	Lines, chalk							1, 373	3	175			
1999	Lines, chalk and reel							67					
2000	Line, chalk ... feet									400			1, 600
2001	Lime ... bushels									391			204
2002	Lime ... pounds												
2003	Lumber, pine ... feet							905, 638	50, 558	387, 059			
2004	Lumber, oak and poplar, assorted ... do							906, 582		84, 000			
2005	Lumber, B. M. ... do												2, 214
2006	Lumber, assorted ... do							175, 301	362, 673	383, 090			2, 248, 959
2007	Lumber, old ... lots							2					
2008	Lumber, oak ... feet							689, 603	31, 784	247, 702			
2009	Lumber, poplar ... do							92, 812		17, 203			
2010	Lumber walnut ... do									4, 504			3, 000
2011	Lead, pig ... pounds								115	1, 017			1, 061
2012	Lead, white, assorted ... do							267½	1, 452	3, 436			

Report showing the disposition of United States military railroad property in the military division of the Tennessee, &c.—Continued.

Running number.	Articles.	Sold at public auction to railroad companies on credit on same terms as authorized by Executive Orders of August 8 and October 14, 1865.						Sold at auction for cash.	Transferred to officers.	Lost or expended in the public service.	Captured property returned to railroad companies.	Captured property returned to individuals.	Balance on hand June 1, 1866.
		Nashville and Northwestern railroad.	Selma and Meridian railroad.	Nashville and Decatur railroad.	New Orleans, Jackson, and Great Northern railroad.	Mississippi and Tennessee railroad.	Mississippi Central railroad.						
2013	Lead, black ... pounds								10	159			
2014	Lead, sugar of ... do							36		12			
2015	Lead, sheet ... do							965	35	1,153			
2016	Lead, red, in oil and dry ... do							500		271			828
2017	Lead, bar and pig ... do												
2018	Lead, red ... do							1,416					
2019	Lead, scrap ... do							187					
2020	Litharge ... do							132	5	33			
2021	Lathes, screw-cutting												
2022	Lathes, complete, 7 feet bed, 9-inch swing								1				1
2023	Lathes, shear and head								1				1
2024	Lathes, engine							2	1			1	
2025	Lathes, hand												1
2026	Lathes, axle												
2027	Lathes, wood turning							1					
2028	Lathes, iron turning												
2029	Lathes, dog, wrought, No. 20												
2030	Lathes, screw-cutting machine, 8 feet chain, feed, with chuck												
2031	Lathes, screw-cutting machine, 10 feet bed, 23-inch swing												
2032	Lathes, screw-cutting machine, with pulleys and shafts												
2033	Lathes, with chuck												
2034	Lathes, 24-inch, universal chuck												
2035	Lathes, 24-inch, White's patent												
2036	Lathes, driving wheel												
2037	Lathes, turning												
2038	Lathes												
2039	Lathes, double-head, 20 feet long, 26-inch swing, with counter shafts, tools, and fixtures											1	

2040	Lathes, screw-cutting, with counter shafts											1	
2041	Lathes, small counter shaft											1	
2041½	Lathes, No. 8											1	
2042	Lathes, double-head, wood											1	
2043	Lathes, iron											1	
2044	Lathes, screw-cutting, 16 feet bed, 15-inch swing								1				
2045	Lathes, shear and head, 10 feet bed, 12-inch swing								1				1
2046	Lathes, small, with screw, gear, and four extra rods												1
2047	Lathes, 30-inch												2
2048	Ladders, mounting							19					
2049	Ladders, shop and step							18	2		2		
2050	Letters ... sets							1					
2051	Letters							3					
2052	Letters and figures, incomplete ... sets							3					
2053	Links, crooked							145					
2054	Links, chain												
2055	Links, coupling ... pounds							1, 045	34				
2056	Links, straight ... do									202			
2057	Links, crooked ... do												556
2058	Links, coupling							11					
2059	Ladles							45	3	1			10
2060	Ladles, tin												235
2061	Ladles, perforated							132					
2062	Ladles, melting							12					
2063	Ladles, iron							188	1				
2064	Ladles, iron ... pounds												
2065	Lifts, window									234			
2066	Lifts, brass sash												72
2067	Links, switch rope ... pounds							1, 753					
2068	Links, straight							1, 178					
2069	Links and pins, coupling ... pounds												
2070	Leather, sole ... do								105	157			
2071	Leather, lace ... sides							2	34	78			
2072	Leather, harness ... pounds							19½		1, 907			
2073	Leather, bridle ... do									225			
2074	Leather, russet ... sides									8			
2075	Leather, burnt ... pounds							311					
2076	Leather, sole ... sides							3					
2077	Leather, assorted ... pounds							50					
2078	Leather, blue, title ... dozen								½	½			½
2079	Levels, spirit							183	29	35			
2080	Levels, pocket							8					12
2081	Levels, machinists'												4
2082	Levels							1					
2083	Levers, hand-car												2
2084	Levers and rods, tank								3				71
2085	Levers, switch							11					
2086	Levers, wrought												
2087	Levers												
2088	Levers, brake												19
2089	Levers, track							1					
2090	Levers, whistle							6					

Report showing the disposition of United States military railroad property in the military division of the Tennessee, &c.—Continued.

Running number.	Articles.	Sold at public auction to railroad companies on credit on same terms as authorized by Executive Orders of August 8 and October 14, 1865.						Sold at auction for cash.	Transferred to officers.	Lost or expended in the public service.	Captured property returned to railroad companies.	Captured property returned to individuals.	Balance on hand June 1, 1866.
		Nashville and Northwestern railroad.	Selma and Meridian railroad.	Nashville and Decatur railroad.	New Orleans, Jackson, and Great Northern railroad.	Mississippi and Tennessee railroad.	Mississippi Central railroad.						
2091	Levers, blacksmiths'							16					
2092	Leaves, steel, for tender springs ... pounds												
2093	Leaf, gold ... packages							49	3	10½			
2094	Ley, concentrated ... cans							5	6	22			
2095	Ley, concentrated ... boxes								2				
2096	Lead, bar ... pounds												
2097	Lead, white ... kegs								18	2			
2098	Lugs, water tank												
2099	Lugs, water tank ... pounds							847					
2100	Laths, pine							200	10,000				
2101	Lake madder ... tubes								5	12			
2102	Laudanum ... pounds									1			
2103	Logs, B. M ... feet									1,745,646			
2104	Lifters, rail							4					
2105	Legs, table							58					
2106	Litters												
2107	Machines, small engine												1
2108	Machines, double engine												1
2109	Machines, hoisting engine												
2110	Machines, straightening												
2111	Machines, drill press												
2112	Machines, wheel press												1
2113	Machines, press boring, cylinder												
2114	Machines, press drilling, vertical, Nos. 62 and 63												
2115	Machines, manifest, suspension												
2116	Machines, pipe-cutting												
2117	Machines, stove-pipe former												
2118	Machines, wooden former												3
2119	Machines, burring							1					
2120	Machines, pinning down												1
2121	Machines, setting down							1					

2122	Machines, swedging							1					
2123	Machines, scanning												1
2124	Machines, scanning, double												1
2125	Machines, bolt header												
2126	Machines, screw cutting							1			1		
2127	Machines, beading							4					
2128	Machines, twyring												2
2129	Machines, tenoning							1					
2130	Machines, wiring												
2131	Machines, squaring												
2132	Machines, grooving							3			1		
2133	Machines, folding							4	1				
2134	Machines, planing, common												1
2135	Machines, planing											2	10
2136	Machines, quartering wheel												1
2137	Machines, quartering wheel, double-headed												
2138	Machines, flooring										1		
2139	Machines, striker												1
2140	Machines, scroll-moulding												1
2141	Machines, boring, assorted							91		2			35
2142	Machines, boring, and augers							44					
2143	Machines, boring and drilling, Bement & Dougherty												
2144	Machines and bits, boring							40					
2145	Machines, boring, No. 32, Bement & Dougherty												
2146	Machines, sawing												
2147	Machines, skiving							1					
2148	Machines, mortising										1		
2149	Machines, mortising and boring, car												
2150	Machines, mortising, and chisels, foot, portable												
2151	Machines, thick edge												1
2152	Machines, rolling							1					
2153	Machines, slotting							1					1
2154	Machines, milling												
2155	Machines, gear cutting							1					
2156	Machines, bolt cutting, taps and dies								1				
2157	Machines, small vertical drill												
2158	Machines, key cutting							1					
2159	Machines, key seat drill, No. 12, complete												
2160	Machines, large vertical drill, intermediate shafts, pulleys and hangers												
2161	Machines, nut tapping											2	
2162	Machines, moulding										3		
2163	Machines, railroad cut-off sawing												1
2164	Machines, stove pipe breaking												
2165	Machines, binders' board cutting												1
2166	Machines, shaping												2
2167	Machines, shaping, 12-inch, No. 20												
2168	Machines, drilling												1
2169	Machines, portable, drilling												
2170	Machines, guttering							1					
2171	Machines, bolt, with taps and dyes												1
2172	Machines, car trimming, common												1

Report showing the disposition of United States military railroad property in the military division of the Tennessee, &c.—Continued.

Running number.	Articles.	Sold at public auction to railroad companies on credit on same terms as authorized by Executive Orders of August 8 and October 14, 1865.						Sold at auction for cash.	Transferred to officers.	Lost or expended in the public service.	Captured property returned to railroad companies.	Captured property returned to individuals.	Balance on hand June 1, 1866.
		Nashville and Northwestern railroad.	Selma and Meridian railroad.	Nashville and Decatur railroad.	New Orleans, Jackson, and Great Northern railroad.	Mississippi and Tennessee railroad.	Mississippi Central railroad.						
2173	Machines, car, wood turning												
2174	Machines, turning, large												
2175	Machines, beading, and extra rolls												
2176	Machines, hoisting							7					
2177	Machines, shingle												
2178	Machines, copper pipe breaking												
2179	Machines, spring setting												
2180	Machines, flue drawing												
2181	Machines, slide lathe												18
2182	Machines, wood lathe												3
2183	Machines, hand lathe												2
2184	Machines, eyelet												1
2185	Machines, double seaming							1					
2186	Machines, boring and turning												
2187	Machines, laying off							1					
2188	Machines, bolt cutting, large, with 7 sets taps and dies, plugs for repairing dies, counter shafts, pulleys and hangers												1
2189	Machines, bolt cutting, with 13 sets taps and dies, counter shafts, pulleys and hangers												1
2190	Machines, mortising, with bits, Rogers's patent												
2191	Machines, planing, compound												
2192	Machines, car planing and matching, complete												
2193	Machines, bolt head, and fixtures												
2194	Machines, planing, 12 feet, with counter shafting, wrenches, tools, &c											1	
2195	Machines, tongue-grooving										1		
2196	Machines, planer, (Daniels's patent)										1		
2197	Machines, circular rip-saw, No. 6										1		
2198	Machines, circular rip-saw, No. 5										1		
2199	Machines, board planer, No. 2										1		

2200	Machines, rabbeting, No. 5										1		
2201	Machines, wheel burring lathe										1		
2202	Machines, surface planing, No. 2												
2203	Machines, ruling								1				
2204	Machines, paper cutting								2				
2205	Machines, gumming												
2206	Machines, bolt cutting												
2207	Machines, car planing												
2208	Machines, wood							1					
2209	Machines, cylinder boring								4		1		
2210	Mills, shingle							3					
2211	Mills, saw, with engine boiler complete							4					
2212	Mills, saw, (O. S. and D. patent)							2					
2213	Mills, saw, (Clemens's patent)							1					
2214	Mills, saw, circular, (Clemens's patent)							2					
2215	Mills, saw, circular, (Lea & Leavitt's patent)							4					
2216	Mills, saw, (H. & Co.'s patent, "A," 2 boilers complete)							1					
2217	Mills, saw, (H. & Co.'s patent, "D," complete)							1					
2218	Mills, saw, stationary, L and D patent, incomplete							1					
2219	Mills, saw, A. B. H. & Co.'s patent, incomplete							1					
2220	Mills, saw												
2221	Mills, steam saw, portable												
2222	Mills, paint, assorted							26					
2223	Mills, borax												
2224	Mills, corn							1					
2225	Mills, boring, counter shafts, pulleys, and hangers												3
2226	Mandrels							6	1				2
2227	Mandrels, saw												
2228	Mandrels, S. P												2
2229	Mandrels, iron, assorted												2
2230	Mandrels, steel-nut												194
2231	Mandrels, steel												36
2232	Mandrels, cast-steel												248
2233	Mandrels, cast							8					7
2234	Mandrels, lathe, steel												
2235	Mallets, assorted							1,086	38	214			16
2236	Mallets, carpenters'							915					
2237	Mallets, lignumvitæ							268					
2238	Mallets, caulking							22					34
2239	Mallets, iron-ring												
2240	Mallets, stonecutters'							19					2
2241	Mallets, tinners'												
2242	Mauls							21					1
2243	Mauls, spike							110	3				
2244	Mauls, carpenters'												278
2245	Mauls, carpenters' top												38
2246	Mauls, carpenters' spike							439					120
2247	Mauls, railroad spike							1,954					
2248	Mauls, wooden							1					
2249	Mauls, iron							2					11
2250	Mauls, bridge							23	3				

Report showing the disposition of United States military railroad property in the military division of the Tennessee, &c.—Continued

Running number.	Articles.	Sold at public auction to railroad companies on credit on same terms as authorized by Executive Orders of August 8 and October 14, 1865.						Sold at auction for cash.	Transferred to officers.	Lost or expended in the public service.	Captured property returned to railroad companies.	Captured property returned to individuals.	Balance on hand June 1, 1866.
		Nashville and Northwestern railroad.	Selma and Meridian railroad.	Nashville and Decatur railroad.	New Orleans, Jackson, and Great Northern railroad.	Mississippi and Tennessee railroad.	Mississippi Central railroad.						
2251	Mauls, dirt									2			
2252	Measures, assorted							201		1			24
2253	Measures, tin, assorted							26	1				4
2254	Measures, tin ... sets												1
2255	Measures, oil ... do												1
2256	Measures, pint							51					
2257	Measures, dry ... sets							1					
2258	Mullers							1					2
2259	Moulds, soldering							5					
2260	Moulds, cast												2
2261	Magazines, powder							1					
2262	Marline, tarred ... pounds							258	10	216			
2263	Matches ... gross							211	33¼	210¾			
2264	Meter, gas												
2265	Metal, Babbitt ... pounds							23	335	511½			
2266	Molasses ... gallons							10					
2267	Moulens, wooden-wreath							1					
2268	Machinery, saw-mill ... box							1					
2269	Machinery, rolling-mill ... pounds							26,500					
2270	Nippers							1					34
2271	Nippers, cutting							77					
2272	Needles, assorted							2		10			16
2273	Needles, tufting												59
2274	Needles, upholsterers'							60					
2275	Needles, harness ... papers									11			
2276	Nozzles								18				1
2277	Nozzles, brass												5
2278	Nozzles, pipe												4
2279	Nozzles, hose							14					
2280	Nozzles ... pounds												30
2281	Nuts, assorted ... do							30,413	1,040				

2282	Nuts, brass	do							500	2,000	4,800			
2283	Nuts, square	do							1,000	3,700	8,519			15,130
2284	Nuts, hexagon	do												30,085
2285	Nuts and washers	do							672					
2286	Nuts and bolts	do							11,430					
2287	Nuts, keeper, and rods													
2288	Nuts, iron								12					
2289	Nails, assorted	kegs							931	51	88¼			47
2290	Nails, finishing, assorted	papers							63	68	438			
2291	Nails, clout	do							317		237			
2292	Nails, tufting								144		664			2,304
2293	Nails, clinch	pounds							268	455	4,878			4,389
2294	Nails, horseshoe	do							1,195		955			
2295	Nails, enamelled	gross							17		41			87
2296	Nails, lining	papers												
2297	Nails, assorted	pounds							1,735					
2298	Nails, plush	gross							36		4			
2299	Nails, finishing	kegs							11					
2300	Nails, cut	do							28	13 2-5	85			1,073 3-5
2301	Nails, finishing	pounds							100		154			
2302	Nails, round-head brass	gross								3				
2303	Nails, cut	pounds							325		1,199			
2304	Nails, copper	do							22½					
2305	Nails, tin	papers							28					
2306	Nails, lining, blued	gross												50
2307	Nails, lining, silver	do							154					
2308	Numbers, key	lots							1					
2309	Numbers	sets												1
2310	Netting, wire	feet							446½	14	1,018½			
2311	Oilers								93					150
2312	Oilers, engine, assorted								385	31	31			
2313	Oilers, spring													06
2314	Oilers, spring-top								44					19
2315	Oilers, spring-bottom								981	13				
2316	Oilers, machine								21					324
2317	Oilers, small													7
2318	Oilers, tin													91
2319	Oil, lard	gallons								1,864	8,489½			
2320	Oil, coal	do								426½	584½			
2321	Oil, lubricating	do							412		271			347
2322	Oil, linseed, raw	do							6	139				
2323	Oil, linseed, boiled	do							15	409½	446 1-5			602
2324	Oil, linseed	do									42 2-5			
2325	Oil	do							40		252			
2326	Oil, head-light	do								73½	56			
2327	Oil, neat's-foot	do							30		89			
2328	Oil, castor	bottles									2½			
2329	Ochre, French, yellow	pounds							50	5	1,045			
2330	Oakum	do							2,150	25	250			
2331	Ornaments, brass													
2332	Planes, rounding								2					
2333	Planes, double-smooth								88					

Report showing the disposition of United States military railroad property in the military division of the Tennessee, &c.—Continued.

Running number.	Articles.	Sold at public auction to railroad companies on credit on same terms as authorized by Executive Orders of August 8 and October 14, 1865.						Sold at auction for cash.	Transferred to officers.	Lost or expended in the public service.	Captured property returned to railroad companies.	Captured property returned to individuals.	Balance on hand June 1, 1866.
		Nashville and Northwestern railroad.	Selma and Meridian railroad.	Nashville and Decatur railroad.	New Orleans, Jackson, and Great Northern railroad.	Mississippi and Tennessee railroad.	Mississippi Central railroad.						
2334	Planes, fore							1,411	17	1			
2335	Planes, jack							1,162	62	25			
2336	Planes, jointer							82	2				
2337	Planes, joint							1					8
2338	Planes, rabbet, assorted							568	19				259
2339	Planes, jack, rabbet							1					
2340	Planes, bead, assorted							382	12				
2341	Planes, bench ... sets												6
2342	Planes, long-jointer							166					
2343	Planes, moulding							1					
2344	Planes, smooth							585					
2345	Planes, sash							11	6				
2346	Planes, match							28					221
2347	Planes, match ... pairs							108	6				
2348	Planes, screw-arm match							178					
2349	Planes, panel-plough												9
2350	Planes, plough							1					59
2351	Planes and bits, plough							59					2
2352	Planes, floor ... sets												
2353	Planes, assorted							1		113			17
2354	Planes, double-iron							38					
2355	Planes, grooving ... pairs												
2356	Planes and set bits									6			6
2357	Planes, joiners' short								16				
2358	Planes, panel plough and bits								2				
2359	Planes ... sets								3				
2360	Planers							1					
2361	Planers ... sets												
2362	Planers, rabbet												
2363	Planers, car, complete												1
2364	Planers, compound adjustment head								1				1

2365	Planers and matcher with counter shafts												1
2366	Planers, iron, to plane 16 ft., 4 ft. square, complete												1
2367	Planers, iron												
2368	Planers, 48-inch												1
2369	Planers, iron, 36 x 36 inches, 28-feet bed, 18-feet platform, (Seller's patent)												
2370	Planers, 5-feet							2					
2371	Planers, 36 x 36 inches, No. 124, (Seller's patent)												
2372	Planers, 36 x 36 inches, No. 125, (Seller's patent)												
2373	Planers, (Seller's patent)							1					
2374	Planers, compound, (Bement & Dougherty)												
2375	Planers, compound								1				
2376	Planers, compound, chuck, No. 14, double, (Bement & Dougherty)												
2377	Planers, 36 x 36 inches												
2378	Planers, link and link-block								1				1
2379	Planers, cast-iron link												
2380	Pulleys, assorted							51	32	33		7	171
2381	Pulleys, complete, assorted												32
2382	Pulleys, upright							27					
2383	Pulleys for main shafts, common												
2384	Pulleys, two-ton												1
2385	Pulleys for paint mill							1					
2386	Pulleys and shafts							1					
2387	Pulleys and chain, 2-ton							8					
2388	Pulleys, iron, 2 feet 10 inches face												5
2389	Pulleys, iron, 2 feet 4 inches face												1
2390	Pulleys, cast iron, assorted ..... pounds												
2391	Pulleys, drawer, No. 10												1
2392	Pulleys and hangers											22	
2393	Pulleys ..... pounds								573				
2394	Pulleys, turned for 3/4, 10 by 12, with set screws									10			
2395	Pulleys, cast-iron								6				390
2396	Ploughs and grooves ..... sets												1
2397	Ploughs												
2398	Pincers, carpenters' ..... pairs												1
2399	Pincers, blacksmiths' ..... do							16					
2400	Pincers, upholsterers' ..... do							18					
2401	Pincers, shoeing ..... do												3
2402	Pincers, assorted ..... do							53	5				
2403	Pincers, boiler-makers' ..... do												
2404	Pencils, carpenters'							30		13			41
2405	Pencils, coloring												54
2406	Pencils, C. H												97
2407	Pencils, artists' red sable												47
2408	Pencils, striping												
2409	Pencils, marking												
2410	Pencils, lettering							68					
2411	Punches							145	14				
2412	Punches, belt							176	1				4
2413	Punches, screws and dies												2
2414	Punches, screw							4					

Report showing the disposition of United States military railroad property in the military division of the Tennessee, &c.—Continued.

Running number	Articles.	Sold at public auction to railroad companies on credit on same terms as authorized by Executive Orders of August 8 and October 14, 1865.						Sold at auction for cash.	Transferred to officers.	Lost or expended in the public service.	Captured property returned to railroad companies.	Captured property returned to individuals.	Balance on hand June 1, 1866.
		Nashville and North-western railroad.	Selma and Meridian railroad.	Nashville and Decatur railroad.	New Orleans, Jackson, and Great Northern railroad.	Mississippi and Tennessee railroad.	Mississippi Central railroad.						
2415	Punches, hollow												
2416	Punches, hydraulic												1
2417	Punches, centre							177					
2418	Punches, steel												132
2419	Punches, lever												
2420	Punches, coppersmiths'												4
2421	Punches, harness							2					1
2422	Punches, spring									1			1
2423	Punches, conductors'												15
2424	Punches, track							20					
2425	Punches, blacksmiths'							97	3				
2426	Punches, tinners'												
2427	Punches, tank hoop												
2428	Punches, clamp												
2429	Punches, boiler-makers'							1					
2430	Punches, iron track ... sets												1
2431	Punches, short							4					
2432	Punches, hound							113					
2433	Presses, drill											1	
2434	Presses, upright drill												
2435	Presses, upright drill, &c												
2436	Presses, hydraulic, with shafts and pulleys												2
2437	Presses, wheel											2	
2438	Presses, hand wheel										1		
2439	Presses, upright drill, and counter shafts											2	
2440	Presses, medium "Franklin"								1				
2441	Presses, ½-medium "Franklin"								1				
2442	Presses, binders' hand								1				
2443	Presses, manifest								1				
2444	Presses, drill, and bits							1					
2445	Plyers ... pairs							1	1				58

2446	Plyers, cutting .... do								3				1
2447	Plyers, common .... do												22
2448	Plyers, upholsterers' .... do												3
2449	Plyers, flat nose .... do							62	2				
2450	Pots, glue							39	8				
2451	Pots, marking							6	12				
2452	Pots, wood paint												8
2453	Pots, tin soldering							22					
2454	Pots, tinners' fire												
2455	Pots, paste												1
2456	Pots, paint .... lot							1					
2457	Pots, cast							40					
2458	Pots, tallow									1			8
2459	Pots, rosin												1
2460	Pots, melting												
2461	Pots, soldering										1		
2462	Pots, paint							39	12				18
2463	Pots, iron								3				1
2464	Pumps, steam							2					
2465	Pumps, steam, Woodland							1					
2466	Pumps, cylinder							1					
2467	Pumps, force, McGowan's							63			5		
2467½	Pumps							2					
2468	Pumps, McGowan, with engine complete							1					
2469	Pumps, force							27	7				101
2470	Pumps, Worthington							4					
2471	Pumps, oil							3					2
2472	Pumps, oil, copper							1		2			
2473	Pumps, engine												2
2474	Pumps, rotary fire							2	1				
2475	Pumps, donkey							2					
2476	Pumps, cistern							1					
2477	Pumps, proving												1
2478	Pumps, Harris												1
2479	Pumps, engine, and boiler, complete												
2480	Pumps, incomplete												
2481	Pumps, steam, with engine, Worthington												
2482	Pumps, test and gauge										1		
2483	Pumps, force, with gearing and shafting											1	
2484	Pumps and fixtures, McGowan							1					
2485	Picks, earth, and handles												7
2486	Picks							2, 028	16				
2487	Picks, tamping							931	2				
2488	Picks, railroad												24
2489	Picks, stone							2					
2490	Pins, wooden .... barrels							3					
2491	Pins, coupling .... pounds							281					
2492	Pins, coupling							101	61				
2493	Pins, turned L. V												
2494	Pins, switch												
2495	Pipes, blast							8					
2496	Pipe, blast .... feet							220					

Report showing the disposition of United States military railroad property in the military division of the Tennessee, &c.—Continued.

Running number.	Articles.	Sold at public auction to railroad companies on credit on same terms as authorized by Executive Orders of August 8 and October 14, 1865.						Sold at auction for cash.	Transferred to officers.	Lost or expended in the public service.	Captured property returned to railroad companies.	Captured property returned to individuals.	Balance on hand June 1, 1866.
		Nashville and Northwestern railroad.	Selma and Meridian railroad.	Nashville and Decatur railroad.	New Orleans, Jackson, and Great Northern railroad.	Mississippi and Tennessee railroad.	Mississippi Central railroad.						
2497	Pipes, copper, with couplings							1					
2498	Pipe, copper ... pounds							301					
2499	Pipe, round							1					
2500	Pipe, sheet iron ... pounds							606					
2501	Pipe, wrought ... feet							22					
2502	Pipe, iron, galvanized ... do							35					
2503	Pipe, galvanized ... pieces							4					
2504	Pipes, copper hose							3					
2505	Pipes, rubber hose							2					
2506	Pipe, iron ... pounds							2, 642					
2507	Plugs, assorted												35
2508	Plugs, gas pipe												582
2509	Plugs, for repairing, dies												7
2510	Plugs, flue												6
2511	Plugs, assorted ... pounds												
2512	Plugs and feathers							300					
2513	Plates, wrought scrap fish bar ... pounds							5, 650					
2514	Plates, engine window							12					
2515	Plates, blacksmiths'												
2516	Plates, chuck												17
2517	Plates, head ... pounds							919		4, 000			3, 623
2518	Plates, face ... do												12, 245
2519	Plates, face							16					
2520	Plates, gas-fitters' screw												9
2521	Plates, screw cutter												4
2522	Plates, screw							8					8
2523	Plates, screws and dies												
2524	Plates, angle							1					4
2525	Plates, surface												1
2526	Plates, turntable ... sets												
2527	Plates and rolls ... do												

2528	Plates, bolster ... pounds												
2529	Plates, assorted ... do												
2530	Plates, die												
2531	Points, glaziers' ... papers							77					
2532	Points, glaziers' ... pounds								6	17			77
2533	Points, frog, steel ... do									50			
2534	Patterns, tin							10					
2535	Patterns, moulders'							2					
2536	Patterns, wheelwrights'							14					
2537	Patterns, sheet iron ... sets							1					
2538	Patterns, assorted												
2539	Patterns, tin ... sets												1
2540	Patterns, sheet iron ... pounds												810
2541	Patterns ... lots							1					
2542	Pikes							1					
2543	Piping, assorted ... feet							25					
2544	Putty ... pounds							48	468	604			
2545	Pilots, locomotive												
2546	Pilots, locomotive, wood								1				12
2547	Paulins							48	4				
2548	Potash, prussiate ... pounds							1, 140	5	154			
2549	Potash ... do									8			
2550	Pipe, for cistern pump ... feet												14
2551	Pipe, water, assorted ... do							6, 194		1, 109		6, 576	
2552	Pipe, water ... pounds												1, 387
2553	Pipe, gum firehose												1
2554	Pipe, gas ... feet							32, 429	1, 212 1-12	7, 637 11-12			
2555	Pipe, lead ... pounds							763	147	540			
2556	Pipe, brass ... feet							587	202½	503½			346
2557	Pipe, nozzle and hose												
2558	Pipe, inside, and netting for engine, No. 30									1			
2559	Pipe, outside, for engine, No. 30									1			
2560	Pipe, inside, for smoke stack												
2561	Pipe, copper ... feet							5					
2562	Pipe, tin ... do							119					
2563	Pipe, iron ... bundles								4				
2564	Pipe, iron ... pieces								5				
2565	Pipe, escape									1			1
2566	Paper, drawing ... quires							41 5-12					
2567	Paper, tracing ... rolls							15½					
2568	Paper, waste ... pounds							5, 049					
2569	Paper, antiquarian ... sheets							6					6
2570	Paper, sand ... quires							44	81 11-12	425			
2571	Paper, emery ... do							21	14 1-12	218¼			
2572	Paper, wrapping ... do							110		183			12
2573	Paper, white drawing ... yards												
2574	Paper, marble ... reams								1				
2575	Paper, brown drawing ... pounds							163	5	72			
2576	Paper, white drawing ... do							156		48			69
2577	Paper, printing ... do												
2578	Pickets							19					
2579	Paint, black ... pounds							119					

Report showing the disposition of United States military railroad property in the military division of the Tennessee, &c.—Continued.

Running number.	Articles.	Sold at public auction to railroad companies on credit on same terms as authorized by Executive Orders of August 8 and October 14, 1865.						Sold at auction for cash.	Transferred to officers.	Lost or expended in the public service.	Captured property returned to railroad companies.	Captured property returned to individuals.	Balance on hand June 1, 1866.
		Nashville and Northwestern railroad.	Selma and Meridian railroad.	Nashville and Decatur railroad.	New Orleans, Jackson, and Great Northern railroad.	Mississippi and Tennessee railroad.	Mississippi Central railroad.						
2580	Paint, chrome yellow ... pounds									17			129
2581	Paint, pink Dutch ... do							180	6	50			119
2582	Paint, mineral ... do							54	1,040	1,400			
2583	Paint, assorted ... do								400				
2584	Paint, mineral ... barrels									1			
2585	Paint, mixed ... pounds							303	350	282¾			457¼
2586	Polish, stove ... papers							206					
2587	Powder, blasting ... pounds							2					
2588	Powder ... kegs							49	1	22			
2589	Powder, blue ... pounds									1			
2590	Plungers, brass pump							1					
2591	Pans, oil							4					8
2592	Packing, hemp ... pounds							442	1,694	1,135			
2593	Packing, gum ... do							3,292½	10	791		210	
2594	Packing, steam ... do							1,103					
2595	Pendants, gas-pipe							27					
2596	Poles, pipe							145					
2597	Pedestals ... pounds												
2598	Pedestals									145			22
2599	Powers, horse							1					
2600	Platforms, railroad car			1				1					
2601	Paris, plaster ... pounds							63		60			50
2602	Pockets, iron												
2603	Pits, transfer and masonry												
2604	Pink, rose ... pounds								14	300			
2605	Pinions, feed								9				
2606	Patterns, for brass castings												840
2607	Patterns, for iron castings												1,131
2608	Plank, oak ... feet									6,000			
2609	Pistons, C. I									4			
2610	Paste, blue ... pots									1			

2610½	Ploughs							1					
2611	Quods, hollow ... pounds												25
2612	Quods, pica, corner ... sets												4
2613	Rules, steel												
2614	Rules, foot												52
2615	Rules, 2-foot												
2616	Rules, pocket							2		1			
2617	Rules, board							48	5				
2618	Rules, boxwood								8				67
2619	Rules, assorted									7			38
2620	Rods, guttering												1
2621	Rods, pipe ram												4
2622	Rods, brake ... pounds							13,063	206	269			
2623	Rods, brass ... do									138			
2624	Rods, switch								4				
2625	Rods, switch ... sets									12			
2626	Rods, switch ... pounds												
2627	Rods, levelling							5					
2628	Rods, tank ... sets												
2629	Rods, copper ... pounds							2,379½					194½
2630	Rods, connecting ... do									735			
2631	Rods, piston, wrought iron												
2632	Rods, nuts, and bolts ... pounds												
2633	Rods, iron, for cars ... do												
2634	Rods, brake												
2635	Rods, brake, and wheel							1					
2636	Rods, piston							11					
2637	Rods, tank							81					
2638	Rods and levers, tank ... sets							2					
2639	Rods and bolts, wrought ... pounds							5,056					
2640	Rods, bridge ... do							80					102,789
2641	Rollers ... pairs												1
2642	Rollers, door							5	20				9
2643	Rollers, boiler-makers' ... sets												
2644	Rollers, timber							133		3			
2645	Rollers, large ... sets										1		
2646	Rollers, small, stove-pipe										1		
2647	Rollers, iron							1					
2648	Ratchets											2	21
2649	Ratchets and dogs ... pounds												
2650	Ratchets and stands							1					
2651	Reamers							19					
2652	Reamers and burrs, steel												
2653	Reamers and drills ... pounds												
2654	Reamers, C. S ... do								30				
2655	Reamers and drills											175	
2656	Reamers, globe							1					
2657	Reamers, tap							2					
2658	Rivets, assorted							37,000		21,500			876,321
2659	Rivets, assorted ... pounds							4,281		12,124			
2660	Rivets, boiler ... do								200	1,275			253
2661	Rivets, tinned							101,000		4,700			

Report showing the disposition of United States military railroad property in the military division of the Tennessee, &c.—Continued.

Running number.	Articles.	Sold at public auction to railroad companies on credit on same terms as authorized by Executive Orders of August 8 and October 14, 1865.						Sold at auction for cash.	Transferred to officers.	Lost or expended in the public service.	Captured property returned to railroad companies.	Captured property returned to individuals.	Balance on hand June 1, 1866.
		Nashville and Northwestern railroad.	Selma and Meridian railroad.	Nashville and Decatur railroad.	New Orleans, Jackson, and Great Northern railroad.	Mississippi and Tennessee railroad.	Mississippi Central railroad.						
2662	Rivets, black and tinned ... pounds									4,000			4,875 1-6
2663	Rivets, seat-back ... do								5	415			283½
2664	Rivets, tank ... do							217					
2665	Rivets, smokestack ... do							190					
2666	Rivets, copper ... do							75¼	60	229			
2667	Rivets, brass ... do									1,911			
2668	Rivets, tinned ... papers							32					
2669	Rivets, iron ... pounds							23,643¼	2,180				
2670	Rivets, car seat, and burrs, brass							136					
2671	Rivets, iron							305,500					
2672	Rivets, iron ... papers									303			
2673	Rivets ... sets							10		2			
2674	Rivets, tinned ... pounds							3,687					
2675	Rivets, brass seat-back							282					
2676	Rope, assorted ... pounds							48,241 1-6	5,736	3,139			
2677	Rope, Manilla ... do							103	305	322			22,623
2678	Rope, 1-inch ... feet												
2679	Rope, 1½-inch ... coils											1	
2680	Rope ... do								½				
2681	Rope ... feet								160				
2682	Rope, bell ... pounds									10			
2683	Rope, old ... do							102,880					
2684	Ropes, small												5
2685	Ropes, guy												4
2686	Ropes, fall												2
2687	Ropes, switch							50	6	10			
2688	Ropes, wire ... coils							3	9				
2689	Rounds and hollows							36	16				
2690	Rounds and hollows ... sets												1
2691	Rounds and hollows ... pairs							14					12
2692	Rounds, chair							85					

2693	Rounds, timber, buggy							112					
2694	Riddles												59
2695	Regulators, upholsterers'												17
2696	Reels, chalk-line							116	1				
2697	Resin ... pounds							239	100	713			
2698	Rubber, block ... do												28
2699	Rammers							38					
2700	Rams, battering												
2701	Riving froe												1
2702	Rings, flush, brass							1, 031	12	467			
2703	Rings, brass, packing ... pounds							1, 350		69			
2704	Rings, packing												
2705	Rings, brass, cylinder												
2706	Rings, water tank												
2707	Rings, piston, for water works ... pounds								90				20
2708	Rings, old brass									86			
2709	Rings, brass packing							288					
2710	Rings, Japan mall ... gross							4					
2711	Rings, Japan harness ... do							5					6½
2712	Rings, breeching							5					
2713	Rings, muffin							12					
2714	Rings, harness ... gross							6 7-12		4			
2715	Red, American India ... tubes									2			
2716	Red, India, in oil ... pounds							120	90	521			5
2717	Red, vermilion ... do									20			
2718	Red, India ... do							216	24				
2719	Red, Venetian ... do							54	40	290			
2720	Red, Italian ... do							206					
2721	Rags ... do							612	9, 510	10, 324			
2722	Reservoirs												
2723	Racks, assorted							1					4
2724	Racks, forge, iron ... pounds								70				
2725	Racks, form							1					
2726	Rasps, assorted							252	3				
2727	Rasps, wood							473	10				30
2728	Rasps, horse							124	90				
2729	Rails, T									175			1, 207
2730	Rolls, steel, for turn-table ... sets							2					
2731	Rests, steady for lathe							4					
2732	Rests, tank, lever							46					
2733	Rests, iron							1					
2734	Rests, arm							1					
2735	Rakes, stable							3					4
2736	Rakes, iron											2	
2737	Reflectors, head-light							19					
2738	Registers, conductors'							2					
2739	Rigging for steam balance							1					
2740	Roofing, patent ... pounds							160	130				
2741	Saws, hand							3, 030	53	132			
2742	Saws, tenon							8	1	2			1
2743	Saws, hack							42	5				
2744	Saws, compass, assorted							180	26	13			

Report showing the disposition of United States military railroad property in the military division of the Tennessee, &c.—Continued.

Running number.	Articles.	Sold at public auction to railroad companies on credit on same terms as authorized by Executive Orders of August 8 and October 14, 1865.						Sold at auction for cash.	Transferred to officers.	Lost or expended in the public service.	Captured property returned to railroad companies.	Captured property returned to individuals.	Balance on hand June 1, 1866.
		Nashville and Northwestern railroad.	Selma and Meridian railroad.	Nashville and Decatur railroad.	New Orleans, Jackson, and Great Northern railroad.	Mississippi and Tennessee railroad.	Mississippi Central railroad.						
2745	Saws, back							112	12	1			1, 140
2746	Saws, rip							411	13				38
2747	Saws, buck							3	4				
2748	Saws, web												1
2749	Saws, cross-cut, assorted							638	9	1			458
2750	Saws, cross-cut, 5-foot								1				
2751	Saws, cross-cut, large												6
2752	Saws, cross-cut, hand												103
2753	Saws, cross-cut, tenon												2
2754	Saws, jig							164	20				
2755	Saws, scroll												19
2756	Saws, circular, 48-inch												
2757	Saws, circular and arbor							1			2		
2758	Saws, brass back							55					
2759	Saws, blue back							1, 295					
2760	Saws, mill							29					
2761	Saws, muley												22
2762	Saws, meat							16					9
2763	Saws, drag												8
2764	Saws, keyhole							8					
2765	Saws, wood							48	26				
2766	Saws and frames, wood												27
2767	Saws, wooden frame												50
2768	Saws, pit												33
2769	Saws, fine												40
2770	Saws, whip							35					
2771	Saws, cut-off, 32-inch												2
2772	Saws, shingle, 36-inch												1
2773	Saws, assorted							6					163
2774	Saws, bright back												25
2775	Saws, panel												86

2776	Saws, cut-off												2
2777	Squares, steel							978	39	1			
2778	Squares, try, assorted							1,218	32	2			
2779	Squares, iron								4				
2780	Squares, centre												13
2781	Squares, framing							23	11	24			
2782	Squares, bevel								7				
2783	Squares, lumber												
2784	Squares								1				1
2785	Squares, head												
2786	Stands, head-light												583
2787	Stands, switch							12		2			
2788	Stands, flag								25				
2789	Stands for machines												
2790	Stands, monkey switch							17					
2791	Stands, target switch												24
2792	Stands, wood switch							8					
2793	Stands, iron												
2794	Stamps, U. S. M. R. R.							1					
2795	Stands, brass lamp							2					
2796	Stands, locomotive lamp ......pounds								583				
2797	Stands, sand box ......do								719				
2798	Stands, California, double								2				
2799	Stands, California, single								3				
2800	Stands, lead								1				
2801	Stands, type								3				
2802	Stands, chain, cast ......pounds												
2803	Stands, gauge lamp												
2804	Stands, flag ......pounds												25
2805	Stamps, U. S.							6					1
2806	Stones, grind, assorted							43	1	10			
2807	Stones, grind, assorted ......pounds							2,277	1,965				
2808	Stones, grind, and fixtures ......sets							10					
2809	Stones, grind, 4 feet diameter, cast iron frame												
2810	Stones, paint and muller							2					
2811	Stones, paint							1					2
2812	Stones, oil							2,151	26	38			
2813	Stones, oil, assorted ......pounds							334					2,003
2814	Stones, whet							8					4
2815	Stone ......lot							1					
2816	Stones, grind, frame, hangers complete												
2817	Stones, mill, and fixtures ......pairs										1		
2818	Stones, imposing								1				
2819	Stones, grind, frames and pulleys												1
2820	Stones, grind, and fixtures												24
2821	Stone, blue ......pounds									15			20
2822	Stone, rotten ......do							410	25	91			17
2823	Stone, pumice ......do								50	265			500
2824	Stone, setting for engine												
2825	Snips ......pairs							3					
2826	Snips, circular ......do							4	1				
2827	Snips, tinners', assorted ......do							13	1				

Report showing the disposition of United States military railroad property in the military division of the Tennessee, &c.—Continued.

Running number.	Articles.	Sold at public auction to railroad companies on credit on same terms as authorized by Executive Orders of August 8 and October 14, 1865.						Sold at auction for cash.	Transferred to officers.	Lost or expended in the public service.	Captured property returned to railroad companies.	Captured property returned to individuals.	Balance on hand June 1, 1866.
		Nashville and Northwestern railroad.	Selma and Meridian railroad.	Nashville and Decatur railroad.	New Orleans, Jackson, and Great Northern railroad.	Mississippi and Tennessee railroad.	Mississippi Central railroad.						
2828	Snips, straight .... pairs												
2829	Shaves, spoke							447	8	12			
2830	Shaves, spoke, wood							91					155
2831	Shaves, spoke, iron							18		13			202
2832	Sets, saw							55	1	4			10
2833	Swedges, creasing							2					
2834	Swedges, bottom												395
2835	Swedges, top												11
2836	Swedges and chisels							247					
2837	Screws, assorted .... gross							813½	245	662			
2838	Screws, round head, brass .... do									82			25
2839	Screws, brass, assorted .... do							62	25	119½			
2840	Screws, brass cap .... do								22	82			51
2841	Screws, round head, blued .... do							266½		131			677½
2842	Screws, blued .... do							865		150			
2843	Screws, hand, assorted							149	56				
2844	Screws, bench							1	5	4			120
2845	Screws, wood bench							213	3	6			
2846	Screws, iron bench							144	6				
2847	Screws, bed							254					18
2848	Screws, lag, assorted							656	749	2,733			
2849	Screws, lag .... pounds							1,752					700
2850	Screws, top												
2851	Screws, fore												1
2852	Screws, hydraulic jack												6
2853	Screws, small steel .... sets												8
2854	Screws, clamp							7					
2855	Screws, large, and 4-inch nuts												
2856	Screws for shaft							1					
2857	Screws, auger .... gross												64
2858	Screws, turn-table							1					

2859	Screws, gimblet, brass .... gross							61					
2860	Screws, tank							16					
2861	Screws							21					
2862	Screws, iron wood .... gross							159					
2863	Screws, head .... sets							16					
2864	Screws, lathe							1					
2865	Screws, tire .... sets												
2866	Screws, hand .... pairs												191
2867	Screws, jack									2			14
2868	Screws, wood .... pounds									150			
2869	Screws, gimlet .... gross									443			1,275
2870	Sticks, creasing												
2871	Sticks, yard							80					
2872	Sticks, composing								8				
2873	Sinks, counter								1				
2874	Sinks, drifts, and calking tools .... pounds												4
2875	Slicks, carpenters'												85
2876	Slicks, large framing												2
2877	Slicks, glass							3					
2878	Scrapers, plumbers'							13					4
2879	Scrapers, box							5					
2880	Scrapers							99	2				
2881	Scrapers, iron							133					
2882	Scrapers, drill							62					
2883	Scrapers, stone							1					
2884	Scrapers, carriage							1					
2885	Scrapers, stove							7					
2886	Scrapers, ash-pan												
2887	Straighteners, axle												1
2888	Sockets, top												1
2889	Sockets, chisel												133
2890	Sockets, gas-pipe									60			680
2891	Shafts and pulleys												1
2892	Shafts												10
2893	Shafts, saw mandril counter							1					
2894	Shafting and pulleys .... pounds												
2895	Shafts with pulleys, counter, shafting, &c ... feet												96
2896	Shafting, assorted .... do							176			368		
2897	Shafting, iron, 2-inch .... pounds												
2898	Shafting .... do							405					
2899	Shafting, 3½-inch, with pulleys and hangers, complete .... feet												
2900	Shafting, 3-inch .... do								528½				
2901	Shafting, 3¼-inch, tinned, 12 feet 6 inches long, with couplings and bolts, complete .... sections								12				
2902	Shafts, counter, with pulleys												1
2903	Shafts, counter										1		
2904	Strainers							1					
2905	Strainers, paint												2
2906	Strainers, pump							120					191
2907	Strainers, copper							70					
2908	Strainers, feed-pipe												

Report showing the disposition of United States military railroad property in the military division of the Tennessee, &c.—Continued.

Running number.	Articles.	Sold at public auction to railroad companies on credit on same terms as authorized by Executive Orders of August 8 and October 14, 1865.						Sold at auction for cash.	Transferred to officers.	Lost or expended in the public service.	Captured property returned to railroad companies.	Captured property returned to individuals.	Balance on hand June 1, 1866.
		Nashville and Northwestern railroad.	Selma and Meridian railroad.	Nashville and Decatur railroad.	New Orleans, Jackson, and Great Northern railroad.	Mississippi and Tennessee railroad.	Mississippi Central railroad.						
2909	Skins, chamois							4	7	42			7
2910	Skins, sheep							12		26			
2911	Skins, bark ... dozen												6
2912	Shellac, gum ... pounds							41	11	98			
2913	Saltpetre ... do							50		18			
2914	Spouts, bent							3, 198		100			
2915	Spouts, tank							35	3				
2916	Spouts, sheet-iron												
2917	Shafts, counter, and 4 pulleys												
2918	Spouts, fluid can							762					
2919	Spouts, tin							151					
2920	Spouts, funnel							56					
2921	Staffs, flag							1, 444					
2922	Staffs, brake												
2923	Steel, assorted ... pounds							10, 378	166	3, 110			
2924	Steel, scrap ... do							37, 613		550			653
2925	Steel, cast ... do							84, 799	$30\frac{3}{4}$	4, 516			
2926	Steel, spring, assorted ... do							11, 329		8, 606			
2927	Steel, square ... do								180	7, 164			73, 756
2928	Steel, octagon ... do									1, 239			8, 060
2929	Steel, frog ... do							12, 120	4, 439	5, 643			
2930	Steel, blister ... do							2, 852		680			
2931	Stocks, screw												9
2932	Stocks, iron												
2933	Stocks, drill							2					
2934	Stocks, iron ... pairs												3
2935	Stocks, roller								21				
2936	Saddles, smoke-stack ... pounds								224				
2937	Saddles for cylinder ... pairs									1			
2938	Stacks, smoke, locomotive												
2939	Stacks, smoke, stationary, 31 feet x 22 inches												2

2940	Stacks, smoke, sheet-iron, boiler frame								1				
2941	Stacks, smoke and cap .... pounds												
2942	Scraps, forge .... do												1,278
2943	Stacks, smoke, sheet-iron												1
2944	Stacks, smoke							17	6				
2945	Stacks, smoke .... feet							301					
2946	Sieves, sand							54	1				
2947	Sieves, moulders'							51					
2948	Strips, parallel												
2949	Strips, parallel .... pounds												
2950	Strips, copper-flue .... do							851					
2951	Spikes, bridge .... do								90	5,934			7,845
2952	Spikes, railroad .... kegs							1,985	500	173			
2953	Spikes, marlin							19					
2954	Spikes, bridge and cut .... kegs							113					
2955	Spikes, railroad							100					
2956	Spikes, railroad .... pounds							10,519	165,000	100,000			
2957	Spikes, cut, assorted .... kegs								2	1			
2958	Spikes, assorted .... pounds							1,000					
2959	Spikes .... kegs												
2960	Scales, spring balance							1	4	1			
2961	Scales, platform, assorted							18	5				
2962	Scales, counter							12	1	1			
2963	Scales and weights												
2964	Scales, warehouse												
2965	Scales, brass scoop												1
2966	Scales, set												3
2967	Scales, beam												
2968	Scales								1				1
2969	Scales, track												
2970	Scales, safety-valve												4
2971	Scales, stone							1					
2972	Scales, spring												3
2973	Scales, platform counter												9
2974	Stretchers, iron							51					
2975	Stretchers, car							10					
2976	Snatches, gate							1					
2977	Springs, assorted .... pounds												1,414
2978	Springs, rubber car .... do									1,432			
2979	Springs, car							1					
2980	Springs, packing												3
2981	Springs, rubber .... pounds								270	70			
2982	Springs, gum							2					
2983	Springs, engine tender .... pounds							21,690					
2984	Springs, spiral .... do							8,467					
2985	Springs, assorted												
2986	Springs, gum .... pounds							14,307	5,179	8,344			
2987	Springs, car .... do							24,657					
2988	Springs, tender												
2989	Springs, engine								2				
2990	Springs, engine .... pounds							12,838	402	402			2,000
2991	Springs, window							256					

Report showing the disposition of United States military railroad property in the military division of the Tennessee, &c.—Continued.

Running number.	Articles.	Sold at public auction to railroad companies on credit on same terms as authorized by Executive Orders of August 8 and October 14, 1865.						Sold at auction for cash.	Transferred to officers.	Lost or expended in the public service.	Captured property returned to railroad companies.	Captured property returned to individuals.	Balance on hand June 1, 1866.
		Nashville and Northwestern railroad.	Selma and Meridian railroad.	Nashville and Decatur railroad.	New Orleans, Jackson, and Great Northern railroad.	Mississippi and Tennessee railroad.	Mississippi Central railroad.						
2992	Springs, large D								4				
2993	Springs, small D								16				
2994	Springs, packing ... pounds												
2995	Shovels							2,200	498			12	
2996	Shovels, railroad												75
2997	Shovels, scoop							14	26				
2998	Shovels, coal												1
2999	Shovels, moulder, steel												
3000	Shovels and scrapers												
3001	Spades							270	4			12	
3002	Screens, sand							2					
3003	Screens, cloth							6					
3004	Screens, zinc							1					
3005	Screens, coal												1
3006	Screens, wire							1					
3007	Spools, chalk line												40
3008	Soap ... pounds							183					
3009	Soap, castile ... do									65			
3010	Soap ... bars								15				
3011	Spanners												3
3012	Sienna, assorted ... pounds							180½	15	60			
3013	Sienna, burnt ... do								12	33			18
3014	Sienna, raw Italian ... do									144			110
3015	Sienna, raw, in oil ... do									20			40
3016	Sienna, raw ... do												10
3017	Springs, brass							84					
3018	Sledges, (12-pound)												3
3019	Springs, patent								40				
3020	Stirrups, log ... pairs												4
3021	Stencils, copper							12					5
3022	Scythes, snath							35					

3023	Scythes, grass							13					
3024	Scythes, brier							14					
3025	Sponge, common ... pounds							397	31	85½			
3026	Sponge, fine ... do								20	1¼			
3027	Sponge ... do												33
3028	Sulphur ... do							307		151			
3029	Sulphur flowers ... do									99			324
3030	Sash, assorted ... lights							1,176		122			
3031	Sash, ... pieces							692		90	39		8
3032	Sash ... lots							1					
3033	Sash, wire							5					
3034	Sash, sky-light							21					
3035	Switches, monkey							14					13
3036	Slides, switch ... sets												119
3037	Slides, track ... pounds							1,217					
3038	Signals, fog ... gross												10
3039	Stools, saddlers'												2
3040	Spaces, pica quod ... pounds												23¼
3041	Staples, iron ... do												
3042	Staples, iron							7	4	78			
3043	Straps, seat, back							22	160				200
3044	Straps, connecting, and brasses											4	
3045	Skivers								17				
3046	Skivers, white								24				
3047	Skids, loading							6					
3048	Sizing, gold ... pounds							2		1			
3049	Shoes, mule ... do									955			200
3050	Shoes, mule									1,200			
3051	Sellars, rod ... pounds								75				
3052	Straps, eccentric ... do								158				
3053	Stems, check valve								189				
3054	Settings, masonry, with iron chimney												
3055	Scrapers, hoe												
3056	Sprinklers, fire												
3057	Squares, plated							6					
3058	Shingles							116,200	300,000	225,600			
3059	Saucers, stove												3
3060	Shackles, engine ... pounds												
3061	Salt ... do									379			
3062	Salts, epsom ... do									10			
3063	Sublimate, corr ... do									1			
3064	Staves, tank ... lots												1
3065	Staves, tank ... pieces												4
3066	Staples, back harness									28			
3067	Settings, masonry												2
3068	Seamers, double roofing							5					
3069	Solder ... pounds							233	74	217			78
3070	Soda, sal ... do												
3071	Swivels							1					
3072	Seats, coach							4					
3073	Seats							7					
3074	Shelving ... lots							2					

Report showing the disposition of United States military railroad property in the military division of the Tennessee, &c.—Continued.

Running number.	Articles.	Sold at public auction to railroad companies on credit on same terms as authorized by Executive Orders of August 8 and October 14, 1865.						Sold at auction for cash.	Transferred to officers.	Lost or expended in the public service.	Captured property returned to railroad companies.	Captured property returned to individuals.	Balance on hand June 1, 1866.
		Nashville and Northwestern railroad.	Selma and Meridian railroad.	Nashville and Decatur railroad.	New Orleans, Jackson, and Great Northern railroad.	Mississippi and Tennessee railroad.	Mississippi Central railroad.						
3075	Shelves, wooden							1					
3076	Syphons and cocks							1					
3077	Spoons, packing							7					
3078	Signs, tin							11					
3079	Signs							7					15
3080	Signs, loco							68					
3081	Shutters, window							24					
3082	Steps, engine							1					
3083	Slides, switch							119					
3084	Staves, tank ... cases							4					
3085	Shimmers, paint							2					
3086	Shoes, horse ... pounds							620					2
3087	Shoes, brake												
3088	Sets, hand-saw												33
3089	Sets, cross-cut saw							13					6
3090	Sets, mill-saw							6					
3091	Sets, lever-saw												13
3092	Sets, blacksmiths' cold												6
3093	Sets, rivet							2	4				3
3094	Sets, iron button							132					
3095	Sets, spring							1					
3096	Sledges, assorted								8				
3097	Sledges and handles							80					
3098	Sledges, blacksmiths'							270	3				
3099	Sledges, heavy												2
3100	Sledges, stone							105					208
3102	Shears, hand ... pairs												3
3103	Shears, tinners' ... do							6	1				
3104	Shears, sheet ... do							21					
3105	Shears, circular ... do												1
3106	Shears, lever ... do								1				

3107	Shears, bench ..... do								2	1			
3108	Shears, squaring ..... do								8				
3109	Shears and punch combined ..... do												
3110	Shears, rotary ..... do							2					
3111	Shears, table, trimmers' ..... do								1				
3112	Shears, table, gauge ..... do								1				
3113	Shears ..... do							4					
3114	Shives, iron							4					
3115	Stakes, square, Weddell												14
3116	Stakes, funnel												2
3117	Stakes, bench							4					
3118	Stakes, tinners'							2	1				
3119	Stakes, needle							1					
3120	Stakes, double seaming												
3121	Stakes, oval-head							1					
3122	Stakes, head							13					
3123	Stakes, pointing							1					
3124	Stakes, beak-horn							4					
3125	Stakes, hatchet							3					1
3126	Stakes, square-head							6					
3127	Stakes, horn-blow												1
3128	Stakes, round-head							2					
3129	Swedges, assorted							229	42	4			
3130	Swedges, square ..... pairs												
3131	Swedges, C. S ..... pounds												261
3132	Swedges, W. I ..... do								51				418
3133	Swedges, B. S							353					
3134	Swedges and fullers												19
3135	Swedges and chisels ..... sets												247
3136	Sleeves, water pipe							26					
3137	Sheives ..... pairs												
3138	Stacks, smoke, stationary												
3139	Shafts, steam, wheel								2				
3139¼	Saws, circular, assorted							88	24				
3139½	Slicks												102
3139¾	Sellar's engine truck								321				
3140	Tools, plumbers' ..... sets												
3141	Tools, blacksmiths', assorted ..... do							23	1			3	2
3142	Tools, blacksmiths' ..... pounds												
3143	Tools, shoeing ..... sets							7					3
3144	Tools, carpenters' ..... do							8					
3145	Tools, carpenters' ..... chests							1					
3146	Tools, turning, assorted											225	260
3147	Tools, wheelwright ..... sets							9					
3148	Tools, wheelwright, and chest, (incomplete)							1					
3149	Tools, grooving												3
3150	Tools, sash, assorted							68	15				59
3151	Tools, French sash, assorted								48				108
3152	Tools, hand							88					20
3153	Tools, planing, steel												395
3154	Tools, boring												44
3155	Tools, boring, steel												

Report showing the disposition of United States military railroad property in the military division of the Tennessee, &c.—Continued.

Running number.	Articles.	Sold at public auction to railroad companies on credit on same terms as authorized by Executive Orders of August 8 and October 14, 1865.						Sold at auction for cash.	Transferred to officers.	Lost or expended in the public service.	Captured property returned to railroad companies.	Captured property returned to individuals.	Balance on hand June 1, 1866.
		Nashville and Northwestern railroad.	Selma and Meridian railroad.	Nashville and Decatur railroad.	New Orleans, Jackson, and Great Northern railroad.	Mississippi and Tennessee railroad.	Mississippi Central railroad.						
3156	Tools, lathe, steel ... pounds								128				
3157	Tools, lathe												
3158	Tools, steel, for turning rolls ... pounds											200	
3159	Tools, saddlers' ... chests												2
3160	Tools, saddlers' ... sets							3					3
3161	Tools, tinners' ... do								1				1
3162	Tools, tinners' ... pounds												
3163	Tools, C. S ... do								105				
3164	Tools, coppersmith ... sets												
3165	Tools, graining ... do							5	1				
3166	Tools, cupping												17
3167	Tools, heading							82	2				134
3168	Tools, slotting												1
3169	Tools, rotary-cutting												
3170	Tools, spring ... sets												1
3171	Tools, calking												8
3172	Tools, flat paint, assorted												6
3173	Tools and chains, W. I ... pounds												
3174	Tools, iron												
3175	Tools, turning ... boxes								1				
3176	Tools, lathe and planer							16					
3177	Trams ... pairs												
3178	Taps and dies ... sets								2			1	7
3179	Taps and dies								3			31	
3180	Taps, steel ... pounds												83
3181	Taps, steel												194
3182	Taps, C. S ... pounds										42		
3183	Taps, machine							50					
3184	Taps							362					
3185	Tips, C. S												
3186	Tanks, oil, assorted							2					

3187	Tanks, engine			2				5					
3188	Tanks, water							8	11		24		
3189	Tanks, locomotive										1		
3190	Tanks, oil, (45 galls)												1
3191	Tanks, oil, (5) galls)												1
3192	Tanks, oil, (75 galls)												1
3193	Tanks, oil, (80 galls)												1
3194	Tanks, tin water, (parts) ... lots							1					
3195	Tongs, roofing ... pairs							6					
3196	Tongs, G. P. ... do							106	1				
3197	Tongs, ice ... do							2					
3198	Tongs, B. S ... do							289	16				
3199	Tongs, tinners' ... sets												1
3200	Tongs, grainers' ... do												1
3201	Tongs, engine ... pairs							3	11				
3202	Tongs, R. R ... do							93					
3203	Tongs, tools, and pokers ... pounds												
3204	Tongs, assorted ... pairs							156	32				106
3205	Tongs, B. S. and R. R							446					
3206	Tin, sheet ... boxes								115	82			
3207	Tin, perforated ... sheets									12			10
3208	Tin, block ... pounds								625	1,112			
3209	Tin, sheet ... sheets							378					
3210	Tin, sheet, and screws ... pounds							300					
3211	Timber ... feet							91,347		500			
3212	Timber, oak ... do			27,912				235,412		58,966			181,535
3213	Timber, square, assorted ... do			97,406						114,000			
3214	Timber, bridge ... do							747,582					
3215	Timber, B. M., assorted ... do									58,707			354,214
3216	Timber, framed ... lots							1					
3217	Ties, cross	2,611		14,605				27,216		1,078			
3218	Tallow ... pounds							951	390	24,263½			
3219	Tallow ... barrels								7	13			6½
3220	Thimbles												7
3221	Thimbles, flue, iron ... pounds								238				
3222	Thimbles, cast ... do							298					
3223	Thermometers												2
3224	Tarpaulins							7					6
3225	Tripods							11					257
3226	T's, gas-pipe							290	26	167			
3227	T's, water-pipe							6					
3228	T's, cast iron									6			
3229	Tubes, blast							11					8
3230	Tubing, copper ... pounds												
3231	Trucks, timber							4			1		
3232	Trucks, warehouse							7		1			
3233	Trucks, engine							3					
3234	Trucks ... pairs									11			
3235	Trucks, car	1		35				50		4	19		
3236	Trucks, car ... pairs								5				
3237	Trucks, tender and locomotive ... pounds							5,336					
3238	Trucks, engine ... pairs												3

Report showing the disposition of United States military railroad property in the military division of the Tennessee, &c.—Continued.

Running number.	Articles.	Sold at public auction to railroad companies on credit on same terms as authorized by Executive Orders of August 8 and October 14, 1865.						Sold at auction for cash.	Transferred to officers.	Lost or expended in the public service.	Captured property returned to railroad companies.	Captured property returned to individuals.	Balance on hand June 1, 1866.
		Nashville and Northwestern railroad.	Selma and Meridian railroad.	Nashville and Decatur railroad.	New Orleans, Jackson, and Great Northern railroad.	Mississippi and Tennessee railroad.	Mississippi Central railroad.						
3239	Trucks, machine ... pairs							3					2
3240	Tires, wrought iron ... pounds					4, 045							
3241	Tires, cast iron								4	16			13
3242	Tires, locomotive							15	4				
3243	Tires, locomotive flange ... pounds							27, 345					
3244	Tires, flange cast iron ... do												
3245	Tires, old ... do												270
3246	Tires, wrought iron							68					
3247	Trowels, masons'							15		1			
3248	Trowels, plasterers'							11					
3249	Tables, circular saw												
3250	Tables, turn												
3251	Tables, turn and foundation										1		
3252	Tables, binders' sewing								1				
3253	Torches, gas							5					
3254	Troughs, flock									1			32
3255	Troughs, guttering												2
3256	Troughs, forge							3					
3257	Tops and screws, lamp							1, 203					
3258	Tops, chimney												7
3259	Tops, turn-table												2
3260	Tops, car-lamp												22
3261	Tops, screw ... gross							$24\frac{3}{4}$					
3262	Tops, tallow, can												
3263	Tops and bottoms, can							1, 109					
3264	Tops and bottoms, car-lamp							24					
3265	Tops and bottoms for turn-table							2					
3266	Type ... founts								134				4
3267	Type ... pounds												971 35-48
3268	Tapes, measuring, assorted							330					
3269	Tripoli ... pounds									101			

3270	Tripoli	papers							113		72			
3271	Tacks, assorted	do							14, 420	84	690			
3272	Tacks, gimp	do							571		181			
3273	Tacks, upholsterers'	do							216		235			731
3274	Tacks, blued	do							12					
3275	Targets								44					
3276	Tickets, mess										2, 000			
3277	Tickets													
3278	Tar, coal	gallons									15			
3279	Tar, coal	barrels												4½
3280	Thread, black	pounds												
3281	Thread, black	bundles								6				
3282	Thread, shoe	pounds							2		5			8
3283	Thread, saddlers'	do												4½
3284	Thread, linen	do									34			
3285	Thread, black	skeins							20					
3286	Twine, hemp	pounds								1½				25
3287	Twine, tufting	do												
3288	Twine, wrapping	do								2	45½			
3289	Twine	balls							8					
3290	Turpentine	gallons							5	195	174½			
3291	Trestles								90					11
3292	Trusses, iron								1					
3293	Torpedoes													
3294	Tongues, frog	pounds												
3295	Templets, switch	sets												
3296	Templets								36					
3297	Transits								4					
3298	Tenders, locomotive								1					
3299	Tincture, iodine	pounds									1½			
3300	Transoms, wrought	do							8, 824					
3301	Testers, gas-pipe								1					
3302	Tiles, fire								38					
3303	Traps, rat								1					1
3304	Tighteners, belt								1					
3305	Triangles								1					1
3306	Tubs, tool								1					
3307	Tags, shipping	lots							1					
3308	Unions, brass, assorted								485		20			
3309	Umber, raw, in oil	pounds									46			
3310	Umber, raw	do							97	21				
3311	Umber, burnt	do								31				
3312	Umber, burnt	tubes								3				
3313	Umber, burnt, in oil	pounds								21	47			46
3314	Vices, assorted								91	15			5	103
3315	Vices, parallel								91					
3316	Vices, bench													
3317	Vices, B. S								15	2				9
3318	Vices, solid box									6			1	
3319	Vices, hand								602					
3320	Vices, solid	pounds							1, 344					
3321	Ventilators								18					

Report showing the disposition of United States military railroad property in the military division of the Tennessee, &c.—Continued.

Running number.	Articles.	Sold at public auction to railroad companies on credit on same terms as authorized by Executive Orders of August 8 and October 14, 1865.						Sold at auction for cash.	Transferred to officers.	Lost or expended in the public service.	Captured property returned to railroad companies.	Captured property returned to individuals.	Balance on hand June 1, 1866.
		Nashville and Northwestern railroad.	Selma and Meridian railroad.	Nashville and Decatur railroad.	New Orleans, Jackson, and Great Northern railroad.	Mississippi and Tennessee railroad.	Mississippi Central railroad.						
3322	Ventilators, tin												12
3323	Ventilators, car							56					
3324	Ventilators, car, lamp							9					
3325	Valves, globe, assorted							403	1	30			18
3326	Valves, tank								3				2
3327	Valves, water, assorted							10					
3328	Valves, angle							40					
3329	Valves, check							10		2			
3330	Valves, engine								51	20			
3331	Valves, brass, pump												
3332	Valves, safety, complete												
3333	Valves, brass, pump ... pounds								79	49			
3334	Valves, brass, check ... do									85			
3335	Valves, brass, steam ... do							12					
3336	Valves, governor									3			
3337	Valves, engine ... pounds									51			
3338	Valves, safety ... do									8			
3339	Vermilion, English "D" ... do							12		189			
3340	Vermilion, American extra ... do							70	9	26			
3341	Vermilion, German ... do									72			
3342	Vermilion, Chinese ... do								24	24			
3343	Vermilion, Chinese ... tubes									12			
3344	Vermilion, scarlet ... pounds							24					
3345	Vermilion, chrome ... do							½					
3346	Vermilion ... do							35					
3347	Varnish, copal ... gallons							45	112	21			
3348	Varnish, coach body ... do							456¾	140	683½			
3349	Varnish, shellac ... do							30½		22½			
3350	Varnish, Japan ... do							35½	133	52½			100
3351	Varnish, demar ... do							30	41½	44½			
3352	Varnish, asphaltum ... do							3	17	3			

No.	Article													
3353	Varnish, white	pounds									84			
3354	Varnish, white	gallons							100					
3355	Verdigriss	pounds							30	6	2			
3356	Vitriol	do							30					
3357	Wrenches, assorted										2			420
3358	Wrenches, monkey, assorted								1,035	396	1		12	
3359	Wrenches, blast pipe													1
3360	Wrenches, tap, assorted								121				15	
3361	Wrenches, ratchet								1					
3362	Wrenches, straight													1
3363	Wrenches, screw													35
3364	Wrenches, bridge								2					10
3365	Wrenches, wheel								4					
3366	Wrenches, key								8					
3367	Wrenches, hose													1
3368	Wrenches, long bar													1
3369	Wrenches, lathe												21	
3370	Wrenches, socket												10	97
3371	Wrenches, spanner								87					92
3372	Wrenches, hand								71					
3373	Wrenches, iron tap	pounds								42				
3374	Wrenches, "S"								336	4				
3375	Wrenches, pipe													57
3376	Wrenches, follower													5
3377	Wrenches, iron								696					
3378	Wrenches, packing													2
3379	Wrenches, post								3					
3380	Wedges, stonemasons'													
3381	Wedges	pounds												
3382	Wedges, iron								41					10
3383	Wedges, steel													10
3384	Wedges								6					54
3385	Wedges, blacksmiths'								27					
3386	Wedges and feathers								158					
3387	Whistles, locomotive								3			3		
3388	Whistles, steam													
3389	Windlass, quaker								2					
3390	Windlass, hand													
3391	Wheels, tender, and truck, on axles	pairs										47		
3392	Wheels, car, with axles													12
3393	Wheels, car, on axles	pairs							108	11				
3394	Wheels and axles	pounds							2,202,752					
3395	Wheels, driving, on axles	pairs												5
3396	Wheels, turn-table	pounds								544				540
3397	Wheels, press gear	do									368			1,168
3398	Wheels, car								396					
3399	Wheels, car	pounds							1,434,231		34			
3400	Wheels, water								1					
3401	Wheels, hand car	pounds							61,911					
3402	Wheels, hand car								22					
3403	Wheels, cog, hand car													
3404	Wheels, car and tender													339

Report showing the disposition of United States military railroad property in the military division of the Tennessee, &c.—Continued.

Running number.	Articles.	Sold at public auction to railroad companies on credit on same terms as authorized by Executive Orders of August 8 and October 14, 1865.						Sold at auction for cash.	Transferred to officers.	Lost or expended in the public service.	Captured property returned to railroad companies.	Captured property returned to individuals.	Balance on hand June 1, 1866.
		Nashville and Northwestern railroad.	Selma and Meridian railroad.	Nashville and Decatur railroad.	New Orleans, Jackson, and Great Northern railroad.	Mississippi and Tennessee railroad.	Mississippi Central railroad.						
3405	Wheels, driving								2				7
3406	Wheels, engine truck									8			
3407	Wheels, truck ... pairs												
3408	Wheels, iron pulley								3				
3409	Wheels, brake ... pounds												
3410	Wheels, brake							6					
3411	Wheels, engine												
3412	Wheels, engine and tender, on axles ... pairs												
3413	Wheels, for counter shaft												
3414	Wheels and axles, hand car ... pairs			25				25					
3415	Wheels, car ... do										85		
3416	Wheels and axles ... sets											8	
3417	Wheels, engine truck, on axles ... pairs											5	
3418	Wheels, bevel								2			2	
3419	Wheels, fly, ten feet								2			1	
3420	Wheels, press gear								1, 168				
3421	Wheels, spur								11				
3422	Wheels, truck								18				
3423	Wheels, car, 24-inch, pattern No. 25												50
3424	Wheels, car, 26-inch, pattern No. 27												50
3425	Wheels, freight car												158
3426	Wheels, balance							5					
3427	Wheels, hand car ... pairs												241
3428	Wheels, hand car, on axles ... pounds							165, 226					
3429	Wheels, ratchet									12			25
3430	Wicks, flat								156	3, 076			3, 432
3431	Wicks, lamp ... pounds								5½	10			
3432	Wicks, lamp ... gross												
3433	Wicking ... balls								72				
3434	Wire, brass ... pounds							570		110			
3435	Wire, telegraph ... do							2, 025		150			

3436	Wire, copper	do							261	57½	295			
3436½	Wire, iron	do							4,612					
3437	Wire, assorted	do												
3438	Wire, tin	do							60					23
3439	Wire	bundles								4	4			
3440	Washers, assorted	pounds							26,505	2,720	3,982			
3441	Washers, cast	do							32,540		1,894			
3442	Webbing	yards							170½					
3443	White, China	pounds							274		96			
3444	White, flake, assorted	do							114	7½	216			
3445	White, flake	tubes								6				
3446	Whiting	pounds							216	525				
3447	Whiting, Spanish	do								200	400			165
3448	Wax, bees	do							167	10	35			
3449	Winches, crane								3		1			
3450	Waste, cotton	pounds							172	1,356	2,132			
3451	Waste, tow	do									257			250
3452	Waste	do								1,215				
3453	Weights	do												
3454	Weights								1					
3455	Weights, sash								24					
3456	Walks, plank								1					
3457	Webbing	bolts								2	3			16
3458	Wrenches, square								1					
3459	Yarn, lubricating, packing	pounds									417			
3460	Yellow, canary	do							36		26			
3461	Yarn, packing	reels									3½			
3462	Yawls								1					
3463	Zinc, slab	pounds									361			
3464	Zinc, sheet	do							172		326			645
3465	Zinc, sheet	pieces							3					

[Enclosure No. 4.]

REPORT OF BREVET MAJOR F. J. CRILLY.

Report showing the disposition of United States military railroad property in the military division of the Tennessee, for which Captain J. H. Clemens, assistant quartermaster, is responsible.

Running No.	Articles.	Amount on hand May 1, 1865.	Transferred to officers.	Expended.	Total transferred and expended.
1	Grain sacks ....number..	1,933	1,933	....	1,933
2	Books, blank, assorted ....do....	1,002	178	1,007	1,185
3	Books, memorandum....do....	79	....	85	85
4	Books, Military Laws....do....	1	....	....	....(*).....
5	Boards, card....do....	197	....	197	197
6	Boxes, pounce....do....	7	....	7	7
7	Clips, paper ....do....	82	82	....	82
8	Clips, letter ....do....	197	263	23	286
9	Clips, broad letter ....do....	7	7	....	7
10	Clips, board ....do....	6	6	....	6
11	Clips, board ....do....	142	32	110	142
12	Cutters, paper ....do....	150	84	66	150
13	Cutters, card ....do....	2	2	....	2
14	Cutters for fasteners ....do....	1	....	1	1
15	Erasers....do....	274	49	225	274
16	Files, paper ....do....	569	222	347	569
17	Files, ad. letter ....do....	45	....	45	45
18	Files, wire....do....	46	12	34	46
19	Inkstands, assorted ....do....	1,047	569	476	1,045
20	Paper, letter ....quires..	30	646	100	746
21	Paper, envelope ....do....	8	....	10	10
22	Pens, extension....boxes..	¼	¼	....	¼
23	Pens, drawing ....number..	6	....	6	6
24	Pens, ruling ....do....	1,109	913	200	1,113
25	Rulers ....do....	556	227	333	560
26	Rulers, caliper....do....	1	....	1	1
27	Racks, pen ....do....	360	237	125	362
28	Tearers, paper ....do....	6	....	6	6
29	Bureaus ....do....	4	2	2	4
30	Baskets, paper....do....	7	11	....	11
31	Boards, black....do....	9	16	....	16
32	Boards, diagram ....do....	7	15	....	15
33	Boards, book ....do....	1	....	1	1
34	Brushes, copying ....do....	48	24	42	66
35	Brushes, counter....do....	183	100	83	183
36	Boxes, post office ....do....	23	11	12	23
37	Boxes, ticket ....do....	20	....	20	20
38	Boxes, paper ....do....	300	1	299	300
39	Balances, letter....do....	1	....	1	1
40	Bell, gong, complete....do....	1	5	....	5
41	Buckets, coal....do....	1	1	....	1
42	Bands, gum ....do....	33	55	....	55
43	Cases, ticket....do....	6	2	4	6
44	Cases, bill-head....do....	1	1	....	1
45	Cases, blank....do....	1	1	....	1
46	Cases, pigeon-hole ....do....	6	6	....	6
47	Chairs, office ....do....	1,316	669	654	1,323
48	Chairs, camp ....do....	6	6	....	6
49	Chart, time-stand....do....	1	1	....	1
50	Closets, picket....do....	1	1	....	1
51	Cupboards ....do....	27	82	....	82
52	Clocks ....do....	86	73	15	88
53	Chests ....do....	9	....	9	9
54	Coolers, water....do....	14	14	....	14
55	Cups, sponge ....do....	1	1	....	1
56	Calendars, office....do....	73	57	17	74
57	Caps, stove pipe ....do....	107	23	165	188
58	Desks ....do....	140	156	....	156
59	Dusters, feather ....do....	251	57	194	251
60	Frame, diagonal ....do....	1	....	1	1
61	Holes, nest pigeon ....do....	6	6	....	6
62	Indexes ....do....	75	....	75	75
63	Lamps, office....do....	380	280	130	410
64	Machines, eyelet....do....	6	1	5	6
65	Press, copying....do....	35	38	....	38

* Balance on hand, 1.

Disposition of United States military railroad property, &c.—Continued.

Running No.	Articles.		Amount on hand May 1, 1865.	Transferred to officers.	Expended.	Total transferred and expended.
66	Pots, watering	number	25	35		35
67	Safes, office	do	43	28	16	44
68	Safes, pay, iron	do	4	3	1	4
69	Safes, field	do	7		7	7
70	Safes, key	do	10		10	10
71	Stands	do	6	19		19
72	Stools	do	41	94		94
73	Stoves, office	do	21	2	21	23
74	Stoves and pipe in car	do	29		29	29
75	Stamps	do	13		13	13
76	Scales, post office	do	1	1		1
77	Shears, bank	pairs	46	10	36	46
78	Shades	number	5	12		12
79	Spittoons	do	63	75		75
80	Table, office	do	205	259		259
81	Thermometers	do	3	4		4
82	Weights, paper	do	387	314	73	387
83	Wardrobes	do	23	29		29
84	Boilers, assorted	do	1, 805	128	1, 677	1, 805
85	Boilers, square copper bottom	do	5		5	5
86	Boilers, with steamers	do	5		5	5
87	Boilers, coffee, assorted	do	1, 892	175	1, 719	1, 894
88	Bowls	do	2, 301	303	1, 998	2, 301
89	Bowls, sugar	do	35	6	29	35
90	Bowls, wash	do	2, 071	3	2, 068	2, 071
91	Boxes, tin	do	1	1		1
92	Boxes, mess	do	47	22	25	47
93	Boxes, ice	do	7	6	1	7
94	Boxes, pepper	do	2, 019	2, 372	721	3, 093
95	Boxes, spice	do	1	1		1
96	Bunks	do	367	369		369
97	Benches	do	92	92		92
98	Buckets, fire	do	56	93		93
99	Buckets, slop	do	2	3		3
100	Bedsteads	do	91	67	24	91
101	Basins, assorted	do	531	1, 202	8	1, 210
102	Boards, wash	do	156	14	142	156
103	Candlesticks	do	1, 159	1, 143	152	1, 295
104	Castors	do	14	10	4	14
105	Carvers	do	4	4		4
106	Carvers and forks	do	1	1		1
107	Cans, molasses	do	3	5		5
108	Cellars, salt	do	31	19	12	31
109	Cups	do	12, 426	5, 192	10, 010	15, 202
110	Cleavers, meat	do	23	14	9	23
111	Cots	do	27	27		27
112	Chest, mess	do	30	30		30
113	Dishes, assorted	do	420	254	166	420
114	Dishes, wash	do	2	2		2
115	Dippers, assorted	do	761	671	172	843
116	Forks	do	777	776	566	1, 342
117	Forks, flesh	do	1, 227	889	362	1, 251
118	Graters	do	215	403		403
119	Gates, molasses	do	30	20	16	36
120	Jugs	do	4	4		4
121	Knives, table	do	980	980		980
122	Knives, butcher	do	2, 183	460	1, 723	2, 183
123	Knives and forks	do	13, 788	6, 118	8, 600	14, 718
124	Knives and forks	sets	903 5-6	1	902 5-6	903 5-6
125	Knives, saw	number	1		1	1
126	Kettles, cast	do	38	38		38
127	Kettles, camp	do	240	239	21	260
128	Ladles	do	101	115		115
129	Mills, coffee	do	823	384	439	823
130	Ovens	do	49	23	26	49
131	Ovens, cast, and lid	do	24	4	20	24
132	Ovens, cast, and lid	pounds	1, 209		1, 209	1, 209
133	Pans, assorted	number	6, 027	6, 015	2, 729	8, 744
134	Pans, dish	do	12	5	7	12
135	Plates, assorted	do	14, 312	11, 251	4, 501	15, 752
136	Platters, tin	do	288		288	288
137	Pipe, stove	feet	536	1, 758		1, 758
138	Pipe, stove	pounds	7, 954		7, 954	7, 954
139	Pipe, stove	joints	4, 265	1, 691	3, 154	4, 845
140	Pots, coffee, assorted	number	16	185	44	229
141	Pots, tea	do	4	22		22
142	Pots	do	10	88		88

Disposition of United States military railroad property, &c.—Continued.

Running No.	Articles.	Amount on hand May 1, 1865.	Transferred to officers.	Expended.	Total transferred and expended.
143	Pitchers, cream .... number..	20	19	1	20
144	Pitchers, water .... do....	13	7	6	13
145	Pitchers, molasses .... do....	74	....	74	74
146	Ranges, with upright boiler .... do....	2	2	....	2
147	Ranges, with furniture .... do....	5	....	5	5
148	Ranges, commissary .... do....	1	....	1	1
149	Spoons, assorted .... do....	46, 779	28, 095	18, 684	46, 779
150	Saucers, tin .... do....	152	522	....	522
151	Saucers and cups .... do....	302	....	302	302
152	Saws, meat .... do....	8	18	....	18
153	Sieves .... do....	205	103	103	206
154	Skillets .... do....	21	21	....	21
155	Skillets and lids .... do....	23	23	....	23
156	Skillets and lids .... pounds..	1, 754	435	1, 319	1, 754
157	Steel, carving .... number..	5	8	....	8
158	Skimmers .... do....	42	45	72	117
159	Shovels, fire .... do....	78	17	63	80
160	Shovels and tongs .... pairs...	1	....	1	1
161	Spiders .... number..	1	2	....	2
162	Stoves, cooking, complete .... do....	723	253	470	723
163	Stoves, heating .... do....	30	25	19	44
164	Stoves, box, wood and pipe .... do....	12	....	12	12
165	Tumblers .... do....	73	15	58	73
166	Ticks, bed .... do....	166	....	166	166
167	Washstands .... do....	51	23	112	135
168	Axles, car .... pounds..	20, 000	101, 575	....	101, 575
169	Brushes, horse .... number..	247	252	....	252
170	Buckets, engine .... do....	324	150	174	324
171	Boxes, wagon .... do....	12	....	12	12
172	Boxes, axle .... do....	80	80	....	80
173	Bells, gong, and hanging .... do....	1	6	....	6
174	Balances, h'vy grad. spring loco .... do....	24	....	24	24
175	Balances, round case loco., grad. to 200 lbs... do....	96	....	96	96
176	Balances, loco. spring .... do....	331	148	183	331
177	Bolsters, wagon .... do....	94	....	94	94
178	Carts, sprinkler .... do....	1	1	....	1
179	Combs, curry .... do....	289	414	....	414
180	Cars, box .... do....	1, 493	1, 662	60	1, 722
181	Cars, freight .... do....	500	500	....	500
182	Cars, caboose .... do....	5	....	5	5
183	Cars, coal .... do....	8	8	....	8
184	Cars, platform .... do....	778	783	2	785
185	Cars, truck .... do....	126	33	93	126
186	Cars, guard .... do....	6	....	6	6
187	Cars, dirt .... do....	3	....	3	3
188	Cars, hand .... do....	197	60	137	197
189	Cars, hospital .... do....	3	3	....	3
190	Cars, passenger .... do....	17	25	1	26
191	Cars, passenger, 2d class .... do....	15	15	....	15
192	Cars, stock .... do....	5	....	10	10
193	Cars, stock and rack .... do....	4	....	4	4
194	Cars, house .... do....	196	....	196	196
195	Cars, baggage .... do....	4	....	4	4
196	Chambers, pumps, and valves .... do....	4	....	4	4
197	Cans, locomotive oil .... do....	54	....	54	54
198	Covers, wagon .... do....	5	5	....	5
199	Cocks, gauge, assorted .... do....	20	24	....	24
200	Engines, dummy .... do....	3	3	....	3
201	Gongs, locomotive, assorted .... do....	15	4	30	34
202	Gauges, steam .... do....	12	31	....	31
203	Locomotive engines and tenders .... do....	184	184	....	184
204	Lines, cart .... pairs...	3	3	....	3
205	Lights, locomotive head .... number..	244	146	98	244
206	Oars .... do....	8	....	8	8
207	Saddles, riding .... do....	2	3	....	3
208	Straps, neck .... do....	2	2	....	2
209	Stretchers .... do....	10	10	....	10
210	Springs, rubber car .... pounds..	12, 000	15, 708	....	15, 708
211	Springs, ambulance .... number..	1	....	1	1
212	Tires, locomotive .... do....	80	80	....	80
213	Tires, locomotive .... pounds..	14, 200	14, 200	....	14, 200
214	Tires, B. O. flange .... do....	8, 000	....	8, 000	8, 000
215	Trucks, timber .... number..	8	4	4	8
216	Wheels, car .... do....	160	1, 308	....	....
217	Wagon for moving portable saw mill .... do....	1	1	....	1
218	Whistles, locomotive, complete .... do....	5	6	....	6
219	Yokes, ox .... do....	148	45	103	148

Disposition of United States military railroad property, &c.—Continued.

Running No.	Articles.	Amount on hand May 1, 1865.	Transferred to officers.	Expended.	Total transferred and expended.
220	Yawls .... number..	2	....	2	2
221	Awls .... do....	167	181	91	272
222	Awls, scratch, handled .... do....	124	124	....	124
223	Axes .... do....	8,542	1,291	7,337	8,628
224	Axes, broad .... do....	927	804	140	944
225	Axes, hand .... do....	915	797	126	923
226	Axes, pick .... do....	392	....	392	392
227	Augurs, steel .... set....	7	8	....	8
228	Augurs, assorted .... number..	2,596	1,563	2,087	3,650
229	Augurs with handles .... do....	30	....	30	30
230	Adzes .... do....	1,393	698	810	1,508
231	Anvils .... do....	22	24	....	24
232	Anvils .... pounds..	62,938½	27,116	35,822½	62,938½
233	Arm racks .... number..	1	....	1	1
234	Angles, bell .... do....	7	....	7	7
235	Apparatus, automatic .... sets...	9	9	....	9
236	Bits, augur .... do....	237	62¼	174¾	237
237	Bits, augur, extra quarters .... number..	32	32	....	32
238	Bits, centre, assorted .... do....	131	....	131	131
239	Bits and augurs .... do....	10	....	10	10
240	Bits, car .... sets...	124	6	120	126
241	Bits, gimlet .... number..	131	144	....	144
242	Bits and braces .... do....	59	36	23	59
243	Bits, ratchet drill .... do....	72	4	68	72
244	Bits, assorted .... do....	2,628	184	3,934	4,128
245	Braces and slides .... do....	2	2	....	2
246	Bars, clothes .... sets...	1	....	1	1
247	Bars, claw .... number..	520	27	495	522
248	Bars, crow .... do....	239	210	110	330
249	Bars, crow .... pounds..	4,558	9,580	....	9,580
250	Bars, pinch .... number..	848	107	741	848
251	Bars, switch .... do...	36	36	....	36
252	Bars, draw .... do....	996	....	996	996
253	Bars, boring, portable .... do....	1	....	1	1
254	Bars, lining .... do....	588	2	586	588
255	Bars, spike .... do....	1	....	1	1
256	Bars, assorted .... do....	3,741	1,096	3,026	4,122
257	Bars, pry .... do....	836	....	836	836
258	Bars, tamping .... do....	1,156	28	1,152	1,180
259	Bars, grate .... do....	136	....	136	136
260	Bars .... do....	14	....	14	14
261	Bellows .... do....	102	80	67	147
262	Bellows, blacksmiths' .... pairs...	3	3	....	3
263	Belting, leather .... feet...	4,587	21,495	....	21,495
264	Blocks, assorted .... number..	5,445	498	4,948	5,446
265	Blocks, rigging .... do....	1	....	1	1
266	Blocks and rollers, assorted .... sets...	4	....	4	4
267	Blocks and sheaves .... do....	9	....	9	9
268	Blocks, double .... number..	19	....	19	19
269	Blocks, rubber .... pounds..	300¼	207	94¼	301¼
270	Blocks, pulley, assorted .... number...	609	5	604	609
271	Blocks, pedestal .... do....	4	....	4	4
272	Bolts, assorted .... do....	1,818	5,260	300	5,560
273	Bolts, hatchet .... do....	12	....	12	12
274	Boxes, tool .... do....	51	....	51	51
275	Boxes, Russia iron .... do....	4	....	4	4
276	Boxes, twine .... do....	19	....	19	19
277	Boxes, filing .... do....	24	....	24	24
278	Boxes, Pitman, complete .... do....	1	....	1	1
279	Boxes, grindstone .... do....	2	....	2	2
280	Boxes, emery .... do....	171	99	216	315
281	Boxes, packing .... do....	5	....	5	5
282	Boxes .... do....	179	293	....	293
283	Brushes, varnish, assorted .... do....	679	50	629	679
284	Brushes, paint, assorted .... do....	771	37	734	771
285	Brushes, fitch, assorted .... do....	144	....	144	144
286	Brushes, sash .... do....	36	....	36	36
287	Brushes, graining .... sets...	1	....	1	1
288	Brushes, artists' .... number..	24	....	24	24
289	Brushes, stove .... boxes...	2	....	2	2
290	Brushes, scrubbing .... number..	549	156	403	559
291	Brushes, car window .... do....	24	1	23	24
292	Brushes, whitewash .... do....	6	5	3	8
293	Brushes, assorted .... do....	1,979	635	1,652	2,287
294	Buckets, water .... do....	2,481	1,651	856	2,507
295	Buckets, covered .... do....	86	....	86	86
296	Buckets, S. I. .... do....	15	....	15	15

Disposition of United States military railroad property, &c.—Continued.

Running No.	Articles.	Amount on hand May 1, 1865.	Transferred to officers.	Expended.	Total transferred and expended.
297	Buckets, paint .... number..	25	54	....	54
298	Buckets, fire .... do....	473	109	376	485
299	Balance, spring .... do....	13	15	1	16
300	Buts, brass, assorted .... pairs...	200	429	....	429
301	Buts, wrought, assorted .... do....	50	50	....	50
302	Bunting, red, English .... yards...	1, 389¼	361	1, 028¼	1, 389¼
303	Barrows, wheel .... number..	1, 224	350	877	1, 227
304	Borers, tap .... do....	12	....	13	13
305	Brackets .... do....	1, 799	121	4, 077	4, 198
306	Boilers, steam .... do....	12	13	....	13
307	Brooms, assorted .... do....	900	1, 314	624	1, 938
308	Blenders .... do....	10	3	17	20
309	Blowers, fire .... do....	3	3	....	3
310	Blowers, assorted .... do....	3	1	4	5
311	Buggies, wood .... do....	32	24	8	32
312	Bodkins .... do....	4	6	....	6
313	Brands, government .... do....	2	....	3	3
314	Bolts, stone .... do....	2	2	....	2
315	Braders, No. 1 .... do....	2	....	2	2
316	Breeching, double .... sets...	1	....	1	1
317	Blades, hack saw .... number..	12	6	22	28
318	Body moulding and Russia iron .... set...	1	....	1	1
319	Burners .... number..	302	1, 007	....	1, 007
320	Buttons, enamelled .... do....	700	21, 592	....	21, 592
321	Beaders with stands .... do....	2	1	1	2
322	Beam, scale .... do....	1	1	....	1
323	Buildings, 20 by 25 .... do....	2	2	....	2
324	Buildings, 20 by 45 .... do....	1	1	....	1
325	Buildings, 25 by 30 .... do....	1	1	....	1
326	Buildings, 20 by 30 .... do....	8	8	....	8
327	Buildings, 25 by 40 .... do....	1	1	....	1
328	Buildings, 18 by 50 .... do....	3	3	....	3
329	Buildings, 20 by 50 .... do....	23	23	....	23
330	Buildings, 18 by 16 .... do...	1	1	....	1
331	Buildings, 16 by 16 .... do....	1	1	....	1
332	Buildings, 15 by 33 .... do....	1	1	....	1
333	Buildings, 15 by 25 .... do....	10	10	....	10
334	Buildings, 25 by 45 .... do....	1	1	....	1
335	Buildings, 60 by 275 .... do....	1	1	....	1
336	Buildings, 16 by 60 .... do....	1	1	....	1
337	Buildings, 32 by 125 .... do....	1	1	....	1
338	Buildings, 25 by 72 .... do....	1	1	....	1
339	Buildings, 31 by 100 .... do....	1	1	....	1
340	Buildings, 31 by 130 .... do....	1	1	....	1
341	Buildings, 25 by 60 .... do....	1	1	....	1
342	Buildings, 40 by 70 .... do....	1	1	....	1
343	Buildings, 20 by 56 .... do....	1	1	....	1
344	Buildings, 50 by 180 .... do....	1	1	....	1
345	Buildings, 18 by 28 .... do....	1	1	....	1
346	Buildings, 18 by 80 .... do....	1	1	....	1
347	Buildings, 45 by 60 .... do....	1	1	....	1
348	Buildings, 20 by 35 .... do....	3	3	....	3
349	Buildings, 20 by 55 .... do....	2	2	....	2
350	Buildings, 12 by 15 .... do....	1	1	....	1
351	Buildings, 12 by 16 .... do....	3	3	....	3
352	Buildings, 12 by 20 .... do....	1	1	....	1
353	Buildings, 12 by 12 .... do....	1	1	....	1
354	Buildings, 15 by 30 .... do....	1	1	....	1
355	Buildings, 16 by 77 .... do....	1	1	....	1
356	Buildings, 19 by 19 .... do....	1	1	....	1
357	Buildings, 20 by 40 .... do....	2	2	....	2
358	Buildings, 20 by 80 .... do....	5	5	....	5
359	Buildings, 20 by 112 .... do....	1	1	....	1
360	Buildings, 40 by 60 .... do....	1	1	....	1
361	Buildings, 45 by 36 .... do....	1	1	....	1
362	Buildings, 46 by 100 .... do....	1	1	....	1
363	Buildings, 11 by 11 .... do....	1	1	....	1
364	Buildings, 11 by 12 .... do....	1	1	....	1
365	Buildings, 11 by 14 .... do....	1	1	....	1
366	Buildings, 12 by 39 .... do....	1	1	....	1
367	Buildings, 12½ by 21 .... do....	1	1	....	1
368	Buildings, 12½ by 24 .... do....	1	1	....	1
369	Buildings, 15 by 20 .... do....	1	1	....	1
370	Buildings, 15 by 110 .... do....	1	1	....	1
371	Buildings, 20 by 60 .... do....	1	1	....	1
372	Buildings, 17 by 40 .... do....	2	2	....	2
373	Buildings, 18 by 26 .... do....	2	2	....	2

Disposition of United States military railroad property, &c.—Continued.

Running No.	Articles.	Amount on hand May 1, 1865.	Transferred to officers.	Expended.	Total transferred and expended.
374	Buildings, 20 by 110..........number..	1	1	....	1
375	Buildings, 20 by 163..........do....	3	3	....	3
376	Buildings, 21 by 40..........do....	1	1	....	1
377	Buildings, 24 by 40..........do....	1	1	....	1
378	Buildings, 25 by 68½..........do....	1	1	....	1
379	Buildings, 25 by 115..........do....	1	1	....	1
380	Buildings, 30 by 70..........do....	2	2	....	2
381	Buildings, 31 by 150..........do....	1	1	....	1
382	Buildings, 31 by 165..........do....	2	2	....	2
383	Buildings, 31 by 230..........do....	2	2	....	2
384	Buildings, 31½ by 31½..........do....	1	1	....	1
385	Buildings, 12 by 14..........do....	1	1	....	1
386	Buildings, 14 by 26..........do....	1	1	....	1
387	Buildings, 32 by 48..........do....	2	2	....	2
388	Buildings, 32 by 50..........do....	1	1	....	1
389	Buildings, 24 by 30..........do....	1	1	....	1
390	Buildings, 24 by 36..........do....	1	1	....	1
391	Buildings..........do....	1	1	....	1
392	Cans, assorted..........do....	1,876	1,805	72	1,877
393	Cans, powder..........do....	8	8	....	8
394	Cans, water, with cocks..........do....	2	2	....	2
395	Cans, oil, assorted..........do....	422	574	91	665
396	Cases..........pairs...	6	6	....	6
397	Cases..........number..	4	6	....	6
398	Chains, assorted..........pounds..	2,930½	1,453	1,477½	2,930½
399	Chains, log..........number..	69	42	74	116
400	Chains, lock..........do....	245	....	245	245
401	Chains, coil, assorted..........do....	41,457	735	40,722	41,457
402	Chains, coil..........feet...	1,404	2,188	....	2,188
403	Chains, cable..........pounds..	7,492	503	6,989	7,492
404	Chains, brass..........number..	1	....	1	1
405	Chains, brass..........feet...	1	....	1	1
406	Chains, 100 feet..........number..	6	1	5	6
407	Chains, jack..........yards..	132	....	135⅓	135⅓
408	Chests..........number..	12	36	9	45
409	Chisels, assorted..........do....	3,957	3,722	377	4,099
410	Chisels, firmer, assorted..........do....	24	....	24	24
411	Chisels, firmer, assorted..........sets...	143	48 5-6	151 4-6	200½
412	Chisels, framing, assorted..........number..	1,689	834	858	1,692
413	Chisels, framing..........sets...	161	5	158	163
414	Chisels, mortising..........number..	10	....	10	10
415	Chisels, cold..........do....	1,221	109	1,112	1,221
416	Chisels, socket..........sets...	50	....	50	50
417	Chisels, socket, firmer, assorted..........number..	108	....	108	108
418	Chisels, chipping..........do....	1,404	101	1,303	1,404
419	Chisels and swedge..........do....	1	....	6	6
420	Copper, ingot..........pounds..	1,080	1,080	....	1,080
421	Copper, soldering..........do....	12	12	....	12
422	Coppers, assorted..........pairs...	5	23	....	23
423	Copperas..........pounds..	50	3,856	....	3,856
424	Cups, oil..........number..	340	52	320	372
425	Cups, with cock..........do....	8	8	....	8
426	Cups, tallow..........do....	108	48	61	109
427	Cups, varnish..........do....	12	3	12	15
428	Cups, pedestal, wrought iron..........do....	4	....	4	4
429	Cups, chimney lamp..........do....	2	10	10	20
430	Chimneys, forge..........pounds..	3,617	....	3,617	3,617
431	Cocks, assorted..........number..	332	421	....	421
432	Cranes, water..........do....	61	50	11	61
433	Cranes, portable..........do....	1	1	....	1
434	Clamps..........do....	125	187	24	211
435	Clamps, copper..........pounds..	3	3	....	3
436	Crank and rollers, with flange..........sets...	11	11	....	11
437	Crank and rollers..........number..	18	57	....	57
438	Crucibles, assorted..........do....	3,913	49	3,879	3,928
439	Cuffs, gov't hand..........pairs...	6	6	....	6
440	Covers, file..........do....	12	....	12	12
441	Covers, flag..........number..	37	69	....	69
442	Covers, wire dish..........do....	4	....	4	4
443	Covers, sand-box..........do....	1	3	....	3
444	Covers, driving wheel..........set....	1	....	1	1
445	Covers, truck wheel..........do....	1	....	1	1
446	Centres..........pounds..	2,700	1,410	1,290	2,700
447	Centres, truck, assorted..........number..	36	....	36	36
448	Combs, steel graining..........sets...	1	2	....	2
449	Combs, army extra..........number..	24	....	24	24
450	Couplings and bands..........sets...	120	120	124	244

Disposition of United States military railroad property, &c.—Continued.

Running No.	Articles.	Amount on hand May 1, 1865.	Transferred to officers.	Expended.	Total transferred and expended.
451	Cutters, lead ... number..	1	1		1
452	Cutters, paper, 28-inch ... do....	1	1		1
453	Calipers, assorted ... do....	59	43	18	61
454 455	Chucks, 24-inch, universal screw, with wrenches ... do....	3	3		3
456	Canisters, assorted ... do....	24	33		33
457	Cape, ⅜-inch ... do....	1		1	1
458	Chucks ... do....	1		1	1
459	Circles, plate glass ... do....	100		100	100
460	Cornice brackets ... do....	75		75	75
461	Chills, frog, complete ... do....	4	11		11
462	Chilled car wheels ... do....	3		3	3
463	Dies ... sets...	10	160		160
464	Dies ... number..	1	59		59
465	Dies and stocks, assorted ... do....	117	67	55	122
466	Dies and stocks, assorted ... sets...	42	42		42
467	Drills ... number..	144	773		773
468	Drills, ratchet, assorted ... do....	35		35	35
469	Drills, suspension, and fixtures ... do....	1		1	1
470	Drills, suspension, No. 9 ... do....	3		3	3
471	Drills, vertical ... do....	2	1	2	3
472	Drills, vertical, and comp'd table ... do....	2		2	2
473	Drills, Packer's patent ... do....	90		90	90
474	Diamonds, glaziers' ... do....	8	4	5	9
475	Drawers, spike ... do....	100		100	100
476	Drivers, screw ... do....	662	317	378	695
477	Dividers ... do....	639	14	638	652
478	Drippers, oil ... do....	11	16	10	27
479	Drippers, brass ... do....	2	2		2
480	Drippers, gauge cock ... do....	1	1		1
481	Dashes, brass ... do....	2		2	2
482	Drums, steam ... do....	3		3	3
483	Drums, Russia iron ... do....	4	4		4
484	Drums, driving wheel, 10½ feet ... ao....	2		2	2
485	Dusters, painters' round, assorted ... do....	88	62	26	88
486	Doors, frames for furnaces ... do....	2	2		2
487	Engines, portable ... do....	4	4		4
488	Engines, stationary ... do....	1	1		1
489	Engines and boilers, stationary ... do....	2	2		2
490	Engines, cylinder, convex, 12 by 20 ... do....	3	3		3
491	Engines, steam ... do....	1	1		1
492	Engines, steam, and boiler, common ... do....	1	1		1
493	Engines, caloric, 18-inch ... do....	2	2		2
494	Engines, gear-cutting ... do....	1	1		1
495	Engines, donkey steam ... do....	2	2		2
496	Engines and boiler, with chimneys, cir. S. M., complete ... do....	6		6	6
497	Elbows, assorted ... do....	698	1,112	863	1,975
498	Escutcheons, brass ... do....	29		29	29
499	Edges, straight ... do....	2	3		3
500	Figures, stencil ... sets...	1	1		1
501	Figures ... do....	1	1	1	2
502	Files, assorted ... number..	88,003	30,433	76,201	106,634
503	Flannel, cotton ... yards...	39	11	98	109
504	Furnaces, for tinners ... number..	5	1	4	5
505	Furnaces, soldering ... do....	1	1		1
506	Formers ... do....	5		5	5
507	Forges, cast iron ... do....	44	44		44
508	Forges, portable ... do....	15	15		15
509	Forges, stationary, complete ... do....	24	8	16	24
510	Frames ... do....	8	8		8
511	Frames, machine saw ... do....	3	3		3
512	Frames, tank ... do....	6		6	6
513	Frames, saw-mill, complete ... do....	1		1	1
514	Funnels, assorted ... do....	108	235		235
515	Fixtures, W. crane ... sets...	7		7	7
516	Pitchers, assorted ... number..	9	8	1	9
517	Forks, long-handled ... do....	12	4	26	30
518	Flanges, small ... pounds..	30		30	30
519	Flanges, deck ... number..	8		31	31
520	Flanges, sheet iron ... do....	1	1		1
521	Flanges, dish ... do....	10		11	11
522	Froes ... do....	2	1	1	2
523	Faucets, oil ... do....	21	21		21
524	Faucets, ambulance keg ... do....	80	12	68	80
525	Fixtures for bells, assorted ... set...	1		1	1
526	Fronts, boiler ... number..	5		5	5

Disposition of United States military railroad property, &c.—Continued.

Running No.	Articles.	Amount on hand May 1, 1865.	Transferred to officers.	Expended.	Total transferred and expended.
527	Fronts, smoke box ... number..	1	....	1	1
528	Flasks, stone, comp't ... do...	6	....	6	6
529	Folders ... do...	4	....	4	4
530	Gauges, assorted ... do...	1,084	881	262	1,143
531	Gauges, assorted ... sets...	25	....	25	25
532	Gouges ... number..	75	105	6	111
533	Grindstones ... do...	5,121	54	5,067	5,121
534	Grindstones ... pounds..	6,687	6,687	....	6,687
535	Grindstones and fixtures ... number..	83	34	49	83
536	Gimlets ... do...	281	76	221	297
537	Gunners' saws ... do...	7	....	17	17
538	Graters ... do...	3	....	3	3
539	Gaskets, assorted ... do...	43	....	43	43
540	Gaskets, assorted ... pounds..	40¼	....	40¼	40¼
541	Gates, oil ... number..	12	6	6	12
542	Galleys, single column, brass lined ... do...	2	2	....	2
543	Galleys, double column, brass lined ... do...	4	4	....	4
544	Galleys, double column, brass lined ... do...	2	2	....	2
545	Galleys, imperial folio slice ... do...	1	1	....	1
546	Galleys, slice ... yards...	1	1	....	1
547	Guards, brass corner ... number..	92	....	188	188
548	Guards, sheet iron ... do...	1	....	1	1
549	Globes, oil ... do...	2	....	2	2
550	Gudgeons, W. W. ... do...	4	....	4	4
551	Hammers, assorted ... do...	5,445	13,039	586	13,625
552	Hammers, stone ... do...	172	87	85	172
553	Hammers, stone ... pounds..	1,328	258	1,070	1,328
554	Handles, axe ... number..	10,987	10,987	....	10,987
555	Handles, assorted ... do...	21,519	4,360	18,681	23,041
556	Hatchets ... do...	1,898	522	2,358	2,880
557	Hatchets, handled ... do...	265	....	265	265
558	Hatchets, shingling ... do...	362	359	3	362
559	Hoes ... do...	29	39	....	39
560	Heads, cutter and boxing, extra set ... do...	1	....	1	1
561	Heads, passenger car lamp ...	24	....	24	24
562	Heads, stove-pipe ... do...	3	....	3	3
563	Heads, wall, assorted ... do...	72	....	72	72
564	Heads, cross, common ... sett...	1	7	....	7
565	Heads, front cylinder, common ... do...	1	1	....	1
566	Hinges, heavy "T" ... number..	30	8	26	34
567	Hooks, belt ... do...	4,322	3,822	500	4,322
568	Hooks, shave ... do...	12	....	12	12
569	Hooks and eyes ... do...	312	258	54	312
570	Holders, driving iron ... do...	2	....	2	2
571	Holders, large drawing ... do...	24	....	24	24
572	Hoods, sheet-iron stove-pipe ... do...	3	....	3	3
573	Hoods, forge ... pounds..	3,000	1,000	2,000	3,000
574	Hoods, iron ... number..	12	....	36	36
575	Haugings, grindstone ... do...	72	72	....	72
576	Heaters ... pounds..	6,000	6,000	....	6,000
577	Horse, stitching ... number..	1	....	1	1
578	Horns, beak ... do...	1	....	1	1
579	Hobs and collars ... set...	1	....	1	1
580	Instruments, levelling ... do...	9	1	8	9
581	Instruments, transit ... do...	6	2	4	6
582	Instruments, drawing ... do...	1	....	2	2
583	Instruments, drawing, cases ... do...	1	....	1	1
584	Iron, assorted ... pounds..	446,000	125,207	370,681	495,888
585	Iron, bar ... do...	54,000	54,000	....	54,000
586	Iron, railroad ... do...	1,600,000	3,236,393	....	3,236,393
587	Iron, scrap ... do...	100,000	673,963	....	673,963
588	Iron, charcoal, assorted ... do...	8,000	235,011	....	235,011
589	Irons, turner ... number..	24	24	....	24
590	Irons, tuyere, complete ... do...	34	151	....	151
591	Irons, double plane ... do...	106	91	15	106
592	Irons, soldering ... do...	24	55	....	55
593	Irons, U. S. branding ... do...	1	....	1	1
594	Irons for transfer table ... pounds..	3,462	....	3,462	3,462
595	Irons for turn-table ... set...	1	....	1	1
596	Injectors ... number..	71	39	32	71
597	Jacks, timber ... do...	106	106	....	106
598	Jacks, car ... pairs..	4	4	....	4
599	Jacks car, with hooks ... number..	36	36	....	36
600	Jacks, lever ... do...	184	184	....	184
601	Jacks, hydraulic ... do...	12	12	....	12
602	Jacks, base, 15 ton ... do...	6	6	....	6
603	Jacks, plain, 15 ton ... do...	6	6	....	6

Disposition of United States military railroad property, &c.—Continued.

Running No.	Articles.	Amount on hand May 1, 1865.	Transferred to officers.	Expended.	Total transferred and expended.
604	Jacks, locomotive, 15 ton....number..	97	97		97
605	Jacks, screw....do....	280	280		280
606	Jacks, claw, assorted....do....	12	12		12
607	Jointers, double....do....	40		41	41
608	Jointers, short....do....	441		441	441
609	Joints, union....do....	7		7	7
610	Knives, drawing....do....	450	245	289	534
611	Knives, putty....do....	132	58	74	132
612	Knives, splitting....do....	2	2		2
613	Knives, shoe....do....	24	10	14	24
614	Knives, palette....do....	42	33	9	42
615	Knives, round....do....	5		5	5
616	Kettles, composition....do....	1	1		1
617	Kettles, glue....do....	33	28	5	33
618	Lights....do....	2, 862	1, 185	• 1, 677	2, 862
619	Lamps, assorted....do....	3, 602	3, 602		3, 602
620	Lanterns, assorted....do....	7, 373	599	6, 839	7, 438
621	Lathes, engine, complete....do....	6	6		6
622	Lathes, double hdd....do....	1	1		1
623	Lathes, driving wheel....do....	1	1		1
624	Lathes, complete....do....	3	3		3
625	Lathes, dove hd. wheel....do....	2	2		2
626	Lathes, hand....do....	1	1		1
627	Lathes, hand, and fixtures....do....	1	1		1
628	Lathes, slides, assorted....do....	8	8		8
629	Lathes, wood....do....	1	1		1
630	Lathes, axle....do....	1	1		1
631	Lathes, l'ge h'vy turning, complete....do....	1	1		1
632	Lathe, boring and drilling, complete....do....	1	1		1
633	Lead....pounds..	600	1, 310		1, 310
634	Levels, assorted....number..	187	166	44	210
635	Lines, sea-grass....do....	28	28		28
636	Locks, pad....do....	500	422	78	500
637	Locks, door, assorted....do....	50	79		79
638	Locks for switches....do....	4		21	21
639	Ladles, copper....do....	1		1	1
640	Ladders, step....do....	2	2		2
641	Levers, rivenning, complete....do....	1		1	1
642	Levers, equalizing, complete....do....	1		1	1
643	Letters....do....	1	1		1
644	Machines, assorted....do....	185	201		201
645	Machines, bit-boring....do....	18		18	18
646	Machines, circular sawing....do....	17		17	17
647	Machines, flooring....do....	1		1	1
648	Machines, foot-morticing....do....	2	1	1	2
649	Machines, gumming....do....	1		1	1
650	Machines, moulding....do....	1		1	1
651	Machines, planing, assorted....do....	8	1	10	11
652	Machines, screw-cutting....do....	3	3		3
653	Machines, bolt-cutting....do....	4		5	5
654	Machines, tenon....do....	2	2		2
655	Machines, tinners....sets...	1	1		1
656	Machines, boring, complete....number..	146	39	110	149
657	Machines, boring, drill, complete....do....	2		2	2
658	Machines, boring and turning, complete....do....	1		1	1
659	Machines, medium size, &c....do....	1		1	1
660	Machines, irregular moulding....do....	1		1	1
661	Machines, car turning....do....	1		1	1
662	Machines, shaping....do....	1		1	1
663	Machines, shaping and moulding, complete..do....	1		1	1
664	Machines, straightening, No. 4....do....	1		1	1
665	Machines, burring....do....	4		4	4
666	Machines, gutter, No. 1....do....	1		1	1
667	Machines, rip-saw....do....	2		2	2
668	Machines, doub. nut tap'g, with fixtures....do....	1		1	1
669	Machines, two-head shaping, complete....do....	2	2		2
670	Machines, milling, No. 4, complete....do....	1		1	1
671	Machines, punching and shearing, complete..do....	1		1	1
672	Machines, car-axle cutting....do....	1		1	1
673	Machines, crab, and fixtures....do....	1		1	1
674	Machines, folding....do....	1		1	1
675	Machines, groove and grooving....do....	1		1	1
676	Machines, vertical and resawing....do....	1		1	1
677	Machines, link planing....do....	1		1	1
678	Machines, double seaming, No. 2....do....	1		1	1
679	Machines, hoisting....do....	10		10	10
680	Machines, bolts, with taps and dies....do....	1	1		1

Disposition of United States military railroad property, &c.—Continued.

Running No.	Articles.	Amount on hand May 1, 1865.	Transferred to officers.	Expended.	Total transferred and expended.
681	Machines, ruling .... number..	1	1	....	1
682	Mallets, printers' .... do....	4	4	....	4
683	Mills, paint .... do....	14	9	5	14
684	Mills, paint, with pullies .... do....	6	6	....	6
685 686	Mills, portable saw, complete, with engines and boilers .... do....	2	2	....	2
687	Mauls, spike .... do....	2,660	1,141	1,519	2,660
688	Mauls, spike and top .... do....	125	....	125	125
689	Mauls, top .... do....	388	....	388	388
690	Mauls, railroad .... do....	1,265	109	1,156	1,265
691	Mauls, carpenter .... do....	231	12	219	231
692	Mauls, bridge .... do....	404	....	404	404
693	Mallets, assorted .... do....	1,387	1,130	342	1,472
694	Measures, assorted .... do....	41	104	....	104
695	Measures, tape, assorted .... do....	832	453	379	832
696	Measures, surveyors' cl. feet .... do....	5	....	6	6
697	Mandrels, cast .... pounds..	670	765	....	765
698	Magazine .... number..	3	2	1	3
699	Metre, connexions .... do....	1	1	....	1
700	Metre, gas .... do....	1	1	....	1
701	Mattocks .... do....	5	....	5	5
702	Muzzles for s'm f. eng .... do....	1	....	1	1
703	Muzzles, copper .... do....	1	....	1	1
704	Mouldings for window caps .... do....	72	....	72	72
705	Nails, clinch .... pounds..	1,208	900	308	1,208
706	Nails, tufting .... number..	7,000	....	7,000	7,000
707	Nuts, assorted .... pounds..	100	2,360	....	2,360
708	Nippers .... pairs...	81	43	49	92
709	Nozzles .... number..	36	36	....	36
710	Needles, upholsterers', assorted .... do....	54	52	2	54
711	Oil, lard .... gallons..	60	7,599	....	7,599½
712	Oil, coal .... do....	1½	186½	2	188½
713	Oilers, engine .... number..	2,771	1,817	1,920	3,737
714	Planes, assorted .... do....	3,254	2,566	1,662	4,228
715	Planes, match .... pairs...	173	13	160	173
716	Planes, ann. match .... sets...	9½	3	6½	9½
717	Planers .... number..	2	2	....	2
718	Plough press .... do....	1	1	....	1
719	Ploughers .... feet...	11	....	11	11
720	Pots, glue .... number..	63	53	14	67
720½	Pots, marking .... do....	48	15	33	48
721	Pots, tar .... do....	79	....	79	79
722	Pots, tallow .... do....	473	2	471	473
723	Pots, varnish .... do....	12	....	12	12
724	Pots, soldering .... do....	21	....	21	21
725	Pots, fire .... do....	22	13	11	24
726	Pots, paint .... do....	12	12	12	24
727	Pots, assorted .... do....	616	161	455	616
728	Paulins .... do....	116	43	81	124
729	Powers, one-horse .... do....	8	6	2	8
730	Presses, hay .... do....	1	....	1	1
731	Presses, drill .... do....	5	9	1	10
732	Presses, wheel .... do....	4	2	2	4
733	Presses, h'lf med'm Frank .... do....	1	1	....	1
734	Presses, h'lf med'm Frank .... do....	1	1	....	1
735	Pulleys, assorted .... do....	84	84	....	84
736	Pulleys, assorted .... pounds..	26,970½	12,324	24,419½	36,743½
737	Pulleys, iron, assorted .... do....	11,550½	11,550½	....	11,550½
738	Pulleys, turned .... do....	338	338	....	338
739	Pulleys, screw .... number..	84	84	....	84
740	Punches, assorted .... do....	222	519	1	520
741	Punches, assorted .... sets...	1	1	....	1
742	Punches and lever .... number..	1	1	....	1
743	Plates, screw .... do....	4	31	1	32
744	Plates, levelling .... do....	1	....	1	1
745	Plates, angle .... pounds..	544	544	....	544
746	Plates and dies for gas-pipe .... number..	12	20	....	20
747	Plates for turn-table .... set....	1	1	....	1
748	Plates and rollers .... do....	1	1	....	1
749	Plates, face, assorted .... number..	10	12	....	12
750	Punches and chisels .... sets....	2	....	2	2
751	Pipes, gum .... number..	12	2	10	12
752	Pipes, brasses .... feet...	1,787	926	861	1,787
753	Pipes, black .... pounds..	3,002	....	4,448	4,448
754	Pipes, copper .... do....	1,500	....	2,494½	2,494½
755	Pipes, iron, assorted .... do....	700	6,433	....	6,433
756	Pipes, steam .... do....	5	1	5	6

Disposition of United States military railroad property, &c.—Continued.

Running No.	Articles.	Amount on hand May 1, 1865.	Transferred to officers.	Expended.	Total transferred and expended.
757	Pumps, assorted ... number..	139	22	117	139
758	Pumps, first class steam ... do....	2	....	2	2
759	Pumps, second class steam ... do....	2	....	2	2
760	Pumps, third class ... do....	3	....	3	3
761	Pumps, steam, complete ... do....	8	....	8	8
762	Pumps, complete ... pairs..	1	1	....	1
763	Putty ... pounds..	500	1,227	....	1,227
764	Picks ... number..	5,202	1,691	4,242	5,933
765	Picks, tamping ... do....	2,429	127	2,302	2,429
766	Picks, railroad ... do....	1,544	....	1,544	1,544
767	Pincers ... pairs..	32	38	3	41
768	Patterns ... set..	1	1	....	1
769	Poles, pike ... number..	26	26	....	26
770	Pendants, assorted ... do....	62	27	68	95
771	Ploughs ... do....	1	....	1	1
772	Plyers ... pairs..	179	89	101	190
773	Pencils, lettering ... number..	186	186	....	186
774	Pencils, striping ... do....	130	130	....	130
775	Pencils, T line ... do....	80	80	....	80
776	Pencils, C. H., assorted ... do....	144	144	....	144
777	Pans, assorted ... do....	587	142	880	1,022
778	Pans, iron oil ... do....	15	15	....	15
779	Platforms ... do....	6	....	6	6
780	Plugs, assorted ... do....	9	628	....	628
781	Pails, covered ... do....	3	3	....	3
782	Points, steel ... pounds..	1,441	120	1,321	1,441
783	Piece, time, lever, 8-inch ... number..	24	....	24	24
784	Piece, top and bottom, for form ... do....	2	....	2	2
785	Plumbs, level ... do....	132	....	132	132
786	Pins, turn ... do....	12	....	12	12
787	Pedestals ... do....	8	163	....	163
788	Quods, hollow ... do....	25	25	....	25
789	Quods, pica corner ... sets..	4	4	....	4
790	Rams, battering ... number..	1	1	....	1
791	Rasps, horse ... do....	102	101	1	102
792	Rasps, wood, assorted ... do....	142	142	....	142
793	Rivets, black, assorted ... papers..	400	400	....	400
794	Rivets, assorted ... do....	268	....	268	268
794½	Rings, flush ... number..	80	136	....	136
795	Riddles, assorted ... do....	5	4	12	16
796	Ropes, switch ... do....	14	19	....	19
797	Ropes, wire ... do....	9	9	....	9
798	Rules, assorted ... do....	538	70	469	539
799	Rules, brass, fronts ... do....	5	....	5	5
800	Rules, brass ... pounds..	2	....	2	2
801	Rules, brass ... feet...	44	....	44	44
802	Rules, brass space, No. 3 ... number..	4	....	4	4
803	Rules, 4-fold ... do....	18	....	18	18
804	Rods, levelling ... do....	2	....	2	2
805	Rods, levelling, and targets ... do....	4	....	4	4
806	Rods, piston, complete ... do....	1	....	1	1
807	Rods, connecting ... sets...	2	2	....	2
808	Rods, reverse, with quods complete ... number..	1	....	1	1
809	Reflectors, time ... do....	4	....	4	4
810	Rollers, iron ... do....	18	18	....	18
811	Rollers, iron ... pounds..	2,520	65	2,455	2,520
812	Rollers, boiler and plate ... sets...	1	1	....	1
813	Rollers, binding, No. 6, set ... number..	1	....	1	1
814	Rollers for turn table ... do....	2	2	....	2
815	Reels, chalk line ... do....	225	96	130	226
816	Rockers, wrought iron ... pairs...	1	....	1	1
817	Regulators, upholsterers' ... number..	24	18	6	24
818	Saws, assorted ... do....	5,306	2,979	2,734	5,713
819	Scales ... do....	83	52	32	84
820	Screws, assorted ... do....	50,000	176,448	....	176,448
821	Screws, jack ... do....	4	3	1	4
822	Screws, bench ... do....	337	222	115	337
823	Screws, running ... do....	2	....	2	2
824	Screws, sag, assorted ... do....	3,066	495	2,571	3,066
825	Screws, sag, assorted ... pounds..	2,500	....	2,500	2,500
826	Screws, hand, assorted ... number..	222	582	....	582
827	Screws on match planes ... pairs...	24	24	....	24
828	Screw clamps, assorted ... number..	51	....	51	51
829	Shafts, counter, and pullies ... feet...	200	200	....	200
830	Shafts, counter, and pullies ... number..	2	2	....	2
831	Shafts, counter, and pullies ... pounds..	3,451	3,451	....	3,451
332	Shafts, steam wheel ... number..	1	1	....	1

Disposition of United States military railroad property, &c.—Continued.

Running No.	Articles.	Amount on hand May 1, 1865.	Transferred to officers.	Expended.	Total transferred and expended.
833	Shafts and planers .... number..	1			
834	Shafts, lifting .... do....	1	1		1
835	Shafting .... pounds..	185, 461	11, 490		
836	Shafting, main .... feet...	270	295		295
837	Shafting pulleys and hangers .... pounds..	15, 708	15, 708		15, 708
838	Shaves, spoke .... number..	224	145	83	224
839	Shaves, draw .... do....	75		75	75
840	Shears .... pairs...	91	3	103	106
841	Shears, bench .... number..				
842	Shears, circular .... do....	5	1	4	5
843	Shears, tinners' .... do....	13	3	10	13
844	Shears, squaring, with framing, No. 10 .... do....	1	1		1
845	Shears, coal, composition .... do....	1		1	1
846	Shears, gauge, table .... do....	1		1	1
847	Shears, lamp .... pairs...	24	4	21	25
848	Shears, hand .... do....	6	6		6
849	Shears and burr .... do....	1		1	1
850	Shears and lever .... do....	1	1		1
851	Shears, squaring, with frame .... do....	1	1		1
852	Scrapers, box .... number..	7	66		66
853	Shovels, assorted .... do....	6, 283	2, 277	4, 022	6, 299
854	Shoes, wrought iron, for equalizing lever .... do....	2		2	2
855	Seines .... do....	37	4	33	37
856	Scoops .... do....	151	67	84	151
857	Slates .... do....	402	407		407
858	Squares and edges, straight .... do....	7		7	7
859	Squares, bevel .... do....	591		589	
860	Squares, try, assorted .... do....	1, 640	197	1, 443	1, 640
861	Squares, steel .... do....	1, 475	480	995	1, 475
862	Squares, iron .... do....	90		90	90
863	Squares, framing .... do....	3, 037	1, 271	1, 767	3, 038
864	Sprinklers .... do....	37	34	4	38
865	Sprinklers, bath .... do....	1		1	1
866	Spades .... do....	416	238	178	416
867	Swedges, bottom .... do....	95	402		402
868	Swedges, top .... do....	92	203		203
869	Swedges, hand .... do....	1	1		1
870	Stones, oil .... do....	1, 440	491	972	1, 443
871	Stones, oil .... pounds..	87	87	87	174
872	Stones, painters' .... number..	4	5		5
873	Stone, composing .... do....	1	1		1
874	Stones, imposing, and frames .... do....	1	1		1
875	Sprinklers, bath .... do....	1		1	1
876	Stones and mullers, painters' .... do....	1		1	1
877	Spikes, railroad .... pounds..	600	80, 900		80, 900
878	Spikes, boat .... kegs...	200	129		
879	Signals, white .... number..	2, 928		2, 928	2, 928
880	Signals, ruby .... do....	390		390	390
881	Signals, fog .... do....	1, 440		1, 440	1, 440
882	Signals, blue .... do....	48		48	48
883	Stoves .... do....	483	524	40	564
884	Stoves, sheet-iron	6	31	22	53
885	Stoves, admiral .... do....	183		183	183
886	Stoves, coal .... do....	27	6	21	27
887	Stoves, cannon .... do....	17		17	17
888	Stoves, diadem .... do....	18		18	18
889	Sets rivets, assorted .... do....	1	27		27
890	Sets, saw .... do....	166	104	74	178
891	Sledges .... do....	2, 266	787	1, 479	2, 266
892	Sledges, blacksmith .... do....	29		29	29
893	Sledges .... pounds..	5, 677		5, 677	5, 677
894	Strainers .... number..	165	203		203
895	Sockets, assorted .... do....	18	742		742
896	Stakes .... do....	321	20	301	321
897	Staffs, flag .... do....	1, 569	202	1, 372	1, 574
898	Snaths, scythe .... do....	36		58	58
899	Scythes .... do....	48	23	25	48
900	Safe, match .... do....	46	55	97	152
901	Safe, tin chimney .... do....	1		1	1
902	Safe, stone pipe .... do....	262	18	376	394
903	Siphons .... do....	70		70	70
904	Stencils, Russia iron .... do....	12	12		12
905	Stencils, copper .... do....	14	14		14
906	Sticks, composing, assorted .... do....	5		5	5
907	Sticks, screwing .... do....	33	9	24	33
908	Sticks, mahogany .... do....	2	2		2
909	Sticks, composing .... do....	8	8		8

Disposition of United States military railroad property, &c.—Continued.

Running No.	Articles.	Amount on hand May 1, 1865.	Transferred to officers.	Expended.	Total transferred and expended.
910	Sticks, yard ....number..	48	113	....	113
911	Spatulas ....do....	12	....	12	12
912	Stands, single, with racks ....do....	2	1	1	2
913	Stands, double, California ....do....	2	....	2	2
914	Stands, roller ....do....	3,000	....	3,000	3,000
915	Stands, lantern ....do....	2	....	2	2
916	Scissors, lamp ....do....	32	6	26	32
917	Slicks, assorted ....do....	281	143	204	347
918	Slickers, glass ....do....	3	....	3	3
919	Stamp, hammer ....do....	6	....	6	6
920	Stamp, hand ....do....	6	....	6	6
921	Shelves, oil can ....do....	2	....	2	2
922	Shaves, pica quod ....pounds..	23¼	23¼	....	23¼
923	Slides and blocks, complete ....set...	1	1	....	1
924	Straps and rods, eccentric ....number..	1	1	....	1
925	Straps, eccentric ....do....	6	6	....	6
926	Snips, assorted ....pairs...	9	18	....	18
927	Seamers, roofing ....set...	2	....	2	2
928	Strips, flue ....number..	506	506	....	506
929	Sheaves ....do....	306	....	306	306
930	Tanks, assorted ....do....	119	21	98	119
931	Taps, metallic ....do....	16	2	14	16
932	Taps, steel, engineers ....do....	66	....	81	81
933	Taps, leather ....do....	36	....	36	36
934	Taps, assorted ....sets...	8	6	2	8
935	Taps and dies ....do....	9	....	9	9
936	Tarpaulins ....number..	24	....	24	24
937	Tools, steel ....do....	2,287	2,812	....	2,812
938	Tools, heading ....do....	82	137	....	137
939	Tools, graining ....sets...	11	5	6	11
940	Tools, tinners' ....do....	1	2	....	2
941	Tools, sash ....number..	2	2	....	2
942	Tools, blacksmiths' ....sets...	25	3	22	25
943	Tools, saddlers' ....do....	2	....	2	2
944	Tools, wheelwrights' ....do....	2	....	5	5
945	Tools, shoeing ....do....	11	1	10	11
946	Tools, carpenters ....do....	1	....	8	8
947	Tongs, assorted ....pairs...	22	22	....	22
948	Tongs, blacksmiths ....do....	150	150	....	150
949	Tongs, gas-pipe ....do....	40	48	....	48
950	Tongs, rail ....do....	6	6	....	6
951	Trowels ....number..	41	44	....	44
952	Trucks ....do....	23	16	15	31
953	Trucks, warehouse ....pairs..	2	2	....	2
954	Ties, cross ....number..	30.000	1,078	28,922	39,000
955	Ties, assorted ....do....	26	143	....	143
956	Torches ....do....	2	2	....	2
957	Targets and quadrants ....pounds..	1,045⅜	....	1,045⅜	1,045⅜
958	Trunks for stencils ....do....	1	....	1	1
959	Types, assorted ....pounds..	971 35-48	971 35-48	....	971 35-48
960	Types, fonts ....number..	138	138	....	138
961	Troughs, bread ....do....	4	....	4	4
962	Thimbles, stove-pipe ....do....	11	19	....	19
963	Thimbles ....pounds..	513	238	275	513
964	Tables, turn ....number..	1	1	....	1
965	Tubes, blasting ....do....	13	8	5	13
966	Vices ....do....	134	134	....	134
967	Vices ....pounds..	23,954¼	33,945	....	33,945
968	Varnish, japan ....gallons..	150	187	....	187
969	Ventilators ....number..	42	41	6	47
970	Wrenches, assorted ....do....	4,214	3,586	825	4,411
971	Wheels, water ....do....	1	1	....	1
972	Wheels, hand ....do....	8	....	8	8
972½	Windlasses ....do....	3	2	1	3
973	Wick ....ball...	1	1	....	1
974	Wedges, iron ....number..	5	8	....	8
975	Wipers ....pounds..	20,000	....	20,000	20,000
976	Winches ....sets...	2	2	....	2

[Enclosure No. 5.]

REPORT OF BREVET MAJOR F. J. CRILLY.

Report showing the disposition of United States military railroad property in the military division of the Tennessee, for which First Lieutenant George Francis Nelson, acting assistant quartermaster, is responsible.

Running No.	Articles.	Amount on hand May 1, 1865.	Transferred to officers.	Expended.	Total transferred and expended.
1	Awls .... number..	1,057	1,125	....	1,125
2	Axes .... do....	2,153	20,048	....	20,048
3	Adzes, railroad .... do....	1,585	1,594	....	1,594
4	Augers, assorted .... do....	4,726	4,749	47	4,796
5	Alcohol .... gallons..	188¼	193½	....	193½
6	Blanks, quartermasters' .... quires..	507	50	457	507
7	Books, blank, assorted .... number..	2,837	2,952	....	2,952
8	Buckets, water .... do....	1,043	1,082	....	1,082
9	Bars, assorted .... do....	956	408	608	1,016
10	Balances, assorted .... do....	178	202	....	202
11	Bellows, blacksmiths' .... do....	49	49	....	49
12	Boxes, dredge .... do....	1,987	1,987	....	1,987
13	Bits, auger, assorted .... do....	332	422	....	422
14	Bits, ratchet drill .... do....	252	252	....	252
15	Blocks, assorted .... do....	503	555	....	555
16	Bevels, sliding T .... do....	585	585	....	585
17	Barrows, wheel .... do....	275	301	....	301
18	Borers, tap .... do....	11	11	....	11
19	Blenders .... do....	16	16	....	16
20	Bodkins .... do....	6	....	6	6
21	Brads, patent .... papers..	1,405	1,645	....	1,645
22	Bolts, assorted .... number..	7,165	36,659	2,385	39,044
23	Blades, hack-saw .... do....	24	24	....	24
24	Butts, assorted .... do....	5,361	5,361	....	5,361
25	Brushes, assorted .... do....	1,772	1,772	....	1,772
26	Bronze, gold .... papers..	19	19	....	19
27	Brass, sheet, assorted .... pounds..	947	2,013	....	2,013
28	Bells, engine signal gong .... number..	9	27	....	27
29	Belting, gum .... feet....	6,093	6,824	....	6,824
30	Bunting, red .... yards...	760	803	....	803
31	Burlaps .... do....	1,000	1,280	....	1,280
32	Chairs, office .... number..	44	44	....	44
33	Clocks, office .... do....	2	2	....	2
34	Cars, box freight .... do....	118	118	....	118
35	Chairs, switch .... do....	83	1,840	....	1,840
36	Chisels, assorted .... do....	2,218	2,323	....	2,323
37	Compasses .... do....	197	255	....	255
38	Cups, assorted .... do....	904	928	....	928
39	Cans, assorted .... do....	873	892	....	892
40	Cases, drawing .... do....	9	9	....	9
41	Clamps .... do....	33	33	....	33
42	Callipers	7	8	....	8
43	Chucks	8	9	....	9
44	Cocks, assorted .... number..	599	772	....	772
45	Covers, assorted .... do....	2,842	2,842	....	2,842
46	Chairs, railroad .... do....	10,454	19,080	....	19,080
47	Candles .... do....	2,387	2,990	....	2,990
48	Cloth, enamelled .... yards...	150	....	156	....
49	Chain, coil .... feet...	1,250	1,250	735	1,985
50	Chalk, white .... pounds..	615	5,238½	....	5,238½
51	Cord, bell .... feet....	300	2,163	....	2,163
52	Copper, sheet .... pounds..	3,926	14,140	....	14,140
53	Dividers .... number..	39	47	....	47
54	Drills, assorted .... do....	197	197	....	197
55	Dies, gas-pipe .... do....	5	5	....	5
56	Dies and stocks .... do....	15	54	....	54
57	Drivers, screw .... do....	672	672	....	672
58	Drippers, oil .... do....	7	7	....	7
59	Demijohns .... do....	1	1	....	1
60	Envelopes .... do....	20,211	36,035	....	36,035
61	Engines, pumping, complete .... do....	1	....	1	1
62	Eyes, bell cord .... do....	144	472	....	472
63	Ears, kettle .... do....	6,408	10,152	....	10,152
64	Elbows, assorted .... do....	373	391	....	391
65	Escutcheons, brass .... do....	24	24	....	24

Disposition of United States military railroad property, &c.—Continued.

Running No.	Articles.	Amount on hand May 1, 1865.	Transferred to officers.	Expended.	Total transferred and expended.
66	Folders or cutters, paper ....number..	15	15	....	15
67	Forks, flesh ....do....	611	615	....	615
68	Fixtures, grindstone ....do....	117	117	....	117
69	Furnaces, assorted ....do....	9	9	....	9
70	Forges, portable ....do....	26	26	....	26
71	Figures ....sets...	1	1	....	1
72	Funnels, tin ....number..	265	265	....	265
73	Forks, rail ....do....	17	17	....	17
74	Fillers, lamp ....do....	110	222	....	222
75	Files, assorted ....do....	44,858	44,858	....	44,858
76	Flannel, assorted ....yards...	319¼	319¼	....	319¼
77	Fuze, safety ....feet...	2,000	2,400	....	2,400
78	Gauges, assorted ....number..	555	555	....	555
79	Gimlets ....do....	79	79	....	79
80	Gummers, saw ....do....	10	10	....	10
81	Gates, oil ....do....	18	18	....	18
82	Gouges, assorted ....do....	23	23	....	23
83	Grease, car ....gallons..	1,885½	....	1,885½	1,885½
84	Governors and valve ....number..	1	....	1	1
85	Hammers, assorted ....do....	2,647	3,357	....	3,357
86	Hatchets, assorted ....do....	2,453	2,453	....	2,453
87	Hods, coal ....do....	28	30	....	30
88	Handles, assorted ....do....	27,919	27,323	1,185	28,508
89	Hooks, cant ....do....	70	100	....	100
90	Hooks, belt ....do....	3,912	3,916	....	3,916
91	Hinges, assorted ....do....	1,088	1,088	....	1,088
92	Hose, rubber ....feet....	4,380	13,802	....	13,802
93	Hay ....pounds..	5,310	....	5,310	5,310
94	Inkstands ....number..	222	267	....	267
95	Injectors, steam engine ....do....	46	46	....	46
96	Iron, assorted ....pounds..	4,908,683	4,908,683	....	4,908,683
97	Jacks, assorted ....number..	248	248	....	248
98	Knives, assorted ....do....	1,994	1,994	....	1,994
99	Knives, table, and forks ....do....	2,400	2,400	....	2,400
100	Knobs, mahogany ....do....	856	1,119	....	1,119
101	Locomotive and tender ....do....	1	1	....	1
102	Letters ....sets...	1	1	....	1
103	Levels, spirit ....number..	111	120	....	120
104	Lines, chalk ....do....	2,041	2,041	....	2,041
105	Lines, sea-grass ....do....	42	42	....	42
106	Lines, tape ....do....	385	389	2	391
107	Lanterns, railroad globe ....do....	2,867	3,572	....	3,572
108	Locks, assorted ....do....	2,692	3,200	....	3,200
109	Leather, assorted ....pounds..	249	258	....	258
110	Leather, lace ....sides...	67	99	....	99
111	Leaf, gold ....papers..	6	8	....	8
112	Lamps, assorted ....number..	855	1,076	....	1,076
113	Links, coupling, assorted ....do....	542	1,398	....	1,398
114	Lead, assorted ....pounds...	400	400	....	400
115	Lye, concentrated ....cans...	63	63	....	63
116	Matting, floor ....yards...	48	48	....	48
117	Machines, slotting ....number..	126	137	....	137
118	Mauls, assorted ....do....	1,832	1,884	....	1,884
119	Mandrels ....do....	3	3	....	3
120	Mills, saw, with engine ....do....	5	5	....	5
121	Mallets, assorted ....do....	1,191	1,191	....	1,191
122	Measures, assorted ....do....	200	314	....	314
123	Marlin, tarred ....pounds..	517	601	....	601
124	Nippers, cutting ....number..	47	47	....	47
125	Nozzles, brass ....do....	4	6	....	6
126	Nails, assorted ....pounds..	103,692	142,200	....	142,200
127	Needles, assorted ....number..	24	24	....	24
128	Oilers, engine, assorted ....do....	1,121	1,211	....	1,211
129	Oil, assorted	6,867¼	5,231	....	1,971
130	Oakum ....pounds..	600	2,150	....	2,150
131	Paper, blotting ....sheets...	785	1,051	12	1,063
132	Paper, cap ....quires...	1,544	1,544	....	1,544
133	Paper, oil ....sheets...	155	155	....	155
134	Presses, letter ....number..	2	2	....	2
135	Pokers ....do....	1	1	....	1
136	Pipe, stove ....feet...	32	78	....	78
137	Pumps, assorted ....number..	104	104	....	104
138	Picks, assorted ....do....	2,076	2,076	....	2,076
139	Punches, assorted ....do....	187	187	....	187
140	Planes, assorted ....do....	2,286	2,286	....	2,286
141	Paulins ....do....	27	27	....	27
142	Powers, horse ....do....	4	4	....	4

Disposition of United States military railroad property, &c.—Continued.

Running No.	Articles.	Amount on hand May 1, 1865.	Transferred to officers.	Expended.	Total transferred and expended.
143	Presses, drill ..number..	2	2	....	2
144	Pincers ..do....	191	185	6	191
145	Packing, gum ..pounds..	1,565	2,548	....	2,548
146	Pencils, slate ..number..	9,126	9,126	....	9,126
147	Pins, coupling ..do....	1,405	1,405	....	1,405
148	Potash, prussiate of ..pounds..	548	566	....	566
149	Pipe, gas ..feet...	15,821	16,342¼	....	16,342¼
150	Pipe, lead ..pounds..	1,192	1,347	....	1,347
151	Pulleys, assorted ..number..	130	130	....	130
152	Racks, pen ..do....	95	98	....	98
153	Riddles ..do....	59	64	....	64
154	Reels, chalk-line ..do....	24	41	....	41
155	Rosin ..pounds..	865	838	307	1,145
156	Rope, assorted ..do....	26,847½	36,812½	....	36,812¼
157	Rivets, assorted ..number..	26,850	1,313,800	9,011	1,322,811
158	Rasps, horse ..do....	646	646	....	646
159	Rings, flush ..do....	849	1,017	....	1,017
160	Shovels, coal ..do....	1	1	....	1
161	Safes, iron ..do....	2	2	....	2
162	Stoves, coal ..do....	17	17	....	17
163	Skimmers ..do....	72	72	....	72
164	Scissors ..do....	41	41	....	41
165	Snips, assorted ..do....	8	8	....	8
166	Slicks, carpenters' ..do....	28	28	....	28
167	Sets, law ..do....	29	29	....	29
168	Saws, assorted ..do....	4,233	4,233	....	4,233
169	Stones, paint, and muller ..do....	1	1	....	1
170	Shaves, spoke ..do....	446	446	....	446
171	Stakes, hatchet ..do....	2	2	....	2
172	Shades, lamp ..do....	36	36	....	36
173	Scales ..do....	16	16	....	16
174	Sieves ..do....	3	3	....	3
175	Stones, oil ..do....	6	6	....	6
176	Sledges, blacksmiths' ..do....	386	386	....	386
177	Scythes ..do....	35	35	....	35
178	Staffs, flag ..do....	788	876	....	876
179	Snathes, scythe ..do....	22	23	....	23
180	Steel, assorted ..pounds..	66,753	69,222	....	69,222
181	Screws, brass ..gross..	638 5-18	3,462	....	3,462
182	Sponge ..pounds..	579	653	....	653
183	Spouts, bent ..number..	1,035	1,035	....	1,035
184	Shears, sheep ..do....	3	3	....	3
185	Stone, rotten ..pounds..	156	156	....	156
186	Skins, chamois ..number..	10	10	....	10
187	Spikes ..pounds..	95,395	250,890	126,766	377,659
188	Stands, switch ..number..	8	8	....	8
189	Stops, car seat ..do....	100	571	....	571
190	Tables, office ..do....	10	17	....	17
191	Tools, assorted ..sets...	41	41	....	41
192	Taps ..number..	81	81	....	81
193	Trowels, assorted ..do....	106	106	....	106
194	Tongs, assorted ..do....	212	212	....	212
195	Transits ..do....	3	3	....	3
196	Tubs, wash ..do....	1	1	....	1
197	Tires, locomotive ..pounds..	40,500	132,500	....	132,500
198	Tacks, assorted ..papers..	54,213	54,213	....	54,213
199	Taps, lamp screw ..number..	2,226	2,226	....	2,226
200	Thread, assorted ..pounds..	3	20	....	20
201	Twine, assorted ..do....	50	47	4	51
202	Tin ..boxes..	50	50	....	50
203	Tools, sash, assorted ..number..	282	282	....	282
204	Turpentine ..gallons..	24½	24½	....	24½
205	Tallow ..pounds..	5,161	5,161	....	5,161
206	Tubes, blasting ..number..	11	11	....	11
207	Unions, brass ..do....	250	250	....	250
208	Vices, assorted ..do....	85	85	....	85
209	Ventilators ..do....	31	31	....	31
210	Varnish, assorted ..gallons..	179	384	....	384
211	Wedges, iron ..number..	15	15	....	15
212	Wrenches ..do....	574	574	....	574
213	Wire, assorted ..pounds..	2,053	4,558	....	4,558
214	Whiting ..do....	602	1,449	....	1,449
215	Wheels, car ..number..	64	158	....	158
216	Washers ..pounds..	2,000	31,940	....	31,940
217	Waste ..do....	2,500	5,897	....	5,897

[Enclosures Nos. 6, 7, 8, and 9.]

REPORT OF BREVET MAJOR F. J. CRILLY.

[No. 6.—Statement showing the original cost and appraised value of 154 locomotive engines sold to railroad companies.

No. 7.—Statement showing the appraised value of property sold to railroad companies.

No. 8—Statement showing the average appraised value of box and flat cars sold to railroad companies.

No. 9.—Copies of orders under which the property was sold.]

Statement showing the original cost and appraised value of 154 *locomotive engines sold to railroad companies in the military division of the Tennessee and Mississippi, under the Executive Orders of August* 8 *and October* 14, 1865.

No. of engine.	From whom purchased.	Original cost.	Appraisement.
14	L. and N. railroad	$15,550 00	$10,500 00
15	do	15,550 00	8,500 00
16	do	15,550 00	10,000 00
17	do	15,550 00	9,000 00
23	C. and E. railroad	9,750 00	7,500 00
25	M. W. Baldwin & Co	14,935 00	16,000 00
26	do	15,192 50	16,250 00
27	do	13,905 00	10,750 00
28	do	13,905 00	11,500 00
29	do	10,004 44	8,500 00
30	do	16,588 15	16,250 00
31	do	17,902 35	16,500 00
32	Schenectady Locomotive Works	15,450 00	15,000 00
33	do	15,765 30	14,500 00
34	Hinckley & Williams	17,850 00	15,500 00
35	do	17,856 00	15,500 00
36	Taunton Locomotive Works	16,016 50	16,000 00
37	do	16,343 37	16,000 00
38	William Mason	16,816 32	16,500 00
39	do	16,816 32	17,000 00
40	Danforth, Cooke & Co	16,275 00	15,500 00
41	do	16,275 00	16,000 00
42	Rogers's Locomotive and Machine Works	16,284 30	16,000 00
44	New Jersey Locomotive Works	16,290 81	16,000 00
45	do	16,290 81	16,500 00
46	do	16,290 81	16,000 00
48	R. Norris & Son	15,450 00	14,500 00
49	do	15,450 00	14,000 00
50	do	15,765 30	13,500 00
51	do	15,765 30	14,000 00
52	do	15,606 05½	14,000 00
53	do	15,606 05½	14,000 00
70	Rogers's Locomotive and Machine Works	20,618 00	15,750 00
71	do	20,600 00	16,250 00
72	do	20,600 00	16,250 00
73	do	20,600 00	16,500 00
74	Schenectady Locomotive Works	17,686 86	17,400 00
75	do	16,646 45	14,500 00
76	do	19,827 50	16,000 00
77	do	19,827 50	16,000 00
78	New Jersey Locomotive Works	20,600 00	14,000 00
79	do	20,600 00	16,500 00
80	Danforth, Cooke & Co	20,600 00	17,000 00
81	do	20,600 00	17,000 00
83	Hinckley & Williams	20,600 00	15,500 00
84	do	20,600 00	15,500 00
85	William Mason	18,540 00	17,000 00
86	do	18,540 00	17,000 00
87	Taunton Locomotive Works	18,620 00	16,500 00
88	do	18,620 00	16,500 00
89	do	18,620 00	16,500 00
90	M. W. Baldwin & Co	22,145 00	19,000 00
91	do	20,857 50	18,000 00
92	do	20,857 50	14,000 00
93	do	20,857 50	18,000 00
94	R. Norris & Son	20,600 00	14,000 00
95	do	18,777 93	14,000 00
96	do	18,777 93	13,500 00
101	Michigan Central Railroad	14,280 00	8,000 00

Statement of the original cost and appraised value of engines, &c.—Continued.

No. of engine.	From whom purchased.	Original cost.	Appraisement.
115	Rogers's Locomotive and Machine Works	$20,618 00	$17,000 00
116	........do	20,600 00	17,000 00
117	........do	20,600 00	16,500 00
118	........do	20,600 00	17,000 00
119	........do	20,600 00	17,000 00
120	........do	20,600 00	17,000 00
121	........do	20,600 00	17,500 00
122	........do	20,600 00	15,000 00
123	........do	20,600 00	17,250 00
124	........do	20,600 00	17,250 00
125	........do	20,600 00	17,000 00
126	........do	20,600 00	16,500 00
127	........do	20,600 00	16,500 00
128	........do	20,600 00	17,500 00
129	........do	20,600 00	17,000 00
130	Danforth, Cooke & Co	20,600 00	16,500 00
131	........do	20,600 00	17,250 00
132	........do	20,600 00	16,750 00
133	........do	20,600 00	17,500 00
134	........do	20,600 00	17,000 00
135	........do	20,600 00	17,000 00
136	........do	20,600 00	17,000 00
137	........do	20,600 00	17,250 00
138	........do	20,600 00	17,000 00
139	........do	20,600 00	17,250 00
140	........do	20,600 00	17,000 00
141	........do	20,600 00	17,000 00
142	New Jersey Locomotive Works	20,600 00	16,500 00
143	........do	20,600 00	16,500 00
144	........do	20,600 00	16,500 00
145	........do	20,600 00	16,500 00
146	........do	20,600 00	16,250 00
147	........do	20,600 00	16,500 00
148	........do	20,690 00	16,250 00
149	........do	20,600 00	16,500 00
150	........do	20,600 00	16,500 00
151	M. W. Baldwin & Co	19,516 15	16,500 00
152	........do	19,516 15	16,500 00
153	........do	19,516 15	16,750 00
154	........do	19,516 15	15,000 00
155	........do	19,516 15	16,500 00
156	........do	19,516 15	16,500 00
157	........do	19,516 15	16,350 00
158	........do	19,516 15	16,500 00
159	........do	19,516 15	16,750 00
160	........do	19,516 15	16,500 00
161	........do	19,516 15	17,000 00
162	........do	19,516 15	16,500 00
163	........do	19,516 15	16,500 00
164	........do	19,516 15	16,500 00
165	........do	19,516 15	16,500 00
166	R. Norris & Son	18,777 93	15,000 00
167	........do	18,777 93	13,500 00
168	........do	18,777 93	14,500 00
169	........do	18,777 93	15,000 00
170	........do	18,777 93	15,000 00
171	........do	18,777 93	15,000 00
172	........do	18,777 93	15,000 00
173	........do	18,777 93	15,000 00
174	........do	18,777 93	15,500 00
175	........do	18,777 93	15,000 00
176	........do	18,777 93	14,250 00
177	........do	18,777 93	13,500 00
178	........do	18,777 93	14,500 00
179	Taunton Locomotive Works	20,600 00	16,750 00
180	........do	20,600 00	16,250 00
181	........do	20,600 00	16,500 00
182	........do	20,600 00	16,750 00
183	........do	20,600 00	13,000 00
184	........do	20,600 00	17,000 00
185	........do	20,600 00	16,500 00
186	William Mason	20,600 00	17,000 00
187	........do	20,600 00	17,000 00
188	........do	20,600 00	17,000 00
189	........do	20,600 00	17,000 00
190	........do	20,600 00	17,000 00
191	........do	20,600 00	16,750 00
192	........do	20,600 00	17,000 00
193	........do	20,600 00	17,400 00

Statement of the original cost and appraised value of engines, &c.—Continued.

No. of engine.	From whom purchased.	Original cost.	Appraisement.
194	Manchester Manufacturing Co	$20,600 00	$16,000 00
195	........do	20,600 00	16,500 00
196	........do	20,600 00	16,250 00
198	Hinckley & Williams	20,600 00	13,000 00
199	........do	20,600 00	16,000 00
200	........do	20,600 00	16,500 00
201	........do	20,600 00	16,500 00
202	........do	20,600 00	16,500 00
203	Portland Manufacturing Co	20,600 00	15,500 00
204	........do	20,600 00	14,500 00
205	........do	20,600 00	15,000 00
206	........do	20,600 00	16,000 00
208	R. Norris & Son	18,540 00	15,500 00
209	........do	18,540 00	15,500 00
210	........do	18,540 00	15,500 00
211	L. C. & A. railroad	13,905 00	12,500 00
	Total	2,932,943 60	2,412,650 00

Total original cost	$2,932,943 60
Total appraised value	2,412,650 00
	520,293 60

Report showing the appraised value of property sold to railroad companies in the military division of the Tennessee and Mississippi, under the Executive Orders of August 8 *and October* 14, 1865, *with the amounts paid thereon, and the balance due and remaining unpaid May* 31, 1866.

No.	Name of company.	Appraised value of property sold.	Total amount of instalments and interest paid by each company.	Balance of principal and interest due and remaining unpaid.
1	Rome Railroad Company	$22, 086 05	$7, 271 62	$15, 645 60
2	Edgefield and Kentucky Railroad Company	114, 772 86	....	119, 597 34
3	Mobile and Great Northern Railroad Company	14, 637 73	4, 193 65	11, 011 62
4	Southwestern Railroad Company	46, 159 89	46, 159 89	....
5	Wills Valley Railroad Company	30, 248 52	1, 302 08	30, 262 27
6	East Tennessee and Georgia Railroad Company	366, 183 02	27, 033 20	357, 250 34
7	Montgomery and West Point Railroad Company	38, 559 66	9, 581 16	30, 509 06
8	Macon and Brunswick Railroad Company	93, 237 50	67, 662 21	26, 547 33
9	Alabama and Florida Railroad Company	51, 912 00	12, 753 55	41, 433 02
10	Muscogee Railroad Company	5, 244 20	1, 318 04	4, 141 79
11	Macon and Western Railroad Company	83, 638 15	81, 282 60	2, 355 55
12	Mobile and Ohio Railroad Company	444, 543 70	158, 872 63	301, 284 77
13	Memphis and Ohio Railroad Company	106, 929 13	18, 212 88	96, 025 23
14	Mississippi and Tennessee Railroad Company	127, 750 52	27, 603 06	101, 849 46
15	East Tennessee and Virginia Railroad Company	265, 655 65	7, 921 20	271, 202 19
16	Memphis and Charleston Railroad Company	547, 494 09	80, 774 44	477, 499 62
17	Memphis, Clarksville, and Louisville Railroad Company	337, 082 36	150 93	350, 261 65
18	Nashville and Chattanooga Railroad Company	1, 566, 551 73	159, 225 16	1, 484, 352 83
19	Nashville and Northwestern Railroad Company	525, 400 26	23, 168 63	530, 079 00
20	New Orleans and Ohio Railroad Company	32, 150 00	....	33, 523 88
21	Tennessee and Alabama Railroad Company	108, 692 68	32, 349 20	81, 461 29
22	Central Southern Railroad Company	77, 186 32	22, 996 43	57, 821 06
23	Tennessee and Alabama Central Railroad Company	84, 143 00	25, 071 06	63, 030 28
24	Nashville and Decatur Railroad Company	135, 171 92	31, 267 01	108, 205 54
25	Mississippi, Gainesville, and Tuscaloosa Railroad Company	33, 476 39	....	34, 981 72
26	Selma and Meridian Railroad Company	146, 318 92	56, 104 14	95, 114 64
27	Southwestern Iron Company	32, 515 00	32, 515 00	....
28	Georgia Railroad and Banking Company	11, 935 05	11, 935 05	....
29	Mississippi Central Railroad Company	78, 460 00	14, 447 49	66, 188 29
30	Alabama and Tennessee River Railroad Company	183, 276 49	15, 416 88	175, 504 06
31	New Orleans, Jackson, and Great Northern Railroad Co.	167, 815 58	49, 900 16	123, 762 54
32	Adams Express Company	4, 361 45	4, 361 45	....
33	Western and Atlantic Railroad Company	472, 944 66	....	495, 924 13
34	Virginia and Tennessee Railroad Company	102, 880 00	....	106, 175 58
35	South Carolina Railroad Company	23, 458 50	....	23, 955 81
36	McMinnville and Manchester Railroad Company	20, 310 00	....	20, 740 57
		6, 503, 182 98	1, 030, 850 82	5, 737, 697 59

RECAPITULATION.

Total appraised value of property sold	$6, 503, 182 98
Total amount of instalments and interest paid by each company	1, 030, 850 82
Balance of principal and interest due and remaining unpaid May 31, 1866	5, 737, 697 59

Statement showing the average appraised value of "box" and "flat" cars sold to southern railroad companies in the military division of the Tennessee, under the Executive Orders of August 8 and October 14, 1865, with the average original cost of the same.

Name of railroad.	Price of box cars.	Price of flat cars.	Remarks.
Memphis, Clarksville, and Louisville	$755 00	$600 00	
Edgefield and Kentucky	800 00	610 00	
Nashville and Chattanooga	847 00	650 00	New lot; appraised separately.
Nashville and Northwestern	830 00	650 00	
Nashville and Decatur Line	825 00	....	
Tennessee and Alabama	826 00	650 00	
Central Southern	835 00	650 00	
Tennessee and Alabama Central	816 00	650 00	
Wills Valley	815 00	650 00	
East Tennessee and Georgia	845 00	650 00	
East Tennessee and Virginia	847 00	650 00	
Rogersville and Jefferson	850 00	650 00	
Western and Atlantic	820 00	650 00	Has many wrecked boxes.
Rome Branch	715 00	530 00	
Macon and Western	790 00	625 00	
Southwestern	839 00	650 00	
Macon and Brunswick	815 00	650 00	
Montgomery and West Point	847 00	....	
Alabama and Florida	847 00	625 00	
Alabama and Tennessee River	855 00	650 00	
Selma and Meridian	805 00	625 00	
Mississippi, Gainesville, and Tuscaloosa	855 00	625 00	
Mobile and Ohio	780 00	....	
New Orleans, Jackson, and Great Western	780 00	....	
Mississippi and Tennessee	730 00	600 00	
Memphis and Charleston	830 00	650 00	
Memphis and Ohio	730 00	600 00	
New Orleans and Ohio	715 00	....	
Mobile and Great Northern	735 00	575 00	
Nashville and Chattanooga	725 00	550 00	Second invoice.
Mississippi Central	710 00	525 00	
Rolling Mill	....	600 00	
Adams Express Company	700 00	....	

NOTE.—The average original cost of these cars was $1,150 for box, and $890 for flats. The average length service was eighteen (18) months.

[General Orders No. 56.]

QUARTERMASTER GENERAL'S OFFICE,
Washington, D. C., September 28, 1865.

The following order, by the President of the United States, in relation to the relinquishment of the government's control over all railroads in the State of Tennessee, and their continuations in adjoining States, now occupied by the United States military authorities, and no longer needed for military purposes, is published for the information of all officers and agents of the quartermaster's department.

M. C. MEIGS.
Brevet Major General, U. S. A., Quartermaster General.

WAR DEPARTMENT,
Washington, August 8, 1865.

GENERAL: It having been determined by the government to relinquish control over all railroads in the State of Tennessee, and their continuations in adjoining States, that have been in charge of, and are now occupied by, the United States military authorities, and no longer needed for military purposes, you are hereby authorized and directed to turn over the same to the respective owners thereof, at as early a date as practicable, causing, in all cases of transfer as aforesaid, the following regulations to be observed and carried out:

1. Each and every company will be required to reorganize and elect a board of directors whose loyalty shall be established to your satisfaction.

2. You will cause to be made out in triplicate, by such person or persons as you may indicate, a complete inventory of the rolling stock, tools, and other materials and property on each road.

3. Separate inventories will be, in the same manner, made of the rolling stock and other property originally belonging to each of said roads, and that furnished by and belonging to the government.

4. Each company will be required to give bonds satisfactory to the government that they will, in twelve months from the date of transfer as aforesaid, or such other reasonable time as may be agreed upon, pay a fair valuation for the government property turned over to said companies, the same being first appraised by competent and disinterested parties at a fair valuation, the United States reserving all government dues for carrying mails, and other service performed by each company, until said obligations are paid; and if, at the maturity of said debt, the amount of government dues, retained as aforesaid, does not liquidate the same, the balance is to be paid by the company in money.

5. Tabular statements will be made of all expenditures by the government for repairing each road, with a full statement of receipts from private freights, passage, and other sources; also a full statement of all transportation performed on government account, giving the number of persons transported, and amount of freight, and the distance carried in each case—all of said reports or tabular statements to be made in triplicate, one each for the Secretary of War, the military headquarters of the department, and the railroad company.

6. All railroads in Tennessee will be required to pay all arrearages of interest due on the bonds issued by that State, prior to the date of its pretended secession from the Union, to aid in the construction of said roads, before any dividends are declared or paid to the stockholders thereof.

7. Buildings erected for government purposes on the line of railroads, and not valuable or useful for the business of said companies, should not form a legitimate charge against such companies; nor should they be charged for rebuilding houses, bridges, or other structures which were destroyed by the federal army

8. You are authorized to give any orders to quartermasters within your division, which you may deem necessary to carry into execution this order.

By order of the President:

EDWIN M. STANTON,
Secretary of War.

Major General GEORGE H. THOMAS,
Commanding Military Division of Tennessee, Nashville, Tennessee.

[General Orders No. 62.]

QUARTERMASTER GENERAL'S OFFICE,
Washington, D. C., October 23, 1865.

The following order by the President of the United States, in relation to executive order of 8th August, 1865, extending the provisions and benefits of the same to all railroads within the limits of the military division of the Tennessee desiring to purchase railroad rolling stock and material from the United States, for the purpose of repairing the losses of the war, is published for the information of all officers and agents of the quartermaster's department.

M. C. MEIGS.
Brevet Major General U. S. A., Quartermaster General.

WAR DEPARTMENT,
Washington, D. C., October 14, 1865.

GENERAL: The provisions and benefits of the executive order of 8th of August are hereby extended to all railroads within the limits of your command desiring to purchase railroad rolling stock and material from the United States, for the purpose of repairing the losses of the war.

You are also authorized to direct the sale to any such railroads of rolling stock, now within the limits of your command, and not needed by the United States for actual use, upon the following conditions, if they are preferred to the terms of the order of 8th August, and the individual security required by you under that order.

You will take care that this property is distributed among the several roads in proportion to their actual needs, and that none is sold to any railroad in excess of the reasonable requirements of its business, or to be used for purposes of speculation, sale, or hire to other roads.

You will require from all such railroad companies satisfactory bonds, in the form herewith enclosed, binding them to the payment to the United States of the full appraised value of the property sold to them, in equal monthly instalments, with the interest at the rate of seven and three-tenths per cent. per annum, within two years, credit being allowed to them, on the first of each month, for any service of military transportation rendered by them during the preceding month, at the established rates now allowed to northern railroads for such service.

Full reports of all sales under this order will be made to the War Department from time to time, as required by existing orders.

The serviceable railroad iron in possession of the quartermaster's department at Chattanooga and Nashville is excepted. It will be sold only for cash at the prices fixed by the War Department.

By order of the President:

EDWIN M. STANTON,
Secretary of War.

Major General GEORGE H. THOMAS,
Com'd'g Mil. Div. of the Tenn., Headquarters, Nashville, Tenn.

BOND.

Know all men by these presents, that the ——— railroad company, duly incorporated by the act of the ——— of the State of ———, by ——— its president, acting for and in behalf of said railroad company, do hereby acknowledge itself and its successors held and firmly bound unto the United States of America in the full and just sum of ——— dollars, lawful money of the United States; for which payment, well and truly to be made to the disbursing quartermaster of the United States military railroads, at his office in Nashville, or to such other disbursing quartermaster as may be designated by the War Department, within two years from the date of these presents, the said railroad company, by its president, hereby binds itself and its successors, firmly by these presents.

Sealed with its corporate seal, attested by the signature of its president, and affixed by the express authority of its directors, this ——— day of ———, in the year of our Lord one thousand eight hundred and sixty ———.

The nature of the above obligation is such that, whereas the above bounden railroad company has purchased and received, or shall receive, from the War Department of the United States, rolling stock, iron rails, cross-ties, chairs, spikes, timber, and other materials for repairing and operating its railroad, in quantities, at prices, and to an amount and value which shall be evidenced by the receipts given for the same by the said railroad company to the proper officer of the said War Department, upon a credit of two years from the date of these presents, payable in equal monthly instalments, with interest, at the rate of 7 3-10 per cent. per annum, within the said two years, either in cash to the disbursing quartermaster of the United States military railroads, at his office in Nashville, or to such other disbursing quartermaster as may be designated for this purpose by the War Department, or in transportation of the troops or military supplies of the United States, under the order of the proper military authorities, at the rates of fare and tolls allowed for such service to northern railroads;

And whereas the said railroad company desires, and by these presents intends, to secure to the United States the complete and punctual payment as aforesaid of the amounts which may be due for the said materials received or to be received by it from the United States:

Now, therefore, if the said railroad company shall well and truly pay as aforesaid, either in cash, in equal monthly instalments, or in transportation as aforesaid, to the United States, within two years from the date of these presents, all that shall be due as aforesaid to the United States on account and in payment for all the materials received as aforesaid from the United States, then this obligation shall be void and of no effect.

But if the said railroad company shall fail to pay to the United States all or any portion of what may be due to the United States, on account of the said materials received from the United States, within two years from the date of these presents, either in cash as aforesaid, or in transportation as aforesaid, or shall fail to pay any of the monthly instalments aforesaid, punctually when due, then this obligation shall remain in full force and effect to the extent that may be necessary to fully repay to the United States the full amount which may be due on account of the said materials so received as aforesaid, and all loss or damage which may have been incurred by the United States by reason of the said railroad company's failure to pay for the same what shall be due therefor when the same shall be due.

And as a further security for such payment and indemnity to the United States, the United States shall have a lien upon the property sold to said company, and in default of such complete and punctual payment of all moneys which may be due on account of the aforesaid purchase of materials, be fully authorized to take possession of and sell said property, and also to place in charge and control of the said company's railroad, an agent of the said United States, who shall be fully empowered, and by these presents is fully empowered, in case of such default as aforesaid, to collect all the revenues of the said company, and apply the same to the payment to the United States of all the moneys which shall be due at the times of such application of such revenues to the United States for any such materials, which shall have been delivered by the United States to the said railroad company, or by reason of any loss or injury to the United States resulting from such default in payment of the same. And the said company shall have no authority to sell or convey out of its possession without the consent of the United States first in writing obtained, any of the property referred to in this agreement; but shall hold and retain the same to the exclusive use of said company, in carrying on the business of transportation of persons and property over its line of road, until the whole is fully paid for as aforesaid.

In witness whereof, the corporate seal of said railroad company is affixed hereto, by authority of its directors, and attested by its president.

——— ———.

Witness:

——— ———

NOTE.—The amount of this bond to be double the valuation of the property sold and delivered. Internal revenue stamps should be affixed, to the amount of fifty cents for every thousand dollars.

No. 2.

LETTER OF MAJOR CRILLY, TRANSMITTING AND EXPLAINING THE ABOVE REPORTS.

OFFICE ASS'T QUARTERM'R, U. S. MILITARY RAILROADS,
Washington, D. C., July 9, 1866.

GENERAL: I have the honor to transmit the papers called for in your indorsement of the sixth ultimo on the Quartermaster General's letter, transmitting the resolution of the House of Representatives, calling for a report of the amount of United States military railroad property on hand May 1, 1865, and the disposition made of the same.

It has not been possible to comply with that portion of the resolution requiring the cost price of each article to be reported. The amount of property was so large, and was obtained from so many different sources, that it would be impossible to trace the items back to their original bills, within the present session of Congress. For the same reason it has also been impossible for me to consolidate the reports of the different officers, before Congress adjourns. The individual reports are therefore forwarded; they are as follows, viz:

1. Report of United States military railroad property in the department of Tennessee and Arkansas, for which Brevet Colonel John Parks, assistant quartermaster, was responsible.

2. Report of United States military railroad property on the roads operated by the United States in the military division of the Tennessee, south of Chattanooga, for which Captain W. R. Hopkins, assistant quartermaster, was responsible.

3. Report of United States military railroad property in the military division of the Tennessee, on all roads operated by the United States centring at Nashville, for which Captain S. R. Hamill, assistant quartermaster, was responsible.

4. Report of the same, for which Captain G. H. Clemens, assistant quartermaster, was responsible.

5. Report of same, for which Lieutenant George F. Nelson, assistant quartermaster, was responsible.

[NOTE.—There was no property sold while Captain Clemens and Lieutenant Nelson had charge of property.]

6. Report showing the cost value of 154 locomotive engines, purchased by the United States for roads operated by government in the military division of

the Tennessee, together with the appraised price fixed to the same by the board convened by Major General George H. Thomas, commanding military division of the Tennessee.

[NOTE.—It is not possible to compare the balance of the locomotives, the original cost not being known to me.]

7. Report showing the money value of the property sold to the different companies, with the amount paid thereon, and the balance of principal and interest due and remaining unpaid.

8. Showing the appraised price of box and flat cars sold to the different companies, together with the average original cost of the same.

9. Copies of the executive orders of August 8th and October 14, under which the property was sold.

Very respectfully, your obedient servant,

T. J. CRILLY,
Brevet Major and A. Q. M. U. S. Army.

General D. C. McCALLUM,
Gen. Man. Mil. Railroads United States, Washington, D. C.

No. 3.

REPORT OF ALL RAILROADS OPERATED AND CONTROLLED BY THE MILITARY RAILROAD DEPARTMENT DURING THE WAR, AND OF ALL RAILROAD PROPERTY ON HAND ON MAY 1, 1865, SUBJECT TO THE CONTROL OF THE MILITARY RAILROAD DEPARTMENT, AND NOT EMBRACED IN THE REPORT OF MAJOR CRILLY; SHOWING HOW THE SAME WAS OBTAINED, HOW AND BY WHAT AUTHORITY DISPOSED OF, WITH COPIES OF THE LETTERS OF THE QUARTERMASTER GENERAL TO THE HON. EDWIN M. STANTON, SECRETARY OF WAR, DATED MAY 19| AND JULY 17, 1865, AND INDORSEMENTS THEREON, AND OF EXECUTIVE ORDERS OF AUGUST 8 AND OCTOBER 14, 1865.

No. 1.—Letter of the Quartermaster General to the Hon. E. M. Stanton, Secretary of War, dated May 19, 1865; letter of the Quartermaster General to the Hon. E. M. Stanton, Secretary of War, dated July 17, 1865; and Executive Orders of August 8 and October 14, 1865.

QUARTERMASTER GENERAL'S OFFICE,
Washington, D. C., May 19, 1865.

SIR: * * * * * * * *

The question of the disposition of the railroads in the States lately in rebellion is a large one, and, after reflection, I have the honor to advise that the following principles be established to govern the action of the quartermaster's department and of the military authorities in disposing of all of them:

1st. The United States will, as soon as it can, dispense with the military occupation and control of any railroad of which the quartermaster's department is now in charge, turn it over to the parties asking to receive it who may appear to have the best claim, and be able to operate it in such manner as to secure the speedy movement of all military stores and troops. The Quartermaster General, upon the advice of the military commander of the department, to determine when this can be done, subject to the approval of the Secretary of War.

2d. No charge tô be made against the railroad for expense of material or expense of operation.

3d. All material for permanent way used in the repair and construction of the road, and all damaged material of this class, which may be left along its route, having been thrown there during the operations of destruction or repair, to be considered as part of the road and given up with it.

4th. No payment or credit to be given to the railroad for its occupation or use by the United States during the continuance of the military necessity which compelled the United States to take possession of it by capture from the public enemy; the recovery of the road from the public enemy, and its return to loyal owners, with the vast expenditure of defence and repair as a full equivalent for its use.

5th. All movable property, including rolling stock of all kinds, the property of the United States, to be sold at auction, after full public notice, to the highest bidder.

6th. All rolling stock and material, the property before the war of railroads, and captured by the forces of the United States, to be placed at the disposal of the roads which originally owned it, and to be given up to these roads as soon as it can be spared, and they appear by proper agents authorized to receive it.

7th. When a State has a board of public works able and willing to take charge of its railroads, the railroads in possession of the quartermaster's department to be given up to the board of public works, leaving it to the State authorities and to the judicial tribunals to regulate all questions of property between rival boards, agents, or stockholders.

8th. Roads not being operated by the United States quartermaster's department not to be interfered with unless under military necessity. Such roads to be left in possession of such persons as may now have possession, subject only to the removal of every agent, director, president, superintendent, or operative who has not taken the oath of allegiance to the United States, which rule should be rigidly enforced.

9th. When the superintendents in actual possession decline to take such oath, some competent person to be appointed as receiver of the railroad, who shall administer the affairs of the road and account for its receipts to the board of directors, who may be formally recognized as the legal and loyal board of managers. This receiver to be appointed as in the case of other abandoned property by the Treasury Department.

10th. I recommend that the governor of the State of Virginia be informed that the War Department will interpose no obstacle to the board of public works of the State taking possession of all the railroads in the State not in use and occupation of the military force of the United States by the quartermaster's department, and that, as soon as the military occupation of any of these roads can be safely dispensed with, the road will be transferred to the charge of the board of public works.

In some of the States the State is a large bond-holder in the roads, and though there may be in such States no board of public works, it is probable that the State authorities will be willing to receive and take charge of the roads; if not, receivers should be appointed by the Treasury Department, upon application at the War Department, to take charge of them as abandoned property.

I have the honor to be, very respectfully,

M. C. MEIGS,
Quartermaster General and Brevet Major General.

Hon. E. M. STANTON,
Secretary of War.

A true extract:

ALEXANDER BLISS,
Lieutenant Colonel, Quartermaster's Department.

A true copy:

D. C. McCALLUM,
Brt. Brig. Gen., Director and Manager Mil. Railroads U. S.

QUARTERMASTER GENERAL'S OFFICE,
Washington, D. C., July 17, 1865.

SIR: I submit herewith an estimate for funds required by the disbursing officer for railroads at Nashville, Tennessee.

The remittances to Nashville, on account of railroads in the southwest, in 1865 are as follows, viz:

In March, on the November, 1864, estimate	$1,805,500
In March, on the December, 1864, estimate	1,000,000
On May 2, on the January, 1865, estimate	1,400,000
On May 2, on the February, 1865, estimate	1,400,000
On May 30, on the April, 1865, estimate	1,400,000
Total	7,005,500

The estimate for March was held back by General McCallum, it being supposed that the sums required on the previous estimates, and that for April, would be sufficient to pay off all his indebtedness to the 30th of June, owing to expected reductions in the establishment.

General McCallum reports (on the 3d instant) that one million dollars will be sufficient on the estimate for March to enable Captain Crilly to pay off his indebtedness.

It will be perceived from the foregoing statement that these railroads have been costing, during the present year, upwards of $1,300,000 monthly, and the expenditures are still going on. These expenditures were necessary during the war, but it appears to me that the government should be relieved from this heavy expenditure by the restoration of the railroads to the companies; and I recommend that this be done as soon as it is possible to make arrangements for the transfer, on the basis of my report of the 19th of May last.

The appropriation for transportation of the army is exhausted, and there is no money in the treasury for army transportation, against which requisitions can be drawn.

Very respectfully, your obedient servant,

M. C. MEIGS,
Brevet Major General U. S. A., Quartermaster General.

Hon. E. M. STANTON,
Secretary of War.

A true copy:

ALEXANDER BLISS,
Lieutenant Colonel, Quartermaster's Department.

[One enclosure.]

WAR DEPARTMENT, *July* 24, 1865.

The recommendation of the Quartermaster General is approved, and he is directed to turn over the roads immediately.

By order of the Secretary of War:

THOS. T. ECKERT,
Acting Assistant Secretary of War.

QUARTERMASTER GENERAL'S OFFICE,
Washington, July 27, 1865.

Respectfully referred to Brevet Brigadier General D. C. McCallum, general manager of the military railroads, together with a copy of the report of the Quartermaster General of May 19, 1865.

General McCallum will at once transfer all the railroads in the military division of the Mississippi, which are controlled at Nashville, in accordance with the recommendations of the Quartermaster General, as approved and directed by the Secretary of War. General McCallum will please report what railroads will remain in the possession of the military authorities when this transfer shall have been accomplished.

By order of the Quartermaster General:

ALEXANDER BLISS,
Lieut. Colonel, acting in charge 4th Division.

A true copy of letter and indorsements:

D. C. McCALLUM,
Bvt. Brig. Gen., Director and Manager Mil. Railroads U. S.

[General Orders No. 56.]

QUARTERMASTER GENERAL'S OFFICE,
Washington, D. C., September 28, 1865.

The following order by the President of the United States, in relation to the relinquishment of the government's control over all railroads in the State of Tennessee, and their continuations in adjoining States, now occupied by the United States military authorities, and no longer needed for military purposes, is published for the information of all officers and agents of the quartermaster's department.

M. C. MEIGS,
Brevet Major General U. S. A., Quartermaster General.

WAR DEPARTMENT,
Washington, August 8, 1865.

GENERAL: It having been determined by the government to relinquish control over all railroads in the State of Tennessee, and their continuations in adjoining States, that have been in charge of, and are now occupied by, the United States military authorities, and no longer needed for military purposes, you are hereby authorized and directed to turn over the same to the respective owners thereof at as early a date as practicable, causing, in all cases of transfer as aforesaid, the following regulations to be observed and carried out:

1. Each and every company will be required to reorganize and elect a board of directors whose loyalty shall be established to your satisfaction.

2. You will cause to be made out in triplicate, by such person or persons as you may indicate, a complete inventory of the rolling stock, tools, and other materials and property on each road.

3. Separate inventories will be in the same manner made of the rolling stock and other property originally belonging to each of said roads, and that furnished by and belonging to the government.

4. Each company will be required to give bonds satisfactory to the government that they will, in twelve months from the date of transfer as aforesaid, or such other reasonable time as may be agreed upon, pay a fair valuation for the government property turned over to said companies, the same being first appraised by competent and disinterested parties at a fair valuation, the United States reserving all government dues for carrying mails, and other service performed by each company, until said obligations are paid; and if, at the maturity

of said debt, the amount of government dues, retained as aforesaid, does not liquidate the same, the balance is to be paid by the company in money.

5. Tabular statements will be made of all expenditures by the government for repairing each road, with a full statement of receipts from private freights, passage, and other sources; also a full statement of all transportation performed on government account, giving the number of persons transported, and amount of freight, and the distance carried in each case—all of said reports or tabular statements to be made in triplicate, one each for the Secretary of War, the military headquarters of the department, and the railroad company.

6. All railroads in Tennessee will be required to pay all arrearages of interest due on the bonds issued by that State, prior to the date of its pretended secession from the Union, to aid in the construction of said roads, before any dividends are declared or paid to the stockholders thereof.

7. Buildings erected for government purposes on the line of railroads, and not valuable or useful for the business of said companies, should not form a legitimate charge against such companies; nor should they be charged for rebuilding houses, bridges, or other structures which were destroyed by the federal army.

8. You are authorized to give any orders to quartermasters within your division which you may deem necessary to carry into execution this order.

By order of the President:

EDWIN M. STANTON,
Secretary of War.

Major General GEORGE H. THOMAS,
Commanding Military Division of Tennessee, Nashville, Tenn.

[General Orders No. 62.]

QUARTERMASTER GENERAL'S OFFICE,
Washington, D. C., October 23, 1865.

The following order by the President of the United States, in relation to Executive Order of August 8, 1865, extending the provisions and benefits of the same to all railroads within the limits of the military division of the Tennessee desiring to purchase railroad rolling stock and material from the United States, for the purpose of repairing the losses of the war, is published for the information of all officers and agents of the quartermaster's department.

M. C. MEIGS,
Brevet Major General U. S. A., Quartermaster General.

WAR DEPARTMENT,
Washington, D. C., October 14, 1865.

GENERAL: The provisions and benefits of the Executive Order of August 8 are hereby extended to all railroads within the limits of your command desiring to purchase railroad rolling stock and material from the United States for the purpose of repairing the losses of the war.

You are also authorized to direct the sale to any such railroads, of rolling stock now within the limits of your command, and not needed by the United States for actual use, upon the following conditions, if they are preferred to the terms of the order of August 8, and the individual security required by you under that order.

You will take care that this property is distributed among the several roads in proportion to their actual needs, and that none is sold to any railroad in excess of the reasonable requirements of its business, or to be used for purpose of speculation, sale, or hire to other roads.

You will require from all such railroad companies satisfactory bonds, in the form herewith enclosed, binding them to the payment to the United States of the full appraised value of the property sold to them, in equal monthly instalments, with interest at the rate of seven and three-tenths per cent. per annum, within two years, credit being allowed to them, on the first of each month, for any service of military transportation rendered by them during the preceding month, at the established rates now allowed to northern railroads for such service.

Full reports of all sales under this order will be made to the War Department, from time to time, as required by existing orders.

The serviceable railroad iron in possession of the quartermaster's department at Chattanooga and Nashville is excepted. It will be sold only for cash at the prices fixed by the War Department.

By order of the President:

EDWIN M. STANTON,
Secretary of War.

Major General GEORGE H. THOMAS,
Commanding Military Division of Tennessee, Nashville, Tenn.

BOND.

Know all men by these presents, that the ——— railroad company, duly incorporated by the act of the ——— of the State of ——— by ———, its president, acting for and in behalf of said railroad company, does hereby acknowledge itself and its successors held and firmly bound unto the United States of America in the full and just sum of ——— dollars, lawful money of the United States; for which payment, well and truly to be made to the disbursing quartermaster of the United States military railroads, at his office in Nashville, or to such other disbursing quartermaster as may be designated by the War Department, within two years from the date of these presents, the said railroad company, by its president, hereby binds itself and its successors firmly by these presents.

Sealed with its corporate seal, attested by the signature of its president, and affixed by the express authority of its directors, this ——— day of ———, in the year of our Lord one thousand eight hundred and sixty ——.

The nature of the above obligation is such that, whereas the above bounden railroad company has purchased and received, or shall receive, from the War Department of the United States rolling stock, iron rails, cross-ties, chairs, spikes, timber, and other materials for repairing and operating its railroad, in quantities, at prices, and to an amount and value which shall be evidenced by the receipts given for the same by the said railroad company to the proper officer of the said War Department, upon a credit of two years from the date of these presents, payable in equal monthly instalments, with interest, at the rate of 7 3-10 per cent. per annum, within the said two years, either in cash to the disbursing quartermaster of the United States military railroads, at his office in Nashville, or to such other disbursing quartermaster as may be designated for this purpose by the War Department, or in transportation of the troops or military supplies of the United States, under the orders of the proper military authorities, at the rates of fare and tolls allowed for such service to northern railroads;

And whereas the said railroad company desires, and by these presents intends, to secure to the United States the complete and punctual payment as aforesaid of the amounts which may be due for the said materials received or to be received by it from the United States:

Now, therefore, if the said railroad company shall well and truly pay as aforesaid, either in cash, in equal monthly instalments, or in transportation as aforesaid, to the United States, within two years from the date of these presents, all that shall be due as aforesaid to the United States on account and in payment for all the materials received as aforesaid from the United States, then this obligation shall be void and of no effect.

But if the said railroad company shall fail to pay to the United States all or any portion of what may be due to the United States on account of the said materials received from the United States, within two years from the date of these presents, either in cash as aforesaid, or in transportation as aforesaid, or shall fail to pay any of the monthly instalments aforesaid, punctually when due; then this obligation shall remain in full force and effect to the extent that may be necessary to fully repay to the United States the full amount which may be due on account of the said materials so received as aforesaid, and all loss or damage which may have been incurred by the United States by reason of the said railroad company's failure to pay for the same what shall be due therefor when the same shall be due.

And as a further security for such payment and indemnity to the United States the United States shall have a lien upon the property sold to said company, and in default of such complete and punctual payment of all moneys which may be due on account of the aforesaid purchase of materials, be fully authorized to take possession of and sell said property, and also to place in charge and control of the said company's railroad, an agent of the said United States, who shall be fully empowered, and by these presents is fully empowered, in case of such default as aforesaid, to collect all the revenues of the said company, and apply the same to the payment to the United States of all the moneys which shall be due at the times of such application of such revenues to the United States for any such materials, which shall have been delivered by the United States to the said railroad company, or by reason of any loss or injury to the United States resulting from such default in payment of the same. And the said company shall have no authority to sell or convey out of its possession, without the consent of the United States first in writing obtained, any of the property referred to in this agreement; but shall hold and retain the same to the exclusive use of said company, in carying on the business of transportation of persons and property over its line of road, until the whole is fully paid for as aforesaid.

In witness whereof, the corporate seal of said railroad company is affixed hereto, by authority of its directors, and attested by its president.

—— ——.

Witness:

—— ——.

NOTE.—The amount of this bond to be double the valuation of the property sold and delivered. Internal revenue stamps should be affixed, to the amount of fifty cents for every thousand dollars.

No. 2.—*Report of all railroads operated and controlled by the United States, at director and general manager, giving the name of the road, number of miles what authority transferred.**

No.	Name of road.	Distance operated.			Estimated
		From—	To—	Miles.	Per mile.
	DEPARTMENT OF VIRGINIA.				
1	Washington and Alexandria....	Washington	Alexandria	7	$57, 142 85 5-7
2	Orange and Alexandria	Alexandria	Mitchell's Station	68	40, 000 00
3	Warrenton Branch.............	Warrenton Junction ...	Warrenton	9	40, 000 00
4	Alexandria, Loudon, and Hampshire.	Alexandria	Vienna	15	30, 000 00
5	Richmond, Fredericksburg, and Potomac.	Aquia Creek...........	Falmouth	15	30, 000 00
6,	Richmond and York River	White House	Fair Oaks	20	15, 000 00
7	South Side	City Point	Burkeville	62	42, 000 00
8	Richmond and Petersburg......	Manchester	Petersburg	22	40, 000 00
9	Clover Hill Branch of Richmond and Petersburg railroad.	Clover Hill Station	Coal Mines	18	20, 000 00
10	Richmond and Danville	Manchester	Danville	140	30, 000 00
11	Norfolk and Petersburg	Norfolk	Blackwater...........	44	50, 000 00
12	Seaboard and Roanoke.........	Portsmouth............	Suffolk..............	17	35, 000 00
13	City Point and Army Line	Pitkin Station, &c......	Humphrey's Station..	18	11, 111 11 1-9
14	Manassas Gap	Manassas Junction.....	Strasburg	62	40, 000 00
15	Winchester and Potomac.......	Harper's Ferry	Stevenson	28	25, 000 00
	Total..................	....	....	545	....
	MILITARY DIVISION OF THE TENNESSEE.				
1	Louisville City................	River Landing	Louisville and Nashville railroad depot.	2	15, 000 00
2	Nashville and Chattanooga	Nashville	Chattanooga.........	151	50, 000 00
3	Shelbyville Branch	Wartrace	Shelbyville	9	30, 000 00
4	Nashville and Decatur	Nashville	Decatur	120	50, 000 00
5	Mt. Pleasant Branch	Columbia	Mt. Pleasant	12	30, 000 00
6	Nashville and Northwestern....	Nashville	Johnsonville	78	30, 000 00
7	Nashville and Clarksville......	......do	Clarksville	62	30, 000 00
8	McMinnville and Manchester ...	Tullahoma	McMinnville	35	30, 000 00
9	East Tennessee and Georgia....	Chattanooga...........	Knoxville	112	30, 000 00
10	Dalton	Cleveland	Dalton	27	30, 000 00
11	East Tennessee and Virginia....	Knoxville	Carter's Station......	110	40, 000 00
12	Rogersville and Jefferson	Junction of East Tennessee and Virginia railroad.	Rogersville	12	25, 000 00
13	Western and Atlantic	Chattanooga	Atlanta	136	40, 000 00
14	Rome	Kingston	Rome	17	20, 000 00
15	Macon and Western............	Atlanta	Rough and Ready....	11	30, 000 00
16	Memphis and Charleston	Decatur, Ala	Stevenson, Ala	80	40, 000 00
		Memphis, Tenn........	Pocahontas	75	45, 000 00
17	Mississippi Central............	Grand Junction........	Tallahatchie River...	48	40, 000 00
18	Mobile and Ohio	Columbus, Ky.........	Crockett's Station....	35	40, 000 00
19	Memphis and Little Rock	Duvall's Bluff	Little Rock, Ark.....	49	30, 000 00
	Total..................	....	....	1, 181	....

* The time of taking possession of the roads is not given, for the reason that the possession thereof was not continuous, being held and abandoned as the United States armies advanced or retreated.

any time during the war, under the direction of General D. C. McCallum, operated, estimated value, how held, date of transfer, and to whom and by

value.	How held.	How disposed of.		
Total.		Date.	To whom delivered.	By whose authority.
$400,000	By right of capture ..	Aug. 8, 1865	W., A., and G. R. R. Co...	By order of Sec'y of War.
2,720,000	......do	June 27, 1865	Board of public works of Va.	Do.
360,000	......do	......do	......do	Do.
450,000	......do	Aug. 8, 1865	......do	Do.
450,000	......do	May 23, 1864	Abandoned	
300,000	......do	June 13, 1864	Track taken up, material removed, and road abandoned.	Lieut. Gen. U. S. Grant.
2,480,000	......do	July 24, 1865	Southside R. R. Co	By order of Sec'y of War.
880,000	......do	July 3, 1865	Board of public works of Va.	By order of Gen. Halleck.
360,000	......do	......do	......do	Do.
4,200,000	......do	July 4, 1865	......do	Do.
2,200,000	......do	July 1, 1865	N. and P. R. R. Co.........	Do.
595,000	......do	......do	S. and R. R. R. Co.........	Do.
200,000	Built by the United States.	June —, 1865	Track taken up and sold by the United States.	By order of Sec'y of War.
2,480,000	By right of capture ..	Nov. 10, 1864	Track removed and road abandoned.	
700,000	......do	Jan. 20, 1866	W. and P. R. R. Co........	Do.
18,775,000				
$30,000	Built by the United States.	Mar. —, 1866	Track taken up............	Do.
7,550,000	By right of capture ..	Sept. 25, ——	N. and C. R. R. Co	Executive orders of August 8 and October 14.
270,000	......do	......do	......do	Do.
6,000,000	......do	......do	T. and A., C. S. and T., and A. C. R. R. Cos.	Do.
360,000	......do	—— —, 1864	{ Track removed by the United States. Road turned over to N. and D. R. R. Co.	By order of Gen. Grant. Executive orders of August 8 and October 14.
2,340,000	27¼ miles by right of capture, 50¾ miles built by the United States.	Sept. 1, ——	N. and N. W. R. R. Co.....	Do.
1,860,000	By right of capture ..	Sept. 23, ——	M., C., and L. R. R. Co....	Do.
1,050,000	......do	....	27 miles and 2,750 feet of track removed and used in repairs of other roads; road abandoned.	By order of Lt. Gen. Grant.
3,360,000	......do	Aug. 28, ——	E. T. and Ga. R. R. Co....	Executive orders of August 8 and October 14.
710,000	......do	......do	......do	Do.
4,400,000	......do	......do	E. T. and Va. R. R. Co....	Do.
300,000	......do	......do	R. and J. R. R. Co.........	Do.
5,440,000	......do	Sept. 25, ——	State of Georgia	Do.
340,000	......do	......do	Rome R. R. Co.............	Do.
330,000	......do	Nov. —, 1864	Track removed and road abandoned.	By order of the general commanding.
3,200,000	......do	Sept. 1, ——	M. and C. R. R. Co.........	Executive orders of August 8 and October 14.
3,375,000	......do	......do	......do	Do.
1,920,000	......do	Aug. 24, 1864	Abandoned	
1,400,000	......do	Aug. 25, ——	M. and O. R. R. Co.........	Do.
1,470,000	......do	Nov. 1, ——	M. and L. R. R. R. Co.....	Do.
45,705,000				

No. 2.—*Report of all railroads operated and*

No.	Name of road.	Distance operated.			Estimated
		From—	To—	Miles.	Per mile.
	MIDDLE DEPARTMENT AND DEPARTMENT OF THE SUSQUEHANNA.*				
1	Western Maryland railroad	Relay	Westminster	29	$25,000 00
2	Hanover Branch railroad	Hanover Junction	Hanover	13	20,000 00
3	Gettysburg railroad	Hanover	Gettysburg	17	20,000 00
4	Franklin railroad	Chambersburg	Hagerstown	22	20,000 00
	Total			81	
	DEPARTMENT OF GEORGIA.				
1	Savannah and Gulf railroad	Savannah	Ogeeche River	11	30,000 00
2	Georgia Central railroad	In and around the city of Savannah.		3	33,333 33⅓
	Total			14	
	DEPARTMENT OF NORTH CAROLINA.				
1	Atlantic and North Carolina railroad.	Morehead City	Goldsboro'	95	30,000 00
2	North Carolina railroad	Goldsboro'	Charlotte	223	30,000 00
3	Wilmington and Weldon railroad.	Wilmington	Weldon	162	30,000 00
4	Raleigh and Gaston railroad	Raleigh	Cedar Creek	25	30,000 00
	Total			505	
	DEPARTMENT OF THE GULF.				
1	New Orleans, Opelousas, and Great Western railroad.†	New Orleans	Brashear City	80	

* No special orders were given relative to relinquishing these roads. The necessity for military occupation having ceased the several companies were allowed to resume control.

† This road was controlled and operated by the quartermaster's department and not by the military railroad department.

controlled by the United States, &c.—Continued.

value.	How held.	How disposed of.		
Total.		Date.	To whom delivered.	By whose authority.
$725, 000	Seized	July 7, 1863	W. M. R. R. Co	
260, 000	......do	Aug. 1, 1863	Hanover Branch R. R. Co	
340, 000	......do	......do	Gettysburg R. R. Co	
440, 000	......do	Oct. 1, 1862	Cumberland Valley R. R. Co.	
1, 765, 000				
$330, 000	By right of capture	June 20, ——	S. and G. R. R. Co	
1, 000, 000	......do	......do	Ga. Cen. R. R. Co	Major General Gilmore.
1, 330, 000				
$2, 850, 000	......do	Oct. 25, ——	A. and N. C. R. R. Co	By order of Sec'y of War.
6, 690, 000	......do	Oct. 22, ——	N. C. R. R. Co	Do.
4, 860, 000	......do	Aug. 27, ——	W. and W. R. R. Co	Do.
750, 000	......do	May 3, ——	R. and G. R. R. Co	
5, 150, 000				
....	......do	Jan. 31, 1866	N. O., O., and Gt. W. R. R. Co.	Executive orders of August 8 and October 14.

No. 3.—*Statement showing the value of property sold to railroad companies in the departments of Virginia and North Carolina on credit, payments made, amount remaining unpaid, and terms of and authority for the sale.*

DEPARTMENT OF VIRGINIA.

Number.	Name of company.	Date of sale.	Value of property sold.	Value of property sold, with interest to June 30, 1866, added.	Total amount of interest and instalments paid by each company to June 30, 1866.	Balance of principal and interest remaining unpaid July 1, 1866.	Amount due for carrying the mails to June 30, 1866, in addition to the foregoing, and which will be retained, as well as all subsequent sums, and applied to the payment of the am'nt due the United States.	Terms of sale.
1	Richmond, Fredericksburg, and Potomac Railroad Company.	July 3, 1865	$7,449 27	$7,449 27	$7,449 27	....	....	On a credit of six months.
2	Petersburg Railroad Company.	July 10 and 20, 1865.	65,000 00	66,706 27	18,012 67	$48,693 60	$4,266 66	On a credit of six months. Time of payment extended twelve months from January 12, 1866, with interest. $20,412 20 to be paid July 12, 1866, in addition to the amount already paid.
3	Virginia Central Railroad Company.	Aug. 1, 1865	70,000 00	74,408 13	20,924 71	53,473 42	3,400 00	On a credit of six months. Time of payment extended eighteen months from February 17. Payable monthly, with interest, at 7 3-10 per cent. from date of purchase.
4	Orange and Alexandria Railroad Company.	Oct. 12, 1865	90,395 74	95,089 02	17,750 45	77,338 57	....	On a credit of six months. Time extended eighteen months from April 12, payable monthly, with 7 3-10 per cent. interest from date of purchase.
4	Orange and Alexandria Railroad Company; two locomotive engines transferred from Wilmington and Weldon Railroad Company.	Nov. 20, 1865	28,500 00	29,823 36	5,404 74	24,418 62	4,575 00	On a credit of eighteen months, payable monthly, with 7 3-10 per cent. interest.
5	Alexandria, Loudon, and Hampshire Railroad Company.	Dec. 30, 1865	62,592 96	64,877 55	....	64,877 75	....	On a credit of two years, payable monthly, with 7 3-10 per cent. interest.
6	Manassas Gap Railroad Company...	Jan. 18, 1866	4,623 51	4,743 23	309 09	4,460 63	....	On a credit of two years, payable monthly, with 7 3-10 per cent. interest.
7	Mobile and Ohio Railroad Company.	Oct. 6, 1865	60,600 00	.... (*)....	.... (*)....	.... (*)....	.... (*)....	On a credit of 12 months, payable monthly, with interest.
	Total....................	....	389,161 48	343,096 83	69,850 93	273,262 59	12,241 66	

* Payments reported by Major Crilly, in connexion with payments for property sold at Nashville.

DEPARTMENT OF NORTH CAROLINA AND ARKANSAS.

1	Wilmington and Weldon Railroad Company.	Sept. 25, 1865	$50,000 00	$52,788 14	$3,000 00	$49,788 14	....	On a credit of six months. Time of payment extended to two years from date of sale, with interest, and payable in fifteen equal monthly instalments.
1	Wilmington and Weldon Railroad Company.	Nov. 20, 1865	31,500 00	32,736 06	10,836 07	21,899 99	$4,204 00	Credit of two years, payable in equal monthly instalments, with 7 3-10 per cent. interest.
2	Atlantic and North Carolina Railroad Company.	Dec. 3, 1865	51,453 93	53,527 67	5,948 84	45,578 83	....	Do. do.
3	Western North Carolina Railroad Company.	Dec. 11, 1865	14,269 82	14,811 51	2,138 35	12,672 16	585 00	Do. do.
	Total............	....	147,223 75	153,863 38	21,923 26	129,939 12	4,789 00	
1	Memphis and Little Rock Railroad Company.	Nov. 1, 1865	153,287 47	160,747 46	....	160,747 46	....	On a credit of eighteen months, with 7 3-10 per cent. interest.

REMARK.—Payment secured by bond for double the value of the property sold.

NOTES.—All sales of property to railroad companies, enumerated on this sheet, were made by order of the Secretary of War.

The amount originally sold to the Wilmington and Weldon Railroad Company was $110,000. Two locomotive engines ($28,500) have, however, been transferred to the Orange and Alexandria Railroad Company, leaving the amount for which the Wilmington and Weldon Railroad Company is responsible, $81,500.

No. 4.—*Schedule of property sold on credit to railroad companies in the departments of Virginia and North Carolina, since May* 1, 1865.

A schedule of railroad property in the possession of and belonging to the United States on the 1st *day of May, A. D.* 1865, *and sold, by order of the Secretary of War, to the Richmond, Fredericksburg and Potomac Railroad Company, on a credit of six months, from July* 3, 1865, *without interest, the company giving their bond in the sum of* $50,000 *to secure payment of the same.*

Date of sale.	Articles.	Cost.	Sold for.
1865.			
July and August.	2,000 pounds railroad spikes	$175 00	$120 00
	147,918 feet pine timber	5,916 72	5,546 93
	47,529 feet hemlock timber	1,901 16	1,782 34
	Total	7,992 88	7,449 27
1866.			
January 3	Paid in full		7,449 27

Railroad property in the possession of and belonging to the United States on the 1st *day of May,* 1865, *and sold on a credit of twelve months to the Mobile and Ohio Railroad Company, upon the terms specified in Executive Order of August* 8, 1865.

Date of sale.	Articles.	Cost.	Sold for.
1865.			
October 6	101 box cars	$126,250 00	$60,600 00

A schedule of railroad property in the possession of and belonging to the United States on the 1st *day of May, A. D.* 1865, *and sold, by order of the Secretary of War, to the Petersburg Railroad Company, on a credit of six months, from July* 10 *and* 20, 1865, *without interest, the company giving two separate bonds in the sum of* $65,000 *each, (being double the value of material purchased,) to secure the payment of the same.*

Date of sale.	Articles.	Cost.	Sold for.
1865.			
July	$800\frac{12}{2240}$ tons railroad iron	$92,000 00	$64,000 21
	14,000 pounds railroad spikes	1,225 00	840 00
	320 cross-ties	160 00	160 00
	Total	93,385 00	65,000 21

NOTE.—The time of payment of the above sum of $65,000 was extended January 12 and 20, for a further period of six months, with interest at the rate of 7 3-10 per cent. per annum, by order of the Secretary of War.

A schedule of railroad property in the possession of and belonging to the United States on the 1st *day of May, A. D.* 1865, *and sold, by order of the Secretary of War, to the Virginia Central Railroad Company, on a credit of six months, from August* 1, 1865, *without interest, the company giving bond in the sum of* $140,000 *as security for the payment of the same.*

Date of sale.	Articles.	Cost.	Sold for.
1865.			
August and Sept.	$842\frac{1073}{2240}$ tons railroad iron	$96,885 08	$67,417 60
	43,040 pounds railroad chairs	4,304 00	2,582 40
	Total	101,189 08	70,000 00

NOTE.—The time of payment of the above sum of $70,000 was extended for the further period of eighteen months from February 17, 1866, with interest at 7 3-10 per cent. per annum from date of purchase, payable in equal monthly instalments.

A schedule of railroad property in the possession of and belonging to the United States on the 1st day of May, A. D. 1865, and sold by order of the Secretary of War on credit to the Manassas Gap Railroad Company on the terms specified in Executive Order of October 14, 1865.

Date of sale.	Articles.	Cost.	Sold for.
1865.			
January 5	4,545 pounds square nuts	$363 60	$363 60
	3,601 pounds hexagonal nuts	351 10	351 10
	1 set switch fixtures	240 00	240 00
	4,079 pounds car coupling	285 53	203 95
	3 Henderson pumps	397 98	375 00
	12 dozen shovels	187 20	156 00
	20 scoop shovels	36 00	25 00
	12 tallow cans	*	6 00
	24 pint oilers	*	5 04
	24 quart oilers	*	15 60
	24 squirt cans	*	1 92
	24 tin torches	*	2 88
	68 clamp screws	*	21 76
	6 notch blocks	19 50	19 50
	6 notch blocks	24 00	24 00
	3 notch blocks	17 25	17 25
	1 notch block	7 00	7 00
	6 tackle blocks	20 25	20 25
	2 tackle blocks	10 00	10 00
	4 tackle blocks	24 00	24 00
	2 tackle blocks	13 00	13 00
	38 buck saws	38 00	33 06
	2 dozen buckets	10 00	5 00
	2 hydraulic jacks	225 00	200 00
	4 screw jacks	34 00	27 00
	3 chain vices	45 00	75 00
	24 picks	38 64	24 00
	$12\frac{1}{2}$ dozen pick handles	30 00	20 63
	3 dozen white lanterns	4 50	72 00
	2 dozen red lanterns	4 00	70 00
	$1\frac{1}{12}$ dozen 16-inch hand bastard files	22 18	22 18
	$\frac{2}{12}$ dozen 14-inch hand bastard files	1 58	1 58
	$\frac{4}{12}$ dozen 13-inch hand bastard files	2 11	2 11
	$1\frac{4}{12}$ dozen 12-inch hand bastard files	7 16	7 16
	2 dozen 9-inch hand bastard files	6 48	6 48
	$9\frac{6}{12}$ dozen 10-inch hand bastard files	36 01	36 01
	$8\frac{2}{12}$ dozen 8-inch hand bastard files	21 97	21 97
	2 dozen 6-inch hand bastard files	3 68	3 68
	4 dozen 4-inch hand bastard files	4 76	4 76
	2 dozen 16-inch hand smooth files	29 70	29 70
	2 dozen 4-inch hand smooth files	19 80	19 80
	2 dozen 12-inch hand smooth files	14 30	14 30
	$4\frac{4}{12}$ dozen 10-inch hand smooth files	20 89	20 89
	2 dozen 12-inch hand dead smooth files	28 60	28 60
	$2\frac{8}{12}$ dozen 10-inch hand dead smooth files	25 71	25 71
	2 dozen 8-inch hand dead smooth files	13 76	13 76
	1 dozen 6-inch hand dead smooth files	5 06	5 06
	2 dozen 16-inch round bastard files	20 90	20 90
	1 dozen 14-inch round bastard files	7 15	7 15
	1 dozen 11-inch round bastard files	4 13	4 13
	1 dozen 10-inch round bastard files	3 45	3 45
	1 dozen 8-inch round bastard files	2 35	2 35
	2 dozen 14-inch half-round bastard files	14 30	14 30
	1 dozen 12-inch half-round bastard files	5 10	5 10
	1 dozen 10-inch half-round bastard files	3 45	3 45
	1 dozen 8-inch half-round bastard files	2 35	2 35
	1 dozen 14-inch half-round bastard files	9 35	9 35
	1 dozen 12-inch half-round bastard files	6 75	6 75
	1 dozen 10-inch half-round bastard files	4 40	4 40
	1 dozen 8-inch half-round bastard files	3 17	3 17

*Manufactured.

Schedule of railroad property, &c.—Continued.

Date of sale.	Articles.	Cost.	Sold for.
1865.			
January 5.......	2 dozen 14-inch mill saw files	$12 66	$12 66
	$1\frac{8}{12}$ dozen 14-inch square bastard files ..	10 55	10 55
	1 dozen 12-inch square bastard files.....	4 55	4 55
	6 dozen $5\frac{1}{2}$-inch taper files.............	11 04	11 04
	9 steam gauges..........................	270 00	225 00
	6 hack saws	5 22	5 22
	15 jig saws	40 65	7 50
	2 18-inch dividers	4 42	3 00
	2 10-inch dividers.......................	4 42	2 00
	2 levels.................................	4 10	2 26
	7 Salter's balances......................	105 00	140 00
	2 second-hand Salter's balances..........	30 00	30 00
	8 18-inch monkey wrenches................	24 96	22 40
	57 2-gallon oil cans	25 65	42 75
	479 pounds Russia iron...................	95 80	95 80
	1,716 pounds tank rivets	205 92	205 92
	50 feet $2\frac{1}{2}$-inch rubber hose	116 00	67 50
	50 feet $2\frac{1}{4}$-inch rubber hose	116 00	52 50
	518 pounds rubber springs................	621 60	207 20
	87 pounds rubber packing.................	147 90	34 80
	38 feet $9\frac{1}{2}$-inch second-hand leather belting	30 02	5 70
	27 feet 6-inch second-hand leather belting	21 33	4 05
	115 pounds waste.........................	48 30	25 30
	97 gallons paraffine varnish.............	58 20	82 46
	11 pounds hemp packing	2 53	2 42
	48 pounds wire...........................	11 52	4 79
	1 carpenter shop.........................	500 00	500 00
	3 large stoves	49 35	36 00
	Total	5,353 84	4,623 51

A schedule of railroad property in the possession of and belonging to the United States on the 1st day of May, A. D. 1865, and sold on credit to the Orange and Alexandria Railroad Company, by order of the Secretary of War.

Date of sale.	Articles.	Cost.	Sold for.
1865.			
June and July...	552,678 feet pine timber.................	$22,107 12	$20,703 16
	$937\frac{5}{8}$ gallons sperm oil..................	2,053 38	2,250 30
	4 1-inch tackle blocks...................	22 20	15 00
	2 $1\frac{1}{4}$-inch tackle blocks..................	14 00	14 00
	1 ice box................................	2 50	2 50
	42 short-handled shovels, second-hand..	54 60	11 13
	7 dozen tin plates.......................	9 24	90
	7 dozen tin cups.........................	6 37	78
	35 pair knives and forks.................	13 30	3 75
	36 table spoons..........................	2 88	42
	$6\frac{1}{2}$ pounds rotten-stone..................	65	39
	$2,229\frac{1}{2}$ pounds waste......................	936 39	490 49
	8 sheets emery cloth	72	24
	2 papers Tripoli	16	08
	12 picks	19 32	5 76
	250 pounds tamping bars..................	30 00	22 50
	48 railroad cold chisels	14 40	7 20
	478 pounds claw bars.....................	57 36	43 20
	260 pounds lining bars	31 20	23 40
	180 pounds spike mauls	270 00	27 05
	1 hospital tent*.........................	....	20 00

* Received from Quartermaster's department.

Schedule of railroad property, &c.—Continued.

Date of sale.	Articles.	Cost.	Sold for.
1865.			
June and July ...	2 track adzes	$5 00	$1 80
	5 track gauges	1 85	1 15
	3 truck cars	150 00	45 00
	5 balls wick	55	55
	2 wall tents*	....	30 00
	2 Sibley tents*	....	30 00
	1 No. 10 cook stove and fixings	26 00	19 00
	1 frying pan	24	50
	1 coffee-pot	90	10
	1 butcher knife	1 09	02
	6 wooden buckets	2 52	54
	24 pounds track cold chisels	4 32	4 32
	4 axe handles	92	56
	3 cant hooks	2 25	2 25
	45 pounds timber bars	5 40	4 05
	5 pounds railroad punches	75	75
	3 timber jacks	2 25	2 25
July to December.	1 hand wash basin	25	08
	1 pepper box	08	03
	1 salt box	08	03
	115 pounds Manilla rope	28 75	25 70
	4 pounds hemp packing	25	23
	48 pounds track cold chisels	8 64	8 64
	18 pick handles	2 48	2 48
	4 maul handles	1 60	1 60
	14 switch locks	28 00	12 88
	22 picks	35 42	10 56
	6 camp kettles	8 52	66
	120 pounds tamping bars	14 40	10 80
	1 Henderson pump, new	132 66	125 00
	35 feet 2-inch gas pipe	15 40	9 63
	3 2-inch L joints	96	45
	3 9-inch rubber tank hose	80 13	51 00
	1 copper strainer	50	50
	12 pike poles	3 60	3 60
	1 hospital tent*	....	20 00
	2 pair 2-inch gas pipe tongs	1 50	1 50
	1 12-inch monkey wrench	3 12	2 00
	1 chipping hammer	1 00	88
	4 pounds hand cold chisels	60	60
	6 pounds gum packing	6 90	3 60
	¼ gallon kerosene oil	21	23
	141 hours' labor	49 35	49 35
	2 1-gallon oil cans	74	70
	1 long spout	65	65
	4 ⅝-bolts 6 inches long	1 00	1 00
	1 frying pan	24	50
	1 No. 10 cooking stove and fixings	26 00	31 00
	1 coffee-pot	90	90
	1 butcher knife	1 09	75
	3 wooden buckets	1 26	69
	1 hand wash basin	25	25
	1 pepper box	08	06
	2 chopping axes	4 02	2 00
	1 tin boiler	4 00	4 00
	1 yawl boat and oars	106 56	86 00
	16 pounds lead pipe	1 60	1 76
	1 18-inch monkey wrench	3 12	2 80
	4 pounds bell cord	2 20	1 16
	1 dozen short-handled shovels	15 60	13 00
	1 ration box	2 50	2 50
	2 coffee-pots	1 80	20
	1 dish pan	24	20

* Received from Quartermaster's Department.

Schedule of railroad property, &c.—Continued.

Date of sale.	Articles.	Cost.	Sold for.
1865.			
July to December.	500 pounds boat spikes	$45 00	$30 00
	41,650 pounds railroad spikes	3,748 50	2,499 00
	2 pounds hemp packing	46	46
	179 pounds solder	89 50	71 60
	1,201 pounds nails	120 10	72 06
	¼ yard Canton flannel	14	15
	1 sheet tin	18	18
	65 pounds lining bars	6 50	6 50
	4 track gauges	2 00	2 00
	20 pounds spike mauls	3 60	3 60
	12 short-handled shovels	15 60	13 00
	6 picks	9 66	6 00
	6 pick handles	83	83
	1 track adze	2 50	90
	1 2-gallon oil can	1 00	1 00
	1 ½-gallon oil can	33	33
	1 chimney	15	15
	24 pounds track cold chisels	3 60	3 60
	1 pint benzine	08	08
	2 pounds packing yarn	46	46
	2⅝ gallons benzine	1 37	1 52
	1 paper Tripoli	04	04
	2 boxes matches	06	06
	7½ pounds emery	68	68
	1 paper Tripoli	04	04
	1 emery can	10	10
	1 box lye	14	14
	½ pound sulphur	05	05
	2 ½-gallon oil-cans	66	66
	3 boxes lye	42	42
	38 pounds wrought-iron	1 62	1 62
	2 lanterns	4 00	4 00
	1 paper Tripoli	04	04
	1,074½ pounds hemp packing	247 13	247 14
	2,000 cross-ties	1,000 00	1,000 00
	8,200 pounds railroad chairs	820 00	492 00
	3 gallons sperm oil	7 20	7 20
	254 pounds iron castings	15 24	4 13
	36,016 feet oak timber	2,160 96	756 33
	4,039 feet ash timber	....	80 78
	21 pounds Babbitt metal	12 81	6 51
	59,335 pounds axle iron	....	3,560 10
	1,476 pounds sheet copper	1,092 24	708 48
	4,470 feet panel pine	312 90	312 90
	342 pounds sheet-iron	253 08	17 53
	1,605 pounds assorted nuts	192 60	144 45
	3,000 feet hemlock plank	87 00	112 50
	1 pilot for engine Geary	35 00	35 00
	54 trucks for freight cars	12,150 00	12,150 00
	1,520 pounds rivets	182 40	182 40
	1 10-ton hydraulic jack	112 50	69 00
	3,430 pounds flues	857 50	857 50
	2,652 pounds boiler iron	....	139 24
	11,553 pounds sheet-iron	1,386 36	592 09
	1,436 pounds angle iron	....	59 30
	189 pounds 1-inch half-round iron	9 45	7 80
	1,915 pounds Russia sheet-iron	689 46	421 30
	16 pounds lampwick	20 64	13 60
	4 dozen 3-inch iron chest locks	27 84	12 00
	8 15-ton hydraulic jacks	816 00	808 00
	10 screw jacks	85 00	160 00
	$22\frac{35}{112}$ boxes leaded tin, 14 by 20 by 10	334 55	334 68
	288 pounds sheet-iron, No. 26	26 64	26 64

Schedule of railroad property, &c.—Continued.

Date of sale.	Articles.	Cost.	Sold for.
1865.			
July to December.	4 boxes 18 by 24 double thick glass	$82 36	$28 00
	3 sides lace leather	11 61	6 00
	20 pounds chrome yellow, in oil	7 00	3 00
	710 pounds engine springs	149 10	32 84
	5 pounds sewing wire	1 20	50
	10 boxes bright tin, 14 by 20	233 70	172 50
	6 boxes bright tin, 10 by 14	140 22	102 00
	6 boxes bright tin, 12 by 12	140 22	99 75
	1 box leaded tin, 14 by 20	23 37	15 00
	20 pounds brass wire	9 00	8 90
	14 pounds copper wire	7 00	7 00
	712 pounds sheet brass	441 44	356 00
	206 pounds borax	142 74	61 80
	2,400 pounds cast-iron drawheads	....	39 00
	49$\frac{274}{2240}$ tons railroad iron	5,647 32	3,928 58
	1 oil pan	300 00	300 00
	168 pounds resin	....	6 72
	1 pair bellows	31 66	25 00
	1,000 pounds pig lead	150 00	100 00
	937 pounds block tin	833 93	374 80
	158 33-inch car wheels	3,630 84	4,424 00
	79 30-inch car wheels	1,815 42	2,054 00
	15 desks	....	150 00
	2 box cars	1,701 48	1,300 00
	30 vices	1,020 00	300 00
	990 pounds grindstones	29 70	19 80
	50 tons assorted iron	5,600 00	4,625 00
	2 tons cast-steel	54	600 00
	7 tons iron	784 00	647 50
	180 feet 9-inch tank hose	....	306 00
	2 24-inch screw jacks	17 00	32 00
	42 gallons boiled linseed oil	66 78	58 80
	80 quires sandpaper	20 00	13 60
	1 hydrostatic wheel press	1,133 00	1,133 00
	3 grindstone boxes	225 00	225 00
	50 feet shafting	400 00	400 00
	2 12-inch universal chucks	70 00	80 00
	1 9-inch universal chuck	30 00	35 00
	3 sets letters and figures	....	21 00
	4,080 pounds iron tools	612 00	612 00
	2,680 pounds steel tools	402 00	402 00
	31 chipping hammers	26 97	26 97
	56 monkey wrenches	174 72	112 00
	4 cranes	....	300 00
	1,100 pounds straightening plates	....	17 88
	1 cast-iron anvil, 700 pounds	161 00	11 38
	2 cast-iron heading anvils, 1,100 pounds	253 00	17 88
	1 pair centres for axles	....	60 00
	6,962 pounds anvil blocks	....	113 13
	2 anvils, 493 pounds	113 39	49 30
	1 bellows	31 63	25 00
	1 forge	29 75	20 00
	1 set blacksmith's tools	....	35 00
	2 large shop stoves	52 00	24 00
	2 test pumps	....	200 00
	1 set injector tools	....	125 00
	1 36-gallon oil-can	....	8 00
	1 saw gummer	21 00	25 00
	1 pair centres for planing taps	....	100 00
	1 set clamps for crank pins	....	75 00
	1 waste washing-machine	....	500 00
	1 drilling machine, including counter-shaft and pulleys	400 00	100 00

Schedule of railroad property, &c.—Continued

Date of sale.	Articles.	Cost.	Sold for.
1865. July to December.	1 boring mill, No. 5, with cutters, including counter-shafts and pulleys, with universal chuck base	$1,957 00	$1,960 00
	1 punching and shearing machine, with dies and punches	1,545 00	1,500 00
	1 hand lathe, 10-feet shears, 16-inch swing, 9-inch universal chuck, slide, rest, and tools	315 00	300 00
	1 slide lathe, 10-feet shears, 8-inch swing, 9-inch universal chuck, and tools		400 00
	1 slide lathe, 12-feet shears, 16-inch swing, 12-inch universal chuck, and tools	635 00	600 00
	1 slide lathe, 12-feet shears, 16-inch swing, 12-inch universal chuck, and tools		500 00
	1 slide lathe, 10-feet shears, 16½-inch swing, 16-inch universal chuck, and tools		400 00
	1 compound planer, 12-inch stroke, and tools	1,200 00	1,200 00
	1 bolt-cutting machine, with dies and taps.		450 00
	1 slotting machine, 12 inch stroke, and tools		1,200 00
	1 stationary engine	6,000 00	5,000 00
	1 stock and dies		100 00
	1 set fluted rammers		500 00
	1 wood-sawing engine	1,300 00	650 00
	1 30-ton hydraulic jack		101 00
	1 15-ton hydraulic jack	112 50	83 00
	1 10-ton hydraulic jack	112 50	83 00
	Total		90,395 74

A schedule of all railroad property in the possession of and belonging to the United States on the 1st day of May, A. D. 1865, *and sold, by order of the Secretary of War, on credit, to the Alexandria, Loudon and Hampshire Railroad Company, on the terms specified in Executive Order of October* 14, 1865.

Date of sale.	Articles.	Cost.	Sold for.
	15 box cars	$12,761 10	$9,750 00
	1 baggage car	450 00	650 00
	7 flat cars	3,334 73	4,480 00
	8 flat cars	3,811 12	4,000 00
	1 stock car	900 00	650 00
	4 gondolas	1,869 56	2,640 00
	3 hand cars	345 00	148 50
	1 truck car	50 00	27 50
	1 iron car	96 00	96 00
	200 pounds Babbitt metal	122 00	62 00
	581 pounds ⅜-inch chain	63 91	79 89
	415 pounds ⅝-inch chain	45 65	31 13
	461 pounds gum springs	499 20	184 40
	165 second-hand car wheels, 33-inch	3,795 00	1,897 50
	20 truck wheels, 26-inch	490 00	300 00
	50 car axles, 18,180 pounds	1,818 00	1,272 60
	50 car axles, 13,000 pounds, second-hand.	1,300 00	390 00
	2,240 pounds straight couplings	156 80	112 00
	1,120 pounds crooked couplings	78 40	56 00
	10 tons cast-steel	500 00	3,000 00

Schedule of railroad property, &c.—Continued.

Date of sale.	Articles.	Cost.	Sold for.
	228 pounds Russia sheet iron	$45 60	$45 60
	711 feet 2-inch wrought pipe	1,322 46	195 53
	24 steel-plated frogs	597 84	1,200 00
	200,000 pounds railroad spikes	17,500 00	11,500 00
	40,000 pounds railroad spikes (old)	3,500 00	1,300 00
	8 car springs, 576 pounds	121 36	26 64
	12 broadaxes	40 08	24 00
	24 track adzes	60 00	48 00
	1 wood-sawing machine	650 00	650 00
	12 switch stands	165 00	360 00
	13,368 pounds iron castings	802 08	217 23
	500 pounds grindstones	20 00	5 00
	2 office stoves	32 90	5 50
	1 rail-punching machine	80 00	100 00
	100 feet 2-inch rubber hose	232 00	90 00
	2,500 pounds boat spikes	225 00	125 00
	5,000 pounds cut spikes	500 00	250 00
	1,000 pounds cut nails, 6*d*	100 00	56 25
	1,000 pounds cut nails, 8*d*	100 00	60 00
	1,000 pounds cut nails, 10*d*	100 00	56 25
	1,000 pounds cut nails, 12*d*	100 00	56 25
	1,000 pounds cut nails, 20*d*	100 00	53 75
	2 hydraulic jacks, 15 tons	225 00	164 50
	4 screw jacks, 28-inch	34 00	41 00
	4 screw jacks, 18-inch	34 00	40 00
	137 pounds new claw bars	13 70	12 67
	125 pounds new tamping bars	12 50	7 50
	206 pounds new pinch bars	20 60	20 09
	50 pounds new spike mauls	75 00	10 00
	362 pounds switch ropes (6)	90 50	79 64
	373 pounds 1¼ switch ropes	93 25	76 70
	716 pounds 1½ switch ropes	179 00	147 23
	125 pounds ¾ switch ropes	31 25	25 70
	41 pounds ½ switch ropes	10 25	8 43
	4 chain vices	60 00	80 00
	2 parallel vices	54 50	40 00
	3 dozen Ames's shovels	46 80	45 00
	1 dozen new shovels	15 60	12 00
	2 dozen pick handles	3 84	5 50
	4 dozen maul handles	7 68	11 00
	1 grindstone frame	6 50	6 13
	1 dozen white lanterns	18 00	36 00
	1½ dozen red lanterns	36 00	21 00
	2 sets blacksmith's tools	61 50	61 50
	2 anvils, 427 pounds	98 21	38 96
	2 bellows	63 26	24 00
	2 new boring machines	14 00	14 00
	2 cross-cut saws	10 90	10 00
	6 handsaws	6 00	7 50
	2½ reams emery cloth	108 02	25 00
	50 quires emery paper	12 00	8 50
	2 1½-inch tackle blocks	11 10	10 00
	2 1¼-inch tackle blocks	11 10	9 00
	4 1-inch tackle blocks	22 20	16 00
	108,885 feet 3-inch pine	4,028 74	2,831 01
	425,000 feet pine timber	17,000 00	9,562 50
	49,530 feet ¾ pine boards	1,832 61	1,857 38
	1 pile-driving engine	3,740 00	525 00
	1 pile-driving screw	450 00	450 00
	Total	87,418 40	62,592 96

A schedule of railroad property in the possession of and belonging to the United States on the 1st day of May, A. D. 1865, *and sold by order of the Secretary of War, on credit, to the Wilmington and Weldon Railroad Company, on the terms specified in Executive Orders of August* 8 *and October* 14, 1865.

Date of sale.		Articles.	Cost.	Sold for.
1865.				
October	5	125 tons railroad iron	$14,375 00	$10,000 00
November	1	500 tons railroad iron	57,500 00	40,000 00
	20	45 flat cars	21,437 55	23,700 00
	20	2 locomotive engines	22,250 00	28,500 00
	20	10 rack cars	4,763 90	5,000 00
	20	5 box cars	4,253 70	2,800 00
		Total	124,580 15	*110,000 00

* The two locomotive engines have been transferred to the Orange and Alexandria Railroad Company, and all instalments and interest due to July 1 paid, to wit, $9,979 74.

A schedule of railroad property in the possession of and belonging to the United States on the 1st day of May, A. D. 1865, *and sold, on credit, to the Western North Carolina Railroad Company, on the terms specified in Executive Order of October* 14, 1865.

Date of sale.		Articles.	Cost.	Sold for.
1865.				
December	11	7,500 pounds railroad spikes	$5,625 00	$450 00
		800 pounds 7-inch boat spikes	72 00	48 00
		2,000 pounds 18d cut nails	180 00	120 00
		2,000 pounds 10d cut nails	220 00	120 00
		1,500 pounds 12d cut nails	165 00	90 00
		19 long-handled shovels	24 70	28 50
		8 dozen Ames's shovels	108 00	120 00
		4,800 pounds railroad chairs	402 00	288 00
		150 feet 12-inch leather belting	270 00	285 00
		150 feet 4-inch leather belting	187 00	85 50
		150 feet 3-inch leather belting	187 00	63 00
		50 rubber springs, 393 pounds	471 60	432 30
		24 rubber springs	52 80	48 40
		4 tires, 3,420 pounds	889 20	752 40
		4 tires, 3,340 pounds	868 40	734 80
		6 box stoves	156 00	60 00
		3 Fairbanks's platform scales	187 71	75 00
		1 counter scale	17 60	15 00
		118 pounds rope	29 50	25 96
		12 26-inch truck wheels	294 00	300 00
		16 pair elliptic springs, 4,800 pounds	1,032 00	960 00
		2 grindstones, 680 pounds	57 80	20 40
		24 bench screws	20 88	18 00
		1 universal chuck	63 50	55 00
		369 pounds tamping bars	44 28	25 83
		549 pounds claw bars	65 88	65 88
		217 pounds spike mauls	65 10	65 10
		24 switch locks, (48 keys)	48 00	24 00
		370 pounds $\frac{3}{16}$ tank iron	22 20	29 60
		125 pounds tank rivets	17 50	18 75
		150 pounds plate washers	33 00	22 50
		6 papers brads	9 00	60
		38 gross screws	39 90	19 00
		440 pounds lay screws	101 20	88 00
		60 pounds wire	13 80	6 00
		750 pounds square nuts	90 00	105 00
		500 pounds hexagonal nuts	90 00	80 00
		440 pounds white lead	88 00	66 00
		150 pounds dry lead	30 00	28 00

Schedule of railroad property, &c.—Continued.

Date of sale.	Articles.	Cost.	Sold for.
1865.			
December 11	56 pounds chrome green	$22 40	$16 80
	72 pounds chrome yellow	30 96	25 20
	48 pounds patent dryer	7 92	7 20
	3 pounds burnt umber	4 80	90
	8 pounds raw sienna	2 50	3 20
	18 pounds light scarlet	9 00	9 00
	12 pounds extra vermilion	42 00	24 00
	2,479 pounds iron	165 26	136 35
December 12	6 sides lace leather	24 00	6 12
	405 pounds waste	113 40	27 33
	2 tape-lines	2 80	3 00
	2 head-lights	210 00	220 00
	46 head-light chimneys	13 34	13 80
	50 feet rubber hose	100 00	116 50
	48 crucibles	156 00	48 00
	108 files, half-round bastard	102 60	108 00
	84 files, flat bastard	79 80	84 00
	12 files, square bastard	11 40	12 00
	24 files, 2d cut	22 80	24 00
	24 engine oilers	16 56	12 00
	20 monkey-wrenches	Captured.	48 00
	36 pairs brass butts	9 00	9 00
	312 pairs cast-iron butts	49 92	19 44
	22 pounds finishing nails	4 40	4 40
	12 brass flush bolts	8 28	3 60
	2 Riddle's "Malden wire"	3 00	3 00
	24 axes	42 00	42 00
	4 broadaxes	13 32	10 00
	2 hydraulic jacks	225 00	120 00
	4 screws, jack	66 64	36 00
	120½ gallons sperm oil	289 20	307 28
	8 boxes tin	186 64	154 00
	24 paint brushes	30 00	18 00
	1 boring machine, complete	Captured.	10 00
	2 crosscut saws	10 00	10 00
	2 reams sand-paper	10 00	15 00
	6 railroad adzes	15 00	12 00
	78 feet gas-pipe	34 32	11 70
	33 pounds rubber packing	49 50	19 80
	12 white lights	18 00	36 00
	4 brass faucets	14 60	3 00
	350 coach screws	42 00	32 40
	200 pounds Venetian red	30 00	30 00
	20 pounds chrome green	8 00	6 00
	1 Stanwood cutter	8 50	3 00
	7 boxes glass	62 13	67 00
	45 pounds rope	11 25	20 25
	1 bench vice	17 17	8 00
	2 vices	34 34	12 04
	526 pounds sheet-iron	63 12	199 88
	62 pounds Russia iron	Captured.	18 60
	418 pounds cast-steel	167 20	104 50
	1,245 pounds spring steel	498 00	199 20
	30 kegs nails	271 50	240 00
	313 pounds nuts, square	65 73	62 60
	300 pounds washers	63 00	54 00
	1 pound Chinese vermilion	3 50	3 60
	5 pounds chrome yellow	2 15	1 25
	112 pounds litharge	22 40	13 44
	25 pounds yellow ochre	3 50	4 00
	25 pounds prussiate potash	20 00	30 00
	10 pounds vermilion	35 00	5 00
	3 pounds burnt umber	4 80	48

Schedule of railroad property, &c.—Continued.

Date of sale.	Articles.	Cost.	Sold for.
1865.			
December 12	40 gallons linseed oil	$51 20	$50 00
	10 pounds spelter	5 20	1 60
	64 pounds antimony	15 36	17 28
	1,457 pounds iron, assorted	97 13½	116 56
	1 set tinners' tools	102 95	180 00
	6 flat cars	2,858 34	3,480 00
	2,000 feet white pine flooring	95 00	120 00
	60 car wheels	Captured.	1,560 00
	Total	19,214 38½	14,269 82

A schedule of railroad property in the possession of and belonging to the United States on the 1st day of May, A. D. 1865, *and sold, by order of the Secretary of War, on credit, to the Atlantic and North Carolina Railroad Company, on the terms specified in Executive Order of October* 14, 1865.

Date of sale.	Articles.	Cost.	Sold for.
1865.			
December 3	3 hand cars	$345 00	$300 00
	600 bushels of coal	300 00	342 86
	4,818 feet white pine flooring	313 17	289 08
	11,567 feet yellow pine flooring	751 85	694 02
	206 pounds block tin	131 84	92 70
	50 feet belting	62 50	22 50
	14 pounds zinc metal	3 08	2 52
	30 pounds block zinc	4 05	5 40
	63 pounds antimony	15 12	37 80
	18 rubber springs	21 60	27 00
	355 pounds waste	99 00	88 75
	25 boxes tin	583 25	625 00
	30 car wheels, (double plated)	870 00	750 00
	2 locomotive engines	18,000 00	29,000 00
	7 box cars	5,955 15	4,340 00
	20 flat cars	9,527 86	11,600 00
	5 rack cars	2,381 95	2,500 00
	50 kegs railroad spikes	450 00	320 50
	30 kegs bridge spikes	270 00	187 50
	3 engine oilers	2 07	1 50
	3 oil cans	1 92	1 50
	1 red light	2 00	3 00
	2 white lights	3 00	6 00
	2 packing wrenches	5 40	50
	3 monkey wrenches	Captured.	6 00
	42 gallons sperm oil	100 80	94 50
	4 pinch bars	9 52	11 20
	1 hydraulic jack	112 50	80 00
	1 carpenter's maul	58	50
	1 hand axe	2 00	60
	2 handled axes	4 12	2 00
	1 cross-cut saw	5 00	2 00
	1 handsaw	2 13	1 50
	1 railroad adze	2 50	1 00
	6 claw bars	18 96	6 00
	6 track mauls	9 96	8 40
	2 chairs	10 90	9 60
	1 tallow can	69	50
	Total	40,388 83	51,461 93

No. 5.—*Schedule of property sold at auction for cash by General H. L. Robinson, assistant quartermaster, and Captain J. D. Stubbs, assistant quartermaster, since May* 1, 1865.

Schedule of railroad property in the possession of and belonging to the United States on the first day of May, A. D. 1865, *and sold at public auction by Brevet General H. L. Robinson, assistant quartermaster.*

Date of sale.		Articles.	Cost.	Am't received.
1865.				
September	11	6 locomotive engines	$139,050 00	$64,950 00
	21	4 locomotive engines	111,240 00	44,200 00
	25	50 freight cars	42,537 00	30,240 00
	27	84 freight cars	71,463 00	45,055 00
October	3	27 locomotive engines	671,550 66	310,610 00
	4	5½ sets car trucks	2,750 00	2,117 50
		14 cars, (platform)	6,669 60	6,550 00
		157 cars, (freight)	133,567 75	88,350 00
	11	2,214$\frac{566}{2240}$ tons railroad iron	287,451 66	161,698 21
	13	10 freight cars	8,507 40	6,100 00
		12 flat cars	5,716 80	5,700 00
		1 passenger car	1,517 68	1,075 00
		1 locomotive engine	27,810 00	11,700 00
		1 set box-car trucks	500 00	300 00
		6 freight cars	5,104 50	2,340 00
		11 flat cars	5,240 40	4,670 00
		2 locomotive engines	21,345 00	21,100 00
		1 locomotive engine	17,810 00	15,000 00
	17	2 locomotive engines	5,300 00	19,000 00
		1 passenger car	1,517 68	1,350 00
		1 hospital car	900 00	670 00
		5 freight cars	4,253 75	2,350 00
		149 tons railroad iron	19,341 69	7,375 50
		26 locomotive engines	256,215 40	294,600 00
		1 stock car	900 00	485 00
		92 freight cars	78,269 00	53,000 00
		32 flat cars	15,244 80	15,200 00
		5 old cars	4,253 70	1,300 00
		4 hospital cars	3,600 00	2,790 00
		185 freight cars	157,388 75	108,800 00
		15 stock cars	13,500 00	7,125 00
		6 stock cars	5,400 00	2,970 00
		45 freight cars	38,283 75	19,600 00
		4 locomotive engines	30,210 00	46,050 00
		2 passenger cars	3,035 36	2,750 00
		1 wreck car	900 00	560 00
		1 pay car	900 00	800 00
		7 stock cars	6,300 00	2,835 00
		3 locomotive engines	20,800 00	19,650 00
		3 baggage cars	1,350 00	1,830 00
		31 freight cars	26,373 25	23,750 00
		26 flat cars	12,386 40	16,640 00
		578$\frac{580}{2240}$ tons railroad iron	75,060 56	41,683 07
		4 locomotive engines	18,500 00	20,050 00
		16 flat cars	7,622 40	7,840 00
		2 locomotive engines	24,720 00	32,900 00
		23 flat cars	10,957 20	12,580 00
		4 freight cars	3,403 00	1,360 00
		1 locomotive engine	5,000 00	1,500 00
		35 flat cars	16,664 00	20,300 00
		15 freight cars	12,761 25	7,500 00
		4 flat cars	1,905 60	2,000 00
		2 passenger cars	3,035 40	1,900 00
November	8	10 freight cars, (5-feet gauge)	12,500 00	5,000 00

Schedule of railroad property, &c.—Continued.

Date of sale.	Articles.	Cost.	Am't received.
1865.			
November 22	1 hydraulic wheel press	$1,133 00	$1,000 00
	1 railroad drill, large		900 00
	1 punching and shearing machine		1,525 00
	4 15-ton jacks	604 72	360 00
	100 claw bars	16 00	270 00
	40 dozen files	398 40	220 00
	6 head-lights, (kerosene)	510 60	390 00
Dec. 12 to 15.	11 old desks and tables		22 55
	1 desk		3 50
	1 counter scale	17 05	5 25
	1 desk		4 25
	1 case drawers		7 00
	69 sash		62 10
	4 sets match planes	19 00	2 60
	1 20-inch circular saw	18 00	10 00
	101 sash		99 99
	4 stocks and dies	177 00	26 00
	2,115 pounds rubber packing	2,432 25	1,247 74
	47 feet second-hand rubber hose	94 00	17 13
	3 head-lights	255 30	69 00
	100 tons wrought scrap iron	15,000 00	4,750 00
	3 forges, portable	89 25	86 00
	1 pair ways		20 00
	2 scows		325 00
	250 pounds curled hair	126 25	125 00
	27 feet leather belting	21 47	6 89
	30 steam gauges	871 95	96 00
	1,011 feet wrought pipe	1,880 46	1,011 00
	1 circular saw		60 00
	1 circular saw		12 50
	1,667 pounds sheet copper	1,239 14	800 16
	294 pounds bar copper	205 26	141 12
	25 pounds sal ammonia	18 50	4 88
	67 pounds oxalic acid	45 23	10 05
	23 pounds copper wire	17 25	8 05
	2,312 pounds roofing felt	173 40	52 02
	852 feet belting leather	677 34	527 53
	15 water tanks	975 00	1,455 00
	37 wheelbarrows	148 00	40 70
	1 desk		6 75
	111 stoves	2,887 11	230 15
	1,200 pounds sheet iron	174 00	110 00
	212 pounds spelter solder	106 00	65 72
	9 boxes tin	210 33	150 75
	6 dozen axes	240 48	85 50
	11,194 pounds boiler iron		587 69
	669 pounds 3-inch chain		91 99
	252 pounds anchors		13 86
	10,945 pounds brass castings	6,348 10	2,832 02
	1 desk		3 00
	1 grindstone	14 52	4 60
	Lot file handles		1 15
	2 chain vices	50 00	18 00
	17 feet second-hand belting	13 51	51
	13$\frac{130}{2240}$ tons cast-steel	10,383 75	3,917 41
	770 pounds blister steel		57 75
	2 dozen chopping axes	80 16	22 50
	10 timber buggies	59 50	10 00
	100 pounds top mauls	150 00	100 00
	40 gallons varnish	288 54	70 00
	142 dozen tin cups	129 22	15 62
	222 dozen tin plates	306 36	28 31
	422 mess pans	101 28	30 60

Schedule of railroad property, &c.—Continued.

Date of sale.	Articles.	Cost.	Am't received.
1865.			
Dec. 12 to 15.	170 dippers	$63 75	$7 23
	410 dozen forks and knives	311 60	92 25
	229 dish pans	....	49 24
	104 tin boilers	....	46 96
	121 slicks	352 50	84 70
	259 pounds pike pole points	....	23 31
	123 grindstones	1,955 70	140 88
	20 springs	....	195 27
	9 water coolers	45 00	27 00
	2 caloric engines	....	415 00
	27,700 pounds railroad spikes, 5-inch	2,093 00	1,419 63
	7,506 pounds old stove pipe	1,989 09	215 80
	11 sets blacksmith tools	....	338 25
	1,261 pounds axles	107 18	31 53
	7,470 pounds brass trimmings	4,708 75	1,120 50
	11,818 pounds scrap brass	7,386 25	2,718 14
	8 tons scrap steel	6,272 00	532 00
	24 feet rubber belting	18 00	4 80
	20 $\frac{400}{2240}$ tons spring steel	18,984 00	2,118 75
	3 box stoves	48 00	7 50
	2 scales	34 10	30 00
	17½ dozen chalk lines	30 36	14 88
	41 screw jacks	348 50	250 00
	44½ tons old car wheels	....	1,846 75
	14 pairs old truck wheels	686 00	429 00
	6 old wheels	137 88	34 00
	32,228 pounds cast chairs	3,222 80	443 14
	9 circular saws	225 00	130 50
	1 spirit level	2 05	1 13
	138 tons old T iron	17,913 78	6,348 00
	41 feet rubber hose	95 12	28 70
	530 feet hose	1,298 50	567 50
	484 pounds brass wire	220 22	215 38
	154 gallons varnish	634 48	215 70
	3½ tons tire iron	....	304 50
	37½ tons axle iron	7,980 00	2,812 50
	3½ tons tire iron	....	304 50
	44 chipping hammers	44 00	25 90
	1 box broken wrenches	....	11 00
	44 chipping hammers	44 00	25 06
	23,040 pounds railroad chairs	2,304 00	691 20
	20 screw jacks	367 00	296 00
	247 gas pipe tongs	869 44	61 75
	13 screw jacks	238 61	192 25
	1 set tinners' tools	....	262 00
	1,350 pounds lead pipe	135 00	151 88
	1 barrel pitch	13 10	4 00
	70 gallons tar	52 50	11 20
	2 barrels pitch	26 20	8 00
	90 pounds white chalk	4 05	1 80
	35 pounds red chalk	....	2 89
	44 pounds steel wire	....	8 80
	1 barrel pitch	13 10	4 00
	93 pounds white chalk	....	1 86
	950 pounds iron wire	228 00	106 88
	2,624 pounds washers	590 40	270 19
	52 pounds Babbitt metal	31 98	16 12
	8½ boxes tin	198 64	129 00
	27 sets grindstone fixtures	57 65	16 88
	2 reams sandpaper	11 00	6 50
	26 pounds Babbitt metal	15 99	8 06
	10 reams emery cloth	405 80	100 00
	1¾ reams sandpaper	9 62	5 64

Schedule of railroad property, &c.—Continued.

Date of sale.	Articles.	Cost.	Am't received.
1865.			
Dec. 12 to 15.	1 scales	....	$12 00
	1 dozen pint oilers	....	2 52
	8 reams emery cloth	$324 64	80 00
	2 marble slabs	27 00	15 50
	26 gallons tar	19 50	4 16
	3 barrels pitch	39 30	12 00
	117 augers	118 17	29 25
	2 scales	....	24 00
	3½ dozen pint oilers	....	8 82
	6 reams paper	....	64 50
	308 quires paper emery	73 92	52 36
	105 saw blades	210 00	36 75
	12 dozen chopping axes	290 16	132 00
	268 gross screws	407 36	58 17
	310 pounds lye	88 35	43 40
	725 pounds soda	68 87	29 00
	2 desks	....	7 50
	1 desk	....	4 50
	1 cupboard	....	4 25
	1 table and drawing board	....	5 25
	1 wardrobe	....	3 75
	2 cupboards	....	6 75
	2 desks and cases	....	22 25
	4 chairs and stools	....	4 25
	Lot car window sash	....	32 00
	3 bedsteads	....	5 25
	7 stoves	182 08	53 25
	9 circular saws	180 00	121 00
	1 stationery engine	....	610 00
	4 pumping engines	....	3,000 00
	Lot cant-hook handles	....	4 00
	1 truck car	115 00	30 00
	105 tons cast-iron scrap	12,936 00	3,832 50
	118¾ tons cast-iron scrap	14,630 00	4,037 50
	114 tons old car wheels	....	5,016 00
	4 locomotive tires	1,647 00	296 78
	1 locomotive tire	411 65	29 40
	8 wheels	183 84	50 00
	56 wheels	1,286 88	840 00
	57,856 pounds railroad chairs	5,785 60	1,771 84
	389,777 pounds castings	13,335 50	6,333 88
	3,100 pounds old files	2,232 00	325 50
	5 dozen mess pans	24 40	14 00
	90 dish pans	....	67 50
	2¾ dozen tallow pots	....	9 62
1865 and 1866.	57½ dozen tin cups	52 32	43 13
Dec. and Jan.	1,000 pounds 5-inch cut spikes	90 00	60 00
	1,000 pounds 6-inch cut spikes	90 00	60 00
	81,494 feet pine timber	3,259 76	3,056 03
	10,000 feet pine timber	400 00	375 00
	47,529 feet hemlock	1,378 87	1,782 34
	56,424 feet pine lumber	2,256 96	2,115 90
	1 desk	....	4 50
	46 tin buckets	....	6 90
	137 gallons linseed oil	219 20	191 80
	1 yawl boat	106 56	86 00
	6 caldrons	210 00	55 00
	14 ventilators and pipes	....	35 00
	1 hand lathe	100 00	40 00
	Lot wooden mauls	....	55
	506¼ tons strap rails	....	30,657 63
	1 pumping engine	....	815 00
	1 pile-driving engine	3,740 00	525

Schedule of railroad property, &c.—Continued.

Date of sale.	Articles.	Cost.	Am't received.
1865–'66.			
Dec. and Jan.	64 feet rubber hose	$148 48	$78 72
	68 feet rubber belting	51 00	5 78
	48 feet leather		15 36
	1 portable saw-mill	1,300 00	1,375 00
	39 vices	1,327 17	312 00
	9,360 pounds frog points		245 70
	10 sets switch stands and fixtures		265 00
	34 pounds antimony	32 98	6 80
	116 gas pipe joints	72 79	21 00
	1 morticing machine		26 00
	1 pipe cutter	11 00	11 00
	1 counter scales	17 05	4 25
	11 clamp screws	5 50	5 50
	2,702 sash		567 42
	135 feet red glass	101 25	28 35
	173 boxes glass		881 35
	13 switch ropes		397 54
	22 water tanks	1,430 00	2,112 00
	2 truck cars	230 00	192 00
	5,678 pounds frog points		567 80
	17,877 pounds axles	2,026 06	1,251 39
	20 patent frogs		290 00
	21,100 pounds boat spikes	2,479 25	1,055 00
	901 pounds chain	90 10	67 58
	500 feet rubber hose	1,160 00	550 00
	3,045 pounds rubber springs	3,654 00	1,582 50
	9 tank hose	242 55	15 30
	3½ dozen boy axes		23 06
	5 hydraulic jacks	750 00	350 00
	3 tons old chain	1,747 20	204 00
	8½ tons bolt iron	1,275 00	612 00
	18½ tons car repair material		1,239 50
	8,906 pounds axles	385 93	267 18
	1,851 pounds grindstones	92 55	46 28
	1 portable forge	30 75	30 00
	4 stoves	104 05	42 00
	108,000 shingles	972 00	918 00
	672 pounds rubber springs	806 40	302 40
	10 sets switch stands	137 50	250 00
	400 feet wire cable	150 00	150 00
	Lot spigots		1 05
	1 set morticing chisels		1 65
	2 buildings		60 00
	36 pounds sole leather	13 68	10 80
	14 skins		56 00
	4 boring machines		42 00
	1 set chisels	8 52	5 00
	2⅙ dozen hatchets	17 55	15 17
	7⅓ dozen garden hoes	88 00	44 00
	2 dozen handled axes	57 60	29 00
	269 augers	271 69	58 52
	9 dozen escutcheons	11 52	90
	1 set chisels	8 52	2 00
	1 building		30 00
	5 buildings		130 00
	4 buildings		50 00
	1 building		30 00
	1 building		70 00
	2 buildings		113 00
Jan. 1866.	Lot miscellaneous tools		273 92
1865–'66.			
Dec. and Jan.	1 blacksmith's fan	125 00	76 00

Schedule of railroad property, &c.—Continued.

Date of sale.	Articles.	Cost.	Am't received.
1865–'66.			
Dec. and Jan.	109 adzes	$299 75	$98 10
	1 platform scales	62 58	10 50
	16 dozen axes	432 00	221 00
	4 coal scuttles	5 00	5 00
	81 dozen tin cups	73 71	54 68
	11 dozen switch locks	231 00	110 00
	29 steel squares	37 70	29 73
	179 gross screws	272 08	45 68
	1 counter scales	17 05	3 50
	13 sashes		6 25
	9 blacksmith's bellows	272 08	58 50
	100 Sibley stoves		1 50
	8 copper boilers		37 60
	19 boring machines	122 50	52 25
	1,744 pounds ox-chain	1,621 92	85 02
	480 augers	484 80	96 00
	26 smooth planes	35 10	5 85
	8,687 pounds lead pipe	868 70	694 96
	14 second-hand padlocks	17 50	3 75
	52 pounds bell cord	28 60	17 16
	400 carriage bolts	26 00	10 00
	83 pairs strap hinges	52 29	15 59
	5 plough planes	42 50	11 00
	7 drawing knives	11 62	2 28
	23 gouges	15 52	92
	22 spirit levels	45 10	13 20
	133 planes	166 25	69 55
	190 chisels		30 88
	11 trowels	19 25	2 20
	149 wrenches	596 00	137 83
	1 signal wagon		82 00
	1 portable forge	29 75	4 00
	4½ dozen side lamps		21 77
	5 5/12 dozen No. 2 kerosene burners	17 16	2 71
	20½ dozen globe valves	705 80	19 00
	87 augers	87 87	24 88
	Lot benches, boxes, &c.		54 00
	1 second-hand cook-stove	26 00	18 00
	1 stockade		200 00
	11 rabbet planes	15 40	1 38
	1 spring balance	10 81	1 25
	14 coffins	98 00	7 00
	1 pair scales	17 05	4 00
	1⅜ dozen 5-inch barrel bolts	1 30	67
	2 5/12 dozen 6-inch brass knob bolts	20 63	2 42
	1 pound tinned rivets	62	25
	26 dozen pairs iron butts	26 00	10 40
	16¼ papers tacks	11 32	8 54
	12½ pounds copper burrs		8 50
	1⅜ dozen bibbs	60 00	20 59
	1 1/12 dozen patent faucets	5 23	1 59
	⅚ dozen try squares	8 20	2 00
	⅙ dozen short spirit levels	6 10	1 34
	8 hollow punches	38 64	4 60
	104 pairs strap hinges	65 52	28 04
	2 dozen painted buckets	10 13	5 00
	14 pounds copper rivets	11 90	9 10
	¾ dozen bibbs	27 00	9 38
	3 dozen fore planes	74 88	40 13
	2¼ gross camel hair pencils	94 50	5 63
	5 gallons varnish	20 60	30 00
	94 pounds lag screws	27 26	5 64

Schedule of railroad property, &c.—Continued.

Date of sale.	Articles.	Cost.	Am't received.
1865–'66.			
Dec. and Jan.	1,612 pounds galvanized iron	$290 16	$233 74
	1 saw gummer	21 00	22 00
	1,064 gross screws	1,617 28	740 29
	1 link machine	....	6 00
	$10\frac{1}{2}$ dozen car-window fasteners	39 06	18 38
	122 pounds finishing nails	24 40	16 17
	1 letter press	23 35	5 00
	$1\frac{1}{3}$ dozen 6-inch tower bolts	....	67
	$\frac{7}{12}$ dozen sail patterns	....	30
	$\frac{1}{4}$ dozen lock cocks	3 99	4 19
	6 sets firmer locket chisels	....	21 00
	$4\frac{7}{12}$ dozen door bolts	....	5 26
	$\frac{1}{4}$ dozen iron braces and bits	45 00	11 38
	394 feet rubber hose	914 08	295 00
	3 cleavers	15 00	1 80
	1 building	....	85 00
	200 pounds Russia iron	72 00	42 00
	17 box stoves	442 17	48 88
	7 office stoves	182 07	11 00
	25 coal scuttles	31 25	12 50
	45 box stoves	1,170 45	33 75
	2 monkey wrenches	6 25	5 60
	400 feet rubber hose	928 00	420 00
	3 hose nipples	....	7 50
	44 cook stoves and fixtures	1,144 44	836 00
	18 anvils (3,487 pounds)	5 94	297 09
	1 pumping engine	....	550 00
	297 blocks	3,415 50	762 46
	5,389 pounds claw bars	502 97	498 48
	845 pounds pinch bars	78 86	82 39
	1,477 bridge wrenches	4,421 00	110 78
	35,851 second-hand track bars	3,346 09	3,226 59
	133 taps and dies	....	101 08
	3 48-inch circular saws	636 00	83 25
	1,301 second-hand lanterns	1,951 50	650 50
	39 box vices	1,326 78	656 33
	13 hydraulic jacks	2,002 00	1,056 75
	2 head lights	170 20	89 00
	11 head light reflectors	....	77 00
	52 timber buggies	309 40	109 20
	$137\frac{1}{2}$ tons wrought scrap iron	43,120 00	7,112 50
	15 tons English T iron	1,947 15	780 00
	$54\frac{1}{4}$ tons second-hand iron	17,012 80	3,797 50
	$178\frac{1181}{2240}$ tons assorted bar iron	55,986 14	16,538 55
	$267\frac{1}{4}$ tons railroad iron	34,694 39	19,726 07
	104,352 pounds railroad chairs	10,435 20	2,959 12
	1 pair ways and hammers	....	116 00
	2 pairs ways framed	....	90 00
	260,733 feet 3-inch pine planks	9,125 65	6,779 06
	544,333 feet pine timber	21,773 32	12,248 62
	113 patent car springs	3,390 00	565 00
	1 steam hammer	2,051 00	1,450 00
	1,041 feet wrought pipe	895 20	286 28
	56,232 pounds old railroad spikes	5,060 88	1,827 54
	13,128 pounds 8-inch boat spikes	1,542 54	574 35
	115,588 pounds 7-inch boat spikes	13,681 59	5,779 40
	8,100 pounds 7-inch cut spikes	899 84	374 63
	34,100 pounds 6-inch cut spikes	3,367 34	1,705 00
	2,100 pounds 10d nails	178 50	112 88
	723 feet leather belting	578 40	130 14
	200 pounds rubber packing	300 00	124 00
	11 boxes 12 by 18 glass	110 00	61 88

Schedule of railroad property, &c.—Continued.

Date of sale.	Articles.	Cost.	Am't received.
1865–'66.			
Dec. and Jan.	16 boxes 18 by 22 glass	....	$104 00
	5,046 pounds old chain	$504 60	353 22
	8 boxes 20 by 24 double thick glass	....	56 20
	23 boxes 9 by 16 ground glass	....	97 75
	900 square feet spark netting	522 00	229 50
	2 marble slabs and mullers	27 00	9 00
	2,552 pounds assorted paints	....	382 80
	$104\frac{1}{2}$ dozen eagle Tripoli	104 50	47 03
	520 pounds pulverized rotten-stone	52 00	26 00
	338 pounds flour emery	37 18	28 73
	43 pounds pulverized pumice stone	4 30	3 33
	2,465 pounds assorted rivets	640 90	295 80
	$3\frac{97}{224}$ boxes 12 by 121 bright tin	82 25	57 07
	$12\frac{81}{224}$ boxes 10 by 14 bright tin	289 50	210 15
	775 boxes lantern glasses	837 00	46 50
	6,364 pounds nuts	1,294 01	551 78
	31 $1\frac{1}{4}$-inch tackle blocks	186 00	155 00
	12 dozen axes	289 44	168 00
	48 patent sheaves	86 80	36 00
	$5\frac{1}{2}$ dozen 1-gallon oil cans	....	20 63
	8 glue pots	10 40	10 80
	202 mallets	117 10	50 50
	1 universal chuck, 12-inch	63 50	40 00
	2 hydraulic jacks, 30-ton	357 84	200 00
	3 circular saws, 10-inch	22 50	9 00
	3 circular saws, 12-inch	27 00	9 00
	$338\frac{3}{4}$ pounds turned iron rivets	94 85	99 93
	27 dozen pairs iron butts, 3-inch	27 00	18 90
	13 dozen pairs iron butts, $2\frac{3}{4}$-inch	13 00	9 10
	$42\frac{1}{6}$ dozen pairs iron butts, $2\frac{1}{2}$-inch	42 30	27 41
	$4\frac{3}{4}$ dozen papers tacks, 8-ounce	4 75	2 50
	1 dozen papers tacks, 7-ounce	1 00	53
	15 dozen papers tacks, 6-ounce	15 00	7 88
	$7\frac{2}{3}$ dozen papers tacks, 5-ounce	7 67	4 03
	$3\frac{1}{3}$ dozen papers tacks, 4-ounce	3 33	1 75
	14 boring machines	91 00	50 40
	49 tackle blocks	372 00	290 00
	1 dozen hand screws, 18-inch	....	5 52
	$1\frac{1}{3}$ dozen hand screws, 15-inch	....	5 60
	27 notch blocks	....	96 00
	128 pounds marlines	75 04	17 92
	$51\frac{1}{2}$ dozen Ames's shovels	1,287 50	664 50
	1,369 pounds steel track mauls	410 70	246 42
	359 pounds track chisels	....	64 62
	387 pounds railroad punches	135 45	54 18
	12 dozen bastard files, 6-inch	....	12 60
	$8\frac{1}{12}$ dozen bastard files, 4-inch	....	6 44
	$\frac{9}{12}$ dozen try-squares, 10-inch	7 38	3 00
	$\frac{8}{12}$ dozen try-squares, $7\frac{1}{2}$-inch	6 56	2 00
	3 hollow punches, $\frac{3}{8}$-inch	16 20	1 35
	4 hollow punches, $\frac{1}{2}$-inch	21 60	2 40
	4 hollow punches, $\frac{5}{8}$-inch	21 60	2 40
	728 pounds chain, $\frac{1}{2}$-inch	119 20	75 53
	$3\frac{3}{8}$ gross gimlets	24 30	16 44
	3 dozen flat varnish brushes, $2\frac{1}{2}$-inch	15 00	10 88
	$4\frac{5}{6}$ dozen flat varnish brushes, 3-inch	24 16	29 42
	$\frac{11}{12}$ dozen paint brushes, 000000	27 50	6 88
	$\frac{3}{4}$ dozen paint brushes, 0000	15 75	8 25
	$\frac{2}{3}$ dozen paint brushes, assorted	13 33	3 67
	$\frac{1}{4}$ dozen varnish brushes, 0000	....	3 00
	15 dirt carts	....	2,850 00
	8 coils wire cable, 3,200 feet	9,600 00	1,440 00
	1 oil tank	....	16 00

Schedule of railroad property, &c.—Continued.

Date of sale.	Articles.	Cost.	Am't received.
1865–'66.			
Dec. and Jan.	39 gallons brown japan and tank	$125 00	$58 50
	31 gallons black japan and tank	101 00	62 00
	42 gallons coach varnish	276 50	168 00
	68 pounds pumice stone	6 80	2 72
	96 pounds muriatic acid	18 24	3 36
	280 pounds borax	221 20	84 00
	24 feet second-hand leather belting, 5-inch	19 08	3 60
	27 feet second-hand leather belting, 7-inch	21 47	5 40
	346 feet rubber hose, 2½-inch	802 72	432 50
	52 feet tank hose, 9-inch	....	88 40
	12 feet second-hand hose, 4-inch	29 40	4 80
	26 feet second-hand hose, 6-inch	63 70	14 30
	22 feet second-hand hose, 9-inch	53 90	9 24
	1,780 pounds log screws, ⅝ by 5-inch	516 20	155 75
	202 pounds railroad rivets, 1⅛ by ⅜-inch	50 50	20 20
	172 pounds tank hose rivets, 1⅛ by ⅜-inch	44 52	17 20
	213 pounds sheet steel	93 90	53 25
	330 pounds sheet brass	206 25	165 00
	1,900 pounds tallow	256 50	114 00
	4 tires, 3,520 pounds	6 54	352 00
	1 planer	....	3,000 00
	1 lathe	4,500 00	3,275 00
	1 boring machine	1,025 00	1,105 00
	2 hand drills	....	158 00
	3,224 pounds axle iron	306 28	193 44
	158 pounds L joints	....	23 70
	15 T joints	....	3 00
	14 union joints, 2-inch	....	7 00
	34 nipples, 1-inch	5 27	2 72
	59 gross brass screws, 1½-inch	91 75	79 65
	26 gross brass screws, ⅝-inch	61 10	7 80
	62 gross round head screws	124 00	62 00
	36 dozen white lanterns	2,183 76	864 00
	2⅙ dozen red lanterns	98 07	75 83
	7½ dozen handsaws	135 00	112 50
	45 crosscut saws, 5½ feet	225 00	146 25
	5 slates	9 45	10 00
	20 slicks, 3-inch	50 00	20 00
	12 dozen maul handles	27 60	15 00
	12 dozen pick handles	30 24	19 80
	12 dozen axe handles	28 80	19 20
	12 dozen Ten Eyck axes	312 48	147 00
	$3\frac{5}{12}$ dozen track adzes	112 75	54 67
	$7\frac{8}{12}$ dozen carpenters' adzes	253 00	115 00
	5 tinners' furnaces	....	10 00
	48¼ dozen handled axes	97 22	675 50
	2 platform cars	1,270 00	800 00
	18 shad-belly bridges	....	252 00
	1,470 pounds blacksmiths' tools	....	121 28
	45 cook-stoves and fixtures	1,170 76	630 00
	1 bell	....	20 00
	2 marline spikes	....	2 20
	1,212 pounds steel tools	484 80	181 80
	821 pounds iron tools	147 78	123 15
	111 handsaws	166 50	94 35
	110 mallets	64 46	7 70
	30 taps	48 84	54 00
	40 chipping hammers	40 00	24 40
	605 pounds railroad forks	....	30 25
	35 pairs strap hinges, 14-inch	22 05	9 80
	19 copper strainers	....	9 50
	162 hinged hasps, 8-inch	88 12	21 06
	150 pounds lampwick	360 00	127 50

Schedule of railroad property, &c.—Continued.

Date of sale.	Articles.	Cost.	Am't received.
1865–'66.			
Dec. and Jan.	10 globe valves, $\frac{3}{4}$-inch	$29 41	$12 50
	1 globe valve, 1-inch	2 94	2 00
	$1\frac{7}{12}$ dozen tape-measures, 100 feet	30 47	17 42
	$2\frac{7}{12}$ dozen monkey wrenches, 15-inch	96 93	46 50
	2 sets chisels, turners'	28 00	10 50
	50 gas-pipe couplings, 2-inch	33 50	5 00
	$6\frac{1}{2}$ dozen caulking irons	39 00	26 00
	$1\frac{7}{12}$ dozen caulking mallets	28 50	9 50
	14 carpenters' stone hammers		21 00
	44 coffee boilers		33 00
	$11\frac{1}{2}$ dozen quart oilers		89 70
	10 dozen tea-kettles		10 00
	$5\frac{10}{12}$ dozen $\frac{1}{2}$-gallon oil cans	48 51	23 33
	169 pounds old brass	94 64	38 87
	14 spiking hammers		21 42
	32 shovels	41 79	11 20
	15 tamping bars		7 50
	4 track gauges		80
	2 raising bars		25 00
	15 lining		24 00
	10 cold chisels	10 00	6 00
	18 picks	29 01	9 00
	4 claw bars		9 20
	2 adzes	5 50	2 20
	2 crank cars	250 00	99 00
	2 water crank pumps	177 30	180 00
	2 tank stoves	52 03	24 00
	2 lamps		1 00
	39,333 feet old timber	1,573 32	737 49
	1 drill press		100 00
	$1\frac{1}{2}$ dozen saw-sets	24 34	1 50
February, '66	2 desks		5 25
	2 scales		6 75
	2 tackle blocks	24 00	14 75
	1 broad rule	2 15	1 00
	2 carboys	7 00	2 00
	11 feet second-hand leather belting, 11-inch	8 76	3 30
	126 feet rubber belting	94 50	18 90
	105 feet rubber hose	243 60	26 25
	1 pump		4 00
	51 feet rubber hose, $\frac{3}{4}$-inch	118 32	11 22
	5 dozen kerosene lamp shades	30 50	4 63
	4 sash planes	8 00	1 60
	19,077 pounds rope	5,341 56	3,922 71
	2 desks		5 50
	1,421 pounds tarred rope	483 14	238 02
	1 skiff		25 00
	21,399 feet old plank	748 96	492 18
	5,752 feet old poplar		143 80
	1,933 feet walnut		183 64
	17,741 feet assorted lumber	709 64	496 75
	1,400 pounds 8d nails	119 00	84 00
	1 cook stove and fixtures	75 00	31 50
	1 portable engine	5,400 00	610 00
	1 portable saw mill	4,300 00	1,325 00
	14 tons old grate bars		143 50
	4,198 feet belting	3,345 80	2,276 84
	2 tables		1 20
	1 building		135 00
	$\frac{1}{2}$ dozen try-squares	4 92	78
	1 slick	2 50	1 25
	3 desks		9 25
	3 watering cans	6 00	1 35

Schedule of railroad property, &c.—Continued.

Date of sale.	Articles.	Cost.	Am't received.
1866.			
February.	201 camp kettles	$286 42	$22 11
	9 coal bunks	11 25	4 05
	45 office stoves	1,170 76	191 25
	6 parlor stoves	156 10	24 00
	1,260 shovels and spades	1,645 56	333 90
	1,220 picks	1,966 64	585 60
	1 pumping engine		275 00
	19 caulking mallets	28 50	8 55
	5 boring machines	32 50	20 00
	5 head-light reflectors		45 00
	1 hay cutter		20 00
	146 sash, 876 pounds		78 84
	2 small cars	100 00	40 00
	2 new dirt cars		150 00
	1 pile-driver and hammer		450 00
	5 floats		100 00
	22,895 feet old tank	698 29	303 36
	5,200 cross-ties	3,099 20	820 00
	107,500 feet old timber	4,300 00	1,075 00
	Lot old plank		250 00
	75,389 feet ash		1,507 78
	3 boilers		600 00
	4,250 nails	361 25	257 13
	838 feet second-hand belting	667 88	180 70
	145 feet second-hand hose		54 38
	443 pounds chain	46 95	33 23
	2 grindstones, 1,940 pounds	29 02	19 40
	258 pounds salt	12 90	1 29
	6 locomotive balances	165 00	2 40
	1 yawl boat	106 56	21 00
	4 skiffs	686 80	76 00
	12 dozen axes	290 16	162 00
	1 dozen switch locks		10 50
	1,000 pounds top mauls		100 00
	29 grindstones	420 79	107 30
	8,797 pounds lining bars	825 71	791 73
	1,310 pounds track chisels		196 50
	85 steel squares	110 50	46 75
	41 bench screws	35 87	16 40
	116 broadaxes	387 44	179 80
	108 saws	162 00	264 60
	5 boring machines	32 50	20 00
	2 platform scales	125 15	14 75
	756 pounds railroad tongs	113 40	49 14
	4 head lights	340 40	240 00
	1,178 pounds top mauls	353 40	129 58
	574 pounds sledges	114 80	78 93
	3,778 pounds spike mauls	1,133 40	576 15
	1,080 chopping axes	2,176 20	734 40
	87 timber jacks		65 25
	77 cant hooks and handles		43 12
	10 iron truck cars		520 00
	5 pairs track wheels	245 00	175 00
	1 engine track		205 00
	6 buildings		1,735 00
	108 gallons turpentine	350 56	87 48
	2 sets morticing chisels	28 00	3 50
	104 wood buckets	41 60	4 68
	92 coffee boilers		7 36
	1 planing machine		150 00
	1 bolt-cutting machine		35 00
	1 switch stand and fixtures		30 00
	104 pounds railroad tongs and forks		6 76

Schedule of railroad property, &c.—Continued.

Date of sale.	Articles.	Cost.	Am't received.
1866.			
February..	155 pounds lining bars	$14 46	$13 95
	40 pounds tamping bars	3 73	2 40
	45 pounds claw bars	4 30	4 16
	65 pounds spike mauls		13 00
	11 pounds sledges	2 20	1 57
	22 pounds cold chisels	8 80	3 30
	1 hand car	115 00	49 50
	1 iron car	2,500 00	52 00
	1 truck car		27 50
	1 saw	1 50	1 25
	2 axes	4 50	2 75
	1 chipping hammer	1 00	75
	1 pair ways and hammers		75 00
	86,667 feet old timber	3,466 68	1,625 00
	441 oil cans, tanks and pumps		97 02
	106 wash basins		7 95
	6 scoops	3 00	1 50
	30 cook stoves	2,250 00	109 50
	21,603 pounds second-hand rope	6,048 84	2,241 31
	99 broadaxes	330 66	159 39
	37 caulking chisels		7 40
	2 counter scales	34 10	4 25
	Lot crockery ware		16 00
	26 meat platters	65 00	20 80
	131 buck saws	131 00	58 95
	94 sash (564 lbs.)		60 63
	103 ox yokes	1,056 36	200 85
	79 track gauges		3 95
	37 truck cars		642 75
	3 large car boilers		9 00
	$2 \frac{1868}{2240}$ tons wrought-iron draw-heads		198 38
	$14 \frac{603}{2240}$ tons bolts	2,450 29	1,291 36
	42 car wheels	965 32	483 00
	51 pairs truck wheels	2,499 00	160 65
	$5\frac{1}{4}$ tons railroad iron	681 52	300 56
	5,100 pounds frog wings		140 25
	268,884 feet assorted hemlock		3 844 93
	113 gross screws	171 87	32 20
	2 derricks		33 00
	14,711 feet pine, $4 \times 1\frac{3}{4}$		441 33
	13,600 laths	408 00	59 50
	10 grindstones, (4,034 lbs.)	201 70	73 57
	39,489 pounds assorted nails	4,143 79	2,244 02
	12 emery wheels	360 00	90 00
	750 pounds resin	75 00	30 00
	100 pounds gum-shellac	132 00	35 00
	600 pounds plate washers	135 00	60 00
	4 screw jacks, (24 inches)	34 00	41 00
	150 cords wood		150 00
	25,249 feet plank		353 49
	2,000 feet oak lumber		28 00
	1 building		600 00
	Lot pine ties		800 00
	15,250 feet pine plank		244 00
	Lot pine ties		150 00
	6,000 feet square timber		600 00
March 9.	2 box freight cars	850 75	265 00
	1 old boiler		460 00
	1 locomotive engine, "J. J. Mare"		1,800 00
	1 locomotive engine, "Vulcan"	9,250 00	1,575 00
	1 locomotive engine, "Chickahominy"	7,800 00	5,000 00
	1 locomotive engine, "Maus"	9,000 00	7 275 00

Schedule of railroad property, &c.—Continued.

Date of sale.	Articles.	Cost.	Am't received.
1866.			
April 4, 10, 11, and 12.	26 cords wood		$58 50
	1 rail bender		10 00
	1 platform scale	$62 57	39 00
	85 truck gauges	148 75	17 00
	1 locomotive engine, W. W. Wright	12,088 72	10,400 00
	1,176 pounds top mauls	1,764 00	99 96
	18 old trucks		2,340 00
	4 pair truck wheels	196 00	200 00
	2 stock cars	1,800 00	1,016 00
	16 sets switch fixtures		320 00
	3 10-ton hydraulic jacks	375 00	174 75
	23 patent frogs		414 00
	3,000 pounds wrought scrap iron		90 00
	9 Henderson pumps	990 00	315 00
	7 tender springs		28 00
	8,291 pounds couplings		290 19
	12,954 pounds tie rods		1,036 32
April 10, 11, 12	389 pounds switch slides		24 34
	5 water strainers		1 75
	1 broken saw		01
	1 ratchet wrench		10 00
	2 vices	68 04	21 00
	790 pounds blacksmiths' tools		49 38
	2 hydraulic jacks	250 00	145 00
	160 pounds steel tools	64 00	22 40
	1 pumping engine	1,800 00	1,100 00
	5 stoves	26 00	15 30
	50 pounds stove pipe	13 50	1 25
	18,046 pounds spike nails		633 82
	3 Henderson pumps	330 00	16 75
	2,005 pounds nuts	601 50	110 28
	4,506 pounds chain couplings		95 76
	3,860 pounds monkey switch fixtures		43 43
	1 telegraph battery		50
	2,238 pounds bolts		111 90
	70 pounds open links		2 10
	53 feet hose	129 85	5 83
	25 pounds oxalic acid	16 75	50
	595 pounds tripods		8 93
	1,309 pounds steel	458 15	109 82
	8,663 pounds iron	476 46	326 54
	17,000 pounds railroad spikes	1,530 00	790 50
	1 rail bender		11 00
	5 frogs	124 55	155 00
	50 feet hose	122 50	10 00
	4 blocks	46 00	3 60
	6 screw jacks	51 00	30 00
	28 ox-yokes	287 00	56 00
	1 pair dividers	2 21	60
	22 feet hose	53 90	3 30
	11 axes	36 74	12 10
	2 pumps		32 25
	½ barrel pitch	6 55	90
	4 pumps		20 00
	5 pumps		32 75
	92 pounds mauls		9 20
	35 buckets	14 00	2 28
	154 feet hose	377 30	33 60
	1 triangle		2 00
	9 monkey wrenches	28 08	1 35
	312 pounds files	258 96	9 36
	1 stock and dies		6 00
	36 boxes		36

Schedule of railroad property, &c.—Continued.

Date of sale.	Articles.	Cost.	Am't received.
1866.			
April 10, 11, 12	3 scales	$51 15	$26 50
	8 screw jacks	68 00	22 96
	48 stove-door buckles		04
	33 files	27 39	2 07
	3 pumps		52 50
	40 gallons resin oil		5 00
	1,739 pounds grindstones	86 95	26 09
	100 tin cups	7 70	50
	1 pair timber wheels		25 00
	320 gallons sperm oil	700 80	544 00
	170 feet gas pipe	75 65	17 85
	200 gallons crude oil		32 00
	50 oil barrels		9 50
	2 coal buckets		20 50
	7 oil cans	7 00	5 25
	1 lot file handles		5 00
	41 lanterns		12 30
	1 refrigerator		13 50
	720 kerosene wicks		4 00
	21 gas shades	31 08	2 92
	36 level tubes	4 60	1 13
	128 chimnies	17 28	6 67
	1 slate	1 90	1 50
	13 lamps	24 89	4 88
	3 5-gallon cans	5 25	2 55
	40 car oilers		16 50
	1 lantern	5 05	1 10
	6 buildings		2,405 00
	2,107 pounds old glass		7 90
	28 oil cans		1 40
	12 dippers	4 53	84
	68 spoons		3 40
	2 pilots		10 00
	1 cupboard		2 50
	1 stationary engine		565 00
	10 trucks		25 00
	20 lamps	4 55	2 00
	1 scale	62 58	50 00
	38 whip-lashes	14 25	5 00
	28 tape-measures	44 94	8 75
	6 squares	5 22	1 00
	12 saws	41 70	11 40
	2 hydraulic jacks	308 00	116 50
	122 chisels	36 60	27 96
	6 wheelbarrows	24 00	6 00
	4 balances	43 24	2 60
	20 flags		10
	38 lights glass		1 43
	5 bench screws	4 37	50
	1 blacksmith's bellows	27 00	18 00
	25 basins	24 72	1 25
	38 pans	19 00	7 60
	4 boilers	4 60	2 20
	4 scuttles	6 00	90
	31 window fasteners	9 61	93
	2 vices	68 00	5 00
	2 anvils	184 78	7 75
	196 spoons		50
	2 scales	34 10	2 00
	8 stoves	208 00	7 75
	1 grindstone		16 00
	24 door bolts		1 50
	92 padlocks	115 00	15 34

Schedule of railroad property, &c.—Continued.

Date of sale.	Articles.	Cost.	Am't received.
1866.			
April 10, 11, 12	375 rim locks		$116 25
	1,178 carriage bolts	$70 68	11 78
	134 files	111 22	24 49
	2 boring machines	13 00	10 50
	12 picks	19 35	10 25
	252 hammer handles	88 20	13 86
	29 mortice gauges		17 52
	2 molasses gates	2 50	70
	17 saw-sets	32 95	1 13
	1 sand sieve		1 00
	6 squares	4 92	1 50
	35 spokeshaves	18 00	6 58
	12 buck saws	12 00	7 50
	3 butcher saws	9 00	2 49
	12 varnish brushes	5 04	11 50
	19 plough planes	161 50	49 50
	5 coal scuttles	1 25	3 75
	106 match boxes		3 18
	10 graters		30
	36 washbasins		7 20
	504 teaspoons		7 00
	9 slates	17 10	2 00
	329 tin pans		48 00
	26 small shovels	6 50	2 60
	250 candlesticks	29 36	8 34
	5 currycombs		63
	1 saw gummer	21 00	1 50
	17 trowels	29 75	11 20
	8 lanterns		4 00
	309 augers	39 39	109 24
	2 water-coolers	10 00	5 25
	23 augers	23 23	5 98
	2 blocks	23 00	75
	19 hammers	21 37	5 13
	54 pounds gas-pipe tongs		4 32
	588 files	488 04	103 68
	288 auger handles	57 60	11 14
	1,314 pounds tents		108 41
	553 pounds rope	160 37	25 54
	1 tank hose	26 98	60
	60 feet belting	11 82	9 30
	21 monkey wrenches	65 66	19 95
	2 stoves	52 02	2 50
	1 refrigerator		1 00
	1 grindstone	14 52	2 50
	1 blackboard		50
	60 hooks and staples		1 65
	11 pairs handles		1 38
	8 locks		32 00
	19 buckets		15 20
	300 pounds oakum	45 00	19 13
	18 feet hose	44 10	9 00
	176 stretchers		16 20
	10 stoves	260 10	15 00
	1 forge	29 75	2 00
	1,931 pounds ox-chain	1,801 62	41 04
	8 pieces webbing	42 00	13 00
	197 pounds bridge wrenches		9 85
	1 counter scales	17 05	1 75
	1 building		98 00
	2 buildings		245 00
	1 cupboard		11 00
	1 building		91 00

Schedule of railroad property, &c.—Continued.

Date of sale.	Articles.	Cost.	Am't received.
1866 April 10, 11, 12	1 cupboard		$3 00
	1 stove	$26 01	3 75
	22 dust-brushes	14 74	2 93
	1 scale	62 58	15 50
	4 blocks	46 00	21 50
	17.000 bricks		102 00
	2 buildings		44 00
	189 locks	110 03	45 94
	384 screw-eyes		1 28
	31 pounds rivets	6 66	3 41
	23 night-latches	19 09	4 79
	31 conductors' punches		7 43
	242 papers saddlers' nails		4 84
	513 files	105 79	58 55
	566 pounds mauls		56 60
	60 ship axes		70 00
	78 broadaxes	260 52	78 00
	1,092 axe handles	218 40	45 50
	24 bead awl handles		50
	18 panel gauges		87
	43 saw-sets	58 05	6 72
	12 nail sets		50
	6 compass saws		2 10
	30 drawing-knives	52 50	11 25
	2 sets turners' gouges	34 00	5 50
	204 yards enamelled cloth	332 52	102 00
	116 hunters' hatchets	76 56	58 00
	3 soldering irons		1 95
	240 shingling hatchets	160 00	120 00
	36 planes	45 00	29 75
	3 scoops		60
	1 cleaver	5 00	1 00
	11 broadaxes	36 74	9 90
	2 circular saws		1 30
	1 letter press	23 33	1 75
	1 clock		19 00
	856 chisels		306 76
	Lot printing presses, type, &c		1,300 00
	1 cutting machine		55 00
	1 ruling machine	262 75	115 00
	214 chimneys	28 89	8 14
	12 counter brushes	8 04	1 63
	1 building		800 00
	53 gouges	33 75	1 13
	26 planes	32 00	14 30
	8 pokers		40
	3 lanterns		1 65
	1 building		27 00
	2 buildings		157 00
	2 buildings		64 00
	1 building		20 00
	1 saloon car		6,850 00
	95 bolts	19 47	5 39
	703 butts	56 24	30 92
	217 papers tacks	17 36	11 10
	50 blocks	575 00	171 13
	500 pounds mauls		38 75
	21 clocks	199 08	56 40
	11 spirit levels	22 55	12 84
	13 paint brushes	32 50	9 66
	3½ packages gold leaf		14 00
	9 sets chisels	76 68	12 60

Schedule of railroad property, &c.—Continued.

Date of sale.	Articles.	Cost.	Am't received.
1866.			
April 10, 11, 12	1 brace and bits	$12 70	$3 13
	156 broad hatchets		117 00
	25,947 feet oak plank	908 14	544 89
	308 feet hose	754 60	215 00
	419 gross screws	369 88	252 55
	38 fore planes	79 04	40 38
	89 jack planes	178 00	59 33
	54 smooth planes	72 90	15 18
	6 sets match planes	28 50	4 50
	14 cross-cut saws	70 00	45 50
	36 axes	72 36	42 00
	185 augers	186 85	66 48
	158 pounds finishing nails		19 51
	9 gross kettle ears		7 20
	7 stoves	182 07	170 00
	48 sash		34 56
	4,100 pounds spikes	410 00	213 75
	500 nails	40 00	25 00
	46 feet shafting		28 98
	1 oil tank		14 00
	1 lot measures		3 00
	20 pounds rivets	5 00	95
	145 pounds washers	31 90	7 61
	53 pounds rubber packing	46 04	26 50
	2 tinners' machines and furnace		35 00
	12 car side lamps	23 20	6 00
	9,243 pounds car repair material		335 06
	1 lot lampblack		5 00
	66 screw-eyes		18
	10 door knobs	2 30	1 67
	16 chest locks	9 36	2 72
	1,252 files	1,039 16	316 33
	300 axes		228 13
	72 broadaxes	240 48	81 50
	312 adze handles	63 96	17 55
	150 buckets	60 00	20 00
	6 rubber buckets		2 70
	1 bucket	40	25
	4 pipe-cutters	44 00	16 50
	1 set grainers' combs	28	70
	2 packages bronze		2 00
	1 truck		20 00
	17 drawing-knives		9 92
	49 slicks	122 50	25 20
	41 gouges	26 03	8 50
	19 hammers		14 25
	18 rabbet planes	25 20	5 85
	44 planes	55 00	21 20
	225 tin plates	24 75	14 06
	54 skimmers	18 90	2 25
	67 butcher knives	73 03	28 62
	568 chisels	965 60	229 34
	1 pump		2 75
	77 track gauges	134 75	1 73
	2 gongs		4 00
	56 torches		2 25
	42 saw-bucks	42 00	5 46
	45 sash		27 00
	18½ gallons varnish	76 22	29 60
	10 hand screws	74	2 90
	166 tin plates	18 26	63
	34 stretcher frames		68

Schedule of railroad property, &c.—Continued.

Date of sale.	Articles.	Cost.	Am't received.
1866.			
April 10, 11, 12	1 lot stove fixtures		$2 00
	1 bath tub		1 50
	1 stove	$26 01	3 75
	24 bedsteads		5 52
	2 tables and cases		6 25
	18 tables		5 40
	1 drawing board and case		8 25
	1 chair		1 50
	12 kegs		50
	84 yards enamelled cloth	136 92	50 40
	4 screw jacks	34 00	11 20
	809 pounds nails	64 72	39 88
	200 belt hooks		1 10
	132 axes		99 00
	120 broadaxes	400 80	140 00
	2 whip-saws		2 75
	414 broadaxe handles	82 80	22 82
	4 steel-plated frogs		120 00
	1,829 pounds old railroad chairs		77 74
	33,931 pounds cast scrap iron		359 67
	3,167 pounds assorted nuts	665 07	190 02
	1,849 pounds chain	184 90	129 43
	10,086 pounds engine springs		458 48
	1,521 pounds car springs		127 39
	4 iron tanks		5 60
	19 fire-buckets	7 60	3 80
	1 anvil		17 08
	1 universal chuck	63 50	21 00
	1 rail-punching machine		25 00
	2 hospital lamps		4 50
	8 boxes		3 20
	11 tender boxes		8 25
	1 boring mill		77 50
	1 platform scale	62 57	36 50
	1 pumping engine		515 00
	2 turn tables		300 00
	2 circular saws		9 82
	9,600 old railroad spikes		432 00
	24 copper belt rivets		12 00
	48 thumb latches		1 50
	101 cabin-door hooks		10 94
	132 sash lifts	9 24	7 15
	25 rivet boxes and rivets		2 25
	24 steam gauges	697 44	324 00
	162 papers brads		9 32
	456 pounds finishing nails		61 56
	13 lamp shears		3 25
	81 yards red bunting	50 22	48 60
	483 assorted files	347 76	136 31
	29 wood rasps	20 88	8 07
	71 pounds gas-pipe joints	44 56	11 36
	45 union joints	27 90	23 50
	1,015 picks		818 92
	24 tamping picks		13 50
	1,368 maul handles	273 60	131 10
	1,494 pick handles	298 80	180 05
	744 axe handles	148 80	99 20
	21 pounds marline	8 19	6 30
	62 pounds spark netting		24 80
	59 reed brooms		26 55
	80 splint brooms		12 00
	8 mops	4 00	1 60

Schedule of railroad property, &c.—Continued.

Date of sale.	Articles.	Cost.	Am't received.
1866.			
April 10, 11, 12	120 pounds assorted mauls		$21 60
	1,800 feet fuze		18 00
	180 oil burners	$46 80	1 88
	16 kerosene burners	4 16	1 47
	82 lamp collars	5 08	1 71
	54 lantern tops		68
	101 scribing awls	8 83	3 37
	27 boxwood gauges		2 70
	13 splitting gauges		2 17
	1 gas-pipe stock and die	43 10	35 00
	4 cast-steel dviiders	8 86	6 00
	7 steel compasses		2 80
	42 assorted hollow punches	226 80	30 00
	248 head-light chimneys	62 00	5 17
	10 back saws	10 00	10 00
	26 tubes colors, assorted		2 38
	39 sash brushes, assorted		7 97
	1 blender brush		50
	3 passenger cars		1,609 00
	37 old trucks		506 25
	342¼ tons old railroad iron	44,427 47	22,214 50
	18 box cars		8,836 00
	4 flat cars		1,600 00
	14 pairs wheels	321 79	280 00
	3 new trucks		735 00
	10¼ tons scrap railroad iron	1,330 55	512 50
	21 truck cars	2,415 00	252 00
	6 pairs truck wheels	147 00	36 00
	19 red flags	9 50	1 50
	15 plated frogs, (steel)		555 00
	1,633 pounds rope	538 89	179 63
	30 varnish brushes, assorted	12 50	16 38
	31 globe valves	1,094 30	202 75
	24 pod augers		5 16
	12 slicks	30 00	9 00
	36 flag covers		1 05
	16 soft hammers		4 80
	20 chipping hammers		5 00
	101 monkey wrenches	315 12	75 75
	18 sash planes	36 00	8 10
	62 torches		13 40
	2 tin buckets		1 10
	10 tallow pots		3 50
	494 pepper and salt boxes	39 52	12 35
	81 camp kettles	115 40	16 88
	12 tin boilers		30 00
	5 watering cans		8 75
	6 ten-gallon oil cans		9 00
	54 oil cans		9 00
	10 teapots		5 00
	12 tin dippers	4 44	1 50
	264 tin cups	20 02	16 50
	5 iron dippers		25
	17 tallow cans		8 50
	95 flesh forks	36 96	3 80
	8 balances	86 48	30 00
	40 jacket lamps		23
	2,080 knives and forks	395 20	78 00
	81 oilstones	16 32	13 77
	10 surveyors' chains		20 00
	2 marline spikes	1 24	70
	1 machine for splicing rope		1 00

Schedule of railroad property, &c.—Continued.

Date of sale.	Articles.	Cost.	Am't received.
1866.			
April 10, 11, 12	28 sickles	....	$3 92
	30 train lamps	....	10 50
	11 bull-eye lamps	....	5 50
	18 tri-color lamps	....	13 50
	495 pounds balance beam fixtures	....	6 81
	3 timber buggies	$17 85	2 40
	2 blocks and hooks	....	8 00
	2 screw jacks	17 00	8 50
	1 locomotive engine—Osceola	9,000 00	10,100 00
April 14	$118\frac{1632}{2240}$ tons railroad iron	15,412 55	8,014 17
10	1 wardrobe	....	1 00
	5 box stoves	130 00	4 25
	6 chairs	....	4 00
	200 pounds rivet iron	....	6 50
	5 windlasses	....	40 00
	1 platform scale	62 57	33 00
	1,481 cross-ties	....	251 77
	15,000 feet old timber	....	90 00
	1 passenger car	....	500 00
	1 old tent	....	3 50
	$4\frac{3}{4}$ dozen screw-drivers	76 38	20 19
	$5\frac{1}{3}$ dozen claw hammers	13 92	84
	1 platform and posts	....	120 00
	1 office stove	26 00	3 00
	$22\frac{1}{8}$ tons railroad iron	2,872 04	1,460 25
	800 pounds chairs	80 00	48 00
	500 pounds spikes	45 00	30 00
	Total	....	2,049,170 63

Schedule of railroad property in the possession of and belonging to the United States on the 1st day of May, A. D. 1865, *and sold at public auction, at Newbern, N. C., by Captain J. D. Stubbs, A. Q. M. and superintendent of military railroads.*

Articles.	Am't received.	HOW OBTAINED.		Price paid.
		Captured.	Purchased.	
		Quantity.	*Quantity.*	
74 hand axes	$43 15	74	....	....
168 broadaxes	184 11	110	58	$193 14
5 handled axes	3 75	....	5	10 30
1,074 assorted axes	849 46	....	1,074	1,782 84
33 hand-car hammered axles	481 60	29	3	30 00
3 hedge anchors	33 50	....	3	81 00
14 anvils	153 44	2	12	1,092 00
1 old anvil	2 55	....	1	91 00
41 carpenters' adzes	29 73	....	41	102 50
162 railroad adzes	134 53	....	162	405 00
15 sets augers	62 80	....	15	15 00
290 augers	71 00	180	110	110 00
2 pounds muriatic acid	08	....	2	38
22 pounds oxalic acid	88	....	22	18 04
25 pounds sal ammonia	1 50	....	25	18 50
35 scratch awls	70	....	35	21 35
6 brad awls	60	....	6	48
206 pounds antimony	22 66	....	206	49 44
12 pounds sheet brass	3 24	....	12	7 44

Schedule of railroad property, &c.—Continued.

Articles.	Am't received.	HOW OBTAINED.		Price paid.
		Captured.	Purchased.	
		Quantity.	*Quantity.*	
2 spring balances	$2 35		2	$3 00
72 wash basins	7 92		72	38 88
25 slide T-bevels	5 00		25	16 75
11 carpenters' benches*	22 00		11	
5 benches*	63		5	
160 ox bows†	3 20		160	
377 tamping bars	85 94	49	328	944 64
38 pinch bars	106 40	32	6	14 28
220 claw bars	235 80	9	241	761 56
31 raising and lining bars	26 35	31		
58 lining bars	60 90	49	9	21 42
6 raising bars	5 70	6		
12 timber bars	2 40	12		
5 wrench bars	7 50	5		
23 assorted bars	16 63 (23 assorted bars and 6 crow-bars together)		23	54 74
6 crow-bars			6	14 28
11 raising, lining, claw, and tamping bars	5 85		11	26 18
24 timber buggies*	35 60		24	
64 double blocks	109 44		64	976 00
10 single blocks	6 80		10	70 00
20 snatch blocks	14 00		20	250 00
2 double tackle blocks‡	2 00		2	
2 sets tackle blocks	2 00		2	11 10
6 triple blocks‡	9 90		6	
2 wrecking blocks‡	43 00		2	
94 head blocks	57 20		94	
1 signal bell	2 50		1	3 50
8 alarm bells	21 20	6	2	
1 circular saw, shafting, leather belting and hanger	50 00			
24 feet leather belting	55 80		24	45 60
50 pounds truck brass	62 00	50		
5 sets car bits	11 25	4	1	5 00
19 bits	9 50		19	9 69
8 paint brushes	2 80		8	9 20
1 hand brush	35		1	82
8 marking brushes	2 00		8	4 80
7 pencil brushes	1 75¾		7	3 50
2 brushes	50		2	90
49 scrub-brushes	5 70		49	22 05
23 dust brushes	6 33		23	18 86
36 whitewash brushes	9 72		36	22 40
337 water buckets	62 59		337	134 80
1 fire bucket	25		1	40
3 car buckets	75		3	1 20
193 pounds borax	48 25		193	90 71
8 blacksmiths' bellows	87 75		8	253 04
424 pairs brass butts	17 32		424	106 00
310 pairs iron butts	4 65		310	24 80
12 brass flush bolts	2 16		12	2 52
39 tons car bolts	2,496 00	39		
117 barrel bolts	4 10		117	7 02
3 lamp boxes*	1 50		3	
3 tool boxes	1 50		3	
114 salt boxes	4 93		114	14 25
353 pepper boxes	8 72		353	44 12
1 tap borer	25	1		
1 draughting-board*	1 05		1	

* Manufactured. † Found and taken up. ‡ Received from unknown source.

Schedule of railroad property, &c.—Continued.

Articles.	Am't received.	HOW OBTAINED.		Price paid.
		Captured.	Purchased.	
		Quantity.	*Quantity.*	
3 tin boilers*	$48	....	3	....
4 wheelbarrows, (old)†	1 00	....	4	....
18 auger bits	1 55	15	3	$1 53
42 brace bits	95	42	....	....
18 iron braces	3 85	14	4	29 40
14 sets braces and bits	39 15	2	12	90 00
10 bedsteads*	2 00	....	10	....
2 bureaus*	13 00	....	2	....
369 time-books	15 68	....	369	154 98
144 blank books	13 45	....	144	43 28
3 letter-press books	9 15	....	3	14 43
2 letter-book water bowls	30	....	2	3 00
2 buildings*	68 00	....	2	....
93,466 railroad chairs	4,191 58	1,000	24	17 52
24 chairs†	6 60	....	7	....
7 clocks	33 25	....	6	34 50
6 office clocks	27 65	....	41	235 75
75 cold chisels	37 50	34	12	9 00
12 blacksmiths' chisels	2 50	....	393	154 75
419 assorted chisels	108 65	26	....	....
2 sets timber chisels	4 68	2	....	....
6 cape chisels	30	6	....	....
70 crucible chisels	47 10	....	70	9 80
186 iron cutters	140 24	....	186	228 78
3 Stanwood cutters	15 00	....	3	25 50
6 car platforms	291 00	....	6	....
9 car trucks	45 00	....	9	708 75
47 flat cars	20,138 34	....	47	22,390 33
16 rack cars	5,820 00	....	16	7,622 24
16 hand cars	176 50	....	16	1,840 00
1 car frame	12 00	....	1	....
1,500 pounds brass castings	465 00	....	1,500	750 00
97 tons car castings*	3,018 60	....	97	....
16 chains‡	23 17	....	16	....
1 pair calipers	10	....	1	....
87 pounds chalk	44	....	87	87
16 pounds carmine	6 75	....	16	2 40
80 pounds assorted colors	36 00	....	80	12 00
4 heater cocks	10 00	....	4	10 16
12 tank cocks	6 00	....	12	15 00
1,874 sheets copper	852 67	926	948	635 16
2,199 tin cups	72 65	....	2,199	219 90
37 candlesticks	71	....	37	4 44
110 oil cans	17 80	....	110	16 50
1 chest*	50	....	1	....
1 medicine chest*	50	....	1	....
5 water-coolers*	9 40	....	5	....
18 pairs compasses	2 06	1	17	6 97
21 pounds bell cord	2 10	....	21	9 66
10 letter-clips, (board)	1 05	....	10	1 30
5 letter-clips, (brass)	65	....	5	7 50
1 calendar	35	....	1	1 75
46 drills	16 25	25	21	68 25
31 screw-drivers	4 27	5	26	31 20
70 tin dippers	3 98	....	70	11 90
8 field and table desks*	30 74	....	8	....
3 desks*	1 10	....	3	....
7 dies	2 00	....	7	....
1 pair dividers	16	....	1	2 21

* Manufactured. † Received from quartermaster's department. ‡ Received from unknown source.

Schedule of railroad property, &c.—Continued.

Articles.	Am't received.	HOW OBTAINED.		Price paid.
		Captured.	Purchased.	
		Quantity.	*Quantity.*	
1 pile-driver, (hand)	$36 00		1	
1 pile-driver, (steam)	375 00		1	$3,750 00
2 fixtures for pile-drivers*	15 00		2	
8 locomotive engines	78,405 00		8	71,060 82
1 upright engine	305 00	1		
69 pounds emery	3 70		69	13 80
280 quires emery cloth	37 10		280	54 40
1 set figures	1 50	1		
45 wood flasks	4 50	45		
2 blacksmiths' forges	30 00		2	
16 railroad forks	8 40		16	
14 lamp-fillers	59		14	4 92
19 flatters	9 67	1	18	
12 top fullers	15 60		12	
2 bottom fullers	7 20		2	
12 grindstone fixtures	11 80		12	
29 funnels†	1 90		29	
28 pewter faucets‡	2 18		28	
10 brass faucets‡	3 15		10	
69 wood faucets	2 76		69	5 86
93 taper files	11 86		93	28 83
128 round bastard files	51 27	44	84	73 08
310 second-cut bastard files	166 90	310		
156 square files	71 68		156	81 12
292 flat bastard files	56 70		292	230 68
156 ½-round bastard files	26 00		156	135 72
475 assorted files	121 42	7	468	369 72
26 files	2 86		26	20 54
48 red flags	1 00		48	48 00
329 pounds steel frogs	40 30		329	
2,100 pounds tarred felt	21 00		2,100	136 50
329 forks	3 20		329	52 64
130 flesh-forks	13 00		130	52 00
103 white globes	4 84		103	30 90
31 pounds chrome green	3 07		31	12 40
20 pounds imperial green	3 20		20	8 00
2 pounds glue	10		2	60 00
10 steam gauges	97 50		10	303 30
27 thumb gauges	49	24	3	1 50
323 track gauges	8 17	124	199	73 63
9 gouges	2 34		9	7 83
24 boxes glass	76 25		24	212 88
6 gimlets	15	6		
10 machinists' hammers	10 00	10		
2 engineers' hammers	1 55	1	1	2 00
2 sets hammers	8 60		2	
2 hand hammers	50	1	1	50
7 curving hammers	5 95	6	1	1 13
41 spike hammers	19 27	34	7	11 90
64 nail hammers	24 28	29	35	17 50
1 backing hammer	50		1	1 00
2 balance beam hooks	3 00	2		
2 fire hooks	82		2	1 50
1 curving hook	35	1		
4 bramble hooks	1 16	4		
28 cant hooks	11 72		28	21 00
17 carrying hooks	4 25	16	1	1 55
274 hatchets	75 35	1	273	384 93

* Purchased with the pile-driver. † Manufactured. ‡ Received from unknown source.

Schedule of railroad property, &c.—Continued.

Articles.	Am't received.	HOW OBTAINED.		Price paid.
		Captured.	Purchased.	
		Quantity.	*Quantity.*	
4 copper hatchets	$2 40	4	....	....
308 axe handles	52 64	....	308	$169 40
192 auger handles	7 68	....	192	28 80
130 broadaxe handles	14 30	....	130	42 90
220 cross-cut saw handles	1 05	....	220	27 50
65 adze handles	5 20	....	65	33 80
94 hand-axe handles	96	....	94	21 62
73 pick handles	73	....	73	11 68
13 file handles	60	....	13	1 62
25 hammer handles	25	....	25	5 50
11 spike maul handles	20	....	11	1 76
2 grubbing hoes	50	....	2	1 10
120 strap hinges	23 30	....	120	105 00
1 hollow and round	6 50	....	1	1 41
1,172 feet rubber hose	1,417 96	....	1,172	2,344 00
25 feet section hose	31 50	....	25	50 00
802 feet suction hose	1,010 52	....	802	3,504 74
25 feet leading hose	31 50	....	25	50 00
100 hasps and staples	4 00	....	100	14 00
371 pen-holders	1 10	....	371	11 13
2,438 pounds hoop-iron	30 48	....	2,438	164 56
42 inkstands	4 59	....	42	21 00
13 caulking irons	2 73	....	13	11 31
9 soldering irons	2 44	6	3	....
60,000 pounds cast scrap iron*	991 07	....	60,000	....
15,808 pounds assorted iron	786 77	2,237	13,571	848 18
3,815 old iron*	109 68	....	3,815	....
$11\frac{1050}{2240}$ tons pig iron†	4,541 75	....	$111\frac{1050}{2240}$	....
1,717½ pounds boiler iron	68 70	1,400	317½	38 10
$521\frac{1973}{2240}$ tons railroad iron	21,635 35	398	$123\frac{1973}{2240}$	14,246 25
1,520 pounds sheet-iron	60 80	862	658	78 96
228 pounds Russia iron	24 77	228	....	....
102,000 pounds wrought scrap iron*	1,890 87	....	102,100	....
6 hydraulic jacks	570 00	4	2	225 00
20 gallons Japan brown	20 00	....	20	86 20
30 gallons baking brown	27 00	....	30	91 80
18 2-quire journals	6 72	....	18	27 00
13 3-quire journals	9 78	....	13	29 25
14 4-quire journals	10 56	....	14	42 00
12 5-quire journals	8 25	....	12	45 00
66 camp kettles	3 90	....	66	138 60
6 tin kettles	64	....	6	4 50
10 iron kettles	3 25	....	10	16 60
77 draw-knives	21 40	19	58	70 18
127 butchers' knives	26 01	....	127	46 99
704½ sets knives and forks	7 00	....	704½	114 56
1,400 mahogany knobs	3 80	....	1,400	28 00
150 pounds sole-leather	22 50	....	150	63 75
126 padlocks	18 75	....	126	44 10
108 brass switch locks and keys	48 60	....	108	216 00
16 cupboard locks	1 60	....	16	4 48
6 rim locks and knobs	3 00	....	6	6 18
6 chest locks	90	....	6	2 28
10 rim dead locks	16 30	....	10	10 30
4 drawer locks	24	....	4	2 16
1 ladder	3 00	....	1	....
138 pounds white lead	13 80	....	138	23 46
105,679 feet white pine lumber	3,153 76	....	105,679	5,019 75

*Found and taken up. †Received from other officers.

Schedule of railroad property, &c.—Continued.

Articles.	Am't received.	HOW OBTAINED.		Price paid.
		Captured.	Purchased.	
		Quantity.	*Quantity.*	
89,066 feet yellow pine lumber	$1,854 93		89,066	$4,230 63
1,550 feet spruce pine lumber	11 24		1,550	43 62
10,582 feet yellow pine flooring	469 36		10,582	634 92
6,000 feet white pine flooring	360 00		6,000	360 00
36 spirit levels	12 80	9	27	54 00
7 head lights	356 25		7	7 35
460 saw logs*	398 90		460	
2 lathes	1,295 00		2	75 00
173 white lights	168 51		173	259 50
15 red lights	17 50		15	30 00
3 blue lights	1 80		3	6 00
2 green lights	1 00		2	4 00
339 tape lines	20 85		339	339 00
6 lanterns	1 26		6	17 64
25 coal-oil lamps	7 63		25	23 00
12 tin hand lamps	1 41		12	13 44
6 pounds lampblack	66		6	2 22
5 pounds black lead	40		5	1 25
1 lounge*	3 75		1	
18 coupling links	3 20		18	12 06
1 set letters	1 75	1		
153 track mauls	192 95		102	176 46
20 spike mauls	26 00		20	34 00
429 carpenter mauls*	210 90		429	
6 bridge mauls	2 70	6		
29 boring machines	83 00		29	203 00
22 tape measures	3 74		22	22 00
23 tin measures*	3 22		23	
28 coffee-mills	17 40		28	31 64
16 tin mugs*	73		16	
23 caulking mallets	2 91		23	34 50
39 Babbitt metal	14 43		39	17 55
42¼ kegs nails	245 75		42¼	380 25
70 pounds finishing nails	7 35		70	14 00
5 nippers	1 30		5	75
4,750 pounds square nuts	427 50		4,750	1,330 00
200 pounds nuts	18 00		200	56 00
1 bake oven*	02		1	
20 gallons linseed oil	22 00		20	32 00
10 gallons resin oil	5 00		10	9 50
70 gallons sperm oil	157 50		70	168 00
50 pounds oakum	3 75		50	8 00
51 S. B. oilers	1 43		51	7 65
112 joints stove-pipe	16 10		112	142 24
130 stove-pipe elbows	16 10		130	52 00
7 sheets oil-paper	35		7	3 50
22 iron pots	8 25	32		
1 drill press	3 25		1	
2,407 pounds gas pipe	577 68	22	2,385	1,049 40
30 pike poles	7 50	30		
167 feet rubber packing	61 79		167	250 50
50 pounds lead pipe	3 50	50		
100 piles	65 00		100	160 00
10 tin pails*	14 85		10	
7 bead planes	1 45	7		
82 fore planes	46 70	3		
4 Grecian moulding planes	1 24		4	5 76
87 jack planes	23 05	2		
37 Babbitt jack planes	12 33		37	10 50

*Manufactured.

Schedule of railroad property, &c.—Continued.

Articles.	Am't received.	HOW OBTAINED. Captured.	HOW OBTAINED. Purchased.	Price paid.
		Quantity.	*Quantity.*	
28 jointer planes	$16 40	21	7	$10 64
2 sets match planes	1 30	....	2	4 80
2 sets movable planes	2 00	....	2	5 60
9 panel plough planes	6 40	7	2	4 80
3 sash planes	1 50	3	....	....
75 smooth planes	24 90	21	54	72 90
3 assorted planes	1 56	2	1	1 35
200 coupling pins	71 70	....	200	130 00
22 punches	2 10	....	22	5 50
5 pokers	53	....	5	5 00
40 die plates	8 45	7	33	148 50
8 glue pots	2 10	1	7	12 81
12 tallow pots	07	12	....	....
16 tamping picks	1 76	....	16	37 60
464 picks	238 85	....	464	733 12
33 rotary hand pumps	973 05	....	33	3,927 00
1 pump	5 00	1	....	....
1 tin pump*	05	....	1	....
1 letter press	8 75	....	1	27 50
32 paulins†	411 25	....	32	....
48 red and blue pencils‡	2 10	....	48	....
24 black pencils	1 05	....	24	3 12
2 plyers	20	....	2	3 50
200 pounds black paint	19 00	....	200	30 00
6½ reams sand paper	17 88	....	6½	32 50
81 bake pans	8 10	....	81	24 30
57 dish pans	6 98	....	57	49 59
1 dust pan	20	....	1	50
11 mess pans	55	....	11	3 74
71 dripping pans	3 55	....	71	61 77
257 assorted tin pans	7 47	....	257	51 40
10 frying pans	2 00	....	10	2 40
18 coffee-pots	3 06	....	18	16 20
1,695 tin plates	5 35	....	1,695	169 50
20 reamers	18 50	20	....	....
5 sets rivets	3 00	....	5	5 70
1,000 pounds boiler rivets	45 00	....	1,000	140 00
10 drill ratchets	6 00	....	10	....
1 mahogany case regulator	35 00	....	1	130 00
1 timber roller	2 30	....	1	75
4 boxes roofing for cars§	10 00	....	4	....
4 switch ropes	32 00	....	4	32 00
9,141 pounds rope	1,813 63	6,070	3,071	767 75
114 feet rope	24 00	....	114	17 10
83 pounds Venetian red	9 60	....	83	12 45
5 pounds India red	20	....	5	75
224 connecting rods	219 31	80	144	....
30 Malden wire riddles	8 22	....	30	45 00
1 rasp	11	1	....	....
280 pounds resin	3 65	....	280	....
13 pen racks	65	....	13	5 59
1 ebony rule	17	....	1	1 07
19 rubber rules	2 53	....	19	20 33
20 boxwood rules	3 25	20	....	....
1 register	55	1	....	....
42 cook stoves and fixtures	240 05	....	42	10 92
1 box stove and fixtures	60	....	1	16
38 assorted stoves, old	1 86	....	38	6 08

* Manufactured. † Received from quartermaster's department. ‡ Received from unknown source. § Found and taken up,

Schedule of railroad property, &c.—Continued.

Articles.	Am't received.	HOW OBTAINED.		Price paid.
		Captured.	Purchased.	
		Quantity.	*Quantity.*	
30 sheaves	$6 13		30	$100 80
40 slicks	32 00		40	100 00
94 try squares	18 22	5	89	42 72
105 steel squares	43 05	24	81	121 50
37 monkey switches	83 25		37	
1 army scales*	8 75		1	
4 bottom swedges	27 00	3	1	
43 top swedges	29 03		43	
7 swedges	8 15	2	5	
1 B. S. shovel	75		1	
425 shovels	137 53		425	565 25
24 scoop shovels	18 83		24	43 20
4 fire shovels	30	4		
2 stocks, dies, and reamers	66 00		2	88 00
153 cross-cut saws	256 50	37	116	580 00
290 handsaws	277 45	102	188	394 80
2 mill saws	8 50		2	10 92
60 buck saws	36 00		60	63 60
1 compass saw	2 00		1	1 20
8 wood bench screws	3 15	5	3	2 61
8 hand screws	1 53	8		
79 jack screws	522 13	52	27	349 82
35 bench screws	38 00		35	47 95
650 coach screws*	29 75		650	
2 hogsheads sea-coal facing	5 50		2	45 00
7 mounted grindstones	16 10		7	59 50
15 grindstones	13 35	4	11	38 83
1,493$\frac{42}{100}$ kegs railroad spikes	8,119 94		1,493$\frac{42}{100}$	12,694 07
91$\frac{75}{100}$ kegs cut spikes	229 38		91$\frac{75}{100}$	1,009 25
734$\frac{57}{100}$ kegs bridge spikes	3,521 10		734$\frac{57}{100}$	6,611 13
1,045 table spoons	4 05		1,045	52 25
472 teaspoons	1 70		472	18 88
120 oil-stones	3 60		120	40 80
1 counter scales	4 00		1	15 00
5 assorted scales	75 00		5	
3 platform scales	30 00		3	187 71
100 pounds sulphur	3 25		100	12 00
13 pounds solder	3 58		13	6 24
15,940 shingles	56 11		15,940	175 34
5,815 pounds spring steel	456 59		5,815	2,326 00
13,000 pounds cast steel	2,157 50		13,000	4,550 00
1,026 pounds cast steel	133 38		1,026	359 10
2,169 pounds spring steel	151 83		2,169	867 60
300 pounds blister steel	15 00		300	105 00
29 stools†	2 34		29	
35 saw-sets	6 30		35	35 00
14 spokeshaves	2 80	5	9	4 50
3 marline spikes	30		3	
115 basting spoons	3 60		115	20 12
5 tin scoops	2 05	3	2	
11 spades	4 25		11	11 00
200 pounds rotten-stone	2 00		200	20 00
19 pounds pumice stone, lump	95		19	2 47
18 pounds pumice stone, ground	59		18	1 80
20 pounds gum shellac	1 20		20	23 00
100 pounds salt	1 00	100		
10 washstands†	4 38		10	
6 slates	60		6	3 60
1 pair letter scales	30		1	4 00

* Found and taken up.

† Manufactured.

Schedule of railroad property, &c.—Continued.

Articles.	Am't received.	HOW OBTAINED.		Price paid.
		Captured.	Purchased.	
		Quantity.	*Quantity.*	
350 slides	$56 00	250	100	$50 00
1 pair shears	05	....	1	1 42
1 field safe	10 00	....	1	95 00
2 scows	64 50	....	2	....
9 sets B. S. tools	107 59	....	9	276 75
9 heading tools	11 00	....	9	....
20 planer tools	14 50	....	20	....
62 pairs lathe tools	21 50	....	62	....
70 tops	16 50	6	64	350 08
24 railroad tongs	9 60	9	15	47 10
5 F. rails tongs	2 00	....	5	15 70
22 pairs G. P. tongs	10 00	....	32	....
55 pairs B. S. tongs	19 25	16	39	....
8 taps and dies	19 00	1	....	....
2 sets pipe taps	32 00	2	....	....
14 water tanks*	199 75	2	12	....
1 log truck	65 00	....	1	....
3 engine tenders	407 00	....	3	....
18 gallons turpentine	14 00	....	18	36 00
5,000 cross ties	550 00	....	5,000	3,250 00
523 papers tacks	20 92	....	523	33 99
250 pieces bridge timber*	447 50	....	250	....
132 boxes tin	949 34	....	132	3,079 56
6 car trucks	9 50	....	6	....
45 pounds twine	4 05	....	45	20 25
16 tables*	7 55	....	16	....
65 lamp tubes	1 46	....	65	2 60
2 trowels	1 05	....	2	3 50
20 pieces tank timber*	7 10	....	20	....
1 set hand-turning tools	2 50	1	....	....
22 wall-tent flies†	....	....	22	....
6 hospital tents†	....	....	6	....
20 "A" tents†	202 00	....	20	....
5 Sibley tents†	....	....	5	....
41 wall tents†	....	....	41	....
39 pounds burnt umber	1 17	....	39	6 24
10 vices	45 23	....	10	171 50
13 bench vices	71 00	....	13	....
100 ventilators	1 40	10	90	....
18 gallons varnish	21 96	....	18	122 40
1 hoisting wheel	2 00	....	1	....
8 tap wrenches	3 80	6	2	2 50
10 screw wrenches	13 00	10	....	....
110 monkey wrenches	108 10	110	....	....
8 assorted wrenches	1 12	....	8	24 00
5 bridge wrenches	2 45	....	5	15 60
1 wheel, wagon tongue and gear	19 00	....	1	222 00
513 pounds of wire	12 70	....	513	117 99
180 pounds wicking	52 30	....	180	225 00
3,170 washers‡	190 20	....	3,170	....
260 pounds whiting	1 00	....	260	10 40
4 double plate car wheels	72 00	....	4	1 16
18 hand-car wheels	76 50	18	....	....
109 new car wheels	1,522 00	109	....	....
401 pounds waste	100 25	....	401	180 45
2 wiper's pails	1 50	....	2	....
144 pounds head-light wick	1 32	....	144	....
3 wardrobes*	7 40	....	3	....

*Manufactured. †Received from quartermaster's department. ‡Found and taken up.

Schedule of railroad property, &c.—Continued.

Articles.	Am't received.	HOW OBTAINED.		Price paid.
		Captured.	Purchased.	
		Quantity.	*Quantity.*	
10 paper weights	$0 50	....	10	$7 00
450 pounds yellow ochre	15 75	....	450	180 00
300 pounds block zinc	24 00	....	300	40 50
Total	192,746 42	....	....	....
*891,719 pounds old railroad iron	17,914 C0	891,719	....	....

* Captured in North Carolina, and sold by General Van Vliet, New York city.

No. 6.—*Schedule of property used in repairing and operating railroads in the department of Virginia and North Carolina since May* 1, 1865.

Schedule of railroad property in possession of and belonging to the United States on the 1st *day of May*, 1865, *and used in repairs of military railroads since that date.*

Articles.	Quantity.	Value.
Acid ... pounds..	19	$11 79
Alcohol ... gallons..	108¾	481 48
Axles and crank-pins ... pounds..	5,131	614 72
Balance, spring ... number..	11	128 88
Basins ... do....	6	1 80
Belting ... feet..	268½	295 10
Benzine ... gallons..	186½	124 56
Bevels ... number..	3	9 15
Beeswax ... pounds..	¾	1 12
Bolts, assorted	....	4 88
Books and stationery	....	3,699 82
Borax ... pounds..	8	3 29
Brass, sheet ... do....	428	312 17
Bricks ... number..	3,624	79 62
Brooms ... do....	299	163 69
Brushes ... do....	398	91 95
Buckets ... do....	76	37 46
Burners ... do....	6	7 00
Buttons, tufting ... gross..	2	1 50
Butts, hinges, &c	....	47 28
Bunting ... yards..	40½	34 43
Candles ... pounds..	387	269 23
Castings, brass ... do....	5,331	3,190 80
Castings, iron ... do....	182,136	14,148 31
Casters ... sets..	24½	23 51
Chain, assorted	....	643 31
Chalk ... pounds..	51	77
Chairs, railroad ... number..	11,202	715 64
Charcoal ... barrels..	341	245 75
Chimnies and candlesticks ... number..	443	64 55
Cloth, enamelled ... yards..	84½	104 38
Cloth and paper, emery	....	106 41
Coal, anthracite ... tons..	175	2,450 00
Coal, Cumberland ... do ..	200	2,600 00
Cocks ... number..	13	28 11
Combs, curry and graining ... do....	15	4 51
Compasses and dividers ... do....	2	3 00

Schedule of railroad property, &c.—Continued.

Articles.	Quantity.	Value.
Copper........pounds..	560	$418 36
Cordage........	....	104 28
Cups, tin, and cans........number..	75	7 40
Cutters, paper and wire........do....	9	14 00
Carpet drapery and tape........	....	56 61
Dippers........number..	18	6 10
Drivers, screw........do....	6	9 16
Duck........yards..	83	311 24
Ears, bucket........gross..	2	5 00
Emery........pounds..	254	26 58
Escutcheons........	....	3 20
Eyes, screw........dozen..	26½	5 26
Fasteners........number..	88	30 96
Files........do....	618	443 19
Fixtures, grindstone........sets..	2	4 07
Flannel........yards..	93½	74 35
Forges........number..	3	66 00
Frogs........do....	31	984 92
Funnels, tin........do....	11	5 33
Gauges, steam........do....	2	60 00
Gimlets........do....	92	1 73
Glass, assorted........	....	168 00
Glue........pounds..	240	78 55
Hair........do....	50	21 50
Hammers and hatchets........number..	7	8 78
Handles, metal........do....	32	20 33
Handles, wood........do....	466	253 16
Hose, rubber........	....	225 79
Hose, water tank........number..	2	53 42
Iron, bar........pounds..	147,936	23,350 32
Iron, railroad........	....	....
Iron, sheet........pounds..	10,101	1,254 93
Joints, hoops, &c........number..	56	13 77
Knives and forks........	....	21 02
Lanterns and lamps........	....	86 14
Lath........number..	4,700	12 20
Lead........pounds..	4	56 00
Leaf, gold........package..	½	5 00
Leather........	....	34 75
Lime........barrels..	½	63
Lines, chalk........number..	15	2 09
Locks, knobs, &c........	....	85 50
Lumber........feet..	1,361,942	147 28
Matches........	....	222 44
Mauls........	....	17 42
Measures, tape and tin........number..	95	107 69
Metal, Babbitt........pounds..	12	9 00
Mops........number..	1	50
Moulds, lantern........	....	60 00
Muslin........yards..	82	41 30
Nails, finishing........papers..	15	3 60
Nails, wrought........pounds..	454	46 21
Needles and palms........dozen..	17	4 08
Netting........feet..	116	145 00
Nuts........pounds..	2,773	443 53
Oil, kerosene........gallons..	359	331 05
Oil, linseed........do....	135½	284 62
Oil, sperm........do....	410½	10,477 75
Pans, water-closet........number..	1	45 00
Packing, hemp........pounds..	470	204 86
Packing, rubber........do....	210	346 40
Paint, assorted........	....	733 37
Paper, sand........	....	6 61
Photograph materials........	....	278 10

Schedule of railroad property, &c—Continued.

Articles.	Quantity.	Value.
Piles .... number..	1,293	$1,864 50
Pipe, gas .... feet..	232½	177 80
Pitch .... barrels..	1	45 38
Plates .... number..	67	8 24
Plates, frog .... do....	11	100 87
Plates and pans .... do....	....	....
Plyers .... do....	11	5 25
Polish, stove .... dozen..	3 1/12	2 92
Potash .... pounds..	107	31 20
Punches .... number..	11	22 75
Resin .... pounds..	1	18
Rivets .... do....	38	15 72
Rules .... number..	32	34 74
Salt .... pounds..	92	2 30
Saws .... number..	21	27 34
Scoops, tin .... do....	26	2 96
Screws, assorted	....	113 69
Shears .... number..	61	84 95
Shingles .... do....	210,650	1,995 87
Sickles .... do....	1	50
Skins .... do....	30	94 67
Soap .... pounds..	205	49 03
Solder .... do....	21	7 38
Spikes and nails .... do....	10,525	919 10
Spikes, railroad .... do....	12,900	804 88
Spoons and skimmers .... number..	17	2 31
Sponge	....	9 03
Springs, assorted .... number..	210	1,960 00
Springs, rubber .... pounds..	1,044	1,193 40
Stamps and solder iron .... number..	3	5 50
Steel .... pounds..	9,861	1,791 62
Stools .... number..	1	75 00
Stone, rotten and pumice .... pounds..	55	5 50
Sulphur .... do....	38½	3 85
Squares .... number..	1	81
Tacks and saddle nails .... papers..	56	3 56
Tallow .... pounds..	149	19 02
Thread	....	6 09
Ties, cross .... number..	94,471	58,020 54
Tin	....	476 18
Tripoli .... dozen..	10	10 00
Turpentine .... gallons..	....	439 13
Tyres .... number..	7	1,963 50
Valves .... do....	20	189 96
Varnish .... gallons..	39	114 50
Washers .... pounds..	621	173 74
Washers and bolts .... do....	16,200	1,944 00
Waste .... do....	5,023	2,080 34
Wheels, emery .... number..	2	60 00
Wheels, engine and car .... do....	131	3,600 74
Wick	....	32 42
Wire .... pounds..	31	15 67
Wood .... cords..	12,074¼	31,288 52
Zinc .... pounds..	405	117 38
Total	....	185,454 49

Schedule of railroad property in the possession of and belonging to the United States on the first day of May, A. D. 1865, and used in repairs of military railroads in North Carolina since that date.

Articles.	Cost.
3 anvils, (1 captured)	....
9 augers, (9 captured)	....
14 sets augers	$168 00
69 scratch awls, (9 captured)	36 00
3 pounds muriatic acid	57
3 pounds oxalic acid	2 46
37 gallons alcohol	173 53
4 pounds sal ammonia	2 80
56 pounds antimony	13 44
13 adzes	32 50
32 broadaxes	106 56
93 axes	154 38
1 kedge anchor	29 00
4 axles	12 84
10 blank books	21 00
59 blank books, memorandum	21 83
2 letter-press books	9 62
90 time-books	37 80
120 water buckets	48 00
6 auger bits, (6 captured)	....
5 spring balances	7 50
6 locomotive balances	237 50
68 washbasins	36 72
2 bedsteads, (manufactured)	....
4 double blocks	41 00
1 snatch block	15 00
6 tackle blocks	42 60
1 tin boiler, (manufactured)	....
65 pepper boxes	42 90
7 salt boxes, (1 captured)	75
1 tool-box, (manufactured)	....
155 brooms	96 10
23 claw bars, (4 captured)	60 04
66 crowbars	157 08
9 raising bars, (5 captured)	9 52
5 lining bars	11 90
5 timber bars, (5 captured)	....
17 tamping bars	40 46
133 assorted bars	316 54
17 grate bars	17 00
9 dusting-brushes	7 38
6 marking brushes	3 60
28 paint brushes	32 20
10 scrub brushes	4 50
29 whitewash brushes	26 10
126 feet leather belting	80 64
10 head blocks	....
10 barrel bolts	2 00
5 brass flush bolts	3 45
156 bolts	31 20
44 pounds borax	20 68
586 brass butts	73 25
274 cast-iron butts	21 92
2 hand bellows	54 66
72 wagon bows, (found and taken up)	....
2 reams quartermaster's blanks	50 00
11 papers brads	16 50
60 pounds brads	10 20
5 bevels	3 35
13 alarm bells	....

Schedule of railroad property, &c.—Continued.

Articles.	Cost.
125 yards red bunting	$131 25
404,060 pounds coal	261 56
890 bushels coal, blacksmiths'	462 80
25 chains, (found and taken up)	....
83 chisels. (12 captured)	95 14
4 sets chisels	34 08
62 iron cutters, (3 captured)	72 57
7 pairs compasses	2 87
1 medicine chest (manufactured)	....
2 mess chests, (captured)	....
6 crucibles	19 44
4 tubes carmine	3 92
40 pounds star candles	15 62
21,900 pounds railroad chairs	1,971 00
63 pounds white chalk	63
10 head-light chimneys	3 00
122 lamp chimneys	10 98
31 pounds chrome green	12 40
15 pounds chrome yellow	6 00
4 quires emery cloth	92
9 yards wire	2 07
16 tubes assorted colors	3 68
164 pounds sheet copper, (74 captured)	60 30
1,000 pounds ingot copper	460 00
49 pounds bell cord	22 54
783 tin cups	78 36
24 brass locks	138 00
1 calendar	1 75
4 wagon covers, (found and taken up)	....
2 curry-combs, (found and taken up)	....
53 sets hose couplings	91 16
27,680 pounds corn, (received from quartermaster's department)	....
35 tin dippers	5 60
12 doubletrees	6 00
2 sets dies and plates	92 24
3 sets screw-drivers	3 60
500 official envelopes	4 90
5 straight edges, (manufactured)	....
9 G. P. elbows	11 25
14 pounds emery	2 80
1 wood faucet	25
1 brass faucet, (received from an unknown source)	....
1 lead faucet, (found and taken up)	....
36 red flags	21 60
730 forks	277 40
2,320 pounds tarred felt	150 80
34 yards cotton flannel	20 40
2,000 feet white pine flooring	120 00
3,000 feet yellow pine flooring	180 00
196 pounds flour	9 50
65 taper files	46 80
18 saw-mill files	14 22
83 assorted files	65 57
26 bastard files	21 58
13 lamp fillers	4 55
7 railroad frogs	174 37
1 gimlet	10
16 boxes glass	141 92
3 white gloves	90
32 lantern glasses	19 20
6 lights glass	60
22 pounds glue	6 60
4 pounds imperial green	1 60

Schedule of railroad property, &c.—Continued.

Articles.	Cost.
3 steam gauges	$90 99
1 track gauge	37
2 thumb gauges	1 00
11 pounds gum shellac	12 65
1 gong	5 46
85 pen-holders	2 55
53,232 pounds hay, (received from quartermaster's department)	....
21 claw hammers	23 52
9 hand hammers	9 00
12 spike hammers	20 40
4 spike hammers	4 20
1 set spike hammers	....
5 adze handles	2 75
4 axe handles	2 20
4 broadaxe handles	2 20
4 sets lifting handles	80
14 pick handles	2 94
11 hammer handles	2 42
22 hatchet handles	4 62
4 saw handles	48
64 assorted handles	35 20
6 hatchets and straight belts	8 40
37 hatchets	52 17
25 hasps and staples	3 50
149 hangers and straps	80 46
1 belt hook, (found and taken up)	....
5 assorted hooks, (3 captured, 2 found and taken up)	....
28 feet 3-inch hose	37 52
1 halter and rope	1 50
381 feet hose	762 00
2 quarts writing ink	3 72
1 bottle writing ink	1 86
36 two-ounce bottles writing ink	5 40
1 quart copying ink	1 66
12 bottles red ink	9 00
4 round irons	8 08
2 caulking irons	1 74
2,632 assorted irons, (1,000 captured)	489 60
200 boiler irons, (200 captured)	....
500 new irons, (500 captured)	....
116 Russia irons, (116 captured)	....
1,825 sheet irons, (100 captured)	207 00
200 old irons	....
2,300 bars railroad iron	41,331 00
12,460 pounds pig iron	....
11 inkstands	5 50
7 two-quire journals	10 50
11 three-quire journals	24 75
7 four-quire journals	21 00
9 five-quire journals	33 75
2 base jacks	....
4 claw jacks	525 00
1 hydraulic jack, (captured)	....
1 toe jack	37 50
13 gallons Japan brown	56 03
7 gallons baking brown	21 42
1 jar	40
17 camp kettles	35 70
978 knives	156 48
39 butcher knives	13 93
4 draw-knives	4 84
88 mahogany knobs	1 76
44 tape lines	44 00
108 chalk lines	31 32

Schedule of railroad property, &c.—Continued.

Articles.	Cost.
550 feet chalk line	....
8 blue lights	$16 00
266 white lights	399 00
2 green lights	4 00
53 red lights	106 00
27 brass switch locks and keys, (captured)	52 00
97 chest locks	36 86
19 cupboard locks	5 32
13 drawer locks	7 02
66 rim and knob locks	67 98
3 car locks	6 00
4 dead locks	8 00
62 padlocks	21 70
11 pounds lampblack	4 07
91 pounds excelsior lead	18 20
300 pounds red and black lead	75 00
198 pounds white lead	33 66
6 sides lace leather	24 00
10 sides sole leather	....
54 pounds sole leather	22 95
7 sides tan leather	34 65
2 head lights	210 00
36 barrels lime, (1 captured)	87 50
17 pounds litharge	3 40
90 saw logs, (manufactured)	....
6,500 feet saw logs, (manufactured)	....
234,494 feet lumber	93,797 60
17 coal-oil lamps	19 04
540 coupling lines	648 00
2 spirit levels	4 00
2 latches	1 66
2 packages gold-leaf	16 00
6 bottles mucilage	1 50
26 carpenters' mauls, (manufactured)	....
285 spike mauls	484 50
35 coffee-mills	39 55
1 mandril	7 15
254 pounds Babbitt metal	114 30
26 pounds zinc metal	3 51
1 mule, (received from quartermaster's department)	....
56½ kegs nails	511 32
1,397 pounds nails	125 73
1 keg nuts, iron	28 63
100 pounds nuts, square	12 00
50 pounds nuts	6 00
50 feet spark netting	62 50
74,732 pounds oats, (received from quartermaster's department)	....
145 pounds oakum	23 92
2 barrels oil	122 24
176 gallons coal oil	176 00
28 gallons linseed oil	53 48
94 gallons kerosene oil	94 00
2,624 gallons sperm oil	6,297 60
3 barrels sperm oil	230 40
62 gallons boiler oil	121 52
16 S. B. oilers	2 40
8 quires envelope paper	5 68
190 quires foolscap paper	76 00
490 quires letter paper	176 40
170 quires note paper	45 90
18 sheets oil-paper	9 00
5¾ reams sandpaper	28 75
½ quire cross section paper	3 00
2 reams emery paper	9 70

Schedule of railroad property, &c.—Continued.

Articles.	Cost.
615 lead pencils	$79 95
418 red and blue pencils	313 50
¼ gross slate pencils	18
3 plates and dies	138 36
3 pairs plyers	5 25
3 iron pokers	3 00
1 glue pot, (captured)	....
57 copper pots	51 30
24 tin pails	18 00
35 bake pans	10 50
1 dish pan	87
7 dripping pans	6 09
5 frying pans	1 20
153 mess pans	52 02
2 assorted tin pans	40
159 picks	251 22
7 tamping picks	16 45
349 tin plates	34 90
1 iron pot	50
2 solder pots	1 80
4 rotary hand pumps	476 00
89 pounds hemp packing	20 47
325 rubber packing	487 50
½ coil yarn packing	16½
30 pounds black paint	4 50
1,506 piles	6,024 00
10 pounds prussiate potash	8 00
1,123 steel pens	11 23
2 gross steel pens	3 12
1 punches	4 00
3 smooth planes	4 05
3 fore planes	6 24
1 sash plane	2 40
120 coupling pins	180 00
300 feet gas pipe	132 00
4 joints stove pipe	5 08
13 pieces rubber	1 95
11 rubber rules	11 77
34 boxwood rules, (14 captured)	15 40
2 ratchets	....
4 Malden wire riddles	6 00
5 pounds Venetian red	75
40 connecting rods, (40 captured)	....
1 box roofing for cars	....
4,187 pounds rope, (200 captured)	1,196 10
⅙ coil bell rope	....
½ barrel resin, (found and taken up)	....
20 pounds resin, (found and taken up)	....
17 pounds iron rivets	2 35
2 pen racks	86
29 reamers	188 50
72 brass rings	26 64
6 slates	11 34
4 rivet sets	4 56
3 saw sets, (1 captured)	2 70
1 try square	48
43 oil-stones, (1 captured)	14 28
3 spoke shaves, (2 captured)	50
4 buck saws	4 24
24 hand-saws	38 40
4 cross-cut saws	20 00
1 rip saw	2 71
2 bench screws, (1 captured)	87
3 hand screws	....

Schedule of railroad property, &c.—Continued.

Articles.	Cost.
82 coach screws, (found and taken up)	....
31 gross assorted screws	$32 86
1,192¾ pounds assorted screws	....
48 timber screws	10 08
3 scoops, (captured)	....
198 shovels	263 34
6 skimmers	2 10
703 table-spoons	38 66
14 basting spoons	2 38
118 teaspoons	4 72
180 pounds salt, (60 captured)	1 36
150 slides, (captured)	....
5 pounds soap-stone	65
72 pounds solder	34 56
38 pounds spelter	19 76
6 kegs spikes	54 00
67,000 pounds hook spikes	6,030 00
405 kegs railroad spikes	3,645 00
30,000 pounds bridge spikes	2,550 00
46 kegs bridge spikes	391 00
1 keg cut spikes	11 00
20 pounds rubber springs	24 00
6,202 pounds steel	1,612 52
6 bars steel	39 00
8 pounds pumice stone	1 06
9 pounds ground pumice stone	90
50 pounds rotten-stone	5 00
35 pounds sulphur	4 20
1 set stock and dies	44 25
2 sledges	3 00
12 spreaders	1 20
18 monkey switches	....
70 gunny sacks, (received from quartermaster's department)	....
1 army scale, (found and taken up)	....
1 skillet	....
4 cook-stoves	104 00
2 camp-stoves, (manufactured)	....
2 anti-friction shieves	6 72
15,940 shingles	159 40
3 tons moulding sand	4 50
33 pounds shellac	37 95
33 pairs B. S. tongs	103 62
4 pairs R. R. tongs, (4 captured)	....
3 pairs T. R. tongs	9 42
100 papers tacks	6 25
2,986 pounds tallow	552 41
791,444 feet timber	51,443 86
69 pieces timber	86 25
6 boxes tin	139 98
150 pounds block tin	94 50
18,320 cross-ties	9,160 00
31 tubes for lamps, (6 captured)	1 00
127 gallons turpentine, (19 captured)	349 92
8 pounds twine	3 60
2 water-tanks	130 00
1 set tools	5 00
5 sash tools	20 00
10 trowels	17 50
4 pounds burnt umber	64
2 vices, (1 captured)	17 15
57½ loads varnish	391 00
100 pounds Venetian red	15 00
4 ventilators, (captured)	....

Schedule of railroad property, &c.—Continued.

Articles.	Cost.
½ package vermilion	$1 75
1 tube vermilion	35
18 pounds vermilion	63 00
15,920 cords wood	55,720 00
64 pounds washers	19 84
5,281 pounds cotton waste	2,376 45
125 pounds whiting	5 00
43 pounds wicking	53 75
85 head-light wicks	31 45
½ ream Manilla wrapping	6 25
36 lamp wicks	36
24 monkey wrenches	76 88
14 screw wrenches	43 40
9 wrenches	47 97
25 pounds annealed wire	5 81
1 wedge iron, (captured)	....
106 car-wheels	3,074 00
15 wheelbarrows	....
116 pounds zinc	15 66

No. 7.—*Schedule of property transferred to officers not connected with military railroads since May* 1, 1865.

Schedule of railroad property in the possession of and belonging to the United States on the 1st *day of May, A. D.* 1865, *transferred to officers not connected with the department of military railroads, department of Virginia, transferred by General H. L. Robinson.*

Date.	Articles.	Cost.	To whom transferred.
1865.			
May 10	7,202 feet timber	$252 07	Geo. T. Browning, Capt. and A. Q. M., Giesboro' Point.
	134 railroad chairs	107 20	Do.
	$16\frac{340}{2240}$ tons railroad iron	1,852 32	Do.
	32 piles	160 00	Do.
	13 kegs railroad spikes	117 00	Do.
May 15	464 railroad wheels	10,796 00	E. A. Morse, Capt. and A. Q. M., New Orleans, La.
July 18	1 pile driver	2,000 00	J. G. C. Lee, Capt. and A. Q. M., Alexandria, Va.
Sept. 4	5,264 cords wood	13,160 00	M. J. Ludington, Col. and Chf. Q. M., Washington, D. C.
Nov. 18	1 ton anthracite coal	10 45	J. M. Moore, Capt. and A. Q. M., Washington, D. C.
	2,000 envelopes	19 60	Do.
	4 glass inkstands	2 00	Do.
	1 letter press	23 33	Do.
	3 rubber rules	3 21	Do.
	6 chairs	*	Do.
	1 desk	*	Do.
	2 tables	*	Do.
	1 coal stove	*	Do.
	2 elbows	*	Do.
	6 feet stove-pipe	*	Do.
	1 sheet zinc	*	Do.
	1 coal hod	83	Do.
	1 stove shake	*	Do.
Dec. 11	16 frame buildings	750 00	J. G. C. Lee, Bvt. Lieut. Col. and A. Q. M., Alexandria, Va.

*Price not known; received from Quartermaster's department.

Schedule of railroad property, &c.—Continued.

Date.	Articles.	Cost.	To whom transferred.
1866.			
Jan. 9	3 truck cars	$150 00	Stuart Barnes, Capt. and A. Q. M., Petersburg, Va.
	16,024 feet matched flooring	640 96	Do.
	5,345 feet car lumber, (prepared)	267 25	Do.
	800 feet oak lumber	48 00	Do.
	34,352 feet 2-inch pine plank	1,305 37	Do.
	14,927 feet 3-inch pine plank	593 08	Do.
	354,652 feet hemlock scantling	10,284 90	Do.
	47,043 feet white pine	1,764 00	Do.
	86,500 shingles	865 00	Do.
	23,220 feet pine timber, 6 by 6	870 75	Do.
	8,000 feet pine timber, 6 by 8	300 00	Do.
	6,874 feet pine timber, 8 by 8	257 77	Do.
	31,978 feet square timber	1,199 17	Do.
	1 claw bar	3 16	Do.
	1 pinch	2 38	Do.
	2 sets double blocks	27 75	Do.
	6 water buckets	2 52	Do.
	1 red lamp	2 00	Do.
	4 white lamps	6 00	Do.
	3 picks	4 83	Do.
	150 feet 1¼-inch rope	....	Do.
	1 cross-cut saw	5 45	Do.
	1 pair scales	17 05	Do.
	2 shovels	2 60	Do.
	2 box stoves and pipes	32 90	Do.
	3 cooking stoves and fixtures	78 00	Do.
	9,714 cross-ties	4,857 00	Do.
Feb. 2	582½ cords 4-foot wood	1,695 00	Geo. A. Flagg, Bvt. Maj. and A. Q. M., Harper's Ferry, Va.
	47,142 feet white pine timber	1,885 68	Do.
	500 feet oak timber	30 00	Do.
	7,500 feet hemlock scantling	217 50	Do.
	11 buildings	3,250 00	Do.
	1 platform, 197 by 27	425 52	Do.
	1 platform, 232 by 22	408 32	Do.
	1 platform, 446 by 25	892 00	Do.
	1 platform, 112 by 16	143 36	Do.

Schedule of railroad property in the possession of and belonging to the United States on the 1st *day of May, A. D.* 1865, *and transferred to officers not connected with military railroads, by Captain J. B. Stubbs, department of North Carolina.*

Articles.	Cost.
1 handled axe	$2 06
3 letter-press books, (received from unknown source)	....
84 time-books	35 28
1 riding bridle, (received from quartermaster's department)	....
2 bedsteads, (manufactured)	....
2 alarm bells	....
1 salt box, (manufactured)	....
2 dusting brushes	1 64
3 marking brushes	60
4 paint brushes	1 15
6 whitewash brushes	90
1 bureau, (manufactured)	....
355 feet leather belting	450 88
190 bushels B. S. coal, (received from unknown source)	....

Schedule of railroad property, &c.—Continued.

Articles.	Cost.
1 board letter clip, (received from unknown source)	
1 calendar, (received from unknown source)	
3 office clocks, (received from unknown source)	
1 water-cooler, (manufactured)	
1 oil can, (manufactured)	
10 pounds chrome green	$4 00
1 field desk and table, (manufactured)	
1 writing desk, (manufactured)	
1 steam pile driver, complete	3,200 00
9 stove-pipe elbows	3 60
1 set fixtures for hauling logs	300 42
2 flesh forks	80
1 steam gauge	30 33
1 horse, (received from quartermaster's department)	
2 belt hooks, (received from an unknown source)	
60 pounds Russia iron	15 00
4 3-quire journals	9 00
4 4-quire journals	12 00
4 5-quire journals	15 00
11 white lights	16 50
100 pounds white lead, (received from an unknown source)	
6 chest locks, (received from an unknown source)	
71,000 feet, board measure, lumber, white pine, (manufactured)	
6,715 feet, board measure, lumber, yellow pine, (manufactured)	
1 portable saw-mill, with engine and boiler	4,300 00
1,598 pounds oats, (received from quartermaster's department)	
42 gallons sperm oil, (received from an unknown source)	
2 quires envelope paper	1 42
18 red and blue pencils, (received from an unknown source)	
1 letter press	27 50
2 tin pails, (manufactured)	
2 bake-pans, (manufactured)	
13 tin pans, assorted	2 60
28 paulins, (received from quartermaster's department)	
55 joints stove pipe, (manufactured)	
1 coffee-pot, (manufactured)	
10 feet smoke-pipe	20 00
4 pen racks	1 72
52 grain sacks, (received from quartermaster's department)	
1 set letter scales	4 00
1 riding saddle, (received from quartermaster's department)	
6 buck saws	6 36
2 hydraulic jacks	225 00
6 basting spoons, (received from an unknown source)	
3 box cars, transferred to Treasury Department, (captured from confederate government)	
6 flat cars, transferred to Treasury Department, (captured from confederate government)	
1 wash stand, (manufactured)	
6 stools, (manufactured)	
6 stoves, assorted, (received from an unknown source)	
5 cook stoves and fixtures	150 00
12 kegs cut spikes	120 00
6 tables, (manufactured)	
53 pounds twine	24 30
2 gallons court varnish	13 60
16 pounds wicking	20 00
Total	6,135 66

No. 8.—*Schedule of captured railroad property on hand May* 1, 1865, *showing how and by what authority disposed of.*

Schedule of captured railroad property in the possession of the United States on the 1st *day of May, A. D.* 1865, *in the department of Virginia, returned to the original owners.*

Articles.	HOW DISPOSED OF.					
	Returned to Orange and Alexandria R. R. Co.	Returned to Manassas Gap R. R. Co.	Returned to Alexandria, Loudon and Hampshire R. R. Co.	Returned to Richmond and York River R. R. Co.	Returned to Norfolk and Petersburg R. R. Co.	Returned to Seaboard and Roanoke R. R. Co.
3,313$\frac{1330}{2240}$ tons railroad iron..tons..	158	538	162$\frac{720}{2240}$	538$\frac{724}{2240}$	1,408	508$\frac{2126}{2240}$
88 car wheels	70	18	....	....	....	....
4 drill presses	3	1	....	....	....	....
1 turning machine	1	....	....	....	....	....
1 wiring machine	1	....	....	....	....	....
1 bolt cutting machine	1	....	....	....	....	....
3 planing machines	1	2	....	....	....	....
2 horn stakes	2	....	....	....	....	....
1 set sheet-iron tools	1	....	....	....	....	....
1 set pipe tools	1	....	....	....	....	....
1 pair shears	1	....	....	....	....	....
5 hammers	2	....	3	....	....	....
100 feet shafting	100	....	....	....	....	....
8 lathes, (assorted)	2	5	1	....	....	....
4 planers, (assorted)	3	....	1	....	....	....
2 locomotive engines	1	....	1	....	....	....
1 stationary engine	....	1	....	....	....	....
1 machine shop and building	....	1	....	....	....	....
1 frame for grindstone	....	1	....	....	....	....
3 circular saws and frames	....	3	....	....	....	....
1 crane for blacksmith forge	....	1	....	....	....	....
32 pairs car wheels and axles	....	32	....	....	....	....
33 cars	....	8	6	....	8	11
1 car body, (old)	....	....	....	....	1	....
10 track bars	....	....	10	....	....	....
6 shovels	....	....	6	....	....	....
6 picks	....	....	6	....	....	....
1 track gauge	....	....	1	....	....	....
98,353 pounds wrought-iron scrap and bars	....	....	....	....	31,959	66,394
5,539 pounds steel springs	....	....	....	....	998	4,541
79,315 pounds castings	....	....	....	....	8,059	71,258
13,173 pounds old tire	....	....	....	....	4,640	8,533
36,582 pounds old axles	....	....	....	....	7,958	28,624
92,416 pounds cast-iron scrap	....	....	....	....	33,080	59,336
155,057 pounds old car wheels	....	....	....	....	42,900	112,157
156,463 pounds old railroad iron	....	....	....	....	....	156,463
2,640 feet old railroad iron, (sidings)	....	....	....	....	....	2,640

A schedule of captured railroad property in the possession of the United States on the first day of May, A. D. 1865, *department of North Carolina, expended, sold, and returned to former owners by order of the Secretary of War.*

Articles.	HOW DISPOSED OF.			
	Expended.	Sold.	Returned to former owners.	Total.
21 anvils	1	2	18	21
74 hand axes		74		74
110 broadaxes		110		110
214 augers	9	180	25	214
9 scratch awls	9			9
340 hammered car axles			340	340
50 hand-car axles		29	21	50
7 driving axles			7	7
230 old wheels and axles			230	230
1 apparatus for welding rails			1	1
3 hand-bellows			3	3
12 carpenters' benches			12	12
2 sets braces and bits		2		2
3 draughting-boards			3	3
14 iron braces		14		14
1 breaker and rope			1	1
42 brace bits		42		42
21 auger bits	6	15		21
4 car bits		4		4
1 salt box	1			1
32 pinch bars		32		32
13 claw bars	4	9		13
5 wrench bars		5		5
17 timber bars	5	12		17
11 raising bars	5	6		11
49 lining bars		49		49
49 tamping bars		49		49
31 raising and lining bars		31		31
1 tap-borer		1		1
135 pounds old brass			135	135
1,924 pounds new brass			1,924	1,924
88 Bristol bricks			88	88
1,200 pounds brass and copper			1,200	1,200
50 truck brasses		50		50
1 horse-power boiler			1	1
1 boiler for locomotive			1	1
1 signal bell			1	1
6 engine alarm bells		6		6
39 tons car bolts		39		39
17 passenger cars			17	17
2 mail cars			2	2
4 baggage cars			4	4
86 box cars			86	86
1 rack car			1	1
68 flat cars			68	68
5 truck cars			5	5
2 cutter bolts			2	2
6 cape chisels		6		6
34 cold chisels		34		34
3 iron cutters	3			3
3 plate chucks			3	3
53 chisels	12	26	15	53
1 set firmer chisels		1		1
1 set framing chisels		1		1
1 pair compasses		1		1

Schedule of railroad property, &c.—Continued.

Articles.	HOW DISPOSED OF.			
	Expended.	Sold.	Returned to former owners.	Total.
2 iron cupolas			2	2
2,280 pounds iron castings			2,280	2,280
1 brass cupola			1	1
300 iron clamps			300	300
2 chests of tools			2	2
1 office clock			1	1
1 crane			1	1
3 large chills with flasks			3	3
6 crucibles			6	6
9 small crucibles with flasks			9	9
3 gong cubes		3		3
625 pounds old railroad chairs			625	625
1 iron cupola			1	1
1 brass cupola			1	1
1,000 pounds railroad chairs		1,000		1,000
½ bale chalk			½	½
1,000 pounds sheet copper	74	926		1,000
1 writing desk			1	1
24 dies		24		24
119 drills		25	94	119
5 screw-drivers		5		5
2 crane derricks			2	2
1 drop derrick			1	1
20 locomotive engines			20	20
4 stationary engines		1	3	4
1 locomotive engine, used as stationary			1	1
1 upright engine for pile-driver		1		1
354 round bastard files		354		354
2 fans			2	2
3 blower and belt fans			3	3
16 B. S. tongs		16		16
1 flatter		1		1
2 jig-saw frames			2	2
1 set figures		1		1
1 set tinners' folders		1		1
313 iron flasks			313	313
72 brass flasks			72	72
45 wood flasks		45		45
2 blower fans			2	2
6 B. S. forges			6	6
8 iron forges			8	8
7 assorted files		7		7
8 R. R. frogs			8	8
7 gimlets		6		6
124 track gauges		124		124
24 thumb gauges		24		24
2 hand hammers		1		1
1 engine hammer		1		1
1 steam hammer			1	1
10 machinists' hammers		10		10
1 trip hammer			1	1
29 nail hammers		29		29
3 fire hooks	3			3
1 hatchet		1		1
2 hammers		2		2
2 hooks for balance beam		2		2
16 carrying hooks		16		16
3 curving hooks		3		3

Schedule of railroad property, &c.—Continued.

Articles.	HOW DISPOSED OF.			
	Expended.	Sold.	Returned to former owners.	Total.
2 bramble hooks		2		2
80 assorted handles			80	80
6 curving hammers		6		6
32 spike hammers		32		32
225 hammer handles			225	225
1 stake-holder		1		1
4 copper hatchets		4		4
1 caulking iron		1		1
6 soldering irons		7		6
20,276 pounds assorted iron	1,000	2,237	16,939	20,276
5,000 pounds bar iron			5,000	5,000
1,600 pounds boiler iron	200	1,400		1,600
2 sheets boiler iron			2	2
4 tons pig iron		4		4
5,000 pounds wrought scrap iron				
50,000 pounds cast scrap iron				
500 pounds new iron	500			
48,314 pounds old cast iron			48,314	
45,262 old scrap iron			45,462	
466 pounds Russia iron	116	*350		
11,000 pounds Scotch pig iron			11,000	
1,862 pounds sheet iron	100	762	1,000	
300 tons old railroad iron			300	
891,719 pounds old railroad iron		891,719		
40 screw jacks		40		40
7 hydraulic jacks		4	2	6
10 small jacks			10	10
19 draw-knives		19		19
17 lathes			17	17
9 spirit levels		9		9
1 set letters		1		1
3 coach lamps			3	3
7 iron foundry ladles			7	7
16 barrels lampblack			16	16
7 brass foundry ladles			7	7
3,596 feet lumber			3,596	3,596
771 pounds bar lead			771	771
130 pounds black lead			130	130
1 brass switch lock and keys	1			1
1 barrel lime	1			1
1 coal mill			1	1
2 boring machines		1 on credit.	1	2
1 dubbing machine			1	1
1 tenoning machine			1	1
1 moulding machine			1	1
1 boring machine, with augers			1	1
3 planing mills			3	3
1 blacking and belt mill			1	1
1 wood-planing machine			1	1
1 iron-planing machine			1	1
2 mortising foot machines			2	2
1 slotting machine			1	1
1 shaping machine			1	1
1 iron punching machine			1	1
1 framing machine			1	1
3 sets machinery for lathes			3	3
1 saw mill complete			1	1

* 62 credit; 60 transferred; 228 for cash.

Schedule of railroad property, &c.—Continued.

Articles.	HOW DISPOSED OF.			
	Expended.	Sold.	Returned to former owners.	Total.
51 track mauls		45	6	51
6 bridge mauls		6		6
3½ kegs nails			3½	3½
700 pounds nails			700	700
12 papers finishing nails			12	12
45 gallons rosin oil			45	45
4 assorted punches			4	4
175 pounds assorted paint			175	175
25 pounds mixed paint			25	25
100 pounds putty			100	100
5 car platforms			5	5
10 plates and dies		7		7
4 drill presses			4	4
2 wheel presses			2	2
2 planers			2	2
1 screw plate and die			1	1
2 glue-pots	1	1		2
2 jack planes		2		2
21 joiner planes		21		21
21 smooth planes		21		21
7 plough panel planes		7		7
7 bead planes		7		7
4 sash planes		4		4
3 fore planes		3		3
1 assorted plane		1		1
12 tallow pots		12		12
22 iron pots		22		22
16 cone plates			16	16
1 pump force, shafting and pulleys			1	1
2 pumps		1	1	2
1 steam pump			1	1
9 pulleys			9	9
44 patterns			44	44
1 plough and irons		1		1
30 pike poles		20		20
10 feet smoke pipe*		10		10
50 pounds lead pipe		50		50
1,320 coupling pins			1, 320	1, 320
15 pounds rosin			15	15
100 pounds rivets			100	100
71 reamers		20	51	51
156 reamers and taps			156	156
34 boxwood rules	14	20		34
1 rasp		1		1
6,970 pounds rope	200	6, 070	{ 175 lbs. 800 ft. }	6, 970
120 connecting rods	40	80		120
1 register		1		1
1 iron safe			1	1
6 fire shovels		4		4
2 sledges		2		2
3 bottom swedges		3		3
1 hand screw		1		1
8 bench screws	1		7	8
1 set stocks and dies			1	1
24 steel squares		24		24
6 try squares	1	5		6

* Transferred.

Schedule of railroad property, &c—Continued.

Articles.	HOW DISPOSED OF.			
	Expended.	Sold.	Returned to former owners.	Total.
102 hand-saws		102		102
37 crosscut saws		37		37
1 compass saw		1		1
1 saw set	1			1
5 wood bench-screws		5		5
7 spokeshaves	2	5		7
10 slicks		10		10
250 slides	150	100		250
1 oilstone	1			1
575 feet shafting and pulleys			575	575
1 shaft and hanger		1		1
4 stakes		4		4
12 jack-screws		10	2	12
2 hydraulic screws*		2		2
7 hand-screws		7		7
5 grindstones and fixtures		4		4
14 grindstones			14	14
1 kitchen safe†				
1 spittoon†				
120 pounds salt	60	60		120
6 scoops	3	3		6
5 circular saws			5	5
4 gig-saws			4	4
1 shape			1	1
3 cotton steelyards			3	3
40 gross screws			40	40
5 pounds soapstone			5	5
112 taps		6	106	112
3 sets taps and dies		2	1	3
16 blacksmiths' tools			16	16
1 pair brass tongs			1	1
1 set iron foundry tools			1	1
1 set brass foundry tools			1	1
1 set hand-turning tools		1		1
13 railroad tongs	4	9		13
22 gas-pipe tongs		22		22
2 pipe taps		2		2
19 gallons turpentine	19			19
25 locomotive tyres			25	25
24 tyres for drivers			24	24
8 pairs car trucks			8	8
2 engine trucks			2	2
6 lamp tubes	6			6
3 water tanks		2	1	3
1 office table			1	1
87 coffee tubes			87	87
100 pounds burnt umber			100	100
1 vice	1			1
36 bench vices		13	23	36
1 hand vice			1	1
1 finisher's vice			1	1
16 ventilators	4	10	2	16
135 monkey wrenches		‡133		135
20 screw wrenches		10	10	20
6 tap wrenches		6		6
125 assorted wrenches			125	125
1 iron wedge	1			1
649 car wheels		§169	480	649

* Transferred. † On hand. ‡ 23 on credit, 110 at cost. § 60 on credit.

Schedule of railroad property, &c.—Continued.

Articles.	HOW DISPOSED OF.			
	Expended.	Sold.	Returned to former owners.	Total.
29 tons car wheels			29	29
11 driving wheels			11	11
18 hand-car wheels		18		18
47 rolls webbing			47	47

NOTE.—All the articles mentioned in the column headed "Sold" are reported in the schedule of property sold at auction, and on credit, and are only mentioned here to show how the property captured was disposed of.

Schedule of captured railroad property in possession of the United States on the first day of May, 1865, *at Savannah, Georgia, returned to the Georgia Central Railroad Company, June* 20, 1866, *by order of Major General H. W. Birge, U. S. A.*

Articles.	Articles returned to former owners.
1 iron safe	1 iron safe.
2 wheelbarrows	2 wheelbarrows.
14 locomotive engines	14 locomotive engines.
10 locomotive tenders	10 locomotive tenders.
50 platform cars	50 platform cars.
11 conductors' cars	11 conductors' cars.
7 passenger cars	7 passenger cars.
113 box cars	113 box cars.
15 baggage cars	15 baggage cars.
12 stock cars	12 stock cars.
480 car wheels	480 car wheels.
117 car axles	117 car axles.
14 wheels on axles	14 wheels on axles.
8 sledge-hammers	8 sledge-hammers.
15 bench vices	15 bench vices.
4 sets blacksmiths' tools	4 sets blacksmiths' tools.
9 jack-screws	9 jack-screws.
1 drill press	1 drill press.
2 bolt-cutters	2 bolt-cutters.
1 horizontal drill machine	1 horizontal drill machine.
1 vertical drill machine	1 vertical drill machine.
2 screw-cutting lathes	2 screw-cutting lathes.
1 sliding lathe	1 sliding lathe.
3 wheel drawing machines	3 wheel drawing machines.
1 pair boiler-makers' shears	1 pair boiler-makers' shears.
2 sets boiler and sheet-iron rollers	2 sets boiler and sheet-iron rollers.
1 pattern-maker's lathe	1 pattern-maker's lathe.
1 stationary engine	1 stationary engine.
6 chalk lines	6 chalk lines.
1 chisel and handle	1 chisel and handle.
10 auger handles	10 auger handles.
10 circular saws	10 circular saws.
33 bench-stops	33 bench-stops.
1 Fairbanks's scale	1 Fairbanks's scale.
96 glass lamp chimneys	96 glass lamp chimneys.
8 oil and turpentine cans	8 oil and turpentine cans.
24 paint brushes	24 paint brushes.
1,175 gross assorted screws	1,175 gross assorted screws.
2,550 wood screws	2,550 wood screws.
7,500 fire bolts	7,500 fire bolts.
3,850 carriage bolts	3,850 carriage bolts.

Schedule of captured railroad property, &c.—Continued.

Articles.	Articles returned to former owners.
4,200 pounds nuts	4,200 pounds nuts.
1,800 pounds washers	1,800 pounds washers.
1,300 pounds bolts	1,300 pounds bolts.
350 pounds cut spikes	350 pounds cut spikes.
4,700 pounds car brasses	4,700 pounds car brasses.
35 bars flat steel	35 bars flat steel.
101 bars round iron	100 bars round iron.
317 bars flat iron	310 bars flat iron.
35 bars square iron	30 bars square iron.
260 iron door bars	260 iron door bars.
4 bundles hoop iron	4 bundles hoop iron.
144 door locks	144 door locks.
400 brass car locks	400 brass car locks.
52 boxes window glass	52 boxes window glass.
60 mineral knobs	60 mineral knobs.
38 pounds finishing nails	38 pounds finishing nails.
168 clothes hooks	168 clothes hooks.
300 belt clasps	300 belt clasps.
40 pairs strap hinges	40 pairs strap hinges.
30 hasps and staples	30 hasps and staples.
100 bell-rope bushings	100 bell-rope bushings.
25 car-hangers	25 car-hangers.
115 bell-rope rollers	115 bell-rope rollers.
528 sash stoppers	528 sash stoppers.
1,320 sash lifters	1,320 sash lifters.
30 lamp bushings	30 lamp bushings.
20 stove bushings	20 stove bushings.
21 ventilators	21 ventilators.
28 sets plated car-seat findings	28 sets plated car-seat findings.
28 sets brass car-seat findings	28 sets brass car-seat findings.
7 pieces India-rubber belting	7 pieces India-rubber belting.
1 piece leather belting	1 piece leather belting.
15 car door plates	15 car door plates.
13 pounds brass wire	13 pounds brass wire.
165 pounds block tin	125 pounds block tin.
24 soldering irons	24 soldering irons.
420 pairs cast butts	420 pairs cast butts.
72 sash fastenings	72 sash fastenings.
120 noiseless pulleys	120 noiseless pulleys.
6 sheets tin	6 sheets tin.
6 assorted files	6 assorted files.
10 time-books	10 time-books.
18 cast-iron uriners	18 cast-iron uriners.
90 car springs, volute	90 car springs, volute.
113 car springs, drop	113 car springs, drop.
45 car springs, bumper	45 car springs, bumper.
180 car springs, India-rubber	180 car springs, India-rubber.
8 car springs, English	8 car springs, English.
16 car springs, steel	16 car springs, steel.
10 shackles	10 shackles.
90 pounds glue	90 pounds glue.
25 pounds borax	25 pounds borax.
50 pounds sulphur	50 pounds sulphur.
171 pounds white lead	171 pounds white lead.
75 pounds umber	75 pounds umber.
260 pounds yellow ochre	260 pounds yellow ochre.
120 pounds lampblack	120 pounds lampblack.
20 pounds pumice stone	20 pounds pumice stone.
150 pounds black lead	150 pounds black lead.
240 pounds Spanish brown	240 pounds Spanish brown.
378 pounds chalk	378 pounds chalk.
120 pounds whiting	120 pounds whiting.
706 pounds fire-proof paint	706 pounds fire-proof paint.

Schedule of railroad property, &c.—Continued.

Articles.	Articles returned to former owners.
160 pounds litharge	160 pounds litharge.
15 pounds India red	15 pounds India red.
33 gallons boiled oil	33 gallons boiled oil.
307 pounds tallow	287 pounds tallow.
85,000 pounds iron scraps	85,000 pounds iron scraps.
53,928 feet sawed timber	53,928 feet sawed timber.
20 feet 2½-inch belting	20 feet 2½-inch belting.
120 feet 7-inch belting	120 feet 7-inch belting.

Of the above-mentioned articles, there were used in repairs of railroads 1 bar round iron, 7 ars flat iron, 5 bars square iron, 40 pounds block tin, and 20 pounds tallow.

No. 9.—*Schedule of property on hand May* 1, 1865, *not yet disposed of.*

Schedule of railroad property in the possession of and belonging to the United States on the first day of May, 1865, *and not yet disposed of in the department of Virginia and North Carolina.*

Articles.	Cost.	Where stored.
2 locomotive engines, ("Governor Nye" and "Reindeer")	$23,350 00	Alexandria, Va.
2 15-ton hydraulic jacks	235 00	Do.
1 tender truck	600 00	Do.
13 stoves	213 85	Do.
412 pounds stove-pipe	107 12	Do.
2 letter presses	46 66	Do.
90 second-hand broadaxes	300 60	Do.
1,941 pounds second-hand chairs	194 10	Do.
69 tons good second-hand railroad iron, (45 pounds)	7,935 00	Do.
1,840 pounds railroad chairs	184 00	Do.
3,432 pounds railroad spikes	308 88	Do.
2 counter scales	34 10	Do.
3 platform scales	187 71	Do.
6 dozen files	51 84	Do.
3 dozen augers	36 00	Do.
1 dozen tin steamers, (manufactured)	....	Do.
4 dozen funnels, (manufactured)	....	Do.
6 lanterns	24 00	Do.
2 clocks	19 00	Do.
1 lot office furniture, (cost not known)	....	Do.
1 lot ash car stuff, (cost not known)	....	Do.
1 lot oars and pike poles, (cost not known)	....	Do.
1 lot old iron and car wheels, (bought with the cars)	....	Aquia creek.
10 letter brass clips	12 60	Newbern, N. C.
2 paper-cutters	2 46	Do.
3 office clocks	36 00	Do.
2 water-coolers, (manufactured)	....	Do.
3 ink erasers	2 16	Do.
1 letter press	23 33	Do.
2 seal presses	16 00	Do.
3 pen-racks	2 31	Do.
4 rubber rulers	4 28	Do.
4 inkstands	2 00	Do.
1 kitchen safe, (captured)	....	Do.
1 spittoon, (captured)	....	Do.
8 paper weights	5 60	Do.

Consolidated statement of sales of United States military railroad property in the military division of the Gulf, with interest, payments, &c., to June 30, 1866, under orders of the Secretary of War and Quartermaster General, as per schedules of property and statements of authority accompanying.

Name of company.	Value of property sold.	Amount of interest to June 30.	Value of property sold, with interest to June 30.	Amount of payments.	Amount due June 30.	Terms of sale and remarks.
New Orleans, Opelousas, and Great Western.	$113,773 45	$4,185 25	$117,958 70	....	$117,958 70	Property sold January 31, 1866. Credit of two years, with interest. Payment secured by bond for $227,546 90.
New Orleans, Jackson, and Great Northern.	33,050 00	743 52	33,793 52	....	33,793 52	Property sold March 10, 1866. Credit of two years, with interest. Payment secured by bond for $66,100.
Alabama and Florida	27,109 04	....	27,109 04	$8,299 28	18,809 76	Expenditures in May, June, and July, 1865. Amount to be stopped against claims for transportation of troops and supplies in favor of this company.
Mobile and Great Northern	3,398 99	....	3,398 99	3,398 99	....	Expenditures in May, June, and July, 1865. Amount to be stopped against claims for transportation of troops and supplies in favor of this company.
Total	177,331 48	4,928 77	182,260 25	11,698 27	170,561 98	

ALABAMA AND FLORIDA RAILROAD AND MOBILE AND GREAT NORTHERN RAILROADS.

Schedule of property in the possession of the United States May 1, 1865, by right of purchase, transferred to said roads, with value of labor in reconstructing road, and authority therefor.

Alabama and Florida	$27,109 04
Mobile and Great Northern	3,398 99
Total	30,508 03

Statement of circumstances and authority under which the railroad property included in the accompanying schedule was transferred to the Alabama and Florida railroad and the Mobile and Great Northern railroad by Captain H. L. Wheeler, 96th U. S. C. I., chief engineer Mobile and Memphis railroad, and acting assistant quartermaster, viz:

[Letter of Captain Wheeler, transmitting abstract, with vouchers of amounts expended on said railroads.]

MOBILE, ALABAMA, *July* 12, 1865.

SIR: I have the honor to enclose herewith an abstract, with vouchers, showing the expenses incurred by the United States government in putting the Mobile and Great Northern and Alabama and Florida railroads in running order during the months of May, June, and July, 1865.

Very respectfully, you obedient servant,

HENRY L. WHEELER,
Captain 96th U. S. C. I., Engineer in charge M. and M. Railroad, and Acting Assistant Quartermaster.

[Letter of the Quartermaster General to the chief quartermaster military division of the Gulf, calling for full report, giving copies of the orders under which these expenditures were incurred.]

QUARTERMASTER GENERAL'S OFFICE,
Washington, D. C., August 21, 1865.

COLONEL: Captain H. L. Wheeler, 96th U. S. C. I., engineer in charge, and acting assistant quartermaster, has forwarded to this office abstracts of expenses incurred by the United States in putting the Mobile and Great Northern railroad, and also the Alabama and Florida railroad, in running order during May, June, and July, 1865.

Your attention is respectfully called to General Orders No. 77, Adjutant General's office, and 24, Quartermaster General's office, 1865. You will please make full report, giving copies of the orders under which these expenditures were incurred and the work done.

By order of the Quartermaster General.

Very respectfully, your obedient servant,

ALEXANDER BLISS,
Lieut. Col. and Quartermaster, acting in charge 4th Division.

Colonel C. G. SAWTELLE,
Chief Quartermaster Mil. Div. of the Gulf, New Orleans, La.

[Extract of reply of the chief quartermaster military division of the Gulf, showing authority' enclosing copies of orders under which the expenditures were incurred, and the work done.]

OFFICE CHIEF QUARTERMASTER, MILITARY DIVISION OF THE GULF,
New Orleans, La., September 19, 1865.

GENERAL: I have the honor to acknowledge the receipt of a letter from your office, bearing date of August 21, 1865, enclosing certain abstracts of expenses incurred by the United States in putting in order the Mobile and Great Northern railroad and the Alabama and Florida railroads, under the direction of Captain Henry L. Wheeler, 95th U. S. C. I., acting assistant quartermaster, &c., and directing me to report under what orders those expenditures were made.

In reply, I have to state that on the 3d of May, 1865, Major General E. R. S. Canby, commanding army and division of West Mississippi, instructed Major General A. J. Smith, then commanding the 16th army corps, with headquarters at Montgomery, to send a competent officer to examine the Great Northern railroad, a copy of which instructions is herewith enclosed. Captain Wheeler seems to have been the officer so designated. I have never been furnished with a copy of the orders or instructions given him by Major General Smith, nor can I ascertain that any reports were made by him, or by General Smith, to General Canby.

About the 12th of May Captain Wheeler came to Mobile, having so far repaired the road as to run a locomotive from Montgomery to Tensas Station, near Mobile, and requested to be informed how he should account for the quartermaster's property expended on the road. The matter was referred to Captain H. C. Hodges, assistant quartermaster United States army, at that time having the immediate charge of the supply of troops and matters pertaining to the quartermaster's department on the Alabama river.

On the 5th of May, 1865, instructions were given by Major General Canby to put the presidents and directors of the railroads in Alabama in charge of the same; copy of which instructions is herewith enclosed. These railroad companies were not, however, in a condition to put their roads in running order without the assistance of the military authorities. I directed that a careful account should be kept of all material used, and expenses incurred in putting these roads in running order, the same to be charged against the roads and paid for by subsequent services rendered in transportation of government freight.

My absence in Texas accounts for my delay in reply to the letter of August 21, referred to above.

I am, general, very respectfully, your obedient servant,

C. G. SAWTELLE,
Colonel and Chief Quartermaster, Military Division of the Gulf.

[Enclosure of foregoing letter.—Order of General E. R. S. Canby.—Extract.]

HEADQUARTERS DIVISION OF WEST MISSISSIPPI,
Mobile, Alabama, May 3, 1865.

GENERAL: * * * * * * * *

The general-in-chief further directs that you send a suitable officer and a sufficient cavalry force along the Alabama and Great Northern railroad all the way from Montgomery to Stockton; the officer will investigate the condition of the road and its rolling stock, and report to these headquarters fully, so as to provide for everything necessary to put the road in running order again. If there is any of the directory at Montgomery, or within your reach, they ought to be sent to these headquarters to confer with the general in regard to the road.

Very respectfully, your obedient servant,

P. J. OSTERHAUS,
Major General, Chief of Staff.

Major General A. J. SMITH,
Commanding 16th Army Corps.

[Indorsement of General Canby on foregoing order.]

Respectfully forwarded to the chief quartermaster's headquarters division of the Gulf. After a thorough examination, no orders or instructions can be found that authorized the expenditures made by Captain Wheeler. The object of the examination ordered was to be prepared to put the road in running order, if the low stage of water in the Alabama river should render it necessary to use this road to supply troops in the interior of Alabama. The general instructions given were to make no expenditures and furnish no material except when the use of the road was necessary for military purposes, and using the authority subsequently delegated to me, I directed that no such expenditures should be made until after the estimates had been approved by the general superintendent of military railroads. See General Order No. 85, department of the Gulf, enclosed herewith.

E. R. S. CANBY,
Major General, &c.

[Order of General Canby.—Enclosure of letter of chief quartermaster military division of the Gulf.]

HEADQUARTERS ARMY AND DIVISION OF WEST MISSISSIPPI,
Mobile, Alabama, May 5, 1865.

The president and directors of the Mobile and Ohio, of the Mobile and Great Northern, and of the Alabama and Florida Railroad Companies, will be put in possession of the offices, depots, locomotives, rolling stock, and all other material and property pertaining to said roads, so far as they may be under the control of the United States military authorities within the limits of this command, and are authorized to put the said roads in working order, and to run under the regulations established by the said president and directory, on such conditions as may be imposed by military authority; but this order will not be construed as barring any questions of private interests that may be involved in this property, or as barring or restraining any legal proceedings that may hereafter be instituted against these companies.

E. R. S. CANBY,
Major General Commanding.

Official:

ALFRED FREDBERY,
Captain and Acting Assistant Adjutant General.

[Letter of the Quartermaster General instructing the chief quartermaster military division of Tennessee to charge the amounts against said roads.]

QUARTERMASTER GENERAL'S OFFICE,
Washington, January 20, 1866.

GENERAL: The following amounts have been reported to this office by Henry S. Wheeler, late captain 96th U. S. C. I. and engineer in charge military railroads, Mobile, Alabama, as chargeable against the respective railroad companies, for expenses incurred in putting the roads in running order, viz:

Alabama and Florida railroad for such expenses incurred during May, June, and July, 1865, $27,109 04.

Mobile and Great Northern railroad for expenses incurred during the same period, $3,398 99.

You will please instruct the quartermaster at Nashville, charged with the settlement of transportation accounts, to withhold payment on any accounts presented by these companies against the government for services rendered, and apply them in discharge of this and any other indebtedness of the companies to the government, until the srme are fully satisfied.

By order of Quartertermaster General.

Respectfully, your obedient servant,

ALEXANDER BLISS,
Brevet Colonel and A. Q. M., in charge 4th Division.

Brevet Major General J. L. DONALDSON,
Chief Quartermaster Mil. Div. Tennessee, Nashville, Tenn.

[Reply of chief quartermaster military division Tennessee to foregoing letter of the Quartermaster General, stating that the amounts will be charged against said roads.]

HEADQUARTERS MILITARY DIVISION OF THE TENNESSEE,
CHIEF QUARTERMASTER'S OFFICE,
Nashville, Tenn., January 24, 1866.

GENERAL: Your letter of January 20, 1866, stating that "the following amounts have been reported to this (your) office by Henry L. Wheeler, late captain 96th U. S. C. I. and engineer in charge military railroads, Mobile, Alabama, as charageable against the respective railroad companies for expenses incurred in putting the roads in running order, viz: Alabama and Florida railroad for such expenses incurred during May, June, and July, 1865, $27,109 04; Mobile and Great Northern railroad for such expenses incurred during the same period, $3,398 99," and directing that "the quartermaster at Nashville be instructed to withhold payment from any accounts presented by those companies against the government for services rendered," has been received, and the disbursing officer of railroad accounts directed to carry out your instructions.

Very respectfully, your obedient servant,

J. L. DONALDSON,
Brevet Major General, Chief Q. M. Mil. Div. Tennessee.

Brevet Major General M. C. MEIGS,
Quartermaster General U. S. A., Washington, D. C.

List of quartermasters' stores transferred to and expended on the Alabama and Florida railroad by Captain H. L. Wheeler, 96th U. S. C. I., engineer in charge M. and M. railroad, and acting assistant quartermaster, in the months of May, June, and July, 1865.

Articles.		Cost when new.	Cost of articles and prices charged.
16⅝ cords wood	per cord	$3 00	$50 25
23,700 pounds coal	per ton	13 00	154 05
16 quires foolscap paper	per ream	6 00	4 80
16 quires letter paper	do	6 00	4 80
½ quire folio post paper	do	15 00	37
150 official envelopes	per thousand	12 00	1 80
150 letter envelopes	do	6 00	90
72 time-books	each	75	54 00
4 three-quire blank books	per quire	1 00	12 00
4 six-quire blank books	do	1 00	24 00
60 memorandum books	each	50	30 00
½ quire note paper	per ream	6 00	15
1 quire blotting paper	do	6 00	30
1 gross steel pens	per gross	1 00	1 00
19 quills	each	06	1 14
30 lead pencils	do	10	3 00
24 pieces office tape	per dozen	1 25	2 50
2 inkstands	each	50	1 00
12 quires quartermaster's blanks	per ream	13 00	7 80
14 mules	each	100 00	1,400 00
36 water buckets	do	68	24 48
18 water buckets	do	1 00	18 00
776 pounds anvils	per pound	12½	97 00
200 pounds blacksmiths' tools, steel	do	30	60 00
300 pounds blacksmiths' tools, iron	do	10	30 00
1,536 pounds blacksmiths' tongs	do	12½	192 00
2 pairs bellows	per pair	50 00	100 00
12 bastard files	each	1 25	15 00
300 pounds lathe tools, steel	per pound	25	75 00
2 oil cans, large	each	2 12½	4 25
4 oil cans, small	do	1 31¼	5 25
60 pounds sledge hammers	per pound	15	9 00
180 pounds vices	do	12½	22 50
3 augers, 1½-inch	each	2 00	6 00
18 augers, 2-inch	do	3 00	54 00
20 auger handles	do	25	5 00
1 boring machine	do	20 00	20 00
20 chisels, 2-inch	do	2 50	50 00
7 chisel handles	do	25	1 75
108 hand saw files	do	25	27 00
4 foot adzes	do	5 00	20 00
36 mill-saw files	per dozen	20 00	60 00
6 steel squares	each	3 00	18 00
50 scratch awls	per dozen	12 00	50 00
630 axes	each	1 65	1,039 50
630 axe handles	do	20	126 00
1 set double blocks	per inch	75	15 00
1 set single blocks	per set	5 00	5 00
10 (257 pounds) bake ovens	per pound	12½	32 12
1 pair engine jacks	per pair	75	75 00
1 half-gallon measure and funnel		....	1 50
74 tin pint cups	each	16½	12 21
240 picks	do	1 50	360 00
240 pick handles	do	16	38 40
1 set platform scales and weights	per set	50 00	50 00
1 surveyor's chain	each	15 00	15 00

List of quartermasters' stores &c.—Continued.

Articles.	Cost when new.	Cost of articles and prices charged.
3 sifters .... each..	$1 00	$3 00
1 sheet-iron sign .... do...	6 25	6 25
240 long-handled shovels .... do...	1 32	316 80
240 short-handled shovels .... do...	1 32	316 80
252 short-handled spades .... do...	1 37	345 24
1 scoop .... do...	1 50	1 50
13 tape lines .... do...	2 00	26 00
37¼ pounds bell line .... per pound..	32	11 92
545 pounds old brass .... do.....	25	136 25
53 feet gum belting .... per foot..	50	26 00
208 pounds brass castings .... per pound..	50	103 00
800 pounds boiler rivets .... do.....	12½	100 00
291 chairs for T-rail .... each..	75	218 25
1,266 cross-ties .... do...	25	316 50
10 chalk lines .... do...	25	2 50
135 feet chain .... per foot..	12½	16 87
20 pounds chain .... per pound..	25	5 00
15 pounds sheet copper .... do.....	60	9 00
36 pounds candles .... do.....	45	16 20
1 escape pipe	....	6 25
2 feed pipes	....	5 75
13 books gold leaf .... per book..	2 00	26 00
1 box glass .... per box..	5 00	5 00
1 ounce gold layer .... per ounce..	1 00	1 00
65,845 feet lumber .... per thousand..	25 00	1,646 12
63 barrels lime .... per barrel..	5 00	315 00
24 lanterns .... each..	1 00	24 00
100 pounds white lead .... per pound..	20	20 00
4,600 pounds nails .... do.....	09	414 00
185½ gallons neat's-foot oil .... per gallon..	2 25	417 37
34 gallons pea-nut oil .... do.....	2 00	108 00
5 quart linseed oil .... per quart..	50	50
17 gallons lard oil .... per gallon..	2 25	83 25
1 pound Prussian blue .... per pound..	2 00	2 00
72 pounds packing yarn .... do.....	40	28 80
2 sable pencils .... each..	1 00	2 00
180 pounds Manilla rope .... per pound..	32	57 60
885 pounds Manilla rope .... do.....	29½	261 07
4 kegs railroad spikes .... per keg..	8 00	32 00
291 bars railroad T-rail iron .... per bar..	16 24	4,725 84
100 pounds tank rivets .... per pound..	12½	12 50
100 gross screws .... per gross..	1 50	150 00
1 quart spirits turpentine .... per quart..	1 00	1 00
50 kegs cut spikes, assorted .... per keg..	9 00	450 00
7 Japanned tins .... each..	1 00	7 00
1 ounce vermilion red .... per ounce..	1 50	1 50
60 pounds butts, wrought iron .... per pound..	12½	7 50
100 washers, assorted .... each..	10	10 00
200 pounds wrought iron .... per pound..	06	12 00
225 pounds sheet gum .... per pound..	1 50	337 50
1 eraser .... each..	1 00	1 00
5 pounds blue smalts .... per pound..	2 00	10 00
76 pounds cotton rope .... do.....	60	45 60
Value of quartermasters' stores transferred and expended	....	15,692 55
Value of labor in reconstructing the road	....	11,416 49
Total amount to be charged to Alabama and Florida railroad	....	27,109 04

List of quartermaster stores expended on the Mobile and Great Northern railroad, under the direction of Captain Henry L. Wheeler, 96th U. S. C. I., engineer in charge of M. and M. railroad, and acting assistant quartermaster, during the month of May, 1865.

Articles.		Cost when new.	Cost of articles and prices charged.
4 quires foolscap paper	per ream..	$6 00	$1 20
4 quires letter paper	do....	6 00	1 20
½ quire folio post	do....	15 00	37
6 quills	each..	06	36
6 lead pencils	do....	10	60
4 pieces office tape	per dozen..	1 25	42
6 quires quartermaster's blanks	per ream..	13 00	3 90
4 pounds candles	per pound..	45	1 80
75 pounds nails	do....	09	6 75
15½ gallons neat's-foot oil	per gallon..	2 25	34 87
5 gallons lard oil	do....	2 25	11 25
5 gallons peanut oil	do....	2 00	10 00
7 cords wood	per cord..	6 00	42 00
6 cords wood	do....	3 00	18 00
300 pounds coal	per ton..	13 00	1 95
7,000 feet lumber	per M..	25 00	175 00
10 pounds bell line	per pound..	32	3 20
10 pounds packing yarn	do....	40	4 00
2 chalk lines	each..	25	50
12 bars T railroad iron	do....	16 24	194 88
12 chairs for T rail	do....	75	9 00
40 cross-ties	do....	25	10 00
40 pounds bolts	per pound..	12½	5 00
200 pounds railroad spikes	do....	08	16 00
Value of quartermaster stores expended		....	552 25
Value of labor in reconstructing road		....	2,846 74
Total amount to be charged the Mobile and Great Northern railroad		....	3,398 99

NEW ORLEANS, OPELOUSAS, AND GREAT WESTERN RAILROAD.

Schedule of property in possession of the United States May 1, 1865, by right of capture and of purchase, transferred to said road, with authority therefor.

Property purchased	$113,773 45
Property captured	173,088 21
Total	286,861 66

Statement of circumstances and authority under which the New Orleans, Opelousas, and Great Western railroad was transferred to the directors of said road by Brevet Colonel J. G. Chandler, acting chief quartermaster, military division of the Gulf, viz:

QUARTERMASTER GENERAL'S OFFICE,
Washington, D. C., August 18, 1865.

COLONEL: The government should be relieved at the earliest possible day of the expenses of maintaining and operating railroads heretofore held by it for military purposes.

You will cause the railroads in the military division of the Gulf to be at once turned over to the several companies or to their representatives, or such other persons or civil authorities as the general commanding the military division shall advise.

In carrying out these transfers you will be governed by the principles recommended by the Quartermaster General in a letter dated May 19, 1865, to the Secretary of War, and by him approved, copy of which is herewith furnished you.

Inventories of the railroad material and supplies, rolling stock, &c., which are the property of the United States, setting forth the amount and estimated value of the articles, will be prepared and forwarded to this office with recommendations as to the most advantageous modes and places of disposition of the same.

Very respectfully, your obedient servant,

M. C. MEIGS,
Quartermaster General, Brevet Major General U. S. A.

Colonel C. G. SAWTELLE,
Chief Quartermaster Mil. Div of Gulf, New Orleans, La.

OFFICE OF CHIEF QUARTERMASTER MILITARY DIVISION OF THE GULF,
New Orleans, Louisiana, February 15, 1866.

GENERAL: In obedience to orders received from the Quartermaster General, dated August 18, 1865, I have transferred the New Orleans, Opelousas and Great Western railroad to the directors, and enclose herewith for file the bond and lists of property transferred. The appraisal was made by two experienced men in railroad matters, and acceptable to myself as well as the railroad company.

Very respectfully, your obedient servant,

J. G. CHANDLER,
Brevet Col. U. S. A., Chief Acting Q. M. Mil. Div. of the Gulf.

Major General M. C. MEIGS,
Quartermaster General U. S. A., Washington, D. C.

List of rolling stock and material to be transferred to the president, directors, and company of the New Orleans, Opelousas, and Great Western railroad, as appraised by Messrs. Pandelly and Shakspeare.

Articles.	Appraised value.
1 locomotive and tender, "Texas"	$9,000 00
1 locomotive and tender, "Nachitoches"	8,000 00
1 locomotive and tender, "St. Mary's"	10,000 00
1 locomotive and tender, "Terrebonne"	6,000 00
1 locomotive and tender, "Tiger"	7,500 00
1 locomotive and tender, "Lafourche"	10,000 00
1 locomotive and tender, "New Orleans"	8,500 00
1 locomotive and tender, "New Iberia"	10,000 00
1 locomotive and tender, "Sabine"	10,000 00
Axles and irons of truck for first-class passenger car	800 00
2 first-class passenger cars, (old)	4,600 00
2 first-class passenger cars, (old)	4,100 00
1 second-class passenger car, (old)	2,100 00

Schedule of railroad property, &c.—Continued.

Articles.	Appraised value.
1 caboose car, No. 7	$950 00
1 caboose car, (old and not in order)	450 00
Irons of trucks, (baggage cars Nos. 1 and 2)	1,200 00
Iron parts of trucks for twenty-four box cars, Nos. 9, 22, 24, 33, 30, 21, 29, 31, 32, 20, 36. 17, 14, 29, 4, 16, 3, 34, 35, 15, 26, 1, 19, 11	8,400 00
4 box cars, Nos. 2, 12, 18, 8, at $450 each	1,800 00
4 box cars, Nos. 37, 6, 25, 23, at $400 each	1,600 00
1 box car, No. 10	300 00
Iron parts of trucks of stock cars Nos. 33, 10, 5, 9, 18, 4, 11, 2, 28, 7, 6, 12, and one in course of construction	4,900 00
Iron parts of trucks of eight wood cars, Nos. 6, 5, 1, 7, 4, 9, 3, 2	2,800 00
1 wood car, No. 8	550 00
1 one-horse car, (old)	200 00
1 stock and 1 platform car, (broken,) appraised at value of trucks and old iron	350 00
Iron parts of trucks of thirty platform cars, Nos. 30, 38, 33, 60, 10, 59, 66, 68, 3, 61, 12, 36, 49, 6, 14, 57, 52, 28, 11, 1, 58, 45, 51, 53, 34, 23, 55, 3, 24, 16	10,500 00
16 platform cars, Nos. 41, 25, 39, 64, 48, 29, 64, 22, 20, 7, 44, 62, 54, 63, 31, 35, at $650 each	10,400 00
3 platform cars, Nos. 27, 13, 20, at $450 each	1,350 00
4 platform cars, Nos. 19, 26, 15, 5, at $350 each	1,400 00
Boutte.	
1 portable engine and boiler	500 00
1 saw-table and mandrel	15 00
84 feet 2-inch gas-pipe	25 20
97 feet 1-inch gas-pipe	19 40
6 hand cars, at $125, (good)	750 00
10 hand cars, at $60, (bad order)	600 00
9 push cars, at $70, (good)	630 00
2 push cars, at $40, (bad)	80 00
Tools in machine shop.	
1 lathe, 14 feet brd., 3 feet swing, screw-cutting	1,050 00
1 lathe, 14 feet brd., 2 feet swing	400 00
1 drill press	600 00
1 planing machine, 11 feet brd., 3 feet wide	1,200 00
1 large lathe, 19 feet brd., 7 feet swing	2,850 00
1 bolt-cutter	175 00
13 taps and dies	80 00
1 lathe, 8 feet brd., 5-inch swing	175 00
1 stationary engine and boiler for running machinery	2,800 00
1 clock	12 00
1 desk	8 00
12 tap wrenchers	13 33
95 assorted taps	120 00
22 drills	18 00
3 counter drills	9 00
20 taps	30 00
21 reamers	36 50
1 ratchet brace	8 00
5 sets of stocks and dies	40 00
1 spirit level	1 50
1 steel chisel bar	2 67
1 wrench	1 50
1 large oil can	2 50
3 fire-pokers	4 00
1 pair tongs	2 00
1 cupboard	7 00
1 surface gauge for planes	6 00
4 parallel bars	12 00
6 lathe tools, 25 pounds, at 50 cents	12 50

Schedule of railroad property, &c.—Continued.

Articles.	Appraised value.
1 cistern, (old)	$75 00
1 brass faucet	2 00
1 pair callipers	6 00
1 block and fall	12 00
1 mandrill, 65 pounds, at 2 cents	1 30
5 swing tools	7 50
3 dogs	6 00
1 old car axle, 310 pounds, at 4 cents	12 40
12 "S" wrenches	18 00
1 spanner	1 50
3 lathe tools	4 50
1 face plate	10 50
40 lathe tools	85 20
559 pounds mandrels, at 6 cents	33 54
4 small drills	2 00
4 boring bars, at $4 each	16 00
4 dogs, at $2 each	8 00
6 cutters	4 75
5 vices	40 00
16 small drills	8 00
40 lathe tools	64 00
8 small taps	10 00
1 boring bar for taper holes	6 00
19 chases, at $1 50 each	28 50
16 steel mandrels	14 00
17 lathe tools	25 50
16 counter borers, at $3 each	48 00
12 drills, at $1 33⅓ each	16 00
2 large ratchet jacks	110 00
12 caulking tools	22 00
10 punches	15 00
6 reamers	14 00
1 stay bolt tap	4 00
7 flue mandrels	12 00
72 car axles, 22,176 pounds, at 4 cents	887 04
24 winches	55 00
1 coppersmith forge and pipe	40 00
1 truck	25 00
1 set rollers for boiler-maker	350 00
1 paint mill	3 50
1 desk	9 00
1 turning lathe, face plates	70 00
Shaft and pulley in blacksmith's machine shop	900 00
1 40-foot turn table	2,033 33
1 stationary engine, about 8 by 14, for lumber wharf	1,000 00
1 large iron tank	250 00
Store-room.	
1 pound raw sienna	25
Blacksmith's shop.	
3 forges, at $60 each	180 00
2 cranes	60 00
49 pair tongs	60 00
3 flatters	4 80
13 fullers	26 00
6 sets hammers	10 00
2 button sets	4 00
11 chisels	9 00
3 anvils	24 00
36 swedges	30 00

Schedule of railroad property, &c.—Continued.

Articles.	Appraised value.
3 cast-iron swedge blocks	$30 00
21 heading tools	27 00
3 sledges and handles	6 00
1 traveller	1 50
6 cup tools	7 00
20 mandrels	17 50
1 vice	8 00
1 framing block	20 00
1 pair callipers	1 75
2 iron rams	16 00
70 car-axles, 21,560 pounds, at 4 cents	862 40
4 iron wrenches	12 00
13 work benches	58 00
15 old steel springs, 3,825 pounds, at 8 cents	306 00
8 old steel springs, 2,120 pounds, at 6 cents	127 20
12 old steel springs, 300 pounds, at 8 cents	24 00
510 pounds blacksmiths' tools, at 8 cents	40 80
2 jack screws	30 00
1 baggage truck	16 00
1 lot patterns	66 67
151 car-axles, 46,508 pounds, at 4 cents	1,860 32
Old car stock, 6,966 pounds, at 3 cents	208 98
30,250 pounds spring steel, (old,) at 3 cents	907 50
5,480 pounds old car stock, at 3 cents	164 40
2,030 pounds old bolts and nuts, at 5 cents	101 50
110 pounds old iron, wrought	2 10
1 press for taking off car-wheels	200 00
370 pounds old tires, at 4 cents	14 80
2 desks	40 00
1 table	9 00
1 armoir	20 00
2 railroad maps	1 50
2 models for steamboats	50
7 freight trucks	70 00
2 four-wheel trucks	30 00
1 portable locker	35 00
8 fire tongs	12 00
6 ash rakes	9 00
7 jack screws	56 00
7 pinch bars	14 00
1 mandrel, 150 pounds, at 4 cents	6 00
3 engine truck-wheels, 1,380 pounds, at 2 cents	27 60
259 car wheels, (burnt,) 119,140 pounds, at 2 cents per pound	2,382 80
101 car axles, 308 pounds each	436 32
9 push-car wheels and five axles, 920 pounds, at 4 cents	36 80
3 old McGowan's pumps and stands	16 00
1 old McGowan's pump and stand	2 00
3 old car-catchers, of wood	15 00
2 old car-catchers, of iron	25 00
1 wheel and stand for bridge	12 00
689 bars railroad iron, (old,) 4,375 yards, 63 pounds to a yard, at 2 cents	5,512 50
60,670 pounds old bridge castings, (burnt,) at 1½ cent	910 05
39,961 pounds wrought-iron from burnt cars and bridges	999 02
7,229 pounds burnt car springs, at 5 cents	361 45
988 pounds steel springs, at 8 cents	79 04
3 ball pumps, (in bad order)	12 00
Total value	173,088 21

G. FANDEBY.
JAMES E. SHAKSPEARE.

Approved:

B. CHANDLER,
Captain and Assistant Quartermaster, Brevet Colonel U. S. A.

List of railroad property transferred to the president and directors of the New Orleans, Opelousas, and Great Western railroad, belonging to the United States government, for the value of which said road has given bond for $227,546 90 to secure payment. Appraisal made by disinterested parties experienced in railroad matters, appointed by Colonel J. G. Chandler, acting chief quartermaster military division of the Gulf.

Date.	Articles.	Appraised value.
1866.		
Jan. 31	1 locomotive and tender, Colonel Holabird	$20,000 00
	1 first-class passenger car, less iron parts of trucks	3,700 00
	2 caboose cars, (Nos. 13 and 1)	2,100 00
	2 baggage cars, (Nos. 1 and 2,) less iron parts of trucks	2,600 00
	24 box cars, (Nos. 9, 22, 24, 33, 30, 21, 27, 31, 32, 20, 36, 17, 14, 29, 4, 16, 3, 34, 35, 15, 26, 1, 9, and 11,) less iron parts of trucks	12,000 00
	16 stock cars, (Nos. 3, 3, 5, 9, 18, 4, 11, 2, 10, 2, 8, 7, 6, 12, and 1,) in course of construction, less iron parts of trucks	6,175 00
	8 wood cars, (Nos. 6, 5, 1, 7, 4, 9, 3, and 2,) less iron parts of trucks	2,600 00
	2 mules and harness	350 00
	30 platform cars, (Nos. 30, 38, 33, 60, 10, 55, 66, 68, 3, 61, 12, 36, 49, 6, 14, 57, 52, 28, 11, 1, 58, 45, 51, 53, 34, 23, 55, 3, 24, and 16,) less iron parts of trucks	9,000 00
	1 steamboat (Kepper) and apparel	4,500 00
	Carpenter shop, 160 by 50, and shingled	5,500 00
	Addition to machine shop	2,000 00
	Saw shed, 25 by 31	125 00
	New blacksmith shop and forges, 44 by 31	1,000 00
	Coal shed and bin	50 00
	Tool-house, 28 by 10	150 00
	Cistern and enclosures in depot	225 00
	Cistern near engine-house	125 00
	Frame on which cistern stands	75 00
	Boutte.	
	Tank-house, 26 by 16, and large cistern	1,000 00
	Platform and shed, 50 by 20, and shed over engine, 62 by 17	600 00
	1 circular saw	12 00
	36 feet 5-inch leather belting	10 80
	1 vice	6 00
	Tigerville.	
	1 portable engine	600 00
	1 counter shaft and pulleys	25 00
	1 saw-table and mandrel	15 00
	1 circular saw	8 00
	52 feet 5-inch leather belting	15 60
	48 feet 2-inch copper pipe	40 00
	1 hogshead for water	2 50
	45 feet 2-inch galvanized pipe, (iron)	22 50
	40 feet lead pipe	10 00
	14 feet India-rubber belting	4 00
	Shed over engine	75 00
	Tank-house and cistern	700 00
	Bayou Bœuf.	
	Dwelling, platform, warehouse, and office, 50 by 24; platform, 26 by 50; storehouse on platform	800 00
	Section 16.	
	Addition to kitchen, 13 by 22	50 00

List of railroad property transferred, &c.—Continued.

Date.	Articles.	Appraised value.
1866.	*Section* 14.	
Jan. 31	Addition to kitchen, 13 by 22	$50 00
	Terrebonne.	
	Warehouse, 60 by 40, and platform	1,300 00
	Platform, 185 by 30, shed thereon	1,800 00
	Station-house	400 00
	Raceland.	
	Station-house and platform	400 00
	Lafourche.	
	1 platform, 75 by 40; 1 storehouse, 12 by 12	450 00
	Bayou des Allesmands.	
	No. 6 section-house, 28 by 24	450 00
	4 hand-car houses	300 00
	6,426 pounds good fish bar iron	257 04
	9,093 pounds bad fish bar iron	181 86
	67,260 pounds bad chair iron	1,345 20
	20,918 pounds good chair iron	627 57
	28 feet 6-inch rubber hose	30 00
	10 feet 6-inch rubber hose	6 00
	14 feet 6-inch rubber hose	3 00
	9 hand-cars, at $125 each	1,125 00
	9 push-cars, at $70 each	630 00
	Partitions and ceilings	125 00
	Tools in machine shop.	
	6 tap wrenches	6 66
	30 taps	45 00
	10 reamers	17 50
	2 ratchet braces	16 00
	1 log slate	75
	2 nut mandrels	1 50
	2 steel chisel bars	5 33
	2 straight-edges	6 00
	1 brass oil-feeder	1 75
	1 oil can	1 50
	1 iron bucket	1 75
	1 18-inch monkey wrench	2 00
	1 pair gas tongs	2 50
	3 pounds oxalic acid	1 20
	10 wooden buckets	5 00
	1 axe	1 00
	1 shovel	1 50
	1 12-inch monkey wrench	2 00
	4 small S wrenches	7 00
	2 cold chisels	2 00
	1 belt-punch	50
	1 oil-feeder	1 00
	1 tallow-can	1 00
	1 squirt-can	75
	1 globe lantern	2 50
	1 padlock	30
	1 cupboard	7 00
	6 lathe tools, 20 pounds, at 50 cents	10 00

List of railroad property transferred, &c.—Continued.

Date.	Articles.	Appraised value.
1866.		
Jan. 31	1 5-feet grindstone, shaft, and pulley	$115 00
	1 frame and box of stone	15 00
	220 pounds bolts and nuts, at 15 cents	33 00
	265 pounds bolts and nuts, at 15 cents	39 75
	20 old files	10 00
	5 pounds copper vice clamps, at 30 cents	1 50
	134 pounds nuts, at 15 cents	20 10
	13 cold chisels	9 75
	44 pounds bolts and nuts, at 15 cents	6 60
	2 monkey wrenches	4 00
	1 gas wrench	2 00
	1 hammer	1 75
	1 squirt-can	50
	5 old files	2 50
	11 cold chisels	14 00
	3 face plates	31 50
	3 machine racks	36 00
	3 boiler-makers' clamps	21 00
	4 centre punches	1 00
	10 lathe tools	18 80
	5 lathe reamers	12 00
	3 cape chisels	1 50
	2 boring bars, at $4 each	8 00
	3 dogs, at $2 each	6 00
	1 single block and fall	4 00
	16 small drills, at 50 cents each	8 00
	10 cold chisels	7 50
	10 lathe tools	16 00
	9 chases, at $1 50 each	13 50
	8 counter borers, at $3 each	24 00
	6 drills, at $1 33⅓ each	8 00
	65 pounds bolts and nuts, at 15 cents	9 75
	1 cupboard	10 00
	1 vice	8 00
	1 boiler maker's forge	30 00
	1 tool cupboard	8 00
	10 punches	15 00
	2 stay-bolt taps	8 00
	5 riveting hammers and handles	10 00
	3 forming blocks	180 00
	1 boiler-maker's bench	16 00
	1 blacksmith's bellows	10 00
	1 anvil	8 00
	1 pair large shears	175 00
	1 large punch	150 00
	1 small punch	75 00
	1 small forge	12 00
	1 goose-neck punch	30 00
	15 wrenches	35 00
	1 pair bellows	12 00
	1 iron ladle	3 00
	41 tamping bars, 416 pounds, at 16 cents	66 56
	35 pounds bolt copper, at 76 cents	24 50
	78 rubber car springs, 5 by 5, 468 pounds	468 00
	172 rubber car springs, 6 by 6, 1,548 pounds	1,548 00
	2 plates glass, 24 inches square	2 50
	100 pounds hemp packing, at 25 cents	25 00
	24⅓ yards canton flannel, at 30 cents	7 30
	100 pounds putty	10 00
	425 pounds tallow, at 16 cents	68 00
	1 old man	25 00
	7 pounds lampblack	3 50
	1 office desk	12 00

List of railroad property transferred, &c.—Continued.

Date.	Articles.	Appraised value.
1866.		
Jan. 31	110 pounds sheet copper, at 65 cents	$71 30
	80 pounds soap	8 00
	8 file handles	2 00
	14 car catches	21 00
	2 pairs canvas tongs	8 00
	5 pieces grass line	2 50
	2½ pounds lampwick	2 50
	¼ gross matches	75
	17 kegs cut nails	119 00
	2 kegs cut spikes	18 00
	21 rubber springs, 6 by 6, 189 pounds	189 00
	7 boxes glass, 20 by 18	84 00
	22 gallons japan varnish	66 00
	3 pounds brass wire	1 80
	35 pounds copper wire	26 25
	30 pounds iron wire	4 20
	24 hand screws	24 00
	100 pounds white lead	16 00
	50 pounds red lead	9 00
	11 gross silver head screws	13 00
	13 quires sandpaper	3 25
	5 jig-saws	6 00
	73 sash-lifts	7 30
	175 pounds yellow ochre	20 62
	45 pounds whiting	6 00
	40 pounds chalk	4 50
	40 pounds glue	12 00
	162 pounds sheet lead	20 25
	4 scrubbing brushes	3 00
	107 papers tacks	16 25
	86 papers finishing nails	12 90
	948 pounds brass castings	474 00
	1 glazier's diamond	1 50
	80 pounds sheet rubber	80 00
	2 small jack screws	14 00
	4 met-car flanges	12 00
	19 glass chimneys	5 70
	43 new files	28 00
	1 press for crank-pins	35 00
	1 desk	9 00
	1 inkstand	1 50
	1 black walnut table	12 00
	2 chairs	6 00
	1 water cooler	5 00
	1 log slate	75
	1 washstand	4 00
	1 bucket	50
	1 stove	6 00
	1 stool	2 00
	26 feet stove pipe	2 60
	2 rulers	1 00
	1 gauge tester	30 00
	3 dogs	6 00
	5 buckets	2 50
	1 saw table	20 00
	1 saw, mandrel, pulley, and boxes	18 00
	1 24-inch saw	10 00
	1 scroll saw table	75 00
	3 circular saws, $\frac{1}{20}$-inch to $\frac{2}{10}$-inch	8 00
	Shafts and pulleys in saw shop	176 00
	Shaft and pulley in blacksmith and machine shops	300 00
	2 40-feet turn tables	4,066 66
	1 rotary pump	250 00
	1 McGowan's pump	150 00

List of railroad property transferred, &c.—Continued.

Date.	Articles.	Appraised value.
	Store-room.	
1866.		
Jan. 31	8 pounds chrome yellow	$2 80
	1 pound Indian red	35
	2 pounds ultra-marine	1 50
	2½ pounds Chateenuc lake	2 50
	5 pounds light vermillion	2 00
	11 pounds drop black	4 40
	1 pound raw umber	25
	10 pounds raw sienna, in oil	2 50
	2 pounds Van Dyke brown	50
	2 pounds burnt sienna	50
	1 pound chrome green	40
	5 pounds burnt umber	1 25
	5 pounds raw sienna	1 25
	132 gallons lard oil	297 00
	10 gallons asphaltum varnish	25 00
	25 gallons copal varnish	100 00
	43 gallons copal varnish	172 00
	1 stove	6 00
	26 feet stove-pipe, cap and flange	3 00
	4 paint buckets	2 00
	3 2½-gallon oil cans	6 00
	15 pounds ground pumice stone	1 80
	1 shop bell, (390 pounds)	234 07
	29 assorted locks	18 00
	50⅓ gross iron screws	50 00
	30¼ gross brass screws	75 00
	53½ pairs wrought and cast butt hinges	18 00
	11 pairs brass hinges	5 50
	38 yards webbing	9 20
	82 papers brads	12 35
	130 feet 4-inch wrought-iron pipe	195 00
	2,493 feet 2-inch gas pipe, (galvanized)	623 20
	18 feet 2½-inch gas pipe	9 05
	13 feet 1½-inch gas pipe	12 00
	177 feet 1-inch gas pipe	26 50
	120 feet 2½-inch copper pipe	120 05
	130 feet 2-inch copper gas pipe	130 00
	5 brass stop-cocks	45 00
	6 2-inch T pipes	4 50
	2 2-inch elbows	1 00
	4 2-inch union couplings	7 00
	Blacksmith's shop.	
	1 forge	60 00
	1 crane	30 00
	1 tilt-hammer	275 00
	1 fan and 75 feet 6-inch gas pipe	225 00
	2 wheelbarrows	8 00
	49 pairs tongs	60 00
	2 flatters	3 20
	13 fullers	26 00
	6 set hammers	10 00
	11 chisels	9 00
	6 punches	6 00
	3 anvils	24 00
	36 swedges	30 00
	2 cast-iron swedge blocks	20 00
	21 heading tools	27 00
	1 hammer and anvil	2 50
	2 sledges and handles	4 00

List of railroad property transferred, &c.—Continued.

Date.	Articles.	Appraised value.
1866.		
Jan. 31	3 shovels	$3 00
	4 log slates	3 50
	3 water buckets	4 00
	20 mandrels	17 50
	1 brass cock	1 50
	70 pounds blister steel	14 00
	1 lock	1 25
	335 pounds angle iron	33 50
	435 pounds Manilla rope, (old and new)	21 75
	270 pounds chain	27 00
	8 blocks	8 00
	1,229 feet belting, (old)	307 25
	30 pounds iron chain	3 00
	Brass foundry.	
	1 brass furnace	25 00
	2 troughs	8 00
	1 tool cupboard	10 00
	13 iron flasks	12 00
	27 wood flasks	18 00
	1 mortar and pestle	6 00
	4 flask weights	12 00
	1 iron ingot mould	1 50
	14 flask clamps	3 50
	5 pairs tongs	9 00
	1 core bench	6 00
	1 spike machine	18 00
	1 cock	1 50
	1 brass pump	8 00
	2 locks	2 00
	1 small block and fall	4 00
	13 work-benches	117 00
	1 bench screw	2 50
	1 lantern	2 00
	1 oil-feeder	75
	1 axe handle	1 00
	100 feet rubber hose	15 00
	1 force pump	60 00
	6 brass cocks	36 00
	1 painter's cupboard	5 00
	13,369 pounds iron, (new, in rack)	935 83
	190 pounds spring steel, at 25 cents per pound	47 50
	13 oak break beams	39 00
	5 cypress carlings	5 00
	5 switch stands	20 00
	10 stanchions	8 00
	1 stove and 28 feet stove pipe	5 00
	1 grindstone and fixtures	12 00
	12 stanchions	9 00
	1 portion of hand car	6 00
	1 boring machine	3 00
	1 spring-balance scale	1 25
	13 brass thimbles	7 00
	4 ventilators	5 00
	1 6-foot cross-cut saw	3 00
	1 truck	6 00
	10 truck beams	30 00
	1 wheelbarrow	6 00
	1 shovel	1 25
	4 car sells	24 00
	1 block and fall	6 00

List of railroad property transferred, &c.—Continued.

Date.	Articles.	Appraised value.
1866.		
Jan. 31	100 feet rope	$10 00
	5 buckets	2 50
	1 step-ladder	6 00
	1 hand-car frame, (oak)	12 00
	1 engine cab	20 00
	1 cupboard	4 00
	2 pounds shellac	1 50
	1 1-gallon oil can	1 25
	14 carpenter's benches	140 00
	15 feet mahogany	2 25
	15 bench screws	15 00
	1 grindstone and fixtures	8 00
	1 stove pipe, 10 feet long	4 00
	1 glue pot	75
	1 lot patterns	33 33
	5 car cushions	7 00
	4 car doors	12 00
	12 freight-car doors	48 00
	2 carpenter benches	25 00
	2 sieves	3 00
	1 mortising machine, (7 bits)	40 00
	32 carlings	32 00
	75 feet white-pine lumber	7 50
	60 feet rosewood	12 00
	1 cupboard	14 00
	97 33-inch car wheels, (new,) 44,620 pounds	2,231 00
	37 30-inch car wheels, (new,) 16,085 pounds	804 25
	27 28-inch car wheels, (new,) 10,800 pounds	540 00
	8 26-inch car wheels, (new,) 2,920 pounds	146 00
	26,290 pounds new castings, at 5½ cents	1,445 95
	1,340 pounds new bolts and nuts, at 15 cents	201 00
	1,750 pounds new castings	96 25
	1,750 feet black walnut, at 12½ cents	217 50
	2,900 feet poplar, at 7 cents	203 00
	3,560 feet cypress, at 3½ cents	124 60
	9,400 feet oak, at 12½ cents	1,175 00
	18,735 feet yellow pine, at 3½ cents	655 72
	9 locks	6 00
	1 cistern next to carpenter shop	90 00
	1 brass faucet	1 25
	1 picket fence around lumber yard	110 00
	17 frames and 18 shutters, with iron gratings	36 00
	1 cistern near the fan of smith's shop	75 00
	Office at depot.	
	1 table in lamp-room	3 00
	3 desks	60 00
	1 table	9 00
	3 stands	7 50
	2 water coolers	14 00
	2 iron safes	450 00
	18 chairs	36 00
	5 stools	10 00
	1 armoir	20 00
	4 paper baskets	3 00
	12 spittoons	4 50
	2 feather brooms	05
	1 eyelet machine	2 00
	16 inkstands	4 00
	13 paper weights	2 00
	1 cup and sponge	50

List of railroad property transferred, &c.—Continued.

Date.	Articles.	Appraised value.
1866.		
Jan. 31	3 deliveries	$0 75
	1 copying press	12 00
	1 cup and brush	50
	1 small vice	4 00
	5 erasers	50
	1 candlestick	10
	5 tin paper cutters	50
	2 folders	30
	3 wooden buckets	1 50
	1 tin bucket	75
	1 coal scuttle	25
	1 garrison flag	42 00
	5 rulers	2 00
	Telegraph office.	
	3 stools and 5 chairs	6 00
	1 desk, 2 chairs, and 1 table	15 00
	2 buckets	1 00
	1 stove and 8 feet pipe	6 00
	1 desk	8 00
	2 chairs	1 00
	2 paper weights	60
	1 inkstand	50
	5 crowbars	8 00
	12 wheelbarrows	24 00
	5 lanterns	2 00
	3 oil cans	3 00
	2 feeders	50
	10 deck buckets	5 00
	2 monkey wrenches	3 50
	12 wrenches	6 00
	2 oil cans	1 00
	1 squirt can	25
	2 feeders	1 50
	1 hose nozzle	5 00
	1 axe	1 25
	1 cupboard	4 00
	70 feet belting, 10 inch	42 00
	20 feet gum belting, 5-inch	8 00
	1 short-handle shovel	1 00
	12 new tarpaulins, at $90 each	1,080 00
	2 desks	12 00
	1 copying press, cup, and brush	10 00
	1 stove and 14 feet pipe	4 00
	1 water bucket	50
	2 inkstands	25
	2 paper files	25
	1 round table	25
	Tools on rolling stock.	
	68 cold chisels	34 00
	28 monkey wrenches	35 00
	7 hand hammers	8 75
	6 corn brooms	05
	43 oil cans	20 00
	10 squirt cans	3 00
	27 oil feeders	13 50
	9 coal-oil lamps	13 50
	7 wood stoves	42 00
	40 feet pipe	6 00
	3 switch ropes, at $4 each	12 00

List of railroad property transferred, &c.—Continued.

Date.	Articles.	Appraised value.
1866.		
Jan. 31	51 axes	$35 70
	35 handles	9 00
	17 water buckets	5 00
	1 tin bucket	50
	4 tallow pots	3 00
	18 brass locks	13 50
	8 padlocks	2 00
	1 hand-lamp	1 50
	41 lanterns	50 00
	22 signal lanterns	35 00
	30 signal flags	5 00
	1 pair dividers	50
	2 water barrels	2 50
	10 brass faucets	12 50
	2 wood faucets	05
	52 crow and claw bars, at $1 each	52 00
	2 wood-barrows	8 00
	1 common hand-barrow	2 50
	8 files	2 00
	4 hand-saw files	20
	19 pick axes	57 00
	17 pick handles	4 20
	16 foot adzes	12 00
	8 foot-adze handles	2 00
	118 tamping bars	156 70
	19 track gauges, (wood)	9 50
	1 track gauge, (iron)	1 25
	23 hoes	10 00
	2 hoes, (bad)	05
	23 handles	8 00
	3 iron straighteners	60 00
	136 jiggers	136 00
	12 water kegs	24 00
	55 switch locks	41 25
	20 switch locks	2 00
	30 spike mauls	18 00
	14 iron punches	5 00
	118 long-handle spades	70 80
	19 long-handle shovels	11 40
	17 short-handle shovels	10 20
	44 scythes	55 00
	44 snaths, 50 cents each	22 00
	16 hand saws	16 00
	22 cross-cut saws	55 00
	4 sandstones	05
	15 grindstones	60 00
	2 grindstones, (bad)	10
	14 fixtures	22 50
	27 track wrenches	30 00
	6 buck saws	3 00
	23 cant hooks	11 50
	12 cant bars	4 00
	9 iron wedges, at 10 cents each	90
	33 brush hooks, at 50 cents each	16 50
	10 hatchets	4 00
	10 hatchet handles	1 50
	2 cook stoves	18 00
	2 cook stoves, (very bad)	3 00
	4 feet pipe	10
	13 augers	6 50
	2 ladders, at $6 each	12 00
	2 boat-hooks	4 00
	1 marking pot and brush	50

List of railroad property transferred, &c.—Continued.

Date.	Articles.	Appraised value.
1866.		
Jan. 31	3 sledge hammers	$3 50
	1 drawing-knife	1 50
	1 tape line, (50 feet)	2 25
	1 tape line, (bad)	05
	12 5 pounds chain, at 10 cents	12 50
	8 car links	3 20
	4 pins	1 00
	7 desks	42 00
	8 chairs	8 00
	5 benches	6 00
	1 ruler	50
	3 paper-cutters	30
	2 inkstands	50
	1 feather duster, (bad)	05
	63 pounds Manilla rope, at 10 cents	6 30
	1 9-inch snatch-block	4 00
	8 pairs iron railroad tongs, at $2 50 each	20 00
	10 iron pulleys, at 40 cents	4 00
	10 broadaxes	29 00
	6 broadaxe handles	1 50
	9 connecting rods, at $1 each	9 00
	3 blocks and tackle	24 00
	2 rope falls, without blocks, at $4 each	8 00
	2 double blocks, at $2 each	4 00
	1 track level, (wood)	3 00
	2,000 shingles	8 00
	13 switch locks on cars	6 00
	Restaurant and passenger depot	300 00
	Shafts and pulleys for working pumps	160 00
		113,773 45

A. B. SEYER, *President.*

NEW ORLEANS, JACKSON AND GREAT NORTHERN RAILROAD.

Schedule of property in possession of the United States May 1, 1865, *by right of capture and of purchase, transferred to said road, with authority therefor.*

Property purchased	$33,050 00
Property captured	7,350 00
Total	40,400 00

Statement of circumstances and authority under which the railroad property included in the accompanying schedules was transferred to the New Orleans, Jackson and Great Northern railroad by Brevet Colonel J. G. Chandler, acting chief quartermaster military division of the Gulf, New Orleans, Louisiana, March 10, 1866, viz:

QUARTERMASTER GENERAL'S OFFICE,
Washington, D. C., August 18, 1865.

COLONEL: The government should be relieved at the earliest possible day of the expenses of maintaining and operating railroads heretofore held by it for military purposes.

You will cause the railroads in the military division of the Gulf to be at once turned over to the several companies or to their representatives, or such other persons or civil authorities as the general commanding the military division may advise.

In carrying out these transfers you will be governed by the principles recommended by the Quartermaster General in a letter dated May 19, 1865, to the Secretary of War, and by him approved, copy of which is herewith furnished you.

Inventories of the railroad material and supplies, rolling stock, &c., which are the property of the United States, setting forth the amount and estimated value of the articles, will be prepared and forwarded to this office, with recommendations as to the most advantageous modes and places of deposition of the same.

Very respectfully, your obedient servant,

M. C. MEIGS,
Quartermaster General, Brevet Major General U. S. A.

Colonel C. G. SAWTELLE,
Chief Quartermaster Mil. Div. of the Gulf, New Orleans, La.

QUARTERMASTER GENERAL'S OFFICE,
Washington, D. C., March 3, 1866.

COLONEL: Your letter of February 10, 1866, presenting request of New Orleans, Jackson, and Great Northern railroad for the return to it of certain property said to have belonged to it, is, with its enclosures, received.

This road or a portion of it, with its appurtenances, was taken possession of by right of capture upon the occupation of the city of New Orleans by the United States forces in 1862.

Its property became the property of the United States by right of capture, and has been used and in part consumed for military purposes.

Such of this property as still remains in possession of the quartermaster's department, and is no longer required for military use, has been, in accordance with the general policy pursued upon grounds of public utility toward railroad companies, ordered to be restored to the company.

It appears that the road was restored to the company in June last. The government does not undertake to restore material which has been consumed or disposed of, such as iron laid down on other roads, &c. Nor does it restore iron and other material which it has taken up and replaced by other equally good or better material.

If any of the property mentioned in enclosed schedule presented by the company and clearly identified as its former property is still in possession of the quartermaster's department, and no longer required for military purposes, it will be, with the exceptions above stated, relinquished to it.

The letter of the treasurer of the New Orleans, Jackson, and Great Northern Railroad Company, with the schedules, are herewith returned.

By order of the Quartermaster General.

Very respectfully, your obedient servant,

ALEXANDER BLISS,
Brevet Colonel and Acting Quartermaster in charge 4th Division.

Brevet Colonel J. G. CHANDLER,
Acting Chief Quartermaster Mil. Div. of the Gulf, New Orleans, La.

OFFICE CHIEF QUARTERMASTER MILITARY DIVISION OF THE GULF,
New Orleans, Louisiana, March 24, 1866.

COLONEL: I have the honor to report the sale of a lot of railroad property to the New Orleans, Jackson and Great Northern railroad, and to enclose the receipt of the agent of said company for the articles sold, with the prices as appraised, and the bond duly executed in accordance with General Orders No. 62, Quartermaster General's office, October 23, 1865.

In accordance with an order from this office this road was advertised for sale, as will be seen by copy of advertisement enclosed.

The property was bid in at the sale, for the reason that there were no bidders present. I then sold it to the company above referred to, under the provisions of the general order above referred to.

I am, general, very respectfully, your obedient servant,

J. G. CHANDLER,
Brevet Colonel United States Army, in charge.

Major General M. C. MEIGS.
Quartermaster General U. S. A., Washington, D. C.

List of captured property transferred by Captain J. B. Dexter, assistant quartermaster United States volunteers, to the New Orleans, Jackson, and Great Northern railroad, as per letter from the Quartermaster General, dated March 3, 1866.

Date.	Articles.	Cost when new.
1866.		
Mar. 10	2 tables	....
	2 sets gas fixtures	....
	1 set drawers	....
	1 book-case	....
	11 ticket cases	....
	3 armoirs	....
	5 desks	....
	1 steam-guage adjuster	....
	1 iron safe	....
	1 passenger car	$2,250 00
	1 passenger car	2,600 00
	1 baggage car	2,000 00
	1 platform car	500 00

Statement of the indebtedness of railroad companies for the purchase of railroad material of the United States, on credit, under Executive Orders of August 8 and October 14, 1865, showing the appraised value of property transferred by the United States, with interest accrued thereon to May 31, 1866, amount payments made, and balance remaining due at that date.

Name of road.	Value of property sold.	Interest to May 31, 1866.	Total indebtedness May 31.	Payments.	Balance.
Wills Valley Railroad Company	$30,248 52	$1,313 75	$31,562 37	$1,300 00	$30,262 27
Edgefield and Kentucky	114,772 86	4,824 48	119,597 34	....	119,597 34
Macon and Brunswick	93,237 50	973 04	94,209 54	67,662 21	26,547 33
Montgomery and West Point	38,559 66	1,516 16	40,075 82	9,566 76	30,509 06
Southwestern	46,159 89	....	46,159 89	46,159 89	....
Rome	22,086 05	816 29	22,902 31	7,256 71	15,645 60
Memphis and Ohio	106,929 13	4,379 67	111,308 80	15,283 57	96,025 23
Memphis, Clarksville, and Louisville	337,082 36	13,329 29	350,411 65	150 00	350,261 65
Mississippi and Tennessee	127,750 52	4,500 89	132,251 41	30,401 95	101,849 46
Alabama and Florida	79,021 04	2,254 77	81,275 81	21,033 03	60,242 78
East Tennessee and Georgia	366,183 02	18,010 29	384,193 31	26,942 97	357,250 34
Muscogee	5,244 20	214 04	5,458 24	1,316 45	4,141 79
Macon and Western	83,638 15	....	83,638 15	81,282 60	2,355 55
Nashville and Chattanooga	1,566,551 73	76,526 33	1,643,078 06	158,725 53	1,484,352 83
Tennessee and Alabama Central	84,143 00	3,958 34	88,101 34	25,071 06	63,030 28
Mobile and Ohio	505,143 70	17,482 65	522,626 35	221,341 58	301,284 77
Mobile and Great Northern	18,036 72	564 08	18,600 80	7,584 18	11,011 62
Memphis and Charleston	547,494 09	9,779 97	557,274 06	79,774 44	477,499 62
Alabama and Tennessee River	183,276 49	7,567 75	190,844 24	15,340 18	175,504 06
Mississippi, Gainesville, and Tuscaloosa	33,476 39	1,504 86	34,981 25	....	24,981 25
Georgia Railroad and Banking Company	11,935 05	....	11,935 05	11,935 05	....
New Orleans and Ohio	32,150 00	1,373 88	33,523 88	....	33,523 88
Nashville and Decatur	135,171 92	4,048 66	139,220 58	31,015 04	108,205 54
Western and Atlantic	472,944 66	22,979 47	495,924 13	....	495,924 13
Central Southern	77,186 32	3,631 17	80,817 49	22,996 43	57,821 06
East Tennessee and Virginia	265,655 65	13,434 96	279,090 61	7,888 42	271,202 19
Southwestern Iron Company	32,515 00	....	32,515 00	32,515 00	....
Adams Express Company	4,361 45	....	4,361 45	4,361 45	....
Nashville and Northwestern Railroad Company	525,400 26	27,723 49	553,123 75	23,044 75	530,079 00
Mississippi Central	78,460 00	2,144 18	80,604 18	14,415 89	66,188 29
New Orleans, Jackson, and Great Northern	200,865 58	6,658 06	207,523 64	49,967 58	157,556 06
Tennessee and Alabama	108,692 68	5,117 81	113,810 49	32,349 20	81,461 29

Selma and Meridian	146,327 92	4,815 21	151,143 13	56,028 49	95,114 64
Virginia and Tennessee	102,880 00	3,295 58	106,175 58	....	106,175 58
Wilmington and Weldon	110,000 00	2,274 21	112,274 21	4,536 57	107,737 64
Atlantic and North Carolina	51,453 93	1,786 05	53,239 98	5,948 04	47,291 94
Western North Carolina	14,269 82	465 06	14,734 88	2,638 35	12,596 53
Petersburg	65,000 00	1,411 80	63,411 80	18,012 67	48,399 13
Virginia Central	70,000 00	3,995 13	73,995 13	4,424 71	69,570 42
Richmond, Fredericksburg, and Potomac	7,449 27	....	7,449 27	7,449 27	....
Orange and Alexandria	90,395 74	4,176 93	94,572 67	8,612 75	85,959 92
Alexandria, Loudon, and Hampshire	62,592 96	1,903 85	64,496 81	....	64,496 81
Manassas Gap	4,623 51	119 72	4,743 23	309 09	4,434 14
McMinnville and Manchester	20,310 00	430 57	20,740 57	....	20,740 57
South Carolina	23,458 50	497 31	23,955 81	....	23,955 81
Memphis and Little Rock	153,287 47	7,459 99	160,746 46	....	160,746 46
New Orleans, Opelousas, and Great Western	113,773 45	2,768 49	116,541 94	....	116,541 94
Total	7,370,196 16	292,027 20	7,662,223 36	1,154,146 56	6,508,076 80

List of railroad property transferred by Captain J. B. Dexter, assistant quartermaster United States volunteers, to the president and directors of the New Orleans, Jackson, and Great Northern railroad, belonging to the United States government, for the value of which said road has given bond for $66,100 to secure payment.

Date.	Articles.	Cost when new.	Cost of articles and prices charged.
1866.			
Mar. 10	21 platform cars ....each..	$550 00	$11,550 00
	5 platform cars ....do...	400 00	2,000 00
	2 wood cars ....do...	600 00	1,200 00
	5 box cars ....do...	650 00	3,250 00
	1 box car ....do...	450 00	450 00
	3 cattle cars ....do...	550 00	1,650 00
	25 coal cars ....do...	300 00	7,500 00
	1 dummy car and engine ....do...	4,000 00	4,000 00
	11 push-cars ....do...	50 00	550 00
	8 hand cars ....do...	50 00	400 00
	1 turn-table ....do...	500 00	500 00
	Total value of railroad property transferred	....	33,050 00

[General Orders No. 62.]

QUARTERMASTER GENERAL'S OFFICE,
Washington, October 23, 1865.

The following order by the President of the United States, in relation to executive order of 8th August, 1865, extending the provisions and benefits of the same to all railroads within the limits of the military division of the Tennessee desiring to purchase railroad rolling stock and material from the United States, for the purpose of repairing the losses of the war, is published for the information of all officers and agents of the quartermaster's department.

M. C. MEIGS,
Brevet Major General U. S. A., Quartermaster General.

WAR DEPARTMENT,
Washington, D. C., October 14, 1865.

GENERAL: The provisions and benefits of the executive order of 8th of August are hereby extended to all railroads within the limits of your command, desiring to purchase railroad rolling stock and materials from the United States, for the purpose of repairing the losses of the war.

You are also authorized to direct the sale to any such railroads of rolling stock now within the limits of you command, and not needed by the United States for actual use, upon the following conditions, if they are preferred to the terms of the order of 8th August, and the individual security required by you under that order:

You will take care that this property is distributed among the several roads in proportion to their actual needs, and that none is sold to any railroad in excess of the reasonable requirements of its business, or to be used for purposes of speculation, sale, or hire to other roads.

You will require from all such railroad companies satisfactory bonds, in the form herewith enclosed, binding them to the payment to the United States of the full appraised value of the property sold to them, in equal monthly instalments, with interest at the rate of seven and three-tenths per cent. per annum, within two years, credit being allowed to them, on the first of each month, for any service of military transportation rendered by them during the preceding month, at the established rates now allowed to northern railroads for such service.

Full reports of all sales under this order will be made to the War Department from time to time, as required by existing orders.

The serviceable railroad iron in possession of the quartermaster's department at Chattanooga and Nashville is excepted. It will be sold for cash, at the prices fixed by the War Department.

By order of the President:

EDWARD M. STANTON,
Secretary of War.

Major General GEORGE H. THOMAS,
Commanding Military Division of the Tennessee,
Headquarters, Nashville, Tennessee.

BOND.

Know all men by these presents, that the ——— railroad company, duly incorporated by the act of the ——— of the State of ———, by ——— its president, acting for and in behalf of said railroad company, does hereby acknowledge itself and its successors held and firmly bound unto the United States of America in the full and just sum of ——— dollars, lawful money of the United States; for which payment, well and truly to be made to the disbursing quartermaster of the United States military railroads, at his office in Nashville, or to such other disbursing quartermaster as may be designated by the War Department, within two years from the date of these presents, the said railroad company, by its president, hereby binds itself and its successors, firmly by these presents.

Sealed with its corporate seal, attested by the signature of its president, and affixed by the express authority of its directors, this ——— day of ——— in the year of our Lord one thousand eight hundred and sixty———.

The nature of the above obligation is such that, whereas the above bounden railroad company has purchased and received, or shall receive, from the War Department of the United States, rolling stock, iron rails, cross-ties, chairs, spikes, timber, and other materials for repairing and operating its railroad, in quantities, at prices, and to an amount and value which shall be evidenced by the receipts given for the same by the same railroad company to the proper officer of the said War Department, upon a credit of two years from the date of these presents, payable in equal monthly instalments, with interest, at the rate of 7 $\frac{3}{10}$ per cent. per annum, within the said two years, either in cash to the disbursing quartermaster of the United States military railroads, at his office in Nashville, or to such other disbursing quartermaster as may be designated for this purpose by the War Department, or in transportation of the troops or military supplies of the United States, under the orders of the proper military authorities, at the rates of fare and tolls allowed for such service to northern railroads;

And whereas the said railroad company desires, and by these presents intends, to secure to the United States the complete and punctual payment as aforesaid of the amounts which may be due for the said materials received or to be received by it from the United States:

Now, therefore, if the said railroad company shall well and truly pay as aforesaid, either in cash, in equal monthly instalments, or in transportation as aforesaid, to the United States, within two years from the date of these presents, all that shall be due as aforesaid to the United States on account and in payment for all the materials received as aforesaid from the United States, then this obligation shall be void and of no effect.

But if the said railroad company shall fail to pay to the United States all or any portion of what may be due to the United States, on account of the said materials received from the United States, within two years from the date of these presents, either in cash as aforesaid, or in transportation as aforesaid, or shall fail to pay any of the monthly instalments aforesaid punctually when due, then this obligation shall remain in full force and effect to the extent that may be necessary to fully repay to the United States the full amount which may be due on account of the said materials so received as aforesaid, and all loss or damage which may have been incurred by the United States, by reason of the said railroad company's failure to pay for the same what shall be due therefor, when the shall be due.

And as a further security for such payment and indemnity to the United States, the United States shall have a lien upon the property sold to said company, and in default of such complete and punctual payment of all moneys which may be due on account of the aforesaid purchase of materials, be fully authorized to take possession of and sell said property, and also to place in charge and control of the said company's railroad an agent of the said United States, who shall be fully empowered, and by these presents is fully empowered, in case of such default as aforesaid, to collect all the revenues of the said company, and apply the same to the payment to the United States of all the money which shall be due at the times of such application of such revenues to the United States for any such materials which shall have been delivered by the United States to the said railroad company, or by reason of any loss or injury to the United States resulting from such default in payment of the same. And the said company shall have no authority to sell or convey out of its possession, without the consent of the United States first in writing obtained, any of the property referred to in this agreement; but shall hold and retain the same to the exclusive use of said company, in carrying on the business of transportation of persons and property over its line of road, until the whole is fully paid for as aforesaid.

In witness whereof, the corporate seal of said railroad company is affixed hereto, by authority of its directors, and attested by its president.

——— ———.

Witness: ——— ———.

NOTE.—The amount of this bond to be double the valuation of the property sold and delivered. Internal revenue stamps should be affixed, to the amount of fifty cents for every thousand dollars.

[General Orders No. 80.]

QUARTERMASTER GENERAL'S OFFICE,
Washington, D. C., December 22, 1865.

Sales to railroad companies under executive orders of August 8 and October 14 (General Orders, Quartermaster General's office, 56 and 62, 1865) will be promptly reported to this office, addressed to R. R. division.

As soon after completion of sale to any railroad as practicable, a statement of the account of such railroad with the United States, accompanied by the receipt of the company for the articles sold, with prices as appraised, and its bond duly executed, will be forwarded for file in this office.

The duplicate of receipt, and a copy of the bond, will be retained by the officer making the sales.

Every payment of instalment and interest, whether in cash or by accepted vouchers, will be reported on the day it is made, with a statement of the balance remaining due to the United States. On all such payments the usual three days' grace will be allowed.

The railroad companies will be credited with the amount of their duly certified vouchers, for any services rendered prior to the month current, whether in excess or not of the monthly instalment due; such credit to date from the receipt by the officer to whom the railroad makes its payments of vouchers duly certified, examined and audited by the proper officer for settlement of transportation accounts.

The accounts of railroad companies will be examined and audited by the proper officers without unnecessary delay; but no payments will be made to any railroad in the States lately in rebellion, except upon the certificate of the officer charged with sales of military railroad property for the military division or department that such road has not incurred any indebtedness to the United States, or if incurred, that its indebtedness has been discharged in full.

If so indebted, the vouchers, duly certified, will be referred to the officer who made the sales, to be credited as above.

The reports herein called for are not intended to supersede those already required by regulations and existing orders.

M. C. MEIGS,
Quartermaster General, Brevet Major General U. S. A.

www.ingramcontent.com/pod-product-compliance
Lightning Source LLC
LaVergne TN
LVHW021309110826
845150LV00003B/532

* 9 7 8 1 4 2 5 5 5 8 6 2 8 *